# The Complete Letters of Sigmund Freud to Wilhelm Fliess 1887–1904

# The Complete Letters of SIGMUND FREUD to WILHELM FLIESS

## 1887–1904

Translated and Edited by
Jeffrey Moussaieff Masson

The Belknap Press of
Harvard University Press
Cambridge, Massachusetts, and
London, England
1985

Printed in the United States of America
10 9 8 7 6 5 4 3 2

This book is printed on acid-free paper, and its binding materials have been chosen for strength and durability.
Library of Congress cataloging information is on last page of book.

# Contents

# Illustrations

# Preface

THE PUBLICATION in German in 1950, then in English in 1954, of *The Origins of Psycho-Analysis*, a selective edition of Sigmund Freud's letters to Wilhelm Fliess, stimulated every reader's desire —including my own—for a full and unabridged edition of these extraordinary documents. I approached Freud's daughter Anna in 1978 and told her of my interest and my certainty that the unpublished letters contained valuable information. She allowed me access to the documents from 1897, and when I was able to show her that they did indeed contain significant material for historians of psychoanalysis, she was willing to consider permitting a complete version of the letters to be published. But it was only when K. R. Eissler, Miss Freud's close friend and trusted adviser, added his voice to mine that she relented fully and agreed to let me prepare a new edition. I did not realize at the time how complicated this task would become, how much effort it would involve, how many countries would have to be visited, how many libraries searched, how many documents tracked down. When I had finished, 133 previously unpublished items in the correspondence had been added to the 168 documents presented, in full or in part, in *Origins*.

It is a hazardous undertaking to edit a work of this magnitude, which is likely to change the image of a great man. Still, I think most readers will agree that a more human, more likable Sigmund Freud emerges from this complete version of his letters to Fliess. It is also true that the fuller rendition of his thinking about some of his key theories contrasts rather starkly with the version that Freud presented to posterity many years later in his published works. This is perhaps inevitable. It is also inevitable that access to works that were never meant to be printed forces the impartial historian to difficult, sometimes unpopular conclusions. In this new edition I have attempted to present the letters as objectively as possible and have refrained from making any interpretations or evaluations of my own.

Anna Freud, once she had made her decision to permit publication of the letters, gave of her time and her knowledge with unfailing generosity. I spent a great deal of time in her house in Maresfield Gardens, London (which had also been her father's home during the last year of his life), reading in Freud's personal library and rummaging through drawers and cupboards for documents that would clarify some of the allusions in his letters to Fliess. I had many conversations with Anna Freud about the letters and their content. Both of us rapidly became caught up in the excitement of meticulously searching Freud's desk and there finding documents long thought lost. I believe that Miss Freud came to realize how much material remained to be discovered and what joy there was in finding some of it. Certainly she shared with me the considerable pleasure to be experienced in the kind of detective work that compiling these letters involved.

My primary gratitude, then, is reserved for the late Anna Freud and her many acts of kindness toward me. Moreover, without the assistance of K. R. Eissler, this project could never have begun. He gave generously of his time and energy and facilitated my access, in the Library of Congress and elsewhere, to a vast storehouse of original documents, many of which have enriched the annotation of this volume.

All those interested in these letters owe a special debt of gratitude to Marie Bonaparte for having rescued the original documents, and to Ernst Kris along with Anna Freud for the first edition of the letters.

Lottie Newman, selected by Anna Freud as the translator, prepared the first draft of the entire translation and compared it against every existing translation. She also made many worthwhile suggestions and excellent criticisms of later drafts. Gerhard Fichtner is responsible for the German text upon which the new translation is based. Needless to say, without his help this volume would not have been possible. He took time from a busy schedule at the University of Tübingen to come to Berkeley, California, where I was working, and offer his scholarly support. Marianne Loring, my research assistant, deserves a large portion of the credit for the final version. Many of the notes too owe a great deal to her research abilities. She has been my intellectual companion over the six years of compiling this work, and it is no exaggeration to say that I could not have managed without her cheerful, unstinting, and skillful help. The book, then, owes its present form to the help of these three people:

Lottie Newman, Gerhard Fichtner, and Marianne Loring. I am more grateful than I can say to all three of them.

I have been supported throughout this work by Mark Paterson, executive director of Sigmund Freud Copyrights. Ilse Grubrich-Simitis has always been ready with valuable advice. Muriel Gardiner has been enthusiastic about the project from the beginning. And the late Elenore Fliess, widow of Wilhelm Fliess's son Robert, became a personal friend during the writing of this book. I regret that she did not live to see the work in print; I know it would have given her much pleasure.

Arthur Rosenthal, director of Harvard University Press, has given strong and consistent support throughout the compilation of this new edition. Vivian Wheeler has been the ideal editor—tactful, helpful, and wise—and it has been a privilege to work with her.

Some of the letters contained in this volume come from the Jewish National and University Library in Jerusalem, where they had been deposited by Fliess's daughter, Pauline Fliess Jacobsohn. Peter Swales called them to my attention, and I am indebted to Mrs. Jacobsohn for permission to use them. Princess Eugenie of Greece kindly allowed use of excerpts from Marie Bonaparte's notebook.

John Broderick, Paul Hefron, and especially Ronald Wilkinson and the staff at the Library of Congress Manuscript Division were ever willing to help me find material difficult of access, and to provide me with copies of whatever I needed.

Albert Dickson, Allan Keiler, and Michael Schröter have made a number of useful corrections in the final translation.

I should like also to thank the following individuals, who have assisted in various ways: Angela Harris, Susan Mango, Annie Urbach, Robert Wallerstein, and Trude Weisskopf.

A work of this magnitude could not have been accomplished without financial aid. For their generous assistance I am grateful to the New Land Foundation, the Fund for Psychoanalytic Research of the American Psychoanalytic Association, the National Library of Medicine, and the National Endowment for the Humanities.

J.M.M.

# Note on Method

THIS TRANSLATION of Freud's letters to Fliess is based on a completely new German text, and it is important to understand the derivation of both the German and the English versions.

Anna Freud made available to me the original transcript of the German holograph of all the letters, as corrected by her and Ernst Kris and published, with omissions, in *Sigmund Freud, Aus den Anfängen der Psychoanalyse.* I obtained photocopies of all the original letters that are housed in the Library of Congress, and of several that are among the papers of the late James Strachey. My colleague Marianne Loring then compared these 284 original letters with the transcript. She and I made many corrections in the transcript, a number of which I discussed with Anna Freud. Later Gerhard Fichtner, director of the Institute for the History of Medicine at the University of Tübingen and a noted authority on Freud, went through the entire set of letters once again and uncovered further errors, both in *Anfänge* and in the improved transcript. Fichtner prepared a new transcript, which Loring and I again reviewed and corrected. Fichtner compared this with the original letters a third time and prepared a final transcript. It is that document from which the present translation derives.

Lottie Newman prepared the first draft of this translation, which Marianne Loring and I revised several times before reaching the present version. Except for occasional amendments, I have followed Strachey's excellent revisions for the first volume of his *Standard Edition of the Complete Psychological Works of Sigmund Freud.*

A comparison of this translation with those previously published in *The Origins of Psycho-Analysis* and in the *Standard Edition* will show that mine often varies in ways that suggest more than a different understanding of the German (although this too is sometimes the case). Frequently the German text Fichtner has established differs from the text printed in *Anfänge.* When the discrepancy seems particularly important, I have noted it; but often I have simply used the correct version. The reader will be able to see the changes by consulting the new German text, for an improved German edition of the letters is being published simultaneously with this volume by S. Fischer Verlag in Frankfurt, under the title *Sigmund Freud, Briefe an Wilhelm Fliess, 1887–1904. Vollständige Ausgabe. Herausgegeben von Jeffrey Moussaieff Masson; Bearbeitung der deutschen Fassung von Michael Schröter; Transkription von Gerhard Fichtner.*

In my annotation I have attempted not to elaborate on the obvious, or to cite information that the reader can easily obtain (for example, by consulting Ernest Jones's three-volume biography of Freud). For this reason I have frequently not reproduced material that is available in Ernst Kris's notes to the earlier edition of the letters, but have simply referred the reader to that edition. Nor have I duplicated Strachey's labors; Strachey's first volume of the *Standard Edition* is particularly helpful in pointing the reader to later works by Freud that expand the ideas first mentioned in these letters.

Freud's own footnotes are signaled by asterisks and other symbols; numbers indicate my own annotation. I have tried to keep the notes to a strict minimum, avoiding the temptation to speculate or to interpret. The reader will find primarily identifications of persons, places, and family events, where these are known; explanations of obscure allusions, political happenings, or literary events; and brief comments on contemporary reviews of works by both Freud and Fliess. Michael Schröter has written a number of additional notes for the German edition of these letters, which he has kindly placed at my disposal. Where I have used them in this edition, I have so indicated.

An occasional Editor's Note explains uncertainties of dating or describes unusual materials. Freud's name and office hours on his letterhead stationery have been dropped as repetitious; the return address and date have been retained. Names of patients are masked, unless they have previously been made public. Bracketed insertions of information in the letters may involve explanations of foreign phrases, additions necessitated by the conversion of German into English, or alternatives to uncertain readings.

I have made a few silent corrections: if Freud made a mistake in grammar or punctuation, for instance, I have not flagged it. Moreover, it seemed pedantic to use brackets to indicate that the translated English required more words than the German. Thus pronouns, often omitted in German, have been included in the English without comment. Gaps and illegible words in the original holograph have been noted, but no liberties have been taken with the tone of Freud's own writing. Any minor changes have been in the interest of clarity.

The section at the back of the book entitled Principal Works Cited contains all publications of Freud and Fliess mentioned in the letters, and any reviews thereof that are cited. The listing of works by other authors is selective and includes, for the most part, present-day authors whose views are mentioned or discussed herein. Writers contemporary with Freud and Fliess, usually only mentioned in passing, are cited in full in the notes.

# The Complete Letters of Sigmund Freud to Wilhelm Fliess 1887–1904

## ABBREVIATIONS OF WORKS CITED

| | |
|---|---|
| *Anfänge* | *Sigmund Freud, Aus den Anfängen der Psychoanalyse. Briefe an Wilhelm Fliess, Abhandlungen und Notizen aus den Jahren 1887–1902.* Edited by Marie Bonaparte, Anna Freud, and Ernst Kris; introduction by Ernst Kris. London: Imago Publishing Company, 1950. |
| *G.W.* | *Sigmund Freud, Gesammelte Werke.* 18 vols. Edited by Anna Freud, with the collaboration of Marie Bonaparte, E. Bibring, W. Hoffer, E. Kris, and O. Isakower. London: Imago Publishing Company, 1940–1952. |
| Jones, *Life* | Ernest Jones, *Sigmund Freud: Life and Work.* 3 vols. New York: Basic Books, 1954–1957. |
| *Letters* | *Letters of Sigmund Freud, 1873–1939.* Edited by Ernst L. Freud; translated by Tania Stern and James Stern. London: Hogarth Press, 1961. |
| *Origins* | *The Origins of Psycho-Analysis: Letters to Wilhelm Fliess, Drafts and Notes, 1887–1902, by Sigmund Freud.* Edited by Marie Bonaparte, Anna Freud, and Ernst Kris; translated by Eric Mosbacher and James Strachey; introduction by Ernst Kris. New York: Basic Books, and London: Imago Publishing Company, 1954. |
| *S.E.* | *The Standard Edition of the Complete Psychological Works of Sigmund Freud.* 24 vols. Edited by James Strachey; translated in collaboration with Anna Freud, assisted by Alix Strachey and Alan Tyson. London: Hogarth Press and the Institute of Psycho-Analysis, 1953–1974. |

# Introduction

SIGMUND FREUD'S LETTERS to his closest friend, Wilhelm Fliess, are probably the single most important group of documents in the history of psychoanalysis. At no time intended for publication, the letters date from 1887 to 1904, a period that spans the birth and development of psychoanalysis. During the seventeen years of the correspondence Freud wrote some of his most revolutionary works: *Studies on Hysteria, The Interpretation of Dreams,* "The Aetiology of Hysteria," and the famous case study of Dora. Never has the creator of a totally new field of human knowledge so overtly and in such detail revealed the thought processes leading to his discoveries. None of the later writings have the immediacy and the impact of these early letters, nor do any reveal so dramatically Freud's innermost thoughts as he was in the very act of creation. The result is an extraordinarily compelling set of writings. They are presented here, for the first time, without any excisions.

At the time the correspondence began, Freud was a thirty-one-year-old lecturer in neuropathology at the University of Vienna. Newly married to Martha Bernays, he had just established his own neurological practice after having studied in Paris for six months with the noted neurologist Jean Martin Charcot. Fliess, twenty-nine, was already a successful ear, nose, and throat doctor in Berlin. In the fall of 1887 he went to Vienna to study with specialists there, and apparently the eminent physician Josef Breuer (1842–1925), then Freud's mentor, colleague, and friend, suggested that Fliess attend Freud's lectures at the university. A few months later, after Fliess had returned to Berlin, Freud wrote the first of a long series of letters that was to chart the origins and evolution of psychoanalysis.

Within five years Freud and Fliess were regular correspondents. In 1890 they began meeting in Berlin, in Vienna (where Fliess's fiancée, Ida Bondy, lived until she and Fliess were married in 1892), and in various Austrian and German towns for what the two men came to call their private "congresses." The relationship grew and deepened: Fliess became Freud's closest friend, and Freud was more open with Fliess than with anyone else in expressing his feelings and thoughts about professional and personal matters.

It is not possible to know for certain what drew the men together. There are obvious similarities: both were Jewish, both were physicians, and both were involved in medical research. More important probably, they found early on that both were interested in aspects of medical science that lay outside the customary channels of research. Both, for instance, visited Paris to work with Charcot. A love of scientific adventure and inquiry seemed to unite them professionally. Moreover, their meetings revealed an uncommon willingness to talk at a personal level and to reveal details of family life. Freud's relentless probing into the psychological consequences of his patients' early sexual experiences was not welcomed by his more conservative medical colleagues, and the ensuing isolation undoubtedly explains the increasing frequency of the letters. For many years Fliess was Freud's only audience.

In an unpublished letter of April 7, 1893, to his sister-in-law, Minna Bernays, Freud described his admiration and affection for Fliess: "He is a most unusual person, good nature personified: and I believe, if it came to it, he would for all his genius, be goodness itself. Therefore his sunlike clarity, his pluck."[1]

Freud was almost reverential toward Fliess. On January 1, 1896, he wrote: "Your kind should not die out, my dear friend; the rest of us need people like you too much. How much I owe you: solace, understanding, stimulation in my loneliness, meaning to my life that I gained through you, and finally even health that no one else could have given back to me."

It is not illuminating to claim, as some have done, that this intense relationship was one of transference—that it was a necessary forerunner of Freud's own self-analysis. Every love relation, which this one certainly was, contains an essential mystery that defies comprehension. Freud himself would later speak of the homosexual component of this friendship,[2] and in fact both men believed that elements of bisexuality are inherent in all individuals.

1. This letter, given me by Freud's daughter Anna, was found at Maresfield Gardens in London, Freud's last home. Translations of all unpublished letters throughout this Introduction are mine.

2. Ernest Jones (*Life* 2:92) quotes a letter of October 6, 1910, from Freud to his friend and colleague Sándor Ferenczi: "You not only noticed, but also understood, that I *no*

The commentary of Robert Fliess, Wilhelm's son, sheds some light here. He wrote to the Freud scholar Siegfried Bernfeld (unpublished letter in English in the Bernfeld Archives at the Library of Congress) on August 28, 1944:

> You are quite right in mentioning the strongly emotional character of the significance of these two men for each other. I have heard a good deal about this from both of them — over a long stretch of years, of course, from my father, and in a long conversation with Freud in 1929, in which he spoke with a frankness apparently not too customary to him in personal matters.

From the correspondence it appears that Freud was the more generous friend, giving himself over to the relationship almost unreservedly, whereas Fliess remained more guarded. Indeed, Freud was so preoccupied with communicating his discoveries that he seemed to have been unaware that, starting at about the turn of the century, Fliess was withdrawing from him and gradually dissolving the friendship.

Marie Bonaparte (1882 – 1962), one of Freud's favorite pupils and analysands, left an account of the deterioration of the relationship in her unpublished notebook:

> The friendship with Fliess began to decline as early as 1900, . . . when Freud published the book on dreams. Freud had not realized this! I taught it to him. His friendship with Fliess made him reluctant to impute envy to Fliess. Fliess could not bear the superiority of his friend. Nor could he tolerate, this time according to Freud, Freud's scientific criticisms . . . Ida Fliess, moreover, . . . out of jealousy, did everything possible to sow discord between the two friends, whereas Martha Freud understood very well that Fliess was able to give her husband something beyond what she could. Fliess, according to Freud, had as passionate a friendship for Freud as Freud had for Fliess.

Some of the emerging difficulty lay in Fliess's stubbornness and possessiveness about his theories. He clung to his scheme of periodicity, by which the major events in man's life supposedly were predetermined. Freud did place some credence in Fliess's claims

---

*longer* have any need to uncover my personality completely, and you correctly traced this back to the traumatic reason for it. Since Fliess's case, with the overcoming of which you recently saw me occupied, that need has been extinguished. A part of homosexual cathexis has been withdrawn and made use of to enlarge my own ego. I have succeeded where the paranoiac fails" (italics in original).

about the significance of the nose. Marie Bonaparte, in a continuation of her notebook, says:

> As for a connection between the nose and the rest of the organism, there is some truth in it. Freud experienced it himself, with respect to his heartburn, which would suddenly disappear after a nasal treatment. He was able to see Fliess in this fashion assuage pain in childbirth. As for bisexuality, if Fliess was the first to talk about it to Freud, he could not pretend to priority in this idea of biology. "And if he gave me bisexuality, I gave him sexuality before that." That is what Freud told me.

Freud's awareness that his debt to Fliess was, after all, not so great came only in later years and presumably was conveyed to no one but Bonaparte. During the years of his friendship with Fliess, Freud believed the two men to be equally interested in theoretical ideas about sexuality. But the fact is that there was a striking divergence, particularly in the crucial area of the emotions provoked by human sexuality. Freud was correct to tell Bonaparte it was he who, however imperfectly, enlightened Fliess on the relevance of sexuality to medical psychology.

The actual end of the friendship was particularly difficult for Freud, and later in his life he seldom spoke of Fliess at all. There is evidence in Freud's letters (some of them unpublished) to his colleagues Carl Jung, Karl Abraham, and particularly Sándor Ferenczi that he discussed Fliess with them—but rarely, and never in the detail that Ferenczi, at least, desired.[3] The late Anna Freud, in a letter to me, wrote that her father never talked to her about Fliess, except very sparingly toward the end of his life, after his letters to Fliess had been discovered. She judged the reason to be that the breakup was still painful to him, even years afterward.

From their writing to their publication, Freud's letters to Fliess have traveled a long and complicated road. In the Fliess Archives in Jerusalem are copies of two unpublished letters from Ida Fliess to Freud,

3. In an unpublished letter to Ferenczi of October 17, 1910, Freud wrote, "You probably imagine that I have secrets quite other than those I have reserved for myself, or you believe that my secrets are connected with a special sorrow, whereas I feel capable of handling everything and am pleased with the greater independence that results from having overcome my homosexuality." On the following December 16, again in an unpublished letter to Ferenczi, Freud mentions Fliess for the last time: "I have now overcome Fliess, about whom you were so curious."

and two unpublished letters from Freud to her.[4] Ida Fliess wrote first, on December 6, 1928, shortly after the death of her husband:

> Esteemed professor:
>
> Whether you will grant me the privilege I admit I do not know, but there is a request I would nevertheless like to submit to you. You perhaps have in your possession letters from Wilhelm addressed to you before your relations became clouded. They probably were not destroyed, although they have lost their meaning to you. If that is the case, would you be good enough and trusting enough, dear professor, to place them in my hands? For I am the person who of all people has the deepest interest in them. I want them for no other purpose, I assure you. If this is not possible, could you at least lend them to me for a short time?
>
> This request has opened an avenue to you that has long been closed to me. I hope that I will be able to approach you once more to give you my heartfelt thanks.
>
> Sincerely yours,
> Ida Fliess

Freud responded immediately, on December 17:

> Esteemed madam:
>
> I hasten to answer your letter, although I cannot at present communicate anything decisive with respect to fulfilling your request. My memory tells me that I destroyed the greater part of our correspondence at some point after 1904. But the possibility remains that a select number of letters were preserved and might turn up after a careful search of the rooms in which I have lived for the past thirty-seven years. I beg you, therefore, to allow me time over Christmas. Whatever I find will be at your disposal, unconditionally. If I do not find anything, you will have to assume that nothing escaped the destruction. Naturally I would be happy to learn that my letters to your husband, for so many years my close friend, have found a fate that will assure their protection against any future use. In view of the circumstances, I express my sympathy in this subdued manner.
>
> Sincerely yours,
> Freud

4. The originals are in the Jewish National and University Library, also in Jerusalem.

This letter suggests that Freud may not have destroyed all the letters he received from Fliess.[5] On December 30, however, he reported:

> Dear madam:
>
> I have found nothing so far and am very much inclined to presume that the entire correspondence has been destroyed. But since I have also not found other things that I certainly intended to preserve, for example the Charcot letters, I do not consider the matter closed. Naturally my promise, should I find something, remains the same.
>
> Sincerely yours,
> Freud

Ida Fliess responded on January 3, 1929, thanking Freud for leaving her "with a glimmer of hope that some day one or more of the letters may be found."

Later Ida Fliess sold Freud's letters to her husband, as we learn in a series of letters from Marie Bonaparte to Freud.[6] The first of these, dated December 30, 1936, reads in part:

> Today a certain Mr. Stahl came to see me from Berlin. He had gotten from Fliess's widow the letters and manuscripts from you that were in Fliess's estate. His widow intended at first to give everything to the National Library of Prussia, but since your works were burned in Germany, she gave up the idea and sold the manuscripts to this Mr. Stahl. He is a writer and art dealer and makes a very good personal impression. Apparently he received offers from America for this collection of your writings, but before he resigned himself to seeing these valuable documents go off to America, he approached me and I decided to buy everything from him. So that they will remain in Europe and in my hands, he even allowed me a lower price—12,000 francs in all—for 250 letters from you (several from

5. Anna Freud assured me that many careful searches of Maresfield Gardens had turned up no additional documents. Yet even as she told me this, I found among the letters there a previously unknown communication from Fliess to Freud. I find it hard to believe that Freud would have destroyed the letters and not remembered that he had done so, given the importance of the friendship to him and the fact that it was not until 1910, by Freud's own account, that he was able to "overcome" the relationship.

6. These letters were published (although with some omissions that have been restored here) by Max Schur in his editor's introduction to volume 2 of *Drives, Affects, Behavior*, the *Essays in Memory of Marie Bonaparte*. I was not able to see the original letters, which are in the Marie Bonaparte Archives of the Library of Congress and sealed until the year 2020. However, I did see the copies sent (presumably by Bonaparte) to Ernest Jones, which are today in the Jones Archives in London.

Breuer), and very long theoretical drafts in your hand in rather large numbers. I am delighted that I was able to do this, for I would regret seeing all of this sent out into the wider world. There can be no doubt that it is yours. I know your handwriting, after all!

Freud's response (January 3, 1937) reiterated that he had either lost or destroyed Fliess's letters, and at the same time confirmed their importance.

My dear Marie:

The matter of the correspondence with Fliess has affected me deeply. After his death his widow asked that I return his letters. I agreed unconditionally, but was unable to find them. I do not know to this day whether I destroyed them, or only hid them ingeniously . . . Our correspondence was the most intimate you can imagine. It would have been highly embarrassing to have it fall into the hands of strangers. It is therefore an extraordinary labor of love that you have gotten hold of them and removed them from danger. I only regret the expense you have incurred. May I offer to share half the cost with you? After all, I would have had to acquire the letters myself if the man had approached me directly. I do not want any of them to become known to so-called posterity . . .

Once more, heartfelt thanks from your

Freud

Four days later Marie Bonaparte replied from Paris:

Mr. Stahl has just arrived and turned over to me the first part of the Fliess papers: scientific essays that were scattered throughout your letters, which he collected separately and put together. The rest, the actual letters, which number about 200 to 250, are still in Germany. He intends to have someone bring them to Paris in a few weeks. The letters and manuscripts were offered to me under the condition that I never, directly or indirectly, sell them to the Freud family, for it was feared that this material, so important for the history of psychoanalysis, would be destroyed. That would not be a definitive reason for me not to discuss the matter with you. Still, you will not be surprised, for you know my feelings and ideas on the matter, that I *personally* have an immense aversion to the destruction of your letters and manuscripts . . .

My idea was the following: to acquire the letters so that they will not be published by just anybody, and to keep them for some years, for example, in a national library — in Geneva, let us say, where there is less reason to fear revolutions or the dangers of war — with the stipulation that they not be seen for eighty or a hundred years after your death. Who could be harmed, even within your own family, should there turn out to be something in the letters?

Furthermore, I do not know what is in the letters. I will not read your letters, if that is your wish — nothing whatever. I have looked at only one letter, which accompanied one of the essays; there was nothing very compromising in it!

Can you really remember after such a long time what is in these letters? After all, you even forgot whether you destroyed the letters from Fliess or hid them . . . The breakup of this friendship must have been so painful.

You probably spoke quite freely about many people, even about your family . . . possibly about yourself [too] you said a great deal.

Moreover, I do not yet have the letters. I will only get them in a few weeks. Could I, at the beginning of March, on my way to Greece, stop in Vienna for a day or two to discuss the matter with you?

I love you . . . and revere you, and that is why I have written to you in this manner.

Marie

P.S. I want to acquire the letters on my own. That will enable us to talk about them more freely.

Stressing the need for Bonaparte to get possession of the letters, Freud emphasized that they were intimate to a remarkable degree (January 10, 1937):

It is disappointing that my letters to Fliess are not yet in your hands, but are still in Berlin . . . However, I tell myself that in eighty or a hundred years interest in the content of this correspondence will be notably less than it is today.

Naturally it is all right with me if you do not read the letters, but you must not believe that they consist of nothing but grave indiscretions. Considering the very close nature of our relationship, these letters naturally deal with anything and everything, factual as well as personal matters. The factual matters concern all the hunches and false paths connected with the birth of analysis, and in this way are also quite personal . . . For these reasons I would be happy to know that this material is in your hands . . .

I accept with thanks your offer to come to Vienna in March, even if only for a few days.

Cordially yours,
Freud

Bonaparte quickly told Freud that the letters were safe (January 12):

I want to reassure you right away about the Fliess letters. They are, though still in Germany, no longer in the hands of "the witch" [Ida Fliess], but already belong to Mr. Stahl, who acquired them from her along with the entire library. They are in his possession, and a friend of his will bring them here.

And on February 10 she wrote again:

Today the letters are to be delivered to me. A woman took them with her to London; they are now in Paris, and I will get them this evening.

In Bonaparte's notebook, which I found in Freud's desk at Maresfield Gardens, London,[7] she wrote:

Freud, when I wrote to him from Paris that Ida Fliess had sold his letters and that I acquired them from Reinhold Stahl, was very moved. He judged this act to be highly inimical on the part of Fliess's widow. He was happy to know that at least the letters were in my hands, and not sent off to someplace in America where they would no doubt have been published immediately . . . Ida Fliess was determined that the letters not reach the hands of Freud . . . I wrote Freud asking for permission to read the letters. At first he wrote saying he would prefer that I not read them. But when later, at the end of February or the beginning of March 1937, I saw him in Vienna and he told me he wanted the letters to be burned, I refused. I asked to read them to be able to judge their content, and Freud agreed. One day he told me: "I hope to convince you to destroy them." Martin and Anna [two of Freud's children] believe, as I do, that the letters should be preserved and later published. Freud was . . . interested in the letter of Thumsee [an Alpine lakeside resort], which I had shown him earlier, and said it was a very important letter [it is dated August 7, 1901]. I will show him still other selected

7. The notebook in Marie Bonaparte's handwriting (dated November 24, 1937) lists the letters to Fliess and gives a brief summary in French (generally not more than a paragraph or two) of the content of each. At the end of the notebook are several pages reporting Bonaparte's conversations with Freud about Fliess.

> letters.[8] He pointed out to me that there were letters missing: all those concerning the break with Fliess . . . and one about a dream relating to Martha Freud. Moreover, four envelopes are empty.[9]

The last portion of this passage is particularly significant: most of the letters relating to the break with Fliess (undoubtedly part of the Stahl packet) were, in fact, eventually sent to the Library of Congress. A few found their way to Maresfield Gardens; presumably Freud kept them when he left Vienna. All are reproduced in full in this volume. The letter concerning a dream about Martha is something of a mystery and has never been found. It is probably the letter that describes the "lost dream," the dream that Fliess persuaded Freud to remove from the *Interpretation of Dreams* and that is often referred to in the subsequent letters. How did Freud know this letter was missing? Did he look at all the letters that Marie Bonaparte purchased? Or had he long before asked Fliess to return the letter, or even to destroy it? There is still a faint hope that the letter will one day be found. It would no doubt be the most important letter of the collection, since it contains the only dream Freud ever analyzed completely.

The extraordinary saga of the letters is continued by Ernest Jones at the beginning of his chapter "The Fliess Period":

> Fortunately she [Marie Bonaparte] had the courage to defy her analyst and teacher, and deposited them in the Rothschild Bank in Vienna during the winter of 1937–1938 with the intention of studying them further on her return the next summer.
>
> When Hitler invaded Austria in March there was the danger of a Jewish bank being rifled, and Mme Bonaparte went at once to Vienna, where, being a Princess of Greece and of Denmark, she was permitted to withdraw the contents of her safe-deposit box in the presence of the Gestapo; they would assuredly have destroyed the correspondence had they detected it . . . When

8. Bonaparte has two sheets titled "List of Letters to Show Freud or Anna Freud in Vienna, Autumn 1937." It is not clear which of the letters Freud actually saw. Marie Bonaparte writes: "Freud saw only those marked in ———, and Anna those in blue." The word that is illegible is probably "red," since some of the letters are annotated with a red line and others with a blue cross.

9. On a separate sheet of paper found in Freud's desk, Bonaparte gives the list of empty envelopes as follows (dated from the postmarks):
August 2, 1896 (from Aussee)
February 12, 1898 (a large envelope)
July 17, 1899 (from Vienna)
December 24, 1899 (from Vienna)

Liste des lettres à montrer
à Freud ou à Anna Freud
à Vienne, en automne 1937
(Freud n'a vu que celles marquées en rouge
et Anna en bleu — ) Vola beaucoup aux
Decouverte de fraude Loco blues

| 1895 | 20 Octobre 1895 | (Anna- Wilhelm?) |
| | 31 Octobre 1895 | (Anna- Wilhelm?) + |
| | 9 Décembre 1895 | (Vasvame d'Anna) + |

| 1896 | 15 Juillet 1896 | (-Maladie du père de Freud) |
| | 26 Octobre 1896 | (Mort du père de Freud) |
| | 2 Novembre 1896 | (Réaction à la mort du père |
| | | Rêve du cercueil mort) |

| 1897 | 21 Septembre 1897 | (Messages de Lez temps passé à ...) |
| | 3 Octobre 1897 | (Auto analyse de Freud, ... ) |
| | 15 Octobre 1897 | (Suite de l'auto analyse! La ... ) |
| | 31 Octobre 1897 | (Rêve aux faux d'Anna + |
| | 14·15 Novembre 1897 | (Rêve de la Théorie sexuelle, |
| | | c'est à dire des jeux cruels) |
| | 3 Décembre 1897 | (Rêve de Rome et de Naples |
| | | ... au dehors! flammes de la |
| | | fers de ... ) |

| 1898 | 9 février 1898 | (Auto analyse - Allemand ... ) |
| | 9 Juin 1898 | (Rêve ... al ... de Theis ) |
| | 20 Août 1898 | (Récit enchanté du ... à la ... ) |
| | 26 Août 1898 | (Freud la félicité d'avoir ... Theis ...) |
| | 31 Août 1898 | (Neudettelsa ) |

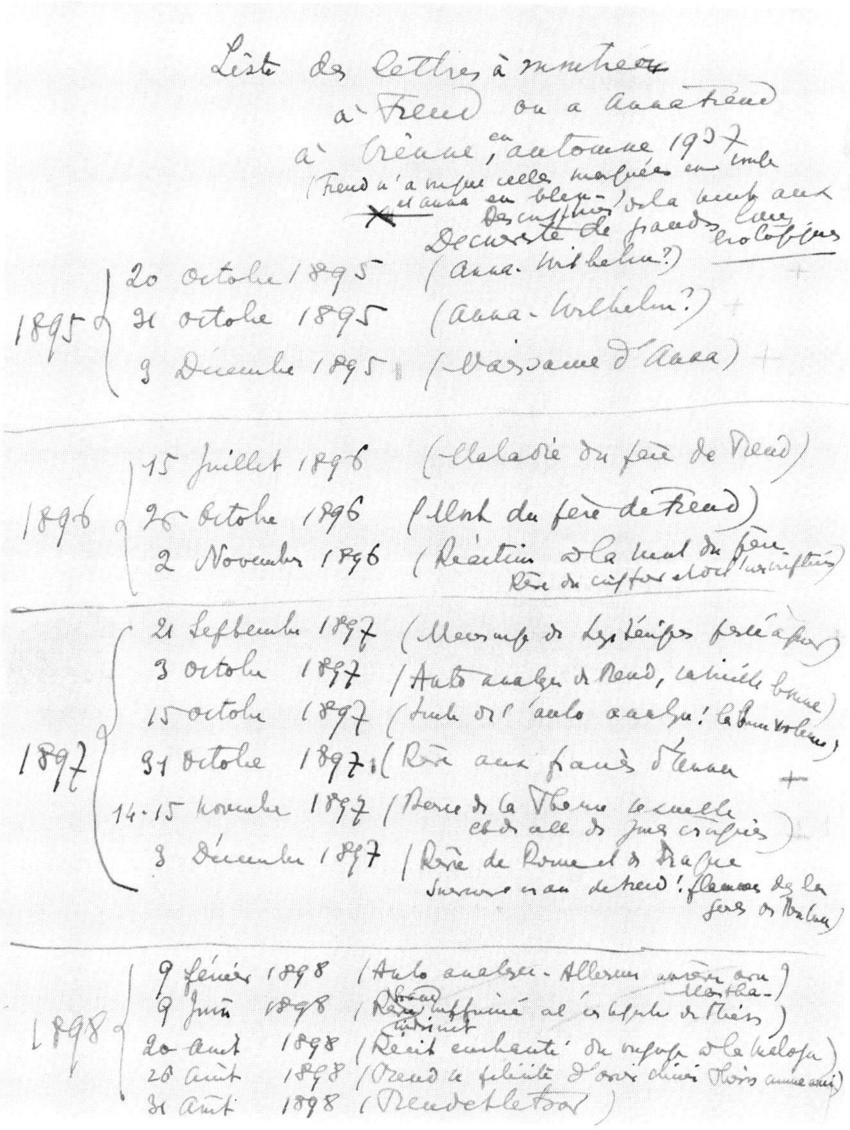

Marie Bonaparte's list of the letters that she intended to show to
Sigmund or Anna Freud. She later annotated the list to indicate which
letters they had actually seen.

1899
- 28 mai 1899 (Freud se décide à publier le livre des Rêves)
- 1 Août 1899 (Premier effet du livre des Rêves sur Fliess)
- 9 novembre 1899 (Fliess se tait après l'envoi du livre des Rêves, 12 jours auparavant)

1900
- 26 Janvier 1900 (Silence persistant de Fliess)
- 1 février 1900 (Silence prolongé de Fliess)
- 11 mars 1900 (Remplacement de la tête de Fliess, après 1 mois de silence) enfants, fièvre
- 23 mars 1900 (Fliess ne peut plus aider Freud...)
- 7 mai 1900 (Freud refuse la splendide isolation préconisée par Fliess)
- 12 juin 1900 (La maison de Freud et la plaque en marbre sur le Rêve)

1901
- 1 Janvier 1901 (N'écris pas si tu n'en éprouves pas le besoin!)
- 7 août 1901 (de l'humanité) (Freud sent que Fliess lui a échappé) n'a pas réussi à collaborer avec Fliess
- 19 Septembre 1901 (Fliess dépeint le psychologue)

24-27 novembre - 1er Décembre 1918 : Lettres de Freud, et de Fliess sur Freud.

5 Juillet 1895 : une lettre de Breuer où il compare Freud à un faucon.

+ +

> she had to leave Paris for Greece, which was about to be invaded, in February 1941, she deposited the precious documents with the Danish Legation in Paris. It was not the safest place, but . . . Paris, together with the Danish Legation, was spared. After surviving all those perils, they braved the fifth and final one of the mines in the English Channel and so reached London in safety; they had been wrapped in waterproof and buoyant material to give them a chance of survival in the event of disaster to the ship.[10]

In the late 1940s Marie Bonaparte gave the original letters to Anna Freud, who had them transcribed and put them at Ernest Jones's disposal during the time he was writing his comprehensive biography of Freud. In 1980 Anna Freud donated the letters to the Library of Congress, where they remain restricted from public view.

The public learned of the letters and the intense friendship of the two men when a German edition of the letters from Freud to Fliess was published in 1950, entitled *Sigmund Freud, Aus den Anfängen der Psychoanalyse. Briefe an Wilhelm Fliess, Abhandlungen und Notizen aus den Jahren 1887–1902.*[11] The editors were Marie Bonaparte (Paris), Anna Freud (London), and Ernst Kris (New York). The book had an excellent and extensive introduction by Kris, an analyst and close friend of Anna Freud, who was related by marriage to both the Fliess and the Rie families.[12] An English translation of the book was published in 1954 as *The Origins of Psycho-Analysis: Letters to Wilhelm Fliess, Drafts and Notes, 1887–1902, by Sigmund Freud.*

In both the German and English editions, only 168 of the 284 letters available to the editors were published. Moreover, passages were deleted in some letters, often with no indication of the omission. The editors explained their choices thus at the beginning of the Editors' Note: "The selection was made on the principle of making public everything relating to the writer's scientific work and scientific interests and everything bearing on the social and political conditions in which psycho-analysis originated; and of omitting or

10. Jones, *Life* 1:316.

11. Actually, there was a reference to the friendship in a paper entitled "The Significance of Freud's Earliest Discoveries" read by Ernst Kris to the sixteenth International Psycho-Analytic Congress in Zurich, August 1949. The paper was published the following year in the *International Journal of Psycho-Analysis.*

12. Oscar Rie, mentioned frequently in these letters, was the Freud children's pediatrician. His wife was Ida Fliess's sister, and his daughter Marianne married Ernst Kris.

abbreviating everything publication of which would be inconsistent with professional or personal confidence."

In this new edition *all* letters—including those located in the Jewish National and University Library in Jerusalem, at Maresfield Gardens, and in Robert Fliess's private collection—are presented, 133 of them for the very first time, and there are no deletions of any kind in the texts.[13] Only the names of patients not previously identified have been disguised with initials (under the system that Freud himself devised). And the 1895 "Project for a Scientific Psychology," Freud's construction of a theory of the mind, has been omitted because it would be difficult to improve on James Strachey's translation, published and still available in his *Standard Edition of the Complete Psychological Works of Sigmund Freud.*

This edition of the Freud-Fliess letters can be profitably read along with several other landmark works. The most important is the first edition of the letters, here called *Origins.* Ernst Kris's introduction to that volume was a milestone in the history of psychoanalysis and is still unmatched today. James Strachey included some excerpts from the Fliess papers in the first volume of *S.E.* and provided a new and improved translation and excellent notes. Strachey is particularly helpful in pointing out later parallels in Freud's published writings, and the reader is invited to consult his volumes. Max Schur, Freud's personal physician and later a well-known psychoanalyst, translated a number of previously unpublished letters to Fliess both in his article "Some Additional 'Day Residues'" and in his book *Freud: Living and Dying.* His interpretation of Freud's relation to Fliess strikes me as the most balanced of the many available. Ernest Jones, in the course of his monumental life of Freud, gives the background to many of the events mentioned in the letters.

In spite of the fact that Freud's life was remarkably devoid of external drama, more has been written about him than about any other thinker of our time, probably because he did so much to alter the contours of the intellectual and emotional age in which we all live. Much of the discussion has focused on Freud's inner life, although virtually everything we know about that life was revealed to us by Freud himself in his published writings. Research on Freud in-

13. The Appendix to this volume indicates which of Freud's letters to Fliess appeared in full in *Anfänge* and in *Origins,* which were given there in excised form, and which are presented for the first time in this edition.

creased enormously with publication of the incomplete edition of his letters to Fliess, because nowhere else did Freud write with such candor, directness, and depth about his innermost thoughts. Now, at long last — nearly a hundred years after they were written — we have a definitive edition of the complete letters. They stand as one of the high points of intellectual achievement and insight of our time.

# Beginnings of the Friendship

Vienna, November 24, 1887
I., Maria Theresienstrasse 8

Esteemed friend and colleague:

My letter of today admittedly is occasioned by business; but I must introduce it by confessing that I entertain hopes of continuing the relationship with you and that you have left a deep impression on me which could easily lead me to tell you outright in what category of men I place you.

Since your departure Mrs. A. has consulted me and caused me some agonizing in coming to a decision. I have finally arrived at the conclusion that her case is not a neurosis; not so much because of the foot clonus+ –(which at present is not in evidence) as because I do not find in her what I consider to be the most important characteristics of neurasthenia (other neuroses really cannot be involved). In the distinction, often so difficult to make, between incipient organic and neurasthenic affections I have been guided by one particular characteristic: in neurasthenia the hypochondriacal alteration, the anxiety psychosis, is never missing and, whether denied or admitted, betrays itself by a profusion of newly emerging sensations, that is, by paresthesias. Our case is almost devoid of such symptoms. She suddenly could not walk, but apart from heaviness in the legs complains of no other sensations — there is none of the pulling and pressing in the muscles, the manifold pains, the corresponding sensations in other parts of the body, and the like. You know what I mean. The so-called dizziness, which began years ago, turns out to have been a kind of fainting spell and not a true *vertige;*[1] that, too, I cannot connect with the neurasthenic swaying when she walks.

On the other hand, as far as the other side of the diagnosis is concerned—that is, the one opposed to organic illness—the following occurred to me. Seventeen years ago the woman had a post-diphtheritic paralysis of the legs. Such an infection of the spinal cord may, in spite of apparently having been cured, leave a residual weak spot in the central nervous system, a starting point for very slowly developing systemic illnesses. I have in mind something similar to the relation between tabes and syphilis. You know, of course, that Marie[2] in Paris attributes multiple sclerosis to preceding acute infections. Mrs. A. was to all appearances in a slowly declining nutritional state, which is the lot of our city women after several pregnancies. In such circumstances the *punctum minimae resistentiae* in the spinal cord began to revolt.

She is in fact doing quite well, better than at any time since the beginning of her illness. This is the result of your diet prescription; there is little left for me to do. I have started galvanic treatment of the back.

Now to other matters. My little one is flourishing; my wife is slowly getting better. I am occupied with writing three papers at the same time, one of which is on the anatomy of the brain.[3] The publisher is willing to bring it out next fall.

With cordial greetings,

Your
Dr. Sigm. Freud

1. Freud uses the French term.

2. Ernst Kris (*Origins*, p. 52n1) says that Freud was acquainted with Pierre Marie's views on the infectious etiology of disseminated sclerosis.

3. The manuscript Freud is referring to has recently come to light. The late Elenore Fliess, Wilhelm Fliess's daughter-in-law, discovered it among her husband's papers and kindly sent it to me. Freud entitled the manuscript "Kritische Einleitung in die Nervenpathologie." It is a purely neurological paper, with no foreshadowing of Freud's psychological interests.

---

Vienna, December 28, 1887

Esteemed friend and colleague:

Your cordial letter and your magnificent gift awakened the most pleasant memories for me, and the sentiment I discern behind both Christmas presents fills me with the expectation of a lively and mutually gratifying relationship between us in the future. I still do not know how I won you; the bit of speculative anatomy of the brain cannot have impressed your rigorous judgment for long. But I am very happy about it. So far I have always had the good fortune of

Sigmund Freud and his fiancée, Martha Bernays.
Taken during a visit to Martha in 1885 as Freud was
en route to Paris. The two were married on September 16
of the following year.

Mathilde, the Freuds' first child, born 1887;
here at age five months.

finding my friends among the best of men, and I have always been particularly proud of this good fortune. So I thank you and ask you not to be surprised if at the moment I have nothing to offer in return for your charming present.

I occasionally hear about you—mostly wonderful things, of course. One of my sources is Mrs. A., who incidentally has turned out to be a case of ordinary cerebral neurasthenia. During the past weeks I have thrown myself into hypnosis and have achieved all sorts of small but noteworthy successes. I also intend to translate Bernheim's book on suggestion.[1] Do not advise me against it; I am already bound by a contract.[2] For recreation I am working simultaneously on two papers, "Brain Anatomy" and "General Characteristics of Hysterical Affections,"[3] to the extent that changing moods and work permit.

My little one is developing splendidly and sleeps through each night, which makes every father proud.

My best wishes; do not let yourself be overwhelmed by work, and when you have some leisure and a reason, think of

Your faithfully devoted
Dr. Sigm. Freud

My wife was delighted with your greetings.

1. Freud translated from the French two books by Hippolyte Bernheim. The first of these, referred to here, is *De la suggestion et de ses applications à la thérapeutique.* Freud's translation appeared in 1888 as *Die Suggestion und ihre Heilwirkung.* The second Bernheim work that Freud translated is *Hypnotisme, suggestion, psychothérapie: Études nouvelles,* with a preface by Bernheim dated Nancy, August 20, 1890. The book was published in German as *Neue Studien über Hypnotismus, Suggestion und Psychotherapie* and does not contain an introduction or notes by Freud.

Referring to the first volume, James Strachey (*S.E.* 1:74) claims that the only footnote "that calls for notice is quoted on pp. 84–85." But this is not so. There is an important footnote signed by Freud (on p. 121 of his translation). Commenting on Bernheim's phrase, "In short, the brain of the newborn is uncompleted anatomically as well as physiologically," Freud writes: "This section contains some statements which are not on the level of present-day science, although correcting them does not interfere with the author's reasoning. Numerous experiments, most recently by Exner and Paneth, prove that the cerebral cortex responds to stimulation even in the newborn animal. Whoever believes that the brain of the newborn 'barely contains a few rudimentary neural tubes' underestimates the structure of this organ to an extraordinary extent."

2. Beyond what Freud tells us in his "Autobiographical Study" (*S.E.* 20:18) and what Ernest Jones reports (*Life* 1:260), not much is known about Freud's studies in Nancy. Some new information is contained in unpublished letters that Freud wrote to his sister-in-law, Minna Bernays, during his stay there. The following excerpt from a letter dated July 28, 1889, is pertinent: "I confess that the thought of staying here until next Saturday . . . makes me sick. True, I spend my mornings very pleas-

antly, since, when I don't sleep through them, I allow myself to be influenced by the miracle of suggestion; but the afternoons are boring." Later in the letter Freud complains of his loneliness in Nancy and ends by saying, "Traveling is very nice, but a person should not be alone—he should have *undici* [eleven] or *dodici* [twelve] people with him, if only it did not cost so much."

3. On the grounds that the second article has a section entitled "General Characteristics," the term Freud uses here, Vogel (1953, p. 484) feels that this is a reference to the article on hysteria, entitled "Hysterie," that Freud wrote for Albert Villaret. Kris, on the other hand, claims that this paper was not published. See also note 2 to letter of May 28, 1888.

Vienna, February 4, 1888

Esteemed friend and colleague:

Would you kindly predate the receipt of this letter; I should have written it long ago, but did not get to it what with work, fatigue, and playing with my daughter. First, I should give you some news about Mrs. A., whose sister is with you at present. The case turned out to be quite simple, an ordinary cerebral neurasthenia, which the sages call chronic cranial hyperemia. This was becoming clearer and clearer, and there was steady improvement with galvanization and *demi-bain* [hydrotherapy] treatment; I thought I could cure her completely with muscular exercises—but then somcthing unexpected happened: she missed her period, became worse soon thereafter; at the time of her next period she missed treatment. Her condition, though presently not very good, allows a great deal of hope. For my part I would have liked to continue the treatment, but do not feel sufficiently certain of its success to take a stand in the face of the anxiety of the woman and her entire family, and against Chrobak's[1] opinion; so I have associated myself with the prophesy that all will be well by the fourth month quite on its own and I am keeping secret my strong doubts about this. Have you had any experience with the influence of pregnancy on such neurasthenias?

It may be that I am in part responsible for this new citizen. I once spoke very strongly and not unintentionally in the patient's presence about the harmfulness of coitus reservatus. Perhaps I am mistaken in the matter.

Of other things, esteemed friend, there is not much. My little Mathilde is thriving and gives us much pleasure and fun. My practice, which, as you know, is not very considerable, has recently increased somewhat by virtue of Charcot's[2] name. The carriage is expensive, and visiting and talking people into or out of things—which is what my occupation consists in—robs me of the best time for work. The brain anatomy is where it was, but the hysteria is progressing and the first draft is finished.

Honorable Christendom is very indecent.[3] Yesterday there was a major scandal in the medical society. They wanted to force us to subscribe to a new weekly journal, which is intended to represent the purified, exact, and Christian views of a few Hofräte [high civil servants] who have long ago forgotten what work is like. Of course, they are succeeding; I feel very much like resigning.

I must hurry off to an entirely superfluous consultation with Meynert.[4] Take care of yourself, and some Sunday write me a few words about yourself.

Your faithfully devoted
Dr. Sigm. Freud

1. Rudolf Chrobak (1843–1910), professor of gynecology at the University of Vienna. In his 1914 essay "On the History of the Psycho-Analytic Movement" (*S.E.* 14:14–15) Freud says that Chrobak sent him a woman patient "to whom he could not give enough time, owing to his new appointment as a university teacher." After eighteen years of marriage the woman was a virgin, her husband being impotent, and Freud remembers Chrobak's taking the man aside and saying: "The sole prescription for such a malady is familiar enough to us, but we cannot order it. It runs:

'Rx Penis normalis
dosim
repetatur'"

According to Jones (*Life* 1:249), this incident is referred to in a letter of May 1886 to Martha. But the letter of May 13, 1886, published in *Letters*, is not about this patient, but about the wife of an American physician whom Freud sent to Chrobak. In an unpublished letter of two days later, Freud tells Martha that the woman, whom he had earlier described as "beautiful and interesting," is to undergo an operation by Chrobak: "The American has already begun his treatment. His wife will be operated on by Chrobak." And in another unpublished letter of May 23, Freud writes to Martha: "My other female patient is in the same sanatorium. She was operated on yesterday."

What we do not know is whether Chrobak operated on this woman because of her presumed hysteria. Nor can we be certain that the patient Freud refers to in his 1914 essay is the same one he is referring to in these letters to Martha. The date of the incident is therefore still a puzzle. Chrobak was made Privatdozent in 1870 and Extraordinarius in 1879, so presumably the incident belongs to the 1880s.

2. Jean Martin Charcot was a renowned French neurologist. Kris (*Origins*, p. 55n1) takes this mention as a reference to Freud's translation of Charcot's *Leçons sur les maladies du système nerveux (Neue Vorlesungen über die Krankheiten des Nervensystems insbesondere über Hysterie)*, which was published in 1886. The French appeared in the following year. See Freud's letter to Martha of December 12, 1885 (*Letters*, no. 88), and his remarks in the "Autobiographical Study" (*S.E.*. 20:12). Freud sent a copy of this book to Breuer, with the dedication: "To my friend Josef Breuer, whom I esteem beyond all other men, the secret master of hysteria and other complicated problems, in quiet dedication from the translator."

In the Freud house in Maresfield Gardens, London, were seven unpublished letters from Charcot to Freud (written between 1888 and 1892). On January 23, 1888,

Charcot writes: "Don't worry, hysteria is making its way and one day it will come to occupy, gloriously and in the full light of day, the important place that is its due." On February 17, 1889: "I have not yet received the Bernheim translation you told me about. One begins to see that there were a lot of exaggerations in the promises of this professor, and in Paris one speaks more of the dangers of hypnotism than of its advantages. Nevertheless, from all this something will remain." On June 30, 1892: "By the way, I am delighted with the notes and criticism which I found at the bottom of the pages of my *Leçons*. It is perfect: long live liberty, as we say here in France."

Evidently Freud sent Cäcilie M., one of the patients mentioned in the *Studies on Hysteria* (*S.E.* 2), to Charcot and on October (?) 26, 1888, Charcot writes to Freud: "The delicate and complete analysis that you made of the physiopsychical phenomena, which are so varied and so complex, sufficiently shows that you have attached yourself to this interesting person just as we attached ourselves during her stay in Paris . . . But I repeat what I said, it is rather psychically that one must act, as you well understood, and it is in this way that one can be useful in this case. I must tell you, furthermore, that the Mrs. X. of today is, in every respect, far superior to what she was before. She is, in fact, and she acknowledges it herself, to a certain extent prepared for the struggle of life, which she was not formerly."

Might this not be the origin of Freud's later famous dictum (for which no source can actually be found) that the goal of analysis is to be able to work and love? What these letters show, and what we did not know before, is the extent of Charcot's receptiveness to Freud's newly emerging ideas. Charcot died in 1893, so it is impossible to know how he would have reacted to the 1895 *Studies on Hysteria*. Would he have recognized it and hailed it as the great successor to his own work? Freud's letters to Charcot have not, as far as I know, survived. In light of these letters, it is curious that Freud writes in the *Psychopathology of Everyday Life* (*S.E.* 6:161), about his translation of Charcot, that "it brings to light an even earlier occasion involving a translation from the French, in which I really did infringe the rights of property that apply to publications. I added notes to the text which I translated, without asking the author's permission, and some years later I had reason to suspect that the author was displeased with my arbitrary action."

3. The incident Freud describes here is given in Sablik (1968). The journal in question was the *Wiener klinische Wochenschrift*. Sablik, however, does not deal with the "Christian" attitude of this new medical journal and how it manifested itself. The first issue appeared on April 5, 1888, and there was nothing obviously Christian about it. Heinrich von Bamberger, the senior editor, was Jewish, as were several other members of the editorial board, including Freud's friend Ernst Fleischl von Marxow (see note 2 to letter of May 6, 1894). The initial editorial speaks, rather ominously, of the "fatherland" and the "honor of the Vienna school." The vote on the subscriptions was 93 to 29 in favor, with Freud evidently among those who rejected the proposal. Curiously, in 1931 Freud was elected an honorary member of the very same society. It seems he never did resign.

4. Freud refers to the Meynert incident in his "Autobiographical Study." His presentation of a case of male hysteria to the Viennese Physicians' Society on October 15, 1886, led to his poor relations with Theodor Meynert (the Viennese psychiatrist) and has been explained in detail by Bernfeld and Bernfeld (1952). See also Dora Meynert (1930), Bernfeld (1951), Lebzeltern (1973), and, for a different point of view, Ellenberger (1970).

In a little-known article never published but reported in the *Internationale klinische Rundschau*, 6 (1892):814–818, 854–856, about lectures on hypnosis and suggestion held April 27 and May 4 in the Wiener medizinischer Klub, Freud writes: "The objection that hypnotic-suggestive therapy is a purely symptomatic treatment is once again perfectly correct, but this would apply to the vast majority of our treatment methods; we have only a very few causal therapies, and in general find ourselves completely satisfied with symptomatic methods [that is, therapy which seeks the relief of symptoms] and the patient does not demand anything other than this from us" (p. 855). Freud was on the verge of creating the first causal therapy in history, though it is not likely that in 1892 he knew it. However, this is probably the year in which he first began using the method of free association.

Unfortunately no other reports of Freud's paper have come down to us. So a tantalizing sentence at the end cannot be further elucidated. Freud is reported to have said, "In hysteria, there is however a case in which hypnosis enables us [to carry out] a real causal treatment, but the speaker does not wish to speak further of it at this time." Could this be a reference to the patient Freud sent to Charcot, who played such a critical role in *Studies on Hysteria* and Freud's developing ideas on the method of psychoanalysis?

---

Vienna, May 28, 1888
I., Maria Theresienstrasse 8

Dear friend and colleague:

I have a small reason for writing to you, though I could have done so long ago without a reason. First of all, then, about this reason: Mrs. A., who since her unmasking as a case of chronic cerebral neurasthenia (if you too want to call it that) and since her miscarriage and the rest has made a splendid recovery with a minimum of treatment and is now very well, sees the summer approaching. Her old preferences attract her to Franzensbad; I recommend a hydropathic cure in the mountains. So she has asked me to refer the matter to you for decision, which I am herewith doing, with all sympathy for you. I had thought of Lake Lucerne, Axenstein, and a number of others. If you agree, send me a card *by return mail* on which you have jotted down the name of one place, and rest assured that this will be the place where Mrs. A. will spend the summer. But please spare me from having to make the decision; this would in no way satisfy her, for the power over the spirits[1] that belongs to you cannot be transferred. Please reply immediately since my promise to write to you is ten days older than this letter.

I have at this moment a lady in hypnosis lying in front of me and therefore can go on writing in peace. We are living rather happily in steadily growing modesty. When our little Mathilde laughs, we imagine that hearing her laugh is the most beautiful thing that could happen to us, and in other respects we are not ambitious and not very industrious. My practice increased somewhat during the winter and spring, is now decreasing again, and barely keeps us alive. Time and leisure for work have been spent on several articles for Villaret,[2] portions of the translation of Bernheim's *Suggestion*, and similar things, not worthy of note. Wait! The first draft of "Hysterical Paralysis"[3] also is finished; uncertain when the second will be. In short, one manages; and life is generally known to be very difficult and very complicated and, as we say in Vienna, there are many roads to the Central Cemetery.

I look upon your efforts, so close to the heroic, without envy but with truly empathic satisfaction. Just keep at it, and take the next step in the organization of your work, that is, finding assistants.— The time for the hypnosis is up.

I greet you cordially.

In all haste, your
Dr. Freud

1. Probably a reference to Goethe's ballad *Der Zauberlehrling* (or possibly to *Faust*), in which only the master of sorcery has the power to call the spirits to his service.

2. The articles in Villaret's *Handwörterbuch der gesammten Medizin* are unsigned, so one cannot be certain which articles are by Freud. Vogel (1953) argues convincingly that the article on "Hysterie" is definitely by Freud. Kris (*Origins*, p. 56n2) writes, "The articles on hysteria and paralysis in children, and perhaps also that on paralyses, can also be claimed for him because of their style and content." Vogel further believes that the article entitled "Hysteroepilepsie" (translated in *S.E.* 1:58–59) is by Freud. He does not believe that the article on "Kinderlähmung" is Freud's, on the grounds that Freud had been concerned, in his neurological publications of this period, with cerebral paralysis, whereas the Villaret article is concerned with spinal paralysis. This argument is not very convincing, especially if one takes into account a lecture by Freud entitled "Über hysterische Lähmungen" given on May 24, 1893, and reported in the *Neurologisches Centralblatt*, 12 (1893):709, where Freud speaks of this distinction. On the other hand, Vogel does believe that the "Lähmung" article is by Freud, because of its similarity to Freud's 1893 French article, "Quelques considérations . . . (see next note).

3. Freud's article, "Quelques considérations pour une étude comparative des paralysies motrices organiques et hystériques," was published by Charcot in his *Archives de neurologie* in 1893, although parts of it were written as early as 1886. It was reprinted in *G.W.*, then translated in *S.E.* as "Some Points for a Comparative Study of Organic and Hysterical Motor Paralyses." Jones (*Life* 1:255–257) tells the story of this paper. When Jones's volume appeared, W. H. Auden wrote him a letter (from the Jones Archives in the Library of the Institute of Psycho-Analysis in London) on November 4, 1953: "You give a wonderful example of his 'historical' insight when you tell how he pointed out to Charcot that the regions affected in hysterias correspond, not to anatomy, but to popular ideas of anatomy. And how typical of the time that Charcot wasn't interested."

Freud's paper was reviewed in 1896 in the *Annales médicopsychologiques* by L. Camuset, who wrote, "In hysterical paralyses, there is no anatomy." In effect, in his original article Freud stated, "In his paralyses and other manifestations, the hysteric acts as if anatomy did not exist, or as if the hysteric had no awareness of anatomy." This was perhaps the first genuine psychological insight into hysteria.

Did Charcot see the article? He died on August 16, 1893. The paper appeared in July. An undated letter from Charcot to Freud (in Maresfield Gardens) reads: "I have just received your comparative study of hysterical and organic paralyses. I have glanced at it and I can see that it must be very interesting. It will be published in the *Archives de neurologie*. I will take care of it as soon as I return." I visited Charcot's library in Paris and found his copy of the pertinent issue of the *Archives*. There, next to the lines I have quoted from Freud, were the only marks in the volume: two heavy markings in the margin. So Charcot did see the article; it was his final glimpse into the psychology of the future, which he had helped to prepare but would not live to see developed.

An unpublished letter to Freud's bride, Martha (February 25, 1886), from Paris warrants quoting: "On Tuesday I had the opportunity to hand over the letter [containing a proposal to write an article] to Charcot, as I already wrote you, but I felt somewhat unwell on Wednesday and did not go to the Salpêtrière [Hospital]. Today he told me to my great joy that it was not so bad, even though he could not accept it [the idea]; he did not want to contradict [me] and thought it important that these matters be spelled out. I should keep at it until it adds up to about 20 printed pages, then send it to him; he wants to publish it in the *Archives de neurologie*. Naturally I am more than merely gratified. I just saw him again and once more he spontaneously brought up the matter, which had clearly pleased him. Altogether he was very charming and gave me the final instructions for the translation. I handed him a photograph of him that I had bought to be autographed. He signed it and gave me another one as a gift. I shall bring you both. Finally he asked if I needed recommendations for Berlin and wrote me two cards, which will probably help me a great deal. I am very pleased with the outcome of our discussions and feel I have not made a bad impression on him."

---

Vienna, August 29, 1888

Esteemed friend:

I have been silent for a long time, but at last my reply turns out to be very impressive: a book, a paper, and a photograph; you cannot expect anything more to accompany a letter. Your own letter contained much that stimulated my thoughts for a long time and that I would have liked to discuss with you. Without reservation I say you are right, yet I cannot do what you request. To go into general practice instead of specializing, to work with all possible means of investigation, and completely to take charge of the patient — that is certainly the only method which promises personal satisfaction and material success; but for me it is too late for that. I have not learned enough to be a medical practitioner, and in my medical development there is a flaw which later on was laboriously mended. I was able to learn just about enough to become a neuropathologist. And now I lack, not youth, it is true, but time and independence to make up for it. Last winter I was quite busy, and that gave me just enough to live on with my very large family and left no time to learn something. The summer was rather bad, left me with sufficient time, but also brought worries that robbed me of my good mood. Moreover, the habit of research, to which I have sacrificed a good deal, my dissatisfaction with what the student is offered, the need to go into detail and exercise critical judgment interfere with my studying. The whole atmosphere of Vienna is such that it does little to steel one's will or to foster that confidence of success which is characteristic of you Berliners and without which a mature man cannot think of changing the basis of his existence. So it seems I must remain what I am; but I have no illusions about the inadequacy of this state of affairs.

The photograph among the enclosures is justified by my recalling a wish you expressed in Vienna and which at that time I could not fulfill. With regard to the *Suggestion* book, you know the story. I undertook the work very reluctantly, and only to have a hand in a matter that surely will deeply influence the practice of nerve specialists in the next years. I do not share Bernheim's views, which seem to me one-sided, and have tried to defend Charcot's point of view[1] in the preface — I do not know how skillfully, but I do know for sure, unsuccessfully. The suggestive (that is, Bernheim's iatrosuggestive theory) acts like a commonplace[2] charm on German physicians who need make no great leap to get from the simulation theory where they stand now to the suggestion theory. In criticizing Meynert,[3] who in his customary impudent-malicious manner spoke out authoritatively on a topic of which he knows nothing, I had to restrain myself because the attitude of all my friends demanded it. Even so, what I have written seems to them daring. I have belled the cat.

At last I am getting near the end of the "hysterical and organic paralyses," which rather pleases me. My part in the Villaret has become less extensive than was to be expected. The paper on brain anatomy has been severely cut; several other bad articles on neurology are not mine! The scientific value of the whole [volume] is not very great.

The "Anatomy of the Brain" is still germinating, as it was at the time you gave me new ideas. That is the extent of my scientific activities. Otherwise things are going well. Since the beginning of July wife and child have been in Maria Schutz on the Semmering, where I too plan to spend a week now. The little one is thriving splendidly.

I was delighted to hear that you have an assistant. Very likely this letter will not find you in Berlin either. Do not work too hard—I would like to remind you of that every day. Take care and think in friendship of

Your sincerely devoted
Dr. Sigm. Freud

1. This letter was written before Freud, along with a patient, went to Nancy to see Bernheim in the summer of 1889. Unfortunately we have very little information about this important visit. Presumably it paved the way for a change of view from the one reported here. Freud is referring to the ideas he writes about in his preface to Bernheim's *De la suggestion* (*S.E.* 1:73), where, it is true, in comparing the school of Paris (Charcot) with that of Nancy (Bernheim and Ambroise Liébeault) he favors Paris.

Freud mentions the visit to Nancy in some detail in the "Autobiographical Study" (*S.E.* 20:17) and more briefly in *Introductory Lectures* (*S.E.* 15:103) and "Some Elementary Lessons in Psycho-Analysis" (*S.E.* 23:285). Strachey's introduction (*S.E.* 1:63–69) to the papers on "Hypnotism" and "Suggestion" is useful.

I have found a previously unnoticed source in *Neue freie Presse,* 6 (1904):10. Th. Thomas, writing on "Magnetische Menschen," makes the following observation: "Professor Freud says: 'Mankind has always harbored the longing to be able to open all secrets with a single key. Such a "key-word" has always been magnetism. It was and remains a word of great suggestive meaning. And it is also understandable that the mysterious power of the magnet, which has distant effects, should also have an effect on our fantasies. A factual effect of the magnet on man, or of man on the magnet, is of course out of the question.'" Since such views are not found in Freud's published writings, I assume that Thomas interviewed Freud.

Freud's statement about this visit to Nancy (*S.E.* 20:17) is significant: "With the idea of perfecting my hypnotic technique, I made a journey to Nancy in the summer of 1889 and spent several weeks there. I witnessed the moving spectacle of old Liébeault working among the poor women and children of the labouring classes. I was a spectator of Bernheim's astonishing experiments upon his hospital patients, and I received the profoundest impression of the possibility that there could be powerful mental processes which nevertheless remained hidden from the consciousness of men." Gregory Zilboorg (1967, p. 369) quotes Bernheim as writing, "In truth, we are potentially or actually hallucinating people during the greater part of our lives."

Bernheim, in fact, sought to show that hysteria and hypnosis were not indissolubly connected, and that the phenomena hypnosis reveals about the mind are valid beyond hysterics, something that Freud later acknowledged to be true and for which he provided the theoretical understanding that was missing in Bernheim's work. Charcot did not believe this, but he did believe that some as yet dimly understood kernel of sexual truth lay behind the phenomena of hysteria. In his book *Les démoniaques dans l'art* he had demonstrated that demoniacal possessions as reflected in art were typical of hysterical individuals. It was this insight about sexuality, never completely understood by Charcot or his school, that seems to have left the deeper impression on Freud. Moreover, we learn from another statement of Freud's that he was not entirely won over by what he saw in Nancy. For in *Group Psychology and the Analysis of the Ego* (*S.E.* 18:89) Freud writes: "Such, too, was the opinion of Bernheim, of whose astonishing arts I was a witness in the year 1889. But I can remember even then feeling a muffled hostility to this tyranny of suggestion. When a patient who showed himself unamenable was met with the shout: 'What are you doing? *Vous vous contre-suggestionnez!'*, I said to myself that this was an evident injustice and an act of violence. For the man certainly had a right to counter-suggestions if people were trying to subdue him with suggestions."

The patient whom Freud took with him to Nancy has not been identified, although Frau Emmy von N. has been suggested. She might, in fact, have been the patient mentioned in Charcot's letter to Freud as having been sent by Freud to Paris. If so, she is the patient whom Freud calls Cäcilie M. in the *Studies on Hysteria.*

2. English in original.

3. On June 2, 1888, Meynert gave a paper entitled "Über hypnotische Erscheinungen" to a meeting of the Gesellschaft der Ärzte in Vienna. It was reported in *Wiener klinische Wochenschrift,* 1 (1888):451–453, 473–476, 496–498, and continued to the last installment on September 13, 1888 (no. 24). In the discussion Wilhelm Winternitz made the following comment: "Hofrat Meynert has proven that suggestion is very powerful; he went beyond that and gave the physiological and anatomical reason for it; he went even further and showed that suggestion has an intense effect in a hypnotic state. It is not clear to me, therefore, why he should reach the conclusion that he cannot justify doing this experiment on sick people when, as he showed us, suggestibility is strong during hypnosis . . . By chance I visited the laboratory of the school of Nancy and there I saw suggestion being used as therapy, and saw that some things were really successful. For instance, in the case of two boys who suffered from incontinence, I saw this weakness disappear as a result of suggestion, etc. In Nancy I saw that it is not hysterics alone who are subject to influence via suggestion."

Vienna, July 21, 1890[1]

Dear friend:

My answer will be as brief as your letter. I have no interest whatsoever in the congress, nor do I intend to participate in it. But your invitation is the loveliest thing and the greatest honor that has happened to me in a long time. I very much look forward to seeing you again, to hearing what you are up to, and to rekindling my almost extinguished energy and scientific interests on yours, and I therefore accept and will write again to let you know when I shall come. You know my feelings and my respect for you; let us chat for a few days. If, however, it was your intention to offer me only lodgings while you yourself would remain devoted to your work, then inform me and I shall not come.

Cordially your
Sigm. Freud

1. Erroneously dated 1891 in *Origins.*

Reichenau, August 1, 1890

Esteemed friend:

Very reluctantly, I write you today that I cannot come to Berlin; I do not care at all about the city or the congress, but I do care that I cannot see you in Berlin. It is not a single major reason that reversed my resolve, but that combination of minor reasons which comes about so easily in the case of a practicing physician and father of a family. It does not work out in any way: not medically, when my most important patient is just now going through a kind of nervous crisis and might get well in my absence; and not as far as the family is concerned, where all sorts of things were happening with the children (I now have a daughter and a son), and my wife who otherwise never wants to stand in the way of small trips really dislikes this particular one, and so on and so forth. In short, it doesn't work out; and since I regard this trip in the sense of a singular treat that I am giving myself, I have been led to forgo this pleasure.

Very reluctantly, because I had expected a great deal from my contact with you. Otherwise quite content, happy if you will, I still feel quite isolated, scientifically dulled, lazy, and resigned. When I talked with you and saw that you thought well of me, I even used to think something of myself, and the picture of absolutely convincing energy that you offered was not without its effect on me. Moreover, medically I undoubtedly would have profited from your presence and perhaps from the atmosphere in Berlin as well, since for many years now I have been without a teacher; I am more or less exclusively involved in the treatment of neuroses.

Could I not see you at some time other than that of the congress in Berlin? Aren't you taking a trip afterward? Or aren't you coming back in the fall? Do not lose patience with me for having left you without a letter in reply and for now declining your invitation, which could not have been more cordial. Let me know of some prospect of seeing you for a few days so that I shall not lose you as a friend.

With cordial greetings,

Your devoted
Dr. Sigm. Freud

---

Vienna, August 11, 1890

Dearest friend:

Splendid! And do you know of anywhere more lovely than Salzburg for this purpose? We will meet there and hike for a few days wherever you want. The date is all the same to me; you decide, please; it will be, I assume, toward the end of August. In view of the obstacles I mentioned to you, it cannot be for more than three or four beautiful days, but have them we shall, and I shall do everything in order not to be kept away again. If you agree to Salzburg, you will probably travel via Munich and not Vienna.

In truly joyful expectation,

Your Sigm. Freud

---

Vienna, May 2, 1891

Dear friend:

Of *that* reviewer and of the result I am indeed proud. I think that the thrust of the review will have contributed not a little to its success.[1] In a few weeks, I shall afford myself the pleasure of sending you a small book on aphasia[2] for which I myself have a great deal of warm feeling. In it I am very impudent, cross swords with your friend Wernicke,[3] with Lichtheim and Grashey, and even scratch the high and mighty idol Meynert. I am very curious to hear what you will say about this endeavor. In view of your privileged relationship to the author, some of it will sound familiar to you. The paper, by the way, is more suggestive than conclusive.

What else are you doing apart from reviewing my work? In my case, "else" means a second boy, Oliver, who is now three months old. Shall we meet this year?

With cordial greetings,

Your
Dr. Freud

1. This is clearly a reference to a Fliess review of some piece by Freud. But no review by Fliess of any of Freud's work has come to light. It is possible that the review was written but never published, or that it was published in an obscure journal that so far has not been found. The *Archiv für Kinderheilkunde* contains a review of Freud's "Über Hemianopsie im frühesten Kindesalter" by a Herr Höltzke of Berlin, who mentions that the two cases Freud reported are the first noticed in the literature. But in view of the sentence at the end of the letter, it is unlikely that Freud is referring to a review by anyone other than Fliess.

2. The reference is to Freud, *Zur Auffassung der Aphasien.*

3. Carl Wernicke (1848–1905) was a prominent neurologist and psychiatrist often mentioned by Freud in connection with aphasia. He was also joint editor (with Theodor Ziehen, whom Freud also mentions in his letter of January 25, 1901) of the *Monatsschrift für Psychiatrie und Neurologie,* in which the Dora case, "Fragment of an Analysis of a Case of Hysteria," was eventually published. Fliess may well have

known him, for he was (according to the 1957 German encyclopedia *Der grosse Brockhaus*) a professor in Berlin from 1885 to 1890 before moving to Breslau.

Freud took the term *überwertig* (supervalent)—which he uses in the Dora analysis—from Wernicke, possibly as a tribute to his editor. Freud also published his paper on screen memories in the *Monatsschrift*.

---

Vienna, August 17, 1891

Dear tardily writing friend:

At last! I was afraid of having spoiled things with you through the aphasia; now I look forward to your appreciation just as much as to your objections.

At present my life is as follows: I am in Reichenau on the Semmering for the whole week; Monday, in Vienna. Tomorrow I am starting out on a one-week tour of the Gesäuse and Dachstein to which I cannot invite you because we would not be alone.[1] Next Monday again in Vienna, then Reichenau, and so on until the first week in September. From September 8 on, we shall no doubt have to stay in Vienna to carry out our move to a new apartment (IX., Berggasse 19).

I am in no way giving up on you, however. I believe this year we may have to arrange it in such a way that you slip *me* in somewhere and at some time between your friends and travel plans and let me know as far ahead as possible that you are coming to Vienna or Reichenau. The only time when *I* am flexible would be the last week in August, and even then I cannot vouch for all eventualities in view of my frequently restricted existence. Nevertheless, write, make suggestions, and firmly hold to the one thing that I immediately want to pin down as the only thing [that matters]—that this year, too, we must see each other and talk.

With cordial greetings,

Your
Sigm. Freud

From Sunday, August 22 on, address: Reichenau, Niederösterreich, or Vienna (*aequo loco*).

1. The Gesäuse is a mountain range in Austria, the Dachstein its highest mountain.

Vienna, September 11, 1891

Dear friend:

Could not notify you sooner because I myself did not know. Now I can tell you that on September 15 I am expecting you, impatiently and joyously, in Vienna, *IX., Berggasse 19* (possibly at the railroad station if you write).

Most cordially your
Dr. Freud

---

Vienna, May 25, 1892[1]

Dearest friend:

I think there is no need at all for you to reply to every one of my silly jokes. I really want to be sure, now, that I can write without expecting a reply from you. All I have to tell you today is that my wife will go to Reichenau on June 1, I shall join her over Whitsun; that I am quite willing to keep out of your way while you are there, but that naturally I am also quite ready to accept the sacrifice and see you, the happy man, and cordially congratulate you for a moment either on Saturday or Tuesday if you already, or still, are there.

By the way, and since nothing more intelligent occurs to me, let me inform you that I was startled to read on your last card a W. Ch. (Wilhelm Christian). I realized only later that you write your first name equivocally.[2]

Cordially,
Your Dr. Freud

Will you quickly think about what you would like for a wedding present. I must know early on.

1. The original of this and nine other letters by Freud to the Fliess family are in Jerusalem, in the department of manuscripts and archives of the Jewish National and University Library. Pauline Jacobsohn, Fliess's daughter, who now lives in Israel, took them with her when she emigrated from Germany. The letters were first brought to my attention by Peter Swales, and the university was kind enough to put them at my disposal for this edition.

2. Michael Schröter has suggested that Fliess's first name, Wilhelm, commonly written "Wilh.," could be misread as W. Ch.

Ida Bondy in 1892, the year in which she and Wilhelm Fliess were married. On the back of the photo is a notation by Elenore Fliess that her mother-in-law was an accomplished amateur pianist and notable hostess, sometimes called "the Duchess" by her son's friends.

Jacob Fliess,
Wilhelm's father.

Fliess's son,
Robert Wilhelm,
as a boy of
about six.

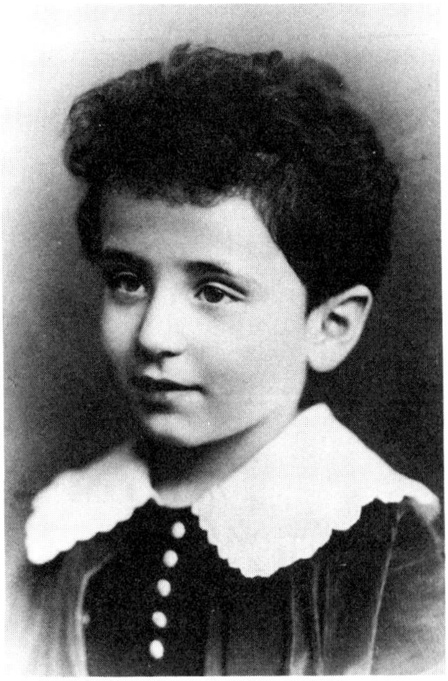

Vienna, June 28, 1892

Dearest friend:

I have had no opportunity other than in memory to refer back to the beautiful evening on which I saw you[1] among yours next to your bride. You know that in the meantime my respect for your diagnostic acumen has only increased further and when in the "upheaval of memory"[2] I happened upon you, the comforting thought welled up in me: he is now well taken care of and in good hands. This certainty also set the tone for my correspondence with you. You will not misunderstand it.

The reason for writing to you is that Breuer has declared his willingness to publish jointly our detailed theory of abreaction, and our other joint witticisms[3] on hysteria. A part of it that I first wanted to write alone is finished, and under different circumstances would certainly have been communicated to you.

The installment of Charcot that I am sending you today has turned out quite well, but I am annoyed that there are several uncorrected accentual and grammatical mistakes in the few French words. Pure sloppiness!

I hear that you are now expecting a return visit. I hope you will do me the favor of giving me a hint of what to send you for the new household as a token of my own and my wife's best wishes for the new house.

Most cordial greetings to you, your Ida, and parents, who received me with such undeserved kindness, from your

Sigm. Freud

Mrs. Gomperz is plaguing me with questions about how she should repay you for your efforts on behalf of Rudi.[4]

1. This is the first letter in which Freud uses the familiar *Du* to Fliess.

2. *Umwälzen der Erinnerung.* Reference unclear.

3. The text printed in *Anfänge* reads *Mitteilungen,* but the manuscript actually says *Witze.*

4. Schröter has identified this as a reference to Rudolf Gomperz (b. 1878).

---

Vienna, July 12, 1892[1]

Dearest friend:

Yesterday afternoon, still tired from my Sunday mountain excursion, as I was contemplating how to get through the evening without moving (at least actively), your father kindly invited me to go with him to the Brühl.[2] I do not need to tell you that I willingly accepted. Everyone was again very cordial out there. I must say that I am really impressed with you, after having seen the choice you made. She is such a "merry hero" of a wife—but these are nice phrases that you do not require from me.

I shall now have more frequent opportunities to pass by the happy house because my prima donna[3] has just moved to the Brühl. I am sure that I shall look in each time; it makes one feel so good.

Our conversations yesterday covered the same ground as your letter today. In August I shall be in Reichenau, only one and a half hours away from you on the same railroad line. Yesterday I requested, successfully, that the two of you spend at least one day in Reichenau. For the sake of my wife, who otherwise could not make Ida's acquaintance and who each time talks about it.

I am of course very much looking forward to the announcement of your book on the nose. I made this suggestion when I thought you badly needed a powerful diversion, but now I am not very happy to have helped you take on a new responsibility during this most turbulent of times. However, it has already happened.

My hysteria has, in Breuer's hands, become transformed, broadened, restricted, and in the process has partially evaporated. We are writing the thing jointly, each on his own working on several sections which he will sign, but still in complete agreement. No one can yet say how it will turn out. In the meantime, I am using a cerebrally dull period to read psychology.

Last week brought me a rare human pleasure: the opportunity to select from Meynert's library what suited me—somehow like a savage drinking mead from his enemy's skull.[4]

I would not have wanted to refrain from my question concerning the wedding contribution since it elicited such warm words from you. But the matter is not settled with this, as you will understand. You rob us of a pleasure if you insist on it.

Now farewell, and quickly bring July to an end.

With cordial greetings,

Your
Sigm. Freud

1. The original of this letter is in Jerusalem. See note 1 to the letter of May 25, 1892.

2. The Bondys, the family of Fliess's wife, lived in the Brühl, a valley just south of Vienna.

3. This patient, whose identity is revealed to Fliess in a later letter, is the same woman whom Freud sent to Charcot (possibly to Bernheim as well) and who is called Cäcilie M. in the *Studies on Hysteria*. See *S.E.* 2:69n1.

4. Meynert died on May 31, 1892. Freud probably paid a condolence visit to the household and was given the choice of some of Meynert's books as a remembrance.

In the *Interpretation of Dreams* (*S.E.* 5:438) Freud writes: "It also reminded me of another incident with him [Meynert] shortly before his death. I had carried on an embittered controversy with him in writing, on the subject of male hysteria, the existence of which he denied. When I visited him during his fatal illness and asked after his condition, he spoke at some length about his state and ended with these words: 'You know, I was always one of the clearest cases of male hysteria.'"

Interesting information about Meynert and Freud's relation to him may be found in the Bernfeld papers in the Library of Congress. See also Lesky (1978, p. 373).

---

October 4, 1892
IX., Berggasse 19

Dearest friend,

Herewith the first proofs of your reflex neuroses.[1] Since it is being printed in Teschen, it might be better for you to get in touch with the printer yourself. I have merely glanced at it here and there and only hope that at some point you will send me the introduction, which for me is the most interesting part.

I almost want to apologize for disturbing your blissful peace (after the patient's departure). Enjoy yourself. I would like to hear only that you and Ida are in good health.

My little ones have been in Vienna for the past eight days, busily engaged in growing; I am writing infantile paralysis part 2, yet another part 2 *si parva licet*,[2] and so forth.

Cordial greetings from house to house.

I may now write

Your Sigm. Freud[3]

1. Fliess, *Neue Beiträge zur Klinik und Therapie der nasalen Reflexneurosen*. The work was reviewed in the *Münchener medizinische Wochenschrift* in 1894.

2. Freud means that it would be hubris to compare his part 2 to Goethe's *Faust*, part 2. The same Latin phrase, *si parva licet componere magnis* (if one dares to compare the small with the great), appears in Freud's letter of October 14, 1900. It is a quotation from Virgil, *Georgica*, 4:176.

3. This was Freud's first use of *Dein* in the signature of a letter.

---

Vienna, October 21, 1892

Dearest friend,

Only a piece of scratch paper, as we agreed. The introductions are always the reason one puts off writing. So you won't think I am disloyal, the following: about three weeks ago I was called to Mr. F., where I found Heitler, the family doctor, with Mr. F. stretched out on the settee. Again pain in walking; discussed your diagnosis; the patient seems to have given up on Berlin. Heitler, ridiculing the diagnosis of flat foot, calls it neuritis. We let him show his feet; I really cannot see anything resembling a flat foot, and must admit that to Heitler, who seems to know all about it from personal experience. On the other hand, I am not ready to contradict you in an area with which I am not familiar and you certainly are; so I fight for you with a lion's courage and at least obtain agreement that he will show his foot to Professor Lorenz so that the latter can say whether or not it is a pes planus. Before we reached this compromise, I had requested that he go to Berlin to see you, as initially he himself had requested. Since that time I have heard nothing, as happens in Vienna, of man, doctor, or foot.

Now let me give you my private opinion. As you know, there is a 3-cm difference in the man's calves and a change in the consistency of the muscle. I do not know whether a pes planus is consistent with such a difference. Be that as it may. As far as I know, in pes planus the pain occurs in the tarsus, increases gradually, and does not subside quickly. In his case things are different: he has pain *only* in the *calf,* which after about five minutes becomes stiff; he then cannot go on, stops, pulls up the foot, shakes it violently a few times, and then he *immediately can again* walk well for a few minutes. That looks just like an ischemic or myositic failure of the muscles, like intermittent claudication, which also occurs in diabetes. I believe therefore that the man can be helped only by prolonged rest and little walking, which of course means that he will not be helped.

The absence of *any* spontaneous pain speaks against neuritis (Heitler). I hope that the man will still come to you and you can solve the interesting problem.

Otherwise, there is very little today. Saturday evening I have a seminar,[1] "jour neuropathologique," which unfortunately for me Breuer also attends. If you again come to Vienna as suddenly as you did at the beginning of 1892, let it be on a Saturday evening.

Best regards to the guest room; I have to remain here and earn some money for my worms.[2] I do not deny that I would like to see house and housewife. Read, my dear couple, Kipling's *Phantom Rickshaw* and *The Light That Failed.* Highly recommended!

My most cordial greetings.

Your Sigm. Freud

1. The German is ambiguous and could mean either that Freud attends or that he gives a seminar once a week. In 1892 Freud did give a weekly seminar entitled "Die Lehre von der Hysterie" (Gicklhorn and Gicklhorn, 1960, p. 151), in which he had four

students! But neither Josef Breuer nor Robert Breuer attended. Presumably, therefore, Freud is referring to a lecture at which he himself had been present.
2. He means his children.

---

October 24, 1892
IX., Berggasse 19

Dearest friend,

It is a real pleasure to be able to carry on a discussion across this great distance. Only three comments. [1] Examined him standing up: yes, hand under the arch did not impress us. You will probably turn out to be right; we were focusing on a severe typical flat foot. [2] That I did not report on sensitivity to pressure on gastrocnemius and tendon — in fact it is severe — was merely an oversight of mine. (3) Claudication is not associated with limping but, according to Charcot's description, with paresthesias, cramps, and having to stop walking.

If only I knew what I could do to get the man to go to Berlin! I have not heard from him since then. If he is now trying other things, he is bound to go back on his own because no one can help him here in Vienna.

Well now, soon again here? Wonderful, but then an evening for just the four of us.

Cordial greetings.

Your Freud

---

October 31, 1892
IX., Berggasse 19

Dearest friend,

Overnight I find myself in the position of having to help an impoverished couple who are close to me[1] move to America. I am giving what I can and asking all my friends to contribute. I shall gladly accept a contribution from you too. I hope you will spare my telling you the details; it is my brother-in-law, whose two girls I am keeping here.

With cordial greetings to *you* and *you*.[2]

Your Dr. Sigm. Freud

Heard nothing from the flat foot.
Charcot installment 2 tomorrow.

1. Freud's sister Anna married Martha's brother, Eli Bernays. According to Jones (*Life* 1:132): "In 1892 Eli visited the United States to ascertain the prospects there, and the year following he fetched his wife to settle in New York. By that time Freud's antipathy had lost all its former intensity. He not only helped his brother-in-law over the financial difficulties of emigrating, but kept one of the two children, Lucia, with his own family for a year until matters could be arranged in the new country."

The two children referred to in this letter are Judith Bernays, born February 14, 1885, in Vienna, and Lucia Bernays, born August 25, 1886, also in Vienna.

Anna Freud-Bernays wrote a little-known book entitled *Erlebtes* (published privately by the Kommissionsverlag der Buchhandlung Heller, in Vienna). No date is given, but from the content it would seem to have been written during the thirties. She died in New York on March 11, 1955. The daughter, Judith, left behind material concerned with her memories of Freud, which is now in the Sigmund Freud Archives.

2. The second "you," meant for Ida, is the polite form *Sie*.

---

Vienna, November 3, 1892

Dearest friend,

Received[1] with many thanks and will see to it that it reaches its destination by the end of the week. There is nothing further to be said about it.

Your
Freud

1. Probably a reference to a contribution from Fliess to the Bernays family. See previous letter.

---

December 18, 1892
IX., Berggasse 19

Dearest friend,

I am glad to be able to tell you that our theory of hysteria (reminiscence, abreaction, and the like) will appear in the *Neurologisches Centralblatt*[1] on January 1, 1893, in the form of a detailed preliminary communication. It has cost enough in battles with my esteemed partner.[2]

You two lost in your happiness, what are you doing? Will we see you both here at Christmas, as rumor has it?

Most cordial greetings.

Your Sigm. Freud

1. Between the first and second parts of the "preliminary communication" of 1893, Freud delivered a lecture to the Wiener medizinischer Klub on January 11 of that year.

Published in the *Wiener medizinische Presse* of January 22 and January 29, it was a shorthand report of the lecture revised by Freud. Strachey (*S.E.* 3:27) translates it as "On the Psychical Mechanism of Hysterical Phenomena."

But there is a report Strachey did not mention, published in *Internationale klinische Rundschau*, 7 (1893):107–110, which differs somewhat from the *Presse* version. At the end of the case presented in *S.E.* 3:34, the *Rundschau* adds what is clearly an authentic phrase of Freud's: "And so psychic pain often becomes transformed into physical pain." The *Rundschau* account also contains a slightly different wording of Freud's famous comment in the *Studies on Hysteria*, "The hysteric suffers mainly from reminiscences." Quoted in italics in the original *Rundschau* report, it undoubtedly stems directly from Freud: "The hysteric suffers, therefore, from memories of psychic traumas which resulted from experiences which could not be fully abreacted, either because the hysteric denies himself one or another means of abreaction, or because the experience took place in a state which was not suitable for abreaction."

2. The German *Herr Compagnon* is somewhat disdainful as well as humorous. Freud's relation to Breuer was a complex one. See the thorough study by Hirschmüller (1978).

# Draft A[1]

[Editor's Note: This is the first in a series of essays (here called drafts) that Freud sent separately to Fliess or enclosed with his letters. Many of the ideas therein appear in Freud's later papers.]

### PROBLEMS

(1) Is the anxiety of anxiety neuroses derived from the inhibition of the sexual function or from the anxiety linked to their etiology?[2]

(2) To what extent does a healthy person respond to later sexual traumas differently from someone predisposed by masturbation? Only quantitatively? Or qualitatively?

(3) Is simple coitus reservatus (condom) a noxa at all?

(4) Is there an innate neurasthenia with innate sexual weakness, or is it always acquired in youth? (From nurses, from being masturbated by someone else.)

(5) Is heredity anything other than a multiplier?

(6) What plays a part in the etiology of periodic depression?

(7) Is sexual anesthesia in women anything other than a result of impotence? Can it of itself cause neuroses?[3]

### THESES

(1) No neurasthenia or analogous neurosis exists without a disturbance of the sexual function.
(2) This either has an immediate causal effect or acts as a predisposition to other factors, but always in such a way that without it the other factors cannot bring about neurasthenia.
(3) Neurasthenia in men, on account of its etiology, is accompanied by relative impotence.
(4) Neurasthenia in women is a direct consequence of neurasthenia in men, through the agency of this reduction in their potency.
(5) Periodic depression is a form of anxiety neurosis, which otherwise manifests itself in phobias and anxiety attacks.
(6) Anxiety neurosis is in part a consequence of inhibition of the sexual function.
(7) Simple excess and overwork are not etiological factors.
(8) Hysteria in neurasthenic neuroses indicates suppression of the accompanying affects.

### GROUPS [FOR OBSERVATION]

(1) Men and women who have remained healthy.
(2) Sterile women, where traumas [resulting from coitus] reservatus in marriage are absent.
(3) Women infected with gonorrhea.
(4) Loose-living men who are gonorrheal, and who are on that account protected in every respect, being aware of their hypospermia.
(5) Members who have remained healthy in severely tainted families.
(6) Observations from countries in which particular sexual abnormalities are endemic.

### ETIOLOGICAL FACTORS

(1) Exhaustion owing to abnormal [forms of] satisfaction. Example: masturbation.
(2) Inhibition of the sexual function. Example: coitus interruptus.
(3) Affects accompanying these practices.
(4) Sexual traumas before the age of understanding begins.

1. The editors of *Origins* note that this draft is undated and suggest the end of 1892. The original German transcript that they used was placed after Freud's letter of December 8, 1895. Somebody wrote, in German, on this same typescript: "According to the handwriting, more likely summer, 1894." Ernst Kris penciled in: "Can hardly belong here! (though 1895!) Belongs earlier?" Evidently the editors changed their minds. Because of the mention of sexual trauma the manuscript may well belong to 1895.

2. Freud wrote, then crossed out, *von dem Bewusstsein der sexuell. Unzulänglichkeit* (from the awareness of sexual inadequacy).

3. Someone wrote here *Kleinheitswahn, sex. Unzulänglichkeit* (delusion of smallness, sexual inadequacy), possibly a reference to anxiety over the size of the penis.

---

January 5, 1893
IX., Berggasse 19

Dearest friend,

I am going to rewrite the piece on the etiology of the neuroses[1] in greater detail for you as the basis for our future work. It will take a while. Mr. F. informed me that after receiving arch supports, he has been walking a little better. The problem has certainly not been corrected properly, but once again you are right.

Cordial greetings to you and Ida.

Your
Sigm. Freud

1. Apparently this is a reference to Draft B, The Etiology of the Neuroses.

---

February 8, 1893
[dated by postmark]

## Draft B. The Etiology of the Neuroses

I am writing the whole thing down a second time for you, dear friend, and for the sake of our common work. You will of course keep the manuscript away from your young wife.

I. It may be taken as a recognized fact that neurasthenia is a frequent consequence of an abnormal sexual life. The assertion, however, which I wish to make and to test by observations is that neurasthenia actually can *only* be a sexual neurosis.

I (along with Breuer) have advocated a similar point of view in regard to hysteria. Traumatic hysteria was known; we then said every case of hysteria that is not hereditary is traumatic. The same holds for neurasthenia: every neurasthenia is sexual.

We will for the moment leave open the question of whether hereditary disposition and, secondarily, toxic influences can produce genuine neurasthenia, or whether what appears to be hereditary neurasthenia also goes back to early sexual exhaustion. If there is such a thing as hereditary neurasthenia, the questions arise whether the *status nervosus* in the hereditary cases should not be distinguished from neurasthenia, what relation it actually has to the corresponding symptoms in childhood, and so on.

In the first instance, therefore, my contention will be restricted to acquired neurasthenia. Then what I asserted above can also be formulated as follows. In the etiology of a nervous affection we must distinguish (1) the necessary precondition without which the state cannot come about at all, and (2) the precipitating factors. The relation between the two can be pictured thus. If the necessary precondition has operated sufficiently, the affection sets in as a necessary consequence; if it has not operated sufficiently, the result of its operation is in the first place a disposition to that affection which ceases to be latent as soon as a sufficient amount of one of the second-order factors supervenes. Thus what is lacking for full effect in the first etiology can be replaced by the etiology of the second order. The etiology of the second order can, however, be dispensed with, whereas that of the first order is indispensable.

This etiological formula, applied to our present case means: sexual exhaustion can by itself alone provoke neurasthenia. If it fails to achieve this by itself, it so predisposes the nervous system that physical illness, depressive affects, and overwork (toxic influences) can no longer be tolerated without [leading to] neurasthenia. Without sexual exhaustion, however, all these factors are incapable of generating neurasthenia: they bring about normal fatigue, normal sadness, normal physical weakness, but they only continue to give evidence of how much "of these detrimental influences a normal person can tolerate."

We shall consider neurasthenia in men and women separately.

*Neurasthenia* in males is acquired at the age of puberty and becomes manifest when the man is in his twenties. Its source is masturbation, the frequency of which runs completely parallel with the frequency of male neurasthenia. One can observe in the circle of one's acquaintances that (at least in urban populations) those individuals who have been seduced by women at an early age have escaped neurasthenia. When this noxa has operated long and intensely, it turns the person concerned into a sexual neurasthenic, whose potency, too, has been impaired; the intensity of the cause is paralleled by a lifelong persistence of the condition. Further evidence of the causal connection lies in the fact that a sexual neurasthenic is always a general neurasthenic at the same time.

If the noxa has not been sufficiently intense, it will have (in accordance with the formula given above) a predisposing effect; so that later, if provoking factors supervene, it will produce neurasthenia, which those factors alone would not have produced. Intellectual work — cerebral neurasthenia; normal sexual activity — spinal neurasthenia, and so on.

In intermediate cases we find the neurasthenia of youth, which typically begins with and runs its course accompanied by dyspepsia and the like, and which terminates at marriage.

The second noxa, which affects men at a later age, makes its impact on a nervous system which is either intact or which has been predisposed to neurasthenia through masturbation. The question is whether it can lead to detrimental results even in the first case; probably it can. Its effect is manifest in the second case, where it revives the neurasthenia of youth and creates new symptoms. This second noxa is *onanismus conjugalis* — incomplete intercourse in order to prevent conception. In the case of men all the methods of achieving this seem to fall in line: they operate with varying intensity according to the earlier predisposition, but do not actually differ qualitatively. Those with a strong predisposition or persistent neurasthenics cannot tolerate even normal coitus; then intolerance of the condom, of extravaginal coitus, and of coitus interruptus take their toll.

A healthy man will tolerate all of these for quite a long time, but even so not indefinitely; after a prolonged time he behaves like the predisposed individual. His only advantage over the masturbator is the privilege of a longer latency or the fact that on every occasion he needs the provoking causes. Here coitus interruptus proves to be the main noxa, which produces its characteristic effect even in the case of an individual who is not predisposed.

*Neurasthenia* in females. Normally, girls are sound and not neurasthenic; and this is true as well of young married women, in spite of all the sexual traumas of this time [of life]. In rarer cases neurasthenia appears in married women and in older unmarried ones in its pure form; it is then to be regarded as having arisen spontaneously and in the same manner. Far more often neurasthenia in a married woman is derived from neurasthenia in a man or is produced simultaneously. In that case there is almost always an admixture of hysteria and we have the common mixed neurosis of women.

The *mixed neurosis* of women is derived from neurasthenia in men in all those not-infrequent cases in which the man, being a sexual neurasthenic, suffers from impaired potency. The admixture of hysteria results directly from the *holding back* of the excitation of the act. The poorer the man's potency, the more the woman's hysteria predominates; so that essentially a sexually neurasthenic man makes his wife not so much neurasthenic as hysterical.

This [hysteria] arises, *along with* neurasthenia in men during the second thrust of sexual noxa, which is by far of greater significance for a woman, assuming that she is sound. Thus we come across far more neurotic men during the first decade of puberty and far more neurotic women during the second. In the latter case this is the result of the noxae due to the prevention of conception. It is not easy to arrange them in order, and in general none of them should be regarded as entirely innocuous to women; so that even in the most favorable case (condom) women, being the more exacting partners, will scarcely escape slight neurasthenia. A great deal will obviously depend on the *two* predispositions: whether (1) she herself was neurasthenic before marriage or whether (2) she was made hystericoneurasthenic during the period of free[1] intercourse [without preventives].

II. *Anxiety neurosis.* Every case of neurasthenia is no doubt marked by a certain lowering of self-assurance, by pessimistic expectation and an inclination to distressing antithetic ideas. But the question is whether the emergence of this factor [anxiety], without the other symptoms being specially developed, should not be detached as an independent "anxiety neurosis," especially since this is to be found no less frequently in hysteria than in neurasthenia.

Anxiety neurosis appears in two forms: as a *chronic state* and as an *attack of anxiety.* The two readily combine: an anxiety attack never occurs without chronic symptoms. Anxiety attacks are more common in the forms connected with hysteria—more frequent, therefore, in women. The chronic symptoms are more common in neurasthenic men.

The chronic symptoms are (1) anxiety relating to the body—hypochondria; (2) anxiety relating to the functioning of the body—agoraphobia, claustrophobia, giddiness at heights; (3) anxiety relating to decisions and memory (therefore one's own fantasies, psychic functioning) with respect to *folie de doute,* obsessive brooding, etc. So far I have found no reason for not treating these symptoms as equivalent. Again, the question is (1) to what extent this condition emerges in hereditary cases, *without* any sexual noxa, (2) whether it is released in hereditary cases by any chance sexual noxa, (3) whether it supervenes as an intensification in common neurasthenia. There is no question but that it is acquired, that is by men and women in marriage, during the second period of sexual noxae, through coitus interruptus. I do not believe that predisposition owing to earlier neurasthenia is necessary for this; but where predisposition is lacking, latency is longer. The causal formula is the same as in neurasthenia.

Rarer cases of anxiety neurosis outside marriage are encountered especially in men. They turn out to be cases of congressus interruptus in which the man is strongly involved psychically with women whose well-being is a matter of concern to him. In such circumstances this procedure is a greater noxa for a man than coitus interruptus in marriage, for this is often corrected, as it were, by normal coitus outside marriage.

I must look upon *periodic mild depression,* an attack of anxiety lasting for weeks or months, as a third form of anxiety neurosis. This, in contrast to melancholia proper, almost always has an apparently rational connection with a psychic trauma. The latter is, however, only the provoking cause. Moreover, this periodic mild depression occurs without *psychic anesthesia,* which is characteristic of melancholia.

I have been able to trace a number of such cases to coitus interruptus; their onset was late, during marriage, after the birth of the last child. In a case of tormenting hypochondria that began at puberty, I was able to establish that an assault took place in the eighth year of life. Another case from childhood turned out to be a hysterical reaction to a masturbatory assault. Thus I do not know whether we have here truly hereditary forms without sexual causes; nor do I know on the other hand whether coitus interruptus alone is to be blamed here, or whether hereditary predisposition can always be dispensed with.

I shall omit *occupational neuroses,* since, as I have told you, changes in the muscular parts have been demonstrated in them.

### CONCLUSIONS

It follows from what I have said that neuroses are entirely preventable as well as entirely incurable. The physician's task is wholly shifted to prophylaxis.

The first part of this task, prevention of the sexual noxa of the first period, coincides with prophylaxis against syphilis and gonorrhea, since they are the noxae that threaten anyone who gives up masturbation. The only alternative would be free sexual intercourse between young men and unattached young women,[2] but this could only be adopted if there were innocuous methods of preventing conception. Otherwise, the alternatives are masturbation, neurasthenia in the male, hysteroneurasthenia in the female, or syphilis in the male, syphilis in the next generation, gonorrhea in the male, gonorrhea and sterility in the female.

The same task — an innocuous means of controlling conception — is set by the *sexual* trauma of the second period; since the condom provides neither a safe solution nor one acceptable to someone who is already neurasthenic.

In the absence of such a solution, society appears doomed to fall victim to incurable neuroses, which reduce the enjoyment of life to a minimum, destroy marital relations, and bring hereditary ruin on the whole coming generation. The lower strata of society, knowing nothing of Malthusianism, are in full pursuit, and in the natural course of events, having arrived, will fall victim to the same fate.

Thus the physician is faced with a problem whose solution is worthy of all his efforts.

By way of preparation I have begun a collection: one hundred cases of anxiety neurosis; likewise I would like to collect a corresponding number of male and female cases of neurasthenia and the much rarer periodic mild depressions. A necessary counterpart would be a second series of one hundred cases of nonneurotics.[3]

If it should turn out that the same disturbances of functions of the nervous system which are acquired through sexual abuse also come about on a purely hereditary basis, it would give rise to the most significant speculations which today are only beginning to dawn on me.

With cordial greetings,

Your
Sigm. Freud

1. Freud originally wrote "normal," then changed it to "free."

2. The German text reads *Mädchen freien Standes,* which Strachey translates as "respectable girls." The term is open to interpretation. Presumably Freud is referring to unmarried young women willing to engage in sexual acts.

3. The original manuscript reads *nicht Nervösen.* In *Anfänge* the *nicht* is mistakenly omitted.

## Draft C. Something of a Report on Motives[1]

Dearest friend,

I need only intimate the great pleasure it gives me to be able to continue our Easter discussion. On the whole I am not sufficiently unbiased to be a real critic of your work. Therefore, only one thing: I like it very much and do not believe that the congress will bring anything of higher importance. But others should tell you all the nice things this lecture deserves. I turn now to comments and suggestions for changes, in compliance with your own wish.

It must have been written on a day that was not entirely free of headaches, because it does not have the precision and succinctness with which you can write. Some items are decidedly too long, for instance, the *formes frustes.* I have marked in blue pencil what should go to the barber's. I have tried to bring out more sharply some of the underlying points.

I would recommend to you a comparison with Ménière's disease and hope that the nasal reflex neurosis will soon be generally known as Fliess's disease.

Now to the sexual question. I believe that in this respect one can act more like a literary businessman. The way you present sexual etiology, you are attributing to the audience a knowledge which it, after all, possesses only in latent form. It knows, and yet behaves as though it knew nothing. Preyer,[2] whose contribution I fully recognize, really has no claim to be given such prominence in a fleeting reference of this sort. So far as I know his works—because actually I treat the literature the way you do—he falls short on two principal points: (1) he divides neurasthenia into separate, reflexively transmitted afflictions of the stomach, intestines, bladder, and so forth; that is, he does not know our etiological formula, nor does he know that in addition to their direct effect, the sexual noxae also have a predisposing one which constitutes the latent neurasthenia. (2) He derives the reflex neuroses from minor anatomical changes of the genitals instead of from changes in the nervous system. Nevertheless, the *urethra postica* may still be a reflex organ similar to the nose. He cuts himself off, however, from any connection to the large point of view.

I think that you cannot avoid mentioning the sexual etiology of neurosis without tearing the most beautiful leaf out of the wreath. So do it immediately in a manner suitable to the circumstances. Announce the forthcoming investigations; describe the anticipated result as that which it really is, something new; show people the key that unlocks everything, the etiological formula; and if in the process you give me a place in this by incorporating a reference such as "a colleague and friend," I shall be very pleased rather than angry. I have inserted such a passage on sexuality for you, merely as a suggestion.[3]

As far as the therapy of the neurasthenic nasal neurosis is concerned, I should not make too pessimistic a pronouncement. Here too there may be residual manifestations that promptly disappear; if there are pure cases of vasomotor reflex neuroses, the purely organic cases probably are quite rare, and the mixed cases probably are typical. That is how I look at it.

I am beginning to sense your obligation to present me with some guidance in examining and assessing the nose — on a later occasion, because one can expect this organ to have a role that is similar to, though more modest than, that of the *retina*. Here, as there, one can observe multiple organic changes, but in addition gain a glimpse of the circulatory conditions inside the head!

I am not clear about the naval cadet. He confessed to masturbating already in the morning; did you establish that the attack followed directly upon a masturbatory excess? Certain fantasies about the possibility of suppressing the impulse to masturbate via the nose, to explain such impulses, to undo anesthesia and the like should remain only fantasies?[4]

Now, "go where glory waits thee."[5]

With cordial greetings to you and Ida,

Your
Sigm. Freud

No misunderstanding. Do not mention any names! Surely you couldn't think of me as so inordinately ambitious.

1. According to Kris, the congress mentioned took place in June 1893, and the discussion Freud is continuing occurred at Easter (April 2–3), so Kris argues that this letter was written sometime between those two dates. However, the envelope reads 8.2. [Feb.] 93, to which Kris comments, *Muss wohl 8/5 heissen* (Must mean May 8). On May 15 Freud mentions having been in Berlin, so this draft must predate that visit. Michael Schröter informs me that in actuality the congress took place April 12–15, and at his suggestion I have moved the draft to its present position.

2. *Origins*, p. 74n1, erroneously refers the reader to the work of A. Preyer. But Kris is thinking of Alexander Peyer (not Preyer) of Zurich. Freud clearly wrote "Preyer" and undoubtedly had in mind Wilhelm Thierry Preyer, three of whose works he owned. The book Freud probably had in mind was *Die Seele des Kindes* (Leipzig: T. Grieben, 2nd ed. 1884), which he not only owned but referred to with respect to the fact that it did not recognize childhood sexuality (see *Three Essays on the Theory of Sexuality, S.E.* 7:174n).

3. In his paper "Die nasale Reflexneurose," read at the Twelfth Congress of Internal Medicine at Wiesbaden, Fliess writes: "For I admit to the expectation that

[we] shall succeed in demonstrating: the etiology of neurasthenia proper, insofar as the latter can be differentiated from other status nervosi, is to be found in *abusus sexualis,* in the misuse of the sexual function. I have joined forces with a colleague and friend for the purpose of proving this by a series of carefully analyzed observations of patients. You know that sexual abuse has always been cited among the causes of neurasthenia. In our view, this factor is the *specific* etiology of neurosis, either in the sense that this etiology by itself is sufficient to transform a healthy nervous system into a neurasthenic one, or in other cases that it represents the necessary precondition for the production of neurasthenia by other such noxae which by themselves are incapable of having this effect" (p. 391). This is, possibly, the passage that Freud wrote for Fliess.

In the *Archives de laryngologie* (also known as the *Archives internationales d'otologie et de rhinologie*) there is an article entitled "Les reflexes d'origine nasale" (Travail lu au Congrès de médecine interne de Wiesbaden) by Wilhelm Fliess, and it is given as an *Autorreferat*—that is, the report was prepared by the author. Fliess writes: "The first group consists of cerebral symptoms: headache, dizziness, anorexia, poor memory, nightmares, and intolerance of alcohol" (p. 266). Two pages later he writes: "If, as happens most frequently, neurasthenia is held responsible [for the ills cited above], one must turn one's attention to it. And, in regard to this, the author agrees with a foreign colleague that sexual abuses are its specific cause."

4. The implications of this important passage, which was omitted in the previous edition of the letters, are uncertain. Freud's question to Fliess is not entirely clear, because the German is somewhat ambiguous. What Freud writes is, *Die Masturbation hatte er schon vormittags eingestanden.* This translates as "Already in the morning he admitted to masturbation," whereas what Freud probably means is "He admitted to having masturbated in the morning." Unfortunately, we learn nothing further about this patient in the course of the correspondence.

5. English in original; from Thomas Moore, "Irish Melodies." The next two lines read:

But, while fame elates thee,
oh! still remember me.

---

Vienna, May 14, 1893

Dear friend,

The bearer of this letter, Mr. F. from Budweis, suffers from left-sided neuralgiform headaches, is intolerant of alcohol, has pain in the sternum, some dizziness, cannot breathe through the nose when reclining, has a dried-out mouth upon awakening, restless sleep, a suspicious shape to his nose—in brief, I do not doubt that it will be a simple matter for you to free him from his troubles.[1]

In another respect he suffered a great deal from pollutions[2] (without masturbation); until recently had very good potency; for the past four years has practiced coitus interruptus because of his wife's stubbornness, without so far suffering any ill effects as a result (precisely because he was not a masturbator), but is very excited, does not feel well after intercourse, and easily develops hysterical choking. For the last ten years has complained about pressure in the bladder region, needs to urinate frequently at night, still has a weekly pollution; a year ago gonorrhea (prostate!).

With cordial greetings,

Your
Dr. Freud

1. It would seem that Freud regularly sent his patients to Fliess, who frequently operated on their noses. It is clear from this letter that Freud shared Fliess's views of the importance of the nose and its relation to the disturbed sexual life of the patient. Apart from the next letter, the patient described here is not mentioned again in the ensuing letters. A "suspicious" nose apparently refers to the swelling believed by Fliess to result from masturbation.

2. Nocturnal emissions.

---

Vienna, May 15, 1893

Dearest friend,

Since my return from Berlin I have not been well until finally an influenza arrived, presented me with the gift of a tonsillar abscess, and then departed, leaving me feeling better and refreshed. The only thing I have been left with is an incomprehensible disinclination to write (dysgraphia), in which I regret to have included you as well. Things are no better today either. I only think that if you haven't made a decision long ago, you should not do it with the 11,000 German doctors,[1] but rather be glad that people leave you time to work undisturbed until the thing is finished.

Yesterday I sent you a man from Budweis who is a brother-in-law of my friend Dr. E. I hope my diagnosis was correct.

The neuroses are somewhat at a standstill, am working more on hysteria. Wernicke apparently will not come [to Vienna].

Our little one is thriving.

Most cordial greetings to you and your wife Ida.

Your
Sigm. Freud

As soon as I have overcome the disturbance, I shall write properly.

1. Michael Schröter believes this to be a reference to the number of physicians who belonged to German medical societies of the day.

# Treatment of Hysteria

Vienna, May 30, 1893

Dearest friend,

I am well again, for it is once again a pleasure to write to you.

I know of no such thing as a department of residential health in Vienna.

The fact that you are inundated with patients demonstrates that on the whole people do know what they are doing. I am curious to know whether you will confirm the diagnosis in the cases I sent to you. I am now making this diagnosis very often and agree with you that the nasal reflex is one of the most frequent disturbances. Unfortunately, I am never sure what to do then. The tie to sexuality too is becoming ever tighter; it is a pity we cannot work on the same cases.

Recently I too encountered something like crossed reflexes. Furthermore, a short time ago I interrupted (for one hour) a severe migraine of my own with cocaine; the effect set in only after I had cocainized the opposite side as well; but then it did so promptly. I see a good possibility of filling yet another gap in the sexual etiology of the neuroses. I believe I understand the anxiety neuroses of young persons who must be presumed to be virgins and who have not been subjected to abuse. I have analyzed two cases of this kind; it was a *presentient dread* of sexuality, and behind it things they had seen or heard and half-understood—thus, the etiology is purely emotional but nevertheless of a sexual nature.

The book I am sending you today[1] is not very interesting. The hysterical paralyses, shorter and more interesting, will appear at the beginning of June.

My family is going to Reichenau tomorrow. I have already enlisted the first pupil from Vienna for the therapeutic polyclinic. Are things working out with the blond youth from Danzig?

Most cordial greetings to you and Ida from our entire house.

Your
Sigm. Freud

I continue, because now I am writing more easily, to submit the following problem to you:

Undoubtedly there exist cases of juvenile neurasthenia *without* masturbation, but *not* without the usual preliminaries of over-abundant pollutions — that is, precisely as though there had been masturbation. I have only the following unproven surmises for the understanding of these cases:

(1) Innate weakness of the genital and nervous systems
(2) Abuse in the prepubertal period
(3) Could it not be that organic changes of the nose produce the pollutions and thereby the neurasthenia, so that here the latter develops as a product of the nasal reflex noxa?

What do you think, and do you know something about it?

1. Freud's "Zur Kenntnis der cerebralen Diplegien des Kindesalters (im Anschluss an die Little'sche Krankheit)." See also the reference to the same work in the letter of May 21, 1894.

---

Vienna, July 10, 1893

Dearest friend,

Had we not agreed on full freedom of interchange, I should have to apologize to you very emphatically today. But you do not once comment on my having been remiss, the reason for which is a hypernormal writing fatigue after an awful writing campaign.

With your question, when and where this year, you anticipated mine by only a few days. Well, the holidays I ordered for myself start at the same time, the middle of August or a little earlier. So our seeing each other presents no difficulties. Where will depend on your choice. I can come for a few days to where you are if it is not an out-of-the-way or too-distant place. Our Tyrol, Brenner, *Suldental,* Toblach, and the like seem to me to offer a sufficient choice of beautiful, high-altitude places to stay. Three days in Reichenau, though, would be even nicer and would also offer something to Martha, who to my pleasure is very enthusiastic about Ida — something that happens rarely in view of her extremely reserved nature. The brief time of the vacation I shall in any case spend in Reichenau with my brood, which gives me the greatest fun.

The hysterical paralyses should have appeared long ago; they probably will be in the August issue; it is quite a short essay, focused to some extent on a single idea. You may remember that I already had the thing when you were my pupil, and I lectured on it in my course at that time. I do not want to burden you with the neuroses; I am now seeing so many neurasthenics that I may well be able to confine this work to my own material in the course of the next two to three years. But I am not for this reason dissolving our partnership. In the first place, I hope that you will explain the physiological mechanism of my clinical findings by your approach; second, I want to retain the right to come to you with all my theories and findings on the neuroses; third, I still look to you as the messiah who, by an improvement of technique, will solve the problem I have pointed out.

Your work on the nasal reflex has in no way been wasted; you yourself must be aware of that. But people need time for everything. I am sending you a small paper from which you can see that the younger generation is referring to you.[1] Perhaps you could realize your intention of presenting your material in Vienna, through Hajek,[2] Schnitzler's son-in-law and successor. It also could be done through Schrötter, if his assistant Koller, one of the best minds in Vienna and a good friend of mine, were not about to leave on a trip. Most likely you will not want to have anything to do with the big names. You can certainly visit Chiari.[3] We will talk more about it. Our work on hysteria has at last received due recognition on the part of Janet[4] in Paris. Since then, not much could be done with Breuer. His time is taken up with weddings, travels, and his practice.

I see that I can scarcely go on writing legibly, therefore I hastily close with assurances that all of us are well, that in spite of lacking information I hope the same is true of you and Ida, and that I am very much looking forward to the realization of our plan as early as this year.

With cordial greetings,

Your
Sigm. Freud

1. Probably a reference to a review by O. Chiari of Fliess's *Neue Beiträge zur Klinik und Therapie der nasalen Reflexneurosen.* This review, in the *Wiener klinische Wochenschrift,* is brief and not particularly laudatory.

2. Marcus Hajek (1861–1941) was the assistant of Johann Schnitzler (1835–1893), father of the physician and writer Arthur Schnitzler (1862–1931) and of Julius Schnitzler (1865–1939). A more positive review by Arthur Schnitzler of Fliess's *Neue Beiträge* appeared in the *Internationale klinische Rundschau* in 1893.

3. Leopold Schrötter Ritter von Kristelli (1837–1908) was the well-known head of the laryngological clinic at the university. Ottokar von Chiari (1853–1918) was his student, as was Karl Koller (1857–1944), Freud's close friend and the man who discovered the anesthetic properties of cocaine (see Bernfeld, 1953; Becker, 1963). For further information on these men and their medical publications and activities, see Lesky (1978).

4. The article to which Freud refers in this letter appeared in *Archives de neurologie,* 26 (1893):29. On the very same page is the end of an article by Pierre Janet ("Quelques définitions récentes de l'hystérie"), which concludes: "The word 'hysteria' should be kept. The name has such a long and beautiful history. If the etymology is too embarrassing it would be better, as M. Charcot so nicely put it, to modify the word 'uterus' rather than the word 'hysteria.'" The coincidence is startling. For more information on the relation between Freud and Janet, see Prevost (1973, p. 62).

---

Vienna, July 24, 1893

Dearest friend,

I intended to quarrel with you for preferring the Carpathians to the Alps, especially since you are going to the mountains, but I recently met your father-in-law at the South Station — God give all children of Israel an old age like his — and heard from him that it will take me only eight hours to get to Csorba instead of sixteen to twenty hours to a high-altitude alpine resort, that it is very beautiful there, and that you have definitely made up your mind, and therefore I yield. Yesterday on Mount Rax a beast stung my right hand; I can barely write because of the edema; I say this only to protect you from a diagnostic error.

I am already quite bored in Vienna and look forward very much to our meeting. In Reichenau everyone is doing fine; all the little rascals are thriving, my wife feels well.

At last the hysterical paralyses have appeared, but I do not yet have any offprints. In the last *Progrès médical*[1] I saw something about the nose. If you cannot get it, I'll send it to you by return mail. This year I have not been to the Brühl at all. The summer is strangely quiet after a medically very eventful half-year.

With cordial greetings to you and your dear wife,

Your faithful
Sigm. Freud

1. *Progrès médical: Journal de médecine, de chirurgie et de pharmacie,* 18 (1893):39–40, carried the summary of a paper by a Dr. Laborde, "Le réflexe nasal dans la syncope chloroformique." The paper was delivered to the Académie de Médecine at its meeting of July 11, 1893. Freud cites it because of the tie-in to Fliess's work on the nose, but in actuality the article had nothing to do with Fliess's theories.

Reichenau, August 13, 1893

Dearest friend,

I had actually planned to be with you by the time this letter arrived and, what is more, with my wife. Then came a household catastrophe, palace revolution, cook and nurse suddenly had to be chased away, and therefore my wife cannot come along. But I myself must also wait until quiet returns, and therefore I am inclined to postpone my trip to you till the second half of the vacation. So be so kind as to let me know now how long you are planning to stay and what your next stops will be. If it is too late for me to come to Csorba, I would simply meet you somewhere else, because a year in which I did not twice have the pleasure of discussing with you all the matters important to me would be terribly incomplete.

I saw your papa in Riedhof and once again I was delighted to see his vigor. I remember that he is with you now, or just has been.

With cordial greetings from house to house and warmest thanks to your dear wife for the lovely suggestion,

Your faithful
Sigm. Freud

From both of us best regards to your mama.

---

Reichenau, August 20, 1893[1]

My beloved friend,

With anyone else I would, first of all, be embarrassed to cancel after I had definitely agreed to come and, second, give different reasons than those which I shall tell you in all frankness. Thus, the following piece of home psychology: I spent the 18th and 19th on a complicated tour around and on Mount Rax with my friend Rie,[2] and yesterday sat in a cheerful mood in the new hut on the mountain when suddenly someone entered the room, completely flushed from the heat of the day, whom initially I stared at as at an apparition and then had to recognize as my wife. Martha has always maintained that climbing was impossible for her and that she did not enjoy staying on the mountain. But now she had followed me, had borne up well under the strain, and was enchanted by the view and the place. She expressed the wish to spend several days with me up here, where the accommodations are excellent, and I felt obliged to afford her this pleasure—which is possible, so to speak, without feeling remote from home, because from up here one can stay in touch with Reichenau by telephone and easily get down in two and a half hours. She had been looking forward to the trip to Csorba so very much. The events at home had shown her how difficult it is to make arrangements for leaving the children; and for the past six years, since child followed child, there has been little room for change and relaxation in her life. I do not believe I can deny her this wish. You can imagine what is behind it; gratitude, a feeling of coming back to life again of the woman who for the time being does not have to expect a child for a year because we are now living in abstinence; and you know the reasons for this as well. Now, this plan does not at all agree with my intention to visit you in Csorba. The month only has eleven more days, of which one would have to be allocated to Vienna and five to my trip. Although she never interferes with a pleasure of mine, and least of all would want to interfere with getting together with you, she nevertheless made the point that I only needed to give up Csorba, and not you, since ten days later I can have you so much nearer in the Brühl and that two ten-hour trips in the heat are no relaxation for me either. In addition, there are two other factors of which she knows nothing: the necessity not to spend much more during these months in which I have no income, and the realization that my head has not yet gotten rid of the obsession with the pursuit of medical ideas and that continuation for a while of the present way of life would be very good for it.

So I shall not come to Csorba. After the preceding arguments, which will certainly strike you as genuine, you will excuse me. But now to the second point. I do, of course, want to see you and talk and work with you for a whole day, and for this purpose want you to set aside a day in September that is convenient for you in Reichenau, Brühl, or Vienna. This year I have already made one trip to see you — no sacrifice, to be sure, but a treat[3] — and so this time would like to make it easier on myself and count on your kind indulgence to make the arrangements that are now necessary. I could come with my wife to the Brühl (Hajek) if it is not easy for you to pay us the promised visit in Reichenau. So be good and make it possible for us. I would hate to have to do without it.

For the rest, the etiology of the neuroses pursues me everywhere, as the Marlborough song follows the traveling Englishman.[4] Recently I was consulted by the daughter of the innkeeper on the Rax; it was a nice case for me.[5] — The best plan would be if you and Ida could spend one or two days with us on the Rax. It is higher than Csorba, 1,700 meters (Thörlhaus), and the food and lodging are excellent.

With the most cordial greetings and wishes for your well-being,

Your
Sigm. Freud

1. I do not believe that Ernst Kris saw this letter, which I found in Freud's desk.

2. Oscar Rie (1863–1931), pediatrician and close friend of the Freud family. He had been Freud's assistant at the Kassowitz Institute, and in 1891 they published a work together: "Klinische Studien über die halbseitige Cerebrallähmung der Kinder." Rie's wife, Melanie, and Fliess's wife, Ida, were sisters.

3. English in original.

4. *Songs of Many Wars*, edited and arranged by Kurt Adler (Howell Soskin, 1943), p. 36, tells us that "an unknown Frenchman wrote this song after Marlborough's victory at Malplaquet in 1709, when word came that the English general had fallen in battle. The fact that Marlborough was very much alive did not keep the ballad from achieving wide popularity. The melody was originally a hunting song of the 17th century; since then it has served almost every nation in the world at one time or another." Schröter points out that Freud is here citing Goethe's *Romische Elegien* 2:9 ff.

5. This is Katharina of the *Studies on Hysteria*.

---

September 14, 1893
IX., Berggasse 19

Dearest friend,

Rosenberg[1] called my attention to the fact that in the *Berliner klinische Wochenschrift*, no. 14, of 1889 there is a series of articles on the nasal reflex neuroses by Scheinmann,[2] which supposedly contain an astonishing number of your findings; as, for instance, the cocaine experiment, the connection with the genital life, the stomach and intestinal troubles, and more of the kind. A true precursor, then. I do not have this volume.

Much luck with your own cure. I certainly expect you to apprise me of everything that happens.

Cordial greetings to you and Ida.

Your
Sigm. Freud

1. Presumably a reference to Ludwig Rosenberg, a pediatrician who figures prominently as Leopold in Freud's dream of Irma's injection. He was the father of Anny Katan, a psychoanalyst, who has informed me (in a letter of September 9, 1980) that Rosenberg was a regular member of the Saturday tarok party, which included Oscar Rie, Alfred Rie, and sometimes Julius Schnitzler, the surgeon. Rosenberg died in 1927.

2. The article that Freud is referring to was given by J. Scheinmann as a paper to the Laryngologische Vereinigung in Berlin, in January 1889, and was published in *Berliner klinische Wochenschrift*, 14 (1889):295 ff., under the title "Zur Diagnose und

Therapie der nasalen Reflexneurosen." It is a thoroughgoing medical overview of all the work done in the area. Of course, the author could not have referred to Fliess, since nothing of Fliess's had been published in 1889. At the end of the article Scheinmann writes, "I can no longer doubt that in cases of nasal hyperesthesia numerous changes in the composition of the blood in the nose are occasioned by the skin and the genital apparatus."

---

Vienna, September 29, 1893

Dearest friend,

I left myself some time so that I could ask you about the success of the operation and whether you have to go back to Bremen once more. That your diagnosis was correct I already knew, since you altogether ruin my critical faculties and I really believe you in everything. I shall be very glad to hear that you are free of headaches. You will then enjoy life so much more. I think it was very nice of Scheinmann to touch upon so many themes and yet leave so much for you. A true precursor with whom one need not be angry. I have the highest expectations for your work if only you will get well so that you can devote yourself to it and to the polyclinic.

I am sending you today an obituary of Charcot that was published at the beginning of September.[1] If I have already sent it to you, then ten thousand apologies. My wife is getting ready to come home. All the children are still well and thriving. Shortly after our epidemic of throat infections, there were several light cases of scarlet fever in Reichenau.

I am still very insufficiently occupied and am correspondingly ill-humored. Breuer is an obstacle to my professional progress in Vienna. He dominates the very circles on which I had counted. His friendship for me, of which he has given indubitable proof, is in evidence far less than I would have expected in "paving the way" for my practice.

I happen to have very few new sexualia. I shall soon start tackling hysteria.

My little nieces' departure for America has been delayed. The days in Reichenau did us such good because they showed us that we exercise a certain attraction for both of you, even when you can have the company of parents and siblings. Thus we are hoping to have another merry get-together before the year is out, in good health on both sides.

With cordial greetings to you and your dear wife,

Your
Sigm. Freud

1. On September 9 Freud published an obituary of Charcot in the *Wiener medizinische Wochenschrift.*

Vienna, October 6, 1893

Dearest friend,

I was just about to get cross over the absence of any news from you when your amiable letter foiled this intention. I still miss in it a positive, heartfelt assurance that you are better, but perhaps it is still too early for this, and God knows what an ordeal the operation was. When you are well again, we shall donate Schaeffer's picture to the therapeutic polyclinic, for I am objective enough to widen my interest in your recovery to the extent of identifying it with the creation of the polyclinic.

Your verdict on my Charcot obituary and the news that you read it to Ida delighted me very much. I knew nothing about the honorable plagiarism by the *Allgemeine L*[1] *Zeitung*. It is very kind of you to respond to my lamentations about business in Vienna, but I really feel it is a disgrace for me to talk about it to you; it only proves the extent to which I sometimes let myself go. Especially in the case of your little sister-in-law I was grateful to Breuer, rather than angry, that he left me out, because I strongly dislike mixing friendship and business; do not, as you know, think anything of my therapy; and gladly avoid the comparison with your medical activities. In the meantime things have become more lively. The sexual business attracts people who are all stunned and then go away won over after having exclaimed,"No one has ever asked me about that before!" It is becoming more and more complicated as confirmation comes in. Yesterday, for instance, I saw four new cases whose etiology, according to the chronology, could only be coitus interruptus. You will perhaps enjoy a short account of them. They are far from being uniform.

(1) Woman, 41; children, 16, 14, *11*, and 7. Nervous for the last twelve years; well during pregnancy; recurrence afterward; not made worse by last pregnancy. Attacks of dizziness with feelings of

weakness, agoraphobia, *anxious* expectation, no trace of neurasthenia, little hysteria. Etiology confirmed, pure [anxiety neurosis].

(2) Woman, 24; children 4 and 2. Since the spring of '93 attacks of pain at night (from back to sternum) with insomnia; otherwise nothing; well during the day. Husband a traveling salesman; was at home for some time during the spring as well as just now. In the summer, while the husband was away, she was perfectly well. Coitus interruptus and great fear of having children. Hysteria, therefore.

(3) Man, 42; children 17, 16, and 13. Well until a year ago; then, on his father's death, sudden anxiety attack with heart failure, hypochondriacal fear of cancer of the tongue; several months later a second attack, with cyanosis, intermittent pulse, fear of death, and so on; since then feels weak, dizzy, agoraphobic; some dyspepsia. This is a case of pure anxiety neurosis accompanied by heart symptoms after an emotional upset; whereas coitus interruptus was apparently tolerated easily for ten years.[2]

(4) Man, 34. Without appetite for the last three years; dyspepsia for the last year; with loss of 20 kg, constipation. When this ceased, violent intracranial pressure at the time of the sirocco; attacks of weakness with associated sensations, hysteriform clonic spasms. In this case, therefore, neurasthenia predominates. One child, 5 years old. Since then, coitus interruptus owing to his wife's illness. At about the same time as his recovery from dyspepsia, normal intercourse was resumed.

In view of such reactions to the same noxa, it takes courage to insist on the specificity of its effects as I define it. Yet it must be so; and there are certain points to go on even in these four cases (pure anxiety neurosis, pure hysteria, anxiety neurosis with heart symptoms, neurasthenia with hysteria).

In case (1), a very intelligent woman, there was no fear of having children; she has a pure anxiety neurosis.

In case (2), a nice, silly little woman, this anxiety was strongly developed; after a short time she initially developed hysteria.[3]

Case (3), with anxiety neurosis and heart symptoms, was a highly potent man who was a heavy smoker.

Case (4), on the contrary, was (without having masturbated) only moderately potent, frigid.

Now imagine what would happen if one were a physician like you, for instance, able to investigate the genitals and the nose simultaneously; the riddle should be solved in no time.

But I am too old, lazy, and overwhelmed with duties to still learn something myself.

With cordial greetings from house to house,

Your
Sigm. Freud

Day before yesterday in trooped wife and children in the best of health.

1. Letter illegible, possibly "C."

2. Kris (*Origins*, p. 78n1) points out that "this case appears, with some further details, in Freud's first and second papers on anxiety neurosis (1895)."

3. The German is *Sie hat nach kurzer Zeit zuerst Hysterie.* Meaning unclear, perhaps that she had her first attack of hysteria.

---

Vienna, October 18, 1893

Dearest friend,

I hope that my confidence in the speediest recovery of your dear wife arrives at your house after that recovery has itself taken place. It cannot be her desire to be ill, so I shall not dwell on that at all. I waited a long time for news of your well-being and was just about to write you of my concern. Generally I am not in the habit of torturing you with obligations to write, but I am so very ignorant that I have no idea of the scope of such an operation.

Today I am already tired of writing; I had a distressing disagreement with Breuer, which occasioned [my writing] many letters.[1] He ended up behaving so graciously that everything is smoothed over; I have just finished my last letter to him, and the one to you I really cannot postpone any longer.

I could write a great deal about the nose and sexuality (two topics). That you see little material of this kind is indeed evidence of its preselection. At present people are not rushing to consult me, yet I see the most beautiful cases and have even made some progress. Next time I shall tell you about an observation of migraine with scotomas in masturbators, unfortunately *without* involvement of the nose. I have established contact here with a Dr. Weil[2] who is much brighter than Laufer;[3] he studied under Schrötter,[4] is a Jew, reads — in short, he would be quite suitable if he were not so ill-mannered. I refer patients to him and urge him to read your writings, and so on. He recently made a remark that I promised to convey to you. He objects to a trifling matter, the case of a woman who in one year had six miscarriages in the second month. He believes this must be a lapse because there was not sufficient time, unless it was a case of dysmenorrhea membranacea, a mistake [in diagnosis] you are unlikely to make.

Not to forget my own interests. The wife of Dr. R. visited me, could not understand why you had not written to me about her, and I promised to remind you. She wants me to give her the treatment you recommended.

I do not in any way intend to pass over my heart condition.[5] At the moment it is much better—no thanks to any merit of mine, because I am smoking heavily owing to all the trouble of which there was a great deal recently. I believe it will soon flare up again, and badly. As far as smoking is concerned, I shall scrupulously follow a prescription of yours; I did this once before when you gave your opinion in regard to it (railroad station—period of waiting). But I did miss it greatly. An acute cold did not aggravate the condition. I observed this symptom complex in a few patients who were *Gast[r]iker [Gestiker?]* and am not yet convinced of its nasal nature. Today I still owe you a great deal.

With cordial greetings to you and your dear wife,

Your faithful
Sigm. Freud

1. I found these letters in Maresfield Gardens. The subject is the financial debt that Freud owes to Breuer. Freud insists on paying it back, and Breuer graciously tells Freud that it is hardly important to him. It is evident that this was a very sensitive issue for Freud. He had also borrowed money from Josef Paneth and from Fleischl. In an unpublished letter to Martha of July 11, 1883, Freud makes this interesting comment, explaining why he cannot travel to Berlin to see Martha: "No discovery gives me the right to go into debt with the expectation of having a great future."

That Freud's attitude toward Breuer's generosity was in the beginning one of happy gratitude is shown clearly in the unpublished letters to Martha. One example (July 18, 1883) suffices: "Breuer has urged me to take a great deal of money for the time when he will be away. If it were anybody but him, I would be ashamed, but he proves himself to be such a trusting friend that his money plays a very secondary role."

2. See letter of April 20, 1895, and Sulloway (1979, p. 152n13). See too Fliess's *Nasale Fernleiden*, p. 42, where Fliess recounts an episode from Weil's practice.

3. Not identified.

4. Leopold Schrötter Ritter von Kristelli (1837–1908). See Lesky (1978, pp. 330 ff., 413 ff.).

5. The German text reads, *Mit meinem Herzbefinden denke ich Dir keineswegs durchzugehen.* Schur (1972, p. 41) translates the passage as "I have no intention of running out on you with my heart condition" and takes it to be a reference to dying. The German can have either meaning, and it is not entirely certain which one Freud intended.

Vienna, November 27,[1] 1893

Dear friend,[2]

The last letter I was able to produce for you immediately thereafter was lost,[3] as we say in Vienna, and then came a period in which I did not feel like writing, my nose was stopped up, and I could not get myself to do it. I again let myself be cauterized, again enjoy working, but otherwise am little satisfied with the success of the local therapy. I am not obeying your order not to smoke; do you really consider it a remarkable boon to live a great many years in misery? But I am very little bothered by the corresponding sensations.

So now it turns out that I have put the news about my own worthy person into the very foreground, as though there were nothing more important to write or ask about. The lost letter contained a lot pertaining to science: nose, sexualia, migraine with scotoma; all this is lost now, but it is nothing to cry about. You could not use the nose stories in any event — guesses[4] without nose mirror findings. The sexual business is becoming more firmly consolidated, the contradictions are fading away, but new material is very meager because of a quite unusual lack of patients during office hours. When I take a case for thorough repair, everything is confirmed and sometimes the seeker finds more than he wishes[5] — especially anesthesia sexualis has many and quite contrary meanings. The anxiety type as seen in Pietsch[6] has become quite clear. I have seen a jolly old bachelor who denies himself nothing and who produced a classic anxiety attack after he let himself be seduced by his thirty-year-old mistress into having intercourse three times in a row. Altogether I have hit upon the idea to tie anxiety not to a psychic but rather to a *physical* consequence of sexual abuse. I was led to this by a wonderfully pure case of anxiety neurosis following coitus interruptus in a totally placid and *totally frigid* woman. Otherwise it does not make any sense.

In every other respect the period of my silence has been quite uninteresting. At home everyone is well; influenza, which is bound to become epidemic again, is just ahead of us. My head misses the usual overwork since I lost Mrs. von K.[7] I am on good terms with Breuer but see little of him. He has registered for my Saturday lecture! Your father-in-law is still bent on finding me a better apartment; recently he proposed one for 3,400 florins to me. This is very kind of him, but I intend to remain here for a while.

This idle talk presupposes that you and your dear wife are both well and that your headaches have cleared up for good since the last operation; otherwise I would certainly have heard from you in the meantime.

Enclosure A ("Enuresis")[8] is rubbish. Enclosure B[9] I cede to you; perhaps you will find something of interest in it. I know K. and am treating members of his family.

With the most cordial greetings to the entire house,

Your
Sigm. Freud

1. Date previously was incorrectly read as 17.

2. Freud uses the German word *Teurer*—literally, valued one or cherished one—which at the time was a common salutation used by close friends. In German today one would say *Lieber*.

3. Freud uses the Viennese colloquialism *verschloffen*.

4. English in original.

5. See Franz F. von Lipperheide, *Sprachwörterbuch* (a book that Freud had in his library), 2nd ed., 1909, p. 184, under "finden": "Man findet häufig mehr, als man zu finden glaubt." This apparently is a German translation of a verse from Corneille's *Le Menteur*, Act 4, scene 1, where Dorante says, "On trouve bien souvent plus qu'on ne croit trouver."

6. See Fliess in *Zur Periodenlehre: Gesammelte Aufsätze*, p. 59: "I cannot suppress here an experience which was written into my heart. Years ago I met the writer Ludwig Pietsch in a florist shop. In his impulsive way he put his arms around me and said: 'I am feeling better than I deserve. I feel happier and fresher than I have felt for years. And, dear friend, if your theories are right, that can only mean that I will soon die, for I feel too good.' My objections did not help. 'Yes, yes, you just don't want to admit it.' The theory really was correct, for soon, on the 27th of November, 1911, the truth of my theory was sealed by Ludwig Pietsch's last breath." See also Fliess's *Ablauf des Lebens*, p. 339, where the date of the meeting (end of October 1911) is given.

7. Cäcilie M., of the *Studies on Hysteria*.

8. No doubt a reference to Freud's "Über ein Symptom, das häufig die Enuresis nocturna der Kinder begleitet," published in the *Neurologisches Centralblatt*. The article is not at all psychological, and Freud even goes so far as to say that the explanation that the phenomenon (hypertonia of the lower extremities) might have to do with fear or shame is not possible. Perhaps this is why Freud disliked the article.

9. There is no clue to what this might have been.

---

Vienna, December 11, 1893

Dearest friend,

My prompt reply to your letter means that I have a few free hours on Sunday and is not a request for reciprocation in kind. Write when you have time and material.

Unfortunately I saw your dear Ida only too briefly and too rarely; on one of the three days I was in Brno, and she spent all three days at the bedside of her mother. I found her looking glorious[1] and she honored me with the admission that already today, her first day, she is bored!! She will not remain Viennese for very long. The transplantation seems to have succeeded. I heard from her that you intend to lecture on my hysterical paralyses, and felt so honored that I thought this must be a misunderstanding.

She further told me of your practical physics, her indignation about it, and I agreed with her without reservation—that is, with the one reservation that I could not maintain this opinion if you yourself convinced me that it was necessary to study this new subject. In spite of this humble uncertainty, I still think that if you were to succeed in improving the coitus devised by God Almighty, everything else would be rubbish in comparison and I would gladly come to Berlin and help you select a place in the Tiergarten[2] for your statue.

The congress is in Rome; there will not be much left over for Vienna; you should speak and write, I think, certainly there and elsewhere. By the way, Scheinmann has been heard from again; his ideas move along very similar lines. Don't you know him? In September the congress of scientists will meet here, and I have been appointed first secretary of the neurological section.

My nose was affected by catarrh; at last it got well again and now I have a clear head and am in a good mood. "Today" I started to restrict my smoking—that is to say, to reduce the continual smoking to a discontinuous, countable amount. I really have the impression that the whole business is organic and cardiac; something neurotic would be much harder to take; one is that indifferent only about organic problems. Moreover, the prohibition of smoking does not agree with the nasal diagnosis. I believe you are fulfilling your medical duty; I shall say nothing more about it and shall obey partially (but not wisely). Two cigars a day—thereby one recognizes the nonsmoker!

I am literally loaded with news about the neuroses and neuropsychoses, but it is all still rather chaotic. Right now I am writing the work on hysteria, which will not be bad. Breuer is too busy to join in doing much. We have a miserable influenza epidemic; my father celebrated his seventy-eighth birthday with a severe attack and now he is a shadow of his former self. In our house everyone is still well. Königstein[3] has been proposed for a professorship; I heartily hope he gets it; he is so upright a man; no one can surpass his standards.

With the most cordial greetings to you and your dear wife,

Your
Sigm. Freud

1. English in original.
2. A park in Berlin.
3. Leopold Königstein (1850–1924), oculist and friend of Freud. For his role in the discovery of the anesthetic property of cocaine, see Bernfeld (1953). Freud's 1886 paper, "Observation of a Severe Case of Hemi-anaesthesia in a Hysterical Male," was based on a case he presented to the Gesellschaft der Ärzte on November 26, 1886, jointly with Königstein. In fact, Königstein became assistant professor in 1900. See Lesky (1978, p. 489).

---

January 4, 1894
IX., Berggasse 19

Dearest friend,

In the last issue of *Revue neurologique* I read an announcement of "Les réflexes d'origine nasale," by a certain W. Fliess in *Arch. internat. de laryng., rhinol., . . . ,* Sept.–Oct. 1893.[1] Could that be you, and you did not send it to me?

Next time you will receive (in manuscript) a piece of the theory of neuroses (phobias, obsessions).[2]

Cordial greetings.

Your
Sigm. Freud

1. The article appeared in *Archives de laryngologie,* 6 (1893):266–269, Travail lu au Congrès de médecine interne de Wiesbaden. It is only a French summary, by Fliess himself, of his longer article in German, "Die nasale Reflexneurose."
2. See note 1 to letter of January 30, 1894. Freud gave a lecture titled "Die Abwehr-Neuropsychosen" to the Verein für Psychiatrie und Neurologie on January 15, 1895. An Autorreferat, "Über den 'Mechanismus der Zwangsvorstellungen und Phobien,'" was published in the *Wiener klinische Wochenschrift.* This one-page report was (later?) expanded to "Obsessions et phobies (leur mécanisme psychique et leur étiologie)," published on January 30.

---

January 16, 1894[1]
IX., Berggasse 19

My dear friends,

Please do not be angry that I did not answer Frau Ida's kind letter sooner. I am very annoyed, in fact furious, that you two are not feeling any better. Your papa, whom I saw on Wednesday, did speak of good news, but I know how reticent he and you are. On the whole I do not think it is nice of you to be living in Berlin, when you are missed daily by the likes of us. Your answer will be that I am not the only one or the closest one who feels that way, but I am one nevertheless.

If the only reason for *his* not writing to me is that he has so much to catch up on now that he is well, I shall be content. If encouraged by a single line, I shall send off a manuscript full of the most beautiful, brand-new discoveries.[2]

Cordial greetings.

Your
F.

1. The original of this letter belonged to Fliess's son, Robert. I obtained it from the late Elenore Fliess, Robert's widow.
2. See note 1 to letter of January 30, 1894.

---

January 30, 1894
IX., Berggasse 19

Dearest friend,

I was glad to have a line from you again, and I am very pleased with the progress of your discoveries.

Herewith the latest [manuscript].[1] Be good enough to forward it to Mendel[2] along with the enclosed letter after you have enjoyed it. Very hectic period now. All well here.

With cordial greetings to you and your dear wife,

Your
Sigm. Freud

1. Presumably the manuscript that Freud sent to Fliess was "Die Abwehr-Neuropsychosen," which was published in the *Neurologisches Centralblatt* later in 1894.
2. Probably Emanuel Mendel, editor of the *Neurologisches Centralblatt* in Berlin.

---

Vienna, February 7, 1894

Dearest friend,

I too am so harassed at present that I am responding to your letter immediately so as not to leave it unanswered for too long. Your appreciation of the theory of obsessional ideas did me good, for I miss you the entire time I am engaged in this kind of work. If you come to Vienna in the spring, you must tear yourself away from the family for a few hours and devote them to an exchange of ideas with me. I still have something *in petto* [in reserve] that is only just dawning on me. You saw that the last paper dealt with affect *transformation* and [affect] *transposition;* in addition, there also is *substitution.* I shall not lift the veil any further as yet.

You are right—the connection between obsessional neurosis and sexuality is not always all that obvious. I can assure you that in my case 2 (urinary urgency), it was not easy to find either; someone who had not searched for it as single-mindedly as I did would have overlooked it. In this case, which I came to know thoroughly during a fattening-up treatment of several months' duration, the sexual [factor] simply dominates the whole scene!—Your case of the disgusted and divorced woman is quite apt to yield the same result on closer analysis.

At present I am engaged in the analysis of several cases that look like paranoia and that have developed according to my theory. The book on hysteria I am doing with Breuer is half-finished; just a few of the total number of case histories and two general chapters are still outstanding.

At home, fortunately, all is well. The little one is turning out to be charming. Her rickets is far more severe than necessary. Breuer became a grandmother *[sic]* on February 3; the granddaughter looks fantastically like him.

I am calmer about your headaches since I received word from Scheffer *[sic]* in Bremen promising full recovery. I was so impertinent as to contact him directly. I do not know whether I have already written you that I will have to serve as the first secretary of the neurological section of the scientific meeting in September. I hope I shall also see you there and sometimes also at our house.

Billroth's death[1] is the event of the day around here. How enviable not to have outlived oneself.

With cordial greetings from all of us to you and your dear, good wife,

Your
Sigm. Freud

1. On Theodor Billroth (1822–1894) and his illness, see *Wiener klinische Wochenschrift,* 7 (1894):123 ff. His achievements in surgery are discussed in Lesky (1978, pp. 435 ff.). Freud took Billroth's courses in clinical surgery in 1877 and 1878 (Bernfeld, 1951).

Vienna, April 19, 1894

Dearest friend,

Your kind letter puts an end to my reserve and my wish to spare you. I feel justified in writing to you about my state of health. The scientific and personal news will then follow at the end.

Since everyone needs the suggestive influence of someone else in order to obtain a respite from his own criticism, I have in fact not had anything warm between my lips since then (today it has been three weeks); and today I can already watch others smoke without envying them and even again imagine life and work without this support. It has not been long since I reached this point; moreover, the misery of abstinence has been far greater than I ever imagined — but that, of course, is obvious.

Less obvious, perhaps, is the state of my health in other respects. Soon after the withdrawal, there were some tolerable days and I began to write down the state of the neurosis problem for you; then suddenly there came a severe cardiac misery, greater than I ever had while smoking. The most violent arrhythmia, constant tension, pressure, burning in the heart region; shooting pains down my left arm; some dyspnea, all of it essentially in attacks extending continuously over two-thirds of the day; the dyspnea is so moderate that one suspects something organic; and with it a feeling of depression, which took the form of visions of death and departure in place of the usual frenzy of activity. The organic discomforts have lessened during the past two days; the lypemanic mood[1] persists, having the courtesy, though, to let up suddenly (as it did last night and at noon today) and leave behind a human being who looks forward with confidence again to a long life and undiminished pleasure in resuming the battle.

It is too distressing for a medical man who spends every hour of the day struggling to gain an understanding of the neuroses not to know whether he is suffering from a logical or a hypochondriacal mild depression. He has to be helped with this. So I actually turned to Breuer last night and told him that in my opinion the heart trouble was not consistent with nicotine poisoning; rather, I presume I have a chronic myocarditis which does not tolerate smoking. I also remember quite well that the arrhythmia appeared rather suddenly in 1889 after my attack of influenza. I had the satisfaction of being told by him that it might be *the one thing or the other* and that I should have myself examined soon. I promised, but know that most of these examinations do not turn up anything. I do not know the extent to which it is at all possible to differentiate between the two, but I think it should be possible to do so on the basis of subjective symptoms and events and that you people know what to make of it all. This time I am especially suspicious of you, because this heart affair of mine is the only one in which I have heard you make contradictory statements. Last time you still explained it as being nasal and said that the percussive signs of a nicotine heart were missing; this time you really show great concern for me and forbid me to smoke. I can understand this only if I assume that you want to conceal the true state of affairs from me, and beg you not to do this. If you can say something definite, just tell me. I have no exaggerated opinion either of my responsibilities or of my indispensability and shall endure with great dignity the uncertainty and the shortened life expectancy connected with a diagnosis of myocarditis; on the contrary, I might even benefit from it in arranging the remainder of my life and enjoying fully what is left to me.

It was painful to realize that in the event of a chronic illness, I could not count on doing scientific work, since I was so completely unable to work. I have not looked at your beautiful case histories; the "present state of the theory of the neuroses" broke off in mid-sentence; everything is as in the castle of Sleeping Beauty when catalepsy suddenly overtook it. As the last few days have undoubtedly brought relief, I hope I shall soon have caught up and shall then report to you.

I shall keep your remark on the diary in mind; you are right. I did not especially like Mrs. Er. either. Perhaps I am doing her an injustice when I classify her as the meat dish "silly goose" and as the vegetable dish "obnoxious root."[2] I can well believe that analysis was disagreeable for her; with this she merely confirmed the idea of "defense"; she also bolted from me the third time. Otherwise I can give her a certificate of good conduct. She is an anesthetic plus a case of unfulfilled longing: melancholia; no question of anxiety; therefore also no intercourse — if I have been informed correctly. Naturally I did not reveal to her that I already knew earlier about the Hofrat.[3] She fancies that no one suspects anything and hates me as a possible source of betrayal.

Otherwise I have nothing new on the theory of the neuroses; but I keep collecting material and expect it will turn out to be something.

The many new things you announce must signify that at last you feel well almost without interruption. I have thought about the etiology of your second headache. I do not quite believe in it. Would you not rather go by the cribriform cells? Rascals and wife are well; the latter is not a confidante of my death deliria. Quite superfluous, in any event.

As soon as I am able to work again, I shall send you a bundle of interesting case histories.

With very cordial greetings to your dear wife and to you, and many thanks for your letter,

Your
Sigm. Freud

1. A state of morbid depression. Incorrectly read in *Anfänge* as *hypomanische*.

2. *Z'widerwurzen*; a south German and Austrian colloquial expression denoting a sulky person.

3. Reference unknown.

---

Vienna, April 25, 1894

My dear friend,

You wrote so kindly that I cannot let you wait until I have something to say, but rather must report on everyday events.

I certainly consider you more competent than anyone else to make a differential diagnosis in these delicate matters; and I once again let myself be confounded in what to make of my condition. Breuer, for example, quietly accepted the possibility of a nontoxic heart condition. Apparently I do not have a dilation of the heart; split heart sounds, arrhythmia, and the like continue despite my abstinence. My libido[1] has long been subdued. One gram of digitalis in two days has considerably diminished the subjective discomforts and apparently also influenced the arrhythmia, which, however, I detect whenever I find some resonance of my pulse. My mild depression, fatigue, inability to work, and the mild dyspnea have become rather worse.

That is the status idem. That I shall not leave this beautiful world without summoning you for a personal farewell has been settled in my mind ever since I began to feel ill. I do not think, however, that I shall be in a position to take you up on your offer in the near future; still, the torture and the useless slipping away of the present hurt me more than any possible unsatisfactory prognosis.

In a few days I shall send you several pages of raw material, a quick sketch of an analysis in which one can see down to the roots of the neurosis. I have not yet been able to pull myself together to make a summary for you, and that annoys me greatly. That was indeed very different in other times. The social and scientific dead calm is causing me all kinds of worries. I feel best when I am in the midst of my daily work. I hope that you, at least, are well. I believe that for a whole hour during these days, I was actually glad about my illness. That must have been when I received your letter.

I cordially greet you and your dear Ida, and my family joins in.

Your
Dr. Sigm. Freud

1. From the context it seems likely that Freud is referring to his desire to smoke, rather than to sexual desire.

---

Vienna, May 6, 1894

My dear friend,

Am herewith returning the "stomachaches"![1] There is little to be said about it except that it is most remarkable and very beautiful. In such cases our late friend E. Fleischl[2] used to say, If you further take into consideration that the matter is even *true,* you will not be able to deny me your recognition. Perhaps I shall manage a few remarks, after all:

(1) Whether the location is right or left, I believe, is not sufficiently mentioned or appreciated.

(2) The theoretical part of it has again turned out to be very short, as did the differential diagnosis. In short, more breadth. How does it happen that not every affection of that particular locus results in stomachaches? I presume there is a connection here with the "neuralgic changes."

I enclose a case history, the form of which is to be excused by my state of health, which I hope will otherwise interest you.

I have not yet been able to finish the "Introduction to the Neuroses." I feel better, at times even much better, but I have not been free of symptoms for as much as half a day, and my mood and ability to work are really at a low ebb. I still think it is not owing to nicotine; having by chance seen *a good deal of the same thing* in my practice last week, I believe it is rheumatic myocarditis, something one never really gets rid of. During the last years I have repeatedly had rheumatic muscle nodes in other parts of the body.

During the summer I should like to go back to anatomy for a while; that is, after all, the only gratifying thing.

I have guests and therefore conclude with cordial greetings to you and your dear wife.

Your
Sigm. Freud

1. No doubt a reference to "Magenschmerz und Dysmenorrhöe in einem neuen Zusammenhang," the first section of which was published in the *Wiener klinische Rundschau* on January 6, 1895. There Fliess asks the question, "But is there in the nose, perhaps, as in the cerebral cortex, a specific localization for the individual distant symptoms in other organs?" Fliess then answers this with a resounding "Yes." This is, I believe, Fliess's own contribution. Similarly, in vol. 8, p. 115, Fliess speaks of "unknown dysmenorrheal pains" and on p. 138 he says that an abortion can be provoked through the nose. In vol. 5, p. 67, he says that a nosebleed stopped when genital bleeding occurred. He mentions a patient from Vienna, M. B——y, twenty-two years old, surely his wife's sister (Melanie Bondy).

2. Ernst Fleischl von Marxow (1846–1891) played an important role in Freud's early life. The story has been told with dramatic flair by Jones (*Life* 1:49, 98) and by Bernfeld (1953), but more research is needed. An important unpublished letter from Freud to Martha of October 28, 1883, gives us additional details (the latter part of the letter was quoted by Jones, *Life* 1:99): "Marthi, you are partly right about Fleischl. Our relationship is not exactly one of friendship, for he has not been a friend to me in the way that Breuer has been. There was always a chasm between us, an aura of unapproachability around him, and when we were together he was always too involved with himself to be able to get close to me. But I admire and love him with the passion of my intellect, if you can allow me this expression. His downfall will move me the way that the destruction of a holy and famous temple would have touched an ancient Greek. I love him not so much as a man but as a precious achievement of creation. And you do not really need to be jealous."

In the Library of Congress I found three letters from Fleischl to Freud (two are dated February 20 and September 16, 1884; the third, congratulating Freud on his docentship, undated, is probably from 1885). They are polite notes thanking Freud for offprints and suggesting changes in an anatomical manuscript that Freud had submitted to the *Berliner Centralblatt.*

Ernst's brother, Otto Fleischl von Marxow, edited his collected papers, *Gesammelte Abhandlungen* (Leipzig: Johann Ambrosius Barth, 1893), which contain a biographical sketch of Ernst by Sigmund Exner. Exner ends with the following paragraphs (my translation):

"It is easy to understand that a man with such brilliant gifts would make a deep impression also on the female sex. He found great pleasure in the frequent company of intellectually gifted women of all ages, since the receptiveness of the female mind to his many-sided interests had a beneficial effect on him. If he did not manage to form a bond for life [with a woman], this was almost certainly due to his premature illness. When I was called, on the 22nd of October, 1891, to Ernst von Fleischl's bedside and saw a corpse in front of me, my first comforting thought was, 'At last he has found rest.' How many times in the last years have I left his room under the shadow of the tragedy that was playing itself out there. Peace had come there now. For those of us who were his friends, Ernst was already lost to us much earlier. Not all at once, but from year to year gradually the relationship of lively mutual friendship turned into deep and one-sided pity.

"We saw one brilliant quality after another begin to pale, becoming suffocated in the dreadful mire of physical suffering. And yet our friend did not live in vain, for the following essays bear witness to the fact that his memory will not be lost to the history of science. But they also allow us to recognize how much more he could have achieved, given his gifts, had his body remained as healthy as his mind."

# Intensification of the Friendship

Vienna, May 21, 1894

Dearest friend,

Dearest in truth, because I find it touching that you should so thoroughly go into my condition at a time when you are either very busy or not well or possibly both. There was a gap in your letters which had begun to look uncanny to me, and which almost induced me to write for information to a young lady in Berlin with whom I am acquainted[1] and who, I hope, is on friendly terms with me as well. Then came your letter with the meticulous refutation of my fantasies that are typical of an intern and a dilettante, but not a word about your own health. I have noted for some time that you bear suffering better and with more dignity than I, who eternally vacillate in my moods.

I promise you a detailed report on my illness next time; I feel better, but far from well; at least I am working again. Today I shall allow myself a good hour and chat only about science with you. It is obviously no special favor of fate that I have approximately five hours a year to exchange ideas with you, when I can barely do without the other—and you are the only other, the *alter.*

Tomorrow I am sending the hen and the five little chicks to Reichenau, and during the sad loneliness that follows—my sister-in-law Minna, otherwise my closest confidante, will depart two weeks later—I shall more often carry out my resolution at least to write to you.

I put part of the neurosis story on paper for you when I was still in my worst period, but now I am stuck. I have a lot to do; in addition, the next installment of the *Leçons du mardi;* the last case history for Breuer; continuing my neurosis collection; thus, I am making no progress.

Was not Marion Delorme a jewel?[2] She will not be included in the collection with Breuer because the second level,[3] that of the sexual factor, is not supposed to be disclosed there. The case history I am writing now — a cure — is among my most difficult pieces of work. You may have it before Breuer if you return it promptly. Among the gloomy thoughts of the past few months was one, in second place right after wife and children — that I shall no longer be able to prove the sexual thesis. After all, one does not want to die either immediately or completely.

I am pretty much alone here in the elucidation of the neuroses. They look upon me as pretty much of a monomaniac, while I have the distinct feeling that I have touched upon one of the great secrets of nature. There is something odd about the incongruity between one's own and other people's estimation of one's intellectual work. Look at this book on the diplegias, which I threw together with a minimum of interest and effort, almost in a frivolous mood. It has been tremendously successful. The reviewers say the nicest things about it; especially the French praise it to high heaven. Only today I came upon a book by Raymond, Charcot's successor, who simply copied this work in an appropriate section, with respectful acknowledgment, of course. And of the really good things, such as the *Aphasia*, the "Obsessional Ideas" which now threaten to appear in print, and the forthcoming "Etiology and Theory of the Neuroses," I can expect nothing better than a respectable failure. It confounds one and makes one somewhat bitter. There are still a hundred gaps, large and small, in the matter of the neuroses; but I am getting closer to an outline and some general perspectives. I know three mechanisms: that of affect transformation (conversion hysteria), that of affect displacement (obsessional ideas), and that of exchange of affect (anxiety neurosis and melancholia). In every case it should be sexual excitation that undergoes these transpositions, but the impetus to them is not in every case something sexual; that is to say, in every case in which neuroses are acquired, it happens as a result of sexual disturbances, but there are people in whom heredity causes a disturbance of their sexual affects and who develop the corresponding forms of hereditary neurosis. The most general viewpoints under which I can classify the neuroses are the four following:

(1) Degeneration
(2) Senility
(3) Conflict
(4) Conflagration

What do these mean?[4]

*Degeneration* means the innately abnormal behavior of the sexual affects; so that conversion, displacement, and transformation into anxiety occur to the degree to which the sexual affects come into play in the course of life.

*Senility* is clear; it is, as it were, degeneration acquired in normal fashion with old age.

*Conflict* coincides with my viewpoint of defense; it comprises the cases of acquired neuroses in persons who are not hereditarily abnormal. What is warded off is always sexuality.

*Conflagration* is a new point of view; it means conditions of what might be called acute degeneration (for example, in severe intoxication, in fevers, in the prestages of paralysis)—catastrophes, that is, in which there occur disturbances of the sexual affects without sexual precipitating causes. Traumatic neurosis might possibly be approached from this point of view.

The core and mainstay of the whole story remain, of course, the fact that as a result of particular sexual noxae even healthy people can acquire the various forms of neurosis. The bridge to a wider conception is built upon the fact that where a neurosis develops without sexual noxa, a similar disturbance of the sexual affects can be shown to have been present from the first. Sexual affect is of course taken in its broadest sense, as an excitation having a definite quantity.

I might bring you my latest example in support of this thesis. A 42-year-old man, strong and handsome, suddenly developed a neurasthenic dyspepsia at the age of 30, with a loss of 25 kilos, and since then has lived in a reduced and neurasthenic state. At the time at which this occurred, he was, to be sure, engaged to be married and emotionally disturbed by his fiancée's illness. Apart from this, however, there were no sexual noxae. He masturbated, perhaps only for a year, from 16 to 17; at 17 he had normal intercourse; hardly ever coitus interruptus; no excesses, no abstinence. He himself ascribes the cause of his trouble to the strain he put on his constitution until the age of 30: to his having worked, drunk, and smoked heavily and led an irregular life. But this strong man, subject to ordinary noxae, was *never* (never from 17 to 30) properly potent: was never able to have intercourse more than once, and besides was through with it quickly, never really exploited his luck with women, never could quickly find his way into the vagina. Where does this curtailment come from? I do not know; yet it is striking that it is present precisely in him. Incidentally, I have treated two of his sisters for neuroses; one of them is among my most beautiful cases of a cure of neurasthenic dyspepsia.

With cordial greetings to you and Ida from your faithful

Sigm. Freud

1. He means Ida Fliess.

2. It is clear that Freud is referring to a patient, perhaps comparing her to Marion Delorme, the heroine in Victor Hugo's play of that name, written in 1829; see Jean Louis Cornuz, ed., *Oeuvres complètes de Victor Hugo* (Paris: Editions Rencontrés, 1967). The play is about a high-class courtesan who falls in love with an ordinary, brave, and very depressive young man of twenty named Didier, who, along with one of the heroine's lovers, is hanged for having fought a duel. It is possible that Freud's reference is to a footnote, added by Hugo to Act 5, scene 6, in the 1836 edition of the text, which stated: "For the reasons already expressed in the preceeding note [where Hugo explains that he had to omit the word 'virginity' since it was too 'impure' for the French public], when the play was performed, instead of:

> offer my nude bosom to the first person
> to come along so that he may rest an hour,

one says:

> sell to the first person to come along,
> love to his liking, naive, tender, artless.

In our view there is nothing more vulgar than the pretense of refinement on the part of a blasé public, expressing fear not so much of the fact but of the word describing it, which would ban all of Molière from the theatre" (p. 359). If this is not Freud's reference, it is at the very least a remarkable coincidence that Freud, too, should complain in the letter that precisely this patient has to be omitted because of the sexual basis of the case history.

3. *Stockwerk*, that is, of a building.

4. In the previously published version of the letters this phrase was thought to apply only to senility. But it is clear from the way Freud wrote the phrase in the original manuscript that he intended it to apply to all four.

---

# Draft D. On the Etiology and Theory of the Major Neuroses

[undated; possibly an outline of the work mentioned at the beginning of the preceding letter]

## I. CLASSIFICATION

*Introduction.* Historical. Gradual differentiation of the neuroses. The course of development of my own views.

### *A. Morphology of the Neuroses*

(1) Neurasthenia and the pseudoneurasthenias
(2) Anxiety neurosis
(3) Obsessional neurosis
(4) Hysteria

(5) Melancholia, mania
(6) The mixed neuroses
(7) Ramifications of the neuroses and transitions to the normal.

### *B. Etiology of the Neuroses*
(provisionally restricted to the acquired neuroses)

(1) Etiology of neurasthenia—type of congenital neurasthenia
(2) Etiology of anxiety neurosis
(3) Etiology of obsessional neurosis and hysteria
(4) Etiology of melancholia
(5) Etiology of mixed neuroses
(6) The basic etiological formula. The thesis of specificity [of etiology]; analysis of the medley of neuroses
(7) The sexual factors according to their etiological significance
(8) Examination [of patients]
(9) Objections and proofs
(10) Behavior of asexual people.

### *C. Etiology and Heredity*

The hereditary types. Relation of etiology to degeneracy, to the psychoses and to predisposition.

## II. THEORY

### *D. Points of Contact with the Theory of Constancy*

Internal and external increase of stimulus; constant and ephemeral excitation.—Summation a characteristic of internal excitation.—Specific reaction.—Formulation and exposition of the theory of constancy.—Intercalation of the ego, with storing up of excitation.

### *E. The Sexual Process in Light of the Theory of Constancy*

Path taken by the excitation in the male and the female sexual process.—Path taken by the excitation in the presence of etiologically operative sexual noxae.—Theory of a sexual substance.—The sexual schematic diagram.

### *F. Mechanism of the Neuroses*

The neuroses as disturbances of equilibrium due to impeded discharge.—Attempts at adjustment, limited in their efficiency.

—Mechanism of the different neuroses in relation to their sexual etiology.—Affects and neuroses.

*G. Parallel between the Neuroses of Sexuality and Hunger*

*H. Summary of the Theory of Constancy and the Theory of Sexuality and the Neuroses*

Place of the neuroses in pathology; factors to which they are subject; laws governing their combination.—Psychical inadequacy, development, degeneration, and the like.

## Draft E. How Anxiety Originates

[undated; envelope of June 6, 1894, may belong to it]

With an unerring hand you have raised the question at the point I feel is the weak one. All I know about it is this: It quickly became clear to me that the anxiety of my neurotic patients had a great deal to do with sexuality; and in particular it struck me with what certainty coitus interruptus practiced on a woman leads to anxiety neurosis. Now, at first I followed various false tracks. I thought that the anxiety from which the patients suffer should be looked on as a continuation of the anxiety felt during the sexual act—that is to say, that it actually was a *hysterical* symptom. Indeed, the connections between anxiety neurosis and hysteria are obvious enough. Two things might give rise to the feeling of anxiety in coitus interruptus: in the woman, a fear of becoming pregnant; in the man, worry that his [preventive] device might fail. I then convinced myself from various cases that anxiety neurosis also appeared where there was no question of these two factors, where it was basically of no importance to these people whether they had a baby. Thus the anxiety of anxiety neurosis was not a continued, recollected, *hysterical* one.

A second extremely important point became established for me from the following observation: anxiety neurosis affects women who are anesthetic in coitus just as much as sensitive ones. This is most peculiar, but it can only mean that the source of the anxiety is not to be looked for in the psychic sphere. It must accordingly lie in the physical sphere: it is a physical factor in sexual life that produces anxiety. But what factor?

To this end I brought together the cases in which I found anxiety arising from a sexual cause. They seemed at first to be quite heterogeneous:

(1) Anxiety in *virginal* people (sexual observations and information, inklings of sexual life); confirmed by numerous instances in both sexes, predominantly female. Not infrequently there is a hint at an intermediate link — a sensation like an erection arising in the genitals.

(2) Anxiety in *intentionally abstinent* people, *prudes* (a type of neuropath), men and women characterized by pedantry and a passion for cleanliness, who regard everything sexual as horrible. The same people tend to convert their anxiety into phobias, compulsions, *folie de doute.*

(3) Anxiety of *necessarily abstinent* people, women who are neglected by their husbands or are not satisfied on account of lack of potency. This form of anxiety neurosis can certainly be acquired and owing to subsidiary circumstances is often combined with neurasthenia.

(4) Anxiety of women living with coitus interruptus, or, what is similar, of women whose husbands suffer from ejaculatio praecox — of people, therefore, who do not obtain satisfaction by physical stimulation.

(5) Anxiety of men practicing coitus interruptus, even more of men who excite themselves in various ways and do not employ their erection for coitus.

(6) Anxiety of men *who go beyond their desire or strength,* older people whose potency is diminishing, but who nevertheless forcibly bring about coitus.

(7) Anxiety of men who abstain on occasion: of youngish men who have married older women, by whom they are in fact disgusted, or of *neurasthenics* who have been diverted from masturbation by intellectual occupation without making up for it by coitus, or of men whose potency is beginning to grow weak and who abstain in marriage on account of sensations *post coitum.*

In the remaining cases the connection between anxiety and sexual life was not obvious. (It could be established theoretically.)

How are all these separate cases to be brought together? What recurs in them most frequently is abstinence. Informed by the fact that even anesthetic women are subject to anxiety after coitus interruptus, one is inclined to say that it is a question of a physical accumulation of excitation — that is, *an accumulation of physical sexual tension.* The accumulation is the consequence of prevented discharge. Thus anxiety neurosis is a neurosis of damming up, like hysteria; hence their similarity. And since no anxiety at all is contained in what is accumulated, the fact can also be accounted for by [saying] that *anxiety* has arisen by *transformation* out of the accumulated sexual tension.

Knowledge acquired simultaneously about the mechanism of melancholia can be interpolated here. Quite particularly often, melancholics have been anesthetic. They have no desire for coitus (and no sensation in connection with it), but they have a great longing for love in its psychic form—one might say, psychic erotic tension; where this accumulates and remains unsatisfied, melancholia develops. This, then, would be the counterpart to anxiety neurosis.

Where physical sexual tension accumulates—anxiety neurosis.

Where psychic sexual tension accumulates—melancholia.

But why this transformation into anxiety when there is an accumulation? At this point one ought to consider the normal mechanism for dealing with accumulated tension. What we are concerned with here is the second case—the case of endogenous excitation. Things are simpler in the case of exogenous excitation. The source of excitation is outside and sends into the psyche an accretion of excitation that is dealt with according to its quantity. For that purpose any reaction suffices that diminishes the inner psychic excitation by the same quantum.

But it is otherwise with endogenous tension, the source of which lies in one's own body (hunger, thirst, the sexual drive). In this case only *specific* reactions are of use—reactions which prevent the further occurrence of the excitation in the end organs concerned, whether those reactions are attainable with a large or small expenditure [of energy]. Here we may picture the endogenous tension as growing either continuously or discontinuously, but in any case as only being noticed when it has reached a certain *threshold.* It is only above this threshold that it is deployed *psychically,* that it enters into relation with certain groups of ideas, which then set about producing the specific remedies. Thus physical sexual tension above a certain value arouses psychic libido, which then leads to coitus, and so forth. If the specific reaction fails to ensue, the physicopsychic tension (the sexual affect) increases immeasurably; it becomes disturbing, but there is still no ground for its transformation. In anxiety neurosis, however, such a transformation does occur, and this suggests the idea that there things go wrong in the following way. The physical tension increases, reaches the threshold value at which it can arouse psychic affect; but for several reasons the psychic linkage offered to it remains insufficient: a *sexual affect* cannot be formed, because there is something lacking in the psychic determinants. Accordingly, the physical tension, not being psychically bound, is transformed into—anxiety.

If one accepts the theory so far, one has to insist that in anxiety neurosis there must be a deficit to be noted in sexual affect, in *psychic libido*. And this is confirmed by observation. If this connection is put before women patients, they are always indignant and declare that on the contrary they now have no desire whatever, and similar statements. Men often confirm the observation that since suffering from anxiety they have felt no sexual desire.

We will now test whether this mechanism fits in with the different cases enumerated above.

(1) *Virginal anxiety.* Here the array of ideas that ought to take up the physical tension is not yet present, or is only insufficiently present; and there is in addition a psychic refusal, which is a secular[1] result of education. This fits in very well.

(2) *Anxiety of prudes.* Here what we have is defense—outright psychic refusal, which makes any working over of the sexual tension impossible. Here too we have the case of the numerous obsessions. This fits in very well.

(3) *Anxiety due to enforced abstinence* is essentially the same, for women of this kind mostly create a psychic refusal so as to avoid temptation. Here the refusal is a contingent one; in (2) it is a fundamental matter.

(4) *Anxiety in women from coitus interruptus.* Here the mechanism is simpler. It is a question of endogenous excitation which does not originate [spontaneously] but is induced, but not in an amount sufficient to be able to arouse psychic affect. An alienation is artificially brought about between the physicosexual act and its psychic working over. If the endogenous tension then increases further on its own account, it cannot be worked over and generates anxiety. Here libido can be present, but not at the same time as anxiety. Thus here *psychic refusal* is followed by *psychic alienation;* tension of endogenous origin is followed by induced tension.

(5) *Anxiety in men from coitus interruptus or reservatus.* The case of coitus reservatus is the clearer; coitus interruptus may in part be regarded as subsumed under it. It is a question once again of psychic diversion, for attention is directed to another aim and is kept away from the working over of physical tension.

The explanation of coitus interruptus, however, probably stands in need of improvement.

(6) *Anxiety in diminishing potency or insufficient libido.* Insofar

as this is not the transformation of physical tension into anxiety owing to *senility,* it is to be explained by the fact that insufficient psychic desire can be summoned up for the particular act.

(7) *Anxiety in men from disgust, or in abstinent neurasthenics.* The former calls for no fresh explanation; the latter is perhaps a specially attenuated form of anxiety neurosis, for a rule this occurs properly[2] only in potent men. It may be that the neurasthenic nervous system cannot tolerate an accumulation of physical tension, since masturbation involves becoming accustomed to frequent and complete absence of tension.

On the whole the agreement is not so bad. Where there is an abundant development of physical sexual tension, but this cannot be turned into affect by psychic working over—because of insufficient development of psychic sexuality or because of the attempted suppression of the latter (defense), or of its falling into decay, or because of habitual alienation between physical and psychic sexuality—the sexual tension is transformed into *anxiety.* Thus a part is played in this by the accumulation of physical tension and the prevention of discharge in the psychic direction.

But why does the transformation take place specifically into anxiety? Anxiety is the sensation of the accumulation of another endogenous stimulus, the stimulus to breathing, a stimulus incapable of being worked over psychically apart from this; anxiety might therefore be employed for accumulated physical tension in general. Furthermore, if the symptoms of anxiety neurosis are examined more closely, one finds in the neurosis disjointed pieces of a major anxiety attack: namely, mere dyspnea, mere palpitations, mere feeling of anxiety, and a combination of these. Looked at more precisely, these are the paths of innervation that the physical sexual tension ordinarily traverses even when it is about to be worked over psychically. The dyspnea and palpitations belong to coitus; and while ordinarily they are employed only as subsidiary paths of discharge, here they serve, so to speak, as the only outlets for the excitation. This is once again a kind of *conversion* in anxiety neurosis, just as occurs in hysteria (another instance of their similarity); but in hysteria it is *psychic* excitation that takes a wrong path exclusively into the somatic field, whereas here it is a *physical* tension, which cannot enter the psychic field and therefore remains on the physical path. The two are very often combined.

That is as far as I have got today. The gaps badly need filling. I think it is incomplete, I lack something; but I believe the foundation is right. Of course it is absolutely not developed enough for publication. Suggestions, amplifications, indeed refutations and explanations will be received *most* gratefully.

Cordial greetings.

Your
Sigm. Freud

1. The manuscript reads *sekular*, not *sekundäres* (secondary) as in *Anfänge*.

2. The German, *da diese sonst nur bei Potenten ordentlich ausfällt*, is not entirely clear, since *ausfallen* can mean both "to succeed" and "to be lacking." *Diese* probably refers to *Angstneurose*. The question then becomes whether a potent man would or would not suffer from an anxiety neurosis. In his 1895 paper "Über die Berechtigung, von der Neurasthenie einen bestimmten Symptomen-Komplex als 'Angstneurose' abzutrennen" Freud speaks of the *frustrane Erregung* (unconsummated excitation) that a man feels when he is not able to have full intercourse. Here, clearly, the man is potent. More generally, a man who is not potent might well fear the obligations of coitus and develop an anxiety neurosis. Freud would probably regard the latter as a psychoneurosis (a hysteria), hence *not* as a form of anxiety neurosis.

---

Vienna, June 22, 1894

Dearest friend,

Your letter, which I have just read, reminds me of the debt which in any case I intended to pay soon. Today I withdrew from my meager practice in order to draft something, but instead I shall write you a rather long letter about "Theory and Life."

I am pleased with your opinion that the anxiety story is not yet quite right; it echoes my own. The essay, for example, has not been seen by anyone else. I will leave it until things become clearer. I have not yet gotten any further, however, and must wait until light dawns upon me from somewhere. I should like to launch a preliminary communication on the justification for differentiating anxiety neurosis from neurasthenia, but there I would have to go into theory and etiology and therefore I would rather not do it. I have further worked out the conversion theory and illuminated its relation to autosuggestion, but this, too, is not complete; I am letting it lie. The book I am doing with Breuer will contain five case histories; an essay by him, from which I wholly disassociate myself, on the theories of hysteria (summarizing and critical); and one by me on therapy, which I have not yet begun.

I am sending you the last case history today; from its style you will notice that I have been ill. The confession of my long-concealed symptoms appears between pages 4 and 5. The material itself is really very instructive; for me, it was decisive.

I shall welcome the summer if it brings what I have been longing for for years — a few days with you without undue interruptions. My plans are as follows; see what you can do with them. On August 1 I shall go to Reichenau; on September 1 I want to go with my wife to Abbazia [Opatija] for eight to ten days, something she very much desires and richly deserves. Most of the time life appears so uncertain to me that I am inclined not to postpone long-held wishes any longer. Other trips will have to be set aside in favor of this one, because this year has been a bad one in several respects: in addition to illness, it has brought financial loss. I could, of course, come for a few days in any event, though I have given up mountain climbing "with a heavy heart" — how meaningful language usage is! If you can arrange matters so that I do not have to travel too far and then can really be alone with you (in this I always include your wife — Martha will not want to leave Reichenau in August), then we shall see each other this year thanks to my reluctance to put up with further delays.

Now follows my case history, the unvarnished truth, with all the details to which a miserable patient attaches importance and which probably do not deserve it.

I have not smoked for seven weeks, since the day of your prohibition. At first I felt, as expected, outrageously bad. Cardiac symptoms accompanied by mild depression, as well as the horrible misery of abstinence. The latter wore off after approximately three weeks, the former abated after about five weeks, but it left me completely incapable of working, a beaten man. After seven weeks, despite my promise to you, I began smoking again, influenced by the following factors:

(1) During this time I saw patients of the same age with nearly identical conditions who either had not smoked at all (two women) or had given up smoking. Breuer, to whom I repeatedly said that I did not consider the affliction to be nicotine poisoning, finally agreed and also pointed to the women. Thus, I was deprived of the motivation that you so aptly characterized in one of your previous letters: a person can give up something only if he is firmly convinced that it is the cause of his illness.

(2) From the first cigars on, I was able to work and was the master of my mood; prior to that, life was unbearable. Nor have I noticed that the symptoms were aggravated after one cigar.

I am now smoking moderately, have slowly increased to three a day; I feel much better than before, actually progressively better; not well, of course. I shall describe the condition:

Some arrhythmia always seems to be present, but intensification to a delirium cordis with oppression occurs only in attacks, now lasting less than an hour and setting in almost regularly after lunch. The moderate dyspnea while climbing steps is gone; the left arm has been free of pain for weeks; the chest wall is still quite tender; stabbing pains, the feeling of oppression, burning sensations have not let up for a day. Objective evidence can *apparently* not be found, but then I really do not know. Sleep and all other functions are entirely undisturbed; I am in good control of my moods; on the other hand, I feel aged, sluggish, not healthy. Digitalis has helped me tremendously (one gram for the second time in three days).

What tortures me is the uncertainty about what to make of the story. It would embarrass me to suggest a hypochondriacal evaluation, but I have no criteria by which to decide this. I am very dissatisfied with the treatment I am receiving here. Breuer is full of apparent contradictions. When I say that I am feeling better, the answer is, You don't know *how* glad I am to hear this. This would lead me to conclude that my condition is serious. When I ask another time what it actually is, I get the answer, Nothing; in any event something that is already over. Moreover, he shows no concern for me at all, does not see me for two weeks at a stretch; I do not know whether this is policy, genuine indifference, or fully justified. On the whole I notice that I am being treated like a patient, with evasion and subterfuge, instead of having my mind set at ease by being told everything there is to tell me in a situation of this kind; that is to say, whatever is known.

It would be a tremendous relief to me had I been able to share your opinion or still share it; even a new period of weaning would be less difficult for me now, but this seems to me a *sacrificio d'intelletto;* for the first time, I have an opinion that differs from yours. With Breuer, it is easier; he voices no opinion.

The example of Kundt[1] did not frighten me very much; he who would guarantee me thirteen years until the age of fifty-one would not have spoiled my pleasure in cigars. My compromise opinion, for which I have no scientific basis, is that I shall go on suffering from various complaints for another four to five to eight years, with good and bad periods, and then between forty and fifty perish very abruptly from a rupture of the heart; if it is not too close to forty, it is not so bad at all.

I would be endlessly obliged to you, though, if you were to give me a definite explanation, since I secretly believe that you know precisely what it is, and that you have been so absolute and strict in your prohibition of smoking — the justification for which is after all relative — only because of its educational and soothing effect.

Well, enough of this now; it is very sad to have to be so preoccupied with oneself when there are so many more interesting things to write about.

I read between the lines that you are not very content with your headaches, and I am angry about our ignorance. You write nothing about your work; evidently you think that I show no interest in it. I ask you to assume that I merely have no opinion about these matters, which indeed are based on facts.

I now see your papa quite often in the Riedhof; he blossoms and beams as always. I too am among those who failed to give medical help to your sister-in-law when she had the attack; moreover, I was harassed and dreamy in my office hour; I clung so closely to the name Singer that the name Bondy did not awaken anything in me; and only two days later it occurred to me that Singer is the name of your cousin, so that it could only have been a sister-in-law of yours.

My children are splendid now; only Mathilde worries me a little. My wife is well and cheerful, but I am not satisfied with the way she looks. The problem is that we are about to become old, somewhat prematurely for the little ones.

Basically, throughout the entire day I actually think only about the neuroses, but since the scientific contact with Breuer has stopped, I have to rely solely upon myself, which is why progress is so slow.

With warm greetings to you and your dear wife,

Your cordially devoted
Sigm. Freud

1. August Kundt (1831–1894), successor to Hermann Helmholtz in the chair of experimental physics at the University of Berlin.

---

[undated; probably follows
June 22, 1894]
IX., Berggasse 19

Dear Wilhelm,

I understand far too little of it to be able to evaluate so certain a rebuttal, but my judgment tells me that I have enough psychological reasons to comply with your orders and so today I am starting a second period of abstinence — which, I hope, will last until we see each other again in August.

Cordial greetings.

Your
S.

---

July 14, 1894

Dearest friend,

Your praise is nectar and ambrosia for me, because I know full well how difficult it is for you to bestow it — no, more correctly, how seriously you mean it when you do bestow it. Since then, preoccupied with abstinence, I have produced very little; another description of anxiety neurosis, which I have just given to Breuer. Miss Elisabeth von R. became engaged in the meantime.

My condition — I now feel obliged not to arouse the suspicion that I might want to hold something back — is as follows: since your letter of Thursday a fortnight ago, abstinence, which lasted eight days; on the following Thursday, in an indescribably bleak moment, one cigar; then again eight days abstinence; the following Thursday one more, since then peace. In brief, a pattern has established itself — one cigar a week to commemorate your letter, which once again robbed me of my enjoyment of tobacco. In practice, this may not be all that different from abstinence.

Since then I have spoken to Oser,[1] who claims to have gone through the same angina nicotina and who spoke with great enthusiasm about the long duration of the condition. Well, that is the second Jew who declares it to be an eel; well, then, it will be an eel?[2]

Condition unchanged. At the end of last week I again had to resort to digitalis; the pulse was again delirious and the asystolic sensation just terrible. With digitalis I am better, but not really comfortable. Should I take digitalis frequently or rarely? I promise to obey.

That I shall visit you both in August is a certainty for me, beyond all obstacles. I am waiting only for the "where."

The day before yesterday an old gentleman[3] asked me in a restaurant, Do you know whether my son-in-law will come to the scientific meeting in Vienna in September? I did not know anything about it. My plans are to go with my wife to Abbazia or Dalmatia before the meeting.

Your headaches leave me hurt and helpless. I would not wait until the middle of August without knowing whether the man will still be in Munich; you will certainly have ascertained this, but I beg you to take care of any treatment that may be required before the vacation. You really do need a holiday urgently.

Cordial greetings to you and your dear wife from

Your faithful
Sigm. Freud

1. Schröter suggests Leopold Oser (1839–1910), who from 1885 was a professor of internal medicine in Vienna.

2. According to Anna Freud, this is a Jewish saying for "so it must be true."

3. Ida's father.

---

Vienna, July 25, 1894

Dearest friend,

Above all, will you please this time allow yourself some time and not leave Munich until your head has had as much relief—complete, I hope—as Gr.[1] is able to give it. This seems to me the most important thing, and I am sure Frau Ida will agree.

If your stay in Munich should be extended, I could visit you right there. I do not know Munich, but promise you I shall not lead you around anywhere and shall not talk of anything serious with you. Or we could select a nice place nearby, so that you could get back to Munich within the hour. Entirely as you wish; I am not at all yet in a position to make proposals, but take all *accidentia* as they come. I have done too long without *ens*.[2] I feel outrageously well; since the last gram of digitalis all symptoms have vanished and that gives me the feeling that they really should not return. I have been very good, however. When I smoke my cigar of the week (for example, today), I no longer relish it at all, and it leaves me with a trace of specific discomfort. I am beginning—something I should have done earlier—to believe you.

Business is not good; it is too hot for science. The only thing August is good for is nature and friendship.

With cordial greetings, the hope for rapid and good reports, and all the thoughts that are still at my disposal,

Your faithful
Sigm. Freud

1. Probably Ludwig Grünwald, an ear, nose, and throat specialist from Munich whom Fliess had publicly praised (this identification courtesy of Michael Schröter).

2. A reference to Aristotle's *ens* (being) and *accidentia*. In other words, Freud wants to be with Fliess.

---

Vienna, August 7, 1894

Dearest friend,

I leave for Salzburg early tomorrow morning. There I shall meet up with my wife and sister-in-law, who plan to visit their mother in Reichenhall, and Friday, Saturday, or Sunday I hope to be with you. I cannot be more precise because it is not yet certain whether or not I shall bring my wife with me to Munich.

I really look forward to seeing you again. If before then you have news for me, please use this address: Salzburg, general delivery.

It has been a bad year for both of us. It is not impossible, however, that during this period both of us will find recovery from afflictions that have lasted for years. I am not feeling nearly so well as a while back, the last time I wrote you. I can see that you are not feeling well because you show so much patience this time. When I think of the many weeks when I felt uncertain about my life, my need to be with you again increases greatly.

With cordial greetings to you and your dear wife and nurse,

Your
Sigm. Freud

---

Reichenau, August 18, 1894

Dearest friend,

Having returned home, after a wonderful reception by the whole bunch of thriving rascals, and with the aftertaste of the beautiful days in Munich—there is again a moment when one can take pleasure in life. A charming letter from your wife which, as it were, demonstrates the gains of the most recent past—Martha will answer it in detail tomorrow—added to easing the transition for us and put before us the entire string of proofs of your love that made up our time together in Munich.

From now on I shall prophesy only good things, and I will be as right about them as I was about my last bad prediction. Above all, I prophesy that we shall have much to write to each other and that frequently. This presupposes that you will be feeling very well. After I had been back for a few hours, a small case of anxiety neurosis that could not be turned away slipped into the house. I am immediately putting it down for you, but do not read it now; rather wait for a free hour and read it together with many others in my collection.

The most cordial greetings to you and Frau Ida! With the feeling that our separation is still far from complete,

Your
Sigm. Freud

---

August 18, 1894

## Draft F. Collection III

[Editor's Note: The headings in this draft appear in Freud's original manuscript, but are not further explained.]

*No. 1*

Anxiety neurosis:
hered. disp.

Mr. K., age 24.

Father treated for senile melancholia; sister, O., good case of complicated anxiety neurosis, thoroughly analyzed; all the K.'s neurotic and comfortably gifted.[1] A cousin of Dr. K. in Bordeaux. — In good health till recently; has slept badly for the last nine months; in February and March woke frequently with night terrors and palpitations; gradually increasing general excitability; letup owing to army maneuvers, which did him a great deal of good. Three weeks ago in the evening a sudden attack of anxiety for no apparent reason, with a feeling of congestion from his chest up to his head. Interpreted [by him to mean that] something dreadful was bound to happen; no accompanying oppression and only slight palpitations. Similar attacks afterward in daytime as well, at his midday meal. Two weeks ago consulted a doctor; improved on bromide, [condition] still continues, but sleeps well. In addition during the last two weeks short attacks of deep depression, resembling complete apathy, lasting barely a few minutes. Improved here in R[eichenau]. Besides this, attacks of pressure at the back of the head.

He himself began with sexual information. A year ago he fell in love with a girl who was a flirt; a huge shock when he heard she was engaged to someone else. No longer in love now. — Attaches little importance to it. — He went on: he masturbated between 13 and 16 or 17 (seduced at school) to a moderate extent, he claimed. Moderate in sexual intercourse; has used a condom for the last two and a half years for fear of infection; often feels tired after it. He described this kind of intercourse as enforced. Notices that his libido has greatly diminished for about a year. Was very much excited sexually in his relations with the girl (without touching her, or the like). His first attack at night (February) was two days after coitus; his first anxiety attack was after coitus on the same evening; since then (three weeks) abstinent — a quiet, mild-mannered, and in other ways healthy man.

1. The German is *gemütlich begabt;* meaning unclear.

---

Reichenau, August 23, 1894

Dearest friend,

You are having severe headaches and are counting on having further surgery; this would sound depressing and annoying to me if I did not fully share your hope that the course you have embarked upon will free you of *your* headaches. Just promise me one thing right now: not to forget the factor that directly precedes the stumbling stone "headache" and that is of a purely nervous nature. Put differently and certainly also more clearly, that you promise me that this time you will let several months pass to allow the scars to heal before you resume work in Berlin. We shall write or talk about this further.

The prospect of spending a few more days together with you both this fall is too beautiful to be given up so quickly. For our trip to Abbazia has become uncertain; I do not think I can get Martha away from here anymore; but I could well make myself free if everything works out. Under special circumstances, for example, if Frau Ida would drop a word that I could be of use in this matter, it would be done immediately. (Naturally, not as your guest!!)

Today two enclosures, because last time I forgot to mention that the epicrisis [critical discussion] will follow, and this, after all, is the only thing that affords a kind of substitute for verbal reporting. In addition, yet another case, which I picked up in the city on Monday. In writing it down I feel as though I were still talking with you. Take your time with the *revanche* until you are *very well.*

All of us are well; upon our return we found that our baby had turned into a little human being and a charming child. Moreover, yesterday was the first lovely day here too. I hope you both will like Garmisch better again. The remark your papa made, that the two of you do not feel comfortable there and probably will not stay on, induced me, quite unjustifiably, though more for psychological reasons, to postpone sending the books. This is to let you know that I *am* sending them.

I would not at all be capable of concern for another fellow who is brimming over with good health as long as I was not feeling well. I could really let you have some of my well-being; it is possible that after this third week I again shall have to take some digitalis; but for the time being, I am still holding up splendidly. On the Thursday after our parting I was forced by circumstances to take a four-hour hike from Weissenbach to Ischl—night, loneliness, pouring rain, hurry—and I tolerated it very well.

With the most cordial greetings and wishes for you and Frau Ida from all of us,

Your
Sigm. Fr.

*Discussion of No. 1*

If one attempts to interpret the case of K., one thing in particular is evident. The man has a hereditary predisposition: his father suffers from melancholia, perhaps anxiety melancholia; his sister has a typical anxiety neurosis with which I am intimately acquainted, which otherwise I should certainly have described as *acquired.* This gives ground for thought on heredity. There is probably only a "*predisposition*" in the K. family and not "*degeneration,*" a tendency to fall ill with greater certainty and more seriously in response to the typical etiology. One may therefore expect that in Mr. K.'s case the slight anxiety neurosis developed from a *slight* etiology. Where is it to be looked for without prejudice?

It seems to me in the first place that it is a question of an *enfeebled* condition of sexuality. The man's libido has been diminishing for some time; the preparations for using a condom are enough to make him feel that the whole act is something forced on him and his enjoyment of it something he was talked into. This is no doubt the nub of the whole business. Now, after coitus he sometimes feels weak; he notices this, as he says, and then, two days after coitus or, as the case may be, on the next evening, he has his first attack of anxiety.

The concurrence of *reduced* libido and anxiety neurosis readily fits in with my theory. What it involves is a weakness of the psychic mastery of the somatic sexual excitation. This weakness has been present for some time and makes it possible for anxiety to appear if there is an incidental *increase* in somatic excitation.

How was the *psychic* enfeeblement acquired? There is not much to be got from masturbation in his youth; it would certainly not have had such a result, nor does it seem to have exceeded the usual amount. His relations with the girl, who excited him very much sensually, seem far better suited to produce a disturbance in the required direction; in fact, the case approaches the conditions in the familiar neuroses of men during [long] engagements. But above all, it cannot be disputed that the fear of infection and the decision to use a condom laid the foundation for what I have described as the factor of *alienation* between the somatic and the psychic. It would be the same as in the case of coitus interruptus. In short, Mr. K. has incurred psychic sexual weakness because he spoiled coitus for himself, and, his physical health and production of sexual stimuli being unimpaired, the situation gave rise to the generation of anxiety. One may add that his readiness to take precautions, instead of finding adequate satisfaction in a secure relationship, points to a sexuality which was from the first of no great *strength*. After all, the man has a hereditary predisposition; the etiology that can be found in his case, though it is qualitatively important, would be tolerated as harmless by healthy — that is, by vigorous — men.

An interesting feature of this case is the appearance of a typically melancholic mood in attacks of short duration. This must be of theoretical importance for anxiety neurosis due to alienation; for the moment I can only make a note of it.

## *No. 2*

Mr. von F., Budapest, age 44.

A healthy man physically, he complains that "he is losing his liveliness and zest, in a way that is not natural in a man of his age." This state — in which everything seems indifferent to him, in which he finds his work a burden and feels morose and weak — is accompanied by severe pressure on the top and also the back of his head. Furthermore, it is regularly characterized by bad digestion — that is, by disinclination for food and by belching and sluggish stools. He also seems to sleep badly.

But the state is evidently intermittent. Each time it lasts for four or five days, then slowly goes away. He notices from the belching that the nervous weakness is coming on. There are intervals of twelve to fourteen days, and he may be well for several weeks. Better periods, even of months' duration, have occurred. He insists that things have been like this for the past twenty-five years. As so often, one has to start by constructing the clinical picture, for he keeps on monotonously repeating his complaints and declares that he has paid no attention to other events. Thus the indeterminate outline of the attacks forms part of the picture, as does their complete irregularity in time. He naturally puts the blame for his state on his digestion. Benedikt wrote down the diagnosis: *cephalea cum digestione tarda.*[1]

Organically sound; no serious worries or mood swings. As regards sexuality: masturbated between the ages of 12 and 16; then very regular relations with women; he was not enormously attracted; married for fourteen years, only two children, the last ten years ago; in the interval and since then, only a condom and no other technique. Potency decidedly diminished in the last few years. Coitus every twelve to fourteen days or so; often, too, with long intervals. Admits that he feels weak and wretched after coitus with a condom; but not immediately afterward, only *two* days later — or, as he puts it, he has noticed that two days later he gets digestive trouble. Why does he use a condom? One should not have too many children! ([He has] two.)

### *Discussion*

A mild but very characteristic case of *periodic depression,* melancholia. Symptoms: apathy, inhibition, intracranial pressure, dyspepsia, insomnia — the picture is complete.

There is an unmistakable similarity to neurasthenia, and the etiology is the same. I have some quite analogous cases: they are masturbators (Mr. A.) and also have a hereditary taint. The von F.'s from Budapest are well known to be psychopathic.[2] Thus the case is one of neurasthenic melancholia; there must be a point of contact here with the theory of neurasthenia.

It is quite possible that the starting point of a minor melancholia like this may always be an act of coitus; an exaggeration of the [importance] of the physiological factor leads to the saying, *Omne animal post coitum triste.*[3] The time intervals would fit. The man is improved by every course of treatment, every absence from home — that is, by every period of relief from coitus. Of course, as he says, he is faithful to his wife. The use of a condom is evidence of weak potency; being something analogous to masturbation, it is a continuous causation of his melancholia.

1. Chronic headaches with slow digestion.

2. Freud is undoubtedly using the word "psychopathic" in the more general sense of suffering from neurosis. Even Pschyrembel's 1964 *Klinisches Wörterbuch* (although not the latest edition) defines psychopaths as "those suffering from a chronic congenital abnormal state of psychic life who themselves suffer from their abnormality or cause others to suffer as a result of it."

3. This is a frequently quoted paraphrase from Aristotle, *De generatione animalium* 1, 18 (725 b). See also Laurence Sterne, *The Life and Opinions of Tristram Shandy, Gentleman*, ed. James Aiken Work (New York: Odyssey Press, 1840), vol. 5, chap. 36; and *Engravings by Hogarth: 101 Prints*, ed. Sean Shesgreen (New York: Dover, 1973), no. 37.

---

Reichenau, August 29, 1894

Dearest friend,

Now this is really too much; are you going to dissolve completely into pus on us? The devil with having surgery again and again; just be done with it once and for all. So that old woman[1] who did not like your headaches years ago, and who wrote that peculiar letter to me, was actually quite right! But what should I do about it? I wish I were a "doctor," as people say, a physician and a great healer so that I could understand such matters and would not have to leave you in strange hands in such circumstances. Unfortunately I am not a doctor, as you know. I must rely on you in this as in everything else; I must hope that you also know how to treat *yourself* and that you can be as successful in *your own* case as in those of others (myself included).

It is not nice either that as a result of this our meeting will fall through. A temporary hope leaves me with an unfulfilled claim.

I am not at all eager to go to Lovrano, but Martha, who otherwise so rarely desires anything, this time insists on the trip and on undertaking it in this way. It also spoiled her pleasure *very* much that Lovrano and our meeting are thus falling to pieces. Besides, I think that if I can be of any service to you, you should test me and see whether I can find the way from Lovrano to Munich. My conscience is searching for some such offer to pacify itself, while I am now anticipating pleasure.

So we shall leave on September 1, Saturday evening, and hope to be in Lovrano, Pension Pankaus,[2] on Sunday morning. Now, however, I must again assume that you are quite fit and rid myself of the accumulation of scientific matters.

I have collected only a few cases this Monday:

*No. 3*

Dr. Z., a physician, age 34. Has suffered for many years from organic sensitivity of the eyes: phosphenes [flashes], dazzle, scotomas, and the rest. This has increased enormously, to the point of preventing his working, in the last four months (since the time of his marriage).

*Background:* A masturbator since the age of 14, apparently continued up to recent years. Did not deflower his wife, potency much reduced; incidentally, divorce proceedings begun.

Clear typical case of *organ hypochondriasis* in a masturbator at periods of sexual excitation. Interesting that medical education reaches such a shallow depth.

*No. 4*

Mr. D., nephew of Mrs. A., who died a hysteric. A highly neurotic family. Age 28. Has suffered for some weeks from lassitude, intracranial pressure, shaky knees, reduced potency, premature ejaculation, the beginnings of perversion: very young girls excite him more than mature ones.

Alleges that his potency has always been capricious; admits masturbation, but not too prolonged; has a period of abstinence behind him now. Before that, anxiety states in the evening.

Has he made a full confession?

A monograph, *Neurologische Beiträge,* by Möbius came out; a collection of older, small essays, very nice, *quite* important for hysteria.[3] He is the best mind among the neurologists, fortunately not on the track of sexuality.

Actually I notice that I have nothing to say! When I get back to Vienna, my editor will certainly press me for articles. Should I then subject Möbius's paper on "Migraine" to a critique?[4] You would have to give me some of your observations for it. Surely you will get the stomach-menstruation business[5] off your back as soon as you feel better? The profession is waiting for this kind of thing.

Cordial greetings and please let me hear from you during this time—*at least a postcard* every three days.

My wife wishes you and your dear wife, whom I believe, she envies a little (governess and housekeeper, doctor with his assistants), the best and the quickest possible passing of these weeks. The same from your faithful

Sigm.

1. Reference unknown.
2. Reading uncertain.
3. Freud is referring to Paul J. Möbius (1853–1907) and his *Neurologische Beiträge.*

*1 Heft: Über den Begriff der Hysterie und andere Vorwürfe vorwiegend psychologischer Art* (Leipzig: Ambr. Abel, 1894). In a chapter written in 1893 or 1894, "Weitere Erörterungen über den Begriff der Hysterie," Janet is praised and there is a long footnote on p. 29 summarizing the Breuer and Freud 1893 paper. Curiously, Möbius does not mention sexuality at all. He has high praise for Charcot: "We were all blind formerly and have learned to see with the help of the works of Charcot" (p. 49). The phrase *pour revenir à nos moutons,* which Freud uses in his letters to Fliess, also occurs (p. 51).

Möbius in this book defends his psychological point of view over that of Meynert and his school. He defends vigorously the reality of the injuries suffered by individuals who had what were then called traumatic neuroses. This important passage clearly impressed Freud: "One should use an admission of simulation only with caution. Not only the feeling of injured honor can cause one to make desperate statements, but the diseased psyche itself. One should not forget that many witches freely confessed their association with the devil and thereby had themselves brought to the stake" (p. 42).

Möbius also reviewed briefly, in *Schmidt's Jahrbuch,* the 1893 paper of Breuer and Freud, "On the Psychical Mechanism of Hysterical Phenomena," and Freud's *Interpretation of Dreams.*

4. Freud actually did so. The review, hitherto unnoticed, was published in the *Wiener klinische Rundschau* in 1895.

5. Undoubtedly a reference to Fliess's article "Magenschmerz und Dysmenorrhöe in einem neuen Zusammenhang," where he writes: "Stomach pain, very common in the case of girls and women, as a result of masturbation. Here, too, as I learned in a case I unfortunately cannot disclose, the path goes through the stomach spot in the nose" (p. 22). This relates to Fliess's view that there are particular spots in the nose that correspond to other organs in the body — an abdominal spot, a genital spot, and so on.

Lovrano, September 13, 1894

Dear friend,

I have been waiting for news for such a long time, but am unwilling to draw any conclusion about what this kind of silence really means. I am very dissatisfied with you, my best friend, but then tell myself that you are certainly doing your best; I could not give you any other advice, and do not have the right to be more impatient than you. I must finally write you to let you know where I am in this world.

We shall leave here on the 15th, Saturday evening, and arrive early on Sunday in Payerbach. Early Monday, the 17th, I shall be in Vienna. There is still a week before the scientific meeting. If you would like to have me for a day in Munich, let me know *quickly.* Here everything has turned out very well, and all will return again, being much better and more cheerful.[1] Weather, on the average, excellent.

Cordial greetings to you and your dear wife; let me hear from you *very* soon.

Your
Sigm. Fr.

1. Freud writes in the margin, next to this sentence, the word "abstinent."

---

December 17, 1894
IX., Berggasse 19

Dear Wilhelm,

I am not writing you much anymore because I hope to see you here very shortly. Your manuscript is at Paschkis';[1] I did not dare to remove the business[2] about labor pains. You can still do it here.

I hope you will have some good days here and we a few beautiful hours.

Cordial greetings from us to you both.

Your
Sigm.

1. Heinrich Paschkis (1849–1923) was editor of the *Wiener klinische Rundschau.*
2. Or "case history."

---

## Draft G. Melancholia[1]

I

The facts on hand seem to be as follows:

(A) There are striking connections between melancholia and [sexual] anesthesia. This is borne out (1) by the finding that in so many melancholics there has been a long previous history of anesthesia, (2) by the observation that everything that provokes anesthesia encourages the development of melancholia, (3) by the existence of a type of woman, very needy psychically, in whom longing easily changes into melancholia and who is anesthetic.

(B) Melancholia develops as an intensification of neurasthenia through masturbation.

(C) Melancholia occurs typically in combination with severe anxiety.

(D) The typical and extreme form of melancholia seems to be the periodic or cyclic hereditary form.

II

In order to make anything of this material, one needs some secure points of departure. These seem to be provided by the following considerations:

(a) The affect corresponding to melancholia is that of mourning—that is, longing for something lost. Thus in melancholia it must be a question of a loss—that is, a loss in *instinctual life.*

(b) The neurosis concerned with eating, parallel to melancholia, is anorexia. The famous *anorexia nervosa* of young girls seems to me (on careful observation) to be a melancholia where sexuality is undeveloped. The patient asserted that she had not eaten, simply because she had *no appetite,* and for no other reason. Loss of appetite—in sexual terms, loss of libido.

It would not be so bad, therefore, to start from the idea: *melancholia consists in mourning over the loss of libido.*

It remains to be seen whether this formula explains the occurrence and characteristics of melancholia. This will be discussed on the basis of the schematic diagram of sexuality.

III

I shall now discuss, on the basis of the schematic diagram of sexuality, which I have often used, the conditions under which the psychic sexual group (ps. S.) suffers a loss in the amount of its excitation. There are two possible cases: (1) if the production of somatic sexual excitation (s. S) sinks or ceases; (2) if the sexual tension is diverted from the ps. S. The first case, in which the production of s. S. ceases, is probably what is characteristic of *genuine*[2] *severe* melancholia proper, which recurs periodically, or of cyclic melancholia, in which periods of increase and cessation of production alternate; it can further be assumed that excessive masturbation—which according to the theory leads to too great an unloading of E. (the end organ)[3] and thus to a low level of stimulus in E.—excessive masturbation extends to the production of s. S. and brings about a lasting reduction in the s. S., thus a weakening of the p. S.[4] This is neurasthenic melancholia. The [second] case, in which sexual tension is diverted from the p. S., while the production of s. S. is not diminished, presupposes that the s. S. is employed elsewhere—at the boundary [between the somatic and the psychic]. This, however, is the precondition of anxiety; and accordingly this coincides with the case of anxiety melancholia, a mixed form combining anxiety neurosis and melancholia.

In this discussion, therefore, the three forms of melancholia, which must in fact be distinguished, are explained.

IV

How does it come about that anesthesia plays this role in melancholia?

According to the schematic diagram [Fig. 1], there are the following kinds of anesthesia.

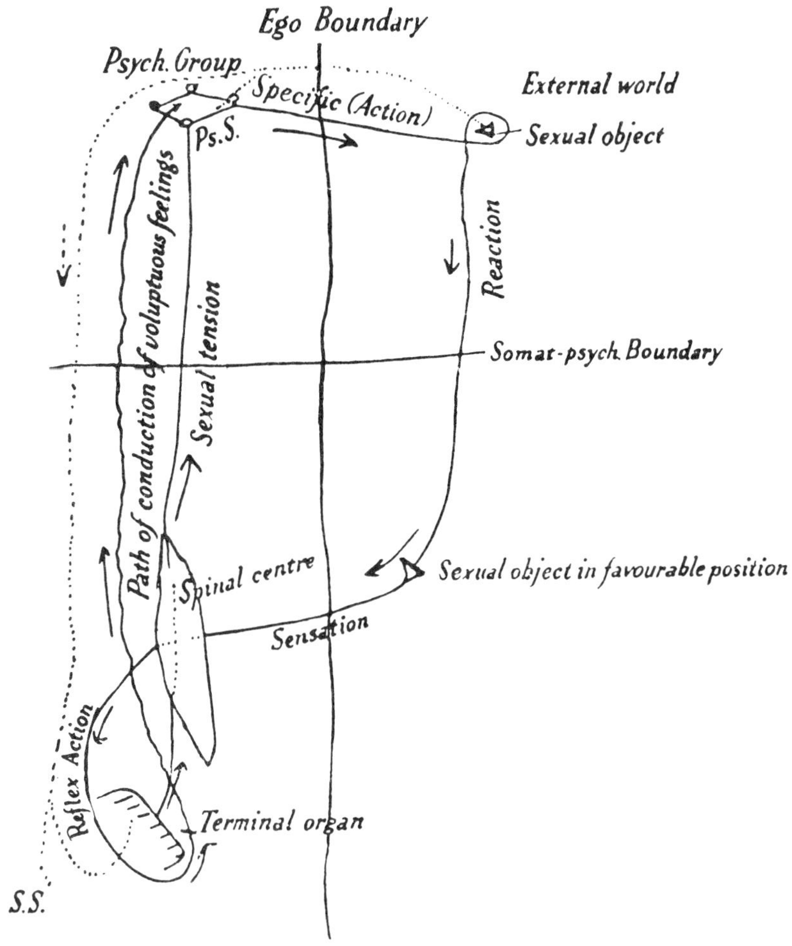


*Figure 1* Schematic Diagram of Sexuality. [In the original all the arrows are drawn in red, except the dotted one at the extreme left.]

Anesthesia always consists, to be sure, in the omission of V. [feelings of pleasure], which ought to be conducted into the ps. S. after the reflex action that unloads the end organ. The feeling of pleasure is measured by the amount of unloading.

(a) The E. is not sufficiently loaded; hence the discharge at coitus is slight and the V. very small: the case of frigidity.

(b) The pathway from sensation to the reflex action is damaged, so that the action is not sufficiently strong. Then the unloading and the V. are also slight: the case of masturbatory anesthesia, the anesthesia of coitus interruptus, and so on.

(c) Everything below is in order; only V. is not admitted to the ps. S. because it is linked with other factors (with disgust—defense): this is hysterical anesthesia, which is entirely analogous to hysterical anorexia (disgust).

To what extent, then, does anesthesia facilitate melancholia?

In case (a), of frigidity, anesthesia is not the cause of melancholia but a sign of a predisposition to it. This tallies with Fact (A)(1) mentioned at the beginning. In other cases the anesthesia is the cause of the melancholia, because the ps. S. is strengthened by the arrival of V. and weakened by its omission. (Based on general theories of the binding of excitation in memory.) Fact (A)(2) is thus taken into account.

Accordingly, it is possible to be anesthetic without being melancholic, because—

Melancholia is related to the omission of s. S.

Anesthesia is related to the omission of V., but anesthesia is a sign of or a preparation for melancholia, since the p. S. is as much weakened by the omission of V. as by the omission of s. S.

V

We must consider why anesthesia is so predominantly a characteristic of women. This arises from the passive role played by women. An anesthetic man will soon cease to undertake any coitus; a woman is not asked. She becomes anesthetic more easily because—

(1) Her entire upbringing works in the direction of not awakening s. S., but of changing all excitations which could have that effect into psychic stimuli—that is, of directing the dotted line [in the schematic diagram, Fig. 1] from the sexual object entirely into the ps. S. This is necessary because if there were a vigorous s. S., the ps. S. would soon acquire such strength intermittently that, as in the case of men, it would bring the sexual object into a favorable position by means of a specific reaction. But in the case of women, it

is required that the arc of specific reaction not take place; instead, permanent specific actions are required of them, which entice the male into the specific action. Thus sexual tension is kept low, its access to the ps. S. so far as possible cut off, and the indispensable strength of the ps. S. defrayed in another way. If, now, the ps. S. gets into a state of longing, then, in view of the low level [of tension] in the E., that state is easily transformed into melancholia. The ps. S. in itself is capable of little resistance. This is the juvenile, immature type of libido, and the demanding, anesthetic women mentioned above [Fact (A)(3)] merely continue this type.

(2) Women [become anesthetic more easily than men do] because they so often approach the sexual act (marry) without love—that is, with less s. S. and tension in the E. In that case they are frigid and remain so.

The low level of tension in the E. seems to contain the main disposition to melancholia. In individuals of this kind every neurosis easily takes on a melancholic stamp. Thus, whereas potent individuals easily acquire anxiety neuroses, impotent ones incline to melancholia.

VI

How, then, can the effects of melancholia be explained? The best description: *psychic inhibition with instinctual impoverishment and pain concerning it.*

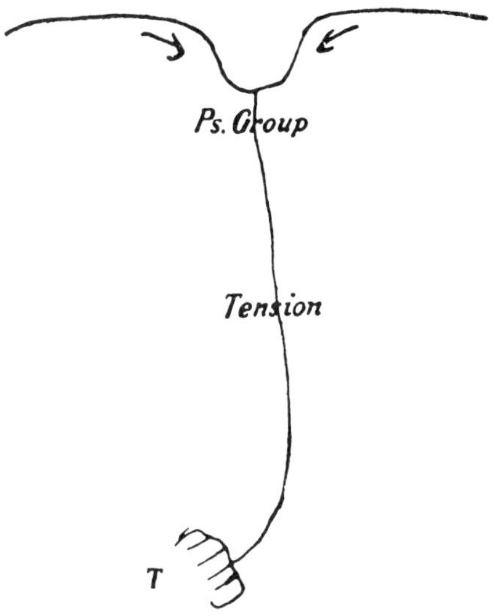

Figure 2

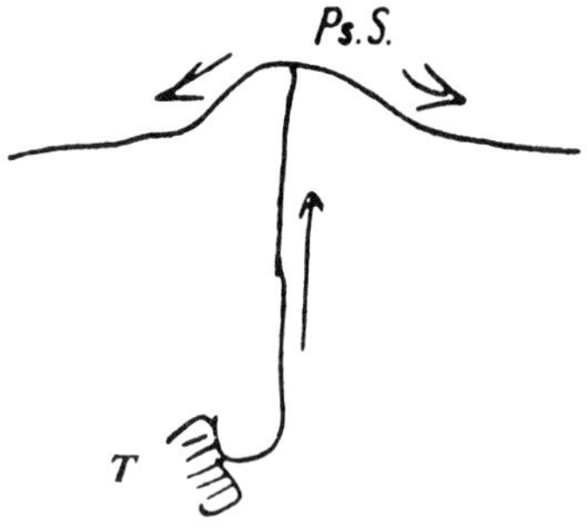

Figure 3

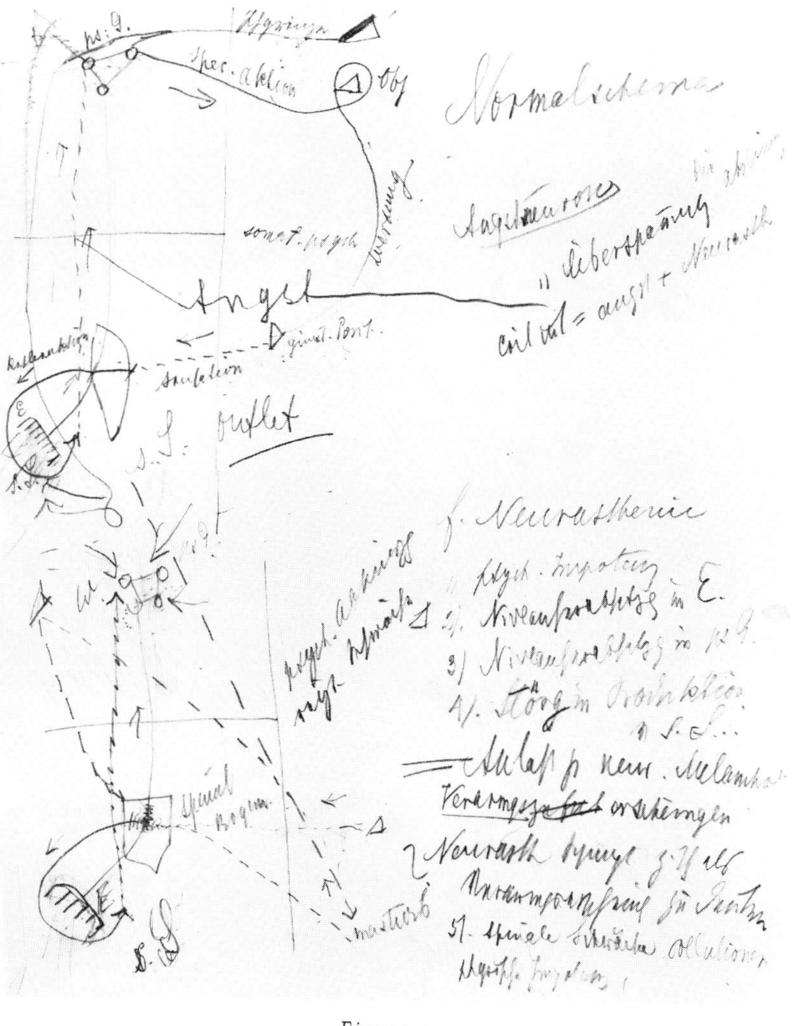


*Figure 4*

One can imagine that, if the ps. S. meets with a very great loss in the amount of its excitation, there may come about *an in-drawing,* as it were, *into the psychic sphere,* which produces an effect of suction upon the adjoining amounts of excitation. The associated neurones must give up their excitation, *which produces pain* [Fig. 2]. The uncoupling of associations is always painful; there sets in, as though through an *internal hemorrhage,* an impoverishment in excitation (in the free store of it) — which makes itself known in the other instinctual drives and functions. As an inhibition, this in-

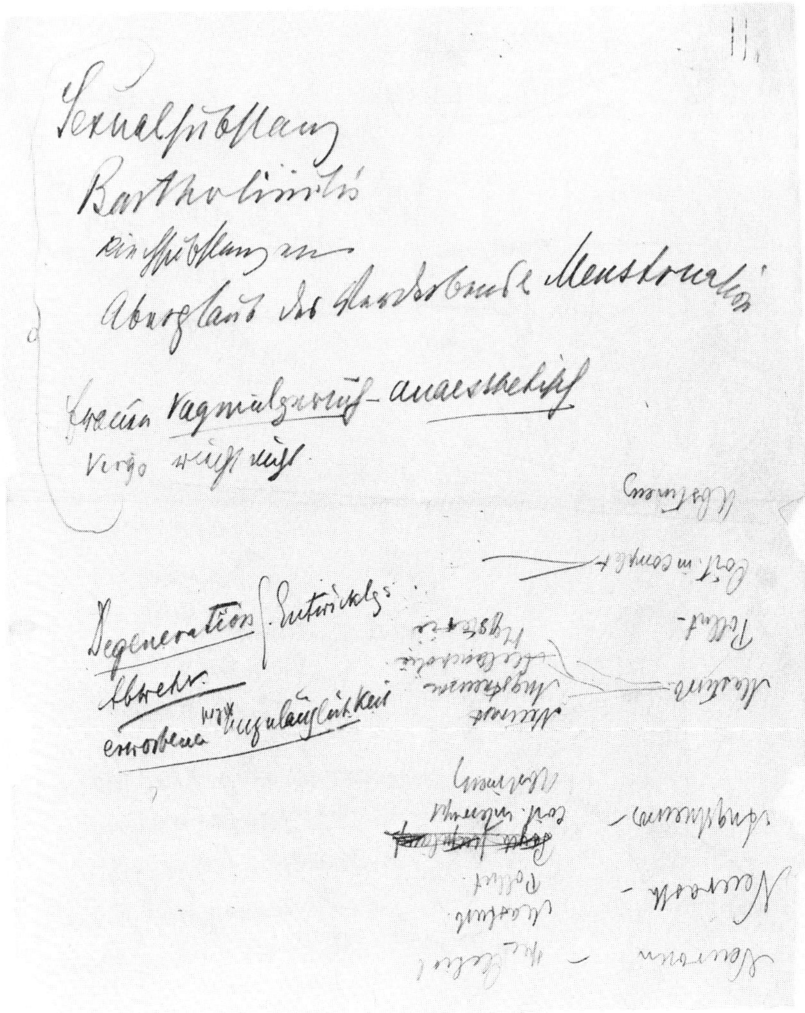

*Figure 5*

drawing operates like a *wound*, in a manner analogous to pain (see the theory of physical pain). A counterpart of this would be mania, where the overflowing excitation is communicated to all associated neurones [Fig. 3]. Here, then, there is a similarity to neurasthenia. In neurasthenia a quite similar impoverishment takes place owing to the excitation running out, as it were, through a hole. But in that case what is pumped empty is s. S.; in melancholia the hole is in the psychic sphere. Neurasthenic impoverishment can, however, extend to the psychic sexual group. The manifestations are in reality so similar that many cases must be sorted out very carefully.

[Editor's Note: Included in the envelope that contained Draft G was another drawing by Freud, which he titled "Normalschema." It was not included in the original German or English editions, probably because it is so difficult to understand. It is reproduced here as Fig. 4, along with its reverse side (Fig. 5), which is evidently an explanation of the drawing.]

1. Undated; according to the editors of *Anfänge* it belongs to an envelope of January 7, 1895.

2. The manuscript reads *genuinen*, not *gemeinen* (common) as in *Anfänge*.

3. The end organ (E.) is the same as the terminal organ (T.) shown in Figs. 1, 2, and 3.

4. Freud uses both "ps. S." and "p. S." to indicate "psychic sexual group."

# The Emma Eckstein Episode

January 24, 1895

Dearest Wilhelm,

I must hurriedly write to you about something that greatly astonishes me; otherwise I would be truly ungrateful. In the last few days I have felt quite unbelievably well, as though everything had been erased — a feeling which in spite of better times I have not known for ten months. Last time I wrote you, after a good period which immediately succeeded the reaction, that a few viciously bad days had followed during which a cocainization of the left nostril had helped me to an amazing extent. I now continue my report. The next day I kept the nose under cocaine, which one should not really do; that is, I repeatedly painted it to prevent the renewed occurrence of swelling; during this time I discharged what in my experience is a copious amount of thick pus; and since then I have felt wonderful, as though there never had been anything wrong at all. Arrhythmia is still present, but rarely and not badly; the sensitivity to external pressure is slight, the sensations being between 0 [zero] and −0. I am postponing the full expression of my gratitude and the discussion of what share the operation had in this unprecedented improvement until we see what happens next.

In any event, I herewith dedicate to you a new insight which is upsetting my equilibrium more than much that happened before and to which I have not yet become indifferent. It is the explanation of paranoia; my inventions are all of such an unpractical nature. *Tell* me your opinion of it; by then I probably will have calmed down.

How would it be if you *first* experimented on the preparation jointly with Gersuny?[1] According to Breuer and Rie, he worked intensively on the matter after he had overcome his initial hesitation.

Now only one more week separates us from the operation,[2] or at least from the preparations for it. The time has passed quickly, and I gladly avoid putting myself through a self-examination to ascertain what right I have to expect so much from it. My lack of medical knowledge once again weighs heavily on me. But I keep repeating to myself: so far as I have some insight into the matter, the cure must be achievable by this route. I would not have dared to invent this plan of treatment on my own, but I confidently join you in it.

Mrs. M. will be welcome; if she brings money and patience with her, we shall do a nice analysis. If in the process there are some therapeutic gains for her, she too can be pleased.

I shall give Paschkis a little push. I think he is behaving badly, but have already had similar experiences in Vienna.

Now I am expecting only a few more lines announcing your arrival.

With cordial greetings to your dear wife from me and Martha,

Yours,
Sigm.

1. Robert Gersuny (1844–1924) was Christian Billroth's former assistant and the first director of the hospital called the Rudolfinerhaus. He was also a well-known plastic surgeon (see Lesky, 1960). From a passage in Freud's letter of March 8, 1895, it would appear that Fliess was operated on by Gersuny, who later played a critical role in the case of Emma Eckstein.

2. In late January or early February Fliess was in Vienna and operated on both Freud and Emma Eckstein. (See note 3 to the letter of March 4, 1895.) The reference here is probably to the impending operation on Eckstein.

## Draft H. Paranoia

[enclosed with letter]

In psychiatry *delusional* ideas stand alongside *obsessional* ideas as purely intellectual disorders, and paranoia stands alongside obsessional insanity as an intellectual psychosis. If once obsessions have been traced back to an affective disturbance and it has been proved that they owe their strength to a conflict, then the same view must apply to delusions and they too must be the outcome of affective disturbances and must owe their strength to a psychological process.

The contrary of this is accepted by psychiatrists, while laymen are inclined to attribute delusional insanity to shattering emotional events. "A man who does not lose his reason over certain things can have no reason to lose."[1]

Now it is in fact the case that chronic paranoia in its classical form is a *pathological mode of defense,* like hysteria, obsessional neurosis, and hallucinatory confusion. People become paranoid over things they cannot put up with, provided they possess the peculiar psychic disposition for it.

In what does this disposition consist? In a tendency toward that which represents the psychic characteristic of paranoia; and this we will consider in an example.

An aging spinster (about thirty) shared a home with her brother and [elder] sister. She belonged to the upper working class; her brother was working his way up to becoming a small manufacturer. Meanwhile they rented a room to a fellow worker, a much-traveled, rather enigmatic man, very skillful and intelligent, who lived with them for a year and was on the most companionable and sociable terms with them. Then the man went away, only to return after six months. This time he stayed for only a comparatively short time and then disappeared for good. The sisters often lamented his absence and could speak nothing but good of him. Nevertheless, the younger sister told the elder one of an occasion when he made an attempt at getting her into trouble. She had been tidying up the rooms while he was still in bed. He called her to his side, and when she unsuspectingly went, put his penis in her hand. There was no sequel to the scene; soon afterward the stranger left.

In the course of the next few years the sister who had had this experience fell ill, began to complain, and eventually developed unmistakable delusions of observation and persecution with the following content. The women neighbors were pitying her for having been jilted and for still waiting for this man to come back; they were always making hints of that kind to her, kept saying all kinds of things to her about the man, and so on. All this, she said, was of course untrue. Since then the patient has only fallen into this state for a few weeks at a time; from time to time she becomes rational, explaining that it is all the result of the excitement; though even in the intervals she suffers from a neurosis which can without difficulty be interpreted as a sexual one. And soon she succumbs to a fresh thrust of paranoia.

The elder sister was astonished to notice that as soon as the conversation turned to the scene of the temptation, the patient denied it. Breuer heard of the case, the patient was sent to me, and I endeavored to cure her tendency to paranoia by trying to reinstate the memory of that scene in its legitimate place. I failed in this. I talked to her twice; in concentration hypnosis got her to tell me everything to do with the lodger; in reply to my pressing inquiries about whether something "embarrassing" had actually happened, I received the most decided negation as an answer; and — saw her no more. She sent me a message to say that it upset her too much. Defense! That was obvious. She *wanted* not be reminded of it and consequently intentionally repressed it.

There could be no doubt whatever about the defense; but she could just as well have acquired a hysterical symptom or an obsessional idea. What was the peculiarity of paranoid defense?

She was sparing herself something; something was repressed. We can guess what it was. Probably she had really been excited by what she saw and by its memory. So what she was sparing herself was the reproach of being a "bad woman." That same reproach she then came to hear from outside. Thus *the factual content remained undisturbed;* what was altered, however, was something in the *placing* of the whole thing. Earlier it had been an internal self-reproach, now it was an imputation coming from outside. The judgment about her had been transposed outward: people were saying what otherwise she would have said to herself. Something was gained by this. She would have had to accept the judgment pronounced from inside; she could reject the one arriving from outside. *In that way the judgment, the reproach, was kept away from her ego.*

The purpose of paranoia is thus to ward off an idea that is incompatible with the ego, by projecting its substance into the external world.

Two questions arise: [1] How is a transposition of this kind brought about? [2] Does it also apply to other cases of paranoia?

[1] Very simple. It is a question of abuse of a psychic mechanism that is very commonly employed in normal life: transposition, or projection. Whenever an internal change occurs, we have the choice of assuming either an internal or an external cause. If something deters us from the internal derivation, we naturally seize upon the external one. Second, we are accustomed to our internal states being betrayed (by an expression of emotion) to other people. This accounts for normal delusions of observation and normal projection. For they are normal so long as, in the process, we remain conscious of our own internal change. If we forget it and are left with only the leg of the syllogism that leads outward, then we have paranoia, with its overvaluation of what people know about us and of what people

have done to us. What do people know about us that we know nothing about, that we cannot admit? *It is therefore abuse of the mechanism of projection for purposes of defense.*

Something quite analogous, indeed, takes place with obsessional ideas. The mechanism of substitution also is a normal one. When an old maid keeps a dog or an old bachelor collects snuffboxes, the former is finding a substitute for her need for a companion in marriage and the latter for his need for—a multitude of conquests. Every collector is a substitute for a Don Juan Tenorio, and so too is the mountaineer, the sportsman, and such people. These are erotic equivalents. Women know them too. Gynecological treatment falls into this category. There are two kinds of women patients: one kind who are as loyal to their doctor as to their husband, and the other kind who change their doctors as often as their lovers. This normally operating mechanism of substitution is abused in obsessional ideas—once again for purposes of *defense.*

[2] Now, does this view also apply to other cases of paranoia?

To all of them, I should have thought. [But] I shall take some examples.

The litigious paranoic cannot put up with the idea that he has done wrong or that he should part with his property. [He] therefore thinks the judgment was not legally valid, [that] he is not in the wrong, and so on. This case is too clear and perhaps not quite unambiguous; maybe it could be resolved more simply.

The *grande nation* cannot face the idea that it could be defeated in war. Ergo it was not defeated; the victory does not count. It provides an example of mass paranoia and invents the delusion of betrayal.[2]

The alcoholic will never admit to himself that he has become impotent through drink. However much alcohol he can tolerate, he cannot tolerate this insight. So his wife is to blame—delusions of jealousy and so on.

The hypochondriac will struggle for a long time until he finds the key to his feeling of being seriously ill. He will not admit to himself that it arises from his sexual life; but it gives him the greatest satisfaction if his ailment is, as Möbius says, not endogenous but exogenous. So he is being poisoned.

The official who has been passed over for promotion requires that there be a conspiracy against him and that he be spied on in his room. Otherwise he would have to admit his shipwreck.

What develops like this need not always be delusions of persecution. Megalomania may perhaps be even more effective in keeping the distressing idea away from the ego. Take, for instance, the faded cook who must accustom herself to the thought that she is permanently excluded from happiness in love. This is the right moment for [the emergence of] the gentleman from the house opposite, who obviously wants to marry her and who is giving her to understand as much in such a strangely bashful but nonetheless unmistakable fashion.

In every instance the *delusional idea* is maintained with the same energy with which another, intolerably distressing, idea is warded off from the ego. Thus they love *their delusions as they love themselves.* That is the secret.

And now, how does this form of defense compare with those that we already know: (1) hysteria, (2) obsessional idea, (3) hallucinatory confusion, (4) paranoia?

To be taken into consideration: affect, content of the idea, and hallucinations. [See Summary.]

(1) *Hysteria.* The incompatible idea is not admitted to *association* with the ego. The content is retained in a segregated compartment, it is absent from consciousness; its affect [is dealt with] by conversion into the somatic sphere. — Psychoneurosis is the only [result].

(2) *Obsessional idea.* Once more, the incompatible idea is not

SUMMARY

| | warded-off Affect | Content of idea | Hallucination | Outcome |
|---|---|---|---|---|
| Hysteria | dealt with by conversion | absent from consciousness | ——— | Unstable defense with satisfactory gain |
| Obsessional idea | retained | absent from consciousness substitute found | ——— | Permanent defense without gain |
| Hallucinatory confusion | absent | absent | friendly to ego friendly to defense | Permanent defense with brilliant gain |
| Paranoia | retained | retained projected out | hostile to ego friendly to defense | Permanent defense without gain |
| Hysterical psychosis | dominates consciousness | | hostile to ego hostile to defense | Failure of defense |

admitted to *association*. The affect is retained; the content is replaced with a substitute.

(3) *Hallucinatory confusion*. The whole incompatible idea—affect and content—is kept away from the ego; and this is possible only at the price of a partial detachment from the external world. One resorts to hallucinations, which are *friendly to the ego* and *support the defense*.

(4) *Paranoia*. The content and the affect of the incompatible idea are retained, in direct contrast to (3); but they are projected into the external world. Hallucinations, which arise in some forms [of the illness], are *hostile to the ego* but support *the defense*.

In hysterical psychoses, in contrast, it is precisely the ideas warded off that gain mastery. The type of these is the attack and *état secondaire*. Hallucinations are *hostile to the ego*.

The *delusional idea* is either a copy of the idea warded off or its opposite (megalomania).

Paranoia and hallucinatory confusion are the two *psychoses of spite or contrariness*.[3] The "reference to oneself" in paranoia is analogous to the hallucinations in confusional states, for these seek to assert the exact contrary of the fact that has been warded off. Thus the reference to oneself always seeks to prove the correctness of the projection.

1. Gotthold Lessing, *Emilia Galotti*, Act 4, scene 7.

2. A reference to the aftermath of the Franco-Prussian War of 1870.

3. *Trotz- oder Justamentpsychosen*. These are Viennese colloquialisms, implying spite and deliberately doing precisely the opposite of what is expected.

February 25, 1895

Dear Wilhelm,

Must immediately send a letter to you. The report on labor pains has appeared in the *Wiener allgemeine Zeitung*,[1] is factual and reasonable, and deserves a correction only insofar as he[2] purports to have been in direct contact with you. Don't be too harsh, please; the public is really entitled to [hear] new things of this sort; and you do not need the cloak of virtue.

Cordially your
S.

1. This article appeared on February 26(!), 1895, on p. 4. The half-column report called "Eine neue medizinische Entdeckung" begins, "In the gynecological clinic of Professor Chrobak, the Berlin physician Dr. Wilhelm Fliess has recently been con-

Emma Eckstein in 1895,
before the operation.

Sigmund Freud (1856–1939)
and Wilhelm Fliess (1858–1928)
in the 1890s.

ducting experiments to eliminate, or at least diminish, labor pain in birth by the use of cocaine on the lower turbinate bone and the so-called tubercula septi of the nose." The phrase Freud is referring to reads, "As Dr. Fliess himself tells us, he has not yet been able to form a conclusive opinion about the significance of the discovery he has made." Curiously, the article continues with, "Dr. Fliess, by the way, is returning to Berlin today," although this is perhaps a reference to when the article was written as opposed to when it appeared.

2. That is, the reporter.

---

Vienna, March 4, 1895

Dearest Wilhelm,

Have left you unconscionably long without a reply; now a great deal has accumulated. To begin with, the picture; it is the only photo that could be considered. I have put in my order for it. Beautiful we are not (or no longer), but my pleasure in having you close by my side after the operation clearly shows.

So, then, your correction; I searched for it several evenings after receiving your letter, it did *not* appear. Breuer thinks there is nothing to be done about it because you are quoted only as asserting that the matter has not been brought to a conclusion, and that you cannot dispute.[1] I believe one should let it go; it is not worth the effort; as long as you have assured Chrobak that you are blameless, all possible harm has been prevented. For the rest, the whole thing does not matter. Naturally, they are now talking a lot about your experiments and spreading the word that they did not succeed. Schauta[2] supposedly did not confirm them. Don't let yourself be impugned.

Third, I know that both of you have influenza or, I hope, soon will have had influenza. I did not send you a telegram inquiring about your health because this, I presume, is reserved for the contact with your mama. I hear that her influenza has recurred. All of us are still well. Otherwise, there are many cases, but light ones.

Fourth, Eckstein's condition is still unsatisfactory:[3] persistent swelling, going up and down "like an avalanche";[4] pain, so that morphine cannot be dispensed with; bad nights. The purulent secretion has been decreasing since yesterday; the day before yesterday (Saturday) she had a massive hemorrhage, probably as a result of expelling a bone chip the size of a heller;[5] there were two bowls full of pus. Today we encountered resistance on irrigation; and since the pain and the visible edema had increased, I let myself be persuaded to call in Gersuny. (By the way, he greatly admired an etching of *The Isle of the Dead* [by Böcklin].) He explained that the access was considerably narrowed and insufficient for drainage, inserted a drainage tube, and threatened to break it [the bone?] open if that did not stay in. To judge by the smell, all this is most likely correct. Please send me your authoritative advice. I am not looking forward to new surgery on this girl.

Fifth, quickly something more pleasant after all this. In his essay on the theories of hysteria (for our book), Breuer cites nasal headaches and the elimination of intercostal pains via [the approach from] the nose as an illustration of effects operating at a distance [from the organ affected]. I congratulate you. He was supposed to give a lecture in my class on Saturday, but he got stuck three times and gave up with apologies. I had to take over for him. I was very concerned, but it was only exhaustion. I visited him on Sunday evening and once again won him over—probably only for a short time—by telling him about the analysis of Eckstein, with which you are not really familiar either. When you are absent and I get the anger out of my system, he again rises a great deal in my estimation. In his essay, by the way, he accepts all my ideas and persistently speaks of conversion and defense, probably because it will not work any other way.

Sixth. Scientifically, there is little that is new. I am hurriedly writing the essay on the therapy of hysteria. Hence the delay [in my writing to you]. Our case of tabes (nose!) has received recognition by Professor Lang[6] and is now considered a feat of diagnostic acumen. Otherwise, nothing but tabes; have nothing to enclose for you. At most a small analogy to Emma E.'s dream psychosis[7] that we witnessed. Rudi Kaufmann, a very intelligent nephew of Breuer's and also a medical man, is a late riser. He has his maidservant wake him, and then is very reluctant to obey her. One morning she woke him again and, since he did not want to listen to her, called him by his name, "Mr. Rudi." Thereupon the sleeper hallucinated a hospital chart (compare the Rudolfinerhaus) with the name "Rudolf Kaufmann" on it and said to himself, "So R.K. is already in the hospital; then I do not need to go there," and went on sleeping!

Seventh. I have not yet been able to speak with Paschkis; I, too, must complain about his not sending proofs, so that everything, from spelling mistakes to printer's errors that destroy the meaning, remains. Perhaps you will come across the short paper on migraine. It contains only two important ideas.

Tomorrow at the Bondys' I shall hear how you all are. Most cordial greetings in the meantime. Tuesday, after your departure, the city was empty in spite of the throngs coming out to honor Albrecht.[8]

All of us and I wish you a speedy recovery.

Your
Sigmund

1. A reference to the article mentioned in the previous letter.

2. Friedrich Schauta (1849–1919), director of the Frauenklinik in the Allgemeine Krankenhaus in Vienna. For more information on him see Lesky (1978, pp. 476 ff.).

3. This is the first mention of the operation performed by Fliess on Emma Eckstein. Max Schur (1966, 1972), who had access to Freud's unpublished letters to Fliess, was the first to write perceptively about this important episode in Freud's career. On the basis of further information, letters from Freud to Eckstein, and publications by Eckstein, I have attempted to determine the significance of this early patient for Freud's theoretical thinking at the time. A detailed discussion of this complex matter is given in Masson (1984).

4. This is a common German humorous expression, generally used in the saying, "Life is like an avalanche, up and down." (An avalanche, of course, moves in one direction only.)

5. A heller is a small coin.

6. Eduard Lang (b. 1841) was a professor of dermatology in Vienna and a specialist in syphilis. The case mentioned in the Dora analysis, "Fragment of an Analysis of a Case of Hysteria" (*S.E.* 7:16n), probably is the one referred to. There Freud writes: "Another physician once sent his sister to me for psychotherapeutic treatment, telling me that she had for years been treated without success for hysteria (pains and defective gait). The short account which he gave me seemed quite consistent with the diagnosis. In my first hour with the patient I got her to tell me her history herself. When the story came out perfectly clearly and connectedly in spite of the remarkable events it dealt with, I told myself that the case could not be one of hysteria, and immediately instituted a careful physical examination. This led to the diagnosis of a not very advanced stage of tabes, which was later on treated with Hg injections (Ol. cinereum) by Professor Lang with markedly beneficial results."

7. I do not know precisely what Freud means by a "dream psychosis." By "we" he presumably is referring to the fact that he examined or saw Emma Eckstein in Fliess's company. When Freud first spoke to Fliess about Eckstein is not known. Since this is the first letter in which she is mentioned, it is likely that she was discussed during one of Freud's meetings with Fliess.

8. Field Marshal Archduke Albrecht (1817–1895), commander in chief of the Austro-Hungarian army, member of the house of Hapsburg, died on February 18, 1895, in Arco, Italy. Freud apparently refers to the crowds drawn by his funeral, which was held in Vienna.

## *Case History* (March 4, 1895) [enclosed with letter]

On the last day you were here, I suddenly discharged several scabs from the right side, the one not operated on. As early as the next day there appeared thick, old pus in large clots, at first on the right side only and soon thereafter also on the left. Since then the nose has again been flooded; only today has the purulent secretion become somewhat less dense. Light but regular symptoms: in the morning a stuffed nose, vile head, not better until large amounts have been discharged; in the interval occasionally migraine; everything, by the way, not very severe. During the first of these days, I noticed with pride that I can climb stairs without dyspnea; for the last three days pain in the heart region, atactic pulse, and beautiful insufficiency. Today, for example, I arrived someplace, found the carriage of the [other] consultant already waiting at the door, ran up the stairs and, once upstairs, was unable to talk for five minutes and had to admit that I was ill, and so forth. Three days ago, after having been massaged, the whole business repeated itself, as in the old days; this morning I once again wanted to die (relatively) young.

Though not designed to make one feel at ease, this information affords some pleasure because it emphasizes once again that the condition of the heart depends upon the condition of the nose. I cannot regard the latter as a new infection; I have the impression that I really still have, as you surmised, a focal pus accumulation (right sphenoid bone), which now happens to feel inclined to produce eruptions like a private Etna, as it were.

But that is no reason for you to come. I shall instead report to you faithfully.

---

March 8, 1895

Dearest Wilhelm,

Just received your letter and am able to answer it immediately. Fortunately I am finally seeing my way clear and am reassured about Miss Eckstein and can give you a report which will probably upset you as much as it did me, but I hope you will get over it as quickly as I did.

I wrote you that the swelling and the hemorrhages would not stop, and that suddenly a fetid odor set in, and that there was an obstacle upon irrigation. (Or is the latter new [to you]?) I arranged for Gersuny to be called in; he inserted a drainage tube, hoping that things would work out once discharge was reestablished; but otherwise he was rather reserved. Two days later I was awakened in the morning—profuse bleeding had started again, pain, and so on. Gersuny replied on the phone that he was unavailable till evening; so I asked Rosanes[1] to meet me. He did so at noon. There still was moderate bleeding from the nose and mouth; the fetid odor was very bad. Rosanes cleaned the area surrounding the opening, removed some sticky blood clots, and suddenly pulled at something like a thread, kept on pulling. Before either of us had time to think, at least half a meter of gauze had been removed from the cavity. The next moment came a flood of blood. The patient turned white, her eyes bulged, and she had no pulse. Immediately thereafter, however, he again packed the cavity with fresh iodoform gauze and the hemorrhage stopped. It lasted about half a minute, but this was enough to make the poor creature, whom by then we had lying flat, unrecognizable. In the meantime — that is, afterward — something else happened. At the moment the foreign body came out and everything became clear to me — and I immediately afterward was confronted by the sight of the patient — I felt sick. After she had been packed, I fled to the next room, drank a bottle of water, and felt miserable. The brave Frau Doktor[2] then brought me a small glass of cognac and I became myself again.

Rosanes stayed with the patient until I arranged, via Streitenfels, to have both of them taken to Sanatorium Loew.[3] Nothing further happened that evening. The following day, that is, yesterday, Thursday, the operation was repeated with the assistance of Gersuny; [the bone was] broken wide open, the packing removed, and [the wound] curetted. There was scarcely any bleeding. Since then she has been out of danger, naturally very pale, and miserable with fresh pain and swelling. She had not lost consciousness during the massive hemorrhage;[4] when I returned to the room somewhat shaky, she greeted me with the condescending remark, "So this is the strong sex."

I do not believe it was the blood that overwhelmed me — at that moment strong emotions were welling up in me. So we had done her an injustice; she was not at all abnormal, rather, a piece of iodoform gauze had gotten torn off as you were removing it and stayed in for fourteen days, preventing healing; at the end it tore off and provoked the bleeding. That this mishap should have happened to you; how you will react to it when you hear about it; what others could make of it; how wrong I was to urge you to operate in a foreign city where you could not follow through on the case; how my intention to do my best[5] for this poor girl was insidiously thwarted and resulted in endangering her life — all this came over me simultaneously. I have worked it through by now. I was not sufficiently clear at that time to think of immediately reproaching Rosanes. It only occurred to me ten minutes later that he should immediately have thought, There is something inside; I shall not pull it out lest there be a hemorrhage; rather, I'll stuff it some more, take her to Loew, and there clean and widen it at the same time. But he was just as surprised as I was.

Now that I have thought it through, nothing remains but heartfelt compassion for my child of sorrows. I really should not have tormented you here, but I had every reason to entrust you with such a matter and more. You did it as well as one can do it. The tearing off of the iodoform gauze remains one of those accidents that happen to the most fortunate and circumspect of surgeons, as you know from the business with your little sister-in-law's broken adenotome and the anesthesia. Gersuny said that he had had a similar experience and therefore he is using iodoform wicks instead of gauze (you will remember your own case). Of course, no one is blaming you, nor would I know why they should. And I only hope that you will arrive as quickly as I did at feeling sympathy[6] and rest assured that it was not necessary for me to reaffirm my trust in you once again. I only want to add that for a day I shied away from letting you know about it; then I began to feel ashamed, and here is the letter.

Beside this, other news really pales. As far as my condition is concerned, you are certainly quite right; strangely enough it is far easier for me to be productive when I have mild troubles of this kind. So now I am writing page after page of "The Therapy of Hysteria."

An odd idea of a different sort I shall entrust to you only after we have Eckstein off our minds. Here influenza is quite widespread, but not very intense. Your mama is not yet quite well either.

I shall soon write to you again and, above all, report in detail on Emma E. Scientifically, otherwise quite desolate. Influenza has been eating up the practice of specialists. That it really took its toll of you I know. Just allow yourself a proper rest afterward. I am determined to do the same if it should strike me.

With cordial greetings,

Your
Sigmund

1. I could not learn anything about Ignaz Rosanes, an ear, nose, and throat specialist in Vienna, except that he was a boyhood friend (ascertained from Freud's unpublished letters to Eduard Silberstein), that Freud treated his wife (see below), and that in 1894 he was director of the Kronprinzessin Stephanie Hospital.

2. It is not clear to whom Freud is referring here. Probably Emma Eckstein was living with one of her brothers or sisters, and the *Frau Doktor* could either be a doctor's wife or a title used by one of Eckstein's sisters.

3. References unknown.

4. *Verblutungsszene;* literally, the scene of bleeding to death.

5. Schur (1966, p. 57) writes: "Freud's use of the word 'anzutun' from 'antun' is quite ambiguous. The correct translation is 'inflict'—used prevalently in the sense of inflicting violence, pain, etc." However, according to the first edition of the Muret-Sanders dictionary (late nineteenth century), as well as the current six-volume

Duden dictionary, the first meaning of *antun* is positive: the example both provide is "to do good to somebody." The second meaning is as Schur gives it. This sentence should not, therefore, be used as evidence of Freud's ambivalence, although much else in the letter can be.

6. The German is *Bedauern,* which could also mean "regret."

---

March 13, 1895

Dearest Wilhelm,

It is a shame that both of us suffer from so much illness when we have so much ahead of us. I am pleased to see something of yours again. I already am accustomed to attributing scantiness and gaps in your report to something bad. I hope that next time you will write more to me and then there will also be something better in it.

Things are finally going well with Eckstein, as they could have without the detour three weeks ago. It does speak well for her that she did not change her attitude toward either of us; she honors your memory beyond the undesired accident.[1]

It has been a dreadful period for me, in almost every respect. The extensive restriction of my professional activities due to the epidemic also was bad for me. The only thing I remember of last week is that I have written fifty-two printed pages on the psychotherapy of hysteria; I shall give you the galley proofs to read. Otherwise, I rarely have felt so low and down, almost melancholic; all my interests have lost their meaning. The letdown following the increasing loneliness after our long time together also must have contributed.

March 15. Today your letter finally arrived, indicating that you are again feeling well. But listen, the two letters from Chrobak are precisely what we know here as an addition to Chrobakian *bonhomie:* pettiness and unreliability. This confirms the reports that are making the rounds. Gersuny says Chrobak always adopts the opinions of those around him. I am indeed convinced that your reply is dignified and that this matter will be settled in a few weeks. What kind of hair-splitting entitles him to say the labor pains have *not* been eliminated by your experiment?

Breuer is like King David; when someone is dead, he becomes cheerful. Previously he had been affected very strongly. Recently, after a polite note from me he indicated that he did not want me to treat him with such exquisite politeness, not him. In his reply he said[2] that it was always easier for me to do so after you had been in

Vienna. Because by then I had gotten enough off my chest and was back in form.

Yesterday Mrs. K. again sent for me because of cramplike pains in her chest; generally it has been because of headaches. In her case I have invented a strange therapy of my own: I search for sensitive areas, press on them, and thus provoke fits of shaking which free her. Formerly, these areas were supraorbital and ethmoid; now they are (for the breast cramps) two areas on the left chest wall, wholly identical with mine. When I press on a point in her axillar, she says she feels it along the entire arm into her fingers. She does not have these pains spontaneously, as I do. By chance Breuer also came and told her that *nevertheless* she must go to Berlin.

Surgically, Eckstein will soon be well, [but] now the nervous effects of the incident are starting: hysterical attacks at night and similar symptoms which I must start to work on. It is now about time you forgave yourself the minimal oversight, as Breuer called it.[3]

How have I been? In a word, like a dog—infamously miserable. Since yesterday evening it has abated; I am again a human being with human feelings; I have an inkling of new ideas and of a few more years of life. It has not been this bad for a long time. The suppuration is now quite inconsiderable; the whole business started with a scab, which came out while you were still present.

Anticipating your wishes, I immediately ordered a dozen of our pictures and can therefore easily send you three more without having to contact the photographer. The number of persons to whom one can give the joint photo is not very large, after all.

Scientifically, I am now acting like the third Littrow[4] in high school. I am pausing. I reported many of my neurotic findings in the psychiatric association and privately, and finally became annoyed at the small measure of understanding; I am withdrawing again. Let them be the ones to know better. The discussion of obsessional ideas has not yet taken place.[5] Krafft is ailing and does not appear in public.

March 20. Events in the interim have interrupted this letter. Today I can continue and conclude. My confession of how bad I am feeling also interfered with my mailing of the letter. Now I can report to you that since the day before yesterday I suddenly feel *very good* again—about the level I was on while you were here. The suppuration stopped a few days ago.

Poor Eckstein is doing less well. This was the second reason for my postponement. Ten days after the second operation, after a normal course, she suddenly had pain and swelling again, of unknown origin. The following day, a hemorrhage; she was quickly packed. At noon, when they lifted the packing to examine her, renewed hemorrhage, so that she almost died. Since then she has been lying in bed again, tightly packed and totally miserable. Gussenbauer[6] and Gersuny believe that she is bleeding from a large vessel—but which one?—and on Friday they want to make an incision on the outside while compressing the carotid artery to see whether they can find the source. In my thoughts I have given up hope for the poor girl and am inconsolable that I involved you and created such a distressing affair for you. I also feel very sorry for her; I had become very fond of her.

With the most cordial greetings to you and Ida,

Your
Sigmund

1. Schur (1972, p. 67) writes: "That Fliess had a gift for impressing his friends and patients with the wealth of his biological knowledge, his far-reaching imagination, and his unflagging faith in his therapeutic abilities can be concluded from the intense loyalty of his patients which was evident from Freud's correspondence with him. Even a patient who, as we shall see, suffered dangerous consequences from a grave 'slip' committed by Fliess remained loyal to him for the rest of her life." In a footnote to this passage Schur writes, "Personal communication." I could not, however, determine the source.

2. Freud undoubtedly meant, "In my reply I said . . ."

3. Max Schur, in an unpublished paper "The Guilt of the Survivor" (copy in the Isakower Archives, Library of Congress), writes as follows: "The previously unpublished correspondence of these months revealed Freud's desperate attempts to deny any realization of the fact that Fliess would have been convicted of malpractice in any court for this nearly fatal error."

4. Reference unclear.

5. In *Wiener klinische Wochenschrift*, 27 (1895):496 is a report of a lecture by Freud, "Über den Mechanismus der Zwangsvorstellungen und Phobien." At the end of the article is a statement that "the discussion has been postponed."

6. Karl Gussenbauer (1842–1903), Billroth's successor. See Lesky (1978, pp. 447 ff.).

---

March 23, 1895
IX., Berggasse 19

Dearest Wilhelm,

I could not make up my mind to send off the letter before I could give you definite news about E. The operation was postponed to Saturday and is just now over. It was nothing, and nothing was done. Gussenbauer palpated the cavity and pronounced everything to be normal; he supposes the bleeding was only from granulation tissue; she is spared any disfigurement. They will continue to pack her [nose]; I shall try to keep her off morphine. I am glad that none of the bad expectations has materialized. Now I hope to hear from you soon again.

Cordial greetings.

Your
Sigm.

---

Vienna, March 28, 1895

Dearest Wilhelm,

I know what you want to hear first: *she* is tolerably well; complete subsidence, no fever, no hemorrhage. The packing that was inserted six days ago is still in; we hope to be safe from new surprises. Of course, she is beginning with the new production of hysterias from this past period, which are then dissolved by me.

I also must accept that you are not yet feeling well; I hope this will not be for long. I think you will soon have worked your way out of it and then tackle the labor pains first. By chance, I recently had a conversation with Chrobak about them. My impression was unfavorable. I would like to see you dispense with all his cases, which, moreover, you do not need. The public will misunderstand [your article on] "labor pains" as "painless birth," which would be claiming too much. These should have been distinguished, and so forth. Make sure that you get well, publish forty cases, and make him a present of his four. I do not know whether I should infect you: I am so very annoyed.

My own condition is not especially bad, but keeps me out of sorts. A pulse so irregular does seem to preclude well-being; the motoric insufficiency has again been intolerable for several days. I should like to accept your proposal, but the present time is obviously not favorable for it. Besides, my practice too is especially poor and then I am, as far as my mood is concerned, mostly useless.

April 2. These past few days I have really felt outrageously indifferent. Writing has been difficult for me — times in which I am not bearable, the most minute intimations of fluctuating mood changes. Now I am my old self again, also vigorous of heart, but wild and yearning to enjoy some of the spring. — Perhaps it is not so important at all how I was and how I am. Otherwise I have little that is serious to report to you. Next time I shall send you a package from an analysis which I am now conducting, because it is so mad. But I do not know whether it can be enjoyed without my comments, whether I should not rather leave it for an hour when we are together.

Psychology is plaguing me a great deal. Löwenfeld launched the first attack on the anxiety neurosis in the *Münchener medizinische Wochenschrift;*[1] I asked him for a reprint so that I can reply (in Paschkis).[2] Naturally, the most obvious objections. Altogether, I miss you very much. Am I really the same person who was overflowing with ideas and projects as long as you were within reach? When I sit down at the desk in the evening, I often do not know *what* I should work on.

She, Eckstein, is doing well; she is a very nice, decent girl who does not hold the affair against either of us and refers to you with great respect.

Stay well, I beg you; give me detailed news of you, and for once without arguing with me. Another time I shall again swamp you with letters and enclosures. You are even-tempered, I am not.

Cordially your
Sigm.

Received your paper with thanks and pride.

1. Leopold Löwenfeld, "Über die Verknüpfung neurasthenischer und hysterischer Symptome in Anfallsform nebst Bemerkungen über die Freudsche Angstneurose." At the end of the article, which was a review of Freud's "Uber die Berechtigung . . . ," Löwenfeld has this interesting comment: "The Freudian theory may well be more or less justified in a large number of cases of anxiety states. My own observations also speak to the fact that anomalies in sexual life are of great significance in the genesis of obsessions and phobias. What I must object to is only Freud's claim of a specificity and a uniformity for the sexual etiology in cases of acquired anxiety states" (p. 285).

Freud's response, "Zur Kritik der 'Angstneurose,'" appeared in the *Wiener klinische Rundschau.*

2. That is, his journal.

Vienna, April 11, 1895

Dearest Wilhelm,

Gloomy times, unbelievably gloomy. Above all, this Eckstein affair, which is rapidly moving toward a bad ending. Last time I reported to you that Gussenbauer inspected the cavity under anesthesia, palpated it, and declared it to be satisfactory. We had high hopes, and the patient was gradually recovering. Eight days later[1] she began to bleed, with the packing in place, something that had not been the case previously. She was immediately packed again; the bleeding was minimal. Two days later renewed bleeding, again with the packing in place, and by then overabundantly. New packing, renewed perplexity. Yesterday Rosanes wanted to examine the cavity again; by chance, a new hypothesis about the source of the bleeding during the first operation (yours) was suggested by Weil. As soon as the packing was partly removed, there was a new, life-threatening hemorrhage which I witnessed. It did not spurt, it surged. Something like a [fluid] level rising extraordinarily rapidly, and then overflowing everything. It must have been a large vessel, but which one and from where? Of course, nothing could be seen and it was a relief to have the packing back in again. Add to this the pain, the morphine, the demoralization caused by the obvious medical helplessness, and the tinge of danger, and you will be able to picture the state the poor girl is in. We do not know what to do. Rosanes is opposed to the ligation of the carotid that was recommended. The danger that she will run a fever also is not far off. I am really very shaken to think that such a mishap could have arisen from an operation that was purported to be harmless.

I do not know whether I should hold this depressing business exclusively responsible for the fact that the condition of my heart remains so much below par for this year of illness. After an interruption of several months, I started to take strophantus[2] again so as to have a less disgraceful pulse, something that so far has failed to materialize. Mood and strength are very *à bas*. I plan to spend Easter with Rie on the Semmering; there I shall perhaps pick up the pieces again.

My scientific work is proceeding, more or less; that is, nothing new, no ideas and no observations. As far as my psychological research is concerned, I have worked myself to the bone and shall now let it rest. Only the book I am writing with Breuer is progressing; it will be ready in about three weeks. The only new thing, the analysis of Mr. F. who perspires in the theater, is quite incomprehensible if I do not elucidate it. I hope I still have a chance to read it to you myself.

Thus far nothing at all has been said about you. I gather you have just begun to feel well again. Just keep it up for a long time now! Your head is well, after all. *That* has been accomplished; may I now really believe it?

With the most cordial greetings to you and your dear wife,

Your
Sigm.

1. Meaning unclear; it could also be "eight days ago." Similarly, two sentences below could be "Two days ago."

2. A drug similar to digitalis.

Vienna, April 20, 1895

Dearest Wilhelm,

The Easter excursion and one day in Abbazia have delayed my reply to your letter. Today I shall send you the second half of the galley proofs of our book; don't let yourself be distracted by the misprints. It pleases me to be able for once to write about something other than our two boring states of health. Your health, indeed, is fortunately no longer on the agenda. We are so ungrateful; how could we have been so timid about the operation and all its attendant dangers? Now one hardly utters a word about the fact that it succeeded and that you are again capable of working. Let me loudly voice my pleasure about it and await a report of your scientific findings.

I did of course immediately inform Rosanes of your recommendations concerning E. At close range many things look different—for instance, the hemorrhages. I can confirm that in their case there could be no question of biding one's time. There was bleeding as though from the carotid artery; within half a minute she again would have bled to death. Now, however, she is doing better; the packing was gently and gradually removed; there was no mishap; she is in the clear.

The writer of this is still very miserable, but also offended that you deem it necessary to have a testimonial certificate from Gersuny for your rehabilitation. For me you remain the physician, the type of man into whose hands one confidently puts one's life and that of one's family—even if Gersuny should have the same opinion of your skills as *Weil*.[1] I wanted to pour forth my tale of woe and perhaps obtain your advice concerning E., not reproach you with anything. That would have been stupid, unjustified, and in clear contradiction to all my feelings.

With regard to my own ailment, I would like you to continue to be right—that the nose may have a large share in it and the heart a small one. Only a very strict judge will take it amiss that in view of the pulse and the insufficiency I frequently believe the opposite. I cannot accept your proposal to come to Berlin *now*. My circumstances are such that I cannot allow myself to spend 1,000 to 1,500 florins, or even only half that amount, on my own health; and I am not sufficiently demoralized to take your suggestion of sparing me the loss. Furthermore, I think I do not have to. If empyema is the main problem, then the aspect of danger is eliminated, and the continuation of the symptoms for a few months will not kill me. But if an affliction of the heart is the essential problem, then all you can do is relieve my symptoms, and I shall then face the danger without warning, which I do not like.

Today I can write because I have more hope; I pulled myself out of a miserable attack with a cocaine application. I cannot guarantee that I shall not come for a day or two for a cauterization or galvanization, but at the moment that too is not possible. What I would like best is for you to agree to want to know nothing further about the heart theme!

I am pleased that I am now entitled to hear from you again, and about many things, and I cordially greet you and your dear wife.

Your
Sigm.

1. See letter of October 18, 1893. Moriz Weil (who was at the Mariahilfer Ambulatorium in Vienna) wrote an article in the *Wiener medizinische Wochenschrift*, 47 (1897):706–710, 761–765, 814–819, 909–913, 965–968, entitled "Zur Pathologie und Therapie der Eiterungen der Nasennebenhöhlen." In it he mentions having had a patient referred to him by Freud. The article ends: "In conclusion allow me to refer to a comment made in 1872 by the great surgeon Langenbeck, which I could just as well have made the motto for this article: We have achieved the insight that *it is less important to discover new operations and new methods of operating than to search for ways and methods to avoid operations*" (my translation; italics in original).

---

April 26, 1895
IX., Berggasse 19

Dear magician,

You seem to be angry when you cloak yourself so assiduously in silence. You are right if you are angry with me for not sending you the galley proofs I announced, an absentmindedness incomprehensible to me; wrong, if it is because of my refusal to come to Berlin. For indeed I shall come as soon as I decently[1] can, in August, as your last patient. Something strange but not unpleasant has happened to me. I put a noticeable end to the last horrible attack with cocaine; since then things have been fine and a great amount of pus is coming out. Evidently I still have an empyema of the sphenoidal bone on the left, which naturally makes me very happy. She [Emma E.] too, my tormentor and yours, now appears to be doing well.

My most cordial greetings.

Your
Sigm.

1. English in original.

---

Vienna, April 27, 1895

Dearest Wilhelm,

Today the letter I expected from you arrived and made me very happy. In it health, work, and progress can finally be found again. I am of course very curious to hear all the news. I hope you are giving first place to the *inertia uteri* [uterine insufficiency],[1] if for no other reason than for the sake of stupid mankind. I thank you very much for your comments on anxiety.[2] The biblical story is striking; I have to look it up and ask a Hebrew scholar about the meaning of the word. Or have you too been one since your youth?

For the rest, the distance and the letter writing are a great misery that cannot be helped at all. Especially if in any case one writes as much as I do and then from time to time becomes acquainted with the *horror calami*.[3] My own condition has taught me this again. Since the last cocainization three circumstances have continued to coincide: (1) I feel well; (2) I am discharging ample amounts of pus; (3) I am feeling *very* well. Thus I want nothing further to do with a heart condition, only the facilitation through nicotine. Really, I have gone through a good deal and nevertheless still cannot get away now, far less so if the diagnosis is harmless than if it is serious. But I shall come and let you help me.

Scientifically, I am in a bad way; namely, caught up in "The Psychology for Neurologists," which regularly consumes me totally until, actually overworked, I must break off. I have never before experienced such a high degree of preoccupation. And will anything come of it? I hope so, but it is difficult and slow going.

Cases of neurosis are now very rare; my practice is becoming more intensive, but diminishing in extent. Various odds and ends. I shall send you, for Mendel, a few pages on a sensory disturbance described by Bernhardt, one from which I suffer myself.[4] Rubbish, of course, just to keep people busy. Löwenfeld attacked me in one of the March issues of the *Münchener medizinische Wochenschrift;*[5] I shall reply in a few pages in Paschkis; and so on and so forth.

I will also have to start on the childhood paralyses for Nothnagel, but my interest is riveted elsewhere.

My heart is in the coffin here with Caesar.[6]

I recall having seen Mrs. A. once. I do of course know her family very well; from the standpoint of differential diagnosis, quite interesting.

G.R. is suffering from very bad headaches — it is a shame you are not here. Eckstein once *again* is in pain; will she be bleeding next? Since the examination A. is doing so well that I cannot expect her to undertake the journey; she is freely discharging pus.

This is the *status praesens* in scientific and private matters.

My cordial greetings, and transfer a good part of them to your dear wife.

Your
Sigm.

1. *Die Wehenschwäche steht Dir wohl auch voran.* The reference (possibly to Fliess's "Magenschmerz und Dysmenorrhöe") and the meaning are unclear.

2. Michael Schröter has pointed out that in *Die Beziehungen zwischen Nase und weiblichen Geschlechtsorganen* Fliess links shame and anxiety, based on a biblical passage.

3. *Calamus* is "writing pen" — therefore, dread of writing.

4. "Über die Bernhardt'sche Sensibilitätsstörungen am Oberschenkel," in which the main case history is autobiographical. Freud also mentions a patient who "put the blame for his suffering on severe emotional upheaval as a result of the illness of his son." An interesting observation for a neurological patient to make!

5. See note 1 to letter of March 28, 1895.

6. English in original. From Shakespeare's *Julius Caesar,* Act 3, scene 2.

---

Vienna, May 25, 1895

Dearest Wilhelm,

Your letter gave me much pleasure and caused me to regret anew what I feel is the great gap in my life — that I cannot reach you in any other way. First of all, I owe you an explanation of why I have not corresponded with your cherished Ida since our meeting. You did not quite guess it. You could have correctly assumed that I would have cried out if there had been something wrong with me. I have felt very well — partly Ia, partly I — and I have a few stupid thoughts on the connections, which I shall append for you (later in this letter). I have had an inhuman amount to do, and after a ten- to eleven-hour period of working with neuroses I have regularly been incapable of picking up my pen to write you a little, when in fact I would have had a great deal to say. The main reason, however, was this: a man like me cannot live without a hobbyhorse, without a consuming passion, without—in Schiller's words—a tyrant. I have found one. In its service I know no limits. It is psychology, which has always been my distant, beckoning goal, and which now, since I have come upon the problem of neuroses, has drawn so much nearer. I am tormented by two aims: to examine what shape the theory of mental functioning takes if one introduces quantitative considerations, a sort of economics of nerve forces; and, second, to peel off from psychopathology a gain for normal psychology. Actually, a satisfactory general conception of neuropsychotic disturbances is impossible if one cannot link it with clear assumptions about normal mental processes. During the past weeks I have devoted every free minute to such work; have spent the hours of the night from eleven to two with such fantasizing, interpreting, and guessing, and invariably stopped only when somewhere I came up against an absurdity or when I actually and seriously overworked, so that I had no interest left in my daily medical activities. It will still be a long time before you can ask me about results. My reading has also been following the same direction. A book by W. Jerusalem, *Die Urteilsfunktion* [The function of judgment], has greatly advanced me; in it I discovered two of my principal ideas: that judging consists in a transference into the motoric sphere, and that internal perception cannot claim to be "evidence."

I derive vast pleasure from working with neuroses in my practice. Almost everything is confirmed daily, new things are added, and the certainty that I have the core of the matter in my hand does me good. I have a whole series of the most peculiar things I could tell you, but it cannot be done in a letter, and in these rushed days my notes are too fragmentary to mean anything to you. I hope to bring enough with me to Berlin so that I can amuse you and hold your interest for the entire time I am your patient.

I felt like shouting when I got your news. If you really have solved the problem of conception, just make up your mind immediately which kind of marble is most likely to meet with your approval. For me you are a few months too late, but perhaps it can be used next year. In any event, I am burning with curiosity to hear something about it. There seems to me to be an urgent need for communicating the labor pain story. Do you already have twenty-five cases? Let Chrobak be a little angry—or a lot, if he prefers.

Breuer, in contrast, is not recognizable. One cannot help but like him again without any reservations. He has accepted the whole of your nose [theory] and is promoting an enormous reputation for you in Vienna, just as he has become fully converted to my theory of sexuality. He is indeed an entirely different fellow from the one we were accustomed to.

Now, to my ideas about the nose. I discharged exceedingly ample amounts of pus and all the while felt splendid; now the secretion has nearly dried up and I am still feeling very well. I propose the following to you: it is neither the congestion nor the flow of pus that determines the distant symptoms. The flow of pus does nothing; pus congestion, infectious swelling, and so forth make for local symptoms and headaches, but not for distant symptoms. The headaches are essentially local symptoms allochirally transposed,[1] probably according to specific logical rules (and according to the law of eccentric projection). For the distant symptoms I would like to hold responsible only a special state of excitation in the nerve endings (such as we may suppose, for example, in the case of scars), which in the extreme corresponds to chronic changes of tissue or to atrophic shrinkage, may be associated with a state of desiccated epithelium, and the like. This condition of the tissue, which develops *after* the flow of pus, infectious swelling, and so forth, is, I believe, the cause of the distant effects and develops, through accommodation on the part of the organs concerned, into these distant effects on the various organs. Heavy pressure and strain from the contact of two segments of mucous membrane, on the other hand, produce neuralgia and pain. Accordingly, three different conditions of the nose tissue would have to be held responsible for three groups of symptoms: pressure, strain; pain, neuralgia, circulatory disturbances; headache; chronic nerve irritation (tissue shrinkage); distant effects. Here I need not defend anything because you can judge, better than I, all the weaknesses as well as the possible merits of this conception. I merely want to place this alongside the localizing tendencies. Discussion of these assertions might possibly result in a classification.

Your well-being, now accomplished, is the condition of everything further. On Monday we shall move to Himmel.[2]

Emma E. is finally doing very well and I have succeeded in once more alleviating her weakness in walking, which also set in again.

With the most cordial greetings to you and your dear wife and a request not to construe the last three weeks as a precedent,

Your
Sigm.

1. As in paresthesia, for example.

2. Himmel (literally, heaven) was a street on the outskirts of Vienna that was the location of Bellevue, the villa mentioned in Freud's letter of June 17, 1895, and from which he wrote to Fliess later in 1895. (Bellevue was also a sanatorium in Switzerland that is alluded to in some of the later correspondence.)

---

Vienna, June 12, 1895

My dear Wilhelm,

Your kindheartedness is one of the reasons I love you. Initially, it seemed to me that you had broken off contact with me because of my remarks about the mechanism of the symptoms distant from the nose, and I did not deem this improbable. Now you surprise me with a discussion that takes those fantasies seriously!

As a reward I want to draw your attention to something more tangible. I have seen and treated here a Mrs. R., who has a one-sided facial spasm and in whose case, with the help of the rather simple-minded Dr. Hajek,[1] I could *almost* demonstrate that the tic can be elicited and removed at only one spot of the nasal mucosa, namely, the entrance to Highmore's antrum. You would certainly have cured the woman. Perhaps I shall succeed in sending this intelligent and pleasant patient to you. Her husband knows you through the pianist Rosenthal.[2] You probably will recall your own conjecture that the points of entry to the accessory nasal sinuses have special dignity. The woman presents a case of very intense headaches that have *subsided,* and she has always suffered from most severe menstrual symptoms. The mother has a diffuse facial tic that I gladly would attribute to irritation resulting from adenoid growth.

Otherwise I have not been successful in my attempts to send people to you in Berlin. A., whom I certainly would have prevailed upon to do so, is *so* free of headaches that no motive exists. Incidentally, she confessed to me that her headaches were *neurasthenic* ones. I really am a kind of Midas, though not a Midas of gold.

You are right in surmising that I am overflowing with new ideas, theoretical ones as well. My theories on defense have made an important advance of which I shall give you an account in a brief paper next time. Even the psychological construction behaves as if it would come together, which would give me immense pleasure. Naturally, I cannot yet say for certain. Reporting on it now would be like sending a six-month fetus of a girl to a ball.

We shall not suffer from a dearth of topics to talk about. "Your battles," it says in *Don Carlos,* "and your God,"[3] and so forth. Now to practical matters: when should I come? You must, first of all, shorten my stay; second, let me off as far as anatomical health is concerned and endeavor only to reinstate functional health insofar as you can separate them. Third, I do *not* want to encroach on your own summer vacation. Perhaps I should come afterward, in September; write to me about it soon because there are other considerations. I am feeling I to IIa. I need a lot of cocaine. Also, I have started smoking again, moderately, in the last two to three weeks, since the nasal conviction has become evident to me.[4] I have not observed any ensuing disadvantage. If you again prohibit it, I must give it up again. But do consider whether you can do this if it is only intolerance and not etiology.

I began *it*[5] again because I constantly missed it (after fourteen months of abstinence) and because I must treat this psychic fellow[6] well or he won't work for me. I demand a great deal of him. The torment, most of the time, is superhuman.

Cordial greetings from all of us, who are feeling very well, to you and your dear wife.

Your
Sigm.

1. Marcus Hajek was the first Jewish full professor of medicine at the University of Vienna. See also note 2 to letter of July 10, 1893.

2. Allan Keiler has informed me that this was Moriz Rosenthal, the last living pupil of Franz Liszt, who resided in Vienna at the time.

3. Friedrich Schiller, *Don Carlos*, Act 2, scene 13.

4. Freud means that he has become convinced of the nasal origin of his cardiac symptoms.

5. Evidently *it* refers to smoking.

6. Freud uses the phrase *psychischen Kerl.*

June 17, 1895
IX., Berggasse 19

My dear,

I grumble, will again be sorely deprived, but cannot do other than obey you. But I have the hope that after careful reconsideration you will again permit it to me. With regard to setting a date, also take my wish into account. I would therefore like you not to postpone your vacation and would prefer to come afterward.

I feel so well that there need be no question of hurry. My heart is wholly with the psychology. If I succeed in this, I will be satisfied with everything else. It will be hard on me that in the meantime I have to keep it to myself.

My family is doing splendidly in Bellevue and all are very well.

With the most cordial greetings to you and your dear wife,

Your
Sigm.

---

June 22, 1895

Hail, cherished Wilhelm!

May your dear, good, and strong wife, in whom hope and fulfillment thus far have always met, become the darling of fate as a mother as well. Martha was joyous as I have rarely seen her. I humbly ask to have my name entered as a poor uncle.

So I shall come early in September. How I shall manage to do without you afterward, I do not know. I am having enough troubles with smoking. Of course I still expect to hear a great deal from you before then. Female curiosity has certainly not yet been satisfied either. *We* are prepared for December/January. Then I will pay my proper respects to your discovery. You would be the strongest of men, holding in your hands the reins of sexuality, which governs all mankind: you could do anything and prevent anything. Therefore I do not believe the second glad tidings; the first I do believe — it is certainly easier.

Cordial greetings and good luck.

Your
Sigm.

---

July 13, 1895

My dear,

Do not understand why you should let yourself be harassed by the R. affair. The boy is normal in other respects. He has a very understanding tutor; he should be with him as much as possible and as little as possible with his family.

Otherwise it is a shame that in regard to my own person you have to depend upon Breuer's ornithological communications.[1] Objectively, I feel very well headwise; nose- and heartwise, only moderately well. I shall certainly come in August/September, as soon as you give the signal. Avid for all your *novis;* I myself shall come laden with rudiments and germinating embryos. My wife and children are quite well. Your news [of Ida's pregnancy] represents for us the very charm of the immediate future. I have no use for headaches on your part in September; I shall be making great demands on you.

Woe unto you if you do not write soon!

Cordial greetings to you and to the entire little family.

Your
Sigm.

1. This is a reference to a letter from Breuer to Fliess. The passage in question (Kris, *Origins*, p. 13n1) says: "Freud's intellect is soaring; I struggle along behind him like a hen behind a hawk." See also Jones (*Life* 1:242).

---

July 24, 1895
IX., Berggasse 19

Daimonie [Demon], why don't you write? How are you? Don't you care at all any more about what I am doing? What is happening to the nose, menstruation, labor pains, neuroses, your dear wife, and the budding little one? True, this year I am ill and must come to you; what will happen if by chance both of us remain healthy for a whole year? Are we friends only in misfortune? Or do we also want to share the experiences of calm times with each other?

Where will you spend the month of August? We are living very contentedly in Himmel.[1]

Most cordial greetings.

Your
Sigm.

1. See note 2 to letter of May 25, 1895. The letters continue to show the Berggasse address, possibly because Freud brought his home stationery to the summer residence.

---

August 6, 1895
IX., Berggasse 19

Dearest,

Am letting you know that after prolonged mental labor I believe I have penetrated to an understanding of pathological defense, and thereby to many important psychological processes. Clinically, it all fitted together long ago, but the psychological theories I needed were arrived at only very laboriously. I hope it is not "dream gold."

It is not anywhere near ready yet, but I can at least talk about it and with regard to many points avail myself of your superior scientific education. It is bold but beautiful, as you will see. I very much look forward to telling you about it—that is, of course, if your treatment leaves me with enough strength. Frau Ida will see to it that I stop when I have tortured you too much.

With the most cordial greetings to the entire little family,

Your
Sigm.

---

Bellevue, August 16, 1895

Dearest Wilhelm,

I was in Reichenau for several days, then was undecided for a few days, but today I can give you a definite account.

Between the 22nd and 24th I shall travel to Venice with my little brother and therefore regret that I cannot simultaneously be in Oberhof since, Breuer notwithstanding, I am not a bird.[1] My motive for coming to this decision, since I had to make *one*, was my concern for the young man who together with me carries the responsibility for two old people and so many women and children. He is a very tortured neurasthenic, escapes my influence too much, and I made an agreement with him whereby he will repay me for my company in Venice by accompanying me to Berlin. It is almost more important to me that you take *him* in hand rather than *me*. Besides, I shall then enjoy the advantage of not being alone in Berlin while you are finding your way back to strenuous work. We can share quarters, live and take walks together, insofar as our noses permit it. I am very eager to bind him closer to me while we are actively pursuing the possibility of finding a husband for our only sister who is not yet provided for (not Rosa, whom you know). So I shall be with you in the first days of September and keep in mind that in spite of all your activities, you will fully participate in the private congress.

With the $\phi\psi\omega$ I have had a strange experience. Shortly after I sounded the alarm with my communication that called for congratulations, and after I had scaled one of the first peaks, I found myself confronted with new difficulties, but without sufficient breath left for new work. So, quickly composing myself, I threw the whole thing aside and am persuading myself that I am not the least bit interested in it. It makes me quite uncomfortable to think that I am supposed to tell you about it. If I saw you every month, I certainly would not do so in September. Well, so be it, since you will demand it, but all the more reason for letting me tell you about things. I do not propose, however, to be reticent about my neurotic novelties.

My troop is doing very well here in rather advantageous circumstances. My wife is, of course, somewhat immobile, but otherwise cheerful. Recently my son Oliver aptly demonstrated his trait of concentrating on what is immediately ahead. An enthusiastic aunt asked him, "Oli, what do you want to become?" He replied, "Aunt, five years, in February." In several other respects as well, the children are very amusing in their different ways.

Psychology is really a cross to bear. Bowling or hunting for mushrooms is, in any event, a much healthier pastime. All I was trying to do was to explain defense, but just try to explain something from the very core of nature! I had to work my way through the problem of quality, sleep, memory — in short, all of psychology. Now I want to hear no more of it.

The soup is on the table, or else I would go on with my lamentations.

I hope all of you are doing *very* well in Thuringia, which I now shall not see. After all, for once the two of you should be allowed to be alone with each other, without work or illness. This has in any event not been the case too often. That is how I finally explained it to myself, that my giving up the Oberhof will be another proof of my friendship for you both.

My most cordial greetings to you, wife and child, and all hopes from your

Sigm.

1. See note 1 to letter of July 13, 1895.

---

Thursday, August 28,[1] 1895
Casa Kirsch, Riva degli schiavoni

Carissimo Guglielmo,

The ridiculous magic of this town has so far kept me from writing to you. There is nothing to be said about it. Today it is inhumanly hot, but the light almost makes up for it. Alexander sleeps in the afternoon, so I can write. We are planning to leave here September 1, and to depart from Vienna on September 3 in the evening. For Berlin, to which I am looking forward tremendously, I have one request. Forgo putting both of us up as your guests and help us find quarters. I am doing this only for his sake; he is shy, sensitive, and does not want to accept anything from you that he does not really have to, since he is a stranger to you. Otherwise, I cannot get him to come along, and he is dear to me and I am uneasy about him. However, I do not want to be deprived of either friend or brother. You can work and I shall lie in wait to take every free hour away from you. He is also strongly opposed to being your guest just now because of your dear Ida. I cannot find fault with that. After all, he does move in different circles of people and ideas, though you will soon find out how capable and noble he is.

Thus, this puts a first restriction on our idyll, though one that I hope will turn out to be a "blessing in disguise."[2] I hope to find you as well as I am, and hope to be at your place and with you so often that I shall not feel deprived. How glad I am to recall the grave concern that dominated my last visit to Berlin.

Tomorrow a little thing made of Venetian glass will be dispatched to our dear hostess; I apologize for it and shall not accept expressions of thanks. It has something about it that, given my uneducated taste and my inability to withstand all that Venetian beauty, moved me to possess it, and then I endeavored to double the pleasure through the address to which I sent it.

Cordially,

Your
Sigm.

1. Date previously was incorrectly read as 29.
2. English in original.

---

Bellevue, September 15, 1895[1]

Dear friends and hosts,

It helps a parting if one immediately thereafter encounters different circumstances that give one something to do. So I felt very fortunate that I had to find my way about Corsica, had to guard against confusing Pelasgians and Phocaeans,[2] and strove to keep in mind the individual traits of the somewhat monotonous heroism of the Corsican gentlemen in all its numerous incarnations. True, there were enough obstacles to this mental activity; side associations constantly distracted my attention. As to the Phocaeans, for example, I was overcome by an insurmountable inclination, which even now has not yet been sufficiently explained, to think of them as "seals."[3] A nasal symptom, probably. In between, my surroundings demanded their due. As to the green hunter, all of us made a careless prediction; he remained a faithful cellmate until Oberhollabrunn and divulged all sorts of things about his "old man," Duke Günther von Schleswig-Holstein, whom he accompanied to Austria on a hunt. Later on I saw the "old man," a disagreeable, very tall and bent-over youth with a scrubby yellow beard. The most interesting figure in this group, however, was the passenger who boarded third. He would have been capable of modifying the opinion of even a Nothnagel concerning the bad manners of the Jews. Above all, he gave evidence of his primitive state of culture and level of education by pronouncing that there was a draft and wishing to shut both windows. My protest just barely kept open the upper third of the window on my side. He nevertheless must have liked my seat because he suddenly sat there until, seizing a favorable opportunity, I reoccupied it without a word of explanation. Later, when I reached for one of my packages and exposed my supply of food, which was certainly sufficient to provoke envy, he exclaimed sorrowfully—without our having been introduced to each other—"Sure, when you come from home, it's easy! Then you can take along whatever you want!" I merely looked at him disdainfully, but was not untouched by the tribute to my hostess that his error implied. The supplies were in fact sufficient for two meals, dinner and breakfast, and in addition I left behind quite a few remnants at the railroad station.

Shortly before Teschen[4] I opened my suitcase to look for paper because it was too dark to read, too early to sleep, and I was considering writing, as well as possible, a first draft of the psychology. While I was rummaging about in my suitcase—which attracted the liveliest attention of Mr. Neighbor—I picked up something unfamiliar and hard, a book, which I did not realize I had; and feeling around further, I had a premonition of additional discoveries. The apprehension rose in me that I could not in good conscience tell the customs official, "Everything belongs to me," and it took a while before I could explain these findings by the assumption of a hereditary disposition to smuggle. In the meantime, I must have had a rather helpless expression because all of a sudden my neighbor said, "Just keep the book in your hand; then *he* will think you are reading it." That was too much for me. I did not pull the emergency brake to stop the train and to let my thanks be conveyed by the conductor, as Miss Mix does in the amusing novella by Hevesi,[5] but thanked him directly and assured him that I was not the least bit in a predicament. From then on I had my peace.

He had to turn his interest thus freed to the "old man," when the latter became visible in a station. "He went and bought himself a glass of beer for six kreuzer," he exclaimed once—a duke and a glass of beer for six kreuzer; obviously he was pained by this contrast. Nothing of any consequence could thereafter occur on this journey.

Minna, who in the city, tried to disarrange my suitcases, maintained that I could not have packed them myself. I remembered that she was right. For lunch, after having bathed and renewed my medical activitics, I went to Bellevue where I found wife and children looking heavier and well-nourished. Since then I have been savoring the last remnants of the beautiful vacation period. The vainglorious happiness was interrupted by copious suppuration. A welcome telegram then appeared in the afternoon, as though in confirmation of my tales about Berlin.

My cordial greetings and thanks to both of you. Next time a sensible letter.

Sigm.

1. Original of letter in Jerusalem. See note 1 to letter of May 25, 1892.

2. Ancient peoples of Asia Minor.

3. The German word is *Seehund* (sea dog), which in both languages can mean veteran seaman. A double pun is probably Freud's intent. Seals belong to the family of Phocidae, whereas the seafaring people he playfully confuses them with are the Phocaeans.

4. A town on the border between Austria and Saxony.

5. Ludwig Hevesi (1843–1910), pseudonym "Uncle Tom," was a minor but popular Austrian/Hungarian writer of travel stories.

---

Bellevue, September 23, 1895

Dearest Wilhelm,

I am writing so little to you only because I am writing so much for you; namely, what I started on the train, a summary account of the $\phi\psi\omega$ which you can take as a basis for your critique, and which I am now continuing in my free time and the pauses between the acts of my gradually increasing medical practice. It already amounts to a sizable volume—scribbles, of course, but nevertheless a basis, I hope, for your additions, for which I have high hopes. My well-rested head is now making child's play of the difficulties previously encountered, such as, for example, the contradiction that conductors reinstate their resistance, whereas neurones generally are subject to facilitation. That fits in very easily if one takes into account the smallness of the individual endogenous stimuli. Other points now are also falling into place, to my greater satisfaction. How much of this progress will on closer inspection again dissolve into thin air remains to be seen. But you gave me a powerful impetus to take the matter seriously.

Apart from the need to adapt the theory to the general laws of motion, which I expect from you, it is incumbent upon me to test it against the individual facts of the new experimental psychology. The capacity of the topic to fascinate me remains as great as ever, to the detriment of all my medical interests and my "infantile paralyses," which are supposed to be finished by the New Year!

I hardly know what else to tell you about; I think I shall probably send you the thing in two parts. I hope your head will do me the favor of finding the imposition, during a refreshed period, as light as a feather. I welcome your attempts at autotherapy with sympathy. My condition is, as you expected it would be, atrocious; increasing discomfort since the last ethmoid operation. If I am not mistaken, today there was a beginning toward improvement.

Ida will probably have read aloud to you that the election results in the third district were 46 to 0, and in the second, 32 to 14 against the Liberals. I voted after all. Our district has remained Liberal.

A dream the day before yesterday yielded the funniest confirmation of the conception that dreams are motivated by wish fulfillment. Löwenfeld has written me that he is preparing a paper on phobias and obsessional ideas on the basis of one hundred cases and has asked me for various bits of information.[1] In reply I warned him that he really ought not take my ideas lightly.

A shame — but one I can explain — that I cannot yet return your paper on labor pains. I also am still waiting for your observations on migraine. I am glad to say that my wife and all the children are doing very well. My most cordial wishes to you, your dear wife, with whom even Alex was very taken, and the expected young one.

Your
Sigm.

1. Apparently the only article by Löwenfeld in this field is "Weitere Beiträge zur Lehre von den psychischen Zwangszuständen," *Archiv für Psychiatrie,* 30 (1898):679–719. Löwenfeld published a book on the topic in 1904, which contains some hitherto unknown letters by Freud, for which see Masson (1984).

---

Vienna, October 8, 1895

Dearest Wilhelm,

By this time news from you had become a necessity for me because I had already drawn the conclusion, in which I am rarely wrong, that your silence meant headaches. I began to feel more comfortable again when—after a long time—I once more held a piece of your scientific material in my hands. So far I have merely glanced at it and fear that respect for so much honest and subtle material will put my theoretical fantasies to shame.

I am putting together all sorts of things for you today—several debts, which remind me that I also owe you thanks, your case history of labor pains, and two notebooks of mine. Your notes reinforced my first impression that it would be desirable to make them into a full-fledged pamphlet on "The Nose and Female Sexuality." Naturally, I was disappointed that the concluding remarks with their surprisingly simple explanations were missing.

Now, the two notebooks. I scribbled them full at one stretch since my return, and they will bring little that is new to you. I am retaining a third notebook that deals with the psychopathology of repression, because it pursues its topic only to a certain point. From there on I had to work once again with new drafts and in the process became alternately proud and overjoyed and ashamed and miserable—until now, after an excess of mental torment, I apathetically tell myself: it does not yet, perhaps never will, hang together. What does not yet hang together is not the mechanism—I can be patient about that—but the elucidation of repression, the clinical knowledge of which has in other respects greatly progressed.

Just think: among other things I am on the scent of the following strict precondition for hysteria, namely, that a primary sexual experience (before puberty), accompanied by revulsion and fright, must have taken place; for obsessional neurosis, that it must have happened, accompanied by *pleasure*.

But I am not succeeding with the mechanical elucidation; rather, I am inclined to listen to the quiet voice which tells me that my explanations are not adequate.

My yearning for you and your company this time came somewhat later, but was very great. I am alone with a head in which so much is germinating and, for the time being, thrashing around. I am experiencing the most interesting things which I cannot talk about and which for lack of leisure I cannot commit to paper. (I am enclosing a fragment for you.) I do not want to read anything, because it plunges me into too many thoughts and stunts my gratification in discovery. In short, I am a wretched hermit. Now, moreover, I am so exhausted that I shall just throw the rubbish aside for a while. Instead, I shall study your "migraine." Furthermore, I am involved in a controversy by mail with Löwenfeld.[1] After I have replied to the letter, you shall get it.

How have I been doing heartwise?[2] Not especially well, but not so badly as during the first fourteen days. This time my attention has not been with it at all. Alexander is a miserable rascal and will write to you. He is doing excellently as far as his head is concerned; he is a different man. He is still complaining, as far as *antipopodisch*[3] is concerned.

My most cordial greetings to Frau Ida and little Paul(inchen).[4] All here are well. Martha has again made herself comfortable in Vienna.

Your
Sigm.

1. The correspondence has not survived. For Freud's relation to Löwenfeld see Masson (1984).

2. *Herzwärts;* literally, in the direction of the heart.

3. Meaning unclear. Possibly a joke based on the child's word *popo* (bottom).

4. Freud means that the baby about to come could be a boy (Paul) or a girl (Paulinchen, little Paula).

## Draft I. Migraine: Established Points

[Editor's Note: According to Michael Schröter, the fragment mentioned in the preceding letter is Draft I, which contains many ideas similar to those in Fliess's *Beziehungen zwischen Nase und weiblichen Geschlechtsorganen.* He has therefore proposed that Draft I be placed in this location.]

(1) *A matter of summation.* There is an interval of hours or days between the instigation and the outbreak of the symptoms. One has a sort of feeling that an obstacle is overcome and that a process then goes forward.

(2) *A matter of summation.* Even without an instigation one has an impression that there must be an accumulating stimulus which is present in the smallest quantity at the beginning of the interval and in the largest quantity toward its end.

(3) *A matter of summation,* in which susceptibility to etiological factors lies in the height of the level of the stimulus already present.

(4) A matter with a *complicated etiology.* Perhaps on the pattern of a chain etiology, where a proximate cause can be produced by a number of factors directly and indirectly, or on the pattern of a surrogate etiology,[1] where, alongside a specific cause, commonplace causes can act as quantitative substitutes.

(5) A matter on the model of menstrual migraine and belonging to the sexual group. Evidence:

(a) Rarest in healthy males.

(b) Restricted to the sexual time of life: childhood and old age almost excluded.

(c) If it is produced by summation, the sexual stimulus too is something produced by summation.

(d) The analogy of periodicity.

(e) Frequency in people with disturbed sexual discharge (neurasthenia, coitus interruptus).

(6) Certainty that migraine can be produced by chemical stimuli: human toxic emanations, sirocco, fatigue, smells. Now, the sexual stimulus too is a chemical one.

(7) Cessation of migraine during pregnancy, when production is probably directed elsewhere.

This would seem to suggest that migraine represents a toxic effect produced by the sexual stimulating substance when this cannot find sufficient discharge. And perhaps one should add that there is a particular path present (whose location must be determined) which is in a state of special susceptibility. The question about this is the question of the localization of migraine.

(8) In regard to this path we have these indications: that organic diseases of the cranium, tumors, and suppurations (without toxic intermediate links??) produce migraine or something most similar; further, that migraine is *unilateral,* is connected with the nose, and is linked with localized paralytic phenomena. The first of these signs is not unambiguous. The unilaterality, localization over the eye, and complication by localized paralyses are more important.

(9) The painfulness of migraine can only suggest the cerebral meninges, since affections of the cerebral *substance* are certainly painless.

(10) If in this way migraine seems to approach neuralgias, this tallies with summation, sensitivity and its oscillations, the production of neuralgias through toxic stimuli. *Toxic neuralgia* will thus be its physiological prototype. The scalp is the seat of its pain and the trigeminal is its pathway. Since, however, the neuralgic change must[2] be a central one, we must assume that the logical center for migraine is a trigeminal nucleus whose fibers supply the dura mater.

Since the pain in migraine is located similarly to that in supraorbital neuralgia, this dural nucleus must be in the neighborhood of the nucleus of the first division. Since the different branches and nuclei of the trigeminal influence one another, all other affections of the trigeminal can contribute to the etiology [of migraine] as concurrent (not as commonplace) factors.

THE SYMPTOMATOLOGY AND BIOLOGICAL POSITION OF MIGRAINE

The pain of a neuralgia usually finds its discharge in tonic tension (or even in clonic spasms). Therefore it is not impossible that migraine may include a spastic innervation of the muscles of blood vessels in the reflex sphere of the dural region. We may ascribe to this [intervention] the general (and, indeed, the local) disturbance of function which does not differ symptomatically from a similar disturbance due to vascular constriction (the similarity of migraine to attacks of thrombosis). Part of the inhibition is due to the pain itself. It is presumably the vascular area of the chorioid plexus that is first affected by the spasm of discharge. The relation to the eye and nose is explained by their common innervation by the first division [of the trigeminal].

1. *Surrogatätiologie* in the manuscript. *Anfänge*, p. 126, and Strachey (*Origins*, p. 116) both read it as *Summierungsätiologie*.
2. The manuscript has no *nur*, as in *Anfänge*.

---

October 15, 1895
IX., Berggasse 19

Dearest Wilhelm,

Crazy, isn't it, my correspondence! For two weeks I was in the throes of writing fever, believed that I had found the secret, now I know that I still haven't, and have again dropped the whole business. Nevertheless, all sorts of things became clear or at least sorted themselves out. I have not lost heart. Have I revealed the great clinical secret to you, either orally or in writing?

Hysteria is the consequence of a presexual *sexual shock*.

Obsessional neurosis is the consequence of a presexual *sexual pleasure*, which is later transformed into [self-] *reproach*. "Presexual" means actually before puberty, before the release of sexual substances; the relevant events become effective only as *memories*.

Most cordially,

Your
[no signature]

Felt rather bad.

Vienna, October 16, 1895

Dearest Wilhelm,

Fortunately I had mailed the little box as well as the letter *before* I received your reproachful lines. Nevertheless, you are right; but I could explain everything to your satisfaction. The feverish work of these last weeks, the enticing hopes and disappointments, a few genuine findings — all that against a background of feeling miserable physically and the usual everyday annoyances and difficulties. If on top of all that I send you a few pages of philosophical stammering (not that I think they are successful), I hope to have put you in a conciliatory mood again.

I am still all mixed up. I am almost certain that I have solved the riddles of hysteria and obsessional neurosis with the formulas of infantile sexual shock and sexual pleasure, and I am equally certain that both neuroses are, *in general*, curable — not just individual symptoms but the neurotic disposition itself. This gives me a kind of faint joy — for having lived some forty years not quite in vain — and yet no genuine satisfaction because the psychological gap in the new knowledge claims my entire interest.

I naturally have not had a moment left for the migraine, but that will still come. I completely gave up smoking again, so as not to have to reproach myself for the bad pulse, and to be rid of the miserable struggle against the craving for the fourth and fifth [cigar]; I prefer struggling right away against the first one. Abstinence probably is not very conducive to psychic contentment either.

Enough about myself now. The result is perhaps still gratifying — that I consider the two neuroses essentially conquered and am looking forward to the struggle with the psychological construction.

The Jacobsen book (*N. L.*)[1] moved me more deeply than anything I have read in the last nine years. I consider the last chapters classic.

I am glad that from your numerous hints I can assume you are really better. — Quickly, some gossip. Robert Breuer,[2] my only follower in Vienna, will soon go to Berlin for several weeks. — At the moment I have a children's party, twenty individuals strong, for Mathilde's birthday.

Last Monday, and the two following, lectures on hysteria at the College of Physicians; very boring.

With cordial greetings to you and your dear wife,

Your
Sigm.

1. Jens Peter Jacobsen (1847–1885), a Danish writer, wrote *Nils Lyhne* in 1880 (translated from the Danish by Hanna Astrup Larsen; New York: American Scandinavian Foundation, 1947). Clearly autobiographical, the book depicts the rather sad, desolate life of this pathologically shy and reclusive man. The second half of the novel is devoted primarily to the losses in his life—mother, father, wife, children. He accepts his fate with a resignation that owes nothing to religion, and finally faces his own death with the same stoicism. Chapter 12 begins with these words: "For the better part of two years Nils Lyhne had roamed about on the Continent. He was very lonely, without kith or kin or any close friend of his heart." Freud presumably is referring to this attitude, but he may also have been moved by the utter isolation in which Lyhne lived; for we know that Freud, too, at this point in his life felt entirely alone.

2. Leopold Robert Breuer (1869–1936), son of Josef Breuer and also a physician. In 1893 and 1894 father and son attended Freud's course, "Ausgewählte Kapitel der Neuropathologie." For information on Breuer's life, see Hirschmüller (1978, pp. 47–48).

Vienna, October 20, 1895

Dearest Wilhelm,

Everything fine except for the three-day migraine. Aside from that regret, this letter is devoted to science.

I was of course terribly pleased with your opinion about the hysteria-obsessional neurosis solution. Now listen to this. During an industrious night last week, when I was suffering from that degree of pain which brings about the optimal condition for my mental activities, the barriers suddenly lifted, the veils dropped, and everything became transparent—from the details of the neuroses to the determinants of consciousness. Everything seemed to fall into place, the cogs meshed, I had the impression that the thing now really was a machine that shortly would function on its own. The three systems of n[eurones]; the free and bound states of Qn [quantity]; the primary and secondary processes; the main tendency and the compromise tendency of the nervous system; the two biological rules of attention and defense; the characteristics of quality, reality, and thought; the state of the psychosexual group; the sexual determination of repression; finally, the factors determining consciousness, as a function of perception—all that was correct and still is today! Naturally, I can scarcely manage to contain my delight.

If I had only waited two weeks longer before reporting to you, everything would have turned out so much clearer. Yet it was only in attempting to report it to you that the whole matter became obvious to me. So it could not have been done any other way. Now I shall not find much time for a systematic presentation. Treatments are beginning, and the cerebral paralyses, which do not interest me at all, urgently need to be done. But a few things I shall nevertheless put together for you: the quantitative postulates, from which you should be able to guess the characteristics of the motion of neurones, and a delineation of neurasthenia and anxiety neurosis based on the premises of the theory. God keep your head free of migraine for me!

If I could talk to you about nothing else for forty-eight hours, the matter could probably be finished. But those are impossibilities.

> Was man nicht erfliegen kann,
> muss man erhinken . . .
> Die Schrift sagt, es ist keine Schande zu hinken.[1]

Other confirmations concerning the neuroses are pouring in on me. The thing is really true and genuine.

Today[2] I launched a second lecture on hysteria, making repression the central point. People liked it, but I shall not have it published.

You will not have any objections to my calling my next son Wilhelm! If *he* turns out to be a girl, *she* will be called Anna.

Most cordial greetings.

Your
Sigm.

1. Kris (*Origins*, p. 130n1) notes that this is a quotation from Rückert's *Makamen des Hariri:*

> What we cannot reach flying,
> we must reach limping; . . .
> The Book tells us it is no sin to limp.

Freud quotes these lines again at the very end of *Beyond the Pleasure Principle.*

2. That is, October 20. The report of the lecture says it was October 21 (which would be correct if it was every Monday: 14 + 7 = 21). Since the letter (according to the envelope) was mailed on October 22, Schröter suggests that Freud may have added this portion of the letter on the 21st. The second lecture was indeed on repression.

---

Vienna, October 31, 1895

Dearest Wilhelm,

Although I am dead tired, I feel obliged to write to you before the month is over. First, to your latest scientific reports which I also welcome as a measure of your headaches.

First impression: amazement that there exists someone who is an even greater fantasist than I am and that he should be none other than my friend Wilhelm. Conclusion: I intend to return the pages to you so they will not get lost. Meanwhile, I found the matter quite plausible and said to myself that only an expert in all fields like you could have come up with it. I was singularly impressed with the sharp glance[1] over all the roofs. I guess I was born to be your claque.

I had better not yet borrow anything against my own million.[2] I really do believe that it hangs together, but I still do not trust the individual parts. I continually exchange them for others and do not yet dare to show the structure to a wise man. What you have in hand has also become partially devalued and is rather intended to be a sample, but I hope it will come off. Now I am pretty much drained[3] and in any case I must put the matter aside for two months, because I have to write about childhood paralyses for Nothnagel before 1896—so far not a word of it is on paper.

I have begun to have doubts about the pleasure-pain explanation of hysteria and obsessional neurosis which I announced with so much enthusiasm. The constituent elements are correct beyond question, but I have not yet put the pieces of the puzzle in the right place.

Fortunately for me, all these theories must flow into the clinical estuary of repression, where I have daily opportunities to be corrected or enlightened. My "bashful" case must be finished by the end of '96. He developed hysteria in his youth and later showed delusions of reference. His almost transparent history ought to clear up a few disputed points for me. Another man (who does not dare to go out in the street because of homicidal tendencies) ought to help me solve another puzzle.

Most recently I have been busy with the delineation of sexual acts, and in the process discovered the pleasure pump[4] (not the air pump) and several other *curiosa,* but for the time being shall not talk about them. The next thing, as a separate unit, will be the migraine, on account of which I made an excursion into the mechanism of sexual acts.

During the past weeks my pleasure in life has been spoiled far less than previously; I even managed to produce a decent common migraine, during which my dear heart was unable to find its rhythm.

"Wilhelm" or "Anna" is very unruly and probably will demand to see the light in November. I hope all is well with your Christmas child.

Recently I perpetrated three lectures on hysteria[5] in which I was very impudent. I am now inclined to be arrogant, especially if you continue to be so delighted.

With cordial greetings to you, Ida, and Paulinchen(?).

Your
Sigm.

Glaucoma?[6]
I should really go and see your family in Joh[annes] Street.

1. Freud refers to a story illustrating the miraculous *Kück* (distant look) of a rabbi in *Jokes and Their Relation to the Unconscious* (*S.E.* 8:63): "In the temple at Cracow the Great Rabbi N. was sitting and praying with his disciples. Suddenly he uttered a cry, and, in reply to his disciples' anxious enquiries, exclaimed: 'At this very moment the Great Rabbi L. has died in Lemberg.' The community put on mourning for the dead man. In the course of the next few days people arriving from Lemberg were asked how the Rabbi had died and what had been wrong with him; but they knew nothing about it, and had left him in the best of health. At last it was established with certainty that the Rabbi L. in Lemberg had not died at the moment at which the Rabbi N. had observed his death by telepathy, since he was still alive. A stranger took the opportunity of jeering at one of the Cracow Rabbi's disciples about this occurrence: 'Your Rabbi made a great fool of himself that time, when he saw the Rabbi L. die in Lemberg. The man's alive to this day.' 'That makes no difference,' replied the disciple. 'Whatever you may say, the *Kück* from Cracow to Lemberg was a magnificent one.' " See also letter of March 10, 1898.

2. According to Brückner (1962, p. 732), this is a reference to Multatuli, whom Freud (*S.E.* 9:246) mentions as one of his favorite authors. Brückner discusses the works of this Dutch writer (Eduard Dowes Dekker, 1820–1887) and Freud's interest in them.

3. *Ausgepumpt;* literally, pumped out.

4. This is a play on words. The German word for "pleasure" is *Lust;* for "air," *Luft.*

5. See Sulloway (1979, pp. 507–509).

6. This word seems not to be in Freud's handwriting.

---

November 2, 1895
IX., Berggasse 19

I'm glad I waited before mailing the letter. Today I am able to add that one of the cases gave me what I expected (sexual shock—that is, infantile abuse in male hysteria!) and that at the same time a working through of the disputed material strengthened my confidence in the validity of my psychological constructions. Now I am really enjoying a moment of satisfaction.

On the other hand, the time has not yet come to enjoy the supreme moment and then sink back.[1] A lot of work still remains to be done on the succeeding acts of the tragedy

by your
Sigm.
who sends cordial greetings.

1. A reference to Faust's last words; see Goethe's *Faust*, part 2.

---

Vienna, November 8, 1895

Dearest Wilhelm,

Your long letters prove to me that you are well. May both—symptom and cause—continue without interruption. I (so as not to forget about it and not to have to talk about it again) have been feeling incomparably better in the last two weeks. I have not been able to maintain complete abstinence; under my load of theoretical and practical worries the increase in psychic hyperesthesia has become unbearable. Otherwise I am following the prescription, and overindulged out of joy only on the day of Lueger's nonconfirmation [as mayor of Vienna].

From now on my letters will lose much of their content. I have packed up the psychological manuscripts and thrown them into a drawer, where they shall slumber until 1896. This came about in the following way. At first I put psychology aside in order to make room for infantile paralyses, which must be finished before 1896. Next I began to write about migraine. The first points I discussed led me to an insight which again reminded me of the topic I had put aside and which would have required a lot of revision. At that moment I rebelled against my tyrant. I felt overworked, irritated, confused, and incapable of mastering it all. So I threw everything away. I now regret that on the basis of these pages you should attempt to form an opinion that would justify my cry of joy at my victory, which must indeed be difficult for you. Don't struggle with it any longer. I hope that in two months' time I shall be able to clarify the whole thing. The clinical solution of hysteria, however, still stands; it is appealing and simple. Perhaps I shall pull myself together and put it down for you soon.

November 10. Along with this I am returning the case histories regarding nose and sex. I need not tell you that I fully agree with your intent. This time you will find I have added little — a few red marks. I hope there will be more when I read the theoretical part. Your sexual-chemical hypotheses really fascinated me. I hope you will succeed.

I am up to my neck in the infantile paralyses, which do not interest me at all. Since I have put the *φψω* aside, I feel beaten and disenchanted; I believe I am not at all entitled to your congratulations.

I now feel a void.

Recently at the College of Physicians Breuer gave a big speech in my honor and introduced himself as a *converted* adherent to the sexual etiology.[1] When I thanked him for this in private, he spoiled my pleasure by saying, "But all the same, I don't believe it." Do you understand this? I don't.

By now Martha is really quite miserable. I wish it were over.

As far as neuroses are concerned, there is a great deal that is interesting, but nothing new; only confirmations. I wish we could talk about it.

With the most cordial greetings to you, mother and (child),

Your
Sigm.

1. Breuer's comments were reported in several publications, among them *Wiener medizinische Blätter,* 18 (1895):716–717 (describing the Vienna College of Physicians meeting of November 4, 1895). Lottie Newman has translated those comments:

"Breuer declares right at the outset of his presentation, which was received with lively applause, that one is mistaken if one expected that he is speaking here as a coauthor, because the entire theory of repression is essentially Freud's property. He is intimately acquainted with a large portion of the cases that constitute the foundation of Freud's theories; he has witnessed the birth of the theory at first hand, though not without some opposition; but he now stands, as a result of Freud's illuminating explanations, as a convert before the assembly.

"If one supposes that Freud's theories are an a priori construction, then this would be a mistake. Much work and a large quantity of observations are contained in Freud's lectures. One might also suppose that the patients labor under the pressuring influence of the physician, that the physician suggests to the patients everything that he wants to hear. This is not so. The speaker has found it enormously difficult to force something on [such] patients. One point on which the speaker does not agree with Freud is the overvaluation of sexuality; Freud probably did not want to say that every hysterical symptom has a sexual background, but rather that the original root of hysteria is sexual. We do not yet see clearly; it remains only for the future, the masses of observations, to bring full clarification to this question; in any event, one must be grateful to Freud for the theoretical hints he has given us.

"Especially in the case of the female sex, the complaint about the underestimation of the sexual factor is justified. It is not right, for example, that in the case of girls who suffer from insomnia, etc., one simply prescribes iron for anemia, without even thinking of masturbation, while in the case of young men we immediately look for pollutions. In this respect we are in a state of hysteria; we repress this feeling which is unpleasant to us. We simply know nothing about the sexuality of girls and women. No physician has any idea what sorts of symptoms an erection evokes in women, because the young women do not want to talk about it and the old ones have already forgotten.

"The objection might also perhaps have been raised that a lack of coherence makes itself felt in Freud's disquisitions; now, there is something to that, but one should not forget that we have provisional conclusions before us, that every theory is a temporary structure."

Vienna, November 29, 1895

Dear Wilhelm,

Impossible to let you wait until the child has made up its mind. Evidently it is insisting on the very day to which, by some kind of reckoning, it can lay a claim. Martha is doing splendidly just now. I hope to hear something similar from you, that is to say, about your wife and Paulinchen, as she is called incognito.

I feel really amazingly well, as I have not since the beginning of the whole business. Moreover, I no longer have any pus, just a lot of mucous secretion. I have, by the way, never doubted the success of your minor surgical interventions, and thus have earned my well-being. I am in top working form, have nine to eleven hours of hard work, six to eight analytic cases a day — the most beautiful things, of course; all sorts of new material. I am entirely lost to science; when I sit down at my desk at 11 P.M., I must paste and patch up the infantile paralyses. I hope to finish them in two months and then be able further to utilize the impressions gained in the course of treatments.

I no longer understand the state of mind in which I hatched the psychology; cannot conceive how I could have inflicted it on you. I believe you are still too polite; to me it appears to have been a kind of madness. The clinical solution of the two neuroses probably will stand up, after some modification.

The children have all come down with colds — an epidemic in the house. Minna came a few days ago for a stay of several months' duration. Of the world I see nothing and hear little. Unfortunately, it is precisely at such times, when I find writing so difficult, that I become acutely aware of the distance between Vienna and Berlin.

In view of your last letters I believe in the improvement of your head[aches] and ask you for further confirmation. *Wernicke*'s pupils, Sachs and C. S. Freund, have produced a piece of nonsense on hysteria (on psychic paralyses), which, by the way, is almost a plagiarism of my "Considérations, etc." in the *Archives de neurologie.* Sachs's postulation of the constancy of psychic energy is more painful.[1]

I hope soon to hear many good things of you, wife, child, and sexuality through the nose.

Most cordial greetings.

Your
Sigm.

As the heart improves, *many* light migraines.

1. See *Origins*, p. 135n2.

Vienna, December 3, 1895
IX., Berggasse 19

Dearest Wilhelm,

If it had been a son, I would have sent you the news by telegram, because he would have carried your name. Since it turned out to be a little daughter by the name of Anna, she is being introduced to you belatedly. Today at 3:15 she pushed her way into my consulting hour, appears to be a nice complete little female who, thanks to Fleischmann's[1] care, did not do her mother any harm. Both are now doing rather well. I hope it will not be long before correspondingly good news arrives from you, and then, when Anna and Paulinchen meet, they ought to learn how to get on very well together.

Your
Sigm.

1. Carl Fleischmann (b. 1859), obstetrician and gynecologist.

# Neuroses Redefined

Sunday, December 8, 1895

Dear Wilhelm,

Many thanks for your letter and all the warmth it contains. When I see your handwriting again, those are moments of great joy, which allow me to forget much of my loneliness and privation. Moreover, from the fact as well as the content of the letter I can infer that you yourself are feeling well, which is a condition for my cheerfully accepting what comes to me in this complicated life.

With excellent care the confinement is proceeding completely undisturbed, even cheerfully!

The little one is guzzling Gärtner's whole milk and is said—I scarcely see her—to accommodate satisfactorily to all demands.

The child, we like to think, has brought an increase of my practice, doubling what it usually is. I have trouble keeping up with it, can decline what appears disadvantageous, and am beginning to dictate my fees. I am simply gaining confidence in the diagnosis and treatment of the two neuroses and believe I can see how the city is gradually beginning to realize that something is to be had from me.

Have I already written to you that obsessional ideas invariably are *reproaches*, while at the root of hysteria there always is *conflict* (sexual pleasure along with possibly accompanying unpleasure)?[1] This is a new way of expressing the clinical solution. Right now I have some beautiful mixed cases of the two neuroses and hope to obtain from them more intimate disclosures on the essential mechanism involved.

I always respect your opinion, even when it concerns my psychological work. It puts me in the mood to take up the matter again in a few months, this time with patient, critical, detailed work. The best you can say about it so far is that it deserves the commendation *voluisse in magnis rebus.*[2] And should I really attract attention to these stammerings by a preliminary communication? I think we should keep it to ourselves and see whether something will come of it. I might have to learn to content myself with the clinical elucidation of the neuroses.

With regard to your revelations in sexual physiology, all I can do is hold in readiness the most eager attention and critical admiration. My knowledge is far too limited for me to join in. But I sense the most beautiful and important things and hope that when the time comes you will not let yourself be dissuaded from publicly expressing your views, even if they are only conjectures. We cannot do without people who have the courage to think something new before they can demonstrate it.

Much would indeed be different if we were not separated by geographic distance.

I am really feeling very well; even the suppuration has become quite insignificant.

I am not dependent on the priority of "psychic constancy." You are right, it can be understood in many different ways.

Visitors — I must stop.

The most cordial greetings to wife and daughter from all of us and

Your
Sigm.

1. Freud clearly means that the conflict in hysteria is between pleasure and unpleasure. He is contrasting hysteria with obsessional ideas.
2. "In great enterprises it is enough to have willed." Propertius, *Elegies*, 10:6.

## Draft J. Mrs. P. J. (Age 27)

[undated; seems to belong to end of 1895]

I

She had been married for three months. Her husband, a traveling salesman, had had to leave her a few weeks after their marriage and had been away for weeks on end. She missed him very much and longed for him. She had been a singer, or at any rate had been trained as one. To pass the time she was sitting at the piano singing, when suddenly she felt sick in her abdomen and stomach, her head swam, she had feelings of oppression and anxiety and cardiac paresthesias;[1]

she thought she was going mad. A moment later it occurred to her that she had eaten eggs and mushrooms that morning, so she thought she had been poisoned. However, the condition quickly passed. Next day the maidservant told her that a woman living in the same house had gone mad. From that time on she was never free of the obsession, accompanied by anxiety, that she too was going to go mad.

The argument runs as follows: I begin with the assumption that her condition at that time had been an anxiety attack — a release of sexual feeling that was transformed into anxiety. An attack of that kind, I am afraid, might take place without any accompanying psychic process. Nevertheless, I do not want to reject the more encouraging possibility that such a process might be found; on the contrary, I take it as the starting point of my work. What I expected was this: she had a longing for her husband — that is, for sexual relations with him; she thus came upon an idea that excited sexual affect followed later by defense; she took fright and made a false connection or substitution.

I began by asking her about the circumstances surrounding the event: something must have reminded her of her husband. She had been singing Carmen's aria "Près des remparts de Séville."[2] I asked her to repeat it for me; she did not even know the words exactly.— At what point do you think the attack came on?— She did not know.— When I applied pressure [to her forehead], she said [it had been] *after* she had finished the aria. That seemed quite possible: it had been a train of thought prompted by the text of the aria.— I then asserted that before the attack there had been thoughts present in her which she might not remember. She [said] she really remembered nothing, but pressure [on her forehead] produced *husband* and *longing*. The latter was further specified, on my insistence, as longing for sexual caresses.—"I'm quite ready to believe that. After all, your attack was only a state of outpouring of love. Do you know the page's song? —

Voi che sapete che cosa è amor,
Donne vedete s'io l'ho nel cor.[3]

There was certainly something besides this: a feeling in the lower part of the body, a cramp and an urgent need to urinate."— She now confirmed this. The insincerity of women starts from their omitting the characteristic sexual symptoms in describing their states. So it had really been an *orgasm*.

"Well, you can surely recognize that a state of longing like that in a young woman who has been left by her husband cannot be anything to be ashamed of."—On the contrary, she said that is the way it is supposed to be.—"Correct; but in that case I can see no reason for fright. You were certainly not frightened about *husband* and *longing*; so we still are missing some other thoughts, which are more appropriate to the fright."—But she added only that she had all along been afraid of the pain that intercourse caused her, but that her longing had been much stronger than her fear of the pain.—At this point we broke off.

II

It was certainly to be suspected that in scene 1 (at the piano), alongside her longing thoughts for her husband (which she remembered), she had entered on another, deep train of thought, which she did *not* remember and which led to a scene 2. But I did not yet know its starting point. Today she arrived weeping and in despair, evidently without any hope of the treatment's succeeding. So her resistance was already stirred up and progress was far more difficult. What I wanted to know, then, was what thoughts that might lead to her being frightened were still present. She brought up all kinds of things that could not be relevant: that for a long time she had not been deflowered (which Professor Chrobak[4] had confirmed to her); that she attributed her nervous states to that and for that reason wished it might be done.—This was, of course, a thought from a later time: until scene 1 she had been in good health.—At last I obtained the information that she had already had a similar but much weaker and more transitory attack with the same sensations. (From this I realize that it is from the mnemic picture of the orgasm itself that the path leading down to the deeper layers starts.) We investigated the other scene. At that time—four years back—she had had an engagement at Ratisbon. In the morning she had sung at a rehearsal and it had been a success; in the afternoon, at home, she had had a "vision"—as if she were "planning" something (a row) with the tenor of the company and another man, and afterward she had had the attack, with the fear that she was going mad.

Here then was scene 2, which had been touched on by association in scene 1. But we must admit that here, too, her memory had gaps in it. There must have been other ideas present in order to account for the release of sexual feeling and the fright. I asked for these intermediate links, but instead I was told her motives. She had disliked the whole of life on the stage.—"Why?"—The brusqueness of the manager and the actors' relations to one another.—I asked for details of this.—There had been an old comic actress whom the young men used to make fun of by asking her if they might come and spend the night with her. —"Something further, about the tenor."— He had pestered her, too; at the rehearsal he had put his hand on her breast. —"Through your clothes or on the bare skin?"— At first she said the latter, but then took it back: she had been in outdoor clothes. —"Well, what more?"— Everything about this relationship, all the hugging and kissing among the players had been abhorrent to her. —"Anything else?"— Once again the manager's brusqueness, and she had only stayed there a few days. —"Was the tenor's assault made on the same day as your attack?"— No; she did not know if it had been earlier or later.— My inquiries with the help of pressure showed that the assault had been on the fourth day of her stay and her attack on the sixth.

Interrupted by the patient's flight.

1. Freud uses the plural.
2. The *seguidilla* from Act 1 of Bizet's opera.
3. Cherubino's *canzonetta* from Act 2 of Mozart's *Marriage of Figaro:*

    You who know what love is,
    Tell me if that is what burns my heart.

4. See note 1 to letter of February 4, 1888.

---

January 1, 1896

My dear Wilhelm,

The first leisure time in the New Year belongs to you— to clasp your hand across these few kilometers and to tell you how glad I was to have your recent news from the family room and study. That you have a son— and with him the prospect of other children; as long as the hope for him was still a distant one, I did not want to admit either to you or to myself what you would have missed. Your kind should not die out, my dear friend; the rest of us need people like you too much. How much I owe you: solace, understanding, stimulation in my loneliness, meaning to my life that I gained through you, and finally even health that no one else could have given back to me. It is primarily through your example that intellectually I gained the strength to trust my judgment, even when I am left alone— though not by you— and, like you, to face with lofty humility all the difficulties that the future may bring. For all that, accept my humble thanks! I know that you do not need me as much as I need you, but I also know that I have a secure place in your affection.

Even if you had not said so explicitly, I would have noticed that your confidence in your therapy was finally borne out in your own case as well. Your letters, as again the last one, contain a wealth of scientific insights and intuitions, to which I unfortunately can say no more than that they grip and overpower me. The thought that both of us are occupied with the same kind of work is by far the most enjoyable one I can conceive at present. I see how, via the detour of medical practice, you are reaching your first ideal of understanding human beings as a physiologist, just as I most secretly nourish the hope of arriving, via these same paths, at my initial goal of philosophy. For that is what I wanted originally, when it was not yet at all clear to me to what end I was in the world. During the last weeks I repeatedly tried to give you *something* in return for your communications, by sending you a short summary of my most recent insights into the neuroses of defense, but my capacity to think so exhausted itself in the spring that now I can accomplish nothing. Nevertheless, I have prevailed upon myself to send you the fragment. A gentle voice has counseled me to postpone the account of hysteria since there are still too many uncertainties in it. You probably will be satisfied with the obsessional [neurosis]. The few notes on paranoia come from a recently started analysis which has already established beyond any doubt that *paranoia really is a neurosis of defense*. Whether this explanation also has therapeutic value remains to be seen.

Your remarks on migraine have led me to an idea, as a consequence of which all my $\varphi\psi\omega$ theories would need to be completely revised — something I cannot venture to do now. I shall try to give you some idea of it, however.

I begin with the two kinds of nerve endings. The free ones receive only quantity and conduct it to $\psi$ by summation; they have no power, however, to evoke sensation — that is, to affect $\omega$. In this connection the neuronal motion retains its genuine and monotonous qualitative characteristics. These are the paths for all the quantity that fills $\psi$; also, of course, the paths for sexual energy. The nerve paths which start from end organs conduct not quantity but the qualitative characteristic peculiar to them; they add nothing to the amount in the $\psi$ neurones, but merely put these neurones into a state of excitation. The $\omega$ neurones are those $\psi$ neurones which are capable of only very little quantitative cathexis. The coincidence between these minimal quantities and the quality faithfully transferred to them from the end organ is once more the necessary condition for the generating of consciousness. I now [in my new scheme] insert these $\omega$ neurones between the $\varphi$ neurones and the $\psi$ neurones, so that $\varphi$ transfers its quality to $\omega$, and $\omega$ now transfers neither quality nor quantity to ψ but merely excites ψ—that is, indicates the pathways to be taken by the free ψ energy. (I don't know whether you can understand this gibberish. There are, so to speak, three ways in which the neurones affect each other: (1) they transfer quantity to one another, (2) they transfer quality to one another, (3) they have an exciting effect on one another in accordance with certain rules.)

According to this view the perceptual processes would *eo ipso* [from their very nature] involve consciousness and would only produce their further psych[ic] effects after becoming conscious. The ψ processes themselves would be unconscious and would only subsequently acquire a secondary, artificial consciousness through being linked with processes of discharge and perception (speech association). Any ω discharge, which my other account required, now becomes unnecessary; hallucination, the explanation of which always raised difficulties, is now no longer a backward movement of excitation to φ, but only to ω. It is much easier today to understand the rule of defense, which does not apply to perceptions but only to ψ processes. The fact that secondary consciousness lags behind makes it possible to give a simple description of the processes of neuroses. I am also relieved of the troublesome question of how much of the strength of φ excitation (of sensory stimuli) is transferred to ψ neurones. The answer is none at all, directly. The Q in ψ depends only on how far the free ψ attention is directed by the ω neurones.

The new hypothesis also fits better with the fact that the objective sensory stimuli are so minimal that it is hard to derive the force of the will from that source in accordance with the principle of constancy. Sensation, however, [in the new theory] brings no Q at all to ψ; the source of ψ energy is the [endogenous] organic paths of conduction.

I also see the explanation of the release of unpleasure, which I need for repression in the sexual neuroses, in the conflict between the purely quantitative organic conduction and the processes *excited* in ψ by conscious sensation.

As regards *your* side of the question, the possibility arises that states of stimulation may occur in organs which produce no spontaneous sensation (though they must no doubt exhibit susceptibility to pressure), but which can by reflex action (that is, through the influence of equilibrium) instigate disturbances arising from other nerve centers. For the thought of there being a reciprocal binding of the neurones or of the nerve centers also suggests that the motor symptoms of discharge are of various kinds. Voluntary actions are probably determined by a transference of Q, since they discharge psychic tension. In addition to this there is a discharge of pleasure, spasms, and the like, which I explain, not by Q's being transferred to the motor center but by its being liberated there because the binding Q in the sensory center coupled with it may have diminished. This would give us the long-sought-for distinction between "voluntary" and "spastic" movements, and at the same time a means of explaining a group of subsidiary somatic effects — in hysteria, for instance.

With respect to the purely quantitative processes of transference to ψ, there is a possibility of their attracting consciousness to themselves — if, that is to say, such conductions of Q fulfill the conditions necessary for producing pain. Of those conditions the essential one is probably the suspension of summation and a continuous afflux [of Q] to ψ for a time. Certain ω neurones then become *hyper*cathected and produce a feeling of unpleasure, and they also cause attention to be fixed at that point. Thus "neuralgic change" would have to be regarded as an afflux of Q from some organ augmented beyond a certain limit till summation is suspended, the two ω neurones hypercathected, and free ψ energy bound. As you see, we have on the way arrived at migraine; the necessary precondition would be the existence of nasal regions in that state of stimulation which you recognized with your naked eye. The surplus of Q would be distributed along various subcortical paths before reaching ψ. Once this has happened, a continuous Q forces its way into ψ and, in accordance with the rule of attention, the free ψ energy flows to the seat of the eruption.

The question of the source of the states of stimulation in the nasal organs now arises. The idea suggests itself that the qualitative organ for olfactory stimuli may be Schneider's membrane and the quantitative organ (distinct from this) may be the *corpora cavernosa*. Olfactory substances — as, indeed, you yourself believe, and as we know from flowers — are breakdown products of the sexual metabolism; they would act as stimuli on both these organs. During menstruation and other sexual processes the body produces an increased Q of these substances and therefore of these stimuli. It would have to be decided whether these act on the nasal organs through the expiratory air or through the blood vessels; probably the latter, since one has no subjective sensation of smell before migraine. Thus the nose would, as it were, receive information about *internal* olfactory stimuli by means of the *corpora cavernosa*, just as it does about external stimuli by Schneider's membrane: one would come to grief from one's own body. The two ways of acquiring migraine —

spontaneously and through smells, or human toxic emanations—would thus be equivalent, and their effects could at any time be brought about by summation.

Thus the swelling of the nasal organs of quantity would be a kind of adaptation of the sense organ resulting from increased internal stimulation, analogous in the case of the true (qualitative) sense organs to opening the eyes wide and focusing them, straining the ears, and so on.

It would not be too hard, perhaps, to transfer this conception to the other sources of migraine and similar conditions, though I cannot yet see how it is to be done. In any case, it is more important to test the idea in relation to the main topic.

In this way a whole number of obscure and ancient medical ideas would acquire life and value.

Enough now! Best wishes for 1896 and let me know very soon how mother and child are. You can imagine how greatly Martha is interested in everything.

Your
Sigmund

## Draft K. The Neuroses of Defense (A Christmas Fairy Tale)

[enclosed with letter]

There are four types of these and many forms. I can only make a comparison between hysteria, obsessional neurosis, and one form of paranoia. They have various things in common. They are pathological aberrations of normal psychic affective states: of *conflict* (hysteria), of *self-reproach* (obsessional neurosis), of *mortification* (paranoia), of *mourning* (acute hallucinatory amentia). They differ from these affects in that they do not lead to anything's being settled, but to permanent damage to the ego. They come about subject to the same precipitating causes as their affective prototypes, provided that the cause fulfills two more preconditions—that it is of a sexual kind and that it occurs during the period before sexual maturity (the preconditions of *sexuality and infantilism*). About preconditions applying to the individual concerned I have no fresh knowledge. In general, I should say that heredity is a further precondition, in that it facilitates and increases the pathological effect[1]—the precondition, that is, that principally makes possible the gradations between the normal and the extreme case. I do not believe that heredity determines the choice of the particular defensive neurosis.

There is a normal trend toward defense — that is, an aversion to directing psychic energy in such a way that unpleasure results. This trend, linked to the most fundamental conditions of the psychic mechanism (the law of constancy), cannot be employed against perceptions, for these are able to compel attention (as is evidenced by their consciousness); it only comes in question against memories and thoughts. It is innocuous where it is a matter of ideas to which unpleasure was at one time attached, but which are unable to acquire any contemporary unpleasure (other than that which is remembered), and in such cases too it can be overridden by psychic interest.

The trend toward defense becomes detrimental, however, if it is directed against ideas which are also able, in the form of memories, to release fresh unpleasure — as is the case with sexual ideas. Here, indeed, is the one possibility realized of a memory's having a greater releasing power than was produced by the experience corresponding to it. Only one thing is necessary for this: that puberty should be interpolated between the experience and its repetition in memory — an event which thus strongly increases the effect of the revival. The psychic mechanism seems unprepared for this exception, and it is for that reason a necessary precondition of freedom from neuroses of defense that no substantial sexual irritation should occur before puberty, though it is true that the effect of such an experience must be increased by hereditary disposition before it can reach a level capable of causing illness.

(Here a subsidiary problem branches off: how then does it come about that under analogous conditions, perversion or simple immorality emerges instead of neurosis?)

We shall be plunged deep into psychological riddles if we inquire into the origin of the unpleasure which seems to be released by premature sexual stimulation and without which, after all, a repression cannot be explained. The most plausible answer will appeal to the fact that shame and morality are the repressing forces and that the neighborhood in which the sexual organs are naturally placed must inevitably arouse disgust during sexual experiences. Where there is no shame (as in a male person), or where no morality comes about (as in the lower classes of society), or where disgust is blunted by the conditions of life (as in the country), there too no repression and therefore no neurosis will result from sexual stimulation in infancy. I fear, nevertheless, that this explanation will not stand up to deeper examination. I do not think that the release of unpleasure during sexual experiences is the consequence of the chance admixture of certain unpleasurable factors. Everyday experience teaches us that if libido reaches a sufficient height, disgust is not felt and morality is overridden; and I believe that the generation of shame is connected with sexual experience by deeper links. In my opinion there must be an independent source for the release of unpleasure in sexual life: once that source is present, it can activate sensations of disgust, lend force to morality, and so on. I hold to the model of anxiety neurosis in adults, where a quantity deriving from sexual life similarly causes a disturbance in the psychic sphere, though it would ordinarily have found another use in the sexual process. As long as there is no correct theory of the sexual process, the question of the origin of the unpleasure operating in repression remains unanswered.

The course taken by the illness in neuroses of repression is in general always the same: (1) the sexual experience (or series of experiences), which is traumatic and premature and is to be repressed; (2) its repression on some later occasion, which arouses a memory of it—at the same time the formation of a primary symptom; (3) a stage of successful defense, which is equivalent to health except for the existence of the primary symptom; (4) the stage in which the repressed ideas return, and in which, during the struggle between them and the ego, new symptoms are formed which are those of the illness proper; (5) a stage of adjustment, of being overwhelmed, or of recovery with a malformation.

The main differences between the various neuroses are shown in the way in which the repressed ideas return; others are seen in the manner in which the symptoms are formed and in the course taken by the illness. But the specific character of a particular neurosis lies in the fashion in which the repression is accomplished.

The course of events in obsessional neurosis is what is clearest to me, because I have come to know it best.

## OBSESSIONAL NEUROSIS

Here the primary experience has been accompanied by pleasure. Whether an active one (in boys) or a passive one (in girls), it was without pain or any admixture of disgust; and this in the case of girls implies a comparatively advanced age in general (about 8 years). When this experience is remembered later, it gives rise to a release of unpleasure; and, in particular, there first emerges a self-reproach, which is conscious. It seems, indeed, as though the whole psychic complex — memory and self-reproach — is conscious to start with. Later, both of them, without anything fresh supervening, are repressed and in their place an *antithetic symptom*, some nuance of *conscientiousness*, is formed in consciousness.

The repression may come about owing to the memory of the pleasure itself releasing unpleasure when it is reproduced in later years; this should be explicable by a theory of sexuality. But things may happen differently as well. In *all* my cases of obsessional neurosis, at a very early age, years before the experience of pleasure, there had been a *purely passive* experience; and this can hardly be accidental. If so, we may suppose that it is the later convergence of this passive experience with the experience of pleasure that adds the unpleasure to the pleasurable memory and makes repression possible. It would then be a necessary clinical precondition of obsessional neurosis that the passive experience happen early enough not to be able to prevent the spontaneous occurrence of the experience of pleasure. The formula would therefore run:

*Unpleasure — Pleasure — Repression*

The determining factor would be the chronological relations of the two experiences to each other and to the date of sexual maturity.

At the stage of the return of the repressed, it turns out that the *self-reproach* returns unaltered, but rarely in such a way as to draw attention to itself; for a while, therefore, it emerges as a pure sense of guilt without any content. It usually becomes linked with a content that is distorted in two ways — in time and in content: the former insofar as it relates to a contemporary or future action, and the latter insofar as it signifies not the real event but a surrogate chosen from the category of what is analogous — a substitution. An obsessional idea is accordingly a product of compromise, correct with regard to affect and category but false owing to chronological displacement and substitution by analogy.

The affect of the self-reproach may be transformed by various psychic processes into other affects, which then enter consciousness more clearly than the affect itself: for instance, into *anxiety* (fear of the consequences of the action to which the self-reproach applies), *hypochondria* (fear of its bodily effects), *delusions of persecution* (fear of its social effects), *shame* (fear of other people's knowing about the objectionable action), and so on.

The conscious ego regards the obsession as something alien to itself: it withholds belief from it, with the help, it seems, of the antithetic idea of conscientiousness formed long before. But at this stage it may at times happen that the ego is overwhelmed by the obsession — for instance, if the ego is affected by an episodic melancholia. Apart from this, the stage of illness is occupied by the defensive struggle of the ego against the obsession; and this may itself produce new symptoms — those of the *secondary defense.* The obsessional idea, like any other, is attacked by logic, though its compulsive force is unshakable. The secondary symptoms are an intensification of conscientiousness, and a compulsion to examine things and to hoard them. Other secondary symptoms arise if the compulsion is transferred to motor impulses against the obsession — for instance, to brooding, drinking (dipsomania), protective ceremonials, *folie de doute,* and so on.

We arrive, then, at the formation of three kinds of symptoms:

(a) The primary symptom of defense — *conscientiousness,*
(b) The compromise symptoms of the illness — *obsessional ideas* or *obsessional affects,*
(c) The secondary symptoms of defense — *obsessional brooding, obsessional hoarding, dipsomania, obsessional ceremonials.*

Those cases in which the content of the memory has not become admissible to consciousness through substitution, but in which the affect of self-reproach has become admissible through transformation, give one the impression of a displacement's having occurred along a chain of inferences: I reproach myself on account of an event — I am afraid other people know about it — therefore I feel ashamed in front of other people. As soon as the first link in this chain is repressed, the obsession jumps onto the second or third link, and leads to two forms of delusions of reference, which, however, are in fact part of the obsessional neurosis. The defensive struggle terminates in general doubting mania or in the development of the life of an eccentric with an indefinite number of secondary defensive symptoms — if such a termination is reached at all.

It further remains an open question whether the repressed ideas return of their own accord, without the assistance of any contemporary psychic force, or whether they need this kind of assistance at every fresh wave of their return. My experiences indicate the latter alternative. It seems that it is the states of contemporary unsatisfied libido that employ the force of their unpleasure to arouse the repressed self-reproach. Once this arousal has occurred and symptoms have arisen through the impact of the repressed on the ego, the repressed ideational material continues to operate on its own account; but in the oscillations of its quantitative power it always remains dependent on the quota of libidinal tension present at the moment. Sexual tension which, because it is satisfied, has no time to turn into unpleasure remains harmless. Obsessional neurotics are people who are subject to the danger that eventually the whole of the sexual tension generated in them daily may turn into self-reproach or rather into the symptoms resulting from it, although at the present time they would not recognize afresh the primary self-reproach.

Obsessional neurosis can be cured if we undo all the substitutions and affective transformations that have taken place, till the primary self-reproach and the experience belonging to it can be laid bare and placed before the conscious ego for judging anew. In doing this we have to work through an incredible number of intermediate or compromise ideas which become obsessional ideas temporarily. We gain the strongest conviction that it is impossible for the ego to direct onto the repressed material the part of the psychic energy to which conscious thought is linked. The repressed ideas—so we must believe—are present in and enter without inhibition into the most rational trains of thought; and the memory of them is aroused too by the merest allusions. The suspicion that "morality" is put forward as the repressing force only as a pretext is confirmed by the experience that resistance during therapeutic work avails itself of every possible motive of defense.

## PARANOIA

The clinical determinants and chronological relations of pleasure and unpleasure in the primary experience are still unknown to me. What I have distinguished is the fact of repression, the primary symptom, and the stage of illness as determined by the return of the repressed ideas.

The primary experience seems to be of a nature similar to that in obsessional neurosis; repression occurs after the memory of it has released unpleasure—how is unknown. No self-reproach, however, is formed and afterward repressed; but the unpleasure generated is referred to the patient's fellow men in accordance with the psychic formula of projection. The primary symptom formed is *distrust* (sensitiveness to other people). This permits the avoidance of self-reproach.

We may anticipate the existence of different forms, according to whether only the affect is repressed by projection or the content of the experience too, along with it. So, again, what returns may be merely the distressing affect or it may be the memory as well. In the second case, with which I am more familiar, the content of the experience returns as a thought that occurs to the patient or as a visual or sensory hallucination. The repressed affect seems invariably to return in hallucinations of voices.

The returning portions of the memory are distorted by being replaced by analogous images from the present — that is, they are simply distorted by a chronological replacement and not by the formation of a surrogate. The voices, too, bring back the self-reproach as a compromise symptom, and they do so, first, distorted in its wording to the point of being indefinite and changed into a threat; and, second, related not to the primary experience but precisely to the distrust — that is, to the primary symptom.

Since belief has been withheld from the primary self-reproach, it is at the unrestricted command of the compromise symptoms. The ego does not regard them as alien to itself but is incited by them to make attempts at explaining them, which may be described as *assimilatory delusions.*

The defense failed instantly upon the return of the repressed in distorted form; and the assimilatory delusions can be interpreted only as the beginning of the alteration of the ego, as a statement of defeat, not as a symptom of secondary defense. The process terminates either in melancholia (a sense of ego smallness), which in a secondary manner grants to the distortion that belief which was denied to the primary reproach, or, which happens more frequently and more seriously, it terminates in protective delusions (megalomania) until the ego has been completely transformed.

The determining element of paranoia is the mechanism of projection involving the refusal of belief in the self-reproach. Hence the common characteristic features of the neurosis: the significance of the voices as the means by which other people affect us, and also of gestures, which reveal other people's emotional life to us; and the importance of the tone of remarks and allusions in them — since a direct reference from the content of remarks to the repressed memory is inadmissible to consciousness.

In paranoia repression takes place after a complicated conscious process of thought (the withholding of belief). This may perhaps be an indication that it first sets in at a later age than in obsessional neurosis and hysteria. The preconditions of repression are no doubt the same. It remains a completely open question whether the mechanism of projection is entirely a matter of individual disposition or whether it is selected by particular temporal and accidental factors.

Four kinds of symptoms:

(a) Primary symptoms of defense,
(b) Compromise symptoms of the return,
(c) Secondary symptoms of defense,
(d) Symptoms of the overwhelming of the ego.

## HYSTERIA

Hysteria necessarily presupposes a primary experience of unpleasure—that is, of a passive nature. The natural sexual passivity of women explains their being more inclined to hysteria. Where I have found hysteria in men, I have been able to prove the presence of abundant sexual passivity in their anamneses. A further condition of hysteria is that the primary experience of unpleasure does not occur at too early a time, at which the release of unpleasure is still too slight and at which, of course, pleasurable events may still follow independently. Otherwise what will follow will be only the formation of obsessions. For this reason we often find in men a combination of the two neuroses or the replacement of an initial hysteria by a later obsessional neurosis. Hysteria begins with the overwhelming of the ego, which is what paranoia leads to. The raising of tension at the primary experience of unpleasure is so great that the ego does not resist it and forms no psychic symptom but is obliged to allow a manifestation of discharge—usually an excessive expression of excitation. This first stage of hysteria may be described as "fright hysteria"; its primary symptom is the *manifestation of fright* accompanied by a *gap* in the psyche. To what age this first hysterical overwhelming of the ego can occur is still unknown.

Repression and the formation of defensive symptoms only occur subsequently, in connection with the memory; and after that *defense* and *overwhelming* (that is, the formation of symptoms and the outbreak of attacks) may be combined to any extent in hysteria.

Repression does not take place by the construction of an excessively strong antithetic idea but by the intensification of a boundary idea, which thereafter represents the repressed memory in the passage of thought. It may be called a *boundary idea* because, on the one hand, it belongs to the ego and, on the other hand, it forms an undistorted portion of the traumatic memory. So, once again, it is the result of a compromise; this, however, is not manifested in a replacement on the basis of some category governed by logic, but by a displacement of attention along a series of ideas linked by temporal simultaneity. Should the traumatic event find an outlet for itself in a motor manifestation, it will be this that becomes the boundary idea and the first symbol of the repressed material. There is thus no need to assume that some idea is being suppressed at each repetition of the primary attack; it is a question in the first instance of a *gap in the psyche*.

1. The German text printed in *Anfänge* has *Affekt*, but the original manuscript clearly reads *Effekt*.

Vienna, February 6, 1896

Dearest Wilhelm,

There has been an unprecedented hiatus in our correspondence. I knew you were occupied with Robert Wilhelmchen, neglecting nose and sex on his account, and I hope he is rewarding you by thriving. I have been toiling, going through one of my quarterly writing attacks, and have utilized it to produce three brief communications for Mendel[1] and a comprehensive presentation for the *Revue neurologique.*[2] Yesterday everything was sent off and, since no one else is doing it, I am applauding myself, am resolving to rest on my self-awarded laurels, and immediately am starting to write to you.

I have spared you the manuscript of the German article because it is identical with part of what I put before you as the Christmas fairy tale. I am terribly sorry that these latest new ideas (the real etiology of hysteria—the nature of obsessional neurosis—insight into paranoia) were spoiled for you by the way I presented them. Everything will be laid before you clearly at our private congress in the summer. I am going to Munich for the psychological congress, from August 4 to 7;[3] will you make me a gift of those days? I am definitely not participating officially.

Annerl is splendid; Martha needed a long time to recover. Mathilde has been isolated with a light case of scarlet fever for the last week . . . So far no second case.

I simply can no longer get along with Breuer at all; what I had to take in the way of bad treatment and weakness of judgment that is nonetheless ingenious during the past months finally deadened me, internally, to the loss. But, please, do not say a word about it that might find its way back here.

Our book had a vicious review by Strümpell in the *Deutsche Zeitschrift für Nervenheilkunde;* on the other hand, it was the subject of a very thoughtful article by Freiherr von Berger in the old *Presse* on February 2, 1896.[4]

Now that everything must have run its course, we ask you for a few words about how your dear wife and my little friend are.

With the most cordial greetings to all three of you,

Your
Sigm.

1. "Further Remarks on the Neuro-Psychoses of Defence" consists of three sections: "The 'Specific' Aetiology of Hysteria", "The Nature and Mechanism of Obsessional Neurosis," and "Analysis of a Case of Chronic Paranoia." Emanuel Mendel was editor of the *Neurologisches Centralblatt* where the articles were published. This paper, along with "On the Aetiology of Hysteria," marks the high point of Freud's belief in the reality of the seduction hypothesis.

2. "L'hérédité et l'étiologie des névroses," published March 30. This paper contains the first use in print of the words "psychoanalysis" and "psychoneurosis" *(psycho-névrose)*, although the latter was used in the 1895 "Project for a Scientific Psychology" (see Introduction). An elaborate summary of the paper is given in *Archives de neurologie,* 2 (1896), ser. 2, 48–50.

3. This was the Third International Congress for Psychology. The invitation made a point of saying, "Female participants in the Congress have the same rights as male participants."

4. The reference is to Adolf von Strümpell's review of the *Studien über Hysterie.* Ellenberger (1970, p. 772) was the first to claim that the review was, with some justifiable criticisms, basically positive. Decker (1977, p. 159) writes: "Strümpell's review of *Studies on Hysteria* was an important basis for the future reception of psychoanalysis in Germany because it was the first lengthy, serious review of Freud's work by a respected medical figure. His remarks were often quoted by other doctors, and his arguments cropped up repeatedly. Strümpell's description of the cathartic method was a fair statement." Sulloway (1979, p. 82) repeats Ellenberger and adds praise of his own: "Both of the two major difficulties raised by Strümpell and Clarke —that of applying the cathartic method and that of distinguishing the hysteric's phantasies from reality—were hardly unreasonable issues in an informed review of *Studies on Hysteria.*"

The reader can decide for himself how accurate these portrayals are. Here is the last third of the review (my translation): "[The therapy] demands, as the authors themselves emphasize, a penetrating inquiry into the most minute details of the private circumstances and experiences of the patient. I do not know whether this sort of intrusion into the most intimate private affairs on the part of even the most experienced physician can under all circumstances be deemed permissible. I find this intrusion most questionable when it concerns sexual relations, and the authors repeatedly stress that frequently and preeminently it does concern those. Second, I cannot suppress my doubts either as to whether what is extracted from hypnotized patients by questioning always corresponds exactly to reality. I fear that in these circumstances some hysterics give free rein to their fantasy and invent stories. It is, then, only too easy for the physician to find himself in a very slippery position. In summary, then, even if I acknowledge, as I said, the success of the method in the capable hands of Mr. Breuer and Mr. Freud, I cannot unconditionally recommend following their method. Above all I have not the least doubt that we can achieve precisely the same thing with sympathetic, direct psychic treatment, without any hypnosis, and without too detailed an investigation of the 'strangulated affect.' "

Alfred Freiherr von Berger (1853–1912), professor of the history of literature at the University of Vienna, and director of the Burgtheater, on February 2, 1896, wrote a review as a "Feuilleton" in the *Morgenpresse,* entitled "Chirurgie der Seele." I have not been able to see the original article, only the reprint of the introduction and the concluding essay. Berger writes that since he saw the book quite by chance the preceding summer, "hardly a day has gone by without my reading some chapter or at least some pages over and over." Why? Because the book speaks to his artistic receptivity *(künstlerische Empfänglichkeit).* In Berger's view this was undoubtedly not the authors' intention: they wished, surely, to point out some truths and be of therapeutic use to their medical colleagues, not write "a beautiful book." Berger, who certainly felt the full force of the book, was the only reviewer to do so. He writes about it in a fine style of his own, in total admiration for the literary, artistic, and scientific achievements of the authors.

Vienna, February 13, 1896

Dearest Wilhelm,

I am so lonely, and therefore so delighted by your letter, that I am using the quiet after today's consulting hours to reply.

First of all, so as not to withhold anything from you: the newest publication is an extract from the so-called Christmas fairy tale I fashioned for you — somewhat more objective and toned down.

I am, of course, very much looking forward to your nose-sex. In the clinics here they are preparing counterarticles against you. I could not find out more than that. The criticism will not affect you any more than Strümpell's criticism affected me; truly, I need no consolation for that one. I am so certain that both of us have got hold of a beautiful piece of objective truth, and we can do without recognition from strangers (strangers to the subject matter) for a long time to come. We shall find many more things, I hope, and correct ourselves before anyone catches up with us. If you do not like Munich, let us meet somewhere else for three scientific days; I certainly will not give up on it.

I would indeed like to have Breuer's letter; in spite of everything, I find it very painful that he has so completely removed himself from my life. He is, by the way, generally ill-humored and not too well.

The article by Berger will follow.

My brother is a strange fellow, but is obviously feeling very well.

My poor Martha is leading a life full of harassments. True, Annerl is doing beautifully and Mathilde suffered so little from her illness that today we are sending her with my sister Dolfi to the Sulz [Valley]; but to make up for it, Martin has fallen ill today, and now it will probably make the rounds. Let us hope the illness will be light. Our living conditions obviously are not very conducive to isolation.

My state of health does not deserve to be a subject of inquiry. Last week there was a recrudescence of the suppuration on the left side, migraines rather frequently; the necessary abstinence is hardly doing me much good. I have rapidly turned gray.

I am continually occupied with psychology — really *meta*psychology; Taine's book *L'intelligence* suits me extraordinarily well. I hope something will come of it. The oldest ideas are really the most useful ones, as I am finding out belatedly. I hope to be well supplied with scientific interests until the end of my life. Apart from that, however, I am scarcely human any longer. By 10:30 in the evening after my practice I am dead tired.

I shall, of course, read *Nose and Sex* without delay and return it. I hope that in this book as well you will discuss some of the basic views on sexuality that we share.

I know nothing at all about your X-ray experiments. Could you send me, on loan, the newspaper [reports] on them?

With cordial greetings to your dear wife and Robert,

Yours,
Sigm.

---

February 23, 1896
IX., Berggasse 19

Dear Wilhelm,

Your manuscript arrived, will be read with the utmost eagerness today, and will be in your hands by the end of the week. Deuticke is out of town; I shall speak to him when he returns and see to it that he writes to you. Mathilde is very well in Sulz; Martin and Ernst had only angina [tonsillitis] without sequelae; the Janus temple is now closed.[1] Annerl laughs all day long. I am somewhat miserable; probably influenza. I cannot guess at what Breuer has contrived with regard to the neurasthenia etiology. I shall write soon again. Today I merely greet all three of you most cordially.

Your
Sigm.

1. The closing of the gates to the temple of the Roman god Janus signified peace.

---

Vienna, March 1, 1896

Dear Wilhelm,

I read through your manuscript at one sitting. I was exceptionally pleased with its plain assurance, the lucid, self-evident connections between the individual themes, the unpretentious unfolding of its riches, and, last but not least,[1] its wealth of glimpses of new riddles and new explanations. At first I read it as though it were meant only for me. With the exception of a single one, there are no marginal notes in red; there was no need for them. You will forgive my not having gone over the case histories again.

In order to be a critic, I must first do violence to myself. I think, then, you should have sent me the last, general chapter at the same time. It cannot be a mere addendum; rather, what you sent me is crying out for it, urgently and loudly. I am also very curious to see it. Furthermore, I think people will be put off by the way in which the charming story of I.F.'s pregnancy periods, with the associated hypotheses of the two halves of the organ and their transfer of functions and interferences, is interpolated like a single glimpse of a distant view in the midst of following along a broad and easy-to-travel road. It is almost reminiscent of the way in which G. Keller in *Der grüne Heinrich* interrupts the narrative of his life story to describe the fate of the poor, crazy, little princess. I would think that for the plebeians for whom the book is intended, it would be better to put this attempt at explanation, which follows the tables, into the general explanatory section; in the context of presenting the facts, it would be sufficient to make a note to the effect that it appears from the nasal findings that the menstrual intervals from July on oscillate between 23 and 33 days, so that later meaningful connections can be made. The following evidence for a 23-day periodicity would then also be on a different level. To be sure, these are the very things which for the two of us are the most interesting by far. But one should not offer the *publico* an opportunity of extending the very limited critical judgment available to it, usually to its own detriment, to the section that is in its entirety devoted to facts. The presentation of what is new and hypothetical in the second section could then also be more extensive. Otherwise I fear *publicus* will jump to the conclusion that this is not the only possible explanation for the series in the case of I.F., especially since the birth did not accord with this series but rather came about as the result of a disturbance. But this can really be grasped only when you have the second section alongside it.

In order to get away from the irksome duty of viewing your work through *publicus'* spectacles, which do not fit me at all, I want to add that some of your random remarks really impressed me. Thus, it occurs to me that the limits of repression in my theory of neuroses — that is to say, the time after which sexual experiences no longer have a posthumous but an actual effect — coincide with the second dentition. It is only now that I dare to understand my anxiety neurosis: the menstrual period as its physiological model; the anxiety neurosis itself as an intoxication, for which an organic process must furnish the physiological foundation. The unknown organ (the thyroid or whatever it may be) probably will not, I hope, remain unknown to you for long. I was greatly delighted with the male menopause[2] as well; in my "Anxiety Neurosis" I boldly anticipated it as the last condition [giving rise to anxiety neurosis] in men.[3] You also seem to have provided, in my stead, an explanation of the periodicity of anxiety attacks, which Löwenfeld demanded from me. Thus, when I read your manuscript, I once again was satisfied with myself, because I reminded myself that I enlisted you as the teacher of medical men. This feat of mine will not be soon forgotten.

I was less angry about Breuer's letter than I had expected to be. I could console myself with the thought that the colorblind turns so quickly into a judge of colors, and I at least could understand why he held a low opinion of the etiology of the n[euroses]: because of my statement that trivial noxae may produce neurosis in persons who, it is true, never masturbated, but who nevertheless exhibit from the beginning a type of sexuality that has the same appearance as if they had acquired it through masturbation. In my mind I have always been uncertain whether one should assume that such cases are due to heredity or, instead, to childhood experiences. In any event, it is an obscure point in the theory, and the opponent rightly makes it into a weak point. The mere fact of this opposition—in an area where no theory can be completely fashioned all at once—shows how superficial are Breuer's conversion and understanding in these matters. He is glad to be able to point to a gap, which is, after all, not identical with a contradiction and even less so with a refutation. The rest of what he says can be reduced to: male masturbation as an etiological factor has been less neglected than female masturbation. Our personal relationship, mended on the surface, casts a deep shadow over my existence here. I can do nothing right for him and have given up trying. According to him, I should have to ask myself every day whether I am suffering from moral insanity[4] or paranoia scientifica. Yet, I regard myself as the psychically more normal one. I believe he will never forgive that in the *Studies* I dragged him along and involved him in something where he unfailingly knows three candidates for the position of *one* truth and abhors all generalizations, regarding them as presumptuous. That everything one enjoys in life has to be paid for so dearly is decidedly not an admirable arrangement. Will the two of us experience the same thing with each other?

Perhaps it will interest you, as an aside, that Martha felt the first movements, with Annerl, on July 10. The birth occurred on December 3. The menstrual period occurred again on February 29. Since puberty Martha has always been regular. The interval between menstrual periods is a little over 29 days, let's say $29\frac{1}{2}$. Now, from December 3 to February 29, there are 88 [days] $= 3 \times 29\frac{1}{3}$:

28
31
29
88 ÷ 3 = $29\frac{1}{3}$ days
−28

From July 10 to December 3, there are $5 \times 29\frac{1}{5}$:

$$\begin{array}{r} 21 \\ 31 \\ 30 \\ 31 \\ 30 \\ \underline{3} \\ 146 \div 5 = 29\frac{1}{5} \\ -46 \\ -\ \ 1 \end{array}$$

Thus, for a period of a little over 29 days, the birth occurred at precisely the right time, and the first movements occurred at the time of the fifth menstrual period.[5]

Most cordial greetings to you, Ida, and W.R.[6]

Your
Sigm.

1. English in original.
2. Possibly Fliess was the first to use this term.
3. Reference to the phrase *Es gibt Männer, die wie die Frauen ein Klimakterium zeigen* (There are men who exhibit a climacteric like women) in the article "On the Grounds for Detecting a Particular Syndrome from Neurasthenia under the Description 'Anxiety Neurosis' " (*S.E.* 3:101–102).
4. English in original.
5. This whole passage is cited verbatim by Fliess in his 1897 book, *Die Beziehungen zwischen Nase und weiblichen Geschlechtsorganen,* as coming from "a friendly colleague." Cf. Sulloway (1979, p. 181).
6. Freud uses W.R. and R.W. interchangeably to designate Fliess's son, Robert Wilhelm.

March 7, 1896

Most assuredly!

Agree with premises and deduction. Life is miserable and very complicated, and we shall have a congress in the spring. For dates, I propose Easter: (1) because we would then have an extra day; (2) because we would still have four weeks to look forward to it; (3) because we would not need to confront our so-called conscience as deserters and epicureans. For the place: Prague, Dresden, Nuremberg, or any other city. In favor of Prague would be that neither of us, I presume, knows it; but the same reasoning also speaks *against* Prague. The same is to be said against Nuremberg or any other German city — namely, that it could arouse an interest independent of the congress and that it is less easily reached from the two starting points for the congress. As far as I know, nothing speaks against Dresden. Will you please comment on these proposed dates (with the third part left uncertain).

I shall bring to the congress:

(1) Toilet articles
(2) Several handkerchiefs
(3) Cordial greetings from all the Freuds
(4) Tremendous anticipation of seeing you again
(5) The dream analysis
(6) The etiology of the neuroses of defense
(7) A psychological conjecture.

Truly seven things, then.[1] Of you I expect at least two:

(1) Evidence for a 23-day period for sexual processes
(2) Evidence for the necessity of a period not exceeding three months in matters of friendship.

In addition, a third one:

(3) A readily comprehensible method that will reform society, with respect to nerves and limbs,[2] by sterilization of sexual intercourse [that is, contraception].

In the expectation that our project will be a beautiful reality, I have cheered up and even have postponed sympathizing with little W.R. The poor fellow, to have to go through all these troubles; but by the time of his first love everything will long since have turned out all right. It will not harm his career. In our family it has been Ernst who for years has had similar experiences. Whatever accidents happened, they have always converged on the boy. In this respect, I hope, W.R. will not imitate him. At present, Martin is in bed with the third throat infection in four weeks! Otherwise, all is well; Annerl is splendid, Martha still somewhat lame; Minna is in Frankfurt, where she has accepted a position.

Yesterday I received an invitation to come to, of all places, Frankfurt, where I am to give the coreport on Little's disease at the scientific meetings in September.[3] One really cannot decline, but it does not suit me in any respect, and I probably will have seen my sister-in-law before then.

Otherwise everything is externally quite monotonous, often disagreeable, and calls for nothing short of an interruption by a private congress.

With most cordial greetings, to W.R. first, then to I.F. and you,

Your
Sigm.

Martha, as you know, suffers from a writing block.

1. *Sieben Sachen* is a German expression meaning everything needed for a certain purpose.

2. Freud changes the German idiom *Reform an Haupt und Gliedern* (reforming head and limbs), meaning total reform, to *Reform an Nerven und Gliedern* (reforming nerves and limbs). He implies that if Fliess discovers a contraceptive method, there will be less nervous disease.

3. This refers to the sixty-eighth meeting of the Gesellschaft deutscher Naturforscher und Ärzte, in Frankfurt, September 21–26, 1896.

---

Vienna, March 16, 1896

Dear Wilhelm,

I have not yet really overcome my depression about the schedule of your headaches. I can perhaps take pleasure in the fact that Easter is far away from the date you underlined as the most critical one. Other than that, I see that unfortunately every third day brings you headaches. But just as emperors exert an indubitable influence on the weather, I have been able to have a favorable influence on your headaches by my presence and therefore hope for good weather for our get-together.

Do not think I am throwing doubt on your periods just because the observations made by you and your wife do not appear to be free of disturbing influences. I merely want to hold you back from giving Mr. Enemy, *publicus*, something that requires him to think—as I unfortunately do constantly—because he customarily takes his revenge for such impositions.

How is R.W.? Very well once again, I hope. Our Annerl is charming; the others for a change are also well.

Science is progressing at a leisurely pace. Today, just as a young poet tends to do, I put this title on a sheet of paper:

*Lectures on the Major Neuroses*
(Neurasthenia, Anxiety Neurosis, Hysteria, Obsessional Neurosis)

for I realize that for the time being I am not getting anywhere in my understanding of the common neuroses, nor do I need to retract anything. So I shall set out to do the work and pull things together. Behind it looms a second and more beautiful work:

*Psychology and Psychotherapy of the Neuroses of Defense*

for which I am allowing myself years of preparation and into which I shall put my whole soul.

I shall bring you one more thing: a case of dipsomania, which resolved itself very obviously according to my schema. I keep returning to psychology; I cannot escape its compelling call. What I have is probably neither a million, nor yet a kreuzer — but a lump of ore containing unknown quantities of precious metal. On the whole I am satisfied with my progress, but am contending with hostility and live in such isolation that one might imagine I had discovered the greatest truths.

I hope our congress will be a real relief and refreshment.

With the most cordial greetings to you, your dear wife and mother of R.W.,

Your
Sigm.

---

Palm Sunday [March 29, 1896?]
IX., Berggasse 19

Dear Wilhelm,

Only eight more days until our congress from which I expect, above all, that it will bring your head clear days. I plan to leave Saturday evening from the Northwest Station and come to Dresden or Schandau, whichever you prefer. Let the weather decide where we shall stay. If you are still free on Tuesday, then I shall be too.

I suspect that you have rediscovered the French thesis concerning the intimate relationship between *nervosisme* [irritability of the nerves] and *arthritisme*, except that you are able to trace the latter to sexual metabolism; I am very curious.

Today I am dead tired after thirteen hours of work, with only a half-hour break since yesterday. I am looking forward enormously to our Easter [congress].

With cordial greetings to your dear wife and R.W., who I hope is well.

Your
Sigm.

(March 26, Rausenberg)

---

Vienna, April 2, 1896

Dear Wilhelm,

Tomorrow your manuscript will wander off to Deuticke. I have just now read through it and was *very* pleased with it. We shall soon be able to discuss it. It does my heart good to see that you are capable of substituting *realia* [realities] for my preliminaries. It may be possible to justify the distinction between neurasthenia and anxiety neurosis in terms of organic processes as well; I made it on the basis of a kind of clinical instinct. I have always conceived of the processes in anxiety neuroses, as in the neuroses in general, as an intoxication, and often also thought of the similarity of the symptoms in anxiety neurosis and Basedow's disease, which perhaps you still can mention. I shall tell you in person about certain practical reservations I have concerning the case history of your I.F. (which you should disguise more so that Ida cannot be identified).

On the whole I am making good progress on the psychology of the neuroses and have every reason to be satisfied. I hope you will lend me your ear for a few *metapsychological* questions as well.

The prospect of Easter has brightened the entire stretch of time for me. Now I hope we shall meet, as you propose, without any obstacles. I shall arrange things according to your telegram; in any event, I shall leave Saturday evening. Will I arrive in Schandau or Dresden *before you?* If both of us are still granted a few more years for quiet work, we shall certainly leave behind something that can justify our existence. Knowing this, I feel strong in the face of all daily cares and worries. As a young man I knew no longing other than for philosophical knowledge, and now I am about to fulfill it as I move from medicine to psychology. I became a therapist against my will; I am convinced that, given certain conditions in regard to the person and the case, I can definitely cure hysteria and obsessional neurosis.

Until we see each other, then. We have honestly earned a few good days.

When you say good-bye to your wife and son for Easter, greet them in my name as well.

Your
Sigm.

---

Vienna, April 16, 1896

Dearest Wilhelm,

I had the same experience; my head full of dates and ideas about summations, proud of having received some recognition, and with a cocky feeling of independence, I returned to a sense of too much well-being and have since then been very lazy because the modicum of misery essential for intensive work will not come back. I can record only a very few ideas arising from my daily work about the in-between realm, as a general reinforcement of the impression that *everything* is as I surmise it to be and thus that everything will be clarified. Among these, a completely surprising explanation of Eckstein's hemorrhages—which will give you much pleasure. I have already figured out the story, but I shall wait to communicate it until the patient herself has caught up.

In accordance with your request, I have started to isolate myself in every respect and find it easy to bear. I have one prior commitment, though—a lecture to be given at the psychiatric society on Tuesday. I have not seen Breuer, nor did I come across him in my practice; I have avoided an unnecessary encounter with him at the home of a patient who at times sees both of us.

I enclose the French publication, which on the whole I like very much, although those people left some misunderstandings that distort the meaning of my draft; I did not receive any galley proofs of it. I expect the German [translation] any day.

Hearing the news of R.W.'s 200 grams, my Annerl immediately gained 210 grams; the other rascals at present are fine. I have booked lodgings in Obertressen near Aussee. I make daily notes about my health, so that they can be used to check special dates.[1] From Martha I obtained [the story of] a good paramenstrual period. As for me, I note migraine, nasal secretion, and attacks of fears of dying, such as today, although Tilgner's cardiac death is most likely more responsible for this than the date.[2] You have helped me a great deal toward moderation in regard to tobacco, just as I feel more resolute and in better shape since our *entrevue*. It was very good for me and very necessary. I shall probably surprise you shortly with psychological scraps; right now I am exceedingly lazy about writing. By the way, any drop of alcohol makes me completely stupid.

Your bits of dates are very nice. All you can say to Mrs. P.'s client is that he should be content with his green needles. You are certainly right with regard to your own motive. *Je n'en vois pas la nécessité.*[3]

Unfortunately I could not get myself to do the infantile paralyses. Does it have to be done? Scold me!

Remembering the beautiful days, I send most cordial greetings to you, I.F., and R.W.

Your
Sigm.

1. *Termin* is literally a fixed point in time and usually implies that something will happen at that particular moment. Here it probably signifies a special or important date.

2. The significance for Freud of sculptor Victor Tilgner's death in 1896 has been well documented by Schur (1972, pp. 100–104).

3. The references in this passage are obscure.

# Isolation from the Scientific Community

Vienna, April 26, 1896

Dear Wilhelm,

You have not written for a long time, which means that either you are feeling so well that you are able to do a lot of work, or you feel quite bad; and this uncertainty of interpretation really ruins the present for me. Since our congress I have felt unburdened scientifically, it is true, but from a personal point of view another one is an urgent necessity for me.

I have a somewhat dull period of time behind me—

April 28, during which a few things happened, and these are also connected with my silence. They are dragging along for such a long time that I do not want to let you wait until they are finished. First of all, Eckstein. I shall be able to prove to you that you were right, that her episodes of bleeding were hysterical, were occasioned by *longing*, and probably occurred at the sexually relevant times (the woman, out of resistance, has not yet supplied me with the dates).

Furthermore, I have become downright obsessed with the problem of neuronic motion. Stimulated by your chemical theories, and after the most unbelievable trials, I have likewise arrived at a chemical conception that instills confidence in me. As soon as the story fits together, you shall have it. When that will be, I do not know, of course.

I have not yet been able to contribute anything in the matter of periods and dates. You probably did not expect much, either. Of all the advice you gave me, I followed the one concerning my isolation most completely. (This reminds me of the anecdote in which a doctor tells an old bon vivant: "Dear friend, from now on, no more wine, women, and song," to which the latter replies, "Very well, I'll stop *singing.*") I have not yet seen Breuer and have given up complaining. A lecture on the etiology of hysteria at the psychiatric society[1] was given an icy reception by the asses and a strange evaluation by Krafft-Ebing: "It sounds like a scientific fairy tale." And this, after one has demonstrated to them the solution of a more-than-thousand-year-old problem, a *caput Nili* [source of the Nile]![2] They can go to hell, euphemistically expressed.

Annerl produced her first tooth today, without discomfort; Mathilde is feeling incomparably better since she has been taken out of school. Oliver, on a recent spring excursion, asked quite seriously why the cuckoo is always calling his own name. I hope that it will not take R.W. as long to find out the secret of name giving.

I assume you received my French paper. The German [translation], I hope, will finally appear in the first days of May.

Cordial greetings, and let me know soon that you did *not* have headaches. That I say so little about this topic is because of my sense of helplessness. Your dear wife also should not entirely forget us.

Your
Sigm.

1. Published in the *Wiener klinische Rundschau*, and subsequently in *S.E.* as "On the Aetiology of Hysteria." See letter of May 30, 1896.

Freud's evaluation is reinforced by the following information: It was the practice of the Verein für Psychiatrie und Neurologie to report both the meetings (with brief summaries) and the discussions. The only exception seems to have been in the case of Freud's paper, which was certainly very poorly received. *Wiener klinische Wochenschrift*, 9 (1896): 420–421 gives the official minutes of the meeting. All that it says is: "Docent Sigm. Freud: Über die Ätiologie der Hysterie." There is no report, no mention of where and when it might be published, and no comment on any discussion. Clearly none took place. As far as I have been able to ascertain, the meeting was reported in only one other journal: *Neurologisches Centralblatt*, 15(1896):709–710, but Freud's paper is not even mentioned by title. Years later Freud remembered the meeting with bitterness. In *On the History of the Psycho-Analytic Movement* (*S.E.* 14:21) he writes: "I innocently addressed a meeting of the Vienna Society for Psychiatry and Neurology with Krafft-Ebing in the chair, expecting that the material losses I had willingly undergone would be made up for by the interest and recognition of my colleagues. I treated my discoveries as ordinary contributions to science and hoped they would be received in the same spirit. But the silence which my communication met with, the void which formed itself about me, the hints that were conveyed to me, gradually made me realise that assertions on the part played by sexuality in the aetiology of the neuroses cannot count upon meeting with the same kind of treatment as other communications. I understood that from now onwards I was one of those who had 'disturbed the sleep of the world,' as Hebbel says."

In Masson (1984) I have speculated in some detail on the effects of this meeting on Freud's later views. Anna Freud (personal communication) told me that she believed her father never attended another meeting of the society. However, according to the membership list for 1899 Freud was still a member. See *Jahrbücher für Psychiatrie und Neurologie*, 18 (1899):390–394.

2. Freud uses this analogy in the etiology of hysteria paper (*S.E.* 3:203): "I believe that this [the importance of early sexual experiences] is an important finding, the discovery of a *caput Nili* in neuropathology."

---

Vienna, May 4, 1896

Dear Wilhelm,

I did know why you did not write. Moreover, it was your special period. But permit me to say that it is atrocious. That in spite of it all you found so many new explanations, while I could contribute nothing to the validity of time periods, only goes to show once more how difficult it is for anyone but the seers to see.

As far as Annerl's tooth is concerned, it is strikingly correct. But Martha had her menstrual periods on March 28 and April 26; in between, on April 13, distinct paramenstrual discomfort. The tooth appeared on April 28; Martha stubbornly used to defend her 28-day periods. The pregnancy resulted in a < 29-day cycle[1] and I think I remember that I had to console her innumerable times because she supposed she was late. There is, then, some detail at the bottom of this which still needs to be added and which, I hope, will be determined by further observation.

I am working on psychology, vigorously and in solitude; I cannot yet send you anything that is halfway finished, no matter how much I reduce my standards concerning what is finished. I believe more and more firmly in the chemical neurone theory; I started with assumptions similar to those you described, but now I am stuck after I ruined my head with it yesterday.

I feel more certain about consciousness and must now make an attempt to deal with this most difficult of all things in my lectures on hysteria.[2] On Saturday I lectured on dream interpretation to the youths of the Jewish academic reading circle; someday you will hear about what it contained; right now I am in no mood for presentations.[3]

I am as isolated as you would wish me to be. Word was given out to abandon me, for a void is forming all around me. So far I bear it with equanimity. I find it more troublesome that this year for the first time my consulting room is empty, that for weeks on end I see no new faces, cannot begin any new treatments, and that none of the old ones are completed. Things are so difficult and trying that it requires, on the whole, a strong constitution to deal with them.

As for Eckstein — I am taking notes on her history so that I can send it to you — so far I know only that she bled out of *longing.* She has always been a bleeder, when cutting herself and in similar circumstances; as a child she suffered from severe nosebleeds; during the years when she was not yet menstruating, she had headaches which were interpreted to her as malingering and which in truth had been generated by suggestion; for this reason she joyously welcomed her severe menstrual bleeding as proof that her illness was genuine, a proof that was also recognized as such by others. She described a scene from the age of fifteen, in which she suddenly began to bleed from the nose when she had the wish to be treated by a certain young doctor who was present (and who also appeared in the dream). When she saw how affected I was by her first hemorrhage while she was in the hands of Rosanes, she experienced this as the realization of an old wish to be loved in her illness, and in spite of the danger during the succeeding hours she felt happy as never before. Then, in the sanatorium, she became restless during the night because of an unconscious wish[4] to entice me to go there; since I did not come during the night, she renewed the bleedings, as an unfailing means of rearousing my affection. She bled spontaneously three times and each bleeding lasted for four days, which must have some significance. She still owes me details and specific dates.

My cordial greetings, and do not forget to write to me as often as your head[aches] permit it.

Your
Sigm.

1. Mathematical sign indicating "less than," but the reading is uncertain; Freud may have meant >, "greater than."

2. According to Schröter, this may be a reference to the course Freud gave on hysteria (see Gicklhorn and Gicklhorn, 1960, p. 152).

3. The manuscript reads *darstellungsunlustig,* not *darstellungslustig* as in *Anfänge.*

4. The unusual German expression *unbewusste Sehnsuchtsabsicht* means literally "an unconscious intent of longing."

---

Vienna, May 17, 1896

Dear Wilhelm,

The wedding excitement[1] is just over. The couple left, reawakening all sorts of memories of September 6. Everyone was delighted; he is an excellent man and has no motive other than long-standing affection, but we all are very tired. Many thanks for your warm congratulations on behalf of the couple and myself. For me it was a ray of sunshine in winter.

The loveliest part of the wedding, by the way, was our Sopherl—with curled hair and a wreath of forget-me-nots on her head.

I hope you are not troubling yourself too much with the remarks against Löw[enfeld]. The relevant line is "lends his own periodicity."[2] Naturally, I cannot find the paper right now.

Most cordial greetings to you and Ida.

Yours,
Sigm.

With the 12th, the courage to face life returned. Critical dates in April: 6 and 12.

1. Freud's sister Rosa (b. 1861) married Heinrich Graf (b. 1852), a lawyer who died in 1908. Rosa died in 1942 at Auschwitz.

2. This exact phrase is not found in Freud's reply to Löwenfeld (although the same idea is; see *G.W.* 1:369) or in Löwenfeld's article. Fliess in his 1897 book defended Freud against Löwenfeld (p. 197n).

---

Vienna, May 30, 1896

Dear Wilhelm,

As the fruit of some tormenting reflections, I send you the following solution to the etiology of the psychoneuroses, which still awaits confirmation from individual analyses.

Four periods of life are to be distinguished:

Ages

| Ia | Ib | A | II | B | III |
|---|---|---|---|---|---|
| Up to 4 years<br>Preconscious | Up to 8<br>Infantile | ////// | Up to 14<br>Prepubertal | ////// | Up to x<br>Maturity |

A and B (from about 8 to 10 and 13 to 17) are the transitional periods, during which repression for the most part occurs.

The arousal in a later epoch of a sexual memory from an earlier one produces a *surplus of sexuality* in the psyche, which operates as an inhibitor of thought and gives the memory and its consequences an obsessive character—uninhibitability.

The period Ia has the characteristic of being *untranslated*, so that the arousal of a Ia sexual scene leads, not to psychic consequences, but to realizations, that is, to a *conversion*. The surplus of sexuality impedes translation.

Surplus of sexuality alone is not enough to cause repression; the cooperation of *defense* is necessary; but without a surplus of sexuality defense does not produce a neurosis.

The individual neuroses have chronological requirements for their sexual scenes:

Chronological Requirements Repression

| | Ia | Ib | A | II | B | III |
|---|---|---|---|---|---|---|
| | Up to 4 | Up to 8 | | Up to 14 | | Up to x |
| Hysteria | Scene | | | Repression | | Repression |
| Obs. neur. | | Scene | | Repression | | Repression |
| Paranoia | | | | Scene | | Repression |

That is, the scenes for hysteria fall in the first period of childhood (up to 4 years), in which the mnemic residues are not translated into verbal images. It is a matter of indifference whether these Ia scenes are aroused during the period after the second dentition (8 to 10) or in thc stagc of pubcrty. Hysteria always results and in the form of *conversion*, since the combined operation of defense and surplus of sexuality impedes translation.

The scenes of obsessional neurosis belong to epoch Ib. They are provided with a translation into words and when they are aroused in II or III, psychic obsessional symptoms are generated.

The scenes for paranoia fall in the period after the second dentition, in epoch II, and are aroused in III (maturity). In that case defense is manifested in disbelief. Thus the periods at which repression occurs are of no significance for the choice of neurosis; the periods at which the event occurs are decisive. The nature of the scene is of importance insofar as it is able to give rise to defense.

What happens if the scenes extend over several age periods? Then the earliest epoch is decisive — or combined forms appear, which it should be possible to demonstrate. Such a combination between paranoia and obsessional neurosis is for the most part impossible, because the repression of the Ib scene effected during II makes new sexual scenes impossible.

Hysteria is the only neurosis in which symptoms are perhaps possible without defense, for even so the characteristic of conversion would remain. (Pure somatic hysteria.)

It will be seen that paranoia depends the least on infantile determinants. It is the neurosis of defense par excellence, independent even of morality and aversion to sexuality (which are what in A and B provide the motives for defense in obsessional neurosis and hysteria) and consequently accessible to the lower classes. It is an affection of maturity. If there are no scenes in Ia, Ib, or II, defense can have no pathological consequences (normal repression). The surplus of sexuality fulfills the preconditions for *anxiety attacks* during maturity. The memory traces are insufficient to take up the sexual quantity released, which should become libido.

The importance of *intervals* between sexual experiences is evident. A continuation of the scenes across a boundary between epochs may perhaps avoid the possibility of a repression, since in that case no surplus of sexuality arises between a scene and the next deeper memory of it.

About consciousness [that is, being conscious], or rather becoming conscious, we must suppose three things:

(1) That with regard to memories, it consists for the most part in the *verbal* consciousness pertaining to them—that is, in access to the associated word presentations;

(2) That it is not attached exclusively and inseparably either to the so-called unconscious or to the so-called conscious realm, so that these names seem to call for rejection;

(3) That it is determined by a *compromise* between the different psychic powers which come into conflict with one another when repressions occur.

These powers must be closely studied and inferred from their results. They are (1) the *inherent quantitative strength* of a presentation and (2) a freely displaceable *attention* which is attracted according to certain rules and repelled in accordance with the rule of defense. Symptoms are almost all *compromise* formations. A fundamental distinction is to be made between *uninhibited* and *thought-inhibited* psychic processes. It is in the conflict between these two that symptoms arise as compromises through which the path to consciousness is opened. In neuroses each of these two processes is in itself rational[1] (the uninhibited one is monoideistic, one-sided); the resultant compromise is *irrational*, analogous to an error in thought.

In every case *quantitative* conditions must be fulfilled, for otherwise the defense by the thought-inhibited process prevents the formation of the symptom.

One kind of psychic disturbance arises if the power of the uninhibited processes increases; another if the force of the thought inhibition relaxes. (Melancholia, exhaustion—dreams as a prototype.)

An increase of the uninhibited processes to the point of being in sole possession of the path to verbal consciousness produces *psychosis.*

There is no question of a separation between the two processes; it is only motives of unpleasure that bar the various possible associative transitions between them.

With this, I shall probably bury the magic wand for this semester. I did not write because I was ill-humored and knew that you too were in a bad period. I already am quite rich with significant dates:

April 6 7
" 12
May 6 7
" 12
" 20
" 29

I again need an infusion of vital strength like the last one in Dresden. This year has exhausted my moral strength.

In defiance of my colleagues I wrote down in full for Paschkis my lecture on the etiology of hysteria. The first installment appears today.

My eldest brother[2] from Manchester has been staying here this week. Next Thursday my family goes to Aussee.

I am very eager to hear from you; what you will have uncovered in the interim! When shall we meet again? How is R.W.? And your dear wife, who in spite of all attempts to influence her, has not been alienated from me?[3] Life is indeed very difficult, don't you think so?

You need not express an opinion on the matters I related at the start; I admitted to you that there is more speculation involved than usual; but it just would not leave me in peace.

My most cordial greetings.

Your
Sigm.

1. Freud uses *korrekt* (correct) and *inkorrekt* (incorrect), probably in the sense of reality-adequate and reality-inadequate.

2. Emanuel Freud (1832–1915) moved to Manchester, England, in 1859 with his wife, Marie (who died in 1923), sons John and Sam, and daughters Pauline and Bertha. John and Pauline figure frequently in Freud's dreams and memories. Sam, a dealer in textiles, died in 1945 in Manchester.

3. See note 1 to letter of August 12, 1896.

June 4, 1896

Dear Wilhelm,

Well! We are to meet this month, and in Berlin at that? What a temptation. Nevertheless, I must resist it. In June I still would lose such and such an amount per day from four patients who can no longer come in July. The head of the household who completely uses up his laboriously earned sixteen to seventeen thousand thus cannot permit himself to do this. Further, against Berlin: did you forget that our congresses should take place neither in Vienna nor in Berlin, because in those two places we are workers who cannot take time off? What I lose by excluding Berlin I shall make up for myself next time, by calling for you at your house, kissing Ida's hand and R.W.'s forehead, and then traveling with you some two to four hours possibly to a place on the Baltic. At the moment it is unfortunately not possible for Martha to come along to neutralize and satisfy your wife. Martha is going with the children to Aussee tomorrow and is without help.

I gather from the gap in your letters that you must have a rather bad period behind you, but how many things you must have found and guessed at! I am thoroughly looking forward to them. You will be disappointed in me. These times have brought me, intellectually and morally, to the very point of losing my strength, and now I have had to put neuroses and the *φψω* aside in order to write about infantile paralyses, which must be finished by the end of August. Since my last letter I have become convinced only of the last explanation—hysteria up to 4 years; the absence of translating word representations also is valid only for this period of life. The Löwenfeld affair is as follows: you must have read his paper. My remark on "coitus periodicity" is part of *my reply* (pp. 9–10). Don't trouble yourself too much with it.

I think, then, that I shall tear myself away in July. If you are against the seashore, then some other town: Magdeburg, Danzig. I really need it, often do not recognize myself—that is how much the experiences with colleagues and patients have taken their toll—which is, after all, really ridiculous. I believe my heart is suffering more from that than from tobacco; it is, by the way, behaving most decently.

I have not seen Breuer again, except for a moment at the wedding; have no further need of doing so.

Eckstein's significant dates unfortunately cannot be obtained because they were not recorded at the sanatorium. Her story is becoming even clearer; there is no doubt that her hemorrhages were due to wishes; she has had several similar incidents, among them actual[1] simulations, in her childhood. Your nose has once again smelled things correctly.[2] Incidentally, she is doing exceedingly well.

Don't let me wait too long for the letter you promised to write in peace and quiet.

Most cordial greetings to all of you.

Yours,
Sigm.

1. The German here is *direkte*.

2. The literal translation of a German idiom meaning to be on the right scent. Here, of course, it is a reference to Fliess's theories about the nose.

---

Vienna, June 9, 1896

Dearest Wilhelm,

I could now say, our next congress is really superfluous because I have nothing to tell you, and what you intimate in your letter you want to tell me I already know. Before you recover from your astonishment, I want to convert the joke and become serious: I really have nothing to tell you (except, perhaps, the resolution of the story of Eckstein and her hemorrhages) and of your discoveries I knew only that you would make them; you did not surprise me; from the claw you showed me in Dresden I was able to form the correct picture of the structure of the future animal. In reality nothing will prevent me from looking forward to the detailed account of your findings as well as to seeing you again. Just a few weeks more; in the meantime I am working on the infantile paralyses and find life away from all that is dear to me very boring.

I did not have any discomfort on my special dates, but instead I am in a very dull period. Therefore I am not properly answering your question: tic and repression? For a difference between compulsion and effect of defense is dawning on me: the significance of the fact that anxiety develops when one tries to suppress the tic and the analogy between tic and hysterical symptoms of childhood from 8 years to puberty; that is, a double form of defense, one automatic and one psychic, initiated by the ego. But no clarity yet.

I do not at all share[1] your astonishment that so far no one has noticed these things. My opinion of the mental capacity of *homo sapiens communis* has long been established, but does not really differ from yours all that much, does it?

Let yourself be further enlightened by R.W. and let me know soon that you, too, are having better days. That remains a dark shadow.

With the most cordial greetings to you, I.F., and R.W.,

Yours,
Sigm.

1. Freud wrote *einteilen;* presumably he meant *teilen,* to share.

---

Vienna, June 30, 1896

My dear Wilhelm,

You taught me that a kernel of truth lurks behind every absurd popular belief, and I can give you an example of this. Certain things should not be mentioned even in jest, otherwise they come true. Thus I wrote to you recently that there was no real need for a congress, and today I have to tell you of a serious obstacle which stands in the way of the next one, or at least in the way of fixing its date. My old father (age eighty-one) is in Baden[1] in a most shaky state, with heart failure, paralysis of the bladder, and so forth. Eagerly waiting for news and traveling to see him were the only things of interest in these past two weeks. Therefore I do not dare make any plans now that would take me a day's journey away from Vienna. To be sure, he is a tremendous fellow,[2] and should he still be granted a span of well-being, as I hope he will, I shall use it for our meeting. I cannot announce my visit today; but could you arrange to take time off if I were to send you a telegram announcing that within twenty-four hours I intend to leave to see you, so that there would still be enough time for you to cable and cancel the trip? Avoiding your significant dates, of course.

I feel a pall has been cast over me, and all I can say is that I am looking forward to our congress as to the slaking of hunger and thirst. I bring nothing but two open ears and one temporal lobe lubricated for reception. I foresee important things—I am that self-seeking—also for my purposes. With regard to the repression theory, I have run into doubts that could be dispelled by a few words from you, in particular about male and female menstruation in the same individual. Anxiety, chemical factors, and so forth—perhaps with your help I shall find the solid ground on which I can cease to give psychological explanations and begin to find a physiological foundation!

I have really been quite inactive as well. The completely uninteresting work on infantile paralyses had to serve as my main focus. Yet I could not help surmising or learning a few things, such as various highly valuable details about somnambulism. I wish I already were with you and relating these things to you.

My family is in a paradise above Aussee (Obertressen) and having a great time. I just came back from there today. As you know, I shall get acquainted with R.W. in 1896. Until then, most cordial greetings to his mama and you and do write *soon* again.

Your
Sigm.

The book on the nose?

1. A spa near Vienna.
2. The German word is *Riesenkerl.*

---

July 15, 1896

My dear Wilhelm,

Just received your letter and was pleased about everything I shall hear from you. A pity, though, that I am not sure when. For the situation is this: the old fellow has paralysis of the bladder and rectum, is failing nutritionally, and at the same time is mentally overalert and euphoric. I truly believe that these are his last days but do not know how long he has and do not dare to leave, least of all for two days and for a pleasure I would like to indulge in fully. To meet you in Berlin, to hear about the new magic from you for a few hours, and then suddenly to have to rush back during the day or night because of news which might turn out to be a false alarm—that is something I really want to avoid, and to this fear I sacrifice the burning desire once again to live fully, with head and heart simultaneously, to be a *zoon politikon* [social animal], and, moreover, to see you.

If the old man's condition no longer presents an obstacle, the temporal circumstances are as follows: from today until July 26 you are in a bad period, and I am frantically trying to "finish" several people and a last flicker of my practice. Therefore, I would rather see you in August, after the 26th, when I begin my vacation (always presupposing that I can do so). Your better week, it seems to me, falls in that period, or did you not last time underline 5 in black for me? In August, then, I could choose *your* time period as well as your location, which I should like to do for the sake of your head[aches]. In September, until the middle of it, I could do the same. You can see that I want to enjoy life.

Freud's mother,
Amalie Nathanson Freud.

Freud's father, Jacob Freud,
in the last year of his life.
He died in October of 1896
at the age of eighty-one.

You must still enlighten me about my condition: well and stupid. The Nothnagel piece[1] is, and will turn out to be, disgusting and will not be finished for some time. Otherwise nothing new, just an urgent need for the introduction of a stimulating current from elsewhere. But I am actually overworked as well; that is, without the capability to grasp anything intellectually. Actually, I am glad I cannot see you in July.

The old man's condition, by the way, does not depress me. I do not begrudge him the well-deserved rest that he himself desires. He was an interesting human being, very happy within himself; he is suffering very little now, and is fading with decency and dignity. I do not wish him a prolonged sickbed, nor do I wish it for my unmarried sister,[2] who is nursing him and suffering in the process. Last Saturday-Sunday I was in Aussee and felt greatly refreshed. Martha is well and cheerful; the rascals are splendid; even Annerl, who for some time had been standing still, is now blossoming with a summation thrust[3] (five teeth). Oli is amusing; he has learned to read and write by listening and spends all day brooding about orthographic problems. An Alpine meadow near us is called "Bärnmoos." He reads this on the first road sign. The second says "Bernmoos," which he notices. At another place, the sign points to "Beerenmos." All of this becomes condensed for him, with the result that he proclaims loudly: "B. can be spelled whichever way one likes, with modified [umlaut]a, one e, and double e; it makes no difference."

With most cordial greetings to I.F. and R.W.,

Your
Sigm.

1. The reference is to "Die infantile Cerebrallähmung," published in Hermann Nothnagel's *Specielle Pathologie und Therapie.*
2. Adolfine Freud (1862–1942).
3. On this term, taken from Fliess, see Sulloway (1979, pp. 179–180).

---

Obertressen, August 12, 1896

My dear Wilhelm,

Not so uncertain. I have just returned from a second little trip to Lichtensteinklamm; the first one was to the Schafberg and Salzburg. I am rapidly recovering. All deliria have the characteristic of victory; I am once again catching myself at creative attempts. Now I soon have to see how you are and hear what I can learn from you. You intend to be in the Brühl the last week of August, which does not help me since I shall not be in Vienna. I stubbornly insist on point 4 of our congress stipulations: congresses are not to be held in either Vienna or Berlin. This doesn't mean anything. As I did in my youth (Hirschbühel, Salzburg, do you remember?), I want to walk and eat with you again as the kind of reanimation that also succeeded in Dresden. (Your dear Ida should skip this passage lest Breuer's seeds begin to ripen in her.[1]) I have time only until the last day of this month, when I want to begin my tour of Italy, of which you approve. Everything is indefinite, though; I cannot give you all the details of the many complications in the plans of this extensive family. It is probably easier for you to come to a decision. Let me know very soon when you will be available, with due consideration for your special dates and other plans, between now and the end of the month, and whether and to what extent the location will be a function of the time of the month. I want this to be a proper, vigorous congress, like the last one, with less complaining and greater receptivity on my part.

It gives me a little satisfaction that you are becoming conservative with regard to your head, to start with. As for the rest, let us experience it together.

I congratulate your boy upon his first tooth and his child's obedience. With us, all are uncommonly well except my recently married sister, who is slowly recovering from a miscarriage. Annerl is dully voracious and has six unobserved teeth, thanks to her unscientific mother. Sopherl, who is three and a half years old, is now in the phase of *beauté*. The boys are naughty and funny; Mathilde is in fine shape, except for a tic which at present is localized in the facial nerve. The old man, strangely, is thriving again.

I would not like to miss the galley proofs; you must admit that in my case undercurrents pass quickly; you, fortunately, do not have any. So, I shall *not* give up *any* of my congress expectations, do you hear? I am again in good shape and look forward to it tremendously.

With a brief greeting until then,

Yours,
Sigm.

Martha sends her warmest to the three of you.

1. In Marie Bonaparte's notebook of November 24, 1937, she writes: "Ida Fliess, de plus, 'ein böses Weib,' fit tout, par jalousie, pour brouiller les deux amis. Tandis que Martha Freud comprenait bien que Fliess pourrait donner à son mari autre chose qu'elle." (Ida Fliess, moreover, "a bad woman," out of jealousy, did everything possible to sow discord between the two friends, whereas Martha Freud understood very well that Fliess was able to give her husband something beyond what she could.) Presumably Freud heard directly from Fliess that Breuer had warned Ida of the

dangers to her in the close friendship of the two men. See the crucial document, Freud's letter to Fliess of August 7, 1901.

---

Obertressen, August 17, 1896

Dearest Wilhelm,

Excellent! The time suits me in every respect. So there remains only the location. Moreover, between here and Brühl or Vienna, I cannot think of another place where one can enjoy life more for just two days than in our lovely Salzburg, where we will also have memories to revive. Don't think that I will have too much of an advantage in getting there; I still have a four-hour train trip. For you, though, starting in Vienna, it will be six hours, which seems to me to speak against it. I would like to spare you the traveling. If you were to come to Aussee, it would be wonderful, but you would have an eight- to nine-hour journey. Linz, Graz, and Wels are very unappealing types of towns.

Result: on August 25, send me a telegram that on the 26th at such and such an hour you will proceed to such and such a place (whichever you like). And I shall follow you there. It could even be *Gastein;* incidentally, from August 23 to 25 I shall be in the Kapruner Valley, which leads to a railroad station at Zell am See. In short, you shall decide and select a beautiful place to your liking or an agreeable town.

I very much look forward to it. Therefore, nothing further today.

Your
Sigm.

---

[a postcard]

August 29, 1896

Were I a believer in the old therapy, I would say that those days were a chalybeate bath for me. My heartfelt thanks to you and greetings to your dear wife. The book is really accurate, courageous, and contains all the essentials that can be known from the historical period.

See you again in September.

Your
S.

Vienna, September 29, 1896

Dear Wilhelm,

I hope you and your wife and son are again installed most comfortably in the beautiful rooms of von der Heydtstrasse; that you are busily observing and calculating new periods of 28 and 23; that Ida is occasionally cursing under her breath about the six children from another family; and that Robert is always eager to reveal new things.[1]

I have not written to you until today because an influenza with fever, pus, and cardiac symptoms suddenly shattered my wellbeing; only today did I begin to have an inkling that health might again be possible. I would like so much to hold out until that famous age limit of approximately fifty-one, but I had one day that made me feel it was unlikely. The infection caught up with me on the last critical date, September 24, so that on September 25 I was hoarse and breathless; at the same time Martin went to bed with a throat infection. But now I can breathe freely again.

On Sunday I had to go and see the daughter of a colleague in Oderberg, where I was closer to you than I usually am. It is this constellation to which I ascribe my making a brilliant diagnosis and recognizing that it was a case of Erb-Goldflam's disease — ptosis ophthalmoplegia with normal pupils, paralysis of the palate and deglutition, paresis of the vagus, weakness of the vocal cords, attacks of choking, aspiration pneumonia, and large variations in the intensity of the symptoms. Several unusual features. Ptosis developed at age 4!; ophthalmoplegia gradually until age 13; the vagus and accessorius symptoms only from puberty to the present (15 years). But then I concluded further that these Erb-Goldflam affections must belong to the group of organic developmental illnesses, of the type resulting from [various] constitutions, which you are only now just envisaging (myxedema, Basedow's disease, acromegaly). The child has a special look, broad nasal septum, light mustache, extreme body length, thyroid not easily palpable, though she has reached puberty. The mother has the same features, strabism. The pictures of the siblings as children immediately remind one of myxedema. Some notion of mine points to your cephalic sexual organ, which I greatly respect. I proposed that they bring the child to Vienna and try organotherapy.[2] What do you say?

How is your book?

Today I learned that a colleague at the university declined to have me as a consultant, with the explanation that I could not be taken seriously; but I have been so fortified by my vacation that I felt nothing at all. Two months ago it would have made me miserable for two days. I have taken the wife of my friend Q. into treatment and it is sheer joy to see once again how everything fits and tallies in hysteria.

Hehn's *Italy*[3] was a delight for the women and for me.

As a result of the intervening circumstances, I have until now seen nothing of Oscar and Mela [Rie], but shall visit your family immediately when they are in the city. My father seems to be on his deathbed; he is at times confused and is steadily shriveling up, moving toward pneumonia and a fateful date.

Most cordial greetings.

Your
Sigm.

1. Sulloway (1979, p. 190) says that "Fliess kept a daily record book in which he recorded his firstborn son's every maturation milestone, affliction, and trace of sexual activity." Fliess, on p. 198 of *Die Beziehungen zwischen Nase und weiblichen Geschlechtsorganen*, writes about sexual observations in young children: "in the case of boys in direct erections of the penis on such days, even in the first months of life!" In the same passage Fliess speaks of blood in the urine of boys as a sign of male menstruation.

That these observations were made on Robert is clear from a passage (noticed by Sulloway as well) in Fliess's 1906 book, *Der Ablauf des Lebens* (2nd ed., 1923, p. 313), where he writes: "The female substance is affected in boys and girls in yet another manner. I noticed that on periodically recurring specific dates my oldest son eliminated blood in his urine and saliva in his first weeks of life (January 1896). I mentioned this in my earlier book, and the shirt and the sheet with those traces [of blood] on them have been kept to this day." The observations of erections were undoubtedly, therefore, made on Robert as well. However, it strikes me as highly unlikely that these communications to Freud played any role in Freud's research at the time.

2. Organotherapy is the treatment of disease by the administration of portions of certain animal organs or extracts thereof.

3. Victor Hehn, *Italien: Ansichten und Streiflichter, mit Lebensnachrichten über den Verfasser*, 5th ed. (Berlin: Bornträger, 1896).

October 9, 1896

Dear Wilhelm,

Martha will probably leave here Sunday morning and hopes to spend the night under your roof. Details will follow. An accident (sprained right hand) suffered by the old woman[1] in Hamburg is hastening Martha's departure from Vienna and therefore also from Berlin to Hamburg. On her return trip she plans to stay with you longer.

My state of health has really not improved very much. The cardiac symptoms in particular do not play a large role; I see no reason to ask you for immediate treatment, especially since it will not be possible to combine it with an earlier date for the wedding. In Johannesgasse everything is moving along. Rie is more collected, it seems to me; the bride makes a better impression; the parents managed to get their way in having a regular fete; and the postponement is being explained as unavoidable.

The condition of my old man will probably keep my participation to a minimum.

You know that I do not laugh at fantasies such as those about historical periods, and I do not because I see no reason for it. There is something to these ideas; it is the symbolic presentiment of unknown realities with which they have something in common.[2] Since not even the organs in that case are the same, one can no longer escape from acknowledging heavenly influences. I bow before you as honorary astrologer.[3]

Your book[4] is probably finished by now. I presume you don't literally intend to give a kick to the man who disdains me.

I am now very satisfied with my cases; another year or two, and I can express the matter in formulas that can be told to everyone. This prospect and the satisfaction with what has already been achieved give me confidence in many a dark hour. My practice is not yet lively at all; a meeting with Breuer at the home of one of his patients was as funny as it was unpleasant. Impossible to get on with him; unfortunately, he isn't looking at all well.

For a time we just did not know what to give Oscar and Mela. Finally, we decided to have the children, of whom he is very fond, photographed for him; and for her, a piece of handiwork from my sister's studio. They are too wealthy for us to have given them other presents. Unfortunately, he was clumsy in initiating the relationship between his bride and his siblings. They are people worthy of all love and respect, especially his sister Ditha.

I break off rather than conclude; I must write about infantile paralyses. My wife will bring the most cordial greetings to your house in a few hours.

Your
Sigm.

P.S. Martha will probably leave on Sunday morning from the North Station and be in Berlin at 9 o'clock (or 8:30?) in the evening.

1. Freud means Martha's mother, Emmeline Bernays.

2. For references to these ideas in Freud's later writings see Schur (1972, p. 108).

3. This is a reference to Fliess's speculations on the relation between astronomical conditions and the creation of organisms, a phrase used by Fliess in the preface (pp.

iii–iv) to *Die Beziehungen zwischen Nase und weiblichen Geschlechtsorganen.* Freud refers to this again later in his life (*S.E.* 18:45). See also Sulloway (1979, p. 402n).

4. This may be another reference to *Die Beziehungen,* in which Fliess defends Freud against Löwenfeld's criticisms (p. 177).

---

October 26, 1896
IX., Berggasse 19

My dear Wilhelm,

There is really no reply possible with such intervals; but it will not remain so.

Yesterday we buried the old man, who died during the night of October 23. He bore himself bravely to the end, just like the altogether unusual man he had been. At the end he must have had meningeal hemorrhages, soporous attacks with unexplained fever, hyperesthesia, and spasms from which he would then awake free of fever. The last attack was followed by pulmonary edema and quite an easy death.[1] All of it happened in my critical period, and I am really quite down because of it.[2]

Next time I shall write more and in greater detail; incidentally, the cocaine brush has been completely put aside.

I learned only this year that your birthday is October 24.

I hope Martha is allowing herself to spend several nice days with you.

Your
Sigm.

1. Fliess, in *Der Ablauf des Lebens,* writes: "Prof. Sigmund Freud in Vienna at one time advised me of the dates of his father's life:

born April 1, 1815
died Oct. 24, 1896 } $29{,}792 = 38 \times 28^2$

Freud senior was born on the same day as Bismarck, who died on July 30, 1898, therefore lived exactly $644 = 23 \times 28$ days longer" (2nd ed., p. 142).

2. In the preface to the second edition of the *Interpretation of Dreams* Freud writes: "For this book has a further subjective significance for me personally—a significance which I only grasped after I had completed it. It was, I found, a portion of my own self-analysis, my reaction to my father's death—that is to say, to the most important event, the most poignant loss, of a man's life" (*S.E.* 4:xxvi).

Vienna, November 2, 1896
IX., Berggasse 19

Dear Wilhelm,

I find it so difficult to write just now that I have put off for a long time thanking you for the moving words in your letter. By one of those dark pathways behind the official consciousness the old man's death has affected me deeply. I valued him highly, understood him very well, and with his peculiar mixture of deep wisdom and fantastic light-heartedness he had a significant effect on my life.[1] By the time he died, his life had long been over, but in [my] inner self the whole past has been reawakened by this event.

I now feel quite uprooted.

Otherwise, I am writing about infantile paralyses (Pegasus yoked)[2] and am enjoying my four cases and especially look forward to the prospect of talking to you for several hours. Lonely, that is understood. Perhaps I shall tell you a few small wild things in return for your marvelous ideas and findings. Less enjoyable is the state of my practice this year, on which my mood always remains dependent. With heart and nose I am satisfied again.

Recently I heard the first reaction to my incursion into psychiatry. From it I quote: "Gruesome, horrible, old wives' psychiatry." That was Rieger in Würzburg.[3] I was highly amused. And, of all things, about paranoia, which has become so transparent!

Your book is still keeping us waiting. Wernicke recently referred a patient to me, a lieutenant who is in the officers' hospital.

I must tell you about a nice dream I had the night after the funeral.[4] I was in a place where I read a sign:

You are requested
to close the eyes.

I immediately recognized the location as the barbershop I visit every day. On the day of the funeral I was kept waiting and therefore arrived a little late at the house of mourning. At that time my family was displeased with me because I had arranged for the funeral to be quiet and simple, which they later agreed was quite justified. They were also somewhat offended by my lateness. The sentence on the sign has a double meaning: one should do one's duty to the dead (an apology as though I had not done it and were in need of leniency), and the actual duty itself. The dream thus stems from the inclination to self-reproach that regularly sets in among the survivors.

I see little of the betrothed couple and the affair, unfortunately, gives me little pleasure. He is more sober and calmer, but his (and your] parents-in-law seem to show little adroitness in handling the relationship. It is not a pleasant topic between us; if you prefer, we shall not talk about it. It's all rubbish, in any event.

My most cordial greetings to I.F. and R.W.; my wife probably is already with you.

Your
Sigm.

P.S. If Martha needs some money for purchases, you will no doubt lend it to her.

1. The German is *er hatte viel in meinem Leben gemacht;* literally, he had made much in my life.

2. "Pegasus im Joche" (1796) was an allegorical poem by Schiller on the subject of poetry.

3. Conrad Rieger, "Über die Behandlung 'Nervenkranker,' " in *Schmidt's Jahrbücher der in- und ausländischen gesamten Medizin,* 251 (1896):173–178, 273–276, says: "I cannot imagine that an experienced psychiatrist could read this essay without feeling total indignation. The reason for this indignation is that the author attributes the greatest importance to paranoid blather with sexual content [on the part of his patients] about purely chance happenings which, even if they were not based merely on imagination, are of no significance whatsoever. This kind of thing cannot possibly lead to anything but a simply dreadful 'old wives' psychiatry' " (my translation). The lack of psychological perception in this passage takes one's breath away, although it has been defended by Sulloway (1979, p. 454). Rieger goes on to say that the best treatment for such patients is physical labor, for they are laboring under the "poison of laziness."

4. Freud repeats this later in *Interpretation of Dreams:* "During the night before my father's funeral" (*S.E.* 4:317).

Vienna, November 22, 1896

Dearest Wilhelm,

The first person to whom I am writing from my new quarters is you, to thank you for your letter and Frau Ida for what she sent. I must assume that she liked doing this work, because one could not explain in any other way why she did it. In return, a little piece of news which should please you, but about which I do not know two things: whether it is true, and whether it is news to you. Little it is not. A colleague who wanted to buy your book at Deuticke's was told by him that it is *out of print* and he [the colleague] told it to my brother. It sounds so unbelievable that I reserve a disclaimer until tomorrow. If you hear nothing tomorrow, then it is so after all.

I hope you do not take it as a damper if I do not in the least restrain my anger about other things I heard. One of the nicest people in Breuer's circle expressed the opinion to me that the 28- and 23-day period is a chance occurrence, after all. Pepi Kaufmann, he said, has very neatly calculated its probability, and the entire circle is constantly calculating — obviously not to confirm your thesis. It would be all right if only they were capable of conversion, but this will not be the case. Vexatious things. By the way, there is no doubt that Rosa A. must be doing *very much* better; recently she even went to the theater with Minna.

I shall be finished with my pain[ful task] for Nothnagel in a few weeks; have been delayed now by the move. My work on hysteria is progressing nicely; I am negotiating about four treatments, none of which is likely to materialize; I do, however, have a lot more to do. What I am lacking completely are high spirits and pleasure in living; instead I am busily noting the occasions when I have to occupy myself with the state of affairs after my death.[1] Again, a topic one should not deal with too extensively if one loves one's friend and only correspondent. The nasal suppuration is markedly improved; just after the first treatment, I once more experienced a temporary intensification of the cardiac pains.

Martha again managed things so splendidly that I did not have to miss a single office hour. Now the disorder is starting upstairs. The second generation is very gratifying.

Let me have a little more time with the Napoleon [book]. I expect it any day, but so far in vain. I have heard nothing from Rie. I do not think they will go from Paris to Vienna via Berlin. The whole affair has again increased my misanthropy.

Write to me soon. Cordial greetings to Frau Ida and little Robert.

Your
Sigm.

1. Meaning unclear.

---

December 4, 1896
IX., Berggasse 19

Dear Wilhelm,

My bad time has run its course in typical fashion; I am fully occupied, with every half-hour taken, and am not in the least interested in life after death. I am dealing with something that cements your work to mine, places my structure on your base, but I have the feeling that I should not yet write about it. A bit of it will be ready in a few days — naturally, only for you. I am curious what you will say.

I am also curious to hear about your lecture and how it was received. I am so isolated here that I hear nothing about your book.

Shamefully, I must renege on one promise. Deuticke and colleagues could not get hold of the Napoleon, and I did not know a more precise title. I do not want to delay you, and ask your permission to substitute something else for it.

Your cousin, Miss G. de B., arrived and seems to have been well prepared because she is very willing. Could you perhaps unobtrusively find out from Ida who in the family or the surroundings has had a speech defect such as stuttering?[1]

The abstinence does me good; I oscillate between one and four [cigars] a day. Essentially I am well, because plenty of work and newly arising possibilities of resolving hysteria satisfy my inner unrest.

Our life has been very comfortable since the new living arrangements. Ida's tables are of great service to me. [I wonder] whether you will approve of my deriving "Ida" from "idea"?

Otherwise the world is full of wild things; stupid ones as well. The latter, however, usually are people. The first things about my work that I can disclose to you are the mottoes. The psychology of hysteria will be preceded by the proud words, *Introite et hic dii sunt;*[2]

the chapter on summation by:
Sie treiben's toll, ich fürcht' es breche
Nicht jeden Wochenschluss macht Gott die Zeche;[3]

the symptom formation by:
Flectere si nequeo superos Acheronta movebo;[4]

and resistance by:
Mach es kurz!
Am jüngsten Tag ist's doch nur ein ———.[5]

I cordially greet you and your little family and remain eager for *rerum novarum* [news] about family and science.

Your
Sigm.

1. Since Freud is asking Fliess to be discreet in his inquiries, it may be assumed that Freud is on the trail of this woman's seducer, and all that he knows about him/her is that the person suffers from a speech defect, which is probably the only thing about the person that the patient can remember.

2. From Aristotle's *De partibus animalium*, 1:5, "Enter—for here too are gods." See Schönau (1968, p. 58). The quotation is used as a motto for Lessing's play *Nathan*

*der Weise.* Freud uses it again in his letter of April 24, 1899, and in his "Autobiographical Study" (*S.E.* 20:13). Fliess uses it on p. 59 of his *Vom Leben und Tod.*

3. Freud is thinking of Goethe's "Sprüche in Reimen." The passage is commented on by Schönau (1968, pp. 80–83).

4. This quote from Virgil's *Aeneid* is treated at length in Schönau (1968, pp. 61–73): "If I cannot bend the higher powers, I will move the infernal regions." It was used by Freud on the title page of his book on dreams (cf. *S.E.* 5:608).

5. The quotation is from Goethe, *Zahmen Xenien,* 9:22:

Cut it short!
On doomsday it won't be worth a ———.

See Schönau (1968, pp. 82–84).

# Periodicity and Self-Analysis

December 6, 1896

Dear Wilhelm,

Today, after having for once enjoyed the full measure of work and earnings that I need for my well-being (ten hours and a hundred florins), I am dead tired and mentally fresh; I shall try to give you a simple report on the latest bit of speculation.

As you know, I am working on the assumption that our psychic mechanism has come into being by a process of stratification: the material present in the form of memory traces being subjected from time to time to a *rearrangement* in accordance with fresh circumstances—to a *retranscription.* Thus what is essentially new about my theory is the thesis that memory is present not once but several times over, that it is laid down in various kinds of indications. I postulated a similar kind of rearrangement some time ago (*Aphasia*) for the paths leading from the periphery [of the body to the cortex]. I do not know how many of these registrations there are—at least three, probably more. This is shown in the following schematic picture, which assumes that the different registrations are also separated (not necessarily topographically) according to the neurones which are their vehicles. This assumption may not be necessary, but it is the simplest and is provisionally admissible.

```
                  I           II          III
   W             Wz           Ub          Vb          Bew[1]
x   x ____ x   x ____ x   x ____ x   x ____ x      x
    x         x   x         x        x         x
                       x
```

*W* [*Wahrnehmungen* (perceptions)] are neurones in which *perceptions* originate, to which consciousness attaches, but which in themselves retain no trace of what has happened. For *consciousness and memory are mutually exclusive.*

*Wz* [*Wahrnehmungszeichen* (indication of perception)] is the first registration of the perceptions; it is quite incapable of consciousness and is arranged according to associations by simultaneity.

*Ub* [*Unbewusstsein* (unconsciousness)] is the second registration, arranged according to other, perhaps causal, relations. Ub traces would perhaps correspond to conceptual memories; equally inaccessible to consciousness.

*Vb* [*Vorbewusstsein* (preconsciousness)] is the third transcription, attached to word presentation and corresponding to our official ego. The cathexes proceeding from this Vb become conscious according to certain rules; and this secondary *thought consciousness* is subsequent in time and is probably linked to the hallucinatory activation of word presentations, so that the neurones of consciousness would once again be perceptual neurones and in themselves without memory.

If I could give a complete account of the psychological characteristics of perception and of the three registrations, I should have described a new psychology. Some material for this is at hand, but that is not my present intention.

I should like to emphasize the fact that the successive registrations represent the psychic achievement of successive epochs of life. At the boundary between two such epochs a translation of the psychic material must take place. I explain the peculiarities of the psychoneuroses by supposing that this translation has not taken place in the case of some of the material, which has certain consequences. For we hold firmly to a belief in a tendency toward quantitative adjustment. Every later transcript inhibits its predecessor and drains the excitatory process from it. If a later transcript is lacking, the excitation is dealt with in accordance with the psychological laws in force in the earlier psychic period and along the paths open at that time. Thus an anachronism persists: in a particular province, *fueros*[2] are still in force; we are in the presence of "survivals."

A failure of translation — this is what is known clinically as "repression." The motive for it is always a release of the unpleasure that would be generated by a translation; it is as though this unpleasure provokes a disturbance of thought that does not permit the work of translation.

Within one and the same psychic phase, and among registrations of the same kind, a *normal* defense makes itself felt owing to a generation of unpleasure. But *pathological* defense occurs only against a memory trace from an earlier phase that has not yet been translated.

It cannot be duc to the magnitude of the release of unpleasure if the defense succeeds in bringing about repression. We often struggle in vain precisely against memories involving the severest unpleasure. So we arrive at the following account. If an event A, when it was a current one, aroused a certain amount of unpleasure, then the mnemic registration of it, A I or A II, has a means of inhibiting the release of unpleasure when the memory is reawakened. The more often the memory recurs, the more inhibited does the release finally become. There is *one* case, however, in which the inhibition is insufficient. If A, when it was current, released a particular unpleasure, and if when it is reawakened it releases fresh unpleasure, then this cannot be inhibited. In this case the memory is behaving as though it were some current event. This case can occur only with sexual events, because the magnitudes of the excitations which these release increase of themselves with time (with sexual development).

Thus a sexual event in one phase acts in the next phase as though it were a current one and is accordingly uninhibitable. What determines pathological defense (repression) is therefore *the sexual nature of the event and its occurrence in an earlier phase.*

Not all sexual experiences release unpleasure; most of them release pleasure. Thus the reproduction of most of them is linked with uninhibitable pleasure. An uninhibitable pleasure of this kind constitutes a *compulsion.* One therefore is led to the following theses. If a sexual experience is remembered in a different phase, a release of pleasure is accompanied by compulsion and a release of unpleasure by repression. In both cases the translation into the indications of the new phase seems to be inhibited (?).

Now, clinical experience acquaints us with three groups of sexual psychoneuroses—hysteria, obsessional neurosis, and paranoia; and it teaches us that the repressed memories relate to what was current—

in the case of hysteria, between the ages of $1\frac{1}{2}$ and 4;
of obsessional neurosis between 4 and 8;
and of paranoia between 8 and 14.

But before the age of 4 there is no repression yet; so the psychic periods of development and the sexual phases do not coincide.

| | $1\frac{1}{2}$ | 4 | 8 | 14–15 |
|---|---|---|---|---|
| Psych. | Ia | Ib | II | III |
| Sex. | I | | II | III |

The following small diagram belongs here:

| Wz<br>Up to 4 | Wz + Ub<br>Up to 8 | Wz + Ub + Vb<br>Up to 14–15 | Ditto |
|---|---|---|---|
| Hysteria current | Compulsion | Repressed in Wz | |
| Obsessional neurosis | Current | Repressed in Ub indications | |
| Paranoia | — | Current | Repressed in Vb indications |
| Perversion current | Current | Compulsion (current) | Repression impossible or not attempted |

For another consequence of premature sexual experiences is perversion, of which the determinant seems to be that defense either does not occur before the psychic apparatus is completed or does not occur at all.

So much for the superstructure. Now for an attempt to set it on its organic foundations. What has to be explained is why sexual experiences, which when they were current generated pleasure, should, when they are remembered from a different phase, generate unpleasure in some people and persist as a compulsion in others. In the former case they must evidently be releasing at a later time an unpleasure that was not released to begin with.

One must also trace the derivation of the different epochs, psychological and sexual. You have taught me to recognize the latter as special multiples of the 28-day female period.[3]

$100\pi = 7\frac{3}{4}$ years, in addition $20\pi = 1$ year, $6\frac{1}{2}$ months
$200\pi = 15$ years $50\pi = 3$ years, 10 months

If I assume that all observed periods are such multiples, then on the one hand the 23-day period remains unutilized, and on the other hand, it remains unexplained why psychic and sexual phases do not coincide (4 years), and why sometimes perversion and at other times neurosis develops.

So I am trying to introduce the notion that it is a male 23-day substance the release of which produces pleasure in both sexes, and a 28-day substance the release of which is experienced as unpleasure.

I then note that I can account for all psychic periods as multiples of 23-day periods ($\pi$) if I *include in the calculation* the period of gestation (276 days = $12\pi$).

$3 \times 12\pi = 1\frac{1}{2}$ years
$6 \times 12\pi = 3\frac{3}{4}$ years
$12 \times 12\pi = 8$ years
$18 \times 12\pi = 12\frac{1}{3}$ years
$21 \times 12\pi = 14\frac{1}{4}$ years
$24 \times 12\pi = 17$ years

This would mean that psychic development occurs according to 23[-day] periods, which would summate to multiples of 3, 6, 12, . . . , 24, in which case the duodecimal system would become effective. The unit would in each case be the *period of gestation,* which equals $10\pi$ or $12\pi$ (approximately). The only result would be that psychic development would progress in accordance with multiples of 3, 6, 12 of the same, whereas the period of gestation *equals* $12\pi$; and sexual development would proceed according to the multiples of 5, 10, 20, whereas this time *equals* $10\pi$.

Two things are noteworthy: (1) that for psychic development, the intrauterine time must be included in the calculation, otherwise it will not work; whereas for sexual development, the calculation can only start with birth. This is reminiscent of the circumstance that during pregnancy there occurs an accumulation of some 28-day substance that is released only at birth; (2) that the 28-day periods are summated more rarely and more highly than the 23-day ones, as though the higher development of human beings were dependent on this characteristic (shame, morality).

The two types of phases thus would interlock as follows:[4]

| | $1\frac{1}{2}$ | $3\frac{3}{4}$ | 8 | $12\frac{1}{4}$ | $14\frac{1}{4}$ | 17 |
|---|---|---|---|---|---|---|
| Psych. | 3T | 6T | 12T | 18T | 21T | 24T |
| Sex. | | | $100\pi$ 10T | | $200\pi$ 20T | |

The fact that there are more psychic phases would fit very well with my assumption of still further translations and innovations of the psychic apparatus. One can also see that the summation in the course of life encompasses ever-greater units of time.

In order to account for why the outcome [of premature sexual experience] is sometimes perversion and sometimes neurosis, I avail myself of the bisexuality of all human beings. In a purely male being there would be a surplus of male release at the two sexual boundaries as well — that is, pleasure would be generated and consequently perversion; in purely female beings there would be a surplus of unpleasurable substance at these times. In the first phases the releases would be parallel: that is, they would produce a normal surplus of pleasure. This would explain the preference of true females for neuroses of defense.

In this way the intellectual nature of males would be confirmed on the basis of your theory.

Finally, I cannot suppress the conjecture that the distinction between neurasthenia and anxiety neurosis, which I detected clinically, is connected with the existence of the two 23-day and 28-day substances.

Besides the two which I postulate here, there might be several of each kind.

It seems to me more and more that the essential point of hysteria is that it results from *perversion* on the part of the seducer, and *more and more* that heredity is seduction by the father. Thus an alternation emerges between generations:

1st generation — perversion

2nd generation — hysteria, and consequent sterility.

Occasionally there is a metamorphosis within the same individual: perverse during the age of vigor and then, after a period of anxiety, hysterical. Accordingly, hysteria is not repudiated sexuality but rather *repudiated perversion.*

Furthermore, behind this lies the idea of abandoned *erotogenic zones.* That is to say, during childhood sexual release would seem to be obtainable from a great many parts of the body, which at a later time are able to release only the 28[-day] anxiety substance and not the others. In this differentiation and limitation [would thus lie] progress in culture, and moral as well as individual development.

A hysterical attack is not a discharge but an *action;* and it retains the original characteristic of every action — of being a means to the reproduction of pleasure. That, at least, is what it is fundamentally; apart from this it puts forward all kinds of other reasons to the preconscious. Thus patients who have had something sexual done to them in *sleep* have attacks of sleep. They go to sleep again in order to experience the same thing and often provoke a hysterical fainting fit in that way.

Attacks of dizziness and fits of weeping—all these are aimed at *another person*—but mostly at the prehistoric, unforgettable other person who is never equaled by anyone later. Even the chronic symptom of a pathological desire to lie in bed is explained in the same way. One of my patients still whimpers in his sleep as he did long ago (in order to be taken into bed by his mother, who died when he was 22 months old). Attacks never seem to occur as an "intensified expression of emotion."

A fragment from my daily experience: One of my patients, in whose history her highly perverse father plays the principal role, has a younger brother who is looked upon as a common scoundrel. One day the latter appears in my office to declare, with tears in his eyes, that he is not a scoundrel but is ill, with abnormal impulses and inhibition of will. He also complains, entirely as an aside, about what surely are nasal headaches. I direct him to his sister and brother-in-law, whom he indeed visits. That evening the sister calls me because she is in an agitated state. Next day I learn that after her brother had left, she had an attack of the most dreadful headaches—which she otherwise never suffers from. Reason: the brother told her that when he was 12 years old, his sexual activity consisted in kissing (licking) the feet of his sisters when they were undressing at night. In association, she recovered from her unconscious the memory of a scene in which (at the age of 4) she watched her papa, in the throes of sexual excitement, licking the feet of a wet nurse. In this way she surmised that the son's sexual preferences stemmed from the father; that the latter also was the seducer of the former. Now she allowed herself to identify with him and assume his headaches. She could do this, by the way, because during the same scene the raving father hit the child (hidden under the bed) on the head with his boot.

The brother abhors all perversity, whereas he suffers from compulsive impulses. That is to say, he has repressed certain impulses which are replaced by others with compulsions. This is, in general, the secret of compulsive impulses. If he could be perverse, he would be healthy, like the father.[5]

It is interesting that the calculation by successive summation yields *nothing*, regardless of whether or not the intrauterine period is included in the calculations.

$$
\begin{array}{lllll}
\text{I.} & 12\pi & = \text{T} & = 276 \text{ days (intrauterine)} \\
& + \\
& 3 \times 12\pi & = 3\text{T} & = 2 \text{ years} + 3 \text{ months (extrauterine)} \\
& + \\
& 6 \times 12\pi & = 9\text{T} & = 6 \text{ years} + 9 \text{ months} \\
& + \\
& 12 \times 12\pi & = 21\text{T} & = 15 \text{ years} + 9 \text{ months} \\
\text{II.} & 12\pi & = & \phantom{=} 9 \text{ months} \\
& + \\
& 3 \times 12\pi & = 4\text{T} & = 3 \text{ years} \\
& + \\
& 6 \times 12\pi & = 10\text{T} & = 7 \text{ years} + 6 \text{ months} \\
& + \\
& 12 \times 12\pi & = 22\text{T} & = 16\tfrac{1}{2} \text{ years}
\end{array}
$$

It works only if the intrauterine $12\pi$ are included in the calculation and in the total summation, as in the last letter.[6] This must have some significance, don't you think?

I am very glad they did not see more in your lecture. So one can just quietly go on cursing them; they are a rather stupid bunch and should leave us alone.

Now a private matter: Oscar and Melanie visited us and made a good impression. I cannot help but like him again. I do *not* want to ask you explicitly about the truth of a rumor which connects Marie B. with Robert Br., but merely indicate that I know about it. I wish them all the best, only I am quite certain that I do not want to meet the Breuer clan. I am fully occupied, ten to eleven hours a day, and correspondingly well, but almost hoarse. Is that excessive strain on the vocal cords or aneurysm?[7] *No* reply needed either. The best thing is to take old Candide's advice: *travailler sans raisonner.*

I really know nothing about a spontaneous resolution of pupillary paralysis in tabes and doubt that something can be found. It is of course a priori very improbable. Certainly, phosphorus?

I have now adorned my room with plaster casts of Florentine statues. It was a source of extraordinary invigoration for me; I am thinking of getting rich, in order to be able to repeat these trips. A congress on Italian soil! (Naples, Pompeii.)

Most cordial greetings to you all.

Your
Sigm.

1. *Bewusstsein*, or "consciousness."

2. A *fuero* was an ancient Spanish law still in effect in some particular city or province, guaranteeing that region's immemorial privileges.

3. Freud uses the Greek letter $\pi$ for "period."

4. In the diagram *T* stands for *Tragzeit*, the period of gestation.

5. See *Three Essays on the Theory of Sexuality*: "Thus symptoms are formed in part at the cost of abnormal sexuality; *neuroses are, so to say, the negative of perversions*" (*S.E.* 7:165). See also letters of January 11 and January 24, 1897, and *S.E.* 7:50.

6. Freud seems to be referring to an earlier portion of *this* letter, perhaps written at a different time, rather than to the preceding letter.

7. *Anfänge* reads *Angstneurose*, but the manuscript clearly has *Aneurysm*, a morbid dilatation of an artery.

---

Vienna, December 17, 1896

Dear Wilhelm,

I guessed the cause of your delay [in writing] and could still notice from your letter that you had had a bad period, which I hope is now past. I am very satisfied, however, with the reception of my fantasies. I know that you put them in the right place, pursue these viewpoints further, and regard me neither as a fantasist because I report on such unfinished things, nor as a fool who for this reason believes himself to be above scrutiny and correction. These are syntheses and working hypotheses,[1] which I trust we may exchange between the two of us without concern. My inner joy in suddenly being struck by an idea obviously was related not to the latent proofs but to finding a common ground for the work we share. I hope it will go so far that we can jointly build something definitive on it, and thereby blend our contributions to the point where our individual property is no longer recognizable. After all, I can collect facts only in the psychic sphere, you in the organological one; the in-between areas will require a hypothesis.

I cannot refrain from writing down for you, without proper order, some further facts and ideas. With regard to thrusts in psychic development we have the calculation based on 3, 6, 12 multiples of the gestation period; however, it may be possible to try another one that fits better with the characteristics of a process of accumulation. Namely, the summation would be calculated, not from the beginning, but starting with each breakthrough. Thus, 1T; next period from then on, 3T (total 4); next period from then on, 6T (total 10T); and so forth.

In this way the periods themselves, rather than the breakthroughs, would be numbered multiples. The same must apply to the 28[-day] π. I have not yet tried this new calculation. (Just done; doesn't work.) The principal idea in this attempt seems to me to be the different deployment of the two substances. I am therefore satisfied that so far you do not have an empirical reason to rule it out. From this position one can further glimpse the following: to begin with, both substances are released simultaneously every day; the differentiation of the sexes brings with it the surplus, and the latter makes itself felt, according to the different formulas of summation, at different times. Now one has to take into consideration the effects of [1] *abnormal production;* (2) *abnormal deployment of the reserves actually present at each particular time;* and (3) the sums attained, that is, the *breakthroughs.* Melancholia and mania (separation of the production) perhaps belong to [1] (production), although this is least clear. The actual neuroses, neurasthenia, and anxiety neurosis would belong to (2), the deployment of the actual reserves. The deployment would, after all, be a multiple one, psychic and somatic, and possibly even directly toxic. Anxiety would arise through the somatic deployment of the female 28-π substance if the sexual discharge is denied to it; and neurasthenia, through somatic deployment of the male substance.

Consequently, the menstrual days should accomplish, by summation, the discharge of the undeployed substances, with the symptoms showing neurasthenic characteristics at the 23-day dates and anxiety characteristics at the 28[-day periods]. When both substances are released simultaneously, mixtures of symptoms would be unavoidable. The toxic effect (resorption) could be considered analogous to mel[ancholia] and mania (not Melanie and Marie).[2]

The pathological manifestation of the effect of the periodic breakthroughs, differentiated according to sex, would show itself in the preconditions giving rise to compulsions and repression. Thus, one would also have to consider:

(1) The daily reserve;
(2) Its increase, in one sense or another, by the summation due on that particular day;
(3) The changes in it [brought about] by the large periods.

The "sign preceding" each special date would be *relative;* that is, according to whether the ♂ or ♀ substance has the ability to block a disease-producing substance.

Hidden deep within this is my ideal and woebegone child—metapsychology. The feeling of pleasure, I think, is a discharge rather than a sensation of intoxication.

Now, without any proper connection, something psychoneurotic. I am very glad you recognize that the elucidation of anxiety is pivotal. I may not yet have told you about the analysis of several phobias. "Anxiety about throwing oneself out of the window" is a misconstruction by the conscious, or rather the preconscious; it relates to an unconscious content in which "window" appears and can be dissected as follows:

Anxiety + . . . window . . .

and be explained thus:

*Unconscious* idea: going to the window to beckon a man to come up, as prostitutes do:

Sexual release arising from this idea

*Preconsciousness:* repudiation; hence, *anxiety* arising from the sexual release.

Out of this content only *window* becomes conscious because this element is raised as a compromise formation by virture of the idea "falling out of the window," which fits in with the anxiety. So they perceive *anxiety about the window* and interpret it in the sense of *falling out;* and even this is not always consciously present. Incidentally, either motive results in the same behavior: they do not go to the window. Think of Guy de Maupassant's *faire de la fenêtre.*[3]

Although I am aware of the inaccuracies and gaps in the superstructure and the inconsiderable stringency of the substructure, I did not want to keep this elaboration from you. First of all, you are not a Breuer to whom one may not show anything unfinished. Second, it is possible that you may do something with it; and third, [it is possible] that you can succeed in thoroughly dissuading me from using your periods in this way. You may be interested to hear how I arrived at it. I noticed that on certain dates, which clearly recur every 28 days, I have no sexual desire and am impotent—which otherwise is not yet the case, after all. Then, when the matter occurred to me, I had a happy day without really knowing why, a sort of blissful aftertaste like after a beautiful dream. Some of the motivation for it appeared subsequently but falls far short of justifying that feeling. Thus, more evidence must be in preparation in the unconscious.

It seems plausible to regard the periodic melancholia/mania as a temporal separation of the otherwise simultaneous release of pleasure and unpleasure.

At the same time I have found all sorts of nice explanations in my field. I actually confirmed a conjecture I had entertained for some time concerning the mechanism of agoraphobia in women. No doubt you will guess it if you think of "public" women. It is the repression of the intention to take the first man one meets in the street: envy of prostitution and identification. I could be satisfied in other respects as well, but so far not a single case is finished; I feel I am still missing an essential piece somewhere. As long as no case has been clarified and seen through to the end, I do not feel sure and I cannot be content. Once this has happened, I shall permit myself to have a good day between two nights of traveling [to visit you].

The explanation of the phase of "clownism" in Charcot's schema of [hysterical] attacks lies in the perversion of the seducers who, by virtue of the compulsion to repeat what they did in their youth, obviously seek their satisfaction by performing the wildest capers, somersaults, and grimaces. Furthermore: the clownism in boys' hysteria, the imitation of animals and circus scenes, which can be explained by the interweaving of childhood games played in the nursery and sexual scenes. Will you believe that the reluctance to drink beer and to shave was elucidated by a scene in which a nurse sits down *podice nudo* [with bare buttocks] in a shallow shaving bowl filled with beer in order to let herself be licked, and so on?

Binswanger has just published a thick handbook of neurasthenia in which the sexual theory—that is, my name—is not even mentioned! I shall take my cold revenge on him as soon as I know how to interpret neurasthenia on the foundation of what I hope will soon be our amalgamated theories.

Most cordial greetings to you, wife, and son.

Your
Sigm.

1. English in original.

2. Melanie and Marie Bondy were twin sisters of Ida Fliess, born in 1872. Fliess tells us this in his *Ablauf des Lebens,* 2nd ed., p. 100.

3. This refers to a short story, "Le Signe," which appeared in 1887 (see *Oeuvres complètes de Guy de Maupassant,* vol. 9, Paris: Louis Conard, 1919). A young married woman "calls" to a passerby from her window, after seeing a prostitute do the same. The expression used (p. 114) is *faire la fenêtre.*

---

December 22, 1896[1]
IX., Berggasse 19

[To Ida Fliess]
Dear friend,

Please accept this contribution to the portrait gallery of his ancestors as a sign that I share your aspirations for the little man, as you are aware from my love for the big one.

With all good wishes,

Your
Dr. Freud

1. The original of this letter was given me by Elenore Fliess, Wilhelm's daughter-in-law.

---

January 3, 1897
IX., Berggasse 19

Dear Wilhelm,

We shall not be shipwrecked. Instead of the channel we are seeking, we may find oceans, the more detailed exploration of which will be left to those who come after us; but if we do not prematurely capsize, if our constitutions can stand it,[1] we shall arrive. *Nous y arriverons.* Give me another ten years, and I shall finish the neuroses and the new psychology. You probably will need less time for your organology. In spite of the complaints you allude to, no New Year has ever found both of us as rich and as ripe. When I happen to be without anxiety, I am still ready to take on all the devils; and you have never known anxiety.

You surely do not believe that my neurotic theories have as flimsy a basis as the comments I am sending you on organology. Here I lack all material and can only guess; in my own field, I rely on the most solid foundation you could imagine. I certainly still have much to learn; thus, the limits of the time periods during which the individual neuroses arise will probably need to be corrected once the cases are terminated. While the work is in progress, it is precisely the neuroses that resist the determination of time more than any other factor. At present everything, it seems to me, is converging more and more on the first period of life, up to three years. This year I have had no further news from a patient with obsessional ideas whom I treated only for seven months. Yesterday I learned from Mrs. F. (who heard it from Professor Sulz [Petz?]) that this man traveled to his hometown in order to ascertain the reality of the things he remembered and that he received full confirmation from his seducer, who is still alive (his nurse, now an old woman).[2] He is said to be doing very well; he is obviously avoiding a complete cure, aided by this improvement. The agreement [of my material] with the perversions described by Krafft [-Ebing] is a new, valuable reality confirmation.

At our next congress I hope there will be important things to talk about. I think by Easter at the latest, maybe in Prague. Perhaps by then I shall have carried one case to completion.

That neuroses do not kill must, I believe, be interpreted as follows: that the two male and female sexual substances are not identical with the others whose vicissitudes you are pursuing, although all of them are released in 23- and 28-[day] thrusts. I would not like to have the border between neurotic and organic blurred. As for your equating migraine and stroke, I feel I could accept your idea only with regard to their form and period, but not with regard to their nature; that is, the identity of the substance. We shall see whether this will stand up.

The section on Therapy will be preceded by the quotation, "*Flavit et dissipati sunt*";[3] that on Sexuality, by the motto, "From heaven through the world to hell,"[4] if that is the correct quotation.

The piece for Nothnagel should be ready in fourteen days. I can also give you some news about G. de B. Your diagnosis was absolutely correct. Herewith the circumstantial evidence:

As a child she suffered greatly from anxiety. At age 8–10 fluor albus (white discharge). As a child she had a painful sensation in the vagina when she beat her little sister. She has the same sensation today when she reads and hears about horrors, cruelties. This youngest sister is the only one who, like herself, loves the father and also suffers from the same illness.

A conspicuous tic; she forms [her lips into] a snout (from sucking).

She is suffering from eczema around her mouth and from lesions that do not heal in the corners of her mouth. During the night her saliva periodically accumulates, after which the lesions appear. (Once before I traced back entirely analogous observations to sucking on the penis.)

In childhood (12 years) her speech inhibition appeared for the first time when, with a *full* mouth, she was fleeing from a woman teacher.

Her father has a similiarly explosive speech, as though his mouth were full.

*Habemus papam!*[5]

When I thrust the explanation at her, she was at first won over; then she committed the folly of questioning the old man himself, who at the very first intimation exclaimed indignantly, "Are you implying that I was the one?" and swore a holy oath to his innocence.

She is now in the throes of the most vehement resistance, claims to believe him, but attests to her identification with him by having become dishonest and swearing false oaths. I have threatened to send her away and in the process convinced myself that she has already gained a good deal of certainty which she is reluctant to acknowledge.

She has never felt as well as on the day when I made the disclosure to her. In order to facilitate the work, I am hoping she will feel miserable again.

The pain in her leg appears to have come from her mother.

At present I am looking forward to the solution of a case that simultaneously affords insight into two psychoses, that of the ill seducer and that of the woman seduced by the patient, who fell ill later. The case also is of organological interest, as you will see. (Oral sexual organs.)

My very best wishes for the New Year; give your dear wife my thanks and my best avuncular greetings to little Robert.

Your
Sigm.

1. This refers to the joke mentioned in the *Interpretation of Dreams* (*S.E.* 4:195). Freud uses it often in the ensuing letters — for instance, in that of July 17, 1899.

2. The Mosbacher translation implies that Freud heard this directly from his patient. Presumably the patient wished to verify the reconstruction, not Freud.

3. "He blew and they were scattered." Freud refers to this in the *Interpretation of Dreams* (*S.E.* 4:213–214), where he writes: "The Armada which sailed against *England*, after whose defeat a medal was struck, bearing the inscription *'Flavit et dissipati sunt'*, since the storm-blast had scattered the Spanish fleet. I had thought, half seriously, of using those words as the heading of the chapter on 'Therapy', if ever I got so far as producing a detailed account of my theory and treatment of hysteria." See also *S.E.* 5:469: "The fact that all the feces disappeared so quickly under the stream recalled the motto: *'Afflavit et dissipati sunt'*, which I intended one day to put at the head of a chapter upon the therapy of hysteria." For the meaning of the phrase in Freud's usage, see Schönau (1968, pp. 79–80).

4. Goethe, *Faust*, Prelude in the Theatre. See *S.E.* 7:161–162: "The highest and the lowest are always closest to each other in the sphere of sexuality: 'vom Himmel durch die Welt zur Hölle.' " For the significance of the passage, see Schönau (1968, pp. 84–85).

5. A victory cry, similar to "Eureka!" — literally, We have a Pope!

---

January 11, 1897
IX., Berggasse 19

Dear Wilhelm,

I am sending you, red-hot, two ideas which occurred to me today and which appear to me to be viable; they are based, of course, on the results of analyses.

(1) The determination of a psychosis (that is, amentia or a confu-

sional psychosis — a psychosis of being overwhelmed, as I called it earlier)[1] as opposed to a neurosis seems to be that sexual abuse occurs before the end of the first intellectual stage, that is, before the psychic apparatus has been completed in its first form (before the age of $1\frac{1}{4}$ to $1\frac{1}{2}$ years). It is possible that the abuse dates back so far that these experiences lie concealed behind the later ones and that they can be revived from time to time. Epilepsy, I believe, belongs to the same period (as in the dispute concerning Sophie, which I told you about). I shall have to deal differently with *tic convulsif*, which I previously assigned to the same stage. Here is how I arrived at this: one of my hysterical male patients (my millionaire) provoked in his eldest sister a hysterical psychosis which ended in a state of complete confusion. I have now traced his own seducer, a man of genius who, however, had had attacks of the severest dipsomania from his fiftieth year on. These attacks regularly started either with diarrhea or with a cold and hoarseness (the oral sexual system!) — that is, with the reproduction of his own passive experiences. Now, until he fell ill himself, the man had been a pervert and consequently healthy. His dipsomania arises through the intensification or, better, *substitution* of the one impulse for the associated sexual one. (The same is probably true of the gambling mania of old F.) Scenes took place between this seducer and my patient, in some of which his little sister (less than a year old) participated.[2] The patient had relations with her later on and she became psychotic in puberty. You may gather from this how a neurosis escalates to a psychosis in the next generation — which is called degeneracy — simply because someone of a more tender age is drawn in. Here, by the way, is the heredity of this case:

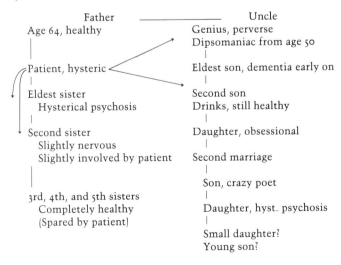

| Father | Uncle |
|---|---|
| Age 64, healthy | Genius, perverse<br>Dipsomaniac from age 50 |
| Patient, hysteric | Eldest son, dementia early on |
| Eldest sister<br>Hysterical psychosis | Second son<br>Drinks, still healthy |
| Second sister<br>Slightly nervous<br>Slightly involved by patient | Daughter, obsessional |
| | Second marriage |
| | Son, crazy poet |
| 3rd, 4th, and 5th sisters<br>Completely healthy<br>(Spared by patient) | Daughter, hyst. psychosis |
| | Small daughter?<br>Young son? |

I hope I shall be able to tell you much else of importance about this particular case, which throws light on three forms of illness.

(2) Perversions regularly lead to zoophilia and have an animal character. They are explained not by the functioning of erogenous zones that later have been abandoned, but by the effect of erogenous *sensations* that later lose their force. In this connection one recalls that the principal sense in animals (for sexuality as well) is that of smell, which has been reduced in human beings. As long as smell (or taste) is dominant, urine, feces, and the whole surface of the body, also blood, have a sexually exciting effect.[3] The heightened sense of smell in hysteria presumably is connected with this. The fact that the groups of sensations have much to do with psychological stratification presumably follows from the distribution in dreams and presumably has a direct connection with the mechanism of hysterical anesthesias.[4]

You see that I am in the full swing of discovery; in other respects, too, I am very well. Now I would like to hear the same from you.

Cordial greetings.

Your
Sigm.

1. See Draft K with letter of January 1, 1896.

2. *Beteiligt*; previously mistranslated as "was present." What Freud meant by her taking part is ambiguous.

3. *Anfänge* reads *Haare* (hair) and *Kopf* (head). However, the manuscript clearly reads *Harn* (urine) and *Kot* (feces), which make better sense in the context.

4. The meaning of this passage is not clear.

January 12, 1897
IX., Berggasse 19

Dear Wilhelm,

Would you please try to search for a case of childhood convulsions that you can trace back (in the future or in your memory) to sexual abuse, specifically to *lictus* [licking] (or finger) in the anus. There must, after all, be some indications or reasons to suspect this where it has occurred. This would then cover the [well-]known functional category in the literature: worm irritation, dyspepsia, and the like. For my newest finding is that I am able to trace back with certainty a patient's attack that merely resembled epilepsy to such treatment by the tongue on the part of his nurse. Age 2 years. — Substitute early infancy and you get the semblance of epileptic psychosis in the reproduction [of the scene]. I have firm confidence in this novelty as well as in yesterday's about the precondition of age in psychosis.

In the case of R.L., who was the subject of the dispute between B. and me, convulsions occurred once prior to age one;[1] two younger sisters are completely healthy, as though the father (whom I know to be a loathsome fellow) had convinced himself of the damaging effects of his caresses.

Cordially,

Your
Sigm.

1. Meaning unclear; could also be "one year ago."

---

January 17, 1897
IX., Berggasse 19

My dear Wilhelm,

You are obviously enjoying the goings-on in my head; that is why I shall let you know every time there is something new. I still think highly of the determination of the psychoses and shall present the material to you soon. You caused me to doubt my explanation of epilepsy, but it is not yet entirely shattered. What would you say, by the way, if I told you that all of my brand-new prehistory of hysteria[1] is already known and was published a hundred times over, though several centuries ago? Do you remember that I always said that the medieval theory of possession held by the ecclesiastical courts was identical with our theory of a foreign body and the splitting of consciousness? But why did the devil who took possession of the poor things invariably abuse them sexually and in a loathsome manner? Why are their confessions under torture so like the communications made by my patients in psychic treatment? Sometime soon I must delve into the literature on this subject. Incidentally, the cruelties make it possible to understand some symptoms of hysteria that until now have been obscure. The pins which make their appearance in the oddest ways; the sewing needles on account of which the poor things let their breasts be mutilated and which are not visible by X-ray, though they can no doubt be found in their seduction stories! Eckstein has a scene [that is, remembers] where the diabolus sticks needles into her fingers and then places a candy on each drop of blood. As far as the blood is concerned, you are completely without blame! A counterpart to this: fear of needles and pointed objects from the second psychic period. In regard to cruelty in general: fear of injuring someone with a knife or otherwise.

Once more, the inquisitors prick with needles to discover the devil's stigmata, and in a similar situation the victims think of the same old cruel story in fictionalized form[2] (helped perhaps by disguises of the seducers). Thus, not only the victims but also the executioners recalled in this their earliest youth.

On Saturday I fulfilled my duty of giving an account of your work on the nose in my course on neuroses, and on Thursday I shall continue it. The five boys[3] properly pricked up their ears. Indeed, it already makes enthralling [material].

As you see, I am doing very well. Why are you not feeling lively now? Oscar and Melanie recently paid us a pleasant visit.

Cordial greetings to your wife and your boy.

Your
Sigm.

Prague at Easter, then.

1. *Hysterie-Urgeschichte,* no doubt a reference to the time of life (in childhood) when seduction occurred.

2. The German reads: "Nun stechen die Inquisitoren wieder mit Nadeln um die Stigmata Diaboli zu finden, und in der ähnlichen Situation fällt den Opfern in Dichtung (vielleicht durch Verkleidungen der Verführer unterstützt) die alte grausame Geschichte ein. So erinnerten sich dabei nicht nur die Opfer sondern auch die Henker an ihre erste Jugend."

The passage is not easy to translate or understand. *Dichtung* here refers to fiction and readily suggests the contrast between *Wahrheit und Dichtung* (truth and fiction), as if Freud were saying that the *Geschichte* was an invention, that is, that the patients have fantasies about seductions. On the other hand, *einfallen* does not imply "invent," the word chosen by Strachey, but rather "thinking of something" or "something comes to mind."

So if Freud had only said *fällt den Opfern die alte grausame Geschichte ein,* he would certainly have meant that an actual event, a seduction, occurs to the patients. By adding *in Dichtung,* he raises the question of whether the stories occurring to the patient were true or invented. The very ambiguity of this passage presages the change in Freud's views that is soon to follow (see letter of September 21, 1897), in the course of which he begins to feel, for the first time, that the stories he heard in his practice were fiction—in other words, invented. But it is also possible that by *in Dichtung* Freud is referring to the fact that the real events return in memory, disguised and distorted. They are worked over, because repression will not allow them free access to memory.

The last sentence is particularly difficult. I think Freud reverts here to his belief in the reality of the seductions and might mean that both the judges and their victims, the witches, had been seduced in childhood. If this interpretation is correct, it clarifies the equally obscure sentence in the next letter, where Freud claims that he now understands the severity of the judges. If they are carrying out an act of vengeance for a seduction in their own past, their severity is merely a distorted form of memory, what Freud was later to call a piece of action. The vengeance the judges extract is to render the passive experience active, inflicting the same torture on the witches that they underwent as children. Presumably the needles then stand for the penis during intercourse (in the case of the judges, anal intercourse). The witches confess to the truth of the event only because they are confessing to a much earlier truth — finally acknowledging that they themselves have been abused.

*Verkleidungen* also is ambiguous. Is it the seducer who disguises himself, or is it the victim who disguises the seducer? The latter interpretation is suggested in Freud's letter of January 24, 1897: "the evildoers, who are, of course, concealed through defense."

3. The course in question was entitled "Vorlesungen über die grossen Neurosen." It was taught twice a week, Wednesday from 7 to 8 P.M. and Saturday from 7 to 9 P.M., during the winter semester 1896–97; see Gicklhorn and Gicklhorn (1960, p. 152). Four of the people taking the course have been identified: Simon Hochenwarter, Arthur Schüller, Peter Stampfl, and Ludwig Teleky. A list of Freud's students from 1886 to 1919 has been compiled by Gicklhorn and Gicklhorn. They prepared a more complete version than the one published, giving the semester of inscription for each student. This unpublished list is in the library of the Sigmund Freud Haus in Vienna.

---

January 24, 1897
IX., Berggasse 19

My dear Wilhelm,

It is nice that you take my requests so seriously. But the case of convulsions is certainly not one of the expected ones. I still believe fully in the matter itself. Most of my hunches *in neuroticis* [in regard to neuroses] subsequently turned out to be true. Incidentally, the whole thing is based on a case in which epileptiform convulsions could with certainty be traced back to similar excitations in later months. I do not yet have new material. The early period before the age of 1½ years is becoming ever more significant. I am inclined to distinguish several periods even within it. Thus I was able to trace back, with certainty, a hysteria that developed in the context of a periodic mild depression to a seduction, which occurred for the first time at 11 months and [I could] hear again the words that were exchanged between two adults at that time! It is as though it comes from a phonograph. The temporal determination of epilepsy (hysterical) and hysterical psychosis therefore lies further back. But there also is a psychotic feature in the periodicity of the mild depression.

The idea of bringing in witches is gaining strength. I think it is also appropriate. Details are beginning to abound. Their "flying" is explained; the broomstick they ride probably is the great Lord Penis. The secret gatherings, with dancing and entertainment, can be seen any day in the streets where children play. I read one day that the gold the devil gives his victims regularly turns into excrement; and the next day Mr. E., who reports that his nurse had money deliria, suddenly told me (by way of Cagliostro—alchemist—*Dukatenscheisser* [one who defecates ducats]) that Louise's money always was excrement. So in the witch stories it is merely transformed back into the substance from which it arose. If only I knew why the devil's semen is always described as "cold" in the witches' confessions. I have ordered the *Malleus maleficarum,* and now that I have put the final touch on the infantile paralyses I shall study it diligently. The story of the devil, the vocabulary of popular swearwords, the songs and customs of the nursery—all these are now gaining significance for me. Can you *without* trouble recommend to me some good reading from your excellent memory? In connection with the dancing in witches' confessions, remember the dance epidemics in the Middle Ages. E.'s Louise was such a dancing witch; he was first, consistently enough, reminded of her at the ballet. Hence his theater anxiety.

Gymnastic feats in the hysterical attacks of boys and the like belong in the category of flying and floating.

I am beginning to grasp an idea: it is as though in the perversions, of which hysteria is the negative, we have before us a remnant of a primeval sexual cult, which once was—perhaps still is—a religion in the Semitic East (Moloch, Astarte). Imagine, I obtained a scene about the circumcision of a girl. The cutting off of a piece of the labium minor (which is even shorter today), sucking up the blood, after which the child was given a piece of the skin to eat. This child, at age 13, once claimed that she could swallow *a* part of an earthworm and proceeded to do it. An operation you once performed was affected by a hemophilia that originated in this way.[1]

Perverse actions, moreover, are always the same—meaningful and fashioned according to some pattern that someday will be understood.

I dream, therefore, of a primeval devil religion with rites that are carried on secretly, and understand the harsh therapy of the witches' judges. Connecting links abound.

Another tributary of the stream is derived from the consideration that there is a class of people who to this very day tell stories like those of the witches and of my patients;[2] they are not believed, although their faith in their stories is not to be shaken. As you have guessed, I mean paranoiacs, whose complaints that excrement is put in their food, that they are maltreated at night in the most shameful way sexually, and so on, are pure memory content.

You know that I make a distinction between delusions of memory and delusions of interpretation. The latter are connected with the characteristic vagueness concerning the evildoers, who are, of course, concealed through defense.

One more detail. In hysteria I recognize the *pater* in the high demands made in love, in the humility in relation to the lover, or in the inability to marry because of unfulfilled ideals. The reason for this is, of course, the height from which the father lowers himself to the child. Compare with this, in paranoia, the combination of delusions of grandeur and fictions of an alienation of parentage. This is the reverse of the coin.

At the same time I am becoming unsure about a conjecture I have hitherto entertained that the choice of neurosis is determined by the period in which it originates; it seems rather to be fixed in earliest childhood. But the decision keeps on oscillating between the period in which it originated and the period in which repression occurs (which is what I presently prefer).

In this abundance of visions it leaves me entirely cold that the board of professors has proposed a younger colleague in my specialty for Extraordinarius [associate professor], thus passing me over, if the news is true.[3] It leaves me entirely cold, but it will perhaps hasten my final break with the university.

With letters such as this one I have exhausted everything before our congress; so instead I shall listen to how the facts of periodicity arrange themselves for you and get the finished substructure from you instead of fantasizing it.

Write to me again soon.

I think I have now passed the critical age.[4] My condition is so much more stable.

Cordially, to you, wife, and child,

Your
Sigm.

1. A reference to the operation on Eckstein.

2. The manuscript reads *meine Patienten*, which makes better sense than *mein Patient* as in *Anfänge*.

3. Freud had presumably heard a rumor to this effect. In fact, on February 13, 1897, the Professorenkollegium recommended four docents for the title of Extraordinarius: Freud, L. Frankl-Hochwart (neuropathology), J. Pal (internal medicine), and R. Limbeck (internal medicine). See Gicklhorn and Gicklhorn (1960, pp. 18–19) and

Eissler (1966, p. 182). Freud probably means Frankl-Hochwart (1862–1914), Privatdozent only since 1891, who in fact obtained the title of Extraordinarius the following year (1898), whereas Freud had to wait until 1902.

4. For Freud's preoccupation with his "critical age" see Schur (1972).

---

February 8, 1897
IX., Berggasse 19

Dear Wilhelm,

Breuer, whom they call the good one, cannot let any opportunity go by when there is a chance of spoiling the most harmless state of contentment. He received my book[1] and thereupon paid a visit to my wife to ask her how the publisher may have reacted to the unanticipated size of this work. The publisher, for whom he is so concerned, and Nothnagel assured me that it did not matter, that the entire work is sure to have splendid sales. The opus really did turn out to be larger than is appropriate to the established size of the series. Confronted with this contrast, I am, however, especially grateful to you for your friendly evaluation—you, the "blunt one"—and merely give expression to my astonishment that you were at all able to look through it in this short time.

That I am the "nobody" in Vienna who believes in your series you undoubtedly know. Brother-in-law Oscar makes very strange compromises between the claims made on him by his relatives and by acquaintances. He is, in equal measure, admiring and rejecting because the authority sitting in judgment in his intellect is strangely impartial. Thus, he is now enthusiastic about my addition of periodic mental development in series of 13. The truth is that I have long since given up my attempt, never intended seriously, to play on your flute. I would rather have you present a concert to me at Easter.

I.K. with the dyspnea (?!?) is not my patient. If you knew Z.v.K.,[2] you would not doubt for a moment that only this woman could have been my teacher. You probably saw a sister-in-law of hers.

I must correct one item I reported to you recently. When I called on Nothnagel a short time ago to present him with a complimentary copy, he told me spontaneously and, for the time being as a secret, that he and Krafft-Ebing would propose me for a professorship (as well as Frankl-Hochwart) and he showed me the document they had signed. He added that if the board did not go along, the two of them on their own would submit the proposal to the ministry. "Being a sensible man," he added, "you are aware of the further difficulties. It may achieve no more than bring up your name for discussion. We all know how little likelihood there is that the minister will accept the proposal."[3]

The proposal may have been brought up at yesterday's meeting. What pleases me in this is that I can go on regarding the two men as decent people; for, seriously, if they had passed me over, it would have been difficult for me to think well of them.

I have not written for a week because work (11½ to 12½ hours daily) has indeed exhausted my strength. In the evening I have been as ready to drop as if I had been chopping wood.

My predictions with regard to this season turned out to be right. I now have ten patients in treatment, including one from Budapest; another one from Breslau is due to arrive. It is probably one hour too much, though otherwise I feel best precisely when I am working a lot. Last week, for example, I earned 700 florins[4]—you don't get that for nothing. Getting rich must be very difficult.

The progress of my work is splendid, but riddles and doubts do of course still abound. I do not want to tell you everything *before* our congress. By then, perhaps, one case will be entirely finished. Until this has been accomplished, there really can be no certainty.

February 11. Pressure of work and two poor[5] days—a rarity nowadays—have delayed me. I had been meaning to ask you, in connection with the eating of excrement [by] [illegible words] animals, when disgust first appears in small children and whether there exists a period in earliest infancy when these feelings are absent. Why do I not go into the nursery and experiment with Annerl? Because working for 12½ hours, I have no time for it, and the womenfolk do not support my researches. The answer would be of theoretical interest. Theory, by the way, appears very remote from me at present. I am postponing all attempts to gain understanding. Even the chronological relationships have become uncertain.

Somnambulism, as we surmised at Dresden, has been correctly understood. The most recent result is the unraveling of hysterical cataleptic fits: imitation of death with rigor mortis, that is, identification with someone who is dead. If she has seen the dead person, then glazed eyes and open mouth; if not, then she just lies there quietly and peacefully.

Hysterical cold shivers = being taken out of a warm bed. Hysterical headache with sensations of pressure on the top of the head, temples, and so forth, is characteristic of the scenes where the head is held still for the purpose of actions in the mouth. (Later reluctance at photographer's, who holds head in a clamp.)

Unfortunately, my own father was one of these perverts and is responsible for the hysteria of my brother (all of whose symptoms are identifications) and those of several younger sisters. The frequency of this circumstance often makes me wonder.

In any case, I shall bring a lot of strange material with me to Prague.

My cordial greetings to you, wife, and child. Mine are doing excellently.

Your
Sigm.

1. "Infantile Cerebral Paralyses," in Nothnagel's volume.

2. Cäcilie M. in *Studies on Hysteria.*

3. The following committee was appointed to nominate Freud for the title of professor extraordinarius (the equivalent of associate professor, although at the time it was far more prestigious than such a position today): Hofräte Nothnagel, von Schrötter, Neusser, Krafft-Ebing, and Ludwig, and Professors Weichselbaum and Exner. A document dated May 10, 1897, in support of Freud's appointment was signed by all the committee members; it is in Krafft-Ebing's handwriting and probably is his work. The fairly long (four printed pages) and detailed account is almost entirely positive. After listing Freud's early work on hysteria, Krafft-Ebing gives a paragraph which, for the following reasons, I believe must have come from Freud:

(a) Freud says that he prepared an account of his work for Krafft-Ebing;

(b) Krafft-Ebing, as we know from his many publications, did not share the views advanced in this paragraph (he never mentions Freud in his otherwise detailed bibliographies);

(c) These *are* Freud's views.

I quote from this document, printed in German in Gicklhorn and Gicklhorn (1960, pp. 94–98; my translation): "The principal theme in creating these works was to gain deeper insight into the mechanism of neurotic processes by the application of a new psychotherapeutic method for which Dr. Breuer gave the idea, in the hope that ways and means for curing such neuroses could be found. In the course of these laborious clinical researches Freud reached surprising results that are extremely important for the etiology of the neuroses. He proved that a major factor in the development of hysterical and neurasthenic conditions, which until then had been totally unintelligible with respect to their etiology, was the existence of anomalies and experiences in the domain of the patient's sexual life and that only their identification and elimination could bring help in individual cases, brilliantly demonstrating this especially in regard to so-called obsessions and phobias."

If we remember that only months before, Krafft-Ebing had listened to these very ideas (in Freud's "Aetiology of Hysteria" lecture of April 21, 1896) and called them a "scientific fairy tale," we can be fairly certain that Krafft-Ebing did not believe what he was saying (and most likely took his statement directly from Freud's report). That he prepared the document at all, from a feeling of collegial responsibility, is commendable. Krafft-Ebing goes on to add these words of mild criticism: "The novelty of this research and the difficulty of verifying it does not allow us, at this point, to judge its importance with certainty. It is possible that Freud overestimates it and that he overgeneralizes the results he obtained." And then Krafft-Ebing says, in what is undoubtedly his own fair judgment, "In any event, his research in this field gives proof of unusual talent and of an ability to guide scientific investigations in new directions."

At the meeting of the medical Professorenkollegium of June 12, 1897, Freud was recommended for the position with twenty-two votes in favor and ten opposed. J. Pal was recommended at the same meeting. Ernst Wertheim would be recommended on February 13, 1897, Josef Ritter O. Metnitz on March 27, and Heinrich Paschkis on July 14, 1897. Freud, as we know (note 3 to letter of January 24, 1897), was not actually appointed until 1902.

4. Gicklhorn and Gicklhorn (1960, p. 19n1) claim they were told by former patients of Freud that at the turn of the century Freud charged 30 gold crowns per session.

5. The literal translation is "badly accentuated."

---

March 7, 1897
IX., Berggasse 19

Dear Wilhelm,

Your wife has risen once again like a meteor in our midst and as usual has outshone everybody and everything, so that next to her the others gave the impression of those eyeless fish that live in the depths of the sea. Unfortunately I saw very little of her; she found me dead tired, a consequence of my present ten- to eleven-hour workday. She let me know that you have found many new things and are looking forward to Easter. The latter, at least, is true in my case as well. It is still a long way off.

I have remained silent for a longer period of time because I noticed that at present you could not answer my letters overflowing with details, because I do not want to deplete myself completely before the congress, and because I was—once again—very tired (overdetermined!). Now I am having a much better time of it. I have not yet finished a single case; am still struggling with the difficulties of treatment and of understanding, which depending on my mood appear to me larger or smaller. On the whole, my constitution is still holding up.

March 17. You surely could not have guessed how very moved I was by your glorious simile of the dying Spartans. It would have impressed me on other occasions as well, but it reached me at precisely the moment when I was ready to give up for lost my Mathilde, who has fallen ill with septic diphtheria, and it comforted me. Today, it seems to me, there has been a decided improvement, which fills us with hope. Uncle Rie really did everything one could and in these circumstances always presents his best side. He and Kassowitz[1] were against the injections recommended by Behring.

I hope that what follows will not spoil the prospect of meeting you in Prague at Easter. For now I close so that I can finally send off this long-delayed letter.

Cordial greetings.

Your
Sigm.

1. Max Kassowitz (1842–1913) was from 1882 to 1906 director of the Öffentliches Kinder-Krankeninstitut, where Freud worked as head of the Nervenkrankheiten section between 1886 and 1896. See Gicklhorn and Gicklhorn (1960) and Lesky (1978, pp. 369 ff.).

March 29, 1897
IX., Berggasse 19

My dear,

Today, after a week-long misery, extending from one special date to the next one, I woke up refreshed. Mathilde is well, except for albuminuria; still in bed. Today everything will be disinfected. The others have remained well.—Cordial thanks for your lecture;[1] it reveals an unbelievable power of condensing thoughts and in twenty minutes leads one through the universe. Can well believe that you needed [to make] the remark about the audience's changing expression.[2] I yearn for the days in Prague. In these bad days my work is a terrible torture for me. How fortunate that I no longer see Br[euer]. He would surely have advised me to emigrate.[3] I am still having the same difficulties and have not finished a single case. I trust Robert has been well again for some time?

With cordial greetings to you and Ida,

Your
Sigm.

1. Freud is referring to a paper entitled "Über Dysmenorrhöe und Wehenschmerz," read at the meeting of the Gesellschaft für Geburtshilfe and Gynäkologie zu Berlin on December 11, 1896—an informal speech rather than a lecture, published in the *Zeitschrift für Geburtshilfe und Gynäkologie.* Here Fliess outlines his periodicity theory. He tells the audience that they know of course about a twenty-eight day period. But the "twenty-three day period, which you are hearing about here for the first time, will, in the future, occupy an equally important place in biology." A slightly paranoid cast and grandiosity are evident in this early lecture.

2. *Mimik.* The passage that Freud refers to concerning the audience's reaction is on p. 366 of Fliess's paper (see preceding note). Fliess evidently interrupted the lecture as follows: "For each one of these series of dates, I could also include the birthdates of the siblings on the mother's side, the uncles and aunts. I see, gentlemen, that this proposal stimulates your laughing muscles in a dubious manner. But I can

reveal to you that we are dealing here with a great law of nature, and I promise you, the time will come when you will be struck dumb by the greatness of this law!"

3. *Welch ein Glück, dass ich Breuer nicht mehr sehe. Er hätte mir schon gerathen auszuwandern.* This passage has been the source of much misunderstanding, because Jones, who cited the passage, mistranslated it. Of Freud he says: " In February [1896] he wrote to Fliess that it was impossible to get on any longer with Breuer, though only a week later he admitted that it was painful to think that Breuer was so entirely out of his life. A year later he was glad he saw no more of him: his very sight would make him inclined to emigrate. These are strong words, and there are stronger ones which need not be reproduced" (*Life* 1:280–281). Jones cites this letter as his source. They are indeed strong words, but they do not belong to Freud.

In notes that Jones wrote on the unpublished Fliess letters (which I saw in the Jones Archives in London), he wrote for this date of March 29: "Lucky don't see Br. more. make me emigrate." This is no doubt the source of the error.

---

April 6, 1897
IX., Berggasse 19

Dear Wilhelm,

Your interpretation of your dream is not that easy [to follow], but the dream should be right. I prefer Nuremberg to Prague, and would prefer even more to associate Venice with your periods if Venice were a city where one could take walks. However, since our congress will have a spring sequel for you — in which I cannot participate because now each day costs me 75 to 90 florins and the days are of no value in September — you should arrange things so that our meeting (the location of which is less important) fits in with your other plans, so that Ida can easily follow you, and so that you need not make a detour in continuing your journey. I shall therefore await your instructions on all counts. I can leave Friday evening and stay away until Wednesday morning at the latest.

Mathilde is well; yesterday for the first time there was no albumin. The child has been very good. Martha will perhaps take her along, if the time when she is to get out of bed is not too close to the departure for Aussee.

The point that escaped me in the solution of hysteria lies in the discovery of a different source, from which a new element of the product of the unconscious arises. What I have in mind are hysterical fantasies which regularly, as I see it, go back to things that children overhear at an early age and understand only subsequently. The age at which they take in information of this kind is, strangely enough, from six to seven months on! Brother-in-law Oscar implored me to drop this one point (probably he has been charged with this mission) and repeatedly asked me what you have to say about this novelty. I herewith give you official notice. I would gladly do without all these complications, but, as you know, *Que messieurs les assassins commencent.*[1] It is like the series [of periods]; if there were only two, they would be accepted more readily.

I have just written my curriculum vitae for Krafft-Ebing, who is writing a report on me.[2] Otherwise, accomplishments are negligible. The work of these weeks has really taxed my capacity to the limit.

I am positively delighted that it is less than two weeks until we meet again.

With the most cordial greetings to you, wife, and child,

Your
Sigm.

1. This is supposedly a quotation from Alphonse Karr (1808–1890), in the periodical *Les Guêpes*, January 1840: "Si l'on veut abolir la peine de mort en ce cas, que MM. les assassins commencent." (If the death penalty is to be abolished in this case, the murderers should be the first to begin [that is, they should cease killing].)

2. This document has not survived. Undoubtedly the substance of it has come down to us in Krafft-Ebing's report. See note 3 to Freud's letter of February 8, 1897.

---

April 12, 1897
IX., Berggasse 19

Dear Wilhelm,

With sorrow I hear that your old friend Siebert is causing you concern by the very illness with which I recently had occasion to become reacquainted; being unable to pronounce a prognosis for him, I am also sorry for myself because of the possibility that this may thwart our congress. I hope, of course, that things may yet turn out well and await your travel instructions, even if they should be conveyed by telegram.

I almost canceled out. Saturday afternoon Martin gave us a fright by suddenly becoming ill with symptoms in the throat, which Oscar did not want to diagnose immediately, whereas Laufer, whom he recommended, pronounced them to be diphtheria. I was shaken; the disinfection had been over for a week, the children were together again, and now we had to be prepared for one after the other taking turns, but would they all survive? In the evening I visited Oscar; a bad guest, of course, but glad to receive his assurance that all the indications pointed instead to a common throat infection.

Next morning Laufer apologized for having frightened us; it definitely was not diphtheria. He still has a fever, of course, but the picture is the same as in the other throat infections with which he periodically comes down. Afterward we recalled that the previous one broke out on February 14, that is, 2 × 28 days.

His illness will be of interest to you in another respect as well. On Friday evening (the day before) he suddenly produced a "poem," about which I hope Martha will write your wife in detail. On Saturday morning the second half of the poem came out; he gave it the title "Summer" and signed it, "Poet Martin Freud." He had scarcely finished neatly writing out the opus when he began to complain, and by evening his temperature already was high. So it was euphoria before the special date.[1] Oli must have had an inkling of this connection when next day he wrote in his essay of the day [diary?]: "Yesterday Martin was a poet; today he is quite ill." Much joy could be had from the little ones if there were not also so much fright. On these occasions I notice with sorrow how far down the overwork and tension of the last years have brought me. Do not imagine that therewith I want to contradict my own etiological theory. I long for a few beautiful days; for several weeks when I happened to have a free hour I did no more than cut open books, play solitaire, study the streets of Pompeii, and the like.

Let me hear from you very soon—only good things on all sides.

With most cordial greetings to you, your dear wife, and son,

Your
Sigm.

1. Although Fliess had not yet published on this topic, he must have told Freud of his belief in the connection between illness, creativity, and death. See his *Zur Periodenlehre*, esp. p. 59, quoted in note 6 to letter of November 27, 1893, with respect to Ludwig Pietsch.

---

Vienna, April 28, 1897

Dear Wilhelm,

Last night I had a dream[1] concerning you. It was a telegraph message about your whereabouts:

Via
"(Venice) Casa SECERNO"
Villa

The way I have written it out shows what seemed obscure and what seemed multiple. "Secerno" was clearest. My feeling about it was annoyance that you had not gone to the place I had recommended to you: Casa Kirsch.[2]

*Report on motives.*—The provoking cause: events from the previous day. H. was here and talked about Nuremberg, saying he knew it very well and used to stay at the Preller. I could not recall it at once, but afterward I asked, "Outside the town, then?" This conversation stirred up the regret I have felt lately at not knowing where you are staying and at having no news of you. For I wanted to have you as my public, tell you some of what I have been experiencing and finding out in my work. But I did not dare to send my notes out into the unknown, because I would have had to ask you to keep them for me as material of value. So it would be the fulfillment of a wish if you would telegraph your address to me. There are all kinds of things behind the wording of the telegram: the memory of the etymological enjoyment you usually give me, my allusion to H. to "outside the town," but more serious things as well, which soon occurred to me. "As though you must always have something special!" says my annoyance. Add to this, first, that you were unable to take any pleasure at all in the Middle Ages, and, further, my persistent reaction to your dream of defense, which tried to substitute the grandfather for the otherwise customary father. In that connection, my constantly tormenting myself about how I can give you a hint to find out who it was who called I.F. *Katzel* [kitten] when she was a child, as she now calls you. Since I myself am still in doubt about matters concerning fathers, my sensitiveness becomes understandable. Thus the dream brings together all the annoyance with you that is unconsciously present in me. Incidentally, the wording means still more:

Via (streets in Pompeii, which I am studying).

Villa (Böcklin's Roman villa).

Our talks about travel, then. Secerno sounds to me like Salerno: Neapolitan—Sicilian. Behind it your promise of a congress on Italian soil.

The complete interpretation occurred to me only after a lucky chance this morning brought a fresh confirmation of paternal etiology.[3] Yesterday I began the treatment of a new case: a young woman whom, for lack of time, I would have preferred to scare off. She had a brother who died insane; and her main symptom (insomnia) first appeared after she had heard the carriage that was taking him to the asylum drive away from the front door. Since then, anxiety at driving in a carriage and a conviction that there would be a carriage accident. Years later, the horses bolted during a drive and she used the opportunity to jump out of the carriage and break her foot. She came today and confessed[4] that she had thought a lot about the treatment and had discovered an obstacle. "What is that?" — "I can make myself out as bad as I must; but I must spare other people. You must allow me to name no names." — "No doubt names are unimportant. What you mean are your relations to people. Here it surely will not be possible to conceal anything." — "I really mean that earlier I should have been easier to treat than today. Earlier I was unsuspecting; but now the criminal significance of some things has become clear to me and I cannot make up my mind to talk about them." — "On the contrary, I believe a mature woman becomes more tolerant about sexual matters." — "Yes, you are right there. When I say that the people who are guilty of such things are noble and high-minded[5] I am bound to think that it is a disease, a kind of madness, and I must excuse them." — "Well then, let us speak plainly. In my analyses the guilty people are close relatives, father or brother." — "Nothing has gone on with my brother." — "Your father, then." And it then turned out that her supposedly otherwise noble and respectable father regularly took her to bed when she was from eight to twelve years old and misused her without penetrating ("made her wet," nocturnal visits). She felt anxiety even at the time. A sister, six years her senior, with whom she talked things over many years later, confessed to her that she had had the same experiences with their father. A cousin told her that when she was fifteen she had had to fend off her grandfather's embraces. Of course, when I told her that similar and worse things must have happened in her earliest childhood, she could not find it incredible. In other respects it is a quite ordinary case of hysteria with the usual symptoms.

Q.E.D.

1. See *S.E.* 4:137.

2. A *pensione* in Venice.

3. Surely a reference to Freud's belief (at this time) that a sexual seduction by the father lies at the heart of neurosis. See letter of December 12, 1897: "Mein Vertrauen in die Vaterätiologie ist sehr gestiegen" (My confidence in paternal etiology has risen greatly).

4. The manuscript reads *beichtet*, not *berichtet* as in *Anfänge*.

5. The manuscript reads *ausgezeichnete, edle Menschen*, not *ausgezeichnet* (as an adverb) *edle Menschen* as in *Anfänge*.

---

Vienna, May 2, 1897

Dear Wilhelm,

In the interim, received postcard and telegram and regret that the congress did not bring you what it brought me — pleasure and renewal. Since then I have been in a continual euphoria and have been working like a young man. As you will gather from the enclosure [Draft L], my acquisitions are becoming consolidated. In the first place, I have gained a sure inkling of the structure of hysteria. Everything goes back to the reproduction of scenes. Some can be obtained directly, others always by way of fantasies set up in front of them. The fantasies stem from things that have been *heard* but understood *subsequently,* and all their material is of course genuine. They are protective structures, sublimations of the facts, embellishments of them, and at the same time serve for self-relief. Their accidental origin is perhaps from masturbation fantasies. A second important piece of insight tells me that the psychic structures which, in hysteria, are affected by repression are not in reality memories—since no one indulges in memory activity without a motive—but *impulses* that derive from primal scenes.[1] I realize now that all three neuroses (hysteria, obsessional neurosis, and paranoia) exhibit the same elements (along with the same etiology) — namely, memory fragments, *impulses* (derived from memories), and *protective fictions;* but the breakthrough into consciousness, the formation of compromises (that is, of symptoms), occurs in them at different points. In hysteria, it is the memories; in obsessional neurosis, the perverse impulses; in paranoia, the protective fictions (fantasies) which penetrate into normal life amid distortions because of compromise.

In this I see a great advance in insight. I hope it strikes you in the same way.

Another confirmation of my protohysteria scenes. In the case of G., I discerned several weeks ago that his mild depression copies a mild depression of his father, which occurred when he himself was not yet quite 2 years old. This could be established in the following way: the father's depression was related to an illness of his which points to an old lues. (The old man actually has bilateral ptosis.) The man underwent a [course of] embrocation treatments that rendered him impotent and disposed him to melancholia. The interruption of marital intercourse was used by another man to force his attentions on the young wife, whereupon the husband, when he learned of his wife's pregnancy, had doubts about the paternity and considered divorce. Now that child is two and a half years younger than my patient; the events related occurred during the first months of the pregnancy, that is, during the period when he was 21 to 24 months old. The following happened: the father, now 62 years old, told his son with whose health he was dissatisfied, "You see, this is what happens when one consults physicians one does not know. In fact, I too was once depressed, thirty-five years ago *when you were not yet 2 years old;* I went to our family physician; he sent me away for six weeks and I was cured."

In other respects, too, we are very well at present. I still want to ask you whether it seems right to have a scraping of the throat and a tonsillectomy performed on Martin under light anesthesia and whether you do not think *Laufer* should be contraindicated. Please give me your opinion; I have become noticeably anxious this year.

On the 15th of May we go to Aussee, where, as you remember, a little guesthouse is waiting for you all. I cannot send you a model made of bread yet. My recovery so far extends only to unconscious work; I cannot yet do it consciously.

I hope that you have finally found the lakes enjoyable. Nor do I easily forgive you the criticism of Venice, but I understand a little of the harmony and the austere structure, built according to the most beautiful proportions, of your psychic processes.

Best wishes to you both for enjoyable days.

Your
Sigm.

1. A reference to Freud's belief that a sexual seduction by the father is the source of neurosis. See his letter of December 12, 1897.

## Draft L

[enclosed with letter]

*The Architecture of Hysteria*

The aim seems to be to reach the earliest [sexual] scenes.[1] In a few cases this is achieved directly, but in others only by a detour via fantasies. For fantasies are psychic facades produced in order to bar access to these memories. Fantasies simultaneously serve the tendency toward refining the memories, toward sublimating them. They are manufactured by means of things that are *heard,* and utilized *subsequently,* and thus combine things experienced and heard, past events (from the history of parents and ancestors), and things that have been seen by oneself. They are related to things heard, as dreams are related to things seen. In dreams, to be sure, we hear nothing; but we see.

### *The Part Played by Servant Girls*

An immense load of guilt, with self-reproaches (for theft, abortion), is made possible by identification with these people of low morals who are so often remembered, in a sexual connection with father or brother, as worthless female material. And, as a result of the sublimation of these girls in fantasies, most improbable charges against other people are contained in the fantasies. Fear of prostitution (fear of being in the street alone), fear of a man hidden under the bed, and so on, also point in the direction of the servant girl. There is tragic justice in the circumstance that the family head's stooping to a maidservant is atoned for by his daughter's self-abasement.

### *Mushrooms*

Last summer a girl was afraid to pick a flower or *even* to pull up a mushroom, because it was against the command of God, who did not wish living seeds to be destroyed. — This arose from a memory of religious scruples[2] of her mother's about precautions during coitus, because thereby living seeds would be destroyed. "Sponges" (Paris sponges)[3] were explicitly mentioned among these precautions. The main content of her neurosis was identification with her mother.

### *Pains*

Not an actual sensation of a fixation, but an intentional repetition of it. The child knocks up against a corner, a piece of furniture, or something similar, and so makes contact *ad genitalia,* in order to repeat a scene in which what is now the painful spot, and was then pressed against the corner, led to fixation.

### *Multiplicity of Psychic Personalities*

The fact of identification perhaps allows us to take the phrase *literally.*

### *Wrapping Up*

A supplement to the mushroom story. The girl demanded that all objects handed to her be wrapped up. (Condom.)

*Multiple Editions of Fantasies—Do they also connect back again [to the original experience]?*

In cases in which patients wish to be ill and cling to their suffering, this regularly happens because the suffering is regarded as a protective weapon against their own libido—that is, because of mistrust in themselves. In this phase the mnemic symptom becomes a defensive symptom: the two active currents combine. At earlier stages the symptom was a consequence of the libido, a provocative symptom: it may be that between the stages fantasies serve for defense.

It is possible to follow the path, the time, and the material of the formation of fantasies, which then closely resembles the formation of dreams. But there is no regression in the form [of representation the fantasies are given], only progression. A relationship among dreams, fantasies, and reproduction.

*Another Wish-Dream*

"I suppose that this is a wishful dream," said E. "I dreamed that, just as I arrived at my house with a lady, I was arrested by a policeman, who requested me to get into a carriage. I demanded more time to put my affairs in order, and so on. It was in the morning, after I had spent the night with this lady."—"Were you horrified?"—"No."—"Do you know what you were charged with?"—"Yes. With having killed a child."—"Has that any connection with reality?"—"I was once responsible for the abortion of a child resulting from an affair. I dislike thinking about it."—"Well, had nothing happened on the morning before the dream?"—"Yes, I woke up and had intercourse."—"But you took precautions?"—"Yes. By withdrawing."—"Then you were afraid you might have made a child, and the dream shows you the fulfillment of your wish that nothing should happen, that you nipped the child in the bud. You made use of the feeling of anxiety that arises after a coitus of that kind as material for your dream."

1. *Urszenen.* Freud means, I believe, the scenes of real seduction—the earliest scenes. "Primal scene," in the later sense of intercourse between parents, is first used in the wolf-man discussion (*S.E.* 18:39n1).

2. The manuscript reads *Skrupel,* rather than *Sprüche* as in *Anfänge.*

3. A form of contraceptive. The German *Schwämme* means both "mushrooms" and "sponges."

May 16, 1897

Dear Wilhelm,

I am now ready to enjoy a nice Sunday evening and thank you for your last letter, which was so very edifying. Bunge[1] was extremely good for me. After all, we do not want to be the only intelligent people in the world; what makes sense to us must also be to the liking of a few capable fellows. Bunge surely makes up for a whole flock of university professors. I spared myself informing you of two miserable critiques that have come to my knowledge since Nuremberg — one of them by an assistant of Chrobak. You can calmly put up with it.

I could tell from your letter that you are mentally refreshed. I hope that now you will remain your old self again for a long time and will let me go on taking advantage of you as a kindly disposed audience. Without such an audience I really cannot work. If you agree, I shall proceed as I did last time and send you whatever notes I have ready, with the request that you return them when I ask. No matter where I start, I always am right back with the neuroses and with the ψ [psychic] apparatus. It certainly is neither personal nor objective indifference if I cannot get my pen to write anything else. Things are fermenting and bubbling in me; I am only waiting for a new thrust. I cannot make up my mind about writing the preliminary outline of the total work you desire; I believe what prevents me is an obscure expectation that shortly something essential will turn up. On the other hand, I have felt impelled to start working on the dream, where I feel so very certain — and in your judgment am entitled to. For the time being I had to interrupt; hurriedly had to prepare an abstract of all my publications[2] for the printer; the vote [on the professorship] is going to take place any day. Now I have finished and am thinking about the dream [book] again. I have been looking into the literature and feel like the Celtic imp: "Oh, how glad I am that no one, no one knows . . . "[3] No one even suspects that the dream is not nonsense but wish fulfillment.

I do not know whether I have already written to you about it; surely yes, and only as a precaution I repeat that now the source of auditory hallucinations in paranoia has been uncovered. The fantasies derive, as in hysteria, from what has been heard and understood *subsequently.*

A proud ship was wrecked for me a few days after my return. My banker, who was furthest along in his analysis, took off at a critical point, just before he was to bring me the last scenes. This certainly also damaged me materially, and convinced me that I do not yet know everything after all about the mainspring of the matter. But refreshed as I was, I easily took it in stride and told myself, so I shall wait still longer for a treatment to be completed. It must be possible and must be done.

Cousin Elise v. G. probably will leave shortly, or at least stop. Her behavior was very odd; it remains to be seen whether it [treatment] was of some use to her and whether she will want to continue. There is no question that the matter has not been finished.

I wanted to send the children to Aussee on the 18th; Martha wanted to stay here until Whitsun. The miserable weather made us postpone it indefinitely. Martin has had another attack of mild *poet*itis, this time somewhat prematurely, thirty-five days after the last poem, but $35 + 56 = 91$ since the last throat infection. By the way, this time the inspiration lasted more than two days; at the same time he lost two teeth, with two days in between. He wrote a poem, "Holidays in the Woods," and then a second, still incomplete one, "The Hunt." That his operation has been done, you can infer from the following verse from his "Conversations of Wise Animals":

"Hare," said the roe.
"Does your throat still hurt when you swallow?"

It was too funny for words when Oli, looking at this production, was indignant about the inevitable spelling mistakes. Really the Xenophon of the *Fliegende Blätter*, when the Greeks again saw the sea and exclaimed in delight, "thalassa" ("one can also say thalata"). Mathilde is now enraptured by mythology and recently wept bitter tears because the Greeks, who used to be such great heroes, suffered such heavy blows at the hand of the Turks. Quite an amusing bunch.

By the way, didn't you meet the Breuers in Bolzano? They left for Bolzano the day I arrived. Four weeks have already gone by since that beautiful first day of Easter.

I now have several new students and a real pupil — from Berlin, a Dr. Gattel,[4] who was an assistant at Levinstein's Maison de Santé and who came here to learn something from me. I promised to instruct him, in the old classical fashion (peripatetically) rather than in the laboratory and on the medical ward, and am curious to see how he will get on. Incidentally, he is half-American and a nephew of Professor Dresenfeld in Manchester.

During the past few days I had all sorts of fine ideas for you, but they have disappeared again. I must wait for the next thrust which will bring them back. Until then I would like to have good and detailed news of you, Ida, and Robert, as well as of how Siebert and your mother are.

Most cordial greetings and good luck in your work.

Your
Sigm.

1. Gustav Bunge (1844–1920), physiologist in Basel.

2. The abstract was published in *S.E.* 3:225–256.

3. The German text reads, "Ach wie bin ich froh, dass es niemand, niemand weiss." This was translated in *Origins* as, "How glad I am that no man's eyes have pierced the veil of Puck's [?] disguise" (p. 201). Freud is quoting from the brothers Grimm — Rumpelstilzchen, whose name nobody knows. Why Freud would call him a Celtic imp is not clear.

4. Felix Gattel, a Berlin physician, may actually have been sent to Freud by Fliess (see Decker, 1977; Sulloway, 1979, p. 513; and Jones, *Life* 1:334). In 1898 Gattel published a sixty-eight-page book, *Über die sexuellen Ursachen der Neurasthenie und Angstneurose* (Berlin: Hirschwald). Möbius gave it a negative review in *Schmidt's Jahrbücher der in- und ausländischen gesamten Medizin,* 259 (1898):214. More damaging was the review by Krafft-Ebing's assistant, P. Karplus (whom Gattel thanks in his preface), in *Wiener klinische Wochenschrift,* 2(1898):689–690, which includes a severe criticism of Freud. (Freud had evidently explained to Gattel that a "seductive" four-year-old girl is only "repeating an act that had previously been perpetrated on her," an idea that Karplus considers outrageous.)

---

May 25, 1897

Dear Wilhelm,

I am sending you herewith the "List of All the Beauties . . . "[1] The decision of the board has been delayed; there was new opposition and consequent postponement at the last meeting. Fortunately my interests lie elsewhere.

The enclosed contains a thrust of ideas which arouse great hope in me. If I manage to get through it, I shall make the familiar visit to Berlin. I estimate that this will not happen until next year.

I was very amused by your analyses of the gestation periods. If only I had the geometry for this algebra! In assuming these differences, you are obviously allowing for the position that it is not the day but the phase from ——— to ——— that determines the event. But then, what does N. [?] 23–28 mean, where 28 is larger than 23? The obscurity arouses the most interesting expectations.

My gang left for Aussee yesterday evening with Minna and arrived, according to reports, in beautiful weather. Martha will stay here until Whitsun.

| | |
|---|---|
| Martin's first throat infection | Sunday February 14 |
| Martin's second throat infection | Saturday April 10 |

(the onset, very probably, was Saturday February 13) = 56 days = 2 × 28

1st poem Dachstein — Friday April 9/Saturday April 10

2nd poem — Friday May 14

next day as well Saturday May 15

a little bit after Sunday May 16

(2 teeth in these 3 days)

3rd poem — Wednesday May 19

(definite decrease in poetic activity)

Most cordially,

Your
Sigm.

Birthday December 7, 1889

1. A phrase taken from Leporello in Mozart's opera *Don Giovanni*. This is the "Catalogue Aria," which refers to the hero's conquests. Here used playfully to refer to Freud's privately printed (by Deuticke) "Inhaltsangaben der wissenschaftlichen Arbeiten des Privatdozenten Dr. Sigm. Freud 1877–1897."

## Draft M. The Architecture of Hysteria

[enclosed with letter]

Probably like this: some of the scenes are accessible directly, but others only by way of fantasies set up in front of them. The scenes are arranged in order of increasing resistance; the more slightly repressed ones come [to light] first, but only incompletely on account of their association with the severely repressed ones. The path taken by [analytic] work first goes down in loops to the scenes or to their proximity, then from a symptom a little deeper down, and then again from a symptom deeper still. Since most of the scenes are combined in the few symptoms, our path makes repeated loops through the background thoughts of the same symptoms [see Fig. 6].

### *Repression*

It is to be supposed that the element essentially responsible for repression[1] is always what is feminine. This is confirmed by the fact that women as well as men admit more readily to experiences with women than with men. What men essentially repress is the pederastic element.

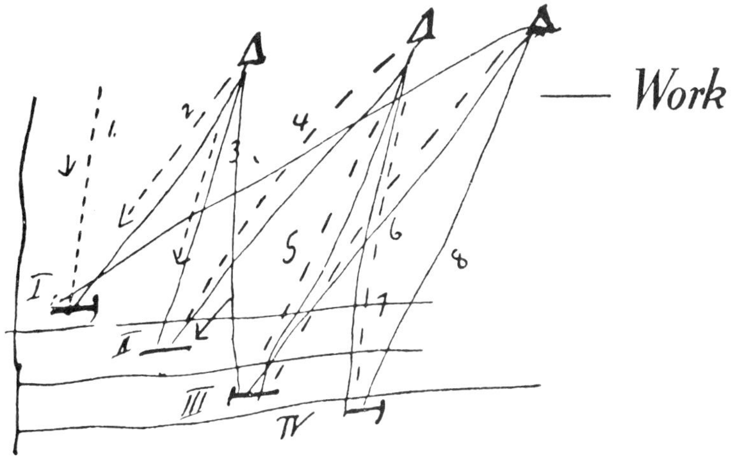


*Figure 6* [In the original all the dotted lines, arrows, and numerals are drawn in red, as well as the word "Work" and the line preceding it.]

*Fantasies*

Fantasies arise from an unconscious combination of things experienced and heard, according to certain tendencies. These tendencies are toward making inaccessible the memory from which symptoms have emerged or might emerge. Fantasies are formed by amalgamation and distortion analogous to the decomposition of a chemical body which is compounded with another one. For the first sort of distortion consists in a falsification of memory by fragmentation in which it is precisely the chronological relations that are neglected. (Chronological corrections seem specifically to depend on the activity of the system of consciousness.) A fragment of the visual scene then combines with a fragment of the auditory one into the fantasy, while the fragment set free links up with something else. Thereby an original connection has become untraceable. As a result of the formation of fantasies like this (in periods of excitation), the mnemic symptoms cease. Instead, unconscious fictions are present which have not been subjected to defense. If now the intensity of such a fantasy increases to a point at which it would be bound to force its way into consciousness, the fantasy is subject to repression and a symptom is generated through a [process of] pushing the fantasy back[2] to its constituent memories.

All anxiety symptoms (phobias) are derived in this way from fantasies. Nevertheless, this simplifies symptoms. A third forward movement and a third method of symptom formation perhaps start from impulse formations.[3]

### *Kinds of Compromise Displacement*

Displacement by association: hysteria.

Displacement by (conceptual) similarity: obsessional neurosis (characteristic of the place where the defense occurs, and perhaps also of the time).

Causal displacement: paranoia.

### *Typical Sequence of Events*

Good grounds for suspecting that the arousing of what is repressed is not left to chance but follows the laws of development. Further, that repression proceeds backward from what is recent, and affects the latest events first.

### *Difference between the Fantasies in Hysteria and Paranoia*

The latter are systematic, all of them in harmony with one another; the former are independent of one another, contradictory as well—that is, insulated, as if automatically generated (by a chemical process). This and neglect of the characteristic of time are no doubt essential for the distinction between activity in the preconscious and the unconscious.

### *Repression in the Unconscious*

It is not sufficient to take into account the repression between the preconscious and the unconscious; we must also consider the normal repression within the system of the unconscious itself.

Very significant, but still very obscure.

There is the soundest hope that it will be possible to determine the number and kind of fantasies just as it is possible with scenes. A romance of alienation (cf. paranoia) is found regularly and serves as a means of illegitimizing the relatives in question. Agoraphobia seems to depend on a romance of prostitution, which itself goes back once more to this family romance. Thus a woman who will not go out by herself asserts her mother's unfaithfulness.

1. The original reads *verdrängende*, rather than *verdrängt* as in *Anfänge.*

2. *Rückdrängung*, a word not found in the dictionary, was formed by Freud in analogy to *Verdrängung*, but implying a backward movement. Thus it could also be interpreted to imply that a symptom is generated by means of a regression or retrogression in which the fantasy is dissolved into its constituent elements.

3. Throughout this section Freud uses *Fantasiebildung* and *Symptombildung*, which Strachey, perhaps guided by the title "architecture," translated as "construction." "Formation," the term used here, is familiar to readers of English from subsequent writings of Freud.

May 31, 1897
IX., Berggasse 19

Dear Wilhelm,

Have not heard anything from you for a long time. Herewith a few scraps washed ashore by the last thrust. I am noting them down for you alone and hope you will keep them for me. I add nothing by way of apology or explanation: I know these are only premonitions, but something has come of everything of that sort; I have had to take back only the bits of wisdom I wanted to add to the Pcs. [preconscious system]. Another presentiment tells me, as though I already knew—but I know nothing at all—that I shall very soon uncover the source of morality. Thus, the whole matter is still growing in my expectation and gives me the greatest pleasure. If only you were nearer, so that I could tell you about it more easily.

Otherwise the feeling of summer is very powerful. Friday evening we plan to go to Aussee for Whitsun. I do not know whether anything worth reporting will still occur to me; I do not want to work on anything[1] any longer; I have laid aside even the dream [book]. Recently I dreamed of [having] overaffectionate feelings for Mathilde, only she was called Hella; and afterward I again saw "Hella" before me, printed in heavy type. Solution: Hella is the name of an American niece whose picture we have been sent.

Mathilde could be called Hella because she recently shed bitter tears over the defeats of the Greeks. She is enthralled by the mythology of ancient Hellas and naturally regards all Hellenes as heroes. The dream of course shows the fulfillment of my wish to catch a *Pater*[2] as the originator of neurosis and thus [the dream] puts an end to my ever-recurring doubts.

Another time I dreamed that I was going up a staircase with very few clothes on. I was moving, as the dream explicitly emphasized, with great agility. (My heart—reassurance!) Suddenly I noticed, however, that a woman was coming after me, and thereupon set in the sensation, so common in dreams, of being glued to the spot, of being paralyzed. The accompanying feeling was not anxiety but erotic excitement. So you see how the sensation of paralysis characteristic of sleep was used for the fulfillment of an exhibitionistic wish. Earlier that night I had in fact gone up the stairs from our ground-floor apartment—without a collar, at any rate—and had thought one of our neighbors might be on the stairs.

Recently Breuer referred [a patient?] to me in the same way he did to you in the sarcoma affair. You see, there is a system in this.

With the most cordial greetings to you, your dear wife and son,

Your
Sigm.

1. The German is *nichts;* misread in *Anfänge* as *nicht.*
2. Incorrectly read previously in the manuscript as *Vater* instead of *Pater.*

# Draft N

[enclosed with letter]

### *Impulses*

Hostile impulses against parents (a wish that they should die) are also an integrating constituent of neuroses. They come to light consciously as obsessional ideas. In paranoia the worst feature of delusions of persecution (pathological distrust of rulers and monarchs) corresponds to these hostile impulses against parents. These impulses are repressed at periods when compassion for the parents is aroused — at times of their illness or death. On such occasions it is a manifestation of mourning to reproach oneself for their death (so-called melancholia) or to punish oneself in a hysterical fashion, through the medium of the idea of retribution, with the same states [of illness] that they have had. The identification which occurs here is, as can be seen, nothing other than a mode of thinking and does not make the search for the motive superfluous.

It seems as though this death wish is directed in sons against their fathers and in daughters against their mothers. A maidservant makes a transference from this by wishing her mistress to die so that her master can marry her. (Observation: Lisel's dream relating to Martha and me.)

### *Relation between Impulses and Fantasies*

Memories appear to bifurcate: one part of them is put aside and replaced by fantasies; another accessible part seems to lead directly to impulses. Is it possible that later on impulses can also derive from fantasies?

Similarly obsessional neurosis and paranoia would derive *ex aequo* [on equal terms] from hysteria, which would explain their incompatibility.

## *Transposition of Belief*

Belief (doubt) is a phenomenon that belongs wholly to the system of the ego (the Cs.) [the conscious] and has no counterpart in the Ucs. [the unconscious]. In the neuroses belief is displaced; it is denied to that which is repressed if it forces [its way] to reproduction and — as a punishment, one might say — transposed onto that which is defending. Titania, who will not love her rightful husband, Oberon, is obliged instead to bestow her love on Bottom, the fantasy ass.

## *Fiction and Fine Frenzy*[1]

The mechanism of fiction is the same as that of hysterical fantasies. For his *Werther* Goethe combined something he had experienced, his love for Lotte Kästner, and something he had heard, the fate of young Jerusalem, who died by committing suicide. He was probably toying with the idea of killing himself and found a point of contact in that and identified himself with Jerusalem, to whom he lent a motive from his own love story. By means of this fantasy he protected himself from the consequences of his experience.

So Shakespeare was right in juxtaposing fiction and madness (fine frenzy).

## *Motives for Symptom Formation*

Remembering is never a motive but only a way, a method. The first motive for the formation of symptoms is, chronologically, libido. Thus symptoms, like dreams, are *the fulfillment of a wish.*

At later stages the defense against libido has made room for itself in the Ucs. as well. Wish fulfillment must meet the requirements of this unconscious defense. This happens if the symptom is able to operate as a punishment (for an evil impulse or because of a lack of trust in one's ability to hinder [sexual desire]).[2] The motives of *libido* and of *wish fulfillment as a punishment* then come together. Here the general tendency toward abreaction, toward a breakthrough of the repressed is unmistakable, and on this the other two motives are superimposed. It appears that at later stages on the one hand more complicated psychic formations (impulses, fantasies, motives) are displaced from the memory, and on the other hand *defense,* arising from the Pcs. (the ego), would seem to force its way into the unconscious, so that defense too becomes *multilocular.*

Symptom formation by identification is linked to fantasies —

that is, to their repression in the Ucs.—in an analogous way to the alteration of the ego in paranoia. Since the outbreak of *anxiety* is linked to these repressed fantasies, we must conclude that the transformation of libido into anxiety does not occur through defense between the ego and the Ucs., but in the Ucs. itself. It follows, therefore, that there is Ucs. libido as well.

The repression of impulses seems to produce not *anxiety* but perhaps depression—melancholia. In this way the melancholias are related to obsessional neurosis.

*Definition of "Holy"*

"Holy" is something based on the fact that human beings, for the benefit of the larger community, have sacrificed a portion of their sexual liberty and their liberty to indulge in perversions. The horror of incest (something impious) is based on the fact that, as a result of communal sexual life (even in childhood), the members of a family remain together permanently and become incapable of joining with strangers. Thus incest is antisocial—civilization consists in this progressive renunciation. Contrariwise, the "superman."

1. The last two words are in English, taken from Shakespeare's *Midsummer Night's Dream*, Act 5, scene 1:

> The poet's eye, in a fine frenzy rolling
> Doth glance from heaven to earth, from earth to heaven;
> And, as imagination bodies forth
> The forms of things unknown, the poet's pen
> Turns them to shapes, and gives to airy nothing
> A local habitation and a name.

2. *Anfänge* reads, "Dies geschieht, wenn das Symptom als Strafe (wegen bösen Impulses), oder aus Misstrauen zur Selbsthinderung wirken kann." Strachey (*S.E.* 1:256) translates it as "This happens if the symptom is able to operate as a self-hindrance, whether by way of *punishment* (for an evil impulse) or from mistrust." In actuality the manuscript reads, "Dies geschieht, wenn das Symptom als *Strafe* (wegen bösen Impulses, oder aus Misstrauen zur Selbsthinderung) wirken kann." This makes much better sense and is clearly a reference to symptom formation, where a symptom is both a gratification of an id impulse and a punishment for that gratification. The passage marks Freud's first insight into this important process.

June 18, 1897

Dear Wilhelm,

Fathomless and bottomless laziness, intellectual stagnation, summer dreariness, vegetative well-being—that is the reason for my neither having replied to your very interesting letter nor having written a new one. Since the last thrust nothing has stirred and nothing has changed; I recall with gratification your mentioning our next congress in your letter, but — so far — you would have to bear the full burden of it alone. I hope you did not think that the majority that proposed me [for the professorship] on June 12 made me too proud to write letters.

In times like these my reluctance to write is downright pathological; for talking I have occasion enough: apart from lectures and six cases, there is my pupil Dr. Gattel, who greatly pleases me by his intelligence and who spends a good deal of time in my company. At the beginning, of course, his own well-controlled neurosis made its appearance. He is very touchy, excessively worried about his future. Initially I took this to be anxiousness, but later it turned out to be a desire for independence and a horror of needing anything from his father. (It is reminiscent of the prostitution romance.) Otherwise, however, he is nice and gallant and, if he sticks to it, I think I shall knock at your door and ask you to take him on as *your* neurological assistant and to introduce him to practice. If he does not come along far enough, then not.

I am very much longing for the end of the season. I plan to be in Aussee again June 26 to 29. Gradually we might begin to tackle the question when we can see each other this summer. I need a new impetus from you; after a while it gives out on me. Nuremberg got me going for two months.

Don't repay me in kind this time, and write to me soon about how your little family is doing and any other interesting news about yourself.

Your
Sigm.

---

June 22, 1897[1]

Dear Wilhelm,

Your letter amused me greatly, especially the remarks about my title. At our next congress you shall call me "Herr Professor"; I mean to be a gentleman like other gentlemen. The truth is that we keep pace wonderfully in suffering, but less so in creativity. I have never before even imagined anything like this period of intellectual paralysis. Every line is torture. But now you are flourishing again; I open all the doors of my senses, though I comprehend nothing; but I am looking forward to the next congress. In Aussee, I hope, and in

August; September is set aside for our trip to Italy (which one day should also be *ours*).

In Aussee I know a wonderful wood full of ferns and mushrooms where you must reveal to me the secrets of the world of lower animals and the world of children. I have never before felt so stupidly expectant in the face of your disclosures, but hope the world will not hear of them before I do and that instead of a short article you will within a year present to us a small book which solves the organic secrets in series of 28 and 23.

Your remark about the occasional disappearance of periods and their reappearance above ground struck me with the force of a correct intuition. For this is what has happened with me. Incidentally, I have been through some kind of neurotic experience, curious states incomprehensible to Cs., twilight thoughts, veiled doubts, with barely a ray of light here or there.

I am all the more pleased that you are working again. We parcel things out like two beggars,[2] one of whom gets the province of Posen; you, the biological; I, the psychological. I must admit that I have recently started a collection of profound Jewish stories.

This summer I had to take on two new cases, which are going quite well. The last one is a 19-year-old girl with almost pure obsessional ideas, who makes me very curious. According to my speculations, obsessional ideas go back to a later psychic age and therefore do not necessarily point to the father, who tends to be the more careful with the child the older the child is, but rather point to the slightly older siblings for whom the child is yet to become a little woman. Now in this case the Almighty was kind enough to let the father die before the child was 11 months old, but two brothers, one of them three years older than the patient, shot themselves.

Otherwise I am dull-witted and ask your indulgence. I believe I am in a cocoon, and God knows what sort of beast will crawl out.

Cordial greetings, and see you soon.

Your
Sigm.

1. Date previously incorrectly read as June 12, 1897.
2. Freud uses the Yiddish word *Schnorrer*.

---

Vienna, July 7, 1897

Dear Wilhelm,

I know that at the moment I am useless as a correspondent, with no right to any claims, but it was not always so and it will not remain so. I still do not know what has been happening in me. Something from the deepest depths of my own neurosis set itself against any advance in the understanding of the neuroses, and you have somehow been involved in it. For my writing paralysis seems to me designed to inhibit our communication. I have no guarantees of this, just feelings of a highly obscure nature. Has nothing of the kind happened to you? For the past few days it has seemed to me that an emergence from this obscurity is in preparation. I notice that in the meantime I have made all kinds of advances in my work, and every now and then an idea once more has occurred to me. The hot weather and overwork no doubt have had their share in this.

I see then that the defense against memories does not prevent their giving rise to higher psychic structures, which persist for a while and then are themselves subjected to defense. This, however, is a most highly specific kind — precisely as in dreams, which contain *in nuce* [in a nutshell] the psychology of the neuroses in general. What we are faced with are falsifications of memory and fantasies — the latter relating to the past or future. I know roughly the rules in accordance with which these structures are put together and the reasons why they are stronger than genuine memories, and I have thus learned new things about the characteristics of the processes in the Ucs. Alongside these, perverse impulses arise; and when, as later becomes necessary, these fantasies and impulses are repressed, the higher determinations of the symptoms already following from the memories make their appearance, as well as new motives for adhering to the illness. I am learning to recognize a few typical cases of how these fantasies and impulses are put together and a few typical determinants for the initiation of repression against them. This knowledge is not yet complete. My technique is beginning to prefer a particular method as being the natural one.

The most certain thing seems to me to be the explanation of dreams, but it is surrounded by a vast number of obstinate riddles. The organological questions await your [solution]: I have made no advances there.

There is an interesting dream of wandering about among strangers, totally or half undressed and with feelings of shame and anxiety. Oddly enough, it is the rule that people do not notice it — for which we must thank wish fulfillment. This dream material, which goes back to exhibiting in childhood, has been misunderstood and worked over didactically in a well-known fairy tale. (The king's imaginary clothes — "Talisman.") The ego habitually misinterprets other dreams in the same way.

What interests me the most in regard to the summer is where and when we will meet. The fact that we shall meet is beyond question.

Dr. Gattel is becoming much attached to me and my theories. His intelligence is quite considerable; he is not free of neurotic sensibility. He is presently engrossed in your papers. I hope you will find him worthy of appreciation and find him helpful when he comes to Berlin.

All is well in Aussee. I am most anxious to hear from you.

Most cordial greetings to the entire family.

Your
Sigm.

---

Vienna, July 20, 1897
IX., Berggasse 19

Dear Wilhelm,

Hail! In these last days I have contemplated how to introduce this letter: that it is nice that we shall get a book rather than an article; that we shall not see each other in August but rather in September at some unspecified time is less nice; and so forth. The argument that the time for it [Fliess's book] has come and that it must come out no doubt is overwhelming, but the uncertainty about whether something with that content can so quickly undergo its [natural] development—in brief, all the scruples involved in my coming between a man and his work as an outsider and dolt, which I so detest—all that stood in the way of the letter I never wrote. Waiting a little is often the best thing. Now everything will turn out nicely. It is charming of Ida to use her influence in this way. Feel free to ask anything of me; I am again out of the clouds and very curious. At the same time my special dates that had been on the decline have appeared again (July 17 ♀ menstruation in its most developed form, with occasional bloody nasal secretion before and afterward). The relative quiet and several minor solutions were very good for me. I shall most energetically try to persuade you not to rush into print. It is taking people a long time to catch up with you; *last week*, I hear, a reviewer in *Lancet*[1] treated you badly. I did not see the issue. You know that this is my present position; nor did I comply with your wish to prepare a preliminary account of the hysteria matter. I am letting things simmer.

I remember Sch. in H. from what you had told me. "Whichever way you throw the cat . . . " So you did achieve your goal of applying mathematics and astronomy to biology! That is an old drive of yours which never would have left you any peace. Well, then, you must give me full details of the results in the beautiful woods, but without any preconceived ideas! I know from school-day memories that the earth rotates a little around the sun — which, however, does not cause dizziness. That is all.

I shall not leave until the end of this week. On July 13 my sister Rosa gave birth to a son, who is called Herman Adolf, is very chipper, and energetically sucks on his mother. The confinement is not free of all sorts of minor complications, and I want to wait and see what happens.

Our travel plans have changed. Umbria and Tuscany instead of Naples; prior to that, September 1 to 8, in Venice with Martha.

With the most cordial greetings to all three of you,

Your
Sigm.

1. Strangely, the *Lancet* issue referred to does not contain a review of Fliess.

---

Aussee, August 5, 1897

Excellenza,[1]

This summer's storms above all, apart from other side effects, interrupted our contact, left us disoriented with respect to each other, and now necessitate a veritable renewal. So: at a certain time before the floods we received the happy news that you would *not* forgo visiting us, or just Martha, in Aussee. Then came the elaboration that Your Excellency would travel ahead and your husband would follow later from Heidelberg. Then came *le déluge*.[2]

And now when the Dachstein in its fabulous gray whiteness is resplendent in front of our windows and the first train (carrying my sister back to Vienna) again departed from our Aussee station, we take the liberty of telling you and of requesting the following.

Above all, we ask for news about how you, Wilhelm, and the little one have been in the interim. We suppose that you have not been in any danger. Further, when are you planning to come to see us? The connection (via Bruck – St. Michael) will have proved to be entirely safe by the time this letter reaches you. Underneath the "when" a "whether" is concealed, which should be relegated to repression and not referred to any further. The little house with two rooms and two windows (similar to Mozart's in which he composed the *Magic Flute*), reserved for you, is still standing. It is the same one in which unfortunately I can only write to you but not entice you [to come].

Furthermore, owing to the complications that so easily arise in life, we are bound by definite dates toward the end of the month. On the 26/27th my brother's vacation starts and with it the three-week trip to Italy. Moreover, this time Martha is to see Venice without any further delay, and originally we had planned to combine the two trips. But a woman does not readily fit in with such general time schedules; for her sake, in particular, I must leave with her alone eight days earlier, at the latest on the 21st or 22nd, and send her back before September 1. Because of my goodness and willingness to make sacrifices, I shall have four weeks in Italy and eight weeks of vacation this year. Thus is virtue rewarded! If Dr. Breuer hears about that!

Everything else I now leave to you. Since the sum total of love extant in this world appears to be constant, a renewed bestowal, a new distribution, will be required of you. Furthermore, this force must be extended over a definite period of time.

I greet you, R.W., and all of yours cordially and expect to hear from Wilhelm as soon as he is back.

Your
Dr. Freud

All the rascals are in good spirits; Annerl is a sight to behold.

1. This letter, addressed to Ida Fliess, is part of the small collection in Jerusalem. See note 1 to letter of May 25, 1892.

2. French in original.

---

Aussee, August 8, 1897
early [in the morning]

Dear Wilhelm,

News at last, and so I am also answering instantly.

We were cut off, but most comfortable and undisturbedly well. It was, by the way, thrillingly beautiful. Now trains are running again via Bruck–southern line; my sister has already taken this route. Three days ago I wrote to your dear wife in Brühl, asking her to give us the dates of her visit. One way or another you will have seen that letter by now. Well, our plans are to leave on the 20th or 21st, make stops along the way to Venice, and at the end of the month meet my brother (and Dr. Gattel) in Venice. It is clear that these decisions were made with a view to Martha's period around September 1 and my brother's vacation time, and that, in the absence of any other clues to go by, we had to make our plans around these fixed dates. I was then most surprised to receive a letter from you from Merano.

Apparently little Robert is now with you as well. I think this is wonderful and can propose several alternatives which hold fast to one thing—that we shall see each other in the next two weeks, which for me is an overdue necessity.

That is, either as you wanted it last time: after Brühl, [that you come] to us in the middle of the month. This has the advantage that you really would be with *us*, could see the children and the scenery, and that Robert could make friends with Annerl. In this case I should like the middle of the month really to be the 15th so that we shall not be rushed in either direction, though our departure for the South could of course easily be postponed for a day or two. Or: you all now do as you like—for instance, stay in the area, meet the parents at Karersee August 15 to 20, and make a date with us for August 21 to 23, wherever you wish. For we shall pass through, plan to spend the night in Innsbruck, and go on to Verona the next day. In between, a meeting on Tyrolean soil (not at Hotel Karer, of course) can be arranged. In that case, too, we can postpone our trip for a few days. Third: you simply travel with us, either from here or (after Verona) from Karersee, if our route does not cover too much of the same territory as your trip in the spring. Make up your mind, then, and let us know quickly. Letters are now so slow that I received your two of August 3 and 5 from Merano only just now on the morning of the 8th. I shall be equally pleased to accept whatever you decide. It involves, after all, an actual wish fulfillment, a beautiful dream about to be realized.

It would be a pity to answer anything else in writing. I am very well and very curious and am trying to prepare myself a little for the trip to central Italy.

Most cordial greetings to the entire little company from your

Sigm.

---

Aussee, August 14, 1897

Dear Wilhelm,

I must keep reminding myself that I did do a good deed yesterday by canceling; otherwise I would regret it too much. But I believe it really was so.

In your first telegram (23rd, Bolzano) you did not indicate how long we could be together. In view of our plans (Martha must return on September 1), it would have been for a short time. So I expressed my disappointment, which you noticed; you then tried to make all sorts of sacrifices to enable us to meet. In the meantime I tried to get used to the idea of our not seeing each other, thought it rather sad, and therefore was truly glad when you decided on the 22nd. At that moment I would have been equally content with any other day. I replied: agreed. Then on the same day your new proposal arrived—that we should travel earlier because you were free until the 19th. From this we gathered, first, that your old folks changed their plan and will leave for Karersee on the 18th instead of on the 15th. (We assume that they too did not do this voluntarily but because of lack of rooms in the hotel on account of the empress' arrival.) Then you would be with them for only two to three days (19th to 22nd) in order to be able to meet with us, and that was the reason, I thought, for your new proposal. But then we were overcome by compassion. Getting from Bolzano to Karersee or Trafoi entails many hours by carriage, and you yourself described Bolzano and how you felt there. We left aside whether the child is with you and Ida—which Martha absolutely wanted to know. If we had chosen the 22nd, then you would have had to put up with: leaving Trafoi on the 18th for Bolzano, from there on the 19th to Karersee, from there on the 22nd back again, and after one or one and a half days off again or back again. Or, on our account, remain with your parents in Bolzano! We assume that you surely would not propose that we take a carriage to Trafoi or back.

If we were to travel earlier, it would be as follows: we could not have left before Monday morning; on the same day we could have gotten no further than Innsbruck, thanks to our train connections; would not have met you until Tuesday afternoon in Bolzano (August 17th), and early on the 19th we would have had to leave you; so we would not even have had two full days. And either you would have left Trafoi earlier for the probably hot and uncomfortable Bolzano or we would have had to come to Trafoi. In this arrangement most of the discomfort probably was on our side. I would then be traveling from August 17 to September 20, for five weeks, which would tax my budget severely, and even then I cannot with certainty count on having a good long talk with you, for which I yearn. More time must necessarily be allowed for a congress with both wives than for one where we are alone. I am not sure how much in these considerations is incorrect and how much, in addition, I have caused myself by my reckless second letter in which I made various kinds of proposals. I saw only that you were ready to make every conceivable sacrifice to enable us to have our get-together, which was thwarted only by the floods; that your wife had to share all the vexations involved in these corrective attempts; and I felt obliged to take the burden from both of you and let you be free again. It won't work out, I said to myself, and one should not want to force anything. You and Ida need not furnish any proof that the failure is not your fault. I am ashamed to confess that I do not regard myself as at all capable of such a large number of small sacrifices.

I only want us to stay in touch during the coming weeks; something perhaps can be improvised. I shall let you know whenever we make any changes in the places where we intend to stay for a longer period of time, if I know where you and Ida are and plan to go. The start of our journey will most likely be on Saturday, August 21.

I now must restrain my curiosity for a while. But if I cannot stand it, I can always come to Berlin over a weekend. This time you are losing nothing at all [by not hearing] my tales. Things are fermenting in me; I have finished nothing; am very satisfied with the psychology, tormented by grave doubts about my theory of the neuroses, too lazy to think, and have not succeeded here in diminishing the agitation in my head and feelings; this can happen only in Italy.

After having become very cheerful here, I am now enjoying a period of bad humor. The chief patient I am preoccupied with is myself. My little hysteria, though greatly accentuated by my work, has resolved itself a bit further. The rest is still at a standstill. That is what my mood primarily depends on. The analysis is more difficult than any other. It is, in fact, what paralyzes my psychic strength for describing and communicating what I have won so far. Still, I believe it must be done and is a necessary intermediate stage in my work.

Now, my cordial greetings to you both, and let the brief disappointment soon be followed by new hope, just as it did in our case.

Your
Sigm.

---

Aussee, August 18, 1897

Dear Wilhelm,

Just received your letter, which proved me right: journeys by carriage, migraine, and August heat. I am pleased that I could at least spare you some discomfort; but it was not done gladly. My cancellation certainly did not have any neurotic motives, but something like a superstition — one should not want to force anything — did contribute, a resolution your banker might likewise have granted a place above his desk. I saw that you were willing to make every possible sacrifice, and yet what might have been arranged would not have matched the long-cherished expectation.

I am writing to you today mainly to ask you to let me know the places where you will be staying in the near future. I do know of two places: Karersee until August 23, and then Brühl. But how long will you be in Brühl, and so on? I am aware recently of having somewhat curtailed my correspondence with you, just because there was the prospect of our getting together. Now that it no longer exists — in my thoughts — I think I want to have the way open again to the old, unjustly scorned technique of exchanging ideas. My handwriting is also more human again; hence my tiredness is receding. Your handwriting, as I see with pleasure, never varies.

Martha is very much looking forward to the trip, though the daily reports of train accidents are not exactly apt to put the father and mother of a family in the mood for it. You will laugh — and rightly so — but I must confess to new anxieties which come and go, but in between last for half a day. Half an hour ago I was pulled out of my fear of the next train accident when the thought occurred to me: W. and I. also are traveling, after all. This put a stop to the tomfoolery. But this must remain strictly between us.

You promised me, by the way, a congress on Italian soil, of which I shall remind you in due time. It is sad how little we have succeeded in overcoming the space between us. At present I know nothing about you, and your advantage consists only in the circumstance that since Easter I have very little new to tell you about.

This time, it is my hope to penetrate somewhat more deeply into the art of Italy. I have some notion of your point of view, which seeks not that which is of cultural-historical interest, but absolute beauty in the harmony between ideas and the form in which they are presented, and in the elementary pleasing sensations of space and color. At Nuremberg I was still far from seeing it. Incidentally, have I already told you that Naples has been dropped and that the journey will take in San Gimignano-Siena-Perugia-Assisi-Ancona — in short, Tuscany and Umbria?

I hope to hear from you very soon, even if only briefly each time. First, write to me here; from the 25th to September 1, to Venice, Casa Kirsch.

The most cordial wishes for an undisturbed, beautiful rest of the summer.

Your
Sigm.

Siena, September 6, 1897

Dear Wilhelm,

From Venice (received your letter) via Pisa, Livorno, to Siena. As you know, in Italy I am seeking a punch made of Lethe;[1] here and there I get a draft. One savors the strange kind of beauty and the enormous creative urge; at the same time my inclination toward the grotesque, perverse-psychological gets its due. I have much to tell you about (which from now on will be a catchword between us). Next goal: Orvieto; in between San Gimignano. It will be difficult for your answer to reach me; so enjoy the signs of life from my journey, which make no demands on you.

Cordial greetings to I.F. [and] R.W.

Your
Sigm

1. The dead drank from Lethe, the river of forgetfulness, upon their arrival in the underworld.

# Theory Transformed

September 21, 1897

Dear Wilhelm,

Here I am again, since yesterday morning, refreshed, cheerful, impoverished, at present without work, and having settled in again, I am writing to you first.

And now I want to confide in you immediately the great secret that has been slowly dawning on me in the last few months. I no longer believe in my *neurotica* [theory of the neuroses]. This is probably not intelligible without an explanation; after all, you yourself found credible what I was able to tell you. So I will begin historically [and tell you] where the reasons for disbelief came from. The continual disappointment in my efforts to bring a single analysis[1] to a real conclusion; the running away of people who for a period of time had been most gripped [by analysis]; the absence of the complete successes on which I had counted; the possibility of explaining to myself the partial successes in other ways, in the usual fashion—this was the first group. Then the surprise that in all cases, the *father*, not excluding my own,[2] had to be accused of being perverse—the realization of the unexpected frequency of hysteria, with precisely the same conditions prevailing in each, whereas surely such widespread perversions against children are not very probable. The [incidence] of perversion would have to be immeasurably more frequent than the [resulting] hysteria because the illness, after all, occurs only where there has been an accumulation of events and there is a contributory factor that weakens the defense. Then, third, the certain insight that there are no indications of reality in the unconscious, so that one cannot distinguish between truth and fiction that has been cathected with affect. (Accordingly, there would remain the solution that the sexual fantasy invariably seizes upon the theme of the parents.) Fourth, the consideration that in the most deep-reaching psychosis the unconscious memory does not break through, so that the secret of childhood experiences is not disclosed even in the most confused delirium. If one thus sees that the unconscious never overcomes the resistance of the conscious, the expectation that in treatment the opposite is bound to happen, to the point where the unconscious is completely tamed by the conscious, also diminishes.

I was so far influenced [by this] that I was ready to give up two things: the complete resolution of a neurosis and the certain knowledge of its etiology in childhood. Now I have no idea of where I stand because I have not succeeded in gaining a theoretical understanding of repression and its interplay of forces. It seems once again arguable that only later experiences give the impetus to fantasies, which [then] hark back to childhood, and with this the factor of a hereditary disposition regains a sphere of influence from which I had made it my task to dislodge it — in the interest of illuminating neurosis.

If I were depressed, confused, exhausted, such doubts would surely have to be interpreted as signs of weakness. Since I am in an opposite state, I must recognize them as the result of honest and vigorous intellectual work and must be proud that after going so deep I am still capable of such criticism. Can it be that this doubt merely represents an episode in the advance toward further insight?

It is strange, too, that no feeling of shame appeared — for which, after all, there could well be occasion. Of course I shall not tell it in Dan, nor speak of it in Askelon, in the land of the Philistines, but in your eyes and my own, I have more the feeling of a victory than a defeat (which is surely not right).

How nice that your letter has arrived just now! It induces me to advance a proposal with which I had intended to close. If during this lazy period I were to go to the Northwest Station on Saturday evening, I could be with you at noon on Sunday and then travel back the next night. Can you clear that day for an idyll for the two of us, interrupted by an idyll for three and three and a half [of us]? That is what I wanted to ask. Or do you have a dear guest in the house or something urgent to do elsewhere? Or, if I have to leave for home the same evening, which would then not be worthwhile, do the same conditions obtain if I go straight to the Northwest Station on Friday evening and stay with you one and a half days? I mean this week, of course.

Now to continue my letter. I vary Hamlet's saying, "To be in readiness": to be cheerful is everything! I could indeed feel quite discontent. The expectation of eternal fame was so beautiful, as was that of certain wealth, complete independence, travels, and lifting the children above the severe worries that robbed me of my youth. Everything depended upon whether or not hysteria would come out right. Now I can once again remain quiet and modest, go on worrying and saving. A little story from my collection occurs to me: "Rebecca, take off your gown; you are no longer a bride."[3] In spite of all this, I am in very good spirits and content that you feel a need to see me again similar to mine to see you.

There remains one small anxiety. What can I still understand of your matters? I am certainly incapable of critically evaluating them; I shall hardly be in a position to comprehend them, and the doubt that then sets in is not the product of intellectual work, like my doubt about my own matters, but is the result of mental inadequacy. It is easier for you; you can survey everything I bring and criticize it vigorously.

I have to add one more thing. In this collapse of everything valuable, the psychological alone has remained untouched. The dream [book] stands entirely secure and my beginnings of the metapsychological work have only grown in my estimation. It is a pity that one cannot make a living, for instance, on dream interpretation!

Martha came back with me to Vienna. Minna and the children are staying in the country another week. They have all been exceedingly well.

My pupil, Dr. Gattel, is something of a disappointment. Very gifted and clever, he must nevertheless, owing to his own nervousness and several unfavorable character traits, be classified as unpalatable.

How all of you are and whatever else is happening between heaven and earth, I hope—anticipating your reply—to hear soon in person.

Cordially your
Sigm.

1. The manuscript previously was misread here. The German text printed in *Anfänge* reads, "die fortgesetzten Enttäuschungen bei den Versuchen, meine Analyse zum wirklichen Abschluss zu bringen," which Strachey correctly translates as "continual disappointments in my attempts at bringing my analysis to a real conclusion." But the original manuscript reads *eine Analyse* (a single analysis), not *meine Analyse*.

2. Strachey (*S.E.* 1:259) resurrected this phrase, "mein eigener nicht ausgeschlossen," which had been omitted in *Anfänge* and *Origins*.

3. Schur (1972, p. 191) writes: "The meaning of this Jewish joke is obvious: 'You were once a proud bride, but you got into trouble, the wedding is off—take off your bridal gown.' " Another interpretation, which I believe to be correct, was suggested

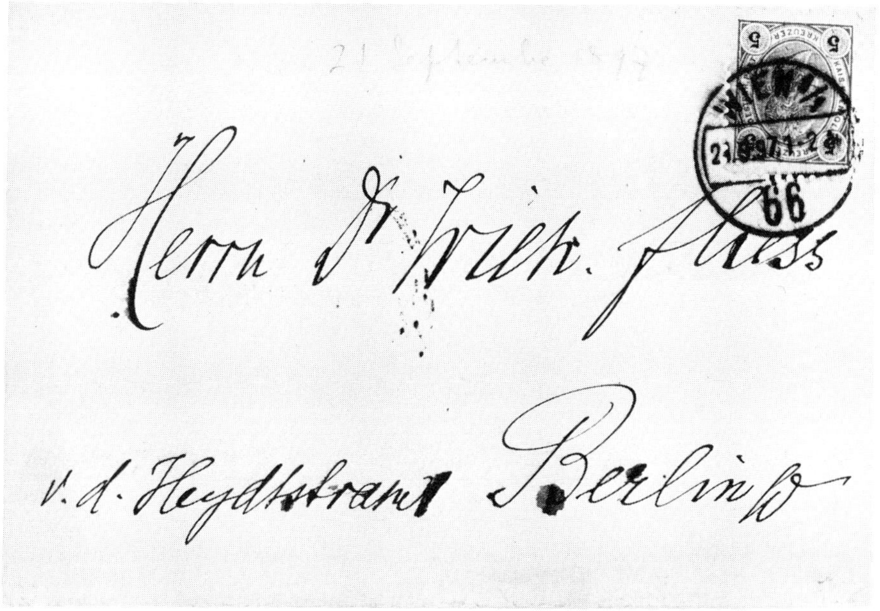


The important letter of September 21, 1897.

Dr. Sigm. Freud
Docent für Nervenkrankheiten a. d. Universität

Wien, 21 Sept 97
IX., Berggasse 19.

Theuerer Wilhelm!

Hier bin ich wieder, seit gestern früh, frisch, heiter, verarmt, derzeit beschäftigungslos u. schreibe Dir zuerst nach hergestellter Wohnbarkeit. Und nun will ich Dir sofort das große Geheimnis anvertrauen, das mir in den letzten Monaten langsam gedämmert hat. Ich glaube an meine Neurotica nicht mehr. Das ist wohl nicht ohne Erklärung verständlich; Du hast ja selbst glaubwürdig gefunden, was ich Dir erzählen konnte. Ich will also historisch beginnen, woher die Motive zum Unglauben gekommen sind. Die fortgesetzten Enttäuschungen bei den Versuchen, meine Analyse zum wirklichen Abschluß zu bringen, das Davonlaufen der eine Zeit lang am besten gepackten Leute, das Ausbleiben der vollen Erfolge, auf die ich gerechnet hatte, die Möglichkeit, mir die partiellen Erfolge anders, auf die gewöhnliche Art zu erklären: dies die erste Gruppe. Dann die Überraschung, daß in sämtlichen Fällen der Vater als pervers beschuldigt werden mußte, mein eigener nicht ausgeschlossen, die Einsicht in die nicht erwartete Häufigkeit der Hysterie, wo jedesmal dieselbe Bedingung erhalten bleibt, während doch solche Verbreitung der Perversion gegen Kinder wenig wahrscheinlich ist. [Die Perversion müßte unermeßlich häufiger sein als die Hysterie, da Erkrankung ja nur eintritt, wo sich die Ereignisse gehäuft haben und ein die Abwehr schwächender Faktor hinzugetreten ist.] Dann drittens die sichere Einsicht, daß es im Unbewußten ein Realitätszeichen nicht gibt, so daß man die Wahrheit und die mit Affekt besetzte Fiktion nicht unterscheiden kann. (Demnach bliebe die Lösung übrig, daß die sexuelle Phantasie sich regelmäßig des Themas der Eltern bemächtigt.) Viertens die Überlegung, daß in der tiefgehendsten Psychose die unbewußte Erinnerung nicht durchdringt, so daß das Geheimnis der Jugenderlebnisse auch im verworrensten Delirium sich nicht verrät. Wenn man so sieht, daß das Unbewußte niemals den Widerstand des Bew. überwindet, so sinkt auch die Erwartung, daß es in der Kur umgekehrt gehen müßte bis zur völligen Bändigung des Unbew. durch das Bew.

Soweit beeinflußt, wurde ich bereit, auf zweierlei zu verzichten, auf die volle Lösung einer Neurose und auf die sichere Kenntnis ihrer Ätiologie in der Kindheit. Nun weiß ich überhaupt nicht, woran ich bin, denn das theoretische Verständnis der Verdrängung und ihres Kräftespiels ist mir nicht gelungen. Es scheint wieder diskutierbar, daß erst spätere Erlebnisse den Anstoß zu Phantasien geben, die auf die Kindheit zurückgreifen, und damit gewinnt der Faktor einer hereditären Disposition einen Machtbereich zurück, aus dem zu verdrängen ich mir zur Aufgabe gestellt hatte – im Interesse der Aufhellung der Neurose.

Wäre ich verstimmt, unklar, ermattet, so wären solche Zweifel wohl als Schwächeerscheinungen zu deuten. Da ich im gegenteiligen Zustande bin, muß ich sie als Ergebnis ehrlicher und kräftiger intellektueller Arbeit anerkennen und stolz darauf sein, daß ich nach solcher Vertiefung solcher Kritik noch fähig bin. Ob dieser Zweifel nur eine Episode auf dem Fortschreiten zu weiterer Erkenntnis darstellt?

Dr. Sigm. Freud
Docent für Nervenkrankheiten
a. d. Universität.

Wien, ..........
IX., Berggasse 19.

Merkwürdig ist auch, daß jedes Gefühl
von Beschämung ausgeblieben ist,
zu dem doch ein Anlaß hätte sein können.
Gewiß, ich werde es nicht in Dan erzählen,
nicht davon reden in Askalon, im
Lande der Philister, aber vor Dir und
bei mir habe ich eigentlich mehr das
Gefühl eines Sieges als einer Nieder-
lage (was doch nicht recht ist).
Wie schön, daß jetzt eben Dein Brief
kommt! Er veranlaßt mich einen Vorschlag
vorauszustellen, mit dem ich schließen
wollte. Wenn ich Samstag abd in dieser
faulen Zeit auf die Nordbahn gehe, kann
ich Sonntag Mittag bei Dir sein u. [illegible]
die nächste Nacht zurückreisen.
Kannst Du Dir den Tag für ein
Idyll zu zweien, unterbrochen durch
eines zu dreien u. dreieinhalb
freimachen? Das wollte ich fragen.

Oder hast Du einen lieben Gast im
Hause oder dringendes auswärts
zu thun? Oder, wenn ich den Abend
nach Hause abreisen muß, was sich
dann nicht lohnen würde, gelten
dieselben Bedingungen, für den
Fall daß ich Freitag abds zur Nordbahn gehe u. 1½ Tage bei Dir bleibe?
Ich meine natürlich diese Woche.
Nun setze ich meinen Brief fort.
Ich variire das Hamlet'sche Wort:
To be in readiness – heiter sein ist
Alles. Ich könnte mich ja sehr unzu-
frieden fühlen. Die Erwartung des
ewigen Nachruhms war so schön
u. des sicheren Reichthums, die volle
Unabhängigkeit, das Reisen, die
Hebung der Kinder über die
schweren Sorgen, die mich um meine
Jugend gebracht haben. Das hing
alles daran, ob die Hysterie
aufgeht oder nicht. Nun kann ich mich
still u. bescheiden bleiben, sorgen

sparen u. da fällt mir aus meiner
Sammlung die kleine Geschichte ein: Rebecca
zieh das Kleid aus, du bist keine Kalle
mehr. Aber ich bin trotz alledem
[illegible] heiter u. zufrieden, daß Du ein
[illegible] Bedürfnis empfindest nach
Wiedersehen wie ich auch.
Ein kleines Stück Angst bleibt übrig. Was
erwarte ich noch von Deiner Kritik?
[illegible]
[illegible]
[illegible] zu begreifen, u. die [illegible]
der dann [illegible] ist nicht wie mein
eigener Zweifel an meiner Lehre
ein Product intellektueller Arbeit
sondern ein Ergebnis [illegible]
[illegible]. [illegible]
[illegible] also wird ich [illegible] über-
sehen u. ein kräftiges Wort darüber
fallen lassen.
Noch etwas muß ich anfügen. In diesem
Sturz aller Werthe ist allein das

Psychologische unberührt geblieben.
Der Traum steht ganz sicher da u. meine
Anfänge metapsych. Arbeit haben
an Schätzung nur gewonnen. Schade,
daß man vom Traumdeuten z. B.
nicht leben kann.
Martha ist mit mir nach Wien gekommen,
Minna u. die Kinder bleiben noch
eine Woche draußen. Sie haben
sich alle ausgezeichnet befunden.
Mein Schüler Dr Gattel war ein Stück
von einer Enttäuschung. Sehr begabt
u. kenntnisreich, muß er doch wegen seiner eigenen
Nervosität u. [illegible] unerfreulicher
Eigenschaften seines Charakters
doch eigentlich als ungenießbar zu
classificieren.
Mit den [illegible] u. was sich sonst
zwischen [illegible] u. [illegible] [illegible],
hoffe ich Deine [illegible]
[illegible] bald selbst zu erfahren.
Herzlichst Dein Sigm

Freud a percé à jour le "mensonge" de l'hystérique. La "séduction régulière paternelle" est un fantasme.

Mais le psychologique et l'interprétation des rêves reste debout —

Et Freud se sent heureux comme — non d'une défaite — mais d'une victoire intellectuelle.

*[postmark:]* Bestellt vom Postamte 22 9 97 11¼–24 N

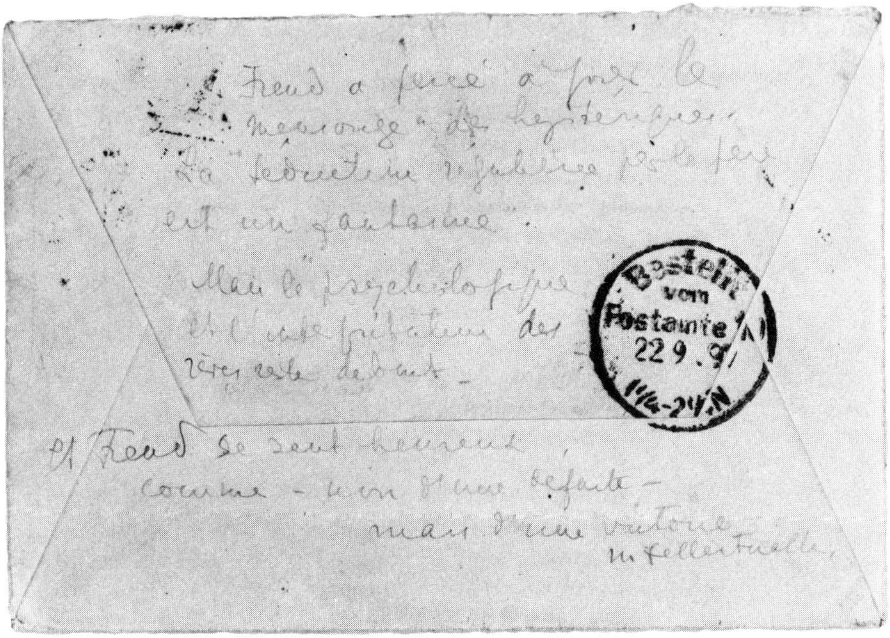

to me by Anna Freud—namely, that Freud, with his theory of the neuroses, had believed himself privileged and happy as a bride. Those days were now over and he had to return to his earlier ordinary status; he had made no discovery. *Kalle* is a slang word that can also be used for a prostitute instead of a bride.

---

September 27, 1897
IX., Berggasse 19

Dear Wilhelm,

Back home after a perfect trip (twelve hours of sleep in an isolation cell), completely without work, refreshed, stimulated, and full of new ideas, I begin with something entirely superfluous—namely, once again expressing the pleasure evoked in me, as old participant and new uncle, by your work, your state of health, your wife, and your child. As for me, I praise the happy decision, to which I have held fast since midsummer, to visit you at your home in Berlin.

My children have not yet returned. I found Martha with a harmless migraine, the first since Bolzano (August 20/21–September 27; for the collector). A new review[1] of I. C. ["Infantile Cerebral Paralyses"] in Wernicke's *Zeitschrift* taught me what beautiful, valuable books I am in the habit of writing.

Most cordial greetings, thanks, and soon more from your

Sigm.

1. The reference is to a long review by a Herr Mann of Breslau, published in the *Monatsschrift für Psychiatrie und Neurologie* (not the *Zeitschrift*, as Freud wrote). It is an extremely positive review, containing among many other praises, "The focal point of this book and its main contribution that cannot be valued highly enough . . . consist in its unsurpassingly clear and comprehensive presentation and critical appreciation of the entire clinical and anatomical material."

---

October 3, 1897

My dear Wilhelm,

My visit has had the advantage of acquainting me with the framework of your current work in its entirety, so that you can relate further details to me. You must not expect a response to everything, and with regard to some of my responses you will not, I hope, fail to take into account that your work is strange to me and my judgment weak. Nevertheless, each time I am grateful to you for every little item that you unselfishly let come my way. For example, your comments on the relationship between infection and conception in mother and daughter seemed to me highly significant because these can after all be explained only by a condition in the eternal life of the protoplasm and not by one in the life of the individual—that is, because they must be dependent on absolute time and not on lifetime. It then occurred to me that this is after all not necessary if the infection in the mother accords with a time period given by the formula $A \times 28$ plus $B \times 23$, and the conception of the daughter by a similar expression, *so* that the difference between the two must again yield a similar formula without there having to exist a special relationship between infection here and conception there. Whether this is nonsense I cannot tell. To do this I would need to know your "timely disposition."

There is still very little happening to me externally, but internally something very interesting. For the last four days my self-analysis, which I consider indispensable for the clarification of the whole problem, has continued in dreams and has presented me with the most valuable elucidations and clues. At certain points I have the feeling of being at the end, and so far I have always known where the next dream-night would continue. To put it in writing is more difficult than anything else for me; it also would take me too far afield. I can only indicate that the old man plays no active part in my case, but that no doubt I drew an inference by analogy from myself onto him; that in my case the "prime originator" was an ugly, elderly, but clever woman,[1] who told me a great deal about God Almighty and hell and who instilled in me a high opinion of my own capacities; that later (between two and two and a half years) my libido toward *matrem* was awakened, namely, on the occasion of a journey with her from Leipzig to Vienna, during which we must have spent the night together and there must have been an opportunity of seeing her *nudam* (you inferred the consequences of this for your son long ago, as a remark revealed to me); that I greeted my one-year-younger brother (who died after a few months) with adverse wishes and genuine childhood jealousy; and that his death left the germ of [self-]reproaches in me. I have also long known the companion of my misdeeds between the ages of one and two years; it is my nephew, a year older than myself, who is now living in Manchester and who visited us in Vienna when I was fourteen years old. The two of us seem occasionally to have behaved cruelly to my niece, who was a year younger. This nephew and this younger brother have determined, then, what is neurotic, but also what is intense, in all my friendships. You yourself have seen my travel anxiety at its height.

I have not yet grasped anything at all of the scenes themselves which lie at the bottom of the story. If they come [to light] and I succeed in resolving my own hysteria, then I shall be grateful to the memory of the old woman who provided me at such an early age with the means for living and going on living. As you see, the old liking is breaking through again today. I cannot convey to you any idea of the intellectual beauty of this work.

The children will return tomorrow morning. Business is still very poor. I fear that if it gets better, it might present an obstacle to my self-analysis. My insight that the difficulties in treatment are due to the fact that in the end one is laying bare the patient's evil inclinations, his will to remain ill, is becoming stronger and clearer. We shall see what happens.

I cordially greet you and your little family, and hope to receive soon again some crumbs from your table.

Your
Sigm.

October 4. The children arrived. The fine weather is gone. Today's dream has, under the strangest disguises, produced the following: she was my teacher in sexual matters and complained because I was clumsy and unable to do anything.

(Neurotic impotence always comes about in this way. The fear of not being able to do anything at all in school thus obtains its sexual substratum.) At the same time I saw the skull of a small animal and in the dream I thought "pig," but in the analysis I associated it with your wish two years ago that I might find, as Goethe once did, a skull on the Lido to enlighten me. But I did not find it. So [I was] a "little blockhead" [literally, a sheep's head]. The whole dream was full of the most mortifying allusions to my present impotence as a therapist. Perhaps this is where the inclination to believe in the incurability of hysteria begins. Moreover, she washed me in reddish water in which she had previously washed herself. (The interpretation is not difficult; I find nothing like this in the chain of my memories; so I regard it as a genuine ancient discovery.) And she made me steal zehners (ten-kreuzer coins)[2] to give them to her. There is a long chain from these first silver zehners to the heap of paper ten-florin notes which I saw in the dream as Martha's weekly housekeeping money. The dream could be summed up as "bad treatment." Just as the old woman got money from me for her bad treatment, so today I get money for the bad treatment of my patients. A special part was played by Mrs. Q., whose remark you reported to me: that I should not take anything from her, as she was the wife of a colleague (he of course made it a condition that I should).

A harsh critic might say of all this that it was retrogressively fantasied instead of progressively determined.[3] The *experimenta crucis* must decide against him. The reddish water would indeed seem to be of that kind. Where do all patients get the horrible perverse details which often are as remote from their experience[4] as from their knowledge?

1. According to Sajner (1968), the woman's name is Monika Zajíc. Cf. Krüll (1979, p. 144). Sajner informs me, in a personal communication, that he has not been able to ascertain any particulars about this woman. When Freud says she was "elderly," it is not clear if he is speaking as a child or as an adult. Anna Freud told me she thought Zajíc may have been in her forties.

2. A zehner is a coin of little value.

3. *Nach vorne* means that the early experiences play a crucial role in determining the present. By *experimenta crucis* Freud no doubt refers to the recovery of memories not available to consciousness.

4. *Erleben* must refer to conscious experience. Freud seems to be saying that the dream revealed a lost memory by providing him with a detail that was not part of his knowledge, nor was it a fantasy. In this rhetorical question he implies that such details speak for the authenticity of the memory; they are recovered, not invented.

---

October 15, 1897
IX., Berggasse 19

Dear Wilhelm,

My self-analysis is in fact the most essential thing I have at present and promises to become of the greatest value to me if it reaches its end. In the middle of it, it suddenly ceased for three days, during which I had the feeling of being tied up inside (which patients complain of so much), and I was really disconsolate until I found that these same three days (twenty-eight days ago) were the bearers of identical somatic phenomena. Actually only two bad days with a remission in between. From this one should draw the conclusion that the female period is not conducive to work. Punctually on the fourth day, it started again. Naturally, the pause also had another determinant—the resistance to something surprisingly new. Since then I have been once again intensely preoccupied [with it], mentally fresh, though afflicted with all sorts of minor disturbances that come from the content of the analysis.

My practice, uncannily, still leaves me a great deal of free time. The whole thing is all the more valuable for my purposes, since I have succeeded in finding a few real points of reference for the story. I asked my mother whether she still remembered the nurse. "Of course," she said, "an elderly person, very clever, she was always carrying you off to some church; when you returned home you preached and told us all about God Almighty. During my confinement with Anna (two and a half years younger), it was discovered that she was a thief, and all the shiny new kreuzers and zehners and all the toys that had been given to you were found in her possession. Your brother Philipp himself fetched the policeman; she then was given ten months in prison." Now look at how this confirms the conclusions of my dream interpretation. It was easy for me to explain the only possible mistake. I wrote to you that she induced me to steal zehners and give them to her. In truth, the dream meant that she stole them herself. For the dream picture was a memory of my taking money from the mother of a doctor—that is, wrongfully. The correct interpretation is: I = she, and the mother of the doctor equals my mother. So far was I from knowing she was a thief that I made a wrong interpretation.

I also inquired about the doctor we had had in Freiberg because one dream concentrated a good deal of resentment on him. In the analysis of the dream figure behind which he was concealed, I also thought of a Professor von Kraus, my history teacher in high school. He did not seem to fit in at all, because my relationship with him was indifferent or even comfortable. My mother then told me that the doctor in my childhood had only one eye, and of all my teachers Professor Kraus was the only one with the same defect! The conclusive force of these coincidences might be weakened by the objection that on some occasion in my later childhood, I had heard that the nurse was a thief and then apparently had forgotten it until it finally emerged in the dream. I myself believe that that is so. But I have another, entirely irrefutable and amusing proof. I said to myself that if the old woman disappeared from my life so suddenly, it must be possible to demonstrate the impression this made on me. Where is it then? Thereupon a scene occurred to me which in the course of twenty-five years has occasionally emerged in my conscious memory without my understanding it. My mother was nowhere to be found; I was crying in despair. My brother Philipp (twenty years older than I) unlocked a wardrobe *[Kasten]*[1] for me, and when I did not find my mother inside it either, I cried even more until, slender and beautiful, she came in through the door. What can this mean? Why did my brother unlock the wardrobe for me, knowing that my mother was not in it and that thereby he could not calm me down? Now I suddenly understand it. I had asked him to do it. When I missed my mother, I was afraid she had vanished from me, just as the old woman had a short time before. So I must have heard that the old woman had been locked up and therefore must have believed that my mother had been locked up too—or rather, had been "boxed up" *[eingekastelt]*—for my brother Philipp, who is now sixty-three years old, to this very day is still fond of using such puns. The fact that I turned to him in particular proves that I was well aware of his share in the disappearance of the nurse.

Since then I have got much further, but have not yet reached any real point of rest. It is so difficult and would carry us so far afield to communicate what I have not yet finished that I hope you will excuse me from it and content yourself with the knowledge of those elements that are certain. If the analysis fulfills what I expect of it, I shall work on it systematically and then put it before you. So far I have found nothing completely new, [just] all the complications to which I have become accustomed. It is by no means easy. Being totally honest with oneself is a good exercise. A single idea of general value dawned on me. I have found, in my own case too, [the phenomenon of] being in love with my mother and jealous of my father, and I now consider it a universal event in early childhood, even if not so early as in children who have been made hysterical. (Similar to the invention of parentage [family romance] in paranoia—heroes, founders of religion). If this is so, we can understand the gripping power of *Oedipus Rex*, in spite of all the objections that reason raises against the presupposition of fate; and we can understand why the later "drama of fate" was bound to fail so miserably. Our feelings rise against any arbitrary individual compulsion, such as is presupposed in *Die Ahnfrau*[2] and the like; but the Greek legend seizes upon a compulsion which everyone recognizes because he senses its existence within himself. Everyone in the audience was once a budding Oedipus in fantasy and each recoils in horror from the dream fulfillment here transplanted into reality, with the full quantity of repression which separates his infantile state from his present one.

Fleetingly the thought passed through my head that the same thing might be at the bottom of *Hamlet* as well. I am not thinking of Shakespeare's conscious intention, but believe, rather, that a real event stimulated the poet to his representation, in that his unconscious understood the unconscious of his hero. How does Hamlet the hysteric justify his words, "Thus conscience does make cowards of us all"? How does he explain his irresolution in avenging his father by the murder of his uncle—the same man who sends his courtiers to their death without a scruple and who is positively precipitate in murdering Laertes?[3] How better than through the torment he suffers from the obscure memory that he himself had contemplated the same deed against his father out of passion for his mother, and—"use every man after his desert, and who should 'scape whipping?'" His conscience is his unconscious sense of guilt. And is not his sexual alienation in his conversation with Ophelia typically hysterical? And his rejection of the instinct that seeks to beget children? And, finally, his transferral of the deed from his own father to Ophelia's? And does he not in the end, in the same marvelous way as my hysterical patients, bring down punishment on himself by suffering the same fate as his father of being poisoned by the same rival?

I have kept my interest focused so exclusively on the analysis that I have not yet even attempted to try out, instead of my hypothesis that in every instance repression starts from the feminine aspect and is directed against the male one, the opposite hypothesis proposed by you. I shall, however, tackle it sometime. Unfortunately, I barely participate in your work and progress. In this one respect I am better off than you are. What I can tell you about mental frontiers *[Seelenende]* of this world finds in you an understanding critic, and what you can tell me about its celestial frontiers *[Sternenende]* evokes only unproductive amazement in me.

With cordial greetings to you, your dear wife, and my new nephew,

Your
Sigm.

1. *Kasten* (box) in Austria is equivalent to *Schrank* and means a wardrobe or closet. The same story occurs in the *Psychopathology of Everyday Life.*

2. *Die Ahnfrau* was F. Grillparzer's first published play (1817). It concerns brother-sister incest and parricide.

3. Actually, Hamlet murders Polonius, not Laertes.

---

Vienna, October 27, 1897
IX., Berggasse 19

Dear Wilhelm,

It seems that I cannot "await"[1] your answer. You certainly cannot offer the explanation for your silence that you have been whirled back with an elemental force to times when reading and writing were bothersome chores for you, as happened to me on Sunday when I wanted to celebrate your not-yet-fortieth birthday with a letter—but I hope it was something just as harmless. As for myself, I have nothing to tell you about except analysis, which I think will be the most interesting thing about me for you as well. Business is hopelessly bad; in general, by the way, right up to the top of the profession, and so I live only for the "inner work." I am gripped and pulled through ancient times[2] in quick association of thoughts; my moods change like the landscapes seen by a traveler from a train; and as the great poet, using his privilege to ennoble (sublimate), puts it:

> Und manche liebe Schatten steigen auf;
> Gleich einer alten, halbverklungenen Sage,
> Kommt erste Lieb' und Freundschaft mit herauf.[3]

And also first fright and discord. Many a sad secret of life is here followed back to its first roots; many a pride and privilege are made aware of their humble origins. All of what I experienced with my patients, as a third [person] I find again here—days when I drag myself about dejected because I have understood nothing of the dream, of the fantasy, of the mood of the day; and then again days when a flash of lightning illuminates the interrelations and lets me understand the past as a preparation for the present. I am beginning to perceive in the determining factors large, general, framing motives, as I should like to call them, and other motives, fill-ins, which vary according to the individual's experiences. At the same time several, though not yet all, doubts about my conception of neurosis are being resolved. An idea about resistance has enabled me to put back on course all those cases of mine that had gone somewhat astray, so that they are now proceeding satisfactorily. Resistance, which finally brings the [analytic] work to a halt, is nothing other than the child's former character, the degenerative character, which developed or would have developed as a result of those experiences that one finds as a conscious memory in the so-called degenerative cases, but which here is overlaid by the development of repression. I dig it out by my work; it struggles; and the person who initially was such a good, noble human being becomes mean, untruthful, or obstinate, a malingerer—until I tell him so and thus make it possible for him to overcome this character. In this way resistance has become something actual and tangible to me, and I wish that instead of the concept of repression I already had what lies concealed behind it as well.

This infantile character develops during the period of "longing," after the child has been removed from sexual experiences. Longing is the main character trait of hysteria, just as actual anesthesia (even though only potential) is its main symptom. During this same period of longing fantasies are formed and masturbation is (regularly?) practiced, which then yields to repression. If it does not yield, then no hysteria develops either; the discharge of sexual excitation for the most part removes the possibility of hysteria. It has become clear to me that various compulsive movements represent a substitute for the discontinued movements of masturbation.

Enough for today; details another time when I have heard good and new things from you. That there is nothing wrong I fortunately know from Oscar and Melanie — who perhaps have already learned something new while I am writing, perhaps not yet.

With the most cordial greetings to you, wife, and child,

Your
Sigm.

1. "*Auswarten*," an Austrian colloquialism.
2. Reading uncertain; probably *alte Zeiten*, or possibly *alle Zeiten* (all times).
3. From the Dedication in Goethe's *Faust:*

And the shades of loved ones appear;
With them, like an old, half-forgotten myth,
First love and friendship.

---

October 31, 1897
IX., Berggasse 19

Dear Wilhelm,

I am so glad to have a letter from you again (the third since Berlin) that I have banished all thoughts of retaliation. And that something whole is shaping itself for you, and biological types are beginning to appear, as well as your parallel between birth and falling ill — all that seems enchanting to me and to hold out a promise of much more in the very near future.

Your nephew — allegedly called Georg, for I have not yet spoken to his father — is all Rie: long, lean, with all the features of the paternal family, not yet masked by baby fat. You must know as much, or more than I, about the details of his birth. Rumor has it that you knew date and sex in advance. I was reassured to learn that her temperature is 36.4[°C] today. On account of my first lecture (eleven students) I could not go there last night; they may, by the way, have been grateful for my not visiting them at that time.

Dr. G.[1] is what you say about him and, above all, still unreliable in his character, made of too poor family material. I have tried to meet in full my obligation as his teacher. He has learned a lot, understands very easily, and progresses well. He makes it all too easy for himself to believe—throws himself into it heart and soul. In view of these pros and cons, I feel toward him as I would toward a wayward son. I wish him the best and must accept his disgrace as mine.

Business here is such that I expect we are facing very bad times, which has been the case in other fields for a long while. Since I have free time, I let myself be persuaded to take on two cases for treatment without a fee. Including myself, that makes three analyses that bring in nothing.

My analysis continues and remains my chief interest. Everything is still obscure, even the problems, but there is a comfortable feeling in it that one has only to reach into one's storerooms to take out what is needed at a particular time. The most disagreeable part of it is the moods, which often completely hide reality. Sexual excitement, too, is no longer of use for someone like me.[2] But I am still pursuing it happily. As regards results, just now there is once more a lull.

Do you believe that what children say in their sleep is part of dreaming? If so, I can present you with the very latest wish dream: Annerl, age 1½ years. She had to starve one day in Aussee because she threw up in the morning, which was blamed on a meal of strawberries. During the following night she called out a whole menu in her sleep: "Stwawberries, high berries, scwambled eggs, pudding." I may have already told you this.

Under the influence of analysis my cardiac symptoms are now very frequently replaced by gastrointestinal symptoms.

Forgive today's idle talk, which is only intended to stress the continuity of our correspondence.

Most cordially,

Your
Sigm.

1. He means Felix Gattel.

2. The German text reads, "Auch die sexuelle Erregung ist für einen wie ich nicht mehr zu brauchen." It may be that Freud is referring to sexual excitement in the context of his self-analysis. When he continues and says, "Ich bin aber noch immer freudig dabei," this is ambiguous and could refer either to sexuality (that he still takes pleasure in it) or, more likely, to the analysis.

Vienna, November 5, 1897
IX., Berggasse 19

Dear Wilhelm,

I have nothing to write really; this happens only during an hour when one could use dialogue and encouragement.

When I last wrote, I did not know anything about the details of Mela's confinement. Since then he [Oscar] has told me about them. I felt very sorry for him; he was terribly shaken and once again has assumed the air of false authority by means of which he silences what is neurotic in him. In the meantime he has become calmer, but the necessity of a laparotomy or of renouncing further offspring will no doubt cast a pall over his mood for some time. The young mother is said to be very cheerful and well now; naturally I have not yet seen her. I spoke briefly with Miss Marie, who is quite smitten with my new nephew—who, as I noticed, increasingly conquers even your cool paternal heart. It is interesting that the literature is now turning so much to the psychology of children. Today I received another book on the subject, by James Mark Baldwin.[1] So one always remains a child of his age, even in what one deems one's very own.

Incidentally, I shudder when I think of all the psychology I shall have to read up on the next few years. At the moment I can neither read nor think. I am completely exhausted by observation. My self-analysis once more is at a standstill; or, rather, it slowly trickles on without my understanding anything of the course it takes. In the other analyses my latest idea about resistance has continued to help me. Recently I had occasion to take up again an old and already published idea about the choice of neurosis, namely, that hysteria is connected with sexual passivity; obsessional neurosis, with activity. Otherwise, it goes slowly, very slowly. Since I can not do anything except analyze and am not fully occupied, I am bored in the evening. My lectures[2] are attended by eleven students who sit there with pencil and paper and hear damnably little that is positive. I play the part of a neuropathological yokel[3] in front of them and comment on Beard, but my interest is elsewhere.

You said nothing about my interpretation of *Oedipus Rex* and *Hamlet.* Since I have not told it to anyone else, because I can well imagine in advance the bewildered rejection, I should like to have a short comment on it from you. Last year you rejected many an idea of mine, with good reason.

Recently I was treated to a stimulating evening by my friend Emanuel Löwy, who is professor of archaeology in Rome. He is a scholar as solid as he is honest and a decent human being, who pays me a visit every year and usually keeps me up until three in the morning. He is spending his fall vacation here where his family lives. Of his Rome . . .

November 10. I am tremendously glad about how you are faring — that your numbers are harmoniously fitting themselves together to form a structure. But I also envy you because once again I do not know at all where I am and am very bored with myself. I shall force myself to write the dream [book] in order to come out of it. The dates of the Bernays family (birthdates) are being put together for you. We are still waiting for a reply from Mama, who is in Merano. I fear some of them will be Jewish dates.

In Oscar something has torn apart as a result of the sad period of waiting. I fear he will now become a complete philistine and give up all hope of further offspring. But don't let him notice anything (in your case, a superfluous reminder).

I am quite seriously thinking of again exploiting you for a day; it works only when we talk, and I greatly miss the intellectual pleasure in understanding something new. With an eye to economy, I would like to know whether you plan to come here at Christmas?

With cordial greetings to you, wife, and child,

Your
Sigm.

P.S. Oli is becoming naughty, exuberant, is doing more poorly in school, and lost his first tooth (Feb. 19, 91).[4]

1. *Mental Development in the Child and the Race* (New York: Macmillan, 1895).
2. See note 3 to letter of January 17, 1897.
3. *Anfänge* has *Naturforscher*, a misreading for *Naturburschen*.
4. This was the birthday of Oliver Freud.

---

Vienna, November 14, 1897

Dear Wilhelm,

"It was on November 12, 1897; the sun was precisely in the eastern quarter; Mercury and Venus were in conjunction —." No, birth announcements no longer start like that. It was on November 12, a day dominated by a left-sided migraine, on the afternoon of which Martin sat down to write a new poem,* on the evening of which Oli lost his second tooth,† that, after the frightful labor pains of the last few weeks, I gave birth to a new piece of knowledge. Not entirely new, to tell the truth; it had repeatedly shown itself and withdrawn again;‡ but this time it stayed and looked upon the light of day. Strangely enough, I have a presentiment of such events a good while beforehand. For instance, I wrote to you once in the summer that I was going to find the source of normal sexual repression (morality, shame, and so forth) and then for a long time failed to find it. Before the vacation trip I told you that the most important patient for me was myself; and then, after I came back from vacation, my self-analysis, of which there was at the time no sign, suddenly started. A few weeks ago came my wish that repression might be replaced by my knowledge of the essential thing lying behind it; and that is what I am concerned with now. I have often had a suspicion that something organic plays a part in repression; I was able once before to tell you that it was a question of the abandonment of former sexual zones, and I was able to add that I had been pleased at coming across a similar idea in Moll. (Privately I concede priority in the idea to no one; in my case the notion was linked to the changed part played by sensations of smell: upright walking, nose raised from the ground, at the same time a number of formerly interesting sensations attached to the earth becoming repulsive — by a process still unknown to me.) (He turns up his nose = he regards himself as something particularly noble.) Now, the zones which no longer produce a release of sexuality in normal and mature human beings must be the regions of the anus and of the mouth and throat. This is to be understood in two ways: first, that seeing and imagining these zones no longer produce an exciting effect, and second, that the internal sensations arising from them make no contribution to the libido, the way the sexual organs proper do. In animals these sexual zones continue in force in both respects; if this persists in human beings too, perversion results. We must assume that in infancy the release of sexuality is not yet so much localized as it is later, so that the zones which are later abandoned (and perhaps the whole surface of the body as well) also instigate something that is analogous to the later release of sexuality. The extinction of these initial sexual zones would have a counterpart in the atrophy of certain internal organs in the course of development. A release of sexuality (as you know, I have in mind a kind of secretion which is rightly felt as the internal state of the libido) comes about, then, not only (1) through a peripheral stimulus upon the sexual organs, or (2) through the internal excitations arising from those organs, but also (3) from ideas — that is, from memory traces — therefore also by the path of deferred action. (You are already familiar with this line of thought. If a child's genitals have been irritated by someone, years afterward the memory of this will produce by deferred action a release of sexuality far stronger than at the time, because the decisive apparatus and the quota of secretion have increased in the meantime.) Thus, there exists a nonneurotic deferred action occurring normally, and this generates compulsion. (Our other memories operate ordinarily only because they have operated as experiences.) Deferred action of this kind occurs also in connection with a memory of excitations of the abandoned sexual zones. The outcome, however, is not a release of libido but of an unpleasure, an internal sensation analogous to disgust in the case of an object.

To put it crudely, the memory actually stinks just as in the present the object stinks; and in the same manner as we turn away our sense organ (the head and nose) in disgust, the preconscious and the sense of consciousness turn away from the memory. This is *repression.*

What, now, does normal repression furnish us with? Something which, free, can lead to anxiety; if psychically bound, to rejection —that is to say, the affective basis for a multitude of intellectual processes of development, such as morality, shame, and the like. Thus the whole of this arises at the expense of extinct (virtual) sexuality. From this we can see that, with the successive thrusts in development, the child is overlaid with piety, shame, and such things, and how the nonoccurrence of this extinction of the sexual zones can produce moral insanity[1] as a developmental inhibition. These thrusts of development probably have a different chronological arrangement in the male and female sexes. (Disgust appears earlier in little girls than in boys.) But the main distinction between the sexes emerges at the time of puberty, when girls are seized by a *non*neurotic *sexual* repugnance and males by libido. For at that period a further sexual zone is (wholly or in part) extinguished in females which persists in males. I am thinking of the male genital zone, the region of the clitoris, in which during childhood sexual sensitivity is shown to be concentrated in girls as well. Hence the flood of shame which the female shows at that period—until the new, vaginal zone is awakened, spontaneously or by reflex action. Hence, too, perhaps the anesthesia of women, the part played by masturbation in children predisposed to hysteria, and the discontinuance of masturbation if hysteria results.

And now for the neuroses! Experiences in childhood which merely affect the genitals never produce neurosis in males (or masculine females), but only a compulsion to masturbate and libido. But since as a rule experiences in childhood have also affected the two other sexual zones, the possibility remains open for males, too, that libido awakening through deferred action may lead to repression and to neurosis. Insofar as memory has lighted upon an experience connected with the genitals, what it produces by deferred action is libido. Insofar as it has lighted upon an experience connected with the anus, mouth, and so on, it produces deferred *internal disgust,* and the final outcome is consequently that a quota of libido is not able, as is ordinarily the case, to force its way through to action or to translation into psychic terms, but is obliged to proceed in a *regressive* direction (as happens in dreams). Libido and disgust would seem to be associatively linked. We owe it to the former that the memory cannot lead to general unpleasure and the like, but that it finds a psychic use; and we owe it to the latter that this use furnishes nothing but symptoms instead of aim-directed ideas. The psychological side of this would not be hard to grasp; the organic factor in it is whether abandonment of the sexual zones takes place according to the masculine or feminine type of development or whether it takes place at all.

It is probable, then, that the choice of neurosis—the decision whether hysteria or obsessional neurosis or paranoia emerges—depends on the nature of the thrust (that is to say, its chronological placing) which enables repression to occur; that is, which transforms a source of internal pleasure into one of internal disgust.

This is where I have got to so far—with all the inherent obscurities. I have resolved, then, henceforth to regard as separate factors what causes libido and what causes anxiety. I have also given up the idea of explaining libido as the masculine factor and repression as the feminine one. These are, in any case, important decisions. The obscurity lies mainly in the nature of the change by which the internal sensation of need becomes the sensation of disgust. I need not draw your attention to other obscure points. The main value of the synthesis lies in its linking the neurotic process and the normal one. There is now a crying need, therefore, for a prompt elucidation of common neurasthenic anxiety.

My self-analysis remains interrupted. I have realized why I can analyze myself only with the help of knowledge obtained objectively (like an outsider). True self-analysis is impossible; otherwise there would be no [neurotic] illness. Since I am still contending with some kind of puzzle in my patients, this is bound to hold me up in my self-analysis as well.

*I was not supposed to know this. It seems his poetic tonsils have been cut.

†The first one was in fact pulled out on the evening of November 9 by the nurse; it might perhaps have lasted till the 10th.

‡Only tall fellows for Sa Majesté le Roi de Prusse.[2]

1. "Moral insanity" in English in original.
2. Freud is referring to the Potsdam guard under Friedrich Wilhelm I, which was recruited wholly from giants.

November 15, 1897

Dear Wilhelm,

More frequently, such one-sided letters; they allow me to forget the distance. Therewith you are only doing what I have always done — writing about what you are engrossed in and leaving aside what you cannot react to. Our conversations used to be like that: each in turn began to speak of what he had to say and did not feel obliged to respond to what he had heard.

My capacity to participate fully in your results increases as they reach perfection, the more the law and idea [behind them] shine through. In the as-yet-uninterpreted numbers I as a layman could not find what appears so promising to you; in your present communication I even found some links to fantasies of my own with which at one time I had wanted to illuminate your discoveries (that 12 as a factor of 23 represents the factor 10 of 28, the former having the male character; the latter, the female one). As you will remember, I also started with the approximate identity of the product

$$12 \times 23 = 10 \times 28 \text{ (period of gestation)},$$

but did not, I admit, know what to do with the difference, which for you became the starting point for further solutions. You surely did not believe that I took those playful attempts seriously or expected you to do so, but I am pleased with the distant relation to your present results.

I can just about imagine the effort it took to let the facts of observation speak in the language of A and P;[1] I carefully suppress further hunches. Care has been taken to make sure that the communication of results will teach nothing to one in whom no indication of the preceding mental work has remained. I am full of hope that at our next meeting it will be easy for me to understand you.

If you cannot come to Vienna — I am still doing so poorly that I do not dare to take off more than one or one and a half days from work at Christmas, and you know that I am far from philistine parsimoniousness — then we could meet in Graz, Reichenau, or the like. But I hold back my proposals because I cannot, as on other occasions, meet you halfway and gladly await whether and what you can manage to do. It will make life easier to be able to look forward to something so close.

I shall ask next time on which side M[elanie]'s tumor is. On my last visit Norbert vividly reminded me of Ramses II, who was found in *persona* several years ago. But he appears to be mentally alert, actively looks about, and still has time, after all, to improve his looks before a few female thrusts come over him.

All are well in my family. Mathilde has a short childhood, is growing rapidly, is becoming completely feminine in character and appearance, and also already shows the first signs of puberty. I enclose the birth dates of the family for you. You will not be able to use them. Thanks to the Jewish calendar, the dates for the birth of my mother, Martha, and Minna are uncertain. The women maintain that one cannot even expect definite Jewish dates from Mama in Merano and did not want to write to her, although I promised it to you. They are altogether unfavorably disposed toward anything that seeks to fathom the secrets of growth, toward your affairs as well as mine.

Now I would like to have a letter from you soon with equally good news about your work and your family. Fortunately I am no longer in the habit of asking how you yourself are.

Most cordially,

Your
Sigm.

1. Algebra and physics, or anatomy and physiology, or astronomy and physics. The first is probably correct, as shown by the letter of July 22, 1899.

---

November 18, 1897
IX., Berggasse 19

Dear Wilhelm,

Mela's tumor is on the right side; Fleischmann, I hear, believes that it can be removed vaginally.

This morning I had a pleasant feeling, as if I had succeeded in something important. But I don't know what it might be. It was in some way connected with the idea that one would have to begin the analysis of hysteria by uncovering the actual, operative motives for accepting the illness, some of which I do know. (For the illness becomes established only when the aberrant libido, having allied itself with such motives, has found, as it were, actual deployment.)

But it cannot be just that. I am telling you all that has happened because feelings of this sort after a time usually prove to have been right and because today has been a mildly accentuated day (tired head, particularly bad lecture).

Most cordial greetings.

Your
Sigm.

---

Vienna, December 3, 1897

Dear Wilhelm,

Last night your dear wife, radiant as always, visited us, bringing the short-lived illusion of all of us being happily together and taking it away again with her departure. Such interruptions of loneliness have a salutary effect by reminding us how difficult renunciation actually is and how wrong one is to get used to it.

December 5. A critical day prevented me from continuing. In honor of the dear visitor, a part of an explanation occurred to me, which she was to have taken back to you. Probably it was not an auspicious day, however; the new idea which occurred to me in my euphoria retreated, no longer pleased me, and is now waiting to be born again. Every now and then ideas dart through my head which promise to realize everything, apparently connecting the normal and the pathological, the sexual and the psychological problem, and then they are gone again and I make no effort to hold onto them because I indeed know that neither their disappearance nor their appearance in consciousness is the real expression of their fate. On such quiet days as yesterday and today, however, everything in me is very quiet, terribly lonely. I cannot talk about it to anyone, nor can I force myself to work, deliberately and voluntarily as other workers can. I must wait until something stirs in me and I become aware of it. And so I often dream whole days away.—All of this is only introductory to our meeting—in Breslau, as Ida proposed, if the train connections suit you. You do know that what happened in Prague proved I was right. When we decided on Prague last time, dreams played a big part. You did not want to come to Prague, and you still know why, and at the same time I dreamed that I was in Rome, walking about the streets, and feeling surprised at the large number of German street and shop signs. I awoke and immediately thought: so this was Prague (where such German signs, as is well known, are called for). Thus the dream had fulfilled my wish to meet you in Rome rather than in Prague. My longing for Rome is, by the way, deeply neurotic. It is connected with my high school hero worship of the Semitic Hannibal, and this year in fact I did not reach Rome any more than he did from Lake Trasimeno. Since I have been studying the unconscious, I have become so interesting to myself. A pity that one always keeps one's mouth shut about the most intimate things.

Das Beste was Du weisst,
Darfst Du den *Buben* doch nicht sagen.[1]

Breslau also plays a role in my childhood memories. At the age of three years I passed through the station when we moved from Freiberg to Leipzig, and the gas flames which I saw for the first time reminded me of spirits burning in hell. I know a little of the connections. My travel anxiety, now overcome, also is bound up with this. Today I am not good for anything. All I can still do is *"Feilen packen,"*[2] as the late Dubois Raymond put it.

Farewell, and let me soon have a sensible answer to this *meschuggene*[3] letter.

Your
Sigm.

Is it true that Robert has not been well?

1. Goethe, *Faust,* Part 1, scene 4, where the text reads, "Das Beste was Du wissen kannst." Here the meaning is "The best you know, you may not tell to *boys.*"
2. Meaning of quotation unclear.
3. Yiddish for "crazy."

Vienna, December 12, 1897

Dear Wilhelm,

Only someone who knows he is in possession of the truth writes as you do. So I look forward with tremendous curiosity to Breslau and shall be all ears. I myself shall not bring anything along. I have gone through a desolate and foggy period and am now suffering painfully from [nasal] suppuration and occlusion; I hardly ever feel fresh. If this does not improve, I shall ask you to cauterize me in Breslau.

I envisage our Breslau trip, on my part, as follows: that I shall leave Saturday morning at 8:00 in order to arrive at 2:30. I don't believe a good night connection can be found. Moreover, traveling at night in an overheated compartment will certainly cost me a [clear] head for the next day. Let me know when you can leave. As things work out, we have to devote two days, Saturday and Sunday, to this excursion, which only enhances my pleasure. One [day] is, after all, far too little. It will be so invigorating for me to chat with you, without a care and seriously, after I have for months again harbored the most *meschugge* matters in my head, without emptying it, and otherwise do not have a sensible person to speak to. Once again, a draft of punch made of Lethe.[1]

Can you imagine what "endopsychic myths" are? The latest product of my mental labor. The dim inner perception of one's own psychic apparatus stimulates thought illusions, which of course are projected onto the outside and, characteristically, into the future and the beyond. Immortality, retribution, the entire beyond are all reflections of our psychic internal [world]. *Meschugge?* Psychomythology.

Let me recommend to you a book by Kleinpaul, *Die Lebendigen und die Toten* [The living and the dead].[2]

May I ask you to bring for me to Breslau the dream examples I sent you (insofar as they are on separate sheets). Last Tuesday I gave a lecture on the dream to my Jewish society (an audience of laymen). It was received enthusiastically. Next Tuesday, the continuation.

My confidence in paternal etiology[3] has risen greatly. Eckstein deliberately treated her patient in such a manner as not to give her the slightest hint of what would emerge from the unconscious and in the process obtained from her, among other things, the identical scenes with the father.[4] Incidentally, the young girl is doing very well.

Recently, the *Meistersinger* afforded me a strange pleasure. A parallel between Breuer and H. Sachs is forced upon me by the circumstance that he too was in the theater. I was sympathetically moved by the "morning dream interpretation melody";[5] I would have liked to add the "*Parnosse*"[6] to "paradise" and "Parnassus." Moreover, as in no other opera, real ideas are set to music, with the tones of feeling attached to it lingering on as one reflects upon them.

Good-bye until Breslau.

Your
Sigm.

But I hope to hear from you and to write to you before then.

1. Same phrase used earlier, in letter of September 6, 1897.

2. Rudolf Kleinpaul, *Die Lebendigen und die Toten in Volksglauben, Religion*

*und Sage* (Leipzig: G. J. Gröschen, 1898). In his preface, written in Leipzig and dated September 25, 1897, Kleinpaul notes that he is writing his book from a psychological point of view, and for the moment acting like a psychiatrist who attempts to see his patient's point of view, even if it means accepting his *idées fixes.*

3. Same phrase used in letter of April 28, 1897, clearly in the sense (both here and there) of the father as the source of neurosis; in other words, the seduction theory.

4. For the significance of this important passage, see Masson (1984, p. 114).

5. "*Morgentraumdeutweise*" was the name given by Hans Sachs in the libretto of Wagner's *Meistersinger* (Act 3) to Walther von Stolzing's prizewinning song.

6. Yiddish for "making a living, nourishment, sustenance."

---

Vienna, December 22, 1897

Dear Wilhelm,

I am in good spirits again and eagerly looking forward to Breslau, that is, to you and your beautiful novelties about life and its dependence on the course of the world. I have always been curious about it, but until now have found no one who could give me an answer. If there now are two people, one of whom can say what life is, and the other can say (almost) what the mind is — and furthermore the two are very fond of each other — it is only right that they should see and talk to each other more frequently. I only want to jot down quickly a few novelties, so that I myself will not have to tell anything and will be able to listen undisturbed.

The insight has dawned on me that masturbation is the one major habit, the "primary addiction," and it is only as a substitute and replacement for it that the other addictions — to alcohol, morphine, tobacco, and the like — come into existence. The role played by this addiction in hysteria is enormous; and it is perhaps there that my major, still outstanding obstacle is to be found, wholly or in part. And here, of course, doubt arises about whether an addiction of this kind is curable, or whether analysis and therapy must come to a halt at this point and content themselves with transforming hysteria into neurasthenia.

With regard to obsessional neurosis, I have found confirmation that the locality at which the repressed breaks through is the *word presentation* and not the concept attached to it. (More precisely, the word memory.) Hence the most disparate things are readily united as an obsessional idea under a single word with multiple meanings. The tendency toward breaking through makes use of these ambiguous words as though it were killing several flies at one blow. Take, for example, the following case. A girl attending a sewing class that soon will come to an end is plagued by the obsessional idea: "No, you mustn't leave; you have not yet *finished;* you must still *make* more; you must still learn all sorts of things." Behind this lay the memory of childhood scenes in which she was put on the pot, did not want to remain there, and experienced the same compulsion:[1] "You mustn't leave; you have not yet *finished*; you must still *make* more." The word "make" permits the later situation to be brought together with the infantile one. Obsessional ideas frequently are clothed in a characteristic *verbal vagueness* in order to permit such multiple deployment. If one takes a closer (conscious) look at it, one finds alongside it the expression "You must still learn more," which perhaps later becomes the fixed obsessional idea and arises through a mistaken interpretation of this kind on the part of the conscious.

All this is not entirely arbitrary. The word "make" has itself undergone an analogous transformation in meaning. An old fantasy of mine, which I would like to recommend to your linguistic sagacity, deals with the derivation of our verbs from such originally coproerotic terms.

I can scarcely detail for you all the things that resolve themselves into—excrement for me (a new Midas!). It fits in completely with the theory of internal stinking. Above all, money itself. I believe this proceeds via the word "dirty" for "miserly." In the same way, everything related to birth, miscarriage, [menstrual] period goes back to the toilet via the word *Abort* [toilet] (*Abortus* [abortion]). This is really wild, but it is entirely analogous to the process by which words take on a transferred meaning as soon as new concepts requiring a designation appear.

The intrinsic authenticity of infantile trauma is borne out by the following little incident which the patient claims to have observed as a three-year-old child. She goes into a dark room where her mother is carrying on[2] and eavesdrops. She has good reasons for identifying herself with this mother. The father belongs to the category of *men who stab women*,[3] for whom bloody injuries are an erotic need. When she was two years old, he brutally deflowered her and infected her with his gonorrhea, as a consequence of which she became ill and her life was endangered by the loss of blood and vaginitis. The mother *now* stands in the room and shouts: "Rotten criminal, what do you want from me? I will have no part of that. Just whom do you think you have in front of you?" Then she tears the clothes from her body with one hand, while with the other hand she presses them against it, which creates a very peculiar impression. Then she stares at a certain spot in the room, her face contorted by rage, covers her genitals with one hand and pushes something away with the other. Then she raises both hands, claws at the air and bites it. Shouting and cursing, she bends over far backward, again covers her genitals with her hand, whereupon she falls over forward, so that her head almost touches the floor; finally, she quietly falls over backward onto the floor. Afterward she wrings her hands, sits down in a corner, and with her features distorted with pain she weeps.

For the child the most conspicuous phase is when the mother, standing up, is bent over forward. She sees that the mother keeps her toes strongly turned *inward*!

When the girl was six to seven months (!!) old, her mother was lying in bed, bleeding nearly to death from an injury inflicted by the father. At the age of sixteen years she again saw her mother bleeding from the uterus (carcinoma), which brought on the beginning of her neurosis. The latter breaks out a year later when she hears about a hemorrhoid operation. Can one doubt that the father forces the mother to submit to anal intercourse? Can one not recognize in the mother's attack the separate phases of this assault: first the attempt to get at her from the front; then pressing her down from the back and penetrating between her legs, which forced her to turn her feet inward. Finally, how does the patient know that in attacks one usually enacts both persons (*self*-injury, *self*-murder), as occurred here in that the woman tears off her clothes with one hand, like the assailant, and with the other holds onto them, as she herself did at the time?

Have you ever seen a foreign newspaper which passed Russian censorship at the frontier? Words, whole clauses and sentences are blacked out so that the rest becomes unintelligible. A *Russian censorship* of that kind comes about in psychoses and produces the apparently meaningless *deliria*.

A new motto:

"What has been done to you, you poor child?"[4]

Enough of my smut.
See you soon.

Your
Sigm.

I shall leave Saturday at eight o'clock as planned.

1. The *Zwang* (compulsion) here surely refers to the external world; for instance, the nurse forcing the little girl to remain on the potty.

2. Meaning uncertain. The German is *ihre Zustände abmacht.*

3. See Richard von Krafft-Ebing, *Psychopathia Sexualis,* ed. Alfred Fuchs, 15th ed. (Stuttgart: Ferdinand Enke, 1918), p. 85.

4. The quotation is from Goethe's *Mignon.* See Eissler (1963, 2:751–764) and Masson (1984, pp. 117–119).

Vienna, December 29, 1897

Dear Wilhelm,

Back home and in harness again, with the delicious aftertaste of our days in Breslau. Bi-bi [bisexuality-bilaterality] is ringing in my ears, but I am still feeling too well for serious work. The first third of the paper for Paschkis is already done, a *Gartenlaube* essay, no more than that.[1]

Otherwise I am resolutely tramping along in the *Dreckology*.[2] A little interpretation came my way in the very first days [after I returned]. Mr. E., whom you know, had an anxiety attack at the age of ten when he tried to catch a black beetle, which would not put up with it. The meaning of this attack had thus far remained obscure. Now, dwelling on the theme of "being unable to make up one's mind," he repeated a conversation between his grandmother and his aunt about the marriage of his mother, who at that time was already dead, from which it emerged that she had not been able to make up her mind for quite some time; then he suddenly came up with the black beetle, which he had not mentioned for months, and from that to ladybug *[Marienkäfer]* (his mother's name was Marie); then he laughed out loud and inadequately explained his laughter by saying that zoologists call this beetle *septem punctata*, or the equivalent, according to the number of dots, although it is always the same animal. Then we broke off and next time he told me that before the session the meaning of the beetle *[Käfer]* had occurred to him; namely: *qué faire?* = being unable to make up one's mind[3] . . . *meschugge!*

You may know that here a woman may be referred to as a nice "beetle." His nurse and first love was a French woman; in fact, he learned to speak French before he learned to speak German. You will remember our discussions about the use of the words "to stick into," "toilet," and the like.

My second and last lecture on the dream is over and was acclaimed enthusiastically by the Jews. Afterward an eager member of the audience asked me whether completely senseless dreams could be interpreted in the same way. This is the value of popular lectures. A physician and colleague could not have asked a more stupid question.

Bild mir nicht ein, ich könnte was lehren
Die Menschen zu bessern und zu bekehren.[4]

What I want now is plenty of material for a mercilessly severe test of the left-handedness theory; I have needle and thread ready.[5] Incidentally, the question that follows from it is the first in a long time on which our hunches and inclinations have not taken the same path.

I have not yet found the time to have a word with my female side.

My nose is behaving itself and conveys its thanks.

Now, a Happy New Year and many meetings in 1898!

Your
Sigm.

1. *Gartenlaube* was a popular journal of light reading. Freud is referring to his "Sexuality in the Aetiology of the Neuroses," published in 1898.

2. Written in Greek in the original; a play on the German *Dreck* (filth).

3. The French *que faire* (what to do?) is here likened to the sound of *Käfer*, hence the accent on *qué*.

4. Goethe's *Faust*, Act 1, scene 1: "I do not pretend I could be a teacher to help or convert a fellow creature" (translated by Bayard Taylor).

5. The reference is to a test to see if a person is left-handed. Fliess believed that people who were left-handed showed the psychological (and physical) characteristics of the opposite sex. In his book *Der Ablauf des Lebens*, a long chapter entitled "On the Significance of Ambidextrous Symmetry" contains sixty-seven brief case histories. At the end is a remarkable passage that reveals a great deal about Fliess's psychology (my translation): "A picture from days long gone surfaces in my memory. I hear singing that moves my heart. I leaf through a small book with enchanting verses. I see a psyche lost in desperate thought. And the creator of all this magnificence was a woman whose exquisite feminine beauty was on everybody's lips, and whose image had been committed to canvas by one of the greatest masters of the brush. But also I see how the fingers of her *left* hand guide the scissors with which she is cutting the material for a beautifully fitting gown, and how the stitching needle soon moves from her right to her *left* hand. How many times did I, teasingly, forbid her to do that! Only today do I know how to interpret these so-called minor flaws whose presence eventually caused her the most severe grief" (italics in original).

---

Vienna, January 4, 1898

Dear Wilhelm,

Little Robert's respectful characterization of Annerl's picture is truly delicious. He is a charming fellow — in case you didn't know.

Today I am sending you No. 2 of the "dreckological"[1] reports, a very interesting journal published by me for a single reader. No. 1, which I am keeping, contains wild dreams that would hardly be of interest to you; they are part of my self-analysis, which is still groping about, entirely in the dark. I would appreciate your returning this to me for future examination, but certainly not right away. As always, the first week after our talks was a very productive one for me. Then followed a few desolate days with rotten mood and pain displaced from my head (or heart) to my legs. As of this morning, a complete clearing. I shall go on striving and erring.

It is of great interest to me that you are so affected by my still negative attitude to your interpretation of left-handedness. I shall try to be objective, for I know how difficult it is.

To me, it seems to be as follows:[2] I literally embraced your stress on bisexuality and consider this idea of yours to be the most significant one for my subject since that of "defense." If I had a disinclination on personal grounds, because I am in part neurotic myself, this disinclination would certainly have been directed toward bisexuality, which, after all, we hold responsible for the inclination to repression. It seems to me that I object only to the permeation of bisexuality and bilaterality that you demand. Initially, I did not take any stand on this idea because I still felt too remote from the subject. On the second afternoon in Breslau I felt as though I had been hit on the head as a result of the nasal reaction; otherwise I should no doubt have been able to turn the doubt I felt into an objection; or, rather, been able to seize upon it [the idea] when you yourself said that each of the two halves probably contains both kinds of sex organs. But where, then, is the femininity, for instance, of the left half of a man if it carries a testicle (and the corresponding lower male/female sexual organs) just like the right one? Your postulate that for all results male and female must unite is already satisfied, after all, in one half!

I had the impression, furthermore, that you considered me to be partially left-handed; if so, you would tell me, since there is nothing in this bit of self-knowledge that might hurt me. It is your doing if you do not know every intimate detail about me; you have surely known me long enough. Well, then, I am not aware of any preference for the left hand, either at present or in my childhood; rather I could say that years ago I had two left hands. There is only one thing I would have you consider: I do not know whether it is always obvious to other people which is their own right and left and where right and left are in others. In my case (in earlier years) it was rather a matter of having to think which was my right; no organic feeling told me. I used to test this by quickly making a few writing movements with my right hand. As far as other people are concerned, I must to this day work out their position and so on. Perhaps this fits in with your theory; perhaps it is connected with the fact that I have an infamously low capability for visualizing spatial relationships, which made the study of geometry and all subjects derived from it impossible for me.

This is how it appears to me. But I know very well, indeed, that it nevertheless may be otherwise, and that the aversion to your conception of left-handedness I have so far felt may rest on unconscious motives. If they are hysterical, they certainly have nothing to do with the subject matter, but merely latch onto a catchword; for example, that I have been up to something that one can only do with the left hand. In that case the explanation will turn up some day, God knows when.

I learned the truth about Q.J. only after my return. If there is really something to him, he will not be hindered by this aberration from amounting to something some day, as little as Meynert was hindered by his drinking of chloroform. The original addiction *[Ursucht]*! The poor boy is the necessary complement to the philistinism and hypocrisy of the entire circle.

You must promise me to expect nothing of the *Gartenlaube*.[3] It will be real chitchat, good enough for the public, but not worth a word between us.

On Wednesday we shall go with your entire family (Bondy, Rie) to a Jewish play by Herzl,[4] in the Carl Theater — a first night, which has already played a role in my dreams.

Where did you get the quotation about the professors and the ears? I would like to appropriate it from you. Recently in a daytime fantasy (of which I am by no means free as yet) I hurled these words at his excellency, the minister of education: "You cannot frighten me. I know that I shall still be a university lecturer when you have long ceased to be called minister."

Farewell, then, and write soon again before I come up with No. 3. On my side of the tunnel it is quite dark, but for you the sun and the stars are shining for this task as well.

Most cordially,

Your
Sigm.

1. Freud uses *Dreckologisch*, that is, pertaining to a collection of filth; written partly in Greek.

2. *Wie ich mir erscheine*; literally, as I appear to myself. Probably an unusual way of saying *wie es mir erscheint*.

3. See note 1 to letter of December 29, 1897.

4. The play was *Das neue Ghetto*, referred to in the *Interpretation of Dreams* (*S.E.* 4:442). See Grinstein (1980, pp. 318–333) for a discussion of this play and Freud's feelings about bilaterality.

January 16, 1898
IX., Berggasse 19

Dear Wilhelm,

I regret that this time our conditions have not remained parallel. I have been well and in good spirits. I hope by now that is true of you too.

Enclosed No. 3 of the DR [dreckology report]. All sorts of little things are teeming; dream and hysteria fit together ever more neatly. The details are now standing in the way of the large problems touched upon in Breslau. One must take it as it comes and be glad that it comes at all. I add the definition of "happiness" (in case I have not already told it to you a long time ago?):

> Happiness is the belated fulfillment of a prehistoric wish. For this reason wealth brings so little happiness. Money was not a childhood wish.

All sorts of other things keep dawning on me and always everything earlier is forgotten. It is too soon to summarize.

Recently Breuer pulled another brilliant stunt. I would think that one should not let his intelligence deceive one about his narrow-mindedness. What I am writing now is sheer craziness. I still owe him money from my student days (2,300 florins, I would estimate). I have never been able to pay it back; it was not until this year that I succeeded in sending him, with a few words of apology, the first installment of 500 florins. Thereupon a letter arrives for my wife, with the return of 350 florins. First, he did not know that the amount had not yet been paid. Second, two years ago I treated his poor niece B., estimated the cost of the treatment to be 500 florins and accepted only 150 florins. Therefore now the return of the rest with a receipt for 500 florins. Thereupon, of course, in a very polite letter which brags a little about my income, I prove to him that he has nothing to do with the affair B., that the amount in this case is completely different, and so forth. Thereupon he in turn: as long as I had not paid, he had not thought about paying either; but since I had started, he could not lag behind. He would keep the money and send me a receipt for 850 florins. All this with the greatest lack of logic, with disdainful condescension and deeply hurt feelings, as well as an unabated need to do good. Just expand a little on this abbreviated [description of the] affair. It is genuine Breuer. It is enough to make one extremely ungrateful for good deeds.

I notice that a dull day has begun, and therefore close. Your last reference to the left foot has considerably changed my disposition about the contested theory. I do not yet have any further material, because I see very few new faces.

I greet you most cordially and herewith announce a new issue.

Your
Sigm.

---

Vienna, January 22, 1898
IX., Berggasse 19

Dear Wilhelm,

Mela is doing very well; she is in good spirits, looks radiant, which on the fourth day after the laparotomy is not a trifle, and seems to be past all worry. You know that I have always had some liking for her, I believe ever since in your honor she played the old damsel who was amazed at the reflex new-roses.[1] Oscar, too, is gradually recovering; he was torn apart;[2] the two nights before the operation apparently were pretty bad because of the excitement. There is very little sense in fate's trying our friend Oscar so severely; he will become ossified quite prematurely. That will be all.

Well, my good spirits ended with a bad migraine on Thursday. Keep the two issues of the DR; I do not know how long it will take for a new one to materialize. Everything has vanished. This nasty habit of my [mental] organization suddenly to rob me of all my mental resources is for me the hardest thing in life to bear. The button business, which has received my fullest recognition, stands out like an oasis in the desert. In the carriage I already convinced myself, by unbuttoning my clothes, that you were right.[3] My practice is not conducive to further testing [of your bilaterality theory]. Recently I had a total of *two* patients in *three* consulting hours! Altogether, this is an abominably bad year.

Ida's remarks about John the Baptist seem to me to be not only clever but also correct. But is the rejection she bases on this fair? Does she not thereby yield too much to her instinctive aversion to everything that is neurotic? John no doubt has *les vertus de ses défauts* [the virtues of his defects] and the reverse; psychoneurosis will no doubt turn out to be in general the reverse of the great psychic achievements of concentration. Christ himself no doubt was a virginal, abstinent visionary. It is noteworthy that obsessional ideas and phobias (as remorse for old sins) are invariably unsociable; it is only abstinence that attracts people, as though they were waiting for [the final distribution of] what has been stored up. Music of the future! Incidentally, John the Baptist has all his deeds (as a sinner) behind him; he is incapable of any new deed (except for measures of protection and repentance).

My anger at Breuer is constantly being refueled. Recently I was disturbed to hear from a patient that mutual acquaintances had said that Breuer severed his relationship with me because he disapproved of the way in which I conduct my life and money matters — a man who earns so much money must save some of it and think of the future. This last remark they have from Breuer himself, who is their family physician. If you want to understand the full extent of his neurotic dishonesty, put the above together with the remark in his letter that he thought my debt to him had already been paid. Did he really think I would start saving money *before* I had paid back my old debts for my education? In all of this, one may always assume that one hears only a small part of the rumors that are being spread about.

Next time, a more pleasant exchange of letters to and fro.

Your
Sigm.

1. Freud's word is *Reflexneu-rosen*, a pun on reflex neurosis and new roses.

2. *Zusammengerissen*; literally, torn together.

3. Undoubtedly a reference to a "test" for left-handedness. Freud may mean that since he is able to unbutton his clothes with his left hand, he is latently left-handed and therefore, in Fliess's view, latently homosexual as well. See note 5 to letter of December 29, 1897.

---

Vienna, January 30, 1898
IX., Berggasse 19

Dear Wilhelm,

As your beautiful quotation surmised so correctly, your letter found me yesterday on a day of wild joyfulness, unfortunately only internal; for there are few external reasons. These mood changes in me are related to dreams and my self-analysis; I understand little of them. Today I am sober again. Your gift of the dream pleased me greatly; it will be a valuable contribution for me. I may publish it?

This morning two things appeared to me to go against the grain. I read your letter more carefully and had to replace my first impression — that you, like me, were too merry to work — with another one — that you have not been well at all.

"In the last few days I have been in the mood for anything but work, will surely come crashing down"—or am I mistaken again and do you mean, after all, a euphoria after which something will happen?[1] But can you really feel too good to work? Or, it just occurs to me, is there something else behind it that I should guess? Do I know the dreaming gravida?[2] Hurrah?!

The second item, which now has lost much of its importance, however (that is, if I have not been mistaken), is Gattel's behavior. He sent me a large treatise[3] in which he deals with the theory of hysteria, with the sexual substance and the like, whereas I had expected from him a report about the anamneses that he elicited in neurasthenics. It is very distressing for me to tell him that even if he has pursued these matters further, he cannot possibly publish them as his own work; and even more distressing that I do not at all agree with his account. But I shall do so [tell him]. "To burden oneself with fools, etc."[4]

A section of the DR is in the process of growing, in order to inform you in due time about the small results of these weeks.

I did not at all intend to write to you about Schenk.[5] Perhaps you do not know that Arthur Schiff[6] is now repeating your cocaine experiments in cases of dysmenorrhea and has confirmed every single detail. I am convinced that one day they will come to realize that you are completely reliable.

At our next congress I shall listen most devoutly; it is surely becoming more rewarding each time.

The symmetry in planes and the numerical ratios of the birth relationships are of course highly impressive. Once you have put these individual occurrences together to form a structure, the wayfarers will be much amazed.[7]

The greatest of all fortunes,[8] it sometimes seems to me, is either good humor or a clear mind. I must now write the last part of my *Gartenlaube* article.

Don't be so parsimonious with such refreshing letters, and make obscure allusions clearer to

Your
Sigm.

1. Fliess believed, mysteriously, that euphoria was a signal of impending disaster. See the quote from his book *Zur Periodenlehre* in note 6 to letter of November 27, 1893.

2. That is, the pregnant woman who had the dream; doubtless a reference to Ida Fliess's pregnancy.

3. The reference is to Felix Gattel's 1898 book, *Über die sexuellen Ursachen der Neurasthenie und Angstneurose.*

4. A quote from Goethe's *Faust,* Part 2:

Da habt ihr's nun!
Mit Narren sich beladen
Das kommt zuletzt dem Teufel selbst zu schaden!

5. On Schenk's book see note 1 to letter of May 1, 1898.

6. Arthur Schiff, "Über die Beziehungen zwischen Nase und weiblichen Sexualorganen," *Wiener klinische Wochenschrift,* 14 (1901):57–65. See note 2 to letter of January 30, 1901. Note that Schiff translated Freud's French article "Obsessions et phobies (leur mécanisme psychique et leur étiologie)" in the *Wiener klinische Rundschau.* See also Fliess's "Aus der Diskussion über die Vorträge des Herrn Siegmund."

7. This is possibly a reference to *Faust,* Act 5, scene 1. Philemon says of the wanderer, who returns to the scene of his youth and finds the land reclaimed from the ocean (translated by Bayard Taylor):

Lass ihn rennen, ihn erschrecken,
Denn er glaubt nicht, was er sieht.

(Let him go, and be affrighted
He'll believe not what he sees.)

8. A quotation from Schiller's *Braut von Messina:* "Das Leben ist der Güter höchstes nicht."

---

Vienna, February 9, 1898
IX., Berggasse 19

Dear Wilhelm,

So I have guessed correctly and congratulate you on the increase in your observational material and the opportunity to predetermine all sorts of things — in addition to everything else. I hope Ida will be equally happy when the current period of suffering is behind her. Mela is very well and is indeed very lovable; I am decidedly partial to her.— Your last A and P[1] experiments are simply uncanny. It probably is not just your good fortune of having married into this family, but others provide similar results.

The reduction of our Easter trip corresponds to the general decline this year. I can, after all, get into a state of real exultation only far away from Madrid! The essential thing, our having a few hours together, does, however, remain certain.

On Sunday I was in Hungary for a consultation. A fifty-year-old lady claimed that she went about on wooden rollers, that her *limbs* were limp like an articulated doll's, and that she would soon start crawling on all fours. I am, by the way, for no accountable reason in a splendid mood and have found my daytime interest. I am deep in the dream book, am writing it fluently, and enjoy the thought of all the "head shaking"[2] over the indiscretions and audacities it contains. If only it weren't necessary to do a lot of reading! I am already fed up with what little literature there is. The only sensible thought occurred to old Fechner[3] in his sublime simplicity: the dream process is played out in a different psychic territory. I shall report on the first crude map of this territory.

I am sending you today a long, finished issue of the DR, which I will perhaps ask you to return soon because of the beautiful dream example. As for the rest, everything is still in a state of latency. My self-analysis is at rest in favor of the dream book. The cases of hysteria are proceeding especially poorly.[4] I shall not finish a single one this year either; and as for the next one, I shall be completely without patient material. Today I finished the *Gartenlaube* article. It is rather impertinent and essentially designed to give offense, in which it undoubtedly will succeed. Breuer will say I did myself a lot of harm. A rumor has it that we are to be invested with the title of professor at the emperor's jubilee on December 2. I do not believe it, but had a delightful dream about it, which unfortunately cannot be published because its background, its second meaning, shifts back and forth between my nurse (my mother) and my wife and one cannot really publicly subject one's wife to reproaches of this sort [as a reward] for all her labor and toil. Quite generally: the best you know, and so on.[5]

Zola keeps us very much in suspense. A fine fellow, someone with whom one could communicate. The lousy[6] behavior of the French reminded me of what you said on the bridge in Breslau about the decay of France, remarks which at first I found quite disagreeable.

Schweninger's[7] performance, here at the talking circus, was a real disgrace! I did not attend, of course; instead I treated myself to listening to our old friend Mark Twain[8] in person, which was a sheer delight.

Farewell and give my greetings to your whole present and future family.

Your
Sigm.

1. See note 1 to letter of November 15, 1897.

2. A reference to *Bilder zur Jobsiade* by Wilhelm Busch. The hero, Hieronymus Jobs, a candidate for admission to the priesthood, evokes repeated *Schütteln des Kopfes* (head shaking) on the part of his examiners.

3. See *S.E.* 4:48.

4. The text reads, "Die Hysteriefälle gehen sogar schlecht voraus." Meaning unclear. Probably Freud meant *schlecht voran.*

5. Goethe, *Faust,* Part 1, scene 4, a quotation Freud used frequently: "The best you know, you may not tell to *boys.*"

6. Freud uses the German *lausig*.

7. Kris (*Origins*, p. 245n4) says: "On February 5th, 1898, Schweninger, Bismarck's well-known doctor, delivered a lecture in dialogue form jointly with Maximilian Harden in which he advocated medical nihilism. He attacked specialization in medicine, made derogatory remarks about the diagnostic value of X-rays and confessed that he envied veterinaries, because their patients could not talk. The climax of his lecture was the phrase: 'The world belongs to the brave, including the brave sick.' "

8. Freud comments on this lecture in a footnote to *Civilization and Its Discontents* (*S.E.* 21:126).

---

Vienna, February 23, 1898
IX., Berggasse 19

Dear Wilhelm,

Interruptions in your letters have the effect of putting me out of humor twice: first, because I then miss the Other even more than usual; second, because I then suspect that the reason is something bad. I did not know, though, that this time your silence was doubly determined.

I thank you for reading and returning the DR, in which I now deposit my novelties. In order not to come to the Easter congress completely empty-handed, not always to be the one who receives, I shall save the sheets that may follow. I believe that nothing major will come up before Easter. I am a bit too worn out for this. Also, my practice has finally picked up; I am more tired than in previous years, when work could not wear me out at all.

Enclosed the *Gartenlaube* article; you will do me the favor of saying *nothing* about it to me.

Several chapters of the dream book already are complete; it is turning out nicely and leads me far more deeply into psychology than I had imagined. All of the new formulations are at the philosophical end; absolutely nothing has come up at the organic-sexual one.

The children are thriving. Recently Annerl complained that Mathilde had eaten all the apples and demanded that her [Mathilde's] belly be slit open (as happened to the wolf in the fairy tale of the little goat). She is turning into a charming child.

Best wishes for a speedy recovery to both of you.

Your
Sigm.

March 5, 1898
IX., Berggasse 19

Dear Wilhelm,

I have heard nothing from you and unfortunately can imagine what this means — one or both [of you is sick] — a very strong reason to get grumpy. We are well, but I am tired from ten to eleven hours of rigorous work, as you can see from my handwriting. I have finished a whole section of the dream book, the best-composed one, to be sure, and am curious about what else will occur to me. Otherwise, no scientific novelties; the DR have been interrupted, since I no longer write them for you.

Inasmuch as Ida's suffering at least serves a good purpose, while yours, if that is the case now, has no purpose whatsoever, I urge you to regain your good spirits soon and then write to me.

Most cordially,

Your
Sigm.

---

Vienna, March 10, 1898
IX., Berggasse 19

Dear Wilhelm,

Your sleepiness now explains to me my own simultaneous state. Our protoplasm has worked its way through the same critical period. How nice it would be if this close harmony[1] between us were a total one; I would always know how you are and would never expect letters without disappointment.[2] I hope your *Kück*[3] has correctly predicted the date on which your Ida can get up; otherwise your Easter trip will be in doubt; I was pleased to see you repeat that it was certain. On the very same day your mother and Marie happened to visit us; but the only one in the family who is flourishing unquestionably is Melanie. I see very little of Oscar (my O.); he seems to sense that he is becoming more and more estranged from me. By now he has no doubt taken the small step that kept him from being a complete philistine.

*Ad vocem Kück* [as to your vision]: It was no small feat on your part to see the dream book lying finished before you. It has come to a halt again, and meanwhile the problem has deepened and widened. It seems to me that the theory of wish fulfillment has brought only the psychological solution and not the biological — or, rather, metapsychical — one. (I am going to ask you seriously, by the way, whether I may use the name metapsychology for my psychology that leads behind consciousness.) Biologically, dream life seems to me to derive entirely from the residues of the prehistoric period of life (between the ages of one and three)—the same period which is the source of the unconscious and alone contains the etiology of all the psychoneuroses, the period normally characterized by an amnesia analogous to hysterical amnesia. This formula suggests itself to me: What is *seen* in the prehistoric period produces dreams; what is *heard* in it produces fantasies; what is *experienced sexually* in it produces the psychoneuroses. The repetition of what was experienced in that period is in itself the fulfillment of a wish; a recent wish only leads to a dream if it can put itself in connection with material from this prehistoric period, if the recent wish is a derivative of a prehistoric one or can get itself adopted by one. It is still an open question how far I shall be able to adhere to this extreme theory and how far I can expose it to view in the dream book.

My seminar was particularly lively this year; even an assistant of Erb's[4] attended. During the period of involuntary interruption when the university was closed, I went on lecturing in my room over a mug of beer and with cigars. As to the next term, I already have two new enrollments in addition to those attending now.

I opened a recently published book by Janet, *Hystérie et idées fixes*,[5] with a pounding heart and put it aside again with my pulse calmed. He has no inkling of the key.

So I go on growing older, contentedly most of the time, watch myself rapidly turning gray and the children growing up, look forward to the Easter holidays, and exercise my patience in waiting for the solution to the problem of the neuroses.

I heard a rumor that R.W., too, is coming with you this year. Shall we then let him get acquainted with the children?

With the most cordial wishes for the speediest recovery,

Your
Sigm.

1. *Verwandtschaftliche Übereinstimmung:* literally, kindred agreement.
2. Freud undoubtedly meant to write that he would never be disappointed.
3. See note 1 to letter of October 31, 1895.
4. Wilhelm Erb (1840–1921), professor of medicine at the University of Heidelberg. Freud makes an interesting reference to Erb in his "Autobiographical Study" (*S.E.* 20:16).
5. Presumably a reference to Pierre Janet, *Névroses et idées fixes*, 2 vols. (Paris: Felix Alcan, 1898). The work includes many citations of the French, German, and English psychiatric literature, but only one reference to Freud (1:124n2, in which Janet mentions Freud's "Obsessions et phobies"). There is almost no mention of sexuality, which may be what Freud is referring to. Further on, however, Janet (2:186–188) describes the seduction of a seven-year-old girl and explains the suicide attempts and hysterical attacks in a fourteen-year-old as due to attempted rape.

# *The Interpretation of Dreams*

Vienna, March 15, 1898
IX., Berggasse 19

Dear Wilhelm,

If I ever underestimated Conrad Ferdinand, I have long since been converted by you through reading his "Himmelstor."[1]

Would you please let me have that passage for the later [book on] hysteria.

I do not in the least underestimate bisexuality either; I expect it to provide all further enlightenment, especially since that moment in the Breslau marketplace when we found both of us saying the same thing. It is only that at the moment I feel remote from it because, buried in a dark shaft, I see nothing else. My productivity in work seems to be a function of the distance from our congresses. At this time I am just plain stupid; I sleep during my afternoon analyses; absolutely nothing new occurs to me any longer. I really believe that my way of life, the eight hours[2] of analysis throughout eight months of the year, devastates me. Unfortunately, my carefree spirit, which would advise me to take a holiday from time to time, does not stand firm in the face of the slim earnings in these times and the prospect of still worse ones. So I go on working like a cab horse, as we say in Vienna. The idea occurred to me that you might like to read my dream study but are too discreet to ask for it. It goes without saying that I would have sent it to you before it goes to press. But since it now has again come to a halt, I can just as well send it to you in fragments. A few explanations about them. This is the second chapter. The first, on the literature, has not yet been written. It is succeeded by:

3. Dream Material
4. Typical Dreams
5. The Psychic Process in Dreaming
6. Dreams and Neuroses

I shall return to the two dreams described here in subsequent chapters, where their still incomplete interpretation will be finished. I hope you will not object to the candid remarks in the dream about the professorship. The philistines here will rejoice at being able to say that with this I have put myself beyond the pale. The thing in the dream that may strike you as odd will find its explanation later on (my ambition). Comments on *Oedipus Rex*, the talisman fairy tale, and possibly *Hamlet*, will find their place. I first must read up on the Oedipus legend[3] — do not yet know where.

While I hesitate to burden you at a time when you feel disinclined to work, I set against this the thought that this thing, with its minimal speculative content, will probably only amuse you in a harmless sort of way.

As far as hysteria is concerned, I am at present completely disoriented. I do, of course, very much want to know whether your hopes concerning the special date were fulfilled and whether we can hold onto our Easter expectations, *without changes*. There is absolutely no question of giving them up.

With the most cordial greetings,

Your
Sigm.

1. The reference is to Conrad Ferdinand Meyer (1825–1898), a Swiss author often cited by Freud. See William G. Niederland, "First Application of Psychoanalysis to a Literary Work," *Psychoanalytic Quarterly*, 29(1960):228–235. Niederland's article contains a translation of the four-verse poem, "Himmelstor," which describes a foot-washing compulsion.

2. The manuscript reads 8, not 9 as in *Anfänge*.

3. In Freud's library in Maresfield Gardens is a scholarly book by L. Constans, *La Légende d'Oedipe: Étudiée dans l'antiquité, au moyen âge et dans les temps modernes en particulier dans le Roman de Thèbes, texte français du XIIe siècle* (Paris: Maisonneuve, 1881). Freud marked those passages in the work having to do with incest (pp. 35–42).

---

Vienna, March 24, 1898
IX., Berggasse 19

Dear Wilhelm,

You will not be surprised if I write to you today about your evaluation of my dream manuscript, which made my day. No doubt you do not want me to compare you with Breuer in any way; such a comparison is forced on me. I think of the underhandedness with which he doled out praise; for example, the style is wonderful, the most ingenious ideas; and the consideration which led him to express his picky objections to the essentials to other people from whom I then heard about them. Again and again I am glad to be rid of him.

Fortunately I can answer your objections by referring to later chapters. I have just stopped before one such chapter, which will deal with the somatic stimuli of dreams. It will also touch upon anxiety dreams, on which light will be shed once again in the last chapter on "Dreams and Neurosis." But in the account you have read I shall include cross-references, to avoid the impression it gave you that the author is making things too easy for himself here.

I do not at all think of this version as final. First I want to put my own ideas into shape, then study the literature in detail, and thereafter insert or revise where this is indicated by my reading. I cannot do the reading until I have finished what I myself have to say, and I can compose the details only in the process of writing. So far another twenty-four pages are finished; but I suspect no other section will turn out to be as amusing and as rounded out[1] as what you have read.

I hope you will tell me more about many particular points when we meet. You shall not refuse me the duties of the first audience and supreme judge. I would like to appropriate your comments on the migraine dreams; I am not familiar with such dreams from my own personal experience and therefore would have omitted them.

Our Easter congress gains even greater value for me in this respect as well, and I am glad to hear that you are adhering to the plan. If at the same time it can be combined with my woeful longing for nature and young greenery, there will be one more wish fulfillment. I know, however, that everything depends on the condition of your dear wife, and if she does not want to be without you or cannot travel with you after all, I shall of course forgo our congress. There are still three weeks between now and then; surely I may expect the most drastic change to occur in this interval.

In my family the girls—Mathilde, Sophie, Anna—have retreated to the state of illness with influenza. The boys are still bearing up. Mathilde frightens us when her glands begin to swell; she has no other symptoms. When Ida is well again, I should like to realize a plan involving Martha and Mathilde in May. Since my sister Marie now lives in Berlin, they will not need to impose upon your hospitality.

Recently Martin described the seduction of a goose by a fox in a poem. The words of wooing were:

I love you from the bottom of my heart.
Come, kiss me;
You could be my favorite
Among all the animals.

Don't you think the structure is noteworthy? Occasionally he composes verses that arouse his audience's indignation, for example,

Father Fox said, We are going to Aussee;
The children look forward to it and drink coffee.

To pacify us, he then said, "When I make up things like that, it is only like making faces."

And Robert Wilhelm? Will you bring him along when you and Ida come to Vienna?

Waiting for the very best news,

Your
Sigm.

1. The manuscript reads *gerundet*, rather than *gründlich* as in *Anfänge*.

---

Vienna, April 3, 1898
IX., Berggasse 19

Dear Wilhelm,

Desolate Easter! Nor can I think of coming to Berlin; for Ida's condition and the fact that your mother is occupying the guest room are not the only hindrances. My own mother is there now as well, with my sister, and I would of necessity have to devote a part of the already short time to her. I shall go somewhere, grumbling about it, perhaps with my brother-in-law, where I shall desperately long for greenery and flowers that do not yet exist, and I shall not be able to hear or to say what I wanted. After each of our congresses I was strengthened anew for weeks, ideas kept crowding in thereafter, the pleasure in hard work was reestablished, and the flickering hope that the way through the underbrush will be found burned quietly and radiantly for a while. Instructive it is not for me, this privation; I always knew what our meetings meant to me.

At odd hours[1] I go on writing the dream book; another section dealing with the sources of dreams and typical dreams is nearly finished, but it is far less satisfactory than the first one and probably needs revision. Otherwise science says nothing whatsoever to me; nor is there an interest alive in me in anything but the dream.

The influenza has run its course, having done little damage and showing no predilection for the male sex. The children are lively and amusing, the women well, the man of the house cranky.

Today I am returning Dr. G.'s work to him, without having exercised any influence on it. It was repugnant to me after my last experience with his theory, which altogether cooled me off further. I am aware that I forced him on you; I hope that you will defend yourself. Fundamentally you are far more good-natured than I am.

Stricker died yesterday;[2] he was an important man, a hard personality, who succeeded in identifying his essentially mean and fanatical bent with scientific aspirations. He was hostile toward me personally. I recall a word of his from the time I worked in his laboratory—the advice never to get involved in petty details, but instead to dare to tackle one of the great problems of life. His pupil Gärtner[3] illustrates the heeding of this advice.

The children want me to play the fine travel game "One Hundred Journeys through Europe" with them today. I shall do so, because the mood for work is not always present.

My lecture bores me; I do not care to lecture on hysteria because I lack the decisive verdict on two important points.

I should love to go to our beautiful Italy again this year, but earnings were bad. I must save.

So, *the* congress is dead; long live the next one! For this purpose it is absolutely essential that the two of you get well at last.

With the most cordial wishes for this outcome,

Your
Sigm.

1. English in original.
2. Salomon Stricker (1834–1898), professor of experimental pathology at the University of Vienna. Part of Freud's work on cocaine was done in his laboratory.
3. Gustav Gärtner (1855–1937) appears in Freud's dream of the "Botanical Monograph." See *S.E.* 4:171, 175–176.

---

Vienna, April 14, 1898
IX., Berggasse 19

Dear Wilhelm,

I think it is a good rule for a correspondent to leave unmentioned what the recipient already knows and to tell him something new instead. I therefore shall pass over having heard that you had a bad time at Easter; you know that anyway. I would rather tell you about my Easter trip, which I took in a grumpy mood, but from which I returned refreshed.[1]

We (Alex and I) left from the South Station on Friday evening and on Saturday morning at ten o'clock we arrived in Gorizia, where we walked in bright sunshine between whitewashed houses, saw trees covered with white blossoms, and could eat oranges and candied fruit. While doing so, we collected memories — the view from the fortress recalls Florence; the *fortezza* itself, San Pietro in Verona and the castle in Nuremberg. The first impression of the Italian landscape that overtakes one — that of missing meadows and woods — naturally was very vivid, as is the case in all transitions. The Isonzo is a magnificent river. On the way we passed three ranges of the Julian Alps. On Sunday morning we had to get up early to take the local Friulian railroad to the vicinity of Aquileia. The former metropolis is a dump; the museum, though, exhibits an inexhaustible wealth of Roman finds: tombstones, amphorae, medallions of the gods from the amphitheater, statues, bronzes, and jewelry. Several priapic statues: a Venus indignantly turning away from her newborn child after having been shown his penis; Priapus as an old man, whose genitals are being covered by a silenus and who henceforth can give himself over to drink; a priapic stone ornament of the penis as a winged animal, which has a small penis in the natural place, while the wings themselves end in a penis. Priapus stood for permanent erection, a wish fulfillment representing the opposite of psychological impotence.

At ten o'clock a little steamer was towed by a strange tug into the Aquileia Canal, just when the tide was at its lowest ebb. The tug had a rope around its body and while in operation was smoking a pipe. I would have liked to bring the steamer back for the children, but since it was the only link between the resort of Grado and the world, it could not be spared. A two-and-a-half-hour trip through the dreariest lagoons brought us to Grado, where at last we were again able to collect shells and sea urchins on the shores of the Adriatic.

We returned to Aquileia the same afternoon, after using our provisions and a choice Istrian wine to have a meal aboard ship. Several hundred of the prettiest Friulian girls had just gathered in the cathedral of Aquileia for the holiday mass. The splendor of the old Romanesque basilica was comforting in the midst of the poverty of modern times. On the way back we saw a piece of an old Roman road that had been cleared in the middle of a field. A modern drunk was lying on the ancient paving stones. On the same evening we got to Divaça on the Carso, where we spent the night so as to visit the caves on the next and last day, Monday. In the morning we went to Rudolf's Cave, a quarter of an hour from the station; it was full of all sorts of strange stalactite formations—giant horsetail,[2] pyramid cakes,[3] tusks growing upward, curtains, corncobs, richly folded tents, hams and poultry hanging from above. Strangest of all was our guide, in a deep alcoholic stupor, but completely surefooted, and full of humor. He was the discoverer of the cave, obviously a genius gone wrong; constantly spoke of his death, his conflicts with the priests, and his conquests in these subterranean realms. When he said that he had already been in thirty-six "holes" in the Carso, I realized he was a neurotic and his conquistador exploits were an erotic equivalent. A few minutes later he confirmed this, because when Alex asked him how far one could penetrate into the cave, he answered, "It's like with a virgin; the farther you get, the more beautiful it is."

The man's dream is one day to come to Vienna, so as to gather ideas in the museums for naming his stalactites. I overtipped the "biggest blackguard in Divaça," as he called himself, with a few guilders, so that he can drink his life away faster.

The caves of Saint Cangian, which we saw in the afternoon, are a gruesome miracle of nature, a subterranean river running through magnificent vaults, waterfalls, stalactite formations, pitch darkness, and slippery paths secured with iron railings. It was Tartarus itself. If Dante saw anything like this, he needed no great effort of imagination for his inferno. At the same time the master of Vienna, Herr Dr. Karl Lueger, was with us in the cave, which after three and a half hours spewed us all out into the light again.

On Monday evening we began the trip home. The following day, when ideas for my work once again occurred to me, I could see that the rest had been good for the apparatus.

Enclose a letter, the history of which is as follows. The last issue of the *Wiener klinische Rundschau* contained a review of your book by a certain Ry,[4] an example of that type of impertinence which is characteristic of absolute ignorance. I wrote Paschkis a harsh letter asking for an explanation. Herewith the loyal but sterile reply. I will do nothing further without having asked you. What would you like to see done? There are several possibilities of obtaining satisfaction.

My self-interest still demands to know when you will be coming to Vienna, so I can figure out when I should send Mathilde with Martha to you for treatment. My first choice would be after Whitsun, because the child has entrance examinations ahead of her. But everything depends upon you. They certainly will not stay in your house this time, because they have my sister in Berlin and the condition of your wife precludes our burdening you.

Well then, let me at last hear something good about you and her. I am waiting for it impatiently.

Your
Sigm.

1. See *S.E.* 4:464, "A Castle by the Sea," for a dream connected with this trip.

2. A plant of the genus *Aquisetum*.

3. Cakes made by dribbling dough onto a turning spit.

4. The review by Ry was published in the *Wiener klinische Rundschau* (my translation; the two bracketed phrases are Ry's insertions):

"*The Relationship between the Nose and the Female Sexual Organs.*" By Dr. Wilhelm Fliess. Verlag von Franz Deuticke, 1897

"After one has laboriously worked one's way through this work, which in view of its meager content is quite voluminous, one retains in memory only a single positive assertion—that it is possible to remove labor pains by the cocainization of certain parts of the nasal mucosa. The reviewer, having made inquiries at obstetrical clinics, learned that experiments in respect thereof—which at the time were also widely discussed in the daily press—did not lead to positive results; therewith any need to deal further with this point of Fliess's work is obviated. The rest of what the book contains has nothing to do with medicine or natural science. For if one nowadays seeks to render such mystical nonsense that aspires to be intellectual wealth capable of discussion, the attempt founders on the realization that it is not the business of science to embark on a critique of the fantasy creations of every author, for such idle disquisitions can be neither refuted nor confirmed. In case anyone should think that thereby the author has been treated unjustly if one refuses to take him seriously, I quote at random a single sentence here for the benefit of such good-natured doubters: 'I saw a $2\frac{1}{2}$-year-old cross-eyed child become straight-eyed after an intervention of this sort [namely, scraping of the tonsils with a fingernail]; since I know [sic!] that the eye muscles of the infant become functional at critical periods, so that the initial strabism characteristic of infants disappears in spurts, I should like to interpret the above observation in the sense that in this case the diseased tonsils inhibited this periodical maturation of the eye muscles' (p. 235). That is indeed disgusting gobbledygook! No wonder that in not a few places the reader of this book has the impression that the author is making fun of him.

"In view of the fact that the publishers' extensive list also contains good scientific products, it should not be difficult for them to wipe out this disgrace."

---

Vienna, April 27, 1898
IX., Berggasse 19

Dear Wilhelm,

It was awkward of me to want to wait until the affair with Paschkis was settled. It is settled now by my having severed my affiliation with the *klinische Rundschau* and having withdrawn my name from the contributors listed on its cover.[1] I intentionally did not send you the review in question. I believe we can now drop this matter.

Your siren's song founders on my plugged ears and tied hands. At present my earnings are so bad that I must not stay away a single day except holidays. It strikes me as funny that I am so dutiful and parsimonious. It must be a sign of old age.

But we must see each other at Whitsun. The refreshing effect of the Easter trip, which was only partially successful in helping me to recover, quickly evaporated. I am very well, but feel dull and now am facing a piece of work, to which I had been looking forward very much, as if I were standing in front of a wall. Do you want me to send you the finished chapter on the dream material? It is to be regarded as far less definitive than the first one.

As to hysteria, I have several things to tell you, which represent clarification and confirmation of my surmise — that initially I defined the etiology too narrowly; the share of fantasy in it is far greater than I had thought in the beginning.

My mother returned today; I have not yet seen her, but heard only that you will take care of poor Mizi,[2] which is very kind of you. I have never advised her to see you because she never asked me about it. None of us has a relationship with her; she has always been isolated and rather peculiar. In her mature years this has manifested itself in pathological parsimony, while the rest of us are all spendthrifts. The three girls are hysterical; the youngest, a rather gifted child, severely so. I doubt the father is innocent in this case either; he is half-Asian, suffers from pseudologica fantastica, though he is otherwise good to his family. All of us (with the exception of my mother, of course) were much relieved when the family moved to Berlin.

We all send most cordial wishes to the birthday girl today and assume that this date coincides with her recovery. This time R.W. will no doubt present his congratulations verbally.

With the most cordial greetings,

Your
Sigm.

1. In the issue of the *Wiener klinische Rundschau* dated May 1, 1898, Freud's name no longer appears on the editorial board.

2. In 1886 Marie Freud (1861–1942) married Moriz Freud (1857–1920), a distant relative. By "half-Asian" presumably Freud refers to the fact that Moriz came from Eastern Europe (Bucharest).

Vienna, May 1, 1898
IX., Berggasse 19

Dear Wilhelm,

What you said about the two hands of the clock of life again sounds so familiar and self-evident that it must be a fabulous novelty and a marvelous truth. May has come, and so at the end of May I shall hear about it. I feel parched; some spring within me has gone dry and all sensibilities are withering. I do not want to give you too detailed a description lest it sound too much like complaining. You will tell me whether it is old age or just one of the many periodic fluctuations.

I have the impression that you might have determined the sex of your next child, so that this time Paulinchen may well become a reality.

Apparently the book by Schenk has already been published;[1] I expect so little of it that I did not try to read it. According to some hints that were dropped in my presence, it is a piece of shortsighted rubbish.

I fancied I knew the date of the birthday better than those who told it to me—which proves that I cannot retain any numbers.

I thank you very much for having been so kind to my old lady. As a result, she came back in high spirits. I always knew that with all your apparent energy, you are one of the most good-natured among all the children of men. You really need not give a thought to Paschkis. The matter deserves nothing better. Nor do I believe that I shall ever regret it. Incidentally, Oscar too spontaneously followed my example.

Enclosed "Caput 3" of the dream. You will find me somewhat unpalatable; I am completely involved in the dream book and completely stupid about it. I have now written the section on psychology in which I had gotten stuck, but I do not like it, nor will it remain. The chapter you have now is stylistically still quite crude and bad in some parts, that is, written without much liveliness. I have left some gaps in regard to the somatic stimuli, which still need to be brought out more sharply. Naturally I expect you to make various vigorous pronouncements about it when we see each other again. The conclusions, I believe, are correct.

I would like to get some vigorous stimulation. I am, as I recently heard someone say about himself, an engine geared to work under a pressure of 10 atmospheres, and under a pressure of 2 atmospheres I overheat. So far this year I have hardly got to the point of feeling tired, while usually by this time I have long been gasping for a holiday. I do not have much, and what I have troubles me less.

Views of the exterior and the entrance to IX., Berggasse 19, where Freud lived and worked from 1891 to 1938.

The Freud family, about 1898, in the garden of the Berggasse home.
Only Mathilde is missing, presumably because she is at school.
From left to right: front row, Sophie, Anna, and Ernst;
middle row, Oliver, Martha, and Martha's sister Minna Bernays;
back row, Martin and Sigmund.

I have never been able to guide my intellectual work; so my leisure, not being used, is wasted.

How refreshing the few days at Whitsun will be for me! Martha does not really want to go to Berlin; she thinks that you can see the child here at Whitsun and you may then, perhaps, recommend the necessary throat operation, which Hajek can carry out here. I am, of course, leaving it up to you and her. The other children with Aunt Minna will already be in Aussee by the time you arrive. Annerl is turning into a charming child; she is of the same type as Martin, physically and mentally. Martin's attempts at poetry, with their self-irony, are highly amusing.

Cordial greetings and I hope to hear from you several times still before Whitsun.

Your
Sigm.

1. Samuel Leopold Schenk (1842–1902), was director of the Embryological Institute in Vienna. See his *Determination of Sex* (authorized translation, London: Werner Co., 1898), p. 173: "If a woman be dieted according to our method, she can reach a stage in which she becomes sexually superior to the man, and her offspring will then be male, in accordance with the law of the cross-heredity of sex."

---

Vienna, May 18, 1898
IX., Berggasse 19

Dear Wilhelm,

I held off because, encouraged by your kind-hearted comments, I wanted to send you another chapter of the dream book before you leave Berlin. I see, however, that I cannot finish it. To my delight the time has passed quickly. I hear that you are coming in ten days.

I shall change whatever you want and gratefully accept contributions. I am so immensely glad that you are giving me the gift of the Other, a critic and reader—and one of your quality at that. I cannot write entirely without an audience, but do not at all mind writing only for you.

My interest in what you are bringing will surely be aroused once you are here. Left to myself, I am of course immersed solely in the dream [book] and desire nothing better for a while. The most difficult task—the unraveling of the psychic process in dreaming—is still ahead of me and will be tackled only after I have been revived by our congress.

You will not see the children; they are leaving for Aussee on

Monday. Martha will stay here with Mathilde so that you can see her. I would gladly save both of them the trip to Berlin because I have very little money this year. If you find that she does not need it [the operation]—her tic, too, is scarcely noticeable—they will go to Aussee very soon after Whitsun. If you would like it, the two of us could go to Graz, a town quite suitable for a congress. It all depends on how long you are staying here and on the willingness of your Viennese family to make sacrifices.

I received Gattel's work yesterday. My impression was not at all entirely unfavorable. I had made no corrections previously and must now read it carefully.

If both of us are simultaneously going through the same life periods, as appeared to be the case on some occasions, you must at present be in a better period. I can now withstand anything. The habit of working on the dream [book] is—after the hysteria torture—extremely good for me.

I very much look forward to hearing more about your specific plans; it has, after all, been almost five months since Christmas.

With the most cordial greetings to I.F., R.W.F., and W.F.,

Your
Sigm.

---

Vienna, May 24, 1898
IX., Berggasse 19

Dear Wilhelm,

I am ready now. The next chapter (formation of dreams) is finished; my interest is freed again. It does not matter to me at all where you want to enjoy my surprise about your *primeurs*[1]—in my usual egoism I did not consider the long train ride to Graz. You could certainly be my guest in the city apartment for those two days, but you really do not know how I loathe the city of Vienna. A little bit of atmosphere and greenery, in conjunction with it [the congress], would be very good for my mood? For this reason I am still going to ask you whether you would like to drive up the Kahlenberg or take a boat to Bratislava, or go to the Thalhof in Reichenau. Unfortunately, I do not have a postal balloon at my disposal; otherwise I would not have done without you for five months.

The children left for Aussee yesterday. Martha and Mathilde will stay here over Whitsun.

In these last days there was more to do and something to be

learned. Nothing that could be served up at our next congress, for which I have nothing but the dream, the dream. I have rarely felt so constricted. I am not writing anymore because I now know that there are only a few more days until I can hear you.

Most cordially until we meet,

Your
Sigm.

1. First wines; here, new work.

---

Vienna, June 9, 1898
IX., Berggasse 19

My dear Wilhelm,

Many thanks for your beautiful picture! My brother made the astute observation that the photographer must know you; this is actually so, as you told me. It will get the place of honor on my desk, the place you hold in my friendship.

Many thanks, too, for your critique. I know that you have undertaken a thankless task. I am reasonable enough to recognize that I need your critical help, because in this instance I myself have lost the feeling of shame required of an author. So the dream is condemned.[1] Now that the sentence has been passed, however, I would like to shed a tear over it and confess that I regret it and that I have no hopes of finding a better one as a substitute. As you know, a beautiful dream and no indiscretion—do not coincide. Let me know at least which topic it was to which you took exception and where you feared an attack by a malicious critic. Whether it is my anxiety, or Martha, or the *Dalles*,[2] or my being without a fatherland? So that I can omit what you designate in a substitute dream, because I can have dreams like that to order.

Martha and Mathilde left last night; since then it has been desolate here. The child had a fever for a day and a half and her tonsils were coated, but ultimately she was lively and in high spirits. Robertchen, by the way, is delightful.

With the continuation of the dream [book] something is amiss[3] (Ida will explain the word to you). True, I have already gotten to page 14, but it is impossible to publish it, perhaps even to show it to someone else. A mere trial run. For it is wretchedly difficult to set out the new psychology insofar as it pertains to the dream; it is of necessity fragmentary, and all the obscure parts which I, in a state of inertia, have so far put off, demand elucidation. I need a lot of patience, a cheerful frame of mind, and a few good ideas. So I am stuck at the relationship of the two systems of thinking; I must deal with them in earnest. For a while I again shall be of no use to anyone. The tension of uncertainty makes for an infamously unpleasant state, which one feels almost physically.

My most cordial thanks to your dear wife for her concerns about the supper — in my case, long since replaced by similar ones. Incidentally, if this interests you diagnostically, there exists the most touching substitute relationship between my migraine and my cardiac symptoms and the like. Since Reichenau I once again do not know whether I have a *cor* [heart trouble]; instead I have a running cold and a very unsteady head. Formerly it was the reverse. So both of them will have to keep going for a while.

I am reading C. F. Meyer with great pleasure. In *Gustav Adolfs Page* I found the idea of deferred action twice: in the famous passage you discovered, the one with the slumbering kiss; and in the episode involving the Jesuit who insinuates himself as little Christine's teacher. In Innsbruck they actually show the chapel where she converted to Catholicism! Otherwise, however, I cannot make head or tail of the arbitrariness of the assumption on which the entanglement rests. The similarity in hand and voice between the page and Lauenburger is in itself so very improbable and is given no further plausible reason.

Next time, a little essay on *Die Richterin*.[4]

Most cordial greetings.

Your
Sigm.

1. This is the first reference to the only *completely* analyzed dream in the *Interpretation of Dreams*, which Freud eventually removed in deference to Fliess's objections. Schur was the first to point this out, and to correct Strachey's error (which arose because Strachey did not know that the dream had been omitted). See Schur (1966, pp. 75–76). The dream is further mentioned in the letters of June 20 and October 23, 1898, and August 1, 1899. There is some hope that the dream may have survived, although Anna Freud definitely believed it lost. According to Marie Bonaparte's notebook, when she told Freud about the Fliess letters, "he pointed out to me that there were letters missing: all those concerning the break with Fliess . . . and one about a dream relating to Martha Freud."

2. *Dalles* is a Yiddish word for "poverty" or "misery."

3. *Es hapert*, a Viennese colloquialism.

4. An 1882 novella by C. F. Meyer.

Vienna, June 20, 1898
IX., Berggasse 19

Dear Wilhelm,

As compensation, a few little things for you. Martin again had a nosebleed exactly on the twenty-eighth day, according to Martha. I, too, am becoming interesting. My head and your head are evidently, even though unsteady, two very different heads, because mine, in spite of all its lability, did not prevent me from having a good period. But I can do something that you cannot do — replace headaches or cardiac pains with ridiculous back pains, which are deceptively like cardiac pains, are precipitated by the same slight provocations, pierce and burn, and extend to several skin areas of the legs, just as the cardiac pains extend into the left arm. An excellent exchange, though!

I came back this morning from Aussee, where I found my poor family with colds and frozen stiff. They do not want to go to Aussee again in spite of its beauties. I find there is enough work here until the end of the month.

I have not yet ceased mourning the lost dream. As if in spite, I recently had a substitute dream in which a house constructed of building blocks collapsed ("We had built a *staatliches* house")[1] and which, because of this connection, could not be used.

DIE RICHTERIN [THE FEMALE JUDGE]

There is no doubt that this has to do with a poetic defense against the memory of a [sexual] affair with the sister. Strange, though, that this [defense] proceeds *exactly* as it does in neurosis. All neurotics create the so-called family romance (which becomes conscious in paranoia); it serves on the one hand the need for self-aggrandizement and on the other as a defense against incest. If the sister is not one's mother's child, one is relieved of all blame. (The same applies if one is oneself the child of other people.) Where does the material for creating the romance — adultery, illegitimate child, and the like — come from? Usually from the lower social circles of servant girls. Such things are so common among them that one is never at a loss for material, and it is especially apt to occur if the seductress herself was a person in service. In all analyses one therefore hears the same story twice: once as a fantasy about the mother; the second time as a real memory of the maid. This explains why in *Die Richterin* — who is in fact the mother — the same story appears twice without changes, a composition one would scarcely regard as a good literary accomplishment. At the end mistress and maid lie lifeless side by side. In the end the maid leaves the house, which is how servant stories usually end, but in the novel it is also the maid's punishment. This part of the romance also serves the purpose of taking revenge on the strict *Frau Mama*, by whom one was possibly surprised in the act and scolded. In the romance, as in the novel, it is the mother who is surprised, judged, and exposed. Taking away the horn[2] is a truly infantile cause of complaint and finding it again is nothing but infantile wish fulfillment. The condition of the sister, her anorexia, is precisely the neurotic consequence of the children's [sexual] relationship, though in the novel it is not the brother but rather the mother who is to blame. Poison in paranoia corresponds exactly to the anorexia of hysteria—and thus to the perversion most common among children. There is even the scare of a "beating" in it (the fear of a beating as a phobia means that the child was beaten). Fighting, which is never missing from a child's love, is also depicted in the novel when the sister is thrown against the rocks, but here the motive for it, in contrast [to what happens in other instances], is a virtue because the little one was too forward. The teacher's role is played by the person of Alcuin. The father appears in the person of Emperor Charles, who in his greatness is far removed from infantile drives, and in another incarnation as the person whose life is poisoned by the mother and who is invariably eliminated in the family romance because he stands in the way of the son. (Wishful dream of the father's death.) Parental quarrels provide the most fruitful material for the romances of childhood. Resentment against the mother is expressed in the novel by turning her into a stepmother. Thus, in every single feature it is identical with the romances of revenge and exoneration which my hysterics, if they are boys, invent about their mothers.

The psychology is proceeding in a strange manner; it is nearly finished, composed as if in a dream and certainly, in this form, not fit for publication, nor intended for it, as the style shows. I feel very timid about it. All its themes come from the work on neurosis, not from that on dreams. I shall do nothing that is definitive anymore before the holidays.

The summer will soon become very boring. Let me hear soon about you and your family. I really dread the 25,600 years.[3]

Most cordially,

Your
Sigm.

1. Schur (1966, p. 75) says: "The words in parentheses represent one of Freud's associations. The word *'staatliches'* is a pun combining the two words: *'stattlich'*—

stately, imposing, grand; and '*staatlich*'—pertaining to the state, to public affairs, to politics." Schur goes on to say that the "pun indicates that the main bone of contention in the rejected dream must have been something 'political,' probably connected with Freud's allusion in the previous letter to 'being without a fatherland.' "

But the phrase is in fact a play on words, the refrain from a students' song, "sung in Jena on November 26, 1819, upon the disbandment of the students' association." The song is entitled "Wir hatten gebauet" and the verse in question reads: "We had built a stately house, and therein placed our trust in God, in spite of weather, storm and dread." It is quoted in Georg Büchmann, *Geflügelte Worte*. I have cited it from the *Allgemeines deutsches Commersbuch*, by Friedrich Silcher and Friedrich Erk, 16th ed. (Strassburg: Moritz Schauenberg, 1873), p. 125.

2. The count's family horn, said to have the power to compel sinners to confess.

3. Meaning unclear.

---

Vienna, July 7, 1898
IX., Berggasse 19

Dear Wilhelm,

Here it is. It was difficult for me to make up my mind to let it out of my hands. Personal intimacy would not have been a sufficient reason; it also took our intellectual honesty to each other. It completely follows the dictates of the unconscious, on the well-known principle of Itzig, the Sunday rider. "Itzig, where are you going?" "Do I know? Ask the horse." I did not start a single paragraph knowing where I would end up. It is of course not written for the reader; after the first two pages I gave up any attempt at stylization. On the other hand, I do of course believe in the conclusions. I do not yet have the slightest idea what form the content will finally take.

I am now living in comfortable laziness and am harvesting some of the fruits of familiarity with the hysterical things. Everything is becoming easy and transparent. On Sunday and Monday, as a consultant, I saw the battlefield of Königgrätz from a distance. I am not going to Aussee yet. At last they are all well down there. For once I am free from pain; when I am well, I am terribly lazy.

I did not do well with [finding for you] the photograph of Archduke Franz Ferdinand. It does not exist in profile; he probably has none—deformation. The only consolation is that a clear family resemblance to old Este is out of the question. He is obliged to carry the title of Este because the inheritance of certain Hapsburgs, who once sat in Este as a parallel branch, devolved on him; and he will divest himself of the title with the inheritance as soon as he becomes emperor and thereby also head of the family. Otherwise he is the emperor's eldest nephew. If this genealogical information is not news to you and you can also use his stupid countenance *en face,* let me know quickly.

Our author's [C. F. Meyer's] most beautiful novel — and the one farthest removed from infantile scenes — seems to me to be *Die Hochzeit des Mönches* [The monk's wedding], which magnificently illustrates the process occurring in later years in the formation of fantasies — a new experience is in fantasy projected back into the past so that the new persons become aligned with the old ones, who become their prototypes. The mirror image of the present is seen in a fantasied past, which then prophetically becomes the present.[1] The secret theme no doubt is unsatisfied revenge and inevitable punishment, continued by Dante into eternity. In the foreground[2] — a slight misinterpretation by the conscious, as it were — is the theme of instability, which takes over once a person has given up his secure supports. Probably common to both the manifest and the latent theme is the feature of going from one prank to the next, as though *Die Richterin* were the reaction to childish misdeeds uncovered in the past, whereas this novel is the echo of misdeeds that remained undetected. The monk is a "frate," a brother. It is as if he had constructed a fantasy before his own marriage and wanted to say: a *frater* like me should not marry lest my childhood love take its revenge on my wife later on.

Most cordial greetings to all three and three-quarters of you.

Your
Sigm.

1. This sentence was mistakenly omitted in *Anfänge* and *Origins.*

2. Lottie Newman points out that Freud uses *vorgeschoben,* and with this one word (subsequently repeated several times) evokes the image and the idea of one thing having been transposed (like a movable scene) in front of something else, which is thereby covered up.

---

Aussee, July 30, 1898
Vienna
IX., Berggasse 19

Dear Wilhelm,

You definitely are far too good company for me. I do not deserve to be given a glimpse of these perspectives. Even though it has been less than a week since I was enchanted by the Kepler of biology, I have already turned into a complete peasant. Unfortunately there are no mushrooms yet, as I convinced myself on a four-and-a-half-hour walk through the woods of the Salzberg; instead, it has been raining and we are freezing—to our heart's content! All science is—I almost wrote "was"—infinitely remote from me, my own of course the farthest. With the ability to turn everything into something desirable—and I still possess remnants of this faculty—I tell myself, this is good and proves the elasticity of my nature. (I can scarcely write, it is so cold.)

Robert is quite right; he suspects that money is a means of unchaining slaves; that one obtains freedom in exchange for money, as one otherwise sacrifices freedom for money.

Couldn't you by now calculate when old Bismarck must die?

Two little trips are dawning for me: one from Landeck via the Engadine to Chiavenna, the other for a stay in Ragusa. The first one, soon; the second one, in September; the first one, with Minna; the second one, with Martha. The first trip really was inspired by your remark that you know very well the land where *Jürg Jenatsch* takes place. But I no longer remember which it is. Graubünden?[1] Certainly not the Engadine. So a certain displacement has occurred; if in leafing through the guide to Switzerland I find the right names, I shall change the route and undo the displacement. I am thinking of leaving on Thursday.

Do not let yourself be deterred from writing to me about the ellipses,[2] although at present I am passing through such an unreasonable segment [of ellipses] of my own. For each should give what he has, without consideration for the other. I am doing the same thing; the lack of constraint is the main attraction of our correspondence.

I would so much like to give you what *you do not* have: a free head [free of headaches]; but you know that this is not possible. The incompleteness of your findings does not trouble me at all; you know that I do not reflect; I receive, enjoy, marvel, and have great expectations.

The period of gestation will soon be over; in view of Ida's condition, this is no doubt a consolation for you. Unfortunately, the vacation too [will soon be over].

Most cordial greetings to you and her.

Your
Sigm.

1. Graubünden Canton, where the Swiss patriot Graubünden was active during the Thirty Years' War. Undoubtedly a reference to C. F. Meyer's novel *Jürg Jenatsch*.

2. See Schur (1972, p. 151n53).

August 1, 1898
IX., Berggasse 19

Dear Wilhelm,

My father always maintained that he was born on the same day as Bismarck — April 1, 1815. In view of the need to convert the date from the Jewish calendar, I never gave much credence to this assertion. So he died after what is probably a typical long life, on October 23/24, 1896; B. on July 30, 1898. B. survived him by 645 days = 23 × 28 + 1. The "1" no doubt is due to my father's error. Therefore the life difference is 23 × 28. You undoubtedly know what that must mean. Another old man, Dittel, — May 15, [18]15 – July 28, [18]98 (early) — is 48 days behind B., and is ahead of Father by 23 × 26 [28?]; off by 1 – 2 days.

With cordial greetings,

Your
Sigm.

---

Aussee, August 20, 1898

Dear Wilhelm,

Your lines revived the pleasures of our trip. It really was glorious — the Engadine composed in simple lines out of a few elements, a kind of post-Renaissance landscape, and Maloja, with Italy beyond, with an Italian air about it (probably merely imposed on it by our expectations). Leprese was for us enchantingly idyllic, also because of the way we were received there and the contrast with the journey up from Tirano. We had to travel that road, which is not exactly level, in a horrible dust storm and arrived up there half-dead. The air made me feel giddy and eager to quarrel, as I have seldom been before. The 1,600 meters did not affect the soundness of my sleep.

Until the last day in Maloja the sun did not trouble us. Then, however, it became hot, even at that altitude, and we didn't have the strength to go to Chiavenna, that is, down to the lakes. I believe that was sensible, because a few days later, in Innsbruck, both of us were in a state of almost paralyzing weakness. Since then it has become increasingly hotter and here, in our beautiful Obertressen, we lie about on all sorts of deck chairs from ten in the morning to six in the evening, without venturing a step beyond the boundaries of our small domain. In Innsbruck I bought a small Roman statuette, which Annerl not inappropriately called "an old child."

Apparently, remote from all intellectual pursuits and hardly able, for example, to understand your beautiful explanations about the duration of the life span of old people, I am at present chiefly occupied with regretting that so much of the vacation is already gone. My keen regret that the two of you are tied to the city during this period is tempered by the thought that you have your trip behind you and that Ida has a beautiful substitute ahead of her.

Yes, I too have skimmed Nansen; my whole household is full of enthusiasm for him — for Martha, the Scandinavians (Grandmother, who is staying with us, still speaks Swedish) obviously revive a youthful ideal which did not materialize in her life; for Mathilde, who until now has been enthralled by the Greek heroes, the transition has been made to the Vikings; and Martin, as usual, reacted to the three volumes of adventure with a not-at-all-bad poem.

I shall be able to make good use of Nansen's dreams;[1] they are completely transparent. I know from my own experience that his psychic state is typical of someone who dares to do something new and relies on his confidence and who, by taking a wrong route, probably discovers something original, but far less than he had anticipated. Fortunately, the secure harmony of your nature keeps you at a distance from that.

I have written to Chiavenna. My cordial greetings to you and your wife. I am not yet reconciled to the distance which separates us during the time we are at work and is so rarely eliminated during our vacations.

Your
Sigm.

1. See *Interpretation of Dreams* (*S.E.* 4:191).

---

Aussee, August 26, 1898

Dear Wilhelm,

Yesterday, from Chiavenna, came the happy news of the unlocking of the mysteries of the universe and of life, of intellectual successes more beautiful than one could dream of. Whether the road to the goal will turn out to be short or long — your intention to call mathematics to your aid would point to the latter — I can sense that the road is open to you; and I rejoice once again that eleven years ago I already realized that it was necessary for me to love you in order to enrich my life. Now, how shall I learn which elements became the new connecting links? It will hardly be possible to see you in September and, as to writing about it, you can only give some indications in outline form. So it will have to wait for our next congress, at which you shall make the first attempt to teach the new science in context to someone who — quite seriously — "is completely stupid and has forgotten everything." If I am not in too bad shape next fall, if the worries about income and analyses do not totally rob me of my inner exaltation, this congress must be long enough to permit the Herr Teacher to take a headache break between his lectures.

What I am doing here? I am getting a little bored in Aussee, where I know all the walks rather well. I cannot do without material altogether. I have set myself the task of building a bridge between my germinating metapsychology and that contained in the literature and have therefore immersed myself in the study of Lipps,[1] who I suspect has the clearest mind among present-day philosophical writers. So far things are going rather well with regard to comprehension and application to my own hypotheses. Naturally, this is a period of few explanations. I am becoming ever more doubtful about the work on hysteria; its value seems smaller, as though I had left out several major factors, and I really dread having to take it up again.

I have at last understood a small point that I had surmised to be so for some time. You know how one can forget a name and substitute part of another one for it; you could swear it was correct, although invariably it turns out to be wrong. That happened to me recently with the name of the poet who wrote *Andreas Hofer* ("Zu Mantua in Banden"). It must be something with an *au* — Lindau, Feldau. Of course, the man's name is Julius *Mosen;* the "Julius" had not slipped my memory. Now, I was able to prove (1) that I had repressed the name Mosen because of certain connections; (2) that infantile material played a part in this repression; (3) that the substitute names that were pushed into the foreground were formed, like symptoms, from both groups of material. The analysis of it turned out to be complete, with no gaps left; unfortunately, I cannot expose it to the public anymore than my big dream. With regard to forgetting, we experienced something like it in Berlin (Emil Hammerschlag).

Farewell. How long until Paulinchen makes her appearance?

Your
Sigm.

1. In his copy of *Grundtatsachen des Seelenlebens* (Bonn: Max Cohen, 1883) by Theodor Lipps (1851–1914), Freud double-marked this line on p. 146: "Wir nehmen vielmehr an, dass unbewusste Vorgänge allen bewussten zu Grunde liegen und sie

begleiten" (We would rather assume that unconscious processes lie at the root of all conscious ones and accompany them). At the top of the page he underlined the heading: "Wirkungen unbewusster Erregungen im Traume" (The effects of unconscious feelings in dreams).

---

Aussee, August 31, 1898

Dear Wilhelm,

At noon today I leave with Martha for the Adriatic; whether we shall stay in Ragusa, Grado, or somewhere else will be decided on the way. "The way to gain riches," according to an apparently eccentric but wise saying, "is to sell your last shirt." The secret of this restlessness is hysteria. In the inactivity here and in the absence of any fascinating novelty, the whole business has come to weigh heavily on my soul. My work now appears to me to have far less value, and my disorientation to be complete; time — another entire year has gone by without any tangible progress in the theory — seems incommensurate with what the problem demands. Moreover, it is the work on the success of which I have staked my livelihood. True, the results have been good, but perhaps only indirectly, as though I had applied the lever in a direction that indeed yields to the line of cleavage of the stuff;[1] what the latter is, however, I do not yet know. So I am running away from myself to gather as much energy and objectivity as is possible, because, indeed, I cannot let the work go.

Things are better in regard to psychology. I found the substance of my insights stated quite clearly in Lipps, perhaps rather more so than I would like. "The seeker often finds more than he wished to find!"[2] Consciousness is only a sense organ; all psychic content is only a representation; all psychic processes are unconscious. The correspondence [of our ideas] is close in details as well; perhaps the bifurcation from which my own new ideas can branch off will come later. So far I have worked my way through less than a third [of his book]. I stopped at "sound relationships." This always vexed me because here I lack the most elementary knowledge, thanks to the atrophy of my acoustic sensibilities. The big news of the day, the czar's manifesto, also touched me personally.[3] Years ago I diagnosed that the young man — fortunately for us — suffers from obsessional ideas, is overly kind, and "unable to bear the sight of blood," like Koko in the *Mikado*,[4] who at the same time is the lord high executioner. Two people would be helped if he and I could be brought together: I'd go to Russia for a year, take away from him just enough so that he no longer suffers, and leave him just enough so that he won't start a war. From then on we have three congresses a year, *exclusively* on Italian soil, and I treat all my patients for nothing. Incidentally, I believe that he, too, acts with mixed motives and that the egoistic side of the manifesto is the intention to gratify himself by securing the peaceful partition of China at this conference.

The most unforgettable thing about the manifesto is its revolutionary language. If such utterances on militarism appeared in editorials in a democratic paper, they would immediately be confiscated in Austria; and in Russia itself [the writer] would be sent to Siberia.

Cordial greetings to you, Ida, Robert, and Paulinchen, and I shall give you further news of our trip.

Your
Sigm.

1. The image is that of splitting wood or rock.

2. Freud uses the same expression in a previous letter, November 27, 1893. See note 5 to that letter.

3. See *Origins*, pp. 263–264n1.

4. The Gilbert and Sullivan operetta.

---

Vienna, September 22, 1898

Dear Wilhelm,

It was no doubt time that I returned home, but I have been back barely three days and all the bad humor of Viennadom has already descended upon me. It is sheer misery to live here and no atmosphere in which the hope of completing something difficult can survive.

I wish you thought less of my masterly skills and I had you close by so that I could hear your criticisms more often. I am not at all in disagreement with you, not at all inclined to leave the psychology hanging in the air without an organic basis. But apart from this conviction I do not know how to go on, neither theoretically nor therapeutically, and therefore must behave as if only the psychological were under consideration. Why I cannot fit it together [the organic and the psychological] I have not even begun to fathom.

A second example of name forgetting resolved itself even more easily.[1] I could not find the name of the renowned painter who did the *Last Judgment* in Orvieto, the greatest I have seen so far. Instead, Botticelli, Boltraffio occurred to me; but I was sure these were wrong. At last I found out the name, Signorelli, and immediately knew, on my own, the first name, Luca — as proof that it had been only a repression and not genuine forgetting. It is clear why Botti*celli* had moved into the foreground; only *Signor* was repressed; the Bo in both substitute names is explained by the memory responsible for the repression; it concerned something that happened in *Bos*nia and began with the words, "*Herr* [*Signor,* Sir], what can be done about it?" I lost the name of Signorelli during a short trip to *Her*zegovina, which I made from Ragusa with a lawyer from Berlin (Freyhau) with whom I got to talking about pictures. In the conversation, which aroused memories that evidently caused the repression, we talked about death and sexuality. The word *Trafio* is no doubt an echo of Trafoi, which I saw on the first trip! How can I make this credible to anyone?

I am still alone; the "household," for whom I already yearn very much, returns at the end of the month. A letter from Gattel, who seeks contact, urges me to come to Berlin because of a patient he is to treat. It is one of those halfway affairs that I might use as an excuse to see you (and the new daughter) again. But it cannot be reconciled with my medical dignity, and I must not provoke gods and men by further travels, but instead wait here patiently for the little sheep to gather.

I hope to hear from you soon how your daughter is behaving and — what interests me especially — how Robert is reacting to his sister. I have heard here that the mother is doing very well.

With the most cordial greetings,

Your
Sigm.

1. See *S.E.* 3:287–297 and *S.E.* 6:2–7.

---

Vienna, September 27, 1898

Dear Wilhelm,

Your letter exudes a truly contagious sense of well-being, which I feel you deserve. With Paulinchen and some work that is going well, you entirely forgot to write about your head, which, after all, also interests me. If I had suspected that in any way whatever you might value the opportunity offered me to go to Berlin with expenses partly paid, I would not have refused. I did not even know that you were informed about it. A situation where I could not stay with you,

Ida confined to bed, and the little one perhaps demanding your attention, left no room for me; on the other hand, I am not at all inclined to facilitate such medical halfway measures. I further had to tell myself that the affair need not be of any value to these people, and that the chance of Gattel's influencing an old man in his melancholia should not be increased by my prediction. For the present it is impossible for me to leave the battlefield.

Gattel has my best wishes for material success; it will improve him because he seems to me to be one of those people who consider first *noblesse,* and then honesty as a luxury item once they have reached a higher level of income; such items, deemed unaffordable, must be left aside when their income is lower. I don't know that you should tell him so many of your most intimate matters. Besides, I envy him for it.

I am hardly alone in my *Katzenjammer* about the lovely trip, which, by the way, was mostly meant for the women; rather, this city really wounds the soul and once again lays bare everything that had begun to heal in two months. I shall adopt the rule, however, not to touch certain points lightly; it must be very distasteful to hear someone complaining all the time. Nor is it the least of my annoyances that I cannot react in any other way.

I turned Signorelli into a little essay, which I sent to Ziehen (Wernicke). If they reject it, I think I shall take up an old idea of yours and offer the thing to the *Deutsche Rundschau.*

I was enchanted by the simile of the rocky path; I accept it by informing you that for the time being I am like an ox on a mountain.[1]

I still have nothing to do; that is, two hours [of treatment] instead of ten. Started a new case, so I am approaching it without any preconceptions. In the beginning, of course, everything fits together beautifully. A 25-year-old fellow who can scarcely walk because of stiffness in the legs, cramps, tremors, and so on. A safeguard against any misdiagnosis is provided by his accompanying anxiety, which makes him cling to his mother's apronstrings like the baby he once was. The death of the brother and the death of the father in a psychosis precipitated the onset of his symptoms, which have been present since age 14. He feels ashamed if anyone sees him walking this way, and he regards that as normal. Prototype: a tabetic uncle with whom he already identified at the age of 13 because of the accepted etiology [of tabes] (leading a dissolute life). Physically, by the way, he is a bear of a fellow!

Please note that the shame is only appended to the symptoms and must correspond to other precipitating factors. He even permitted [me to] clarify that his uncle, after all, is not at all ashamed of his gait. The connection between shame and gait was a correct one years ago when he had gonorrhea, which was of course noticeable in his gait, as well as even earlier when constant (aimless) erections interfered with his walking. Besides this, the cause of his shame lay deeper. He told me that last year when they were living by the river Wien (in the country), it suddenly began to rise; he was seized by a terrible fear that the water would come into his bed, that is, flood his room, and that during the night. Please note the ambiguity of the expression; I knew that the man had been a bed wetter as a child. Five minutes later he spontaneously told me that while he was at school he still regularly wet his bed and that his mother had threatened she would come and tell the teacher and all his classmates about it. He had felt tremendous anxiety. So that is where the shame belongs. The whole story of his youth on the one hand has its climax in the leg symptoms, and on the other releases the affect belonging to it, and the two now[2] become joined in his inner perception. The whole submerged childhood story must be inserted in between.

Now, a child who regularly wets his bed until his seventh year (without being epileptic or the like) must have experienced sexual excitation in his earlier childhood. Spontaneous or by seduction? There it is, and it must also contain the more specific determination in regard to the legs.

You see, if need be, I could say to myself, "It is true I am cleverer than all the coxcombs . . . ," but the sad sentence that follows does not fail to apply to me either: "I lead my people around by the nose and see that we can know nothing."[3]

Who is Lipps? A professor in Munich, and in his terminology he says exactly what I arrived at in my speculations about consciousness, quality, and so forth. I was studying his *Grundtatsachen des Seelenlebens* [Fundamentals of the life of the soul] until I began traveling; must find my way back to it now.

The children are expected back from Aussee in the next few days.

Martha has colitis, which bothers her a lot; she is in good hands, I believe, with Dr. Bloch, whom I esteem highly.

In conclusion, a poem by Martin on the church festival in Aussee (market):

Among the beautiful church festival sights
Are some things really laughable!
A green mouse that runs backward,
A monkey, and both his hands missing;
A clock made of tin that always stands still,

A shuttlecock with its skin peeling;
Tasteless candy, small ones and big ones
In the most charming of boxes.
Yes, at a church festival there are things;
So he who has them can really laugh.

Cordial greetings to you, Ida, Robert, and Paulinchen.

Your
Sigm.

1. A common German saying denoting helplessness.
2. The original letter reads *nun*, not *nur* as in *Anfänge*.
3. From the soliloquy at the beginning of Goethe's *Faust*.

---

Vienna, October 9, 1898

Dear Wilhelm,

The well-being that shines forth from your letters does one good and communicates itself. Just watch how soon Paulinchen will turn out to be a reincarnation of your sister, although by her name you have aligned her with the other family.

My mood, critical faculty, subsidiary ideas — in short, all mental accessories — have been buried under an avalanche of patients that descended on me a week ago. Being hardly prepared for it and having been spoiled by the vacation, I felt at first as if I had been knocked flat; now I feel lively again, but have no energy left. All my strength is concentrated on my work with patients. The treatments start at nine o'clock — before that two short calls — and last until one-thirty; from three to five a pause for consulting hours, the office being alternately empty or full; from five to nine treatments again. I am definitely expecting another case — ten to eleven psychotherapies a day. Naturally, I am speechless and half-dead in the evening. But Sunday is almost free. I move things around, test them, and make changes here and there; I am not entirely without new leads. If I happen to hit on anything, you shall hear about it. Half of my patients now are men of all ages, fourteen to forty-five years.

Martha is better locally, but tired and does not look especially well. Throughout the whole summer there was a breakdown of intestinal activity, constipation, which occasionally ended in an explosive evacuation; at the end in Aussee and then on the trip. The colics occur more frequently and are more painful; her appetite is disturbed only during these periods; between them it is good. Her stool during the colic attacks is alternately hard, glassy, and diarrheic. She is now drinking Karlsbader water and is to stay on a restricted diet, have oil enemas, and so forth, but she has never been a good patient. Yet since she started treatment, she has not had a colic attack.

Mathilde is going to a (private) school this year. The young ones are quite well.

Ziehen accepted the little paper[1] in a friendly fashion: your advice seems to me to be very good; but before I act on it, I need some new observations to clarify several main points.

Leonardo — no love affair of his is known — is perhaps the most famous left-handed person. Can you use him?

Most cordial greetings.

Your
Sigm.

1. "The Psychical Mechanism of Forgetfulness."

---

Vienna, October 23, 1898
IX., Berggasse 19

Dear Wilhelm,

This letter is meant to reach you on your most important date of all and across the distance to bring good wishes for your happiness from me and my family. This wish which — as its nature and not human misuse requires — relates to the future has as its content: the preservation and development of present possessions as well as the acquisition of new gains in children and insights; finally, the avoidance of every vestige of suffering and illness other than that which a man urgently needs to spur on his powers and to contrast with the good.

These are no doubt fine times for you, about which little needs to be said. It would be the same for me if during the last influenza epidemic I had not been left with an infection that deprives me of my good mood, makes breathing through the nose difficult, and the aftereffects of which I no doubt have to fear.

Martha is doing very well; Mathilde is tolerating and enjoying school better than we had hoped. My resources are no longer taxed by work lasting from 9 A.M. to 9 P.M.; indeed, when there is a free hour I feel unoccupied. Once again there is a glimmer of light on the horizon, as though this year I shall be in a position to find my way back to the truth from grave errors.[1] But as yet there is no light —

and I do not want to talk about it, so as not to spend myself before our meeting, on which I have been counting for some time.

I am not sufficiently collected, to be sure, to do anything in addition, other than possibly studying the topography of Rome, the yearning for which becomes ever more tormenting. The dream [book] is lying still, immutably; I lack the incentive to finish it for publication, and the gap in the psychology as well as the gap left by the [removal of the] thoroughly analyzed sample [dream] are obstacles to bringing it to a conclusion which so far I have not been able to overcome. In other respects I am completely lonely; this year I even gave up lecturing so as not to have to talk about anything that I still hope to learn myself.

My sister Rosa gave birth to a girl on October 18; both are well.

I have learned one lesson, however, which makes an old man of me. If ascertaining the few points required for explanation of the neuroses entails so much work, time, and error, how can I ever hope to gain an insight into the whole of mental activity, which was once my proud expectation?

From the vantage point of this recognition, I received the first volume of Kassowitz' *Allgemeine Biologie* with a sad and envious smile. Do not buy the book; I shall send you my copy.

With the most cordial greetings,

Your
Sigm.

1. In *Anfänge* the critical word *zurück* is left out. The manuscript reads, "von schweren Irrtümern den Weg zurück zur Wahrheit zu finden." Freud is talking of finding his way *back* to the truth, with the clear implication that he already had such a truth in the past. As the text was printed, one might have assumed that Freud was speaking of the seduction hypothesis as the serious error, and his hope that he would be led to new discoveries by abandoning it. The translation in *Origins* contains an additional error, reading: "I have a glimmer of hope that in the course of the next year I shall be in a position to find my way out of serious mistakes to the truth." But with the addition of the omitted word, *zurück*, it becomes more likely that Freud is referring to the seduction theory as correct, and he hopes *this* year (not *next* year) to come back to this theory. However, against my interpretation is the letter of November 7, 1899: "Last year's gain, fantasies, have stood the test splendidly."

---

Vienna, October 30, 1898
IX., Berggasse 19

Dear Wilhelm,

After having sent off my last letter with the wishes for your happiness, I reproached myself for having deviated from the traditional formula, which seeks to eradicate every last vestige of suffering or illness. I wanted to sound rational and provide a place and a positive function for that which in any event cannot be avoided. This was nonsense, because wishing does not become reasonable by any correction of this sort. In my inattentive reading I overlooked your first intimation, that you planned to let yourself in for new experimental tortures, and I was therefore greatly surprised to get the news of your operation so soon thereafter. I thank you cordially for the care you took to assure that the same news you sent to your family would also reach me. Incidentally, I spoke to your sister-in-law Marie herself today, because it is the first birthday of little Norbert (who is very sweet). I now hope to hear how soon you got over it all and shall certainly be able to convince myself that it led to a considerable improvement in you. If you needed anything other than rest and I were in a better mood and better general physical condition, I would have used the holidays for a trip to Berlin; but since I have a cold and am engrossed in my own expectations, I would bring you neither invigoration nor enjoyment. I am completely focused on one subject; fortunately there is work, and I want to know what will come out of it. Your flattering words poured sunshine over the situation for a day, but soon they appeared false to me because of your personal affection for me and your intention to console me.

I will not trouble you in matters of Gattel and I hope he too will spare you.

No doubt you will soon be able to read. Kassowitz will be sent off to you tomorrow. I shall write brief letters more frequently.

With the most cordial greetings from all of us to all of you,

Your
Sigm.

---

Vienna, November 6, 1898
IX., Berggasse 19

Dear Wilhelm,

As a consequence of the secret biological sympathy of which you have often spoken, both of us felt the surgeon's knife in our bodies at about the same time, and on precisely the same days moaned and groaned because of the pain; I, because of lesser pain — evidently because I could not stand greater pain, as this sample proved to me. I learned that here there exists a sphere of sensibility as rich and diverse in its elements and construction as that of sounds or colors, though there is little prospect of using this material of sensations in a similar way; it hurts too much.

In my case it was a large furuncle on the raphe scroti which reminded me of my kinship with you. I nevertheless worked the whole day. The number of patients is still increasing; one is supposed to be kind, superior, witty, original, and that is somewhat difficult at this time.

Since yesterday I am doing well, or walking well, and I have reason to assume that the same kind of change has taken place in you as well. I hope to hear from you soon that your recent resolute decision really brought you the desired improvement. I also know that after a period of suffering a new, great, and beautiful discovery can be expected of you.

My very best and most cordial thanks to your dear wife and nurse. One day I must see the children and see them again.[1]

Now, speedy progress!

Your
Sigm.

1. Freud probably means, "I must see the new child and the other one again."

---

November 16, 1898
IX., Berggasse 19

Dear Wilhelm,

Are you up by now? For some time, I hope. I see and hear no one; the last letter, the one from your dear wife, made me extraordinarily happy; it sounded as though the worst was over. I find it very expedient that surgeons never take the pain they cause into account; if they did, they obviously would not find the courage for many a thing. I still shudder — an echo — at your heroism in the early period of our friendship. I could tolerate nothing at all.

I had a difficult time; today is the first good day, perhaps only an *intervallum lucidum.* And, by comparison, these are minor things one should not even mention. I was not prevented from working either.

I greatly long for news.

Most cordially,

Your
Sigm.

November 30, 1898
IX., Berggasse 19

My dear Wilhelm,

It is very unreasonable of me, nor do I understand it fully; I am relating it to you as a phenomenon that evidently I am angry with you because you are doing poorly. I would dearly like to be critical of the operation, but am unable to do so because I understand too little about it; also, with my "raison" I would probably say you were right. So pull me out of this ridiculous situation by telling me *truthfully* that you are doing well and are steadily getting better. At Christmas, if you have no better visitors, I want to come to see you—but harmlessly without a manuscript, even without any inquisitiveness on my part, simply to see you and chat with you. I can stay with my sister, who lives not far from you. Then we shall talk of better times when we shall be able to travel again. I hope you understood that my furuncles were trumpeted so much only as a damper.

Most cordial greetings to you and your dear wife.

Sigm.

---

December 5, 1898

Dear Wilhelm,

That was a pleasant surprise, your reply crossing my letter. Of course, I'll be party to it. If only nothing turns up to prevent it. Then we will once again properly ventilate the inner man; in my case, he needs it; he is showing a few *Knetscher.*[1] As for the rest, wherever you would like to go, as long as it's not the same place we have been before. I am not making any proposals today for the simple reason that I don't know of anything special.

I have a lot of work this month too, and it tires me just as much. All sorts of doubts about the "constitution," which you also raised. In view of your illness I have also forgone, as you have noticed, our interchange of ideas into which so much has gone; a new piece of resignation. Occasionally I have longed for a strong and sweet drop of the juice of grapes—even if it cannot be a "punch made of Lethe"[2]—but I was ashamed of acquiring a new vice.

The literature (on the dream) which I am now reading makes me completely stupid. A horrible punishment for those who write. In the process everything of one's own diffuses. I often cannot remember what I have found that is new, since everything about it is new. The reading stretches ahead, with no end in sight. Enough of that! I celebrated the release [demise] of our dear C. F. Meyer by acquiring the volumes I lacked—*Hutten, Pescara, Der Heilige.* I believe I now equal your enthusiasm for him. I could scarcely tear myself away from *Pescara.* I would very much like to know something about his life story and also the sequence of his works, which I need for interpreting.

It is nice, however, that you are well again, are making plans as I am making "programs." Pain is soon forgotten, after all.

So, until we see each other again! We still shall exchange a few letters before then; a tiny reprint of mine will no doubt reach you in Berlin.

Your
Sigm.

Rechnitzer[3] did not want me to recommend a Viennese rhinologist; he wants to see you.

1. Yiddish for "wrinkles."

2. See letters of September 6, 1897, and April 24, 1899.

3. Possibly Leopold Rechnitzer, whose name appears on a membership list of the Vienna Psycho-Analytic Society in 1910.

---

December 7, 1898

Dear Wilhelm,

In order to avoid a third crossing [of letters], I am answering by return mail. I believe you, as always—that you face the prospect of better times—and my "angriness"[1] clearly is diminishing. So if you come, and since you evidently do not want to travel too far, we shall soon have settled the choice of place for the congress. In Berlin we would have less of each other; I would profit quo ad [with respect to] Paulinchen and my sick sister. As to my miserable mood, which I probably cannot conceal from you, two other factors are responsible, apart from the previously mentioned one that made me angry: the monotony of the heavy burden of work and the awful tedium of the literature on dreams, which nevertheless must be read. At any rate, it is a change from the usual. The children are thriving, the household is doing well. Vienna and the conditions here are almost physically repulsive to me. No doubt this simply means that one is growing old, becoming nervous, and the constitution is slackening. It has always been very open to being refreshed by psychic impressions. Therefore I am *tremendously* looking forward to Christmas.

Greet your wife and children for me!

Your
Sigm.

1. Freud uses the neologism *Bösigkeit.*

December 20, 1898

Dear Wilhelm,

I hope you will call me at noon on Sunday and tell me when you will be free. What I would like best is, of course, if the two of us could get away from Vienna, even if only half an hour from here (Baden). Warned by various indications, however, I do not dare to propose a firm "program." Your head, your preferences, and consideration for your family will be decisive. My wife hopes to see you both here on Wednesday evening for a small party. I am more modest; all I ask is that you be free on Monday, because on Tuesday and so forth I suppose I have to put on the yoke again, to earn the 70 florins which are now to be had every day.

Rarely have three months of separation seemed as long to me as these last ones. You write nothing about the state of your health, apparently so as not to hurt me. There I am in the habit of being less considerate.

I shall be glad to hear of your demolition and reconstruction plans; mine have indeed become more modest. All sorts of things displease me in life. The zoon politikon [political animal] is unsatisfied. Vienna stinks to high heaven and I cannot bear the stench. It is silly that all these things occur to me when at last I once again have an occasion to rejoice.

My little trifle, "The Painting by Signorelli" [published as "The Psychical Mechanism of Forgetfulness"], has appeared in print, though not yet as a reprint.[1]

I have not discovered in myself any further inclination to work.

You will get one of Martin's new poems to May, beginning with lines that really can be sung:

> May beetles fly in bluish air
> Flowers forever spread the sweetest of scents . . .

See you in a few days.

Your
Sigm.

1. *S.E.* 3:289–297.

Vienna, January 3, 1899
IX., Berggasse 19

Dear Wilhelm,

So I am the first to give news of himself after all. After the fall of the meteor gleams a light that brightens the gloomy sky for a long while thereafter. For me it is not yet extinguished. In this brightness, then, I suddenly glimpsed several things, and then even the first professional vexations of the New Year could not disturb my good mood.

In the first place, a small bit of my self-analysis has forced its way through and confirmed that fantasies are products of later periods and are projected back from what was then the present into earliest childhood; the manner in which this occurs also emerged—once again by a verbal link.[1]

To the question "What happened in earliest childhood?" the answer is, "Nothing, but the germ of a sexual impulse existed." The thing would be easy and a pleasure to tell you, but writing it out would take half a sheet[2] so [I shall keep it] for our congress at Easter, together with other elucidations of the story of my early years.

In the second place, I have grasped the meaning of a new psychic element which I conceive to be of general significance and a preliminary stage of symptoms (even before fantasy).

January 4. I got tired yesterday, and today I cannot go on writing along the lines I intended because the thing is growing. There is something to it. It is dawning. In the next few days there certainly will be some additions to it. I shall write you then, when it has become transparent. I want to reveal to you only that the dream schema is capable of the most general application, that the key to hysteria as well really lies in dreams. I now also understand why in spite of all my efforts I have not yet finished the dream [book]. If I wait a little longer, I shall be able to present the psychic process in dreams in such a way that it also includes the process in the formation of hysterical symptoms. So let us wait.

Something pleasant about which I had meant to write you yesterday was sent to me—from Gibraltar by a Mr. Havelock Ellis, an author who concerns himself with the topic of sex and is obviously a highly intelligent man because his paper, which appeared in *Alienist and Neurologist* (October 1898) and deals with the connection between hysteria and sexual life, begins with Plato and ends with Freud; he agrees a great deal with the latter and gives *Studies on Hysteria,* as well as later papers, their due in a very sensible manner. He even quotes Gattel. At the end he retracts some of his praise.

But something remains, and the good impression can no longer be erased. Should I get ready to warn our Oscar, or do we still wait for a while?

Now look at what happens. Here I live in ill humor and in darkness until you come; I get things off my chest; rekindle my flickering flame at your steadfast one and feel well again; and after your departure, I again have been given eyes to see, and what I see is beautiful and good. Is that only because the special date had not yet come? Or could not one of the many days available for all purposes be fashioned into the special date by means of the psychic influences affecting the one who is waiting? Must not some place be left for that, so that the [dynamic] force is not ruled out by the time [element]?

Most cordial greetings to you and yours.

Your
Sigm.

1. Kris (*Origins*, p. 271n1) suggests that this refers to Freud's 1899 paper, "Screen Memories."

2. A printed sheet (or signature) at the time had sixteen pages.

# Fantasy or Reality?

Vienna, January 16, 1899
IX., Berggasse 19

Dear Wilhelm,

You will immediately have understood what occasioned this letter. My work and the sirocco made me so miserable that I went with the two women to "Ancora Verde,"[1] seeking restoration in a bottle of barolo. I have just returned. All sorts of comfort come from the wine and so I am writing to you now.

If after ten hours of talking I were not so lazy about writing—as you can see from my uneven script—I could really compose a small essay for you about the minor advances of the wish theory, because since the 3rd of January the light has not gone out completely, nor the certainty that I have put my finger on an important nodal point. But perhaps it is better if I save and collect, so that at our Easter congress I shall not again stand before you as a poor beggar, enticing you with nothing but announcements of things to come.

A few other things of minor significance have yielded results as well—for instance, that hysterical headaches rest on an analogy in fantasy which equates the top with the bottom part of the body (hair in both places—cheeks *[Backen]* and buttocks [*Hinterbacken;* literally, hindcheeks]—lips *[Lippen]* and labia [*Schamlippen;* literally, shamelips]—mouth = vagina), so that an attack of migraine can be used to represent a forcible defloration, and yet the entire ailment once again represents a situation of wish fulfillment. The necessary conditions of the sexual become clearer and clearer.[2] In one woman patient (whom I have set right with the key of fantasy)[3] there were constant states of despair with a melancholic conviction that she was of no use, was incapable of anything, and so on. I always thought that in her early childhood she had witnessed an analogous state, a genuine melancholia, in her mother. This was in accordance with the earlier theory, but two years brought no confirmation of it. Now it has turned out that when she was a girl of fourteen she discovered that she had atresia hymenalis [an imperforate hymen] and was in despair that she would be of no use as a wife. Hence, melancholia—[that is,] fear of impotence. Similar states, in which she cannot make up her mind to choose a hat or a dress, go back to her struggle at the time when she had to choose her husband.

With another woman patient I have convinced myself that there really is such a thing as hysterical melancholia and identified its characteristics. I have also noted how the same memory appears in the most numerous translations and I have gained a first glimpse of how melancholia comes about through summation. This patient is, moreover, totally anesthetic—as she should be, according to an idea dating back to the earliest period of my work on the neuroses.[4]

I heard about a third woman in the following, interesting way: a man of high standing and vast wealth (a bank director), about sixty years old, came to see me and talked to me about the peculiarities of a young woman with whom he is having an affair. I threw out a guess that she was probably completely anesthetic. On the contrary, she has from four to six orgasms during one coitus. But—at the very first approach she is seized with a tremor and immediately afterward falls into a pathological sleep, during which she talks as though she were in hypnosis, even carries out posthypnotic suggestions; complete amnesia for all this. He is going to marry her off, and she will certainly be anesthetic with her husband. The old gentleman, because of the possible identification with the immensely wealthy father of her childhood, evidently has the effect of being able to set free the libido attached to her fantasies. Instructive!

You have received the Palolowurm.[5] These are good preparations for what you have to say.

At last children and wife are once again well. Annerl suddenly recovered one morning and since then has been delightfully cheeky.

Farewell, cordially greet wife and children, and let me have news of you soon.

Your
Sigm.

1. An Italian restaurant.

2. "Die Bedingung des Sexuellen stellt sich immer schärfer und schärfer." Does Freud mean that sexuality is always the conditioning factor of a neurosis?

3. The "key of fantasy" refers to Freud's belief that he had discovered that the key

to neurosis lay not in real events (such as seductions) but in fantasies (for instance, of seduction by the father).

4. Freud's early theory stressed real events. He is saying here that he believed the child witnessed real depression in the mother and identified with her. But he now thinks that the fantasies of puberty (in this case that she could not be a wife) seek out, as a rationalization, earlier experiences that never happened.

5. Schröter points out that Fliess mentions this worm in his 1906 book, *Der Ablauf des Lebens* (pp. 308–311).

---

Vienna, January 30, 1899

Dear Wilhelm,

From what I hear, you have been in Warsaw. I hope it did you good and cost someone else a lot of money. My delay in writing is explained as follows: I had completed a letter to you a week ago because I believed I had made a real discovery. But doubts set in as I was writing; I decided to wait and was right because the thing was not correct; that is to say, there was something to it, but it had to be reinterpreted with application to quite another area.

You probably do not know how much your last visit raised my spirits. I am still living on it. The light has not gone out since then; bits of insight are dawning now here, now there—a genuine reinvigoration by comparison with the desolation of last year. What is rising out of the chaos this time is the connection to the psychology contained in the *Studies on Hysteria*—the relation to conflict, to life: clinical psychology, as I should like to call it. Puberty is becoming ever more central; fantasy as the key holds fast.[1] Yet there is still nothing big or complete. I diligently make notes of all that is worthwhile so as to present it to you at our congress. I need you as my audience.

For relaxation I am reading Burckhardt's *History of Greek Civilization*, which is providing me with unexpected parallels. My predilection for the prehistoric in all its human forms has remained the same.

On day 28 Mathilde had another throat infection, after which she lost a tooth; then she grew again and—is miserable. Her mother, incidentally, did exactly the same thing before the onset of her menstrual periods.

February 3. I could not resolve to send off this letter as if it were completed, and was waiting for new material. But nothing came. Everything is now going in the pages on which I make notes for our congress, and neither my interest nor my energy is sufficient for anything else. Today, after twelve hours of work and earnings of 100 florins, I am again at the end of my strength. All yearnings of the soul are asleep; that is, just as art thrives only in the midst of prosperity, so does yearning thrive only in leisure. I merely anticipate what you will say about my notes, which will give you a better insight than ever before, though there is nothing of *first* rank in them. In any case, I know you do not like making long-term plans.

Otherwise nothing new here. I expect good news of you, wife, and children.

Your
Sigm.

1. This became Freud's position. The first published reference to his change of views about the etiology of the neuroses occurs in a letter he wrote to Leopold Löwenfeld, which was published in the latter's *Die psychischen Zwangserscheinungen* (Wiesbaden: J. F. Bergmann, 1904), p. 297.

---

Vienna, February 6, 1899
IX., Berggasse 19

Dear Wilhelm,

First crossing! We had the feeling you express at about the same time.

You will not get so quickly from medicine to industrial enterprises (sugar factory); the public will see to that. I hear it with great pleasure. You will certainly have to tell me about Warsaw.

I do not see cases of the kind you ask about, simply because I see none but my daily patients, upon whom I shall indeed manage to live for quite a long, first period of work.[1] They provide me with what is typical; I hope I shall no longer need to trouble myself about the corollaries. I do remember cases of tuberculosis accompanied by anxiety, even dating back to earlier periods, but they did not leave any special impression on me.

Poor Schiff as you present him reminds me of one of the most annoying aspects of our modern medicine. The art of deceiving a patient is certainly not very necessary. But what has the individual come to, how negligible must be the influence of the religion of science, which is supposed to have taken the place of the old religion, if one no longer dares to disclose that it is this or that man's turn to die? Breuer's spirit lives in these arts. The Christian at least has the last sacrament administered a few hours beforehand. And Shakespeare says, "Thou owest Nature a death."[2] I hope that when my time comes, I shall find someone who will treat me with greater respect and tell me when to be ready. My father was fully aware of it, did not talk about it, and retained his beautiful composure to the end.

For a long time we have not had a period as devoid of external events as this one. This is a blessing as far as family affairs are concerned, because such new things are rarely desirable. The work is progressing slowly, never without results, but now for a long time again without taking a surprising turn. The secret dossier is getting thicker and thicker and literally longs for its opening at Easter. I myself am getting curious about when Easter in Rome will be possible.

I am still perfectly serious about a change of profession and residence, in spite of all the improvements in my practice and income. On the whole, things really are too awful. A pity that these plans are just as fantastic as "Easter in Rome." Fate, otherwise so colorful, so eager to provide novelties and surprises, has simply forgotten your friend in his lonely corner.

Recently I went to Spiegelgasse to see Oscar. I found only Norbert, who told me a long story that I unfortunately did not understand; but he behaved very intelligently and so I left, consoled.

Now I hope you will not wait for a new crossing. Cordial greetings to you and all your family.

Your
Sigm.

I am deep in Burckhardt's *History of Greek Civilization.*

1. This could also mean "who will keep me occupied for quite a long period."
2. Quoted by Freud in German. The original reads, "Why, thou owest God a death" (*I Henry IV*, Act 5, scene 1).

---

Vienna, February 19, 1899
IX., Berggasse 19

Dear Wilhelm,

Well, the same thing is happening to you; so I need not feel ashamed. You too start letters on the 11th which you are able to continue only on the 16th, and on the 16th you can write of nothing but the tremendously huge work which is all too hard for the powers of a poor human being, which demands every stirring thought, and which gradually consumes all other faculties and susceptibilities — a sort of neoplastic tissue infiltrating the human and finally replacing it. My lot is barely better — or worse. In my case, work and gainful activities coincide; I have turned completely into a carcinoma. The neoplasm in its most recent stages of development likes to drink wine. Today I am supposed to go to the theater; but this is ridiculous — like an attempt to graft onto the carcinoma. Nothing can adhere to it, so from now on the duration of my life span is that of the neoplasm.

My last generalization has held good and seems inclined to grow to an unpredictable extent. Not only dreams are wish fulfillments, so are hysterical attacks. This is true of hysterical symptoms, but probably applies to every product of neurosis, for I recognized it long ago in acute delusional insanity. Reality — wish fulfillment — it is from these opposites that our mental life springs. I believe I now know what determines the distinction between symptoms that make their way into waking life and dreams. It is enough for the dream to be the wish fulfillment of the repressed thought, for dreams are kept at a distance from reality. But the symptom, set in the midst of life, must be something else besides: it must also be the wish fulfillment of the repressing thought. A symptom arises where the repressed and the repressing thought can come together in the fulfillment of a wish. The symptom is the wish fulfillment of the repressing thought, for example, in the form of a punishment; self-punishment is the final substitute for self-gratification, which comes from masturbation.

This key opens many doors. Do you know, for instance, why X.Y. suffers from hysterical vomiting? Because in fantasy she is pregnant, because she is so insatiable that she cannot bear being deprived of having a baby by her last fantasy lover as well. But she also allows herself to vomit, because then she will be starved and emaciated, will lose her beauty and no longer be attractive to anyone. Thus the meaning of the symptom is a contradictory pair of wish fulfillments.

Do you know why our friend E., whom you know, blushes and sweats as soon as he sees one of a particular category of acquaintances, especially at the theater? He is ashamed, no doubt — but of what? Of a fantasy in which he figures as the deflowerer of every person he meets. He sweats as he deflowers, working very hard at it. An echo of the meaning [of this symptom] finds a voice in him, like the resentment of someone defeated, every time he feels ashamed in the presence of someone: "Now the silly goose thinks I am ashamed. If I had her in bed, she would see how little embarrassment I feel!" And the period during which he turned his wishes into this fantasy has left its mark on the mental complex that produces the symptom. It was the period when he studied Latin. The auditorium of the theater reminds him of the classroom; he always tries to get the same regular seat in the front row. The entr'acte is the school "breather" *[Respirium]*, and the "sweating" stands for "*operam dare*"[1] in those days. He had an argument with the teacher about that phrase. Moreover, he cannot get over the fact that later, at the university, he failed to pass in botany; now he carries on with it as a "deflorator." To be sure, he owes his capacity for breaking into a sweat to his childhood, when his brother poured sudsy water over his face when he was in his bath (at age three); a trauma, though not a sexual one. And why was it that at Interlaken, when he was fourteen, he masturbated in such a strange position on the toilet? It was only to get a view of the Jungfrau;[2] and since then he has never gotten to see another—at all events *ad genitalia*. He has avoided this intentionally, to be sure, else why does he seek to have affairs only with actresses? How "ingenious" and yet indeed, "man with all his contradictions"![3]

Most cordially,

Your
Sigm.

1. "To make every effort."
2. A mountain in Switzerland; literally, the virgin.
3. From C. F. Meyer, *Hutten's letzte Tage*. The quotation reads:

Ich bin kein ausgeklügelt Buch,
Ich bin ein Mensch mit seinem Widerspruch.

This is also quoted by Freud in his "Analysis of a Phobia in a Five-Year-Old Boy."

---

Vienna, March 2, 1899
IX., Berggasse 19

Dear Wilhelm,

"Writing he has completely forgotten."[1] Why? And with a plausible theory of forgetfulness fresh in his memory as a warning?

Could it be that once again our letters are crossing? Well, this letter will stay here for another day.

Things are going almost uniformly well for me. I can hardly wait for Easter to show you in detail a principal part of the story of wish fulfillment and of the coupling of opposites. I am experiencing much pleasure with old cases and have begun two new ones, though not the most favorable. The realm of uncertainty is still enormous, problems abound, and I understand theoretically only the smallest fraction of what I am doing. Yet every few days things become clearer — now here, now there; I have become modest and count on long years of work and patient collecting, with the help of a few useful ideas after vacation and our meetings.

Rome is still distant; you do know my Roman dreams.

March 3. Life is otherwise incredibly devoid of content. Nursery and consulting room — in these times there is nothing else; if both are doing well, enough has been sacrificed to the envy of the gods in other respects. Annerl has had an intestinal flu and is not recovering; no other victims. The weather changes every twenty-four hours, from snowstorms to intimations of spring. Sunday still is a fine institution, although Martin maintains that he feels Sundays are getting fewer and farther between. Easter really is not so far away anymore. Are your plans fixed yet? I am already itching to travel.

*Pour revenir à nos moutons.*[2] I can very clearly distinguish two different intellectual states in myself. In one I retain very well everything that my patients tell me, even invent new things in the course of the work, but outside of it can neither think nor work on anything else. In the second, I draw conclusions, make notes, even am interested in other things, but am really farther away from things and am not paying close attention while I work with patients. Occasionally a second part of the treatment is dawning on me — to provoke their feelings in the same way as their associations, as though this were quite indispensable. The main result of this year's work appears to me to be the surmounting of fantasies; they have indeed lured me far away from what is real.[3] Yet all this work has been very good for my own emotional life; I am apparently much more normal than I was four or five years ago.

I have given up my lectures this year in spite of very sizable enrollments and do not plan to resume them in the near future. I have the same horror of the uncritical adulation of the very young that I used to have of the enmity of their elders. Besides, the whole thing is not ripe — *nonum praematur in annum*![4] Pupils à la Gattel are easy to come by; in the end they regularly ask to be treated themselves. I also have a secondary purpose in mind — the realization of a secret wish that may become ripe at about the same time as Rome. Thus, if Rome becomes possible, I shall give up the lectureship. But, as I said, we are not yet in Rome.

I sorely miss news of you. Does it have to be so?

Most cordially, and with regards to your dear wife,

Your
Sigm.

1. Reference unclear.

2. A much-used phrase taken from *Pathelin*, a fifteenth-century French farce, author unknown. The plot revolves around a trial having to do with stolen sheep. The plaintiff, who has been duped by the accused as well as by the lawyer of the accused in a separate incident, confuses the two problems. He is constantly exhorted by the judge, "Revenez donc à vos moutons!"

3. Eric Mosbacher's translation in *Origins* is, "The outstanding feature of the year's work seems to me to have been the solution of the phantasy problem. I have let myself be lured a long way from reality" (p. 280). This is what one expects Freud to mean. (See his letter of November 7, 1899: "Last year's gain, fantasies, have stood the test splendidly.") But the German does not say that: "Die Überwindung der Phantasien scheint mir das Hauptergebnis der heurigen Arbeit zu sein; sie haben mich doch weit weg vom Wirklichen gelockt."

4. From Horace: "Let it be kept quiet till the ninth year."

---

March 19, 1899
IX., Berggasse 19

Dear Wilhelm,

One of the three long weeks before Easter is fortunately over; it sapped almost my entire store of energy. Now the anxious expectation: whether anything will interfere with it. I inspected Mela today; she looks radiant — and not in accord with any special date. The children all have a cough and complain of earaches. I hope the influenza does not open the door to any other epidemic. I take your not writing as proof that you are not well; by then you will have recovered again. In my work everything is surging to and fro, but I shall not attempt anything new until the meeting with you has turned my thoughts to the laws of the universe and the Easter vacation has not [?] made me more capable of entertaining new points of view. Not long ago I saw Schnitzler's *Paracelsus*;[1] was amazed at how much a poet knows.

In expectation, with most cordial greetings,

Your
Sigm.

1. The reference is to a short, one-act play that describes the return of Paracelsus to Basel at the beginning of the sixteenth century and his meeting with a woman, Justina, still beautiful, whom he had loved as a student. She is now married to Cyprian. Paracelsus hypnotizes her, and in an altered state of consciousness she tells her husband, Anselm (a young Junker), her sister Cacilia, and Paracelsus the truth she has always withheld: that she had been in love with Paracelsus and would have left with him had he returned to take her; moreover, she was on the verge of sleeping with Anselm as a farewell to her youth. The play, a lovely work, is about dreams, truth, madness, and love.

*Paracelsus* was published in Arthur Schnitzler, *Die dramatischen Werke* (Frankfurt: S. Fischer, 1962), 1:465–498.

---

Vienna, March 27, 1899

Dear Wilhelm,

So the second of the three long weeks separating us from Easter is gone, never to return, and it is possible to wait out the fortunately small number of days until we see each other again. Mela's baby no longer is an obstacle; a warm wind arrived today; the epidemics seem to have kept away; so everything will no doubt be favorable. I shall leave Friday evening and be in Innsbruck at 9:30, take rooms in the Sonne or in the more elegant Tirolerhof, whichever you prefer, and fetch you for lunch if you arrive on the express train at 12:45. Then we shall have—and this is the only shadow—barely forty-eight hours for ourselves. I could manage to add Tuesday, but you cannot because of the boat at Genoa.

If only I find you as well as last time in Baden! Your latest news did not please me. You should really spend the six months of your post[operative] treatments in a germ-free environment.

I am dead tired every single evening, but still quite capable of recovering. As a consequence of my getting there a few hours earlier, I shall meet you fully refreshed. I do not know whether in the next few days I shall muster the strength to bring order to the material earmarked for you, or whether you will again have to make do with fragments—the latter, it seems to me. But you will doubtless confirm that it has begun to dawn in my darkness since fall. I have emerged from several blind alleys.

No doubt you will also broaden my view so that I shall once again be able to comprehend something of heaven and earth, in addition to the psychological. I need it badly.

My little Annerl is well again, and the other animals also are growing and grazing properly once more. My brother has taken a big step forward; he has become a partner in the enterprise in which up to now he had been the editor.

These are the most important news items. You realize, no doubt, that I am scarcely able to write any longer. I am waiting for another card from you, and then the Easter congress in Innsbruck.

Most cordially,

Your
Sigm.

April 13, 1899
IX., Berggasse 19

Dear Wilhelm,

It makes me feel good to contemplate that you are now doing so well and can enjoy recalling a beautiful past without regretting that it is over. I do not want to disturb the idyll by giving you any discordant news, for example, about my difficult struggle with unyielding work. But then I have nothing further to report. All of us are well; we are still looking for lodgings in the country; my work load has not increased, as it did before Easter; I feel lazy and comfortable. In view of my diminishing income I have put aside a secret plan: to investigate what you have left over of Naples for me in September. If chance wills it, you will suddenly come upon my brother.

I hope to hear from you. Please convey my most cordial greetings to your traveling companion.

Your
Sigm.

---

April 24, 1899
IX., Berggasse 19

Dear Wilhelm,

Thanks for your announcement of the nectar; its place of origin and the hour when it was bought and the person who ordered it will be appreciated repeatedly. Since drinking alone is merely a vice, you will permit me to empty a glass apiece for Wilhelm, Ida, Robert, and Paulinchen.

A postcard of "mysterious" content awaits you in Florence. It makes reference to Innsbruck, as you will recall. Since then I have been ill-humored, at odds with my work and everything connected with it. Spring storms, according to your certainly optimistic conception—harbingers of birth. Therefore, I gladly will drink the punch made of Lethe.[1]

Alexander has returned, he too saturated with wine. How very much I should like to write here about some work that means something to me.

*Introite et hic dii sunt.*[2]

Or have I not ceded this to you?

Continue to have the happiest of journeys!

Your
Sigm.

1. See note 1 to letter of September 6, 1897.
2. Fliess, in fact, uses this phrase! See note 2 to letter of December 4, 1896.

---

Vienna, May 25, 1899
IX., Berggasse 19

Dear Wilhelm,

A contented letter from you containing evidence of your being well and the promise that you will attempt a first presentation of your earthshaking formulas were a long-missed pleasure and a good omen for the approaching season, in which we shall have to exchange letters for an indeterminate period of time. I still carry in my pocket the instructions on how to handle the "wine of the gods," so that I can faithfully execute them when the time comes.

And now my news. On the Sunday before Whitsun—6 weeks, $28 + \frac{28}{2}$ days, since the migraine in Innsbruck—the mild depression prevailing in the intervening period (including a new migraine) really stopped, suddenly and for no reason, and gave way to an unfounded sense of well-being. Business is in a steady decline, low enough to justify Oscar's blackest apprehensions; three new contacts have already been broken off; a fourth, of no more value, is about to do the same; I foresee all sorts of difficulties, yet remain in the best of spirits. On the day on which things turned, we (that is, Minna and I) were invited by Oscar and Mela. We liked your friend Dernburg very much and let our wrath be aroused by his tolerant evaluation of our Lueger.[1] Your first brother-in-law, Oscar, and I treated him badly on account of this. D. wanted to persuade us that here all is very well, replete with the best "possibilities," and that we are unfair in complaining so bitterly. I still think we know better. Mela's menu unfortunately was sparse, cauliflower and chicken, both of which I detest with all my heart; not one of the refreshing new things of the season; my womenfolk always maintain that she has a distinct inclination to parsimony when she entertains. Since then, though, I relish life again. I used the week before Whitsun to write the essay on "Screen Memories,"[2] which I am sending off to Jena today. While producing it, I liked it immensely—which does not augur well for its future fate. Sunday evening I went to Reichenau where my sister Rosa[3] is now staying, with

Mathilde as her guest. Monday morning, together with brother-in-law Heinrich, I climbed the Rax as in the good old days; three and a half hours going up, two and a half coming down. Only the Rax has become much higher since the last time I climbed it, by at least 500 meters. My heart took it splendidly, but I could eat nothing the following day, and even today my lower parts still feel like lead with a few fiery liquid knots in them.

I had the opportunity to meet friend Gärtner at a consultation with a family ten days ago. Schiller describes him aptly (in "Ring des Polycrates") as "Schaute mit vergnügten Sinnen."[4] After he had behaved incredibly foolishly there, on the way home he pulled his newest dagger from his garment and put it at his fingertips. . .[5]

I would like to imagine that it is possible to introduce the dream [book];[6] I do not yet know how. If in June and July things continue as they are now, with two and a half patients a day, I shall have to write it. What else would I do with my time?

The boys were ill again; are now playing, dressed in uniforms, in the garden.

Most cordial greetings to your dear wife and both children.

Your
Sigm.

1. Karl Lueger (1844–1910), mayor of Vienna, elected in 1897.

2. Published as "Über Deckerinnerungen" in the *Monatsschrift für Psychiatrie und Neurologie.*

3. See note 1 to letter of May 17, 1896.

4. The line Freud quotes (he "gazed with pleasure") is from the first stanza of Schiller's ballad, written in 1797.

5. Reference unclear.

6. Freud actually writes, "Den Traum will ich ihn [?] beginnen," which makes no sense. Possibly the *ihn* is *nun.*

---

Vienna, May 28, 1899
IX., Berggasse 19

Dear Wilhelm,

Yes, indeed, we are still alive, in spite of all the "head shaking,"[1] and intend to make the most of it. Your presentation should mark one day on the calendar in red, because — and this you do not know — it was humanly impossible to remember the powerful stuff on the basis of an oral communication or even to have an overview of it. The "Screen Memories" are in Jena with Ziehen; the wine has arrived and is resting, according to your directions; but the dream [book] is suddenly taking shape, without any special motivation, but this time I am sure of it.[2] I have decided that I cannot use any of the disguises, nor can I afford to give up anything because I am not rich enough to keep my finest and probably my only lasting discovery to myself. In this dilemma I behaved like the rabbi in the story of the cock and the hen. Do you know it? A husband and wife who owned one cock and one hen decided to celebrate the holidays by roasting a fowl, but they could not make up their minds which was to be sacrificed and therefore turned to the rabbi. "Rebbe, what are we to do? We have only one cock and one hen. If we kill the cock, the hen will pine; and if we kill the hen, the cock will pine. But we want to eat a fowl on the holiday; rabbi, what are we to do?" The rabbi: "So kill the cock." — "But then the hen will pine." — "Yes, that's true; so kill the hen." — "But rabbi, then the cock will pine." — The rabbi: "So let him pine!"

So the dream [book] will be. That this Austria is supposed to perish in the next two weeks made my decision easier. Why should the dream perish with it? Unfortunately, to frighten one off, the gods have placed the [dream] literature before the presentation. The first time I got stuck in it. This time I shall fight my way through; there is nothing of consequence in it anyway. No other work of mine has been so completely my own, my own dung heap, my seedling and a *nova species mihi* on top of it. After the literature, there will be deletions, insertions, and the like, and the whole thing should be ready for the printer by the end of July, when I go to the country. I may possibly try to change publishers if I find that Deuticke does not want to pay much for it or is not very eager to have it.

The ten analyses are in no hurry [to come]. I now have two and a half! Four prospects did not materialize; otherwise, dead silence. Strangely enough, this leaves me cold. Lately my technique has been near perfect.

The boys produced a slight throat infection after two days of fever. Ernst still has a lot of pain from his presumed stomach dilatation; he is to be shown to Kassowitz. Friday they (Minna and the children, except Mathilde) are off to Berchtesgaden.

I gave myself a present, Schliemann's *Ilios*,[3] and greatly enjoyed the account of his childhood. The man was happy when he found Priam's treasure, because happiness comes only with the fulfillment of a childhood wish. This reminds me that I shall not go to Italy this year. Until next time!

With the most cordial greetings to you, wife, son, and daughter,

Your
Sigm.

1. See note 2 to letter of February 9, 1898.

2. Not "dreams" (as in *Origins*), but "the dream" — that is, Freud's 1900 book, the *Interpretation of Dreams.*

3. Heinrich Schliemann (1822–1890), *Ilios: Stadt und Land der Trojaner* (Leipzig: F. A. Brockhaus, 1881).

June 9, 1899
IX., Berggasse 19

Dear Wilhelm,

A sign of life! The "silence of the forest"[1] is the clamor of a metropolis compared to the silence in my consulting room. This is a good place to "dream." The literature contains some specimens which for the first time make me wish that I had never had anything to do with it. One of them is named Spitta (to spit[2] = to vomit). I am over the hill now. Naturally one gets ever deeper into it, and there comes a point when one has to break off. The whole matter again resolves itself for me into a commonplace. Invariably the dream seeks to fulfill *one* wish that has assumed various forms. It is the wish to sleep! We dream in order not to have to wake up, because we want to sleep. *Tant de bruit* . . . [3]

The children went to Berchtesgaden Tuesday evening. Kassowitz said nothing; only said that it was nothing. After eating, Ernstl complains, "It hurts"; and in the last days he could not be induced to eat because then "it hurts." Martha and Mathilde will follow on June 20. Because I have been in England and Hamburg, I have seen a bit of the ocean, but not enough.

I have begun analyzing a friend (Mrs. A.), a first-rate woman — have I never mentioned her to you? — and once more am able to convince myself how splendidly everything fits. Otherwise I am resigned. I have enough to live on for another few months. I saw Oscar, Mela, and Oscar II just before your mother's departure. Strange that I cannot really get cross with the second Oscar either: he obviously resembles Ida too much. I am swamped with psychological literature — it has a depressing effect on me, giving me a feeling that I know nothing when I had thought I had grasped something new. That this activity of reading and abstracting cannot be endured for more than a few hours a day is another misfortune. So I often ask myself whether you really gave me good advice or whether I should curse you for it. There is only one possible compensation: you must give me something refreshing to read in your introduction to biology.

Most cordial greetings to you and all of you.

Your
Sigm.

1. *Das Schweigen im Walde* is the name of a painting by Böcklin — a forest scene with a woman riding a unicorn. The expression *Dann ist Schweigen im Walde* refers to the lack of response to something.

2. English in original.

3. *Tant de bruit pour une omelette.* According to Voltaire, the phrase was uttered by the French poet Desbarreaux (d. 1675).

---

Vienna, June 16, 1899
IX., Berggasse 19

Dear Wilhelm,

I do occasionally react with a heavy mood to periods such as this one, in which I barely manage to have two working sessions a day, and to dull my senses I consume far too much literature on the dream, after which I really do not know where I am at. That is why I did not immediately respond to your joyous and interesting news. He is indeed a little Italian; some of the fire of Italian wine will circulate in his veins — or a touch of Greek beauty will rest on her features; in short, the impressions made on the mother will not fail to have an influence on his development.

The heavenly marsala is already on our table, but we drink it only in drops; Martha counted the bottles and took charge of them lest in my loneliness I succumb to the consolation of drink. Mother and child will depart on Tuesday, the 20th. As every year, I plan to stay here until July 25th; the following day is Martha's birthday. The prospect of seeing you at the seashore next fall is nice enough, although I fear that this year my wings are bound. But there is still time until then. For the first time, moreover, we have to be back in Vienna on September 14, on account of the children who will be going to school.

The motto did not suit you. I am searching for another one. Robert's contributions will be accepted gratefully.

I was very surprised by the letter from L.D. I do not know a Dr. Noak, though he could well be a "pupil" of mine. If he can bring about such changes in four months, he knows more than his teacher. He may in his simplemindedness have found a simpler way, or he may be dealing with simpler people.

On Sunday there is the wedding at the Königsteins. The daughter is marrying an army physician from Kaschau in Hungary. We shall lend our assistance throughout the day. They are the only warm friends we have here. I do not want to get close to Oscar; he tries very hard to be cordial on every occasion, but he is rigid and you know what he is like in other respects, and occasionally you are even too hard on him. From him, by the way, I have the news, which pleased me very much, that your treatment again did your mother a lot of good. No doubt you are right about the "therapy of discomforts."[1] The announcement that you are engaged in research perhaps may mean, instead of writing? And postponement of the date on which I can read something of yours?

Today I could no longer bear reading the *Coscienza nel Sonno*[2] [Conscience during sleep]. We went to the Prater, first to Urania to hear a lecture on iron, and then to the Krieau for supper. It was a glorious early summer day, but little sunshine within. Perhaps the wish-fulfilling dream is wresting itself out of the darkness.

With most cordial greetings to you and the small family growing and thriving,

Your
Sigm.

1. *Beschwerdentherapie.* Meaning unclear.
2. Giovanni Dandolo, *La Coscienza nel Sonno: Studio di Psicologia* (Padua: Angelo Droghi, 1889).

---

Vienna, June 27, 1899
IX., Berggasse 19

Dear Wilhelm,

Many thanks for the long letter, which I hardly deserve. It is my lot to wait, and in resignation I have given up my habit of complaining about the unbridgeable distance. I hope the path you have taken will lead you even farther and even deeper, and that as the new Kepler you will unveil the ironclad rules of the biological mechanism to us. Indeed you have your calling in life.

You do not mention how your wife is. Since you are an optimist and I am a pessimist, I should probably draw unfavorable inferences from this? I want to postpone it for a while, though. That your mother-in-law is doing so well is no doubt a triumph of reason and a disgrace for the Viennese "intellectual aristocracy."

I am tired and very much looking forward to the four days from June 29 to July 2 that I shall spend at Berchtesgaden. The writing business goes on — once I managed to write as much as a *signature* in a single day; the chapter is becoming more drawn out and will be neither nice nor fruitful. It is, however, a duty to do it. In the process I get no fonder of the subject.

On June 25 Mathilde made her entry into womanhood, somewhat prematurely. At the same time I received a poem about the journey from Martin — at least, it arrived at the same time — but certainly at the same time I had a migraine from which I thought I would die.[1] It is the third of this kind and is absolutely awful.

I am gradually becoming accustomed to the wine; it seems like an old friend. I plan to drink a lot of it in July.

Tomorrow I shall send the first signatures to the printer; perhaps others will like it more than I do. "I do not like it," to paraphrase Uncle Jonas.[2] My own dreams have now become absurdly complicated. Recently I was told that on the occasion of Aunt Minna's birthday Annerl said, "On birthdays I am mostly a little bit good." Thereupon I dreamed the familiar school dream in which I am in *sexta* [sixth grade] and say to myself, "In this sort of dream one is mostly in sixth grade." The only possible solution: Annerl is my *sexta* [sixth] child! Brr . . .

The weather is foul. As you see, I have nothing to write about, am not cheerful, and do not want to distract you from your beautiful findings by telling you about my small neurotic interests. Therefore, a cordial good-bye for today!

Your
Sigm.

1. Freud is attempting to support Fliess's theory that important events of this kind (a woman's first period) are predetermined, and are "critical dates," on which something significant will also happen to other family members. Freud appears somewhat tired of the whole exercise, for in providing Fliess with the evidence of Martin's poem he seems to realize suddenly that the date of composition is the critical date, and this could not be related to Mathilde's period; hence the lame substitution of his own migraine.

2. Reference to a joke, "How is your wife?" — "A matter of taste. Personally, I don't like her." Freud uses it again in his letter of September 11, 1899.

July 3, 1899

Dear Wilhelm,

It is frightening when mothers become shaky; they stand between us and our demise. But then, you write, things are better; for both mothers.

I and all of us are especially glad that this time the younger mother is feeling well. Practice must count for something.

The author of "the extremely important book on dreams which unfortunately is not yet sufficiently appreciated by scientists" felt wonderful for four days in Berchtesgaden *au sein de sa famille* [in the midst of his family], and only a remnant of shame kept him from sending you *no* postcard of the Königsee. The house is a little jewel of cleanliness, solitude, and views; the women and children feel very comfortable there and look wonderful. Annerl is becoming downright beautiful by way of naughtiness. The boys are already civilized human beings, capable of enjoyment. Martin is a strange bird; sensitive and good-natured in his personal relationships, completely wrapped up in a humorous fantasy world of his own. For example, we passed a little cave in the rocks. He bent down and asked: "Is Mr. Dragon at home? No, only Mrs. Dragon. Good day, Mrs. Dragon. Mr. Dragon flew to Munich? Tell him that I shall visit him soon and bring him some candy." This was occasioned by the name Drachenloch [Dragon's Hole], which is between Salzburg and Berchtesgaden. Oli classifies mountains here, just as he does the city railroad and tram lines in Vienna. They get on very well and without jealousy.

Martha and Minna are now reading Hehn's letters to a Mr. Wichmann, and since you know everything and also lived on Wichmann Street, they want you to tell them who this Mr. W. was. I gave them to understand that you have more important things to do at the moment.

Do you know what this excursion vividly reminded me of? Of our first meeting in Salzburg in '90 or '91 and our walking tour over the Hirschbühel to Berchtesgaden, where at the railway station you witnessed one of my finest attacks of travel anxiety. In the visitors' book on the Hirschbühel you are described in my own handwriting as a "universal specialist from Berlin." Between Salzburg and Reichenhall you were, as usual, blind to the beauties of nature and instead raved about the Mannesmanns' tubes.[1] At the time I felt somewhat overwhelmed by your superiority; this I felt distinctly. Furthermore, I vaguely sensed something I can express only today: the faint notion that this man had not yet discovered his calling, which later turned out to be the shackling of life with numbers and formulas. Neither was there at that time any thought of the other calling, and if I had started talking about Miss Ida Bondy, you would have asked, Who is she? Please give my family's most cordial greetings to the lady in question.

Your
Sigm.

1. Seamless tubes invented by the Mannesmann brothers, German industrialists.

---

Vienna, July 8, 1899
IX., Berggasse 19

Dear Wilhelm,

In Aussee there was a folk poet whose saying we still frequently quote: Things never turn out as we intend, they always turn out as they will. I was prepared for a long separation after Innsbruck, and now I shall probably see you very soon, although the occasion is highly undesirable.

You know that two nights of traveling are no more difficult for me than, for instance, for your father-in-law. The simplest thing would have been to leave this evening if I had not promised Oscar to visit him tonight in Hacking[1] where the (repetition of a) cancellation would certainly have aroused his suspicion. Since something that is not going to change is involved, I think it is only right that you choose or designate the day. Not all days will be equally suitable for you, whereas for me it makes very little difference whether it is a weekday or a Sunday. If it is a matter of one day, I can hide it so well here that except for Alexander no one will notice my absence at all.

I know, of course, that I shall not be able to do very much for you; moreover, the psychiatric significance of the event is diminished by the circumstance that it has to do not so much with new psychic formations as with physical decline. But these are not arguments against [my coming]; rather, you will let me know whether and when; after all, all means of communication are open to you from tomorrow, Sunday, on.

Let me acknowledge your share in the dream [book] by enclosing the *proof* of the first page. A strange feeling, in the case of such a child of sorrow! I have great difficulties with it; I cannot manage more than two hours a day without calling on Friend Marsala for help. "He" deludes me into thinking that things are not really so bleak as they appear to me when sober. Sunshine, too, has disappeared again; it did not accompany me from Berchtesgaden. As a political animal I have in solitude all the same symptoms. Every time something changes, I feel better.

See you soon, then!

Most cordially,

Your
Sigm.

1. A suburb of Vienna.

---

July 13, 1899
IX., Berggasse 19

Dear Wilhelm,

On Saturday I blessed my decision to postpone [the trip] when I met the old man at Rie's and heard that he was going to travel to Heringdorf and so on. My coming at that time would have been a real inconvenience for you. It has been a long time since then and I have not heard from you whether I should come and when. Naturally, I am ready any day. I cannot believe that a letter has been lost. Impatiently waiting to hear from you,

Most cordially,

Your
Sigm.

---

Vienna, July 17, 1899[1]
IX., Berggasse 19

Dear Wilhelm,

I am indeed quite open to the argument of *carpe diem*, but I think I shall not immediately follow the course you desired. Everything is different once you do not need me — and that, looked at from another viewpoint, really pleases me. I have to take into consideration that I am tired and ill-humored; that I am hardly in condition to open my eyes and ears as wide as your new findings surely deserve; that the longing for my "worms" [children] already bothers me greatly; and that between Sunday evening (the time of my departure) and Martha's birthday (for which I need to do some errands in Salzburg) there is not sufficient leisure to spend more than a day with you. If the need has been eliminated, I can easily postpone the trip until September, a time when, more alert than now, I shall need to complain less to you — at least, let us hope so.

So do not expect me now, unless — and I hope this will not be the case — there is some change in the condition of the dear patient, in which case you should simply summon me by telegram.

I still need to take care of 115 little chores here; I have finished the big one. Chapter 1 of the dream [book] has been set in type and is waiting to be proofread. And my part of the annual report, too, goes off to Berlin today.

A few farewell visits, tidying up, paying bills, and so on, and I am shipshape. On the whole it was a year that was triumphant and that resolved doubts; the only astonishing thing is that when long-awaited things happen, we no longer take pleasure in them. Clearly, my constitution is slackening, and who knows how much farther Karlsbad is[2] — and Rome, I might say. In addition to my manuscript, I am taking the Lasalle and a few works on the unconscious with me to Berchtesgaden. I have given up — reluctantly — [the idea of] traveling. In my good hours I indulge in fantasies about new works, great and small. A motto for the dream [book] has not turned up since you killed Goethe's sentimental one. A reference to repression is all that will remain.

*Flectere si nequeo superos, Acheronta movebo.*[3]

Titles from my fantasies are:

On the psychopathology of everyday life
Repression and wish fulfillment
(A psychological theory of the neuropsychoses)

So much about myself.

I am going to Hacking today to say good-bye and expect to hear something about your family there. Otherwise, there is a grain of disappointment in it; I would gladly have let myself be forced to see you and your family again, and among them the little miss for the first time.

The ancient gods still exist, because I obtained a few recently, among them a stone Janus who looks at me with his two faces in a very superior manner.

So, most cordial greetings and I hope I shall find news of you waiting for me at Berchtesgaden.

Your
Sigm.

1. Freud wrote in error 17.IX.99.
2. Reference to a joke, first used in letter of January 3, 1897.
3. Motto used on the title page of the *Interpretation of Dreams*. See Freud's letter of December 4, 1896. "If I cannot bend the higher powers, I will move the infernal regions" (*Aeneid* 7:312).

Vienna, July 22, 1899
IX., Berggasse 19

Dear Wilhelm,

I leave this evening. With the approach of the special date I have become lively and cheerful. Of course, I reproach myself for not having come to Berlin. You did not insist on it firmly enough. But September is definite, although I am not entirely in agreement with your program and would much rather get acquainted with your geometry—which I can comprehend altogether more easily—before your algebra.

In reply to your questions: Martha's birthday is Wednesday, July 26. In regard to the dream [book] things are as follows: it lacked a first chapter, an introduction to the literature, which—unless I am very much mistaken—you also asked for in order to lighten the rest. This was written, was a bitter task for me, and did not turn out very satisfactorily. Most readers will get stuck in this thorny thicket and never get to see the Sleeping Beauty[1] behind it. The rest, with which you are familiar, will be revised, though not very drastically. Sections dealing with the literature will be taken out; a few specific references to the literature which I have only just come upon will be scattered throughout; new dream examples will be inserted as illustrations—none of which amounts to very much. Then the last psychological chapter must be written anew: the wish theory, which, after all, provides the link with what follows; some hypotheses about sleep; coming to terms with anxiety dreams; the interrelations between the wish to sleep and the suppressed. All of it, perhaps, by way of allusions.

Now, I do not understand what you want to see, and when. Am I to send you this first chapter? And then the continued revisions, before I send them to the printer? You would be taking on a great burden without any pleasure if you still took pains with it. There has been no change in regard to the conditions of publication. Deuticke did not want to let the book go, so I decided not to betray in any way what a difficult decision this was for me. At any rate, a part of the first third of the large task will have been accomplished, that of placing the neuroses and psychoses in [the sphere of] science by means of the theory of repression and wish fulfillment. (1) The organic-sexual; (2) the factual-clinical; (3) the metapsychological in it. The work is now in its second third; we still need to discuss the first part thoroughly; when the third (Rome, Karlsbad) has been attained, I shall be glad to take a rest. The confidence you express is always extremely beneficial to me and has had a stimulating effect for a long time.

Now, I would like to have detailed news about you and your family soon. I shall write from B. as often as I feel inclined to it, and that will not be seldom.

With most cordial greetings,

Your
Sigm.

Tell your dear wife that her observational talent proves to be brilliant. Little Norbert, whom I recently again heard crying while he was being fed, is exquisitely hysterical, in love — but with his father rather than his mother, as he should be; at the same time he is anxious, subdued, and definitely lagging behind in his speech development. By the way, he does not look at all well, and has symptoms of rickets.

1. Freud uses the words *Dornengestrüpp* and *Dornröschen* (literally, thorny rose).

---

Riemerlehen, August 1, 1899[1]
Vienna
IX., Berggasse 19

Dear Wilhelm,

I am sending you the first proofs of the introductory (literature) chapter in two envelopes at the same time. If there is anything you object to, send me that page with your remarks; there is still time to use them, until the second or third proofs. I cannot tell you how much good your lively interest in this work does me. Unfortunately, this chapter will prove to be a hard test for the reader.

Things are incomparably beautiful here; we take walks, long and short, and all of us are very well, except for my occasional symptoms. I am working on the completion of the dream book in a large, quiet, ground-floor room with a view of the mountains. My old and grubby gods, of whom you think so little, take part in the work as paperweights for my manuscripts. The loss of the big dream that you eliminated is to be compensated for by the insertion of a small collection of dreams (harmless, absurd dreams; calculations and speeches in dreams; affects in dreams). Only the last, psychological chapter needs to be reworked, and that I shall perhaps tackle in September and send you in manuscript form or — bring with me. It occupies my full interest.

There are some mushrooms here as well, though not yet many. The children naturally join in the hunt for them. The birthday of the mistress of the house was duly celebrated, among other things by a family excursion to Bartholomäussee [Königssee]. You should have seen Annerl on the Königssee! Martin, who lives entirely in his fantasy world here, built himself a *malepartus*[2] in the woods and said yesterday, "I do not actually believe that my so-called poems are really good." We did not disturb him in his moment of insight. Oli is again practicing the exact recording of routes, distances, names of places and mountains. Mathilde is a complete human being and of course altogether feminine. All of them are doing fine.

I presume you have tried in vain to convince Father Pineles that both of us are prophets. He is otherwise a likable and fine, knowledgeable man who has become closer to me because he is a relative of my old friend Professor Herzig. He has inhaled too much of the clinical air, which contains a variety of potent toxins. I hear that Breuer commented on my last work (forgetting), saying once again he was not surprised that no one thought anything of my work if I left gaps of that sort. He thought I had failed to demonstrate how I visualized the connections between death and sexuality. Once the dream book is ready and published, he will be able to be appalled by the contrary, by the abundant indiscretions. Only if chance will have bestowed a title on me (most unlikely) will he crawl on his stomach.

The farther the work of the past year recedes, the more satisfied I become. But bisexuality! You are certainly right about it. I am accustoming myself to regarding every sexual act as a process in which four individuals are involved. We have a lot to discuss on this topic.

A good deal of what you say in your letter distresses me greatly. I wish I could help.

Give my most cordial greetings to your whole family and do remember Riemerlehen, where I am.

Most cordially,

Your
Sigm.

1. While away on vacation, Freud apparently wrote this and occasional other letters on his home letterhead stationery.

2. The den of Reynard the Fox.

B[erchtesgaden]
Riemerlehen, August 6, 1899

Dear Wilhelm,

When are you not right? Once again you put into words what I had dimly been thinking to myself, that this first chapter is apt to deter a lot of readers from going on to the following chapters. But there is little to be done about it — except for putting a note in the preface, which we shall construct when everything else is done. You did not want the literature in the body of the work and you were right; nor at the beginning and you are right again. You feel about it as I do; the secret probably is that we do not like it at all. But if we do not want to hand the "scientists" an ax with which to slaughter the poor book, we must put up with it somewhere. The whole thing is planned on the model of an imaginary walk. At the beginning, the dark forest of authors (who do not see the trees), hopelessly lost on wrong tracks. Then a concealed pass through which I lead the reader — my specimen dream with its peculiarities, details, indiscretions, bad jokes — and then suddenly the high ground and the view and the question: which way do you wish to go now?

There is of course no need to return the proofs I am sending to you. Since you did not take exception to anything in Chapter 1, I shall finish it in the galleys. Nothing else has yet been set in type. You shall receive the proofs as soon as they arrive and the new parts will be marked in them. — I have inserted a large number of new dreams, which I hope you will not delete. *Pour faire une omelette il faut casser des oeufs.*[1] Incidentally, only *humana* and *humaniora;*[2] nothing really intimate, that is, personally sexual. Breuer, too, has been kept at a distance as much as possible. In the last few days I have been very pleased with the work. "I like it, " says Uncle Jonas,[3] which, according to experience, is a bad omen for its success. With your permission I shall put Robert's dream among the hunger dreams of children, after Annerl's menu dream. We shall replace "mutual"[4] with "naughtiness" *[Unart].* At some point the "bigness" in children's dreams must indeed be considered; it is related to children's yearning to be big; to be able for once to eat a bowlful of salad like Papa: the child never has enough, not even of repetitions. Moderation is the hardest thing for the child, as for the neurotic.

Conditions are ideal for me here, and I feel correspondingly well. I take walks only in the morning and the evening; the rest of the time I sit at my work. One side of the house is always delightfully shady when the other is blazing hot. I can well imagine what it is like in town, but not how the "mothers" who are keeping you chained to Berlin are doing. Your work apparently has changed into a pupa for me; will I be able to catch it as a butterfly, or will it fly too high for me?

Today, on a superb Sunday marred only by leaden tiredness, I must unfortunately go to Reichenhall to greet a few of my wife's relatives from Munich. Otherwise I am very sedentary. True, there are mushrooms every day. But on the next rainy day I shall tramp on foot to my beloved Salzburg, where I actually unearthed a few Egyptian antiquities last time. These things put me in a good mood and speak of distant times and countries.

J. J. David[5] visited me several times in Vienna; he is an unhappy man and a not inconsiderable poet. Does Ida know any of his writings?

With the most cordial greetings and thanks for your cooperation in the Egyptian dream book,[6]

Your
Sigm.

1. "To prepare an omelet, one must break eggs."
2. "Of men and their concerns."
3. See letter of June 27, 1899.
4. The reading *Mutuale* is uncertain. In the *Interpretation of Dreams* Freud considers the egoism of children and its connection to the egoism of dreams. He includes Robert's dream in this section. The reference here is undoubtedly to the sentence, "Am Abend des Traumtages war er aber unartig" (On the evening of the dream day he had been naughty).
5. Jacob Julius David (1859–1906) reviewed the *Interpretation of Dreams* in *Die Nation*. The piece is beautifully written and, unlike the more "scientific" reviews, extremely sympathetic. David speaks of Freud's "uncommonly honest search for the truth" and of producing in everyone an "uncanny feeling of being, for a large part of his life, delivered over to a dark power which arbitrarily does what it will with us, and which turns the purest man into a sinner, and visits upon the purest woman images the very thought of which colors her cheeks with shame."
6. This is a joke of Freud's, comparing his book to dream interpretation in ancient Egypt.

---

[Riemerlehen]
Vienna, August 20, 1899
IX., Berggasse 19

Dear Wilhelm,

I have been here for four weeks now and lament that this lovely time is passing so quickly. In another four weeks my vacation will be over, and it is not enough for me. I work wonderfully well here, in peace, without additional worries, in a state of almost total well-being; in between I run out for walks and enjoy the mountains and woods. You must indulge me because I am completely immersed in my work; cannot write about anything else. I am far along in the chapter on "dream work" and have replaced—I think to advantage—the whole dream you deleted with a small collection of dream fragments. Next month I shall start the last, philosophical chapter, which I dread and for which I shall again have to do more reading.

The typesetting is progressing slowly. Whatever came in I sent you yesterday. Please send back only the proofs to which you take exception and write your comments in the margin. Also, later on, when it is possible for you, correct any quotations or references; I have no literary sources available here, of course.

After five hours of work today I have something like a writer's cramp in my hand. The rascals are making an unholy row in the meadow—except that Ernst is laid up with a bad insect bite, like the one Ida had when we were in Reichenau. Ever since the boy lost a front tooth, he has been continually hurting himself; he is full of wounds, like Lazarus, yet at the same time totally reckless and as though anesthetic. I ascribe it to a slight hysteria. He is the only one whom the former nurse treated badly.

Martha and Minna, both very well (at least alternately), are just now in the village. Alexander was here for four days; he will lecture on tariff rates at the Export Academy and will be given the title and rank of professor extraordinarius after one year—much earlier in fact than I. The soap bubble that prematurely burst for you would have been the most beautiful of all. Just imagine the joy of our welcome if for once we had both of you entirely to ourselves here, with far and wide no family obligations to weigh on you. Once again it was not meant to be. "Tomer doch?"[1] the Jew asks in such cases.

My hand refuses to function today. More very soon, and most cordial greetings.

Your
Sigm.

1. Yiddish for "Perhaps after all?"

---

B., August 27, 1899

Dear Wilhelm,

Many thanks; I have just received the two pages from Harzburg, which will of course be copied exactly when the revised proofs come back to me. You will have several more occasions to red-pencil similar instances of superfluous subjectivity. Your looking through the proofs is indeed a tremendous reassurance to me.

I am completely useless in all other respects, which you will understand easily. Nothing but the dream [book]. I took a stack of writing paper in manuscript form (including fifty-six new pages, dream interpretations, examples) to the post office yesterday and already the need for preparatory work on the last and most thorny chapter, the psychological one, is making itself felt; but I do not yet know how to delineate and organize it. I should also do some reading for it; the psychologists will in any case find enough to rail at, but a thing like this turns out just as it will. Every attempt to make it better than it turns out by itself gives it a forced quality. So it will contain 2,467 mistakes — which I shall leave in it.[1]

I have never regretted the brevity of my vacation so much as this year. In three weeks it will all be over; and then the worries begin again whether some negroes [*sic*] will turn up at the right time to still the lion's appetite, and thus the mood for writing will be gone. Moreover, the summer is so lovely one cannot work all day long. So I shall certainly not finish it, which is a terrible thought.

You will find Robert's dream later on, in the section on egoism in dreams. Things are going very well here; it is a fair, uninterruptedly beautiful summer. A bit of Italy would be a nice ending to it, but this probably will not come about.

What would you think of ten days in Rome at Easter (the two of us, of course) if all goes well, if I can afford it, and have not been locked up, lynched, or boycotted on account of the Egyptian dream book? A long-standing promise! Learning about the eternal laws of life for the first time in the Eternal City would not be a bad combination.

I expect you are back in Berlin; nice that you had a few days at least for a visit to Harzburg with all the children.

No other correction could have delighted me so much as your first one — that I have confused the dates of the suppuration.[2] Only it is related in the present tense; do you really want me to correct it in a note? This seems to me to be such an excellent example of what one achieves if one does not stop to break off the train of thought before reaching the point to which the account had led. And naturally all those bunglers and impotent people never say a word about this.

You will have to leave me some scope for my "venom" in the interpretations of dreams. It is good for the constitution to get things off one's chest.

Most cordial greetings; during the next few weeks I shall have to trouble you more than enough with my mailings.

Your
Sigm.

1. We know from a later letter (of September 24, 1900) that Freud asked Fliess to return a postscript to this letter (explaining the figure 2,467), which is why the sheet was not among the letters Fliess kept. Freud used the content in the *Psychopathology of Everyday Life* (*S.E.* 6:242).

2. Michael Schröter suggests that this refers to a passage in the *Interpretation of Dreams* (*S.E.* 4:117) where Freud, in analyzing the "specimen dream" (Irma's injection) mentions Fliess: "But he suffered himself from suppurative rhinitis, which caused me anxiety." In the German text (*G.W.* 2/3:122) Freud uses the present tense, "But he himself suffers from nasal suppurations" (Er leidet aber selbst an Naseneiterungen). Schröter feels that Fliess asked Freud to change the verb from "suffers" to "suffered," to show that the rhinitis was past, something he no longer suffered from. Freud, curiously (and correctly, since at the time of writing it was still true), did not make the change.

---

B., September 6, 1899

Dear Wilhelm,

Today is your wedding day, which I remember very well. But bear with me a little longer. I am completely into the dream [book], am writing eight to ten pages a day, and have just got over the worst in the psychology—it was agonizing. I do not even want to think about how it has turned out. You will tell me whether it can stand at all, but in the galley proofs; reading the manuscript is too much drudgery, and everything can still be changed. In the end I did put more into it than I intended; one always does as one goes deeper, but I am afraid it is—bunk;[1] or, as you would say, *Quatsch* [nonsense]. And then they'll really let me have it! When the storm breaks over me, I shall escape to your guest room. You will find something to praise in it in any event, because you are as much on *my* side as the others are *against* me.

I have just now received sixty galleys, which I am sending to you in the same mail. I am almost ashamed of exploiting you in this way, and you will not need my reciprocal service in biology because you can rely on your own sense of discrimination and are dealing with light, not darkness; with the sun, not the unconscious. But please do not try to tackle the whole thing all at once; send me the galleys on which you exert your censorship in several batches, so that I receive your corrections before I send off mine; I shall return the complete set. There is a tremendous amount of new material in it, which I shall mark for you in color. I have avoided sexuality, but filth is unavoidable and asks to be treated humanely. Do not bother with common printer's errors, but if you find errors in quotations, stylistic problems, or bad similes, do mark them. If only someone could tell me whether there is any real value to the whole thing!

It has been lovely here; perhaps I shall yet manage a few free days. My style has unfortunately been bad because I feel too well physically; I have to feel somewhat miserable to write well. — But now about other things. Everyone here is very well; they grow and thrive, most of all the little one. I do not like to think about the coming season.

No more today; the rest is always the same. Cordial greetings and thanks.

Your
Sigm.

Do you know David? And Friedjung's history of 1859–1866?[2]

1. *Stuss*, a colloquialism from the Yiddish.

2. Heinrich Friedjung (1851–1920) is considered by many to be Austria's foremost historian. *Der Kampf um die Vorherrschaft in Deutschland, 1859 bis 1866* was first published in German in two volumes, in 1897. A. J. P. Taylor wrote that it is "undoubtedly Friedjung's greatest work, for in it he combined the accuracy and the gift of vivid narrative, which stamps all his work, with a deep emotional comprehension of both parties in the struggle." See Taylor's introduction to the one-volume English version, *The Struggle for Supremacy in Germany, 1859–1866*, translated and abridged by Taylor and W. L. McElwee (London: Macmillan, 1935).

---

B., September 11, 1899

Dear Wilhelm,

Heartfelt thanks for your efforts. I had myself already noticed a few careless passages and some that were confusing because of omissions, but the other improvements will be faithfully transferred. *Der Vierundzwanzigste Februar* [The twenty-fourth of February] is a tragedy of fate by Houwald.[1] Unfortunately a further package containing thirty galleys is going off today, by no means the last.

I have finished; that is to say, the entire manuscript has been sent off. You can imagine the state I am in, the increase of my normal depression after the elation. Perhaps you do not read *Simplicissimus*, which I regularly enjoy. In it there is a conversation between two army friends: "Well, comrade, so you have become engaged;

your fiancée no doubt is charming, beautiful, witty, and sweet?" "Well, that's a matter of taste; *I* do not like her." That is exactly how I feel now.[2]

With regard to the psychology, I shall rely on your judgment whether I should revise it once more or take the risk of leaving it in its present form. The dream material itself is, I believe, unassailable. What I dislike about it is the style, which was quite incapable of noble, simple expression and lapsed into facetious circumlocutions straining after metaphors. I know that, but the part of me that knows it and knows how to evaluate it is unfortunately the part that does not produce.

It is certainly true that the dreamer is too witty, but it is neither my fault nor does it contain a reproach.[3] All dreamers are equally insufferably witty, and they need to be because they are under pressure and the direct route is barred to them. If you deem it necessary, I shall insert a remark to that effect somewhere. The ostensible wit of all unconscious processes is intimately related to the theory of the joke and the comic.

The news about your mother and your work pleases me greatly. When shall I be able to hear something about the latter? Apparently soon, if you actually can foresee the conclusion of the first draft. But then from the very beginning, without taking anything for granted!

Am I to come to Berlin? I still waver. I am deeply depressed, would gladly revitalize myself, but know of nothing that would attract me, apart from Berlin. Italy is too far, the time too short. Here fall has set in. The foothills are covered with snow. I feel as I usually do after your departure from too brief a meeting. I dread Vienna, and I would dread it three times over, returning from Berlin. *Meschugge*, as you see; and at present I am obviously unbearable, would talk only about dreams, and would still be there too early for the unveiling of life.[4] So let me go on wavering for a while. In any case, I could come only after September 15 because of our wedding anniversary.

The outcome [of the Dreyfus affair] in France also saddened and embittered me. Respects are due the action of the German government! There is no question on whose side the future lies.

All the Breuers are here. So far we have met only once. I hope that will be all.

Give your dear wife and children my most cordial greetings. Perhaps we really shall see each other.

Your
Sigm.

1. Ernst Christoph von Houwald (1778–1845) wrote several such tragedies, in which someone dies as the result of a past crime, often involving incest or parricide. The plays were particularly popular during the romantic movement in Germany. The one Freud refers to here was actually written by Z. Werner in 1809.

2. Berlin dialect. *Anfänge* prints the text incorrectly and omits *jetzt*. See note 2 to letter of June 27, 1899.

3. The manuscript has *involviert*, not the *motiviert* of *Anfänge*.

4. The German is *Enthüllung des Lebens*. The reference might be to Fliess's theories, or to the birth of his child.

---

B., September 16, 1899

Dear Wilhelm,

I have not heard from you in a long time, but it is hardly your fault. You too probably expected news from me, especially a decision on whether I would come. Well, you know what happened. We once again were completely cut off from the world for several days; now we can at least communicate by telegram, but have not seen a newspaper since Wednesday morning, and trains are still running rather infrequently and not without risk.

I can disclose my intention to you, now that it has become impossible to carry it out. In my last letter I made my coming seem more uncertain than I really felt about it. Actually I had planned to leave here for Munich on Friday morning (Thursday was our wedding anniversary) and to go from Munich to Berlin on Saturday and pay you a surprise visit on Sunday. At the same time Minna was to go to her mother in Hamburg. In Munich we still would have been together. Then came the five days of rain, the news that all connections between here and Salzburg, here and Reichenhall, Reichenhall and Munich, and so on, and so on, were disrupted in several places, and thus the nice plan had to be dropped. It is the second time that floods have interfered with our getting together. I must take into account that I can get to Vienna only by a long detour and want to try doing so on Tuesday morning. We have already been informed of the first accident since the resumption of train service, by a special edition of the *Berchtesgaden Anzeiger*.

So this lovely summer has had a nasty aftermath. Naturally, nothing has happened to us ("naturally" refers to the location of our house); nor has much happened in Berchtesgaden. But the roads are thoroughly ruined. Yesterday I went on foot (four hours; impassable by carriage) to Salzburg, parts of which are flooded.

I have actually not yet overcome my ill humor (which this time was enormous after completing the manuscript — [and] which cer-

Wilhelm Fliess in later years,
close to the time of his death in 1928.

Josef Breuer and his wife, Mathilde.
The first Freud child was named for Mrs. Breuer.

tainly was not merely feigned to facilitate surprise)—but, as one always does in such cases, I resigned myself and put it aside. I have also been interrupted while correcting the proofs. Fall has really started, and Breuer is just as much locked in here as I am, so that we are bound to meet daily, on which occasions the ladies on both sides make a great show of tenderness to each other. Another reason to wish one were somewhere else. If I did not anticipate a poor season and were not even more intolerant of Vienna in view of the two factors [?] in Germany, I would be still more irritated about the extension of my stay here.

I cannot predict when you will actually receive this letter. In any case, do not write to me here any longer, but let me know in Vienna whether the improvement of your dear mother's health has continued and how you and all your family are. From Vienna I shall very soon have to inundate you with additional mailings, among which will also be a new reprint ("Screen Memories"), which I expect in September.

The traveler to Rome-Karlsbad who hopes to meet you at his destination thus is once more not very hopeful. But you are quite used to that in me, just as I am used to finding the opposite mood in you.

With the most cordial greetings,

Your
Sigm.

---

Vienna, September 21, 1899
IX., Berggasse 19

Dear Wilhelm,

Here I am after a horrible thirty-two-hour journey through water, sitting again in the familiar place, with seven signatures of proofs in front of me and no medical news, and warmly welcomed by your kind letter with its good reports. I find a kind of substitute for our foiled meeting in the heightened liveliness of our correspondence and hope that you will also often think of the living while you are digging for the dead. As you correctly surmised, my ill humor fell away from me—not after a migraine, but rather after a nice series of similar conditions. Yet I believe my self-criticism was not wholly unjustified. Somewhere inside me there is a feeling for form, an appreciaton of beauty as a kind of perfection; and the tortuous sentences of my dream book, with their parading of indirect phrases and squinting at ideas, deeply offended one of my ideals. Nor am I far wrong in regarding this lack of form as an indication of insufficient mastery of the material. You must have felt exactly the same thing, and we have always been too honest with each other for either of us to have to pretend in front of the other. The consolation lies in its inevitability; it simply did not turn out any better. However, I am sorry that I must ruin my favorite and best reader by giving him proofs, because how can one like anything that one has to read in proofs? Unfortunately I cannot do without you as the representative of the Other—and again have sixty more pages for you.

And now for another year of this strange life in which one's good mood is no doubt the only thing of real value. Mine is fluctuating; but, as you see, as it says on the coat of arms of our dear Paris:

*Fluctuat nec mergitur.*[1]

A patient with whom I have been negotiating, a "goldfish," has just announced herself—I do not know whether to decline or accept. My mood also depends very strongly on my earnings. Money is laughing gas for me. I know from my youth that once the wild horses of the pampas have been lassoed, they retain a certain anxiousness for life. Thus I came to know the helplessness of poverty and continually fear it. You will see that my style will improve and my ideas will be more correct if this city provides me with an ample livelihood.

This time you are not troubling yourself with checking quotations and the like, are you? I once again have all the necessary literary aids. My central accomplishment in interpretation comes in the [enclosed] installment, the absurd dreams. It is astonishing how often you appear in them. In the *non vixit* dream I am delighted to have outlived you; isn't it terrible to suggest something like this—that is, to have to make it explicit to everyone who understands?

My wife and the children are staying in Berchtesgaden until the end of September. I still have not made the acquaintance of Paulinchen.

Most cordial greetings.

Your
Sigm.

1. "It floats but it does not sink."

Vienna, September 27, 1899
IX., Berggasse 19

Dear Wilhelm,

For the record:

Sept. 11 — inexplicable ill humor
Sept. 12 — cardiac weakness with a mild headache
Sept. 14 - 18 — bad days, moody; cardiac fatigue
Tuesday, Sept. 19 — headache without cardiac pain (traveling)
Since then, rather good days
Today, Sept. 27, initially a trace of a headache without other manifestations.

What you objected to means, *bowing* to one's superior is a remnant of that old presentation.

I cannot make out whether you want me to delete the last sentence, the concluding tirade, or emphasize it by putting it in bold type. It is in accord with my need to let it fade away.

For the rest, I do not find it unpleasant to have someone who has a word of praise where it is appropriate instead of invariably telling one the most unpleasant things. For that I thank you especially.

I am speeding up the proofs because I learned that a consummate fool, a certain *Ch. Ruths*,[1] is on the track of something and in 1898 already announced an analysis of dream phenomena. I hope that by October everything will have been taken care of. For the time being I have almost nothing to do; so I have the leisure to complete it.

From a distance I am following your death records with great interest. I know that for the present your theory does not concern itself with *fathers;* otherwise it would indeed be risky to include in the calculations other than the eldest children of noble families. Ever since you stopped writing about your findings, I miss something in your letters. As for my science, you will be left in peace for a while. I am empty and spent; I even gave away the nice double-wish theory of the neuroses for the dream book. Every Tom, Dick, and Harry will soon be in a position to know as much about it as I do.

My family is still in Berchtesgaden, does not complain much about the weather, but will return at the end of the week. In yesterday's newspaper (September 26) you may have seen the announcement of the courses Alexander will give at the Export Academy as a professor of tariffs. If only none of his former infections is slumbering in the womb of time! You undoubtedly guessed which part of the interpretation of the "Autodidasker" dream I withheld.

The goldfish (L. von E., an S. by birth and as such a distant relative of my wife) has been caught, but will still enjoy half her freedom until the end of October because she is remaining in the country. In addition, I have one other patient, who also will not start until late in October. Otherwise I am free except for stray patients turning up in the consulting room, and there are never many of those.

Let me hear from you soon again. And now forget the drudgery you had with the dream book, so that you can leaf through it once more when it is published.

With my most cordial greetings to wife and children,

Your
Sigm.

1. Christoph Ruths (1851–1922), author of *Inductive Untersuchungen über die Fundamentalgesetze der psychischen Phänomene* (Darmstadt: H. L. Schlopp, 1898). The work Freud refers to apparently was never published.

---

Vienna, October 4, 1899
IX., Berggasse 19

Dear Wilhelm,

Your justification is unassailable; but I had complained without reproach. I know very well that you used to give me a hint of everything, which in fact presented serious difficulties to my understanding. Now you write only about great, very great things; true, you prepared me for their quality and I shall retain a personal relationship to them, even though I cannot stand godfather to them, as you did to the dream book, but rather play at a distance, in Nestroy's words, "first cousin to a world-historical event." Your triumph will ultimately be in some measure mine, because my judgment followed you and your works; you know that not many others followed at the time.

But in amazement I ask you whether you finished so quickly that your Anonymous and my dream book can simultaneously see the light of day? For I am counting on at most two weeks; you shall have the volume on your desk for your birthday. I only have to read several *third* proofs, about a third of the whole. Perhaps you did not expect it so early, but unfortunately I have a lot of time. I am so unoccupied that I can take care of each sheet immediately.

You accurately describe the painful feeling of parting with something which has been one's very own. That must have been what made this work so distasteful to me. Now I like it—certainly not much, but a lot better. It was even distressing for me because I had to surrender not only my intellectual but also my emotional property. The book on hysteria is still a long way off. At times like these no desire to work stirs in me.

At present my son Martin is not writing any poems. I believe I reported to you from Berchtesgaden that he said: "I do not actually believe that my so-called poems are really good." This pronouncement marked a turning away from the preceding creative period. Now he is rather at a loss and depressed since he was sent to the fifth grade in school, where his lack of everyday practical abilities is conspicuous. In order to get acquainted he asked the boy sitting next to him what his name was. The answer was Marie; and another introduced himself as Minna. This must have given him a first inkling of how difficult it can be to get along with one's "fellow men."

Life and illness have moved in once more. The first victim was Ernst, but he is all right again. The others still are well.

My mood is holding up valiantly. I shall tell you the date of my next breakdown for your calculations. What is involved is really primary periodic fluctuations, because two weeks of inactivity and a fifth to a quarter income would surely be sufficient as external etiology.

Your brother-in-law Oscar, to whom I gave a few sheets at his request, is at the head of the line of critics. He has the "most serious misgivings" about publication. I think this time we should collect opinions.

I can tell you as a secret that Gretel Breuer really did become engaged to Arthur Schiff. I heard about it from a patient in treatment and therefore must treat it as a secret; otherwise I know of no reason to do so.

The most cordial greetings to you, wife, and children, and good luck for all of this year's expectations.

Your
Sigm.

---

Vienna, October 9, 1899
IX., Berggasse 19

Dear Wilhelm,

Why should I avoid an occasion for a new letter? You do not have to reply immediately. So, I misunderstood you. But now the chance of our coming out together is even less. For your book on the duration of life will long have been banned by the time the first lines of hysteria are written down, because the latter will keep us waiting a long time and it is possible that other things will come first.

You should not regret that this gave you the opportunity to speak of your work once again. I now know better than ever where you are stopping. At the next congress we shall not talk about dreams at all but once more discuss biological periods. Where and when will it be? Do you have any ideas? At Easter again? I am more distant than ever from Rome and Karlsbad.

Can you imagine that I have been impelled by obscure inner forces to read psychological writings, and I feel more at home with them than before. Recently I had the satisfaction of finding part of my hypothetical pleasure-unpleasure theory in an English writer, Marshall.[1] Other authors I stumble on are totally unfathomable to me, however. My mood, too, is still holding up. Putting it all in the dream book must have done me good. A mild migraine – ill humor occurred on October 6. In reply to your remarks concerning the acceleration of my practice, I should like to point out that there also exist local trains, secondary lines, as in the *Fliegende Blätter.* They are supposed to be especially common in Krähwinkel and its surroundings. Things are as follows. Even if in November, for instance, I were to be fully occupied, my income this year, with the lean period from May 1 to the end of October (six months) is insufficient to cover our expenses. I must look around for something else, and I have now taken a step in a definite direction. During the summer I would like to become associated with a hydropathic establishment and look for rooms near it. One place is going to open on the Kobenzl in 1900, I hear, and the director suggested to me last year that for this reason I should make sure to obtain lodgings in Bellevue (both are in the Kahlenberg area). So I have written to this man again. The children's attendance at school will in any case force us to give up the long summer vacation.

In this year's promotions (a batch of five professors at the end of September), our group (Königstein, I, and the others) has once again been passed over.

Martin appears to have become acquainted with yet another Margarethe; prior to going to school he produced a great many anxiety rituals, but now appears to have become adjusted. Our home is haunted by some kind of illness which refuses to show itself completely. Oli is the current victim (the fourth).

All but three sheets of the dream book have been printed. The preface I once showed you stays in. The last sentence concerning the "future," to which you took exception, has been elaborated and thereby made intelligible.

With most cordial greetings to all of you,

Your
Sigm.

1. Henry Rutgers Marshall, *Pain, Pleasure and Aesthetics: An Essay Concerning the Psychology of Pain and Pleasure, with Special Reference to Aesthetics* (London: Macmillan, 1894).

---

October 11, 1899
IX., Berggasse 19

Dear Wilhelm,

*Psychic apparatus ψ*
*Hysteria—clinical*
*Sexuality. Organic*

Oddly enough, something is at work on the lowest floor. A theory of sexuality may be the immediate successor to the dream book. Today several very strange things occurred to me, which I do not yet properly understand at all. As far as I am concerned, there is no question of deliberation. This method of working moves along by fits and starts. God alone knows the date of the next thrust, unless you have figured out my formula. If more comes along, we shall scarcely be able to avoid discussion and collaboration. Wild things, by the way, some of which I already surmised during the stormy first epoch of productivity.

Again ye come, ye hovering forms.[1]

According to an earlier calculation of yours, a productive period, 1900–1901 (every seven and a half years), lies ahead of me.

Farewell.

Your
Sigm.

Oscar is beginning to show enthusiasm.

1. From the Dedication to Goethe's *Faust:* "Ihr naht Euch wieder, schwankende Gestalten."

October 17, 1899
IX., Berggasse 19

Dear Wilhelm,

What would you say if masturbation were to reduce itself to homosexuality, and the latter, that is, male homosexuality (in both sexes) were the primitive form of sexual longing? (The first sexual aim, analogous to the infantile one—a wish that does not extend beyond the inner world.) If, moreover, libido and anxiety both were male?

Cordially,

Your
Sigm.

---

Vienna, October 27, 1899
IX., Berggasse 19

Dear Wilhelm,

Thanks for the kind words in response to my sending you the dream book. I have long since become reconciled to the thing and await its fate in—resigned suspense. If the book did not arrive in time to be on your birthday table, as I had wanted it to be, the reason is the circumstance I had not taken into account, that the post office would accept it only as parcel post. We had timed sending it off as if it were a registered letter. So perhaps it reached you too late: in other respects it will surely arrive too soon. Incidentally, it has not yet been issued; only our two copies have so far seen the light of day.[1]

Now, as to the other five books I am contemplating—we shall have to take our time with them. A long life,[2] material, ideas, freedom from serious interference—and who knows what else; even an occasional strong push from a "friendly quarter." For the time being the thread is broken again; hence no answer to your questions. I am searching for the right point of attack. Pathological phenomena are in many cases compromise formations in the sexual sphere as well, and are unsuitable for resolution.

My good mood persists unshaken in these bad times, but I am lazy again and have no ideas. At home an epidemic of colds is still claiming new victims. Finally, we really are worried about Ernst, who every few days since his arrival in Vienna has developed a temperature under a variety of pretexts, has diarrhea, looks awful, and notwithstanding it all is so spirited that he will never admit to being ill.

October 28. Last night I once again visited Oscar and Melanie after a long time, that is, for a taroc game; otherwise I frequently show up there in the daytime; my weak spot for both of these ordinary human beings is well known to you. Fortunately, I escaped dinner—cauliflower and chicken, both abominations. Oscar announced his objections to my *Hamlet* interpretation, which occurred to him after an evening at the theater. Your sister-in-law Marie is beginning to look peaked, like girls who are waiting. In addition, I occasionally visit Norbert; I am sorry that he is still full of anxiety, in love with his father, and talking very little. The little one is not flourishing, but is cheerful.

I have every reason to assume that Arthur Schiff is engaged to Gretel Breuer (a big secret, of course). But I guess at all sorts of things. So your nasal findings may find official recognition in the not too distant future. Political marriage.

You see that as soon as one does not want to talk about one's worries or one's unborn science, one lapses into gossiping. Enough of it.

If anything begins to stir again in the sexual theory, I shall surprise you with a few enigmatic lines. In the meantime I wish both of you all the happiness for what this year—and century (for the unformed [child])[3]—will yet bring you. In December, I assume?

With the most cordial greetings,

Your
Sigm.

1. The book, which Fliess's son Robert took with him to America, has come into my possession. There are very few markings by Fliess, presumably because he had already made his comments in the proofs Freud had been sending him. However, he does note two places where Freud uses Viennese grammatical constructions rather than standard German ones.

2. The German is *Lebenszeit;* literally, lifetime.

3. *Für den Ungebildeten.* Presumably Freud is referring to the child about to be born.

November 5, 1899
IX., Berggasse 19

Dear Wilhelm,

One cannot say that you are excessively communicative. I do not want to follow your example, even though a depressing uniformity makes it more difficult to communicate. The book at last came out yesterday. The name of Hannibal's father—as I always knew and suddenly remembered recently—was Hamilcar, not Hasdrubal. Practice and children alike are ailing. I am reporting to you a pathological ill humor on November 3, a gorgeous migraine on November 4 (that is, the following day).

I would have liked to write to you about the sexual theory, because I have something that is plausible and confirmed in practice; it is only that I do not yet have the slightest idea what to do with the †††[1] female aspect, and that makes me distrust the whole thing. Otherwise, explanations come slowly, now here, now there, as the day permits—on the whole, rather leisurely. Among them, as a choice morsel: I now understand how premonitory dreams arise and what they mean.[2] For the rest, I should like to hear from you soon and also how your dear wife and children are.

Cordially,

Your
Sigm.

1. Freud draws three crosses. This sign was sometimes chalked on the inside of doors in peasant houses to protect against danger.

2. See Freud's "Premonitory Dream Fulfilled." The manuscript is dated November 10, 1899.

Vienna, November 7, 1899
IX., Berggasse 19

Dear Wilhelm,

Very surprised by and very grateful for your announcement and your letter, which elevated the first good day of this season to an outstanding one. I would gladly take the detour via a foreign country to gain renown. A German [patient] is especially welcome; your diagnosis, her age, everything appears to be highly promising. But she should come soon because—how strange—the very same day two other prospective patients contacted me, one an exceedingly demanding woman from Warsaw who has been with Krafft [-Ebing], and a Viennese woman; they both may turn up and will probably come to a decision in the course of this week. On the other hand, nothing may come of either one.

A practical question: so far I have placed foreign patients in the Pension Vienna on Maximilian Square (Frankgasse 8); it is run by a doctor's widow, who is very decent and if necessary will even help with the patients to some extent. People have been reasonably satisfied. There also are more elegant homes[1] in the area, in my vicinity.

Depending on the nature of the case, one hires a simple or a more genteel nurse; no doubt unavoidable in the case of women and girls. I heard about Pension Vienna from D.F. some time ago. I would assume that more can be done here than at Binswanger's[2] —how much, though, really depends on the case. My speculations on the sexual theory have yielded a new and powerful impetus in analysis this year, but somewhere there still is a lack of clarity and a corresponding therapeutic gap. Last year's gain, fantasies, have stood the test splendidly: predisposition has been given far more scope, without thereby escaping analysis. A riddle is lurking in the region of affects.

The book has just been sent out. The first tangible reaction was the termination of the friendship of a dear friend, who felt hurt by the mention of her husband in the *non vixit* dream.[3] Minna quotes the countesses Wallenstein and Terczky after their reception at the Viennese court: we can expect further ostracism. J. J. David (the writer) promised a review in the *Nation.*

Our letters crossed. Your silence had baffled me. I hope that some time you will also write, *in between* two letters of referral.

The siege of colds is over; only Ernst still has a slight fever. My brother, who has become docent at the Export Academy, is also lecturing at the Oriental Academy now and generally seems to be regarded as the leading authority on the Austrian tariff system. It does him good. His material position is still unstable.

I want to confide in you that we are beginning to entertain the idea of giving up our town apartment and moving to the outskirts. Perhaps we shall manage to avoid it. The summer problem remains unsolved.

Hoping to receive good news soon about your three children,

Most cordially your
Sigm.

1. English in original.

2. The following comment on Robert Binswanger and his sanatorium is from Hirschmüller (1978, p. 152): "The Bellevue Sanatorium in Kreuzlingen was founded by Ludwig Binswanger Senior and after his death in 1880 was taken over by his son, Robert Binswanger. It enjoyed the reputation of being one of the best and most modern private sanatoria for nerve and mood illnesses. The clientele was international and belonged primarily to the higher strata of society. It was run strictly according to the principle of nonrestraint and great value was placed on the contact of the patients with healthy people, such as the family of the directing physician." Freud knew about the sanatorium through Breuer, who had sent Anna O. and other patients there. Freud, too, later referred his own patients there.

3. This is a reference to Betty Paneth, wife of Josef Paneth (1857–1890), who succeeded Freud as Brücke's assistant at the Vienna Physiological Institute. The passage

that Mrs. Paneth might well have objected to occurs in the *Interpretation of Dreams* (*S.E.* 5:484): "There had been a time when I had had to reproach my friend Josef [Paneth] for an attitude of this same kind: *'Ôte-toi que je m'y mette!'* He had followed in my footsteps as demonstrator in Brücke's laboratory, but promotion there was slow and tedious. Neither of Brücke's two assistants was inclined to budge from his place, and youth was impatient. My friend, who knew that he could not expect to live long, and whom no bonds of intimacy attached to his immediate superior, sometimes gave loud expression to his impatience, and, since this superior [Fleischl] was seriously ill, P.'s wish to have him out of the way might have an uglier meaning than the mere hope for the man's promotion."

---

Vienna, November 9, 1899
IX., Berggasse 19

Dear Wilhelm,

So I was right, after all, to be struck by your silence and regard it as ominous. I was well on the way to formulating an explanation for myself; I discarded it, however, because I know you to be free of all nervous *Schigan*.[1] I felt that something in the dream book had very much put you off. I think, however, that among friends it is not necessary to adhere too strictly to the stipulation that each should apprise the other only of favorable events. Where would this leave us if fate is not favorably inclined? I have always behaved differently; for weeks I have been complaining to you whenever I had reason to, risking the danger of alienating you, yet expecting that you would not be alienated; though I surely would much rather tell you about happy and hopeful things.

If it is a question of something you wish to keep secret from your family and larger circles, you need only give the word — as you did this time. I know how to keep quiet when there is a reason, and have not failed to prove it on this occasion.

So, poor Paulinchen is suffering so much, and I do not even know her. My sister's little one, who was so wretched and run down half a year ago, is now full of vigor and mischief; and so, in a case like this one, our first and foremost thought is that children get over most things. When Mathilde had diphtheria for the second time, a medical university colleague came to the house at number 19. He inquired, as the concierge told us later, whether the Freud girl was already dead. That was very Christian. But the girl is still alive and is growing appropriately in length and fortunately also in width. An epidemic of feverish colds raged through all the others, and some of them also had diarrhea. The worst of it was that a few did not have enough with one attack. Just today Sophie once again began to have diarrhea and a fever, while the sore throats and colds of the others are on the wane. For the past two weeks, moreover, Ernst has had an elevated temperature in the afternoon for no apparent reason. The two mothers insist — just to make me anxious — that he resembles too closely their brother Isaac, who died of tuberculosis.

As to the premonitory dream that I have unraveled and the little piece of sexual theory, I would gladly write to you about them and certainly shall do so once your head is free again and my hand functions better. For I am undoubtedly in a phase of a mild writer's cramp, as you may have noticed from my handwriting, which is intensified by making notes on the results of my four analyses every evening. Today it would be almost impossible for me to write anything with pleasure.

I expect to hear from you soon, even if you write only briefly, and also that wife and child are doing very well.

With most cordial greetings and the ever-present regret that we live so far apart,

Your
Sigm.

1. Yiddish for "madness."

---

November 12, 1899[1]
IX., Berggasse 19

Dear Wilhelm,

I am glad that your dear Paulinchen pulled through. Since I am far more inclined to pessimistic expectations than to their opposite, I had been deeply saddened. After having been given up to die, she may now reach a ripe old age, as the wisdom of the old saying has it.

I shall, of course, make all the necessary arrangements for accommodations and care of Miss G.,[2] as I do for all foreign patients. Nothing seems to have come of the other two; I have heard no more from them. People keep on pointing out to me odd mistakes in the dream book. Schiller's birthplace is given as Marburg[3] instead of Marbach; I have already told you about Hannibal's father, whose name I gave as Hasdrubal instead of Hamilcar. These are not lapses of memory, however, but rather are displacements, symptoms. Critics find nothing better to do than to highlight these instances of carelessness, which are nothing of the sort.

At last everyone is well again.

Now that the danger has passed, surely you will let me know what it was that the child suffered from.

Most cordially,

Your
Sigm.

1. Freud wrote in error 12.IX.99.

2. In the Library of Congress are two letters from Freud to the patient mentioned in this letter. The first, dated August 14, 1911, begins with an ironic sentence: "First of all I want to express my respect for you for having achieved the following piece of nonsense: you have attempted to convert your parents, with a joint age of 150, to analytic literature!" The second letter is dated March 25, 1914, and is a request for news of the patient. It ends. "Your old friend, Freud."

3. Cf. *S.E.* 6:217–219.

---

Vienna, November 19, 1899[1]
IX., Berggasse 19

Dear Wilhelm,

On Sunday, the 12th, in the afternoon I again fell ill, for reasons unknown to me, with ill humor that continued, intensified with heart and head migraines, and terminated completely with a head migraine on Thursday, so that since then I have not only been well but downright merry. I want to keep this periodic mild depression under observation; its meaning is entirely unclear to me. The attack was shorter than the previous one, which I likewise reported to you faithfully.

I spent Thursday in Budapest, summoned by a patient, but it did not turn out to be particularly remunerative. I returned Friday morning to find Miss G., accompanied by Miss E. Today I gave her the first lecture. Naturally, I as yet know nothing about her other than what Miss E. has told me. She is still a rough lump of unhappiness, appears to be obstinate and withdrawn, and is covered with a thick institutional patina, which will need to be scraped off first. The disparity in living conditions compared to the institution naturally will at first make her very dissatisfied. There they tried to cure her with common sympathy and by interesting her in art folios (Hirth collection), for the rest leaving her to her fantasies. Well, we shall see. If she sticks with it, you will hear everything about this case, for which I am indebted to you.

She has taken a room in one of the boardinghouses I mentioned, but is discontent there. I shall stay out of it, because I would exhaust myself trying to satisfy her demands, which in part are neurotic and in part inappropriate in Vienna. The best would be a sanatorium of my own; but this I do not have.

I quite like Miss E. Well, we shall see.

It is a thankless task to enlighten mankind a little. No one has yet told me that he feels indebted to me for having learned something new from the dream book and for having been introduced to a world of new problems.

"Very interesting"; that they then regard as condescension.[2] The only gratifying reaction was a letter, which I enclose for you, from Dr. Gomperz, Jr.,[3] who is now studying my method of dream interpretation with me in the evening. I need do no more than mention to you that the very first attempt immediately yielded overabundant material. He will come again tomorrow. Am I gaining a pupil in him? He would be a better sort than the previous ones.

At home everyone is well, except that Annerl has a running cold. Martin is quickly becoming tougher in school and so far is not making much progress. His spelling and arithmetic make it quite uncertain whether he will be accepted in high school next year. Incidentally, he is now fantasizing in drawings and is in full possession of his humor.

The science is resting, as it always does when I am preoccupied with the details of treatment. With regard to the sexual theory, I still want to wait. An unborn piece remains attached to what has already been born.

But now I want to hear soon about Paulinchen and your wife and the other two children. A pity that business is so poor that I am immobilized. I would have liked to come to Berlin for just a day. I could tell you all sorts of funny things about Vienna.

And Rome? And Karlsbad? And our long-promised congress on classical soil? I go on putting new layers of resignation over my yearning. I shall be glad to hear from you that one day it will come true.

Most cordially,

Your
Sigm.

1. Freud wrote in error 19.IX.99.

2. The German is *Sehr interessant, das halten sie dann für Herablassung.*

3. Freud had a long-standing relationship with the Gomperz family. He had been requested by Theodor Gomperz, a well-known professor of philology in Vienna, to translate John Stuart Mill and in 1892 was treating his wife, Elise Gomperz. In a letter to his son Heinrich Gomperz (1873–1943), who became a professor of philosophy, the father writes: "Mama seems, through hypnosis, really to be on her way to a cure. If only the treatment were not itself so strange and so little tested" (November 13, 1892).

The letter is quoted by Robert A. Kann in *Theodor Gomperz: Ein Gelehrtenleben im Bürgertum der Franz-Josefs-Zeit* (Vienna: Österreichische Akademie der Wissenschaften, 1974), p. 234.

For Heinrich Gomperz' relation to Freud, see his autobiographical remarks in *The Personalist*, 24 (1943):254–270. There Gomperz writes: "I had known Sigmund Freud even in preanalytic times, and have always greatly admired his creative originality and his psychological penetration without, however, ever having been fully convinced of the soundness of all of his views. When his *Interpretation of Dreams* was first published in 1899 I offered myself as 'victim' for testing his theory and for several months, during the second half of that year, we tried to interpret my dreams according to the method he had just worked out. The experiment proved a complete failure. All the 'dreadful' things which he suggested I might have concealed from myself and 'suppressed' I could honestly assure him had always been clearly and consciously present in my mind. In short, I offered no 'resistance' and I have learned later that Freud had told a disciple he had met with two persons only whose dreams he had been unable to analyze and that I had been one of them. I am nevertheless convinced that many of the psychic mechanisms discovered by him really play a remarkable part in our lives and in a few cases I have myself been able to effect surprising 'cures' by using some of his methods."

I have a letter from Gomperz to Freud, dated May 5, 1931, in which he writes: "My memories of you go back, in fact, before 1899, and only recently did I come across letters you wrote to my mother in 1893, which I found in her bequest, and which enlightened me about a family secret, which I was in any event on the track of already."

A series of letters between Freud and Gomperz is at Maresfield Gardens; even though some of them date from 1899, they do not provide any further details about the "dream experiment" that Gomperz describes in his autobiography. It seems that Freud did not actually treat Gomperz, but was hoping to turn him into a student who could use his method of dream interpretation.

---

Vienna, November 26, 1899
IX., Berggasse 19

Dear Wilhelm,

Let me for once be more optimistic than you. I only wanted to know whether Paulinchen's was the type of illness that, after her recovery, would cast a shadow over her future prospects. Since it was cholera infantilis or something like it, I take the liberty of treating the coincidence with utter contempt. Stemming from good blood, she too will grow and thrive. I look forward to seeing her sometime in the now-enlarged children's room.

Miss G. is a tough nut, but the work is of course not unpromising, since I have learned all sorts of new things. I am keeping a kind of diary on her, which later on should afford you a glimpse into the technique and the nature of the case—as an attempt to show my gratitude to you. My own efforts at enlisting [new patients] really have had no results. The pseudocure by the sanatorium is atrocious — I should have preferred her ill and demoralized. She is beginning to get bored and has all sorts of resistances in readiness. She is not yet properly engaged [in analysis]. Interesting that she is of Jewish extraction on both sides.

The dream book has not yet occasioned any outcries. The sales so far supposedly are satisfactory. My philosopher, Harry G.,[1] is very amusing. Supposedly he believes nothing whatsoever, but has all sorts of beautiful and witty ideas and gradually is opening up; recently he lost a crown [coin] here — that is, in a symptomatic action he left it here as an honorarium because he feels embarrassed to "exploit" me. His dreams constantly quote my dreams, which he then forgets, and so forth. Interpreting dreams appears to be more difficult for others than I had indicated.

Dr. Seb. Löwy[2] must have felt directly referred to in many passages that struck home. I would be very interested in learning whether a nonneurotic person can make anything of the book.

Nothing has yet been decided about the summer. I am contemplating an approach (to Winternitz), which, being a petition, I keep postponing. The hope of maintaining the status quo also keeps cropping up. In this country it is very difficult to bring about changes.

I have actually profited from my mild depressions since they have begun to occur periodically; during the interim periods I feel more consistently well than ever before. Inasmuch as you are interested in them, I shall let you know the dates of the subsequent occurrences.

Otherwise, things are slumbering and preparing themselves. *Sexual Theory and Anxiety* is the title of my next work, which deep down must have progressed further than I know because I feel so very confident. All I really could tell you about is a rather incomplete segment.

In contrast, I am delighted to read in your letters that your work is progressing clearly and lucidly, in full light; but this way of working doubtless would not suit my subterranean matter.

Children and wife are well. Miss E., who went with them to the Prater today, will certainly give you and your wife a detailed account.

With the most cordial greetings,

Your
Sigm.

1. Freud uses the English, presumably a joking reference to Heinrich Gomperz' real name.

2. Schröter suggests Sebastian Levy, a Berlin physician and friend of Fliess (see Fliess's *Ablauf des Lebens*, p. 77). The reading could also be "Leb. Löwy."

---

Vienna, December 9, 1899
IX., Berggasse 19

Dear Wilhelm,

My thirst for personal data about you is somewhat assuaged by your recent presence here. So I feel free to turn to scientific matters.

I may recently have succeeded in gaining a first glimpse of something new. The problem confronting me is that of the "choice of neurosis." When does a person become hysterical instead of paranoid? In my first crude attempt, made at a time when I was still trying to take the citadel by force, I thought it depended on the age at which the sexual trauma occurred—the person's age at the time of the experience. That I gave up long ago; but then I was left without a clue until a few days ago, when I saw a connection with the sexual theory.

The lowest of the sexual strata is autoerotism, which dispenses with any psychosexual aim and seeks only locally gratifying sensations. It is then succeeded by alloerotism (homo- or heteroerotism), but certainly continues to exist as an undercurrent. Hysteria (and its variant, obsessional neurosis) is alloerotic, since its main path is identification with the loved one. Paranoia again dissolves the identification, reestablishes all the loved ones of childhood who have been abandoned (compare the discussion of exhibitionistic dreams), and dissolves the ego itself into extraneous persons. So I have come to regard paranoia as a forward surge of the autoerotic current, as a return to a former state. The perversion formation corresponding to it would be the so-called idiopathic insanity. The special relations between autoerotism and the original "ego" would throw a clear light on the nature of this neurosis. At this point the thread breaks off again.

Two of my patients have almost simultaneously come up with [self-]reproaches following the nursing and death of their parents and have shown me that my dreams about this were typical. The reproach is in every instance bound to attach itself to revenge, spiteful glee, taking satisfaction in the ill person's excretory difficulties (urine and stools). Truly a neglected corner of psychic life.

L. is progressing, but will probably remain a slow worker. However, I see no reason to fear that failure will occur at some point.

December 14. It is rare, indeed, that you should have written before I did. The bleakness of the last few days prevented me from finishing. A Christmastime during which one must refrain from buying things rather dampens one's mood. We are well aware that Vienna is not the right place for us. Discretion required my not taking you away from your family too much. The older claim was opposed by the more intimate one. So my saying good-bye at the station served only as a symbol.

Your news of the dozen readers in Berlin pleases me greatly. I must have some readers here as well; the time is not yet ripe for followers. There is too much that is new and unbelievable, and too little strict proof. I did not even succeed in convincing my philosopher, though he was providing me with the most brilliant confirmatory material. Intelligence is always weak, and it is easy for a philosopher to transform inner resistance into logical refutation.

Once again there is the prospect of a new case in the immediate future. Except for my cold, health reigns among us. I shall write again before he/she arrives at your home.

Most cordial greetings to all of you.

Your
Sigm.

---

Vienna, December 21, 1899
IX., Berggasse 19

Dear Wilhelm,

One more cordial greeting before Christmas, usually one of our times for a congress. I am not without *one* happy prospect. You are familiar with my dream which obstinately promises the end of E.'s treatment (among the absurd dreams), and you can well imagine how important this one persistent patient has become to me. It now appears that the dream will be fulfilled. I cautiously say "appears," but I am really quite certain. Buried deep beneath all his fantasies, we found a scene from his primal period (before twenty-two months) which meets all the requirements and in which all the remaining puzzles converge. It is everything at the same time—sexual, innocent, natural, and the rest. I scarcely dare believe it yet. It is as if Schliemann had once more excavated Troy, which had hitherto been deemed a fable. At the same time the fellow is doing outrageously well. He demonstrated the reality of my theory in my own case, providing me in a surprising reversal with the solution, which I had overlooked, to my former railroad phobia. For this piece of work I even made him the present of a picture of Oedipus and the Sphinx. My phobia, then, was a fantasy of impoverishment, or rather a hunger phobia, determined by my infantile greediness and evoked by my wife's lack of a dowry (of which I am so proud). You will hear more about all of this at our next congress.

Otherwise there is little news. The book has had one single review, in the *Gegenwart;*[1] as a critical evaluation it is empty and as a review it is inadequate. It is just a bad patchwork of my own fragments. However, I am willing to forgive everything because of the one word "path-breaking." Otherwise the attitude of people in Vienna is quite negative; I do not believe that I shall succeed in getting a review published here. We are, after all, terribly far ahead of our time.

The new patient whom I definitely expected has disappeared again. So your woman from Hamburg remains the only new case. She is still boring much of the time, but in between occasionally valiant. I recently replied to a letter from her father.[2] For the time being it is a hard way to make a living.[3]

I have heard that Breuer vouched for me at E.'s. If things work out, he will have had a share in it.

At the moment I have no strength left for theoretical work, so I am terribly bored in the evening. This year I am also learning what freezing is like, something I had managed to avoid so far. I can hardly write for the chill in my cellar hole.

This last page is given over to curiosity, how you and your family, especially Paulinchen, are doing. I hope a period of thriving has begun for her.

C.Q. is still doing poorly. I believe, though, that she has only a cardiac hysteria. I witnessed her first attack, when her father was still alive, and I know what I saw.

Gersuny's wife, I hear, is dying. Oscar visits Mathilde every day because of an abscess. Otherwise the rascals are well and lively. Martin tolerates school well, and Oli is at his best, accomplishing everything without effort.

So I am growing older, patiently awaiting further developments. A congress would be a welcome interruption — but for a change on Italian soil.

Cordial greetings.

Your
Sigm.

1. The review, by Carl Metzentin, appeared in *Gegenwart* under the title "Über wissenschaftliche Traumdeutung." The essay concludes: "At the end of his path-breaking work, he himself is far from overestimating the value of the dream for gaining knowledge of the future, and is of the opinion that naturally there can be no question of that. But dreams are useful for giving us knowledge of the past."

2. On Freud's relation to L.G. and her father, see note 2 to letter of November 12, 1899.

3. *Es bleibt derzeit ein saures Brot;* literally, It remains at present sour bread.

---

December 24, 1899
IX., Berggasse 19

Dear Wilhelm,

Yet another cordial Christmas greeting! So once again you have a headache, something you are no longer used to. I too am still plagued by my cold. Mathildchen has a temperature that, according to Oscar, is not connected with her furuncle, which has subsided; it is spoiling the joy of Christmas for her. I shall be glad to send a copy of the book to Carus Sterne[1] and refer to his article in *Prometheus,* as you seem to advise.

In regard to the sexual theory, just be patient. It will assuredly come. Out of context it sounds so wild. I believe I have once again found something about anxiety. (There still are strange ebbs and flows; at times they carry me to the crest of certainty, and then everything flows away again and I am back on dry land. I do believe, however, that the sea is gaining.) Following your advice, I am letting it grow naturally.

Send me word about Paulinchen together with the announcement of the new arrival.

All the best for next week!

Your
Sigm.

1. Pen name for Ernst Ludwig Krause (1839–1903), author of *Die Krone der Schöpfung: 14 Essays über die Stellung des Menschen in der Natur* (Vienna and Teschen: Karl Prochaska, n.d.). He speaks of "unconscious memories." See his *Gesammelte kleinere Schriften,* 2 vols. (Leipzig: Ernst Günther, 1885).

---

December 29, 1899
IX., Berggasse 19

Hail

To the valiant son who at the behest of his father appeared at the right time,

To be his assistant and fellow worker in fathoming the divine order.

But hail to the father, too, who just prior to the event found in his calculations

The key to restraining the power of the female sex

And to shouldering his burden of lawful succession;

No longer relying on sensory appearances, as does the mother,

He calls upon the higher powers to claim his right, conclusion, belief, and doubt;

Thus, at the beginning, there stands, hale and hearty, equal to the exigency of error, the father

In his infinitely mature development.

May the calculation be correct and, as the legacy of labor, be transferred from father to son and beyond the parting of the centuries

Unite in the mind what the vicissitudes of life tear apart.

---

Vienna, January 8, 1900
IX., Berggasse 19

Dear Wilhelm,

I am glad to have news of my friend Conrad.[1] On the basis of these few samples of his behavior, it is my judgment[2] that he is a good boy. Whether he adopts his name as a guiding principle for his future activities[3] or else the strange circumstances of his birth celebrated by me, I believe I can predict that there is something capable and reliable about him, and that he will succeed in whatever he sets out to do. I reserve the pleasure of making his personal acquaintance once he is over the worst.

The new century, the most interesting thing about which for us may be that it contains the dates of our deaths, has brought me nothing but a stupid review in the *Zeit* by Burckhard,[4] the former director of the Burgtheater (not to be confused with our old Jacob).[5] It is hardly flattering, uncommonly devoid of understanding, and — worst of all — to be continued in the next issue. Even Oscar Rie thinks that these are the sorts of objections one raises *before* one has read the book.

I do not count on recognition, at least not in my lifetime. May you fare better! At least you can address yourself to a more respectable, educated audience, at home with ideas. I have to deal in obscure matters with people I am ten to fifteen years ahead of and who will not catch up with me. So all I seek is quiet and some material comfort. I am not working, and there is silence in me. If the sexual theory comes, I shall listen to it. If not, then not. In the evenings I read prehistory and the like, without any serious purpose; otherwise my only concern is to bring my cases, in good spirits, closer to a solution. L.G. is beginning to move and gives me great pleasure; of course the work will take a long time. She was in a splendid muddle. In E.'s case, the second genuine scene is coming up after years of preparation; and it is one which may *perhaps* be confirmed objectively by asking his elder sister. Behind it a third, long-suspected scene approaches.

At noontime yesterday Martin suddenly took to his bed with a fever; today he has otitis media and today Oli has — mumps. So all sorts of things are in store for us. Mathilde has recovered, but is quite run down. In all other respects the rascals are very gratifying. My cold is rushing ahead of me; it has already become immortal.

It is sad that things here keep on going downhill. Can you believe it, on January 1, when the crown currency was introduced, there were no postcards to be had; they were to cost five hellers; the post office nevertheless collected postage due for the use of the old ones with the two-kreuzer stamp; nor were supplementary one-heller stamps available. The new five- and ten-crown coins will not be issued until the end of March. That is Austria in a nutshell. Someday you will have to take some of my sons to Berlin for my sake, to send them out into the world.

Now, do not let such a long interval (December 24 to January 7 = 14= 28/2) happen again, and give our cordial greetings to your dear wife as the happy mother of three.

Your
Sigm.

1. Fliess's new son.

2. *Urteilen*, not *mitteilen* as in *Anfänge*.

3. Conrad means courageous helper, adviser.

4. Max Burckhard, "Ein modernes Traumbuch." *Die Zeit* was a popular daily newspaper of which Burckhard was the editor. Kris (*Origins*, p. 307n2) writes that the review was "an ironic and malicious journalistic distortion of Freud's ideas." Ellenberger (1970, p. 784) says that it was "an extensive and learned, though somewhat glib, review. Actually it was by no means negative."

5. Jacob Burckhardt, one of Freud's favorite authors, was a well-known scholar, philosopher, and historian from Basel. Freud had six of Burckhardt's books in his personal library, and specifically mentions the pleasure he had in reading *Griechische Kulturgeschichte*, 4 vols. (Berlin: W. Spemann, 1898–1902), which he took with him to London.

January 12, 1900
IX., Berggasse 19

Dear Wilhelm,

All I want to do is to reply to your kind inquiries. Martin escaped without a perforation; after otitis and a sore throat, he is lively once again. Oli looks somewhat quadrangular, but in other respects is merry. No new case. Bleakness otherwise.—I imagine that the autoerotic period before the age of one and a half must be the proper playing field for education. For this reason I am not sorry for Conrad. My youngest child, L.G., is coming along well.

Best wishes for the resurrection!

Your
Sigm.

I must have already told you that "bedmania" represents hysterical confinement.

---

Vienna, January 26, 1900
IX., Berggasse 19

Dear Wilhelm,

I assume that being preoccupied with three generations of blood relatives, you find little time to write and therefore I shall not wait any longer. In my case the dearth of material requiring communication runs counter to writing. The children either have measles or are about to come down with it. Martin is almost done with it; Ernst, like his predecessor, has had a sore throat with fever for three days; he is now merry and will be regarded as due in the next few days. To judge by her looks, Annerl will be the next one. Mathilde is staying with her grandmother so as not to have to miss school. Thus our lives are even more lonely than normal.

Nothing is happening, really. When I remind myself that I have had only one new case since May 1899, one you know, and that again I am to lose four patients between April and May, I am not exactly in a cheerful mood. How I shall manage I do not yet know, but I am determined to stick it out. My not wanting to complain is another reason for my writing less often. The book has not been mentioned since the review in the *Zeit*,[1] which was lacking in understanding but unfortunately not in impertinent disrespect. For the summer we are again trying to get rooms at Bellevue in Grinzing; I have given up as hopeless the project of finding summer work.

The analytic treatments[2] are going well and are no longer as strenuous as they used to be. I am quite satisfied even with G.; it is of course the beginning of a long stretch of work. My difficulties with her parents are, to be sure, the natural consequence of the lack of authority or title. The patient herself, I would imagine, is by now fascinated.

New ideas come slowly, but there never is total stillness. In the case of F., there is again a delay and a darker region, but the earlier findings still stand. I am collecting material for the sexual theory and am waiting for a spark to set the accumulated material on fire.

We are now reading a book (by Frey)[3] on the life of your C. F. Meyer. He does not know about the inner side [of Meyer's life], or discretion holds him back from discussing it. There is not much to read between the lines either.

Now all that remains is curiosity about how you and your no-longer-small family are. Waiting for news of them, with cordial greetings

Your
Sigm.

1. See note 4 to letter of January 8, 1900.
2. *Die Arbeiten;* literally, the works.
3. Adolf Frey (1855–1920). His book was *Conrad Ferdinand Meyer: Sein Leben und seine Werke* (Stuttgart: J. G. Cotta, 1900). Frey says of Meyer's sister that "she alone is familiar with every moment of his life."

---

Vienna, February 1, 1900
IX., Berggasse 19

Dear Wilhelm,

So my premonition of something ominous turned out to be right. I find it sad that the interval is so short. But perhaps the two attacks belong together and there will be uninterrupted well-being afterward. It is very painful; I know nothing further about it either.

Martin took to bed on January 14,[1] his illness starting acutely between two and three in the afternoon. He has remained the only case and is well again. This time the series of observations breaks off abruptly. Perhaps another time.

If we lived in the same city—this would have to be Berlin, though, not Vienna—much would have turned out differently, and I believe I would never have gotten into such straits (or would have gotten out of them quickly). That is why I have so often regretted our separation. Unfortunately this does not change anything. Perhaps hard times are ahead, both for me and for my practice. On the whole, I have noticed that you usually overestimate me greatly. The motivation for this error, though, disarms any reproach. For I am actually not at all a man of science, not an observer, not an experimenter, not a thinker. I am by temperament nothing but a conquistador — an adventurer, if you want it translated — with all the curiosity, daring, and tenacity characteristic of a man of this sort. Such people are customarily esteemed only if they have been successful, have really discovered something; otherwise they are dropped by the wayside. And that is not altogether unjust. At the present time, however, luck has left me; I no longer discover anything worthwhile.

A kind and perceptive, somewhat diffuse review of the dream book appeared in number 17 of the *Nation*; it is by J. J. David,[2] a personal acquaintance. I promised Löwenfeld to finish a short extract of the book by summer as an issue of *Grenzfragen des Nerven- und Seelenlebens.*[3]

I find science ever more difficult. In the evening I would like something that cheers, refreshes, and clears things away, but I am always alone.

The Hohenzollern sample is amusing. Naturally, an ignoramus immediately has all sorts of questions that will have to wait for an ideal congress. Why does lawful regularity bring out the *difference?* I expect that my share in your work would have been very different had I lived in Berlin. Thus we are becoming estranged from each other through what is most our own.

L.G. is at present in a continuous rage, but very funny at the same time. I understand her very well because I too could explode with rage. I have just acquired Nietzsche, in whom I hope to find words for much that remains mute in me, but have not opened him yet. Too lazy for the time being.

Remember that I regularly develop the gloomiest expectations when your letters fail to arrive, and write soon to

Your
Sigm.

1. Fliess wrote above the date, "$5 \times 28^2 - 10 \times 23$."
2. See note 5 to letter of August 6, 1899.
3. *Über den Traum.* First published as part of the series Freud mentions, then separately in 1911.

Vienna, February 12, 1900
IX., Berggasse 19

Dear Wilhelm,

If I am restraining my need for a more frequent exchange of ideas with you just now, it is to spare you my complaints while you are affected by your mother's continuing illness. Wishes for her improvement no doubt are superfluous; I should like to be able to help you, if it were possible to be of any help in these matters. It is doubtless a form of aging, but certainly no less painful for this reason. At the same time the three grandchildren are blossoming.

I come close to reproaching myself for writing to you only about myself. Much that could be said cannot be put in writing.

My practice has picked up during the past week. The period in which I saw only one patient in five consulting hours (in all five) seems to be over. Today I even started a new case, though of course I do not know whether it will last. Today, too, my depression has lifted. If I could only tell you what constant changes my thoughts undergo in relation to my work, that is, what errors I still find to correct, and how difficult it all is, you would probably make allowances for my neurotic swings of mood,[1] especially if you also took into account my financial worries.

Minna left Saturday evening for Hamburg to visit her mother, who will turn seventy this year and who at the moment is in bed with influenza. She plans to stay away for three weeks; if the old lady is well, the last week is reserved for Berlin. Naturally, she will not fail to visit you, so that she can report to me on the children and give you my cordial greetings. Martha is having a very good time of it, as are the children, who really are developing well. My brother, whose renown as an expert has grown steadily and who is being called upon by the government to act as a confidential consultant in all official investigations and the like, is nevertheless beginning to realize that all of it is just exploitation. He will not even get the title of professor, which he has earned by lecturing at the Export Academy; nor will he be taken into the civil service. Everything in Austria is Austrian. He is working too hard, and you know my fears for his future. He is now thirty-four years old.

I am not at all reluctant to learn more about nasal therapy from you when we find the opportunity for it one day, but it is very difficult to carry out anything new here and there is a difficulty in myself as well. You have no idea how hard it is for me to learn anything, and how easy it seems when you know how to do it.

On the whole I am farther away from Rome than at any time since we met, and the freshness of youth is very markedly on the decline. The journey is long, the stations at which one is thrown out are very numerous, and we are left with "if I can stand it."[2]

Farewell and write very soon again to

Your
Sigm.

1. Freud uses the word *Eigenschwankungen* (self-fluctuations).
2. See note 1 to letter of January 3, 1897.

February 22, 1900
IX., Berggasse 19

Dear Wilhelm,

You are an optimist; fate makes you incorrigible!

I am glad to hear that your mother is considerably better. My mother-in-law in Hamburg is not doing very well.

A splendid migraine on February 18 completed my own full recovery. The new patient soon departed again! I, too, have heard of W. James by name, as an authority. I won't let the ghosts move me for some time to come.

A rumor has it that you two will come to Vienna in March. It is no doubt premature to talk about it.

Miss G. is really in harness now — an excellent but slow piece of work.

With the most cordial greetings to all of you,

Your
Sigm.

March 1, 1900
IX., Berggasse 19

Dear Wilhelm,

The wind has just now blown a strange book by E. Jonas onto my table. Titled *Symptomatologie und Therapie der nasogenen Reflexneurosen,* . . . (Liegnitz: Carl Seyffarth, 1900), it appears to be monotonously optimistic and presents as new and true much that I, amazed and half-believing, heard from you. It is at any rate lacking in systematic insight and cites no names, not even yours. I imagine you would be interested in it?

Cordially,

Your
Sigm.

# Decline of the Friendship

Vienna, Sunday, March 11, 1900
IX., Berggasse 19

Dear Wilhelm,

At last a long letter from you! I have not heard from you since February 15; I was the one who wrote last, and apparently you did not receive a card I sent you at the beginning of March in which I called your attention to a book by Jonas on nasogenous reflex neuroses.[1] In view of my increasing lack of freedom and your being tied down, and the dismal material that always forces its way into my pen; with the prospect of being pushed even farther from you and your family by the impending Breuerization[2]— it would be utterly senseless to try to deny the influence of such circumstances and that of the women, at any rate, on our relationship — in short, in view of all these considerations I have resolved to reduce my claims on you. This is the reason for my prolonged silence, which I could make out to be waiting for an answer from you.

Now I am glad to hear so much from you, because I imagine you would be just as sorry as I if our correspondence were to dwindle and our meetings stop. I was astonished to see that three weeks had passed since I wrote to you. The time slipped by so imperceptibly, almost comfortably, under my new regimen, of which you shall hear. The children have all been well, Martha has felt better than usual, and my health has been excellent — regulated by a regularly recurring slight Sunday migraine. I have been seeing the same people every day, and last week I even started a new case, which is still in the trial stage and perhaps once again will not go beyond it. I have been virtually cut off from the outside world; not a leaf has stirred to reveal that the *Interpretation of Dreams* has had any impact on anyone. It was only yesterday that a rather friendly article in the feuilleton of a daily newspaper, *Wiener Fremdenblatt*, caught me by surprise. L.G. is unquestionably better and in full harness; she will manage with a companion during the afternoon hours, has tolerated the first visit by G.R. well, and will soon let herself be persuaded to see more people. Minna is still in Hamburg, occupied with nursing; she will not be back soon. It is still questionable that she will stop in Berlin.

My patients most of the time are doing well. Now is my busy time, 70 to 80 florins daily; about 500 florins a week. To judge by past experience, it will come to an end at Easter. I could not arrange anything for the summer. Altogether it is impossible to do anything, and everything is just a waste of energy. That is the key to the situation.

I would like to go away for three days at Easter and most of all would like to see you. But I am suffering from a bad case of spring fever, hungering for sunshine, flowers, a bit of blue water, just like a young man. I hate Vienna almost personally and, unlike the giant Antaeus,[3] I gather fresh strength as soon as I lift my foot from the hometown soil. For the children's sake I shall have to give up distance and mountains this summer, and will constantly have to bear the view of Vienna from Bellevue; I do not yet know whether I shall be able to afford a trip in September and therefore would very much like to nibble at the splendors of the world at Easter. But Alexander, my nearest and cheapest travel companion, after a catarrh and influenza already has yielded to his longing for the South this month; he went to Bolzano, Merano, and Gries, where he squandered his Easter vacation, and will not want to accompany me. So I really do not yet know whether Easter will bring me anything at all.

If you want to hear still more about me, listen to this. After last summer's exhilaration, when in feverish activity I completed the dream [book], fool that I am, I was once again intoxicated with the hope that a step toward freedom and well-being had been taken. The reception of the book and the ensuing silence have again destroyed any budding relationship with my milieu. For my second iron in the fire is after all my work—the prospect of reaching an end somewhere, resolving many doubts, and then knowing what to think of the chances of my therapy. Prospects seemed most favorable in E.'s case—and that is where I was dealt the heaviest blow. Just when I believed I had the solution in my grasp, it eluded me and I found myself forced to turn everything around and put it together anew, in the process of which I lost everything that until then had appeared plausible. I could not stand the depression that followed. Moreover, I soon found that it was impossible to continue the really difficult work in a state of mild depression and lurking doubts. When I am not cheerful and collected, every single one of my patients is my tormentor. I really believed I would have to give up on the spot. I found a way out by renouncing all conscious mental activity so as to grope blindly among my riddles. Since then I am working perhaps more skillfully than ever before, but I do not really know what I am doing. I could not give an account of how matters stand. In my spare time I take care not to reflect on it. I give myself over to my fantasies, play chess, read English novels; everything serious is banished. For two months I have not written a single line of what I have learned or surmised. As soon as I am free of my trade, I live like a pleasure-seeking philistine. You know how limited my pleasures are. I am not allowed to smoke anything decent; alcohol does nothing for me; I am done begetting children; and I am cut off from contact with people. So I vegetate harmlessly, carefully keeping my attention diverted from the subject on which I work during the day. Under this regimen I am cheerful and equal to my eight victims and tormentors.

On Saturday evenings I look forward to an orgy of taroc, and every second Tuesday I spend among my Jewish brethren, to whom I recently gave another lecture. Until Easter I am in this way secure; then several treatments will be broken off and another period of greater discomfort will begin.

Well, by now you will have had enough. If ever I should meet you in Rome or Karlsbad, I shall ask you to forgive me for the many complaints I have scattered on the way.

But greet your wife and children very cordially for me, and do come yourself to Vienna for the seventieth birthday.

Your
Sigm.

1. But Fliess did receive the card; see preceding letter dated March 1, 1900.

2. The second daughter of Josef Breuer, Margarethe (1872–ca. 1942), on May 27, 1900, married Arthur Schiff (1871–1939). This information comes from Hirschmüller (1978, p. 48). See note 6 to letter of January 30, 1898.

3. Son of Poseidon and Earth, Antaeus was a wrestler who, when thrown onto the Earth, his mother, derived new strength.

Vienna, March 23, 1900
IX., Berggasse 19

Dear Wilhelm,

I must write to you at length again, after all. Otherwise what would you think? First of all, my most cordial thanks for your hospitality to Minna. At last I have some proper information about your household: that your mother is well again, which is contrary to my expectations and therefore doubly welcome; how beautiful and how tiny your dear Paulinchen is; and how robust Conrad appears; to say nothing of our old friend Robert and his *apta dicta* [bons mots]—now I once again have a good picture of them all. I heard with great satisfaction that your interest in my dream-child remains undiminished and that you are lending a hand in urging it upon the *Rundschau* and its indolent reviewers.[1] For after a good deal of wavering in my mind, I have come down on the side of being very grateful to you for standing godfather to it and considering it to be good and genuine. It has become a consolation to me in many a gloomy hour to be able to leave this book behind. True, its reception—at least the reception it has had so far—has certainly not given me any joy. Understanding for it is meager; praise is doled out like alms; to most people it is evidently distasteful. I have not yet seen a trace of anyone who has an inkling of what is significant in it. I explain this by telling myself that I am fifteen to twenty years ahead of my time. Then, of course, the usual qualms associated with forming a judgment about oneself set in.

There has never been a six-month period in which I so constantly and so ardently longed to be living in the same place with you and that which is yours[2] as the one that has just passed. You know that I have been going through a deep inner crisis; you would see how it has aged me. I was therefore deeply moved when I heard of your proposal that we meet again this Easter. Anyone who did not understand the more subtle resolution of contradictions would think it incomprehensible that I am not rushing to assent to the proposal. In fact it is more likely that I shall avoid you—not only because of my almost childish yearning for spring and the beauties of nature, which I would willingly sacrifice for the gratification of having you near me for three days. But there are other, inner reasons, an accumulation of imponderables, which, however, weigh heavily on me (from the natural habitat of madness,[3] you will perhaps say). Inwardly I am deeply impoverished, I have had to demolish all my castles in the air, and I am just now mustering enough courage to start rebuilding them again. During the catastrophic collapse you would have been invaluable to me; in the present stage I would scarcely be able to make myself intelligible to you. I conquered my depression with the aid of a special diet of intellectual matters and now, thanks to the distraction, it is slowly healing. If I were with you, I could not avoid trying to grasp everything consciously and describe it all to you; we would talk reason and science; your beautiful and positive biological discoveries would arouse my innermost (impersonal!) envy. The upshot would be that I would go on complaining to you for five days and return all upset and dissatisfied to my summer, for which I shall probably need all my composure. No one can help me in the least with what oppresses me; it is my cross, I must bear it; and God knows that in adapting to it, my back has become noticeably bent.

During the summer or fall, no later, I shall see you, talk with you, and explain all the riddles of Count Oerindur to you.[4] You will be able to convince yourself that the matter is merely complicated, not at all *meschugge*—although the abominable work with all its demands would excuse some of that too. Then we also shall discuss the pros and cons of nasal therapy, preferably right on the object. At present I could not in any event go to Berlin. Family obligations would not leave me an hour's peace. My eldest sister Anna and her four children have just arrived there from New York. I do not know what this means and suspect nothing good. I have never had any special relationship with her, as I had, for instance, with Rosa, and her marriage to Eli B. has not exactly improved it. I know only one of her four children and if I were not a helpless beggar and could be an uncle, I would increase my colony of children here by a few little ones.

I do not know what this trip means: a severe illness of Anna's, wealth, extravagance, or a catastrophe threatening her husband? Enough; Mother went there two days ago. Rosa and her husband are going next week; Alexander could not resist the temptation of going to Berlin for a weekend; and I believe everyone is doing it out of concern as much as love. My plan for Easter is to go with Alexander to Trent and from there to Lake Garda, to catch a few nice glimpses of spring while traveling such a long way. We shall set off three weeks from now if nothing interferes, and live for four full days as students and tourists, as we always do.

L.G. is certainly greatly improved. You will hardly expect her to admit to it herself, but her ability to cope and the psychic changes leave no doubt about it. She is passive by nature; it is astonishing how poorly she makes use of her time; she still is constantly intoxicated, has migraines, fatigue, erotic images, and so on, but she is beginning to talk; she keeps up her contact with G.R., was my guest one evening, and will be invited regularly. A good-natured and fine person, at a deeper layer gynecophilic, attached to the mother [?];[5] for this reason it is possible for male images to occur as symptoms.

Last week we heard a lecture by G. Brandes on reading.[6] The topic was nothing special, the lecture strenuous, the voice jarring, the pronunciation foreign—but the man was refreshing. The whole thing must have seemed pretty outlandish to the worthy Viennese;

essentially he uttered nothing but affronts to the audience. Such a rigid view of life is unknown to us here; our petty logic and our petty morality are, after all, very different from those in the North. I reveled in listening to it; Martha, in whom ambition is a very important trait, persuaded me to send a copy of the dream book to his hotel. So far he has not shown any reaction to it; perhaps he will really read it once he is home.

Cordial greetings to you and Ida and the children. I hope to hear from you soon and to write to you several times before Easter.

Your faithful
Sigm.

1. The *Deutsche Rundschau* had not published a review of the *Interpretation of Dreams.*

2. The German is *dem Deinigen,* not *den Deinigen* as in *Anfänge.* Probably a reference to Fliess's work.

3. *Schigan.* This term was also used in letter of November 9, 1899.

4. Alexander Grinstein has written a paper on the significance of this comment, "Freud and Count Oerindur: A Preliminary Communication." Count Oerindur was the protagonist of a play written by Adolphus Müllner (1774–1829), *Guilt; or, the Gipsy's Prophecy; a Tragedy,* translated by W. E. Frye (London: 1819, private printing). According to Schur (1972, p. 206), a condensed version of one of the stanzas from the play had become an idiomatic expression, *Erklärt mir, Oerindur, diesen Zwiespalt der Natur* (Explain to me, Oerindur, this contradiction of nature), referring to ambivalence. Presumably Freud is referring to some contradictory feelings of his own toward Fliess, saying that it is not crazy *(meschugge),* but can be explained by reference to Count Oerindur's notion of loving and hating somebody at the same time.

5. *Mutterlieb;* meaning unclear.

6. Georg Brandes (1842–1927) was a Danish author who also wrote in German and was on friendly terms with Arthur Schnitzler and Theodor Gomperz. The letters between Brandes and Schnitzler were edited and annotated by Kurt Bergel as a Ph.D. dissertation, "Der Briefwechsel Georg Brandes und Arthur Schnitzler" (University of California, 1948). According to Bergel (p. 220), Brandes told G. C. Moore-Smith that there was nothing to be had from dreams, and as proof said he had dreamed twice that he was a woman! When he was eighty-three, he said that Freud's theories were "disgusting," but altered his opinion of Freud as a person when he met him in 1925; see *Living Age,* 332 (1927):642. Whether Brandes' opinion of dreams came from reading the book that Freud took to his hotel is not known; he does not mention it in his correspondence with Schnitzler.

---

Vienna, April 4, 1900
IX., Berggasse 19

Dear Wilhelm,

The expression of feelings can be postponed, but business matters need to be attended to. Therefore let me reply immediately that I have no intention of writing a short dream [book] for the *Rundschau*—for a number of reasons: first, because after the big work it would be a very disagreeable task; second, because I have promised an essay of this kind to Löwenfeld and therefore cannot send it anywhere else; third, because it would violate the principle of differentiation which manifests itself in one man's writing a book and another's reviewing it and which, in addition, gives the reader the benefit of the review and the author the chance to gauge the effect of his work on a stranger; fourth and finally, the *Rundschau* should not be forced to publish a review against its will. An unwilling reviewer quickly turns into an odious one. That seems to have been the secret of Burckhard's review in the *Zeit*,[1] which in its utter stupidity killed the book in Vienna. Fifth, I want to avoid anything that might resemble an advertisement. I know that what I am doing is odious to the majority of people. As long as I behave perfectly correctly, my worthy opponents are unsure; only when I am doing exactly what they are doing will they feel certain that I am doing nothing better than they. It was for reasons such as these that I refrained some time ago from reviewing your book, which otherwise I would very much have liked to do. These fellows shall not say that we are flattering each other in public. So I think the most advisable course is quietly to accept the *Rundschau*'s refusal as an undeniable sign of public opinion.

Mathilde is in bed with chicken pox and is accordingly not very ill; the others are all well. Thanks to Minna's visit we are informed about the minor accidents in your household. L. is progressing rather well. E. will terminate treatment at Easter, having benefited enormously, I hope. I am still too lazy to work things out for myself. I had to send my last new case away after two weeks—it was a case of paranoia.[2]

With the most cordial greetings to you, wife, daughter, and sons,

Your
Sigm.

1. See note 4 to letter of January 8, 1900.
2. See note 6 to letter of April 25, 1900.

---

Vienna, April 16, 1900
IX., Berggasse 19

Dear Wilhelm,

Herewith the greeting as ordered from the land of sunshine. For, once again, I did not get there. The journey, planned to take us to

Trent and Lake Garda, had to be shortened to begin with because my companion was afraid of the twenty-two-hour return trip, and I had to admit he was right. Then we heard that the area where we wanted to go had had a lot of snow, almost as much as we had at home. Then Friday turned into a miserably wet day. Then Martin suddenly became ill, and I decided to stay. Finally, on Saturday the weather was tolerable, but all five children — following Mathilde — were in bed with chicken pox. It is nothing serious, of course, but nevertheless such an accumulation of unpleasantness that I am quite glad I am still at home.

You are completely right, my wishes are not very flexible; so after a partial renunciation, I soon stop enjoying the "entire funeral." That is what happened here as well.

In the meantime you all have been in Dresden; domestic troubles of a minor sort — fortunately forgotten more quickly. Strange, how things are parceled out. We do have every conceivable kind of thing happening to us, but nothing quite like that. The household is running smoothly and people are devoted and stay on. Each social stratum thus has its particular complaints.

E. at last concluded his career as a patient by coming to dinner at my house. His riddle is *almost* completely solved; he is in excellent shape, his personality entirely changed. At present a remnant of the symptoms is left. I am beginning to understand that the apparent endlessness of the treatment is something that occurs regularly and is connected with the transference. I hope that this remnant will not detract from the practical success. I could have continued the treatment, but I had the feeling that such prolongation is a compromise between illness and health that patients themselves desire, and the physician must therefore not accede to it. The asymptotic[1] conclusion of the treatment basically makes no difference to me, but is yet one more disappointment to outsiders. In any case, I shall keep an eye on the man. Since he had to suffer through all my technical and theoretical errors, I actually think that a future case could be solved in half the time. May the Lord now send this next one. L.G. is doing very well. There is no longer any chance of a failure.

Occasionally something stirs toward synthesis, but I am holding it down.

Otherwise Vienna is Vienna, that is, extremely disgusting. If I closed with "Next Easter in Rome," I would feel like a pious Jew. So I say rather, "Until we meet in the summer or fall in Berlin or where you will."

Most cordial greetings.

Your
Sigm.

1. In the sense of not reaching the goal.

---

Vienna, April 25, 1900
IX., Berggasse 19

Dear Wilhelm,

Well, do you realize now that Rome cannot be forced? I frequently have fatalistic convictions of this kind which serve my inertia very well. I am really not making any headway. Upon receipt of your letter a resolution to spend a few days with you by the ocean in August flashed through my mind; a large overpayment by Miss R. had somewhat enriched me that day. But if the Lord subtracts these sums somewhere else in the next few moments, then nothing will come of it after all. I am sure you had a more pleasant time with your wife in Dresden than you might have had with me in Weimar. I certainly would not have come; the sight of the five sick children was too pitiful, harmless as the matter was on the whole.

Yesterday I gave a lecture on Zola's *Fécondité*[1] before my society.[2] I am always ill prepared; actually I start only an hour before — much as one writes a German composition in school. During the night from Monday to Tuesday, I dreamed inordinately of this lecture.[3] I explained that I had to go home to fetch the book, did not find the way, and got lost; the weather was miserable, I made no headway; and during all these delays I worked out part of the talk. The obstacles, therefore, were only pretexts to gain time for working on it. The brethren, moreover, were unkind and scornful of me — conduct that is apt, quite surely, to reduce my interest in the success of the lecture. The "miserable weather" is borrowed from a patient who at the moment arouses my liveliest interest because I finally — in the sixth season — am on the track of her secret. Mistakes in technique prevented me from finding it sooner.

Spring has arrived here as well. The trees in front of my window have delicate reddish leaves. I am curious about what spring will bring forth in you; I am content with a mood of equanimity and physical well-being. I forgot to write to you that my fears that my eldest sister's trip from New York to Berlin were due to an imminent catastrophe appear to have been unfounded; something else unfathomable is behind it. On the other hand, my youngest sister's husband (in New York) is fatally ill.

In the last issue of Wernicke's *Monatsschrift* (for which I also write) is the first part of an article by Dr. Warda of Blankenburg. "A Case of Hysteria, Presented According to the Cathartic Method of

Breuer and Freud."[4] I have not yet read it carefully. The man obviously knows only the little that is in the *Studies* and works rather laboriously with my conceptual creations from the Sturm und Drang period — retention, defense, conversion — and also with the unfortunate "hypnoid"[5] that was forced upon me.

The patient whom I treated for fourteen days and then dismissed as a case of paranoia has since hanged herself in a hotel room (Mrs. Margit Kremzir).[6]

I have not succeeded in getting a new patient. The last one who did not show up was a twelve-year-old boy, a grandson of the painter Alt. Although we had agreed on his coming weeks ago, he supposedly fell ill on the day he was to start.

Most cordial greetings to your entire house and further news as soon as there is some.

Your
Sigm.

1. Emile Zola, *Les quatre Evangiles — Fécondité*, in *Les Oeuvres complètes*, notes and commentary by Maurice Le Blond (Paris: François Bernouard, n.d.). On p. 62, "Dr. Boutan . . . maintains that women are ruined and grow old not because of pregnancies, but because of measures taken to prevent them." And on p. 18, Zola speaks of "girls who are seduced [but] cannot denounce the father as the seducer."

2. B'nai B'rith.

3. This dream does not seem to be cited in Freud's published writings.

4. W. Warda, "Ein Fall von Hysterie, dargestellt nach der kathartischen Methode von Breuer und Freud," *Monatsschrift für Psychiatrie und Neurologie*, 7 (1900):301–318, 471–489. The work is a long, day-by-day account of 102 sessions of a psychotherapy which consisted in abreaction, hypnosis, and suggestion. By abreaction Warda understood that he should ask the patient what occurred to her with respect to each of her many symptoms. At one point the patient asks him, "Should I recount my entire bleak childhood?" Warda has very little to say, but some of the patient's "interpretations" are striking, for example, her explanation that the feelings of physical *pressure* come from a lack of freedom in her childhood and a yearning to be away from the pressures of that period of her life (p. 315). Warda seems to have found it hard to follow her. His understanding of Freud was certainly very limited, but the material he provided was, for the time, unusual.

5. For a discussion of this idea in the *Studies on Hysteria* and Freud's later ideas about it, see Hirschmüller (1978, pp. 221–224) and Strachey's introduction to *S.E.* 2:25. In the Dora case (*S.E.* 7:27n) Freud writes: "I should like to take this opportunity of stating that the hypothesis of 'hypnoid states' — which many reviewers were inclined to regard as the central portion of our work — sprang entirely from the initiative of Breuer. I regard the use of such a term as superfluous and misleading, because it interrupts the continuity of the problem as to the nature of the psychological process accompanying the formation of hysterical symptoms." As early as the *Studies* (*S.E.* 2:286) Freud began to look skeptically at the theory of hypnoid states. Finally, in his *Five Lectures* (*S.E.* 11:20) Freud writes, "Breuer's theory of hypnoid states turned out to be impeding and unnecessary, and it has been dropped by psycho-analysis to-day."

6. In the *Neue freie Presse,* April 20, 1900, under "Kleine Chronik," is a short notice: "Tired of Life. This morning a woman from Hungary, here to consult various professors because of a severe stomach ailment, hanged herself in a hotel in the city out of desperation about her hopeless state." The next day, Saturday, the same paper on p. 4 carried an announcement of the death of Margit Kremzir (maiden name, Weiss de Szurda).

Vienna, May 7, 1900
IX., Berggasse 19

Dear Wilhelm,

Many thanks for such cordial words! They are so flattering that I might almost believe part of them—if I were in your company. However, I see things a little differently. I would have no objection to the fact of splendid isolation[1] if it were not carried too far and did not come between you and me as well. On the whole—except for one weak point, my fear of poverty—I have too much sense to complain and at present I feel too well to do so; I know what I have and I know, in view of the statistics of human misery, how little one is entitled to. But no one can replace for me the relationship with the friend which a special—possibly feminine—side demands, and inner voices to which I am accustomed to listen suggest a much more modest estimate of my work than that which you proclaim. When your book[2] is published, none of us will be able to pass judgment on its truth, which, as with all great new achievements, is reserved for posterity. The beauty of its conception, though, the originality of its ideas, its simple coherence, and the assurance of the author will create an impression that will give you the first compensation for your arduous wrestling with the demon. It is different with me. No critic (not even the stupid Löwenfeld,[3] the Burckhard of neuropathology[4]) can see more clearly than I the disparity arising from the problems and the answers to them; and it will be a fitting punishment for me that none of the unexplored regions of psychic life in which I have been the first mortal to set foot will ever bear my name or obey my laws. When it appeared that my breath would fail me in the wrestling match, I asked the angel to desist; and that is what he has done since then. But I did not turn out to be the stronger, although since then I have been limping noticeably. Yes, I really am forty-four now, an old, somewhat shabby Jew, as you will see for yourself in the summer or fall. My family nevertheless wanted to celebrate the day. My own best consolation is that I have not deprived them of all future achievements. They can have their experiences and conquests, to the extent that may be in their power. I have left them a foothold for a start, but am not leading them to the peak from which they could climb no farther.

On Saturday I start the lecture on dreams. In ten days we shall move to Bellevue. Rumor has it that your wife will soon come to Vienna.

My state of health is tolerable now. Vienna has suddenly become unpleasantly hot. L.G. has been very good during the past month. So the game has been won after all. One new case: a psychically impotent man, probably only for the summer. There are a few other prospects that have not yet matured.

In general, things are stirring somewhat.

With the most cordial greetings to all of you,

Your
Sigm.

1. English in original.

2. Either *Über den ursächlichen Zusammenhang von Nase und Geschlechtsorgan*, published in 1902, or—more likely—*Der Ablauf des Lebens*, published in 1906.

3. On Leopold Löwenfeld and his relation to Freud, see letter of October 8, 1895. In Masson (1984) I have discussed Löwenfeld's influence on Freud's thinking about the seduction theory. It is clear from Löwenfeld's books that the two men engaged in a lively correspondence (which has not survived). I have recently learned that in the second edition (1899) of Löwenfeld's book *Sexualleben und Nervenleiden: Die nervösen Störungen sexuellen Ursprungs* (Wiesbaden: J. F. Bergmann), Löwenfeld wrote: "By chance, one of the patients on whom Freud used the analytic method came under my observation. The patient told me with certainty that the infantile sexual scene which analysis had apparently uncovered was pure fantasy and had never really happened to him" (p. 195). This passage may have played a role in Freud's abandonment of the seduction theory.

4. See note 4 to letter of January 8, 1900.

---

Vienna, May 16, 1900
IX., Berggasse 19

Dear Wilhelm,

Since you have not written for an eternity, you leave me no alternative but to tempt you with a letter out of turn. In any event, there has been a slight break: an evening patient has left me—my most difficult case, and the most certain as far as etiology is concerned. For four years I could not get close to it. Moreover, it was the only case Breuer sent me. He kept sending the girl back to me whenever I had chased her away in utter despair. Last year I finally began to get on good terms with her, and this year at last I succeeded. I found the keys; that is to say, I could convince myself that the keys found elsewhere fitted her and, as far as the short time (December until now) permitted, I have deeply and fundamentally influenced her condition. She took leave of me today with the words, "What you have done for me is invaluable." She told me that when she confessed her extraordinary improvement to Breuer, he clapped his hands and exclaimed again and again, "So he is right after all!" In this little scene you can recognize the worshiper of success, who professes faith in one of the most popular religions of the world, to which all weak characters adhere. Why did he for years proclaim that I was wrong? It is very nice indeed that one can enjoy oneself twice with each mistake—the first time by having been wrong, which gives one a feeling of superiority, and then by admitting that one has been wrong, which makes one appear noble to oneself and others. A poor devil, foolish and obdurate like one of us, loses out on these pleasures. But having so often complained to you, I do not want to deprive you of the news of my little triumph.

Only three students attend my lectures—Hans Königstein, Miss Dora Teleky,[1] and a Dr. Marcuse from Breslau. The bookseller complains that the *Interpretation of Dreams* is "moving slowly." The *Umschau* of March 10 contained a short, friendly, and uncomprehending review.[2] For me, however, nothing counts but my work, and I am prepared to become entirely single-minded if only I can carry it through.

My youngest sister's husband died in New York on May 6. We have not yet had a letter from the widow. I never met him at all; he is supposed to have been very kind. It was a short and happy marriage.

And what about you? Are you still in Chapter 1? Would you allow a tentative first place in your summer plans to the possibility of our spending a few days together at the North Sea? You know that only total lack of funds or illness would prevent me from carrying out this intent. Do you know of any obstacles on your side?

I shall be immensely happy to see your dear wife here. Give my greetings to the three little ones. Mela is looking gratifyingly well a few days before she is due. I went there today.

Most cordially,

Your
Sigm.

1. On Dora Teleky see Masson (1984, pp. 249–250).

2. The review, by C. Oppenheimer, states that the *Interpretation of Dreams* is "a highly interesting, not to say strange, book!" and claims that at first the associations appear to be farfetched, or stale jokes *(Kalauer)*.

Vienna, May 20, 1900
IX., Berggasse 19

Dear Wilhelm,

Naturally I shall never mention the North Sea again if you are on such bad terms with it; I had no inkling. I wished it were the Mediterranean, but it will be what you want, if only it can be. Now comes the dead period of which I am afraid — that is, in which I am afraid of myself. Yesterday the fourth patient said good-bye on the most cordial terms, in excellent shape, with Böcklin's *Selected Paintings* as a parting present.[1] This case gave me the greatest satisfaction and is perhaps complete. So things have gone well this year. I have finally conquered. But what am I going to do now? I still have three and a half persons — that is, sessions — a day. Not enough toys for the whale.[2] Woe is me when I am bored. All sorts of things can go wrong. I cannot work. I am permeated with laziness; the kind of work I have been doing from October until now is very unlike that which leads to writing, and very unfavorable to it. I have not started the little dream pamphlet for Löwenfeld. I do not even stick to my *allotriis* [hobbies] but alternate between chess, art history, and prehistory; nothing is permitted to continue for very long. I would like to disappear for a few weeks to someplace where nothing like science exists — that is, apart from the congress with you. If only I had money or a travel companion for Italy!

My brother-in-law seems to have succumbed to a heart ailment of unknown origin, possibly connected with a latent kidney problem. He was an uncommonly handsome, large, and strong man, who is said never to have been ill before. He was born in Zwittau in Moravia and went to America thirteen years ago. I have met his family; they are poor but capable and good people. They will do their best to provide for the widow and the child. There will be something left for us to do as well.

I was afraid that you too might come to Vienna at Whitsun, because my eldest brother from Manchester wrote that he will visit us during this time. He is no longer a young man; I think he is sixty-eight(!) years old, though he is very youthful in appearance.

I have asked myself why it is that I cannot finish with Breuer, and a recent instance of forgetting provided me with the answer. I had promised Miss L. that I would buy her a small iron strongbox in which she could keep her valuables, but I continually forgot about it. Eventually she reminded me, and I went out shopping for it. I remembered a store, Tanczos, and had the most distinct visual memory of a window in which a small box was to be seen. It must have been somewhere in an easy-to-find location in the inner city. But I was absolutely unable to find this place on my walk. So I resolved to look it up in the telephone book or the register of business firms before my next walk. But then I forgot about it again on five successive days. Finally I forced myself to remember and looked up the address. And where is the place of this window with the iron box? Brandstätte [Street], across from Breuer, where I must have seen it several thousand times. This is easy to interpret.[3]

Most cordial greetings. As yet I know nothing about Rie 3, as of May 22, evening.[4]

Your
Sigm.

1. From the German text it is not clear whether the patient gave this book of reproductions to Freud, or whether Freud gave it to her. The former seems more likely.

2. *Dem Walfisch die rote Tonne hinwerfen* (Throw a red barrel to the whale) is an old German proverb, meaning give someone something to do so he will not create mischief. See K. F. W. Wander, *Deutsches Sprichwörter-Lexikon* (Leipzig: F. A. Brockhaus, 1867).

3. See *Psychopathology of Everyday Life* (*S.E.* 6:137–138), where Freud also describes this incident, but says the shop was in the building where Breuer ("M.") lived.

4. Marianne Rie Kris was born on May 27, 1900.

---

May 26, 1900
IX., Berggasse 19

Dear Wilhelm,

Because it tallies with your calculations, I am reporting to you that after a long and good period I had an awful migraine on Thursday, May 24, and have been tired and miserable since then. I am so ill-humored that I am considering giving up the daily trip to Bellevue, where we have been since Wednesday, to withdraw to my Berggasse loneliness. This would not be the first temporal congruence if there were not more general reasons for it this time.

Bellevue is XIX/5, but I am expecting your letters at the old address. That Paulinchen reacted positively to the thrust is very gratifying.

Cordial greetings.

Your
Sigm.

Vienna, June 12, 1900
IX., Berggasse 19

Dear Wilhelm,

We have had family visitors. My eldest brother, Emanuel, arrived the day before Whitsun with his youngest son, Sam (who already is over thirty-five), and stayed until Wednesday evening.[1] He brought with him a real air of refreshment because he is a marvelous man, vigorous and mentally indefatigable despite his sixty-eight or sixty-nine years, who has always meant a great deal to me. He went on to Berlin, which is now the family headquarters, together with Dolfi, who had brought the New Yorker's (Anna's) three little girls to Vienna, from which they will go (this evening) with Rosa to Lake Ossiach for the summer. The three girls are thirteen, eight, and six years old and are charming children, real beauties, precocious like American girls, and very engaging. So occasionally one gets a good impression of one's family. Naturally, distress is not far behind. Pauline, the young widow, embarked on the *Pretoria* for Hamburg the day before yesterday(?).

Ernst has been ill again with a sore throat and fever for four days. His energy is inexhaustible. Even when he has a temperature of 38.5, he still shouts: "One could not possibly feel better; I want to get up." The rascal becomes docile and compliant only when his temperature climbs to 39.5. This manic vivacity and wildness sometimes strike me as uncanny, like that of a consumptive.

Otherwise life at Bellevue is turning out to be very pleasant for everyone. The evenings and mornings are enchanting; the scent of lilac and laburnum has been succeeded by that of acacia and jasmine; the wild roses are in bloom and everything, as I too notice, happens suddenly.

Do you suppose that someday one will read on a marble tablet on this house:

Here, on July 24, 1895,
the secret of the dream
revealed itself to Dr. Sigm. Freud.[2]

So far there is little prospect of it. But when I read the more recent psychological books (Mach's *Analyse der Empfindungen,* 2nd ed., Kroell's *Aufbau der Seele,* and the like[3]), all of which have a direction similar to my work, and see what they have to say about the dream, I am indeed pleased, like the dwarf in the fairy tale, because "the princess does not know."[4]

I did not get another new case; or rather, I mean that in exchange for the latest one, I lost one that had started in May, so I am back where I was before. But this one is beautiful — a thirteen-year-old girl whom I am supposed to cure instantly, and who for once shows me on the surface what I usually endeavor to unearth beneath superimposed layers. I do not need to tell you that it is precisely the same thing. We shall discuss the child in August, unless she is snatched away from me prematurely. For in August I shall definitely see you, unless I am disappointed in my expectation of 1,500 kronen on July 1. What is more, I am able to come to Berlin in any event — if Pauli does not cost me too much money — and get some fresh air and new energy for 1900 – 1901 in the mountains or in Italy. A bad mood is no more productive than saving is.

I have heard about Conrad's accident and the happy outcome. Now I am again entitled to news about you and yours.

Most cordial greetings to you and them.

Your
Sigm.

1. See note 2 to letter of May 30, 1896.

2. Such a plaque was indeed placed there on May 6, 1977.

3. Ernst Mach (1838 – 1916), *Die Analyse der Empfindungen und das Verhältnis des Physischen zum Psychischen*, 2nd ed. (Jena: Gustav Fischer, 1900; 1st ed., 1886). Breuer is mentioned, but not Freud. The Kroell reference is to *Der Aufbau der menschlichen Seele, eine psychologische Skizze* (Leipzig: Wilhelm Engelmann, 1900).

4. No doubt a reference to the Grimms' *Rumpelstilzchen*. See note 3 to letter of May 16, 1897.

Vienna, June 18, 1900
IX., Berggasse 19

Dear Wilhelm,

My last letter dealt only with myself and now you force me to write about myself again, since you withhold more detailed information about your family from me. I have some notion of your difficulties with "Miss";[1] you say nothing about Conrad. So everything is left for August, when I shall most certainly speak with you, and I must once again write about myself, as though I were no longer interested in anything else.

After Ernst, who recovered quickly, the epidemic of throat infections claimed Martin, who today is beginning to totter about like a shadow. Mathilde seems to be next, but has no fever; the others are still blooming. Our stay at Bellevue naturally lacks everything that makes distance from the metropolis so delightful. There just is no such thing as a dry thaw.

I have authenticated the date of July 24, 1895, however. The dream is dated the same way in the book, July 23–24, and I know that it was the first time I grasped the general principle, just as I know that I analyzed the dream the following day. Can you put the date to use?

I was of course pleased with the review in the *Berliner Tageblatt.*[2] The first voice of someone who is impressed and who demonstrates some understanding, although incomplete; because the last remark —that a scientific technique cannot be based on it and the method cannot be taught—is incorrect. At least two of my patients have learned it as well as I. I would very much like to know who the reviewer is. He cannot really be far removed from medical circles.

Life here is very boring and I am gradually losing my sharp ear and the equanimity I need. Another patient from Zitomir in Russia, from which a woman patient came two years ago, has announced his coming; but I shall hardly continue working beyond August 1 on his account. The little thirteen-year-old girl is very interesting and will give us much to discuss. L.G. is doing excellently; last Sunday she spent the entire afternoon with us at Bellevue, stayed for three meals, and behaved superbly. I hope I can gradually begin to direct my attention to the remaining problems and difficulties, though only after the vacation break, to be sure.

I have in front of me the announcement of:[3]

*Sexuelle Osphresiologie* by Dr. Alb. Hagen.

Chapter 1 is "General Survey," which includes "genital zones" of the nose (the behavior of the nose during puberty, during menstruation, and so on). I hope he acknowledges the source of his wisdom. I also came across your name in the text of the recently published *Mimik auf Grund voluntarischer Psychologie.* (I forget the name of the author.)

I hope this summer is over soon. I need to get away once more and see something. One dries up so easily with the unavoidable restriction of one's interests throughout the year. True, it is not yet Rome —oh optimist!—but at least Berlin, and perhaps also some part of the mountains with my wife. *Vederemo!* [We shall see!]

All the most cordial greetings to you and your entire house from

Your
Sigm.

1. Fliess's daughter Pauline, or the governess.

2. The short review in the *Berliner Tageblatt und Handels-Zeitung* of June 6 calls the book "strange and wonderful."

3. Alb. Hagen, *Die sexuelle Osphresiologie. Die Beziehung des Geruchssinnes und der Gerüche zur menschlichen Geschlechtstätigkeit* (Charlottenburg: H. Barsdorf, 1901).

Vienna, July 1, 1900
IX., Berggasse 19

Dear Wilhelm,

So day is really breaking! But I am not as indifferent to it as you are. Your case always seemed to me far more depressing. In my case I can readily explain people's resistance in terms of the discomfort evoked by the subject. But your subject matter is clean and impersonal, and the only possible explanation is people's aversion to anything new that could be true, and this explanation is really too dismal. Let us take an additional factor into consideration. When the publications which will label your findings as classic appear and the scientific community demonstrates its well-known sheeplike nature in that it will generally accept what it had previously rejected, won't you then have a certain feeling of satisfaction when you imagine Hofrat Chrobak and his clinical assistants endeavoring to see only what they originally saw and then denying it to themselves and to others? Such spiteful glee, such satisfied thirst for revenge plays an important role in my case; so far I have savored too little of this delicious fare. So I am joining you in nibbling a spoonful of your meal. There is an additional factor that explains why, faced with the same judgment, we can behave so differently. Both of us probably set equally little store on the approval of our worthy contemporaries, but you are not dependent on it because you also pull teeth, cut noses, and do other things that they remunerate without getting into conflict with you. But I am supposed to make my living precisely from the opinion of the very same people whose opinion I despise. I probably would be as unconcerned as you are if I were equally independent.

I shall certainly see you during this vacation and at the place you designate. What is still questionable for me is whether it is possible at the beginning of August. I shall probably go with my wife to Trafoi for a week in August and must then avoid the period during which she is not capable of enjoyment. I did not get the money on which I had counted after all, but shall not let this prevent me from traveling. I have already become rather dull, irritable, and morose and respond to everything that does not go smoothly, as with my main cases, with all-too-intense a resonance. In addition, the heat these days is killing. It is time to stop. We shall still be able to negotiate the time of our meeting. Things in your house will settle down, and then I shall be able to ask you about your summer plans.

This is the year of revenants! My old friend Lustgarten from New York is here again; he has been very kind to my poor sister and wants me to meet him in the mountains in August. My sister arrived on July 1, still under the shock preceding mourning, miserable and haggard, with an exuberantly wild four-and-a-half-year-old girl. Several things make sense, if one reflects.

Write soon.

Most cordially,

Your
Sigm.

---

Vienna, July 10, 1900
IX., Berggasse 19

Dear Wilhelm,

It is easily explained and solved after all. Since you could not at that point give me a definite date and I had one, I postponed our congress to later during the vacation. Now that you have disclosed your plans, I can only reply that they suit me splendidly. I can be in Innsbruck on July 31 and remain with you there until August 4; the women can follow on August 4 and I shall then go to Landeck with Martha, whence we can take a carriage to Trafoi. If no child falls ill, no bridge collapses, there is no other mishap — that is how it will be. I have to overcome a slight sense of regret that once again I shall not have an opportunity to see the children and that you will see me at the height of exhaustion and ill humor, but the main thing is that we shall get together; every postponement entails risks. You did not tell me anything about your further plans, so I do not know whether anything else might have been possible during this vacation. So this is settled and I look forward to it after not having had anything to look forward to for a long time.

I remain very curious to learn the details of your rehabilitation as well as everything else that you promise me, though I cannot vouch to reciprocate. I am totally exhausted by my work and everything connected with it that is germinating, enticing, and threatening. The summer, by the way, was not too bad. The question of obtaining summer work, which appeared to be a problem a year ago, has now settled itself. On the one hand, it is not necessary; on the other, I would not have had the strength for it. The big problems are still wholly unresolved. Everything is in flux and dawning, an intellectual hell, with layer upon layer; in the darkest core, glimpses of the contours of Lucifer-Amor.

Whether or not people like the dream book is beginning to leave me cold and I am beginning to bemoan its fate. This one drop has obviously not made the stone any softer. Moreover, I have not heard about any further reviews and the occasional acknowledgments I receive in personal contacts turn out to be more offensive than the usual silent condemnation. I myself have so far not found anything in need of correction. It is true and no doubt remains true. I have postponed the short essay on the dream until October.

At any rate, our meeting on July 31 or, at the latest, August 1 is a ray of light. Let us stick to it. We can still discuss the details. It may be possible to fit in a place other than Innsbruck on the same route. But that does not really matter.

With cordial greetings to your dear wife and children,

Your
Sigm.

---

[postcard showing a commemorative plaque of Goethe]

Tarbole su lago di Garda
September 5, [1900]

For a change, a picture postcard in honor of the old man from your Sigm.

---

Vienna, September 14, 1900
IX., Berggasse 19

Dear Wilhelm,

Astonished that you stayed away longer than we did. I have been in Vienna since September 10. I am very glad you had such a good time. It was extremely nice for me, too. I shall compress my report about the six weeks. After we [Fliess and Freud] parted, we [Martha and Freud] drove to Trafoi. It was a cold, bad journey until we got there. But then Trafoi richly rewarded us; the *Gasthaus zur schönen Aussicht*[1] was comfortable and [the food was] ample. We repeatedly took the beautiful Stilfser road. Then we traveled — all our intermediate trips took place during thunderstorms and under other aggravating circumstances — to Sulden, where two of the most glorious days came our way just when we had despaired of the weather. The Schaubach hut to which we walked on "slippery ice" was imposing. Today I no longer know why I did not carry out my intention of thanking you from there for having recommended it. We then went via Merano for a stopover to the Mendola, where we met Lustgarten and other Viennese friends. It was sweltering, and [we were] lazy there. For a change we took a day's carriage ride through the Nons Valley (Clès), a treasure trove of antiquities. Martha then left for home via Bolzano and absolutely insisted that I follow Lustgarten to Venice to act as his guide. I did so, but there to my surprise I met my brother-in-law Heinrich and Rosa, who after a day and a half in Venice took me along with them to Berghof on Lake Ossiach. I was right in the swing of tramping around and was amenable to everything. In Berghof I found my sister Anna with the American children, who look just like my own, and a day later Uncle Alexander arrived unexpectedly. Finally—we have now reached August 26—came the relief. I mean Minna, with whom I drove through the Puster Valley to Trentino, making several short stops along the way. Only when I was completely in the South did I begin to feel really comfortable; under ice and snow something was missing, though at the time I could not have defined it. The sun was very amiable in Trentino, in no way as intolerable as in Vienna. From Trentino we made an excursion to the extraordinarily beautiful Castel Toblino. That is where the choice *vino santo* grows, which is pressed only at Christmas. There I also saw my beloved olive tree again. Minna wanted a taste of a high-altitude sojourn; therefore we went over a spectacular mountain road to Lavarone (1,200 meters), a high plateau on the side of the Valsugano, where we found the most magnificent forest of conifers and undreamed-of solitude. The nights began to be cool, however, so I headed directly for Lake Garda, as you must have known from the card from Torbole. We finally stopped for five days at Riva, divinely accommodated and fed, luxuriating without regrets, and untroubled—unless the meeting of the Society of Professors at the Hotel du Lac is to be regarded as a "trouble." Present: Sigm. Mayer (from Prague), whose assistant I was to have been, Tschermak, Jodl, Felsenreich from Vienna, Dimmer from Graz, Hildebrand from Innsbruck. We kept away. Two long boat trips took us one time to Salo and the other to Sirmione, where I climbed around in the ruins of what is purported to be Catullus' villa.

On September 8 I took Minna to Merano, where she is supposed to stay for either a few weeks or a few months to cure her pulmonary apicitis [inflammation]. I believe I have told you that the recurrence of this affliction, for which she was sent to Sicily at the age of seventeen, casts a shadow on the immediate future. I arrived feeling outrageously merry and well in Vienna, found my family in good spirits, and on the very same day was back in harness. Contrary to expectations, there was work; the first 200 florins were earned quickly. Let us see what will come next.

So far only two of my important cases are back, F. and L.—the latter after she had conducted herself splendidly with her parents, which earned me a very gracious letter from her father, G. The rest involves all sorts of doings. As far as the psychosis of one of my long-standing patients is concerned, I must be prepared for a great deal.

Unfortunately I learned that Mela was seriously ill. I found Oscar in bad shape and I am really glad that tomorrow, Saturday, the transport from Brühl to the town apartment is to take place. There is nothing good to report about the two old people either, as you already know. Oscar has a difficult year ahead of him. He still found time to be indignant about my having been passed over again, for in fact—one August day all those proposed were elevated to professors with the single exception of my humble self. I was so little affected by it that I remembered it only via Oscar. But at least Königstein got it.

The first day also brought a minor idea concerning the psychological roots (or one of the roots) of superstition.[2] This is how I got to it: I hired a carriage and asked the coachman to take me to Ditrichsteingasse. I wanted to see whether the old lady who is now in her ninety-first year and will not, after all, reach one hundred, was back in Vienna. The driver took me to the wrong street, even though previously he had taken me to the right place on numerous occasions. I now said, "If I were superstitious, I would take this as an omen indicating that she will die during the year. But since I have nothing to do with the coachman's mistake, it is an accident as far as I am concerned." I am now on my guard against taking the accident as psychologically significant. If I myself had gone astray instead of the driver, it would be called an "accident" by someone else. I knew that I wanted to express something by this mistake. If we attribute significance to an external accidental happening, we project to the outside our knowledge that our inner accident is invariably intentional (unconsciously). This dark knowledge therefore is the source of our belief in the appropriateness of accidents, hence of superstition.

Otherwise I am still quite lazy. I am expecting Martha and the children to return home tomorrow. Today is the first day I have not been to Bellevue.

With the most cordial greetings and hoping to hear from you soon,

Your
Sigm.

1. Literally, the inn with a nice view.
2. This incident is reported in the *Psychopathology of Everyday Life* (*S.E.* 6:256–258).

---

September 24, 1900

Dear Wilhelm,

Many thanks for your letter and the clipping; am replying to the latter today. I *must*, after all, take an interest in *reality* in sexuality, which one learns about only with great difficulty. Am slowly writing the "Psychology of Everyday Life" (to be in error—madness).[1] To my regret, I will even have to ask you to return a letter from Berchtesgaden to me, the one that contains the analysis of a number chosen at random.[2] I have fewer objections to the way the theologians go about it than to the indignant introductions of our writers, even by von Krafft-Ebing. Could recommend C. Rieger's *Castration* to you as a counterpart.[3]

I am miserable with a sinus cold.

Cordial greetings.

Your
Sigm.

1. Freud means that the sound of the German *Irren* (to err) reminds him of *Irre* (madmen).
2. See note 1 to letter of August 27, 1899, where this is referred to.
3. Conrad Rieger was professor of psychiatry at the University of Würzburg. The book referred to is *Die Castration in rechtlicher, socialer und vitaler Hinsicht* (Jena: Gustav Fischer, 1900). See note 3 to letter of November 2, 1896.

# Dora and *The Psychopathology of Everyday Life*

Vienna, October 14, 1900
IX., Berggasse 19

Dear Wilhelm,

You now have wife and child back home again, and you surely know that I saw and spoke to both of them for a moment. Robert was superb and with his divinely crude candor — not directed at me — reminded me of Paul Hammerschlag.[1] *Si parva licet componere magnis.*[2] May he retain it for a long time. Your wife obviously took the difficulties of her sick mother very much to heart. It really is something indescribably distressing, and when I heard that there were unnamed reasons against the journey to Berlin, I wondered whether it would not be best to persuade you to have nothing further to do with the treatment. She does not lose anything thereby, because what you want cannot happen. And perhaps she may gain something, because Breuer might do on his own what he would never do on request. I know him; he cannot be influenced, and it is not possible to break with him.

But I am personally far too involved to have a reliable opinion. As you said yourself, you are now asking my pardon for all sorts of thoughts you had about my relationship with him, and Ida has never before so quickly and so frequently agreed with me in all sorts of things — which inwardly must be a displacement of the one unadmitted correction. I wish there had been a more harmless occasion to be proved right. So I must take great pains not to look like an agitator. I really suffered a great deal before I tore myself away from him; an additional factor was the difficulty I had in gaining some understanding of his behavior, which you can now do without trouble.

Your wife with her fine flair stressed a remark that Breuer made directly to her: Mama has said that she likes taking digitalis if he gives it to her. That really is the essential thing for him. Through a lucky card game, not through knowledge or ability, he won the game of life and made his fortune. Woe to the one who dares attack him!

Enough of this. I hope to hear from you about what is happening. I myself am writing the dream [essay] without real pleasure and am becoming a professor by way of absentmindedness while collecting material for the "Psychology of Everyday Life."[3] It has been a lively time and has brought a new patient, an eighteen-year-old girl, a case that has smoothly opened to the existing collection of picklocks.[4]

For the "Psychology of Everyday Life" I would like to borrow from you the nice motto, *Nun ist die Welt von diesem Spuk so voll* . . .[5] Otherwise I am reading Greek archaeology and reveling in journeys I shall never make and treasures I shall never possess.

The children are well; the news from Merano favorable.

With most cordial greetings,

Your
Sigm.

P.S. There was a stupid review of the dream [book] in the *Münchener allgemeine Zeitung* on October 12.[6]

1. Paul Hammerschlag was the son of Freud's teacher, Samuel Hammerschlag, about whom Freud wrote an interesting obituary. In 1893 the younger Hammerschlag married Bertha Breuer (1870–1962), the eldest daughter of Josef and Mathilde Breuer. See Hirschmüller (1978, p. 48).

2. See note 2 to letter of October 4, 1892.

3. At some point Freud changed the title of this article from "Psychology of Everyday Life" to "Psychopathology of Everyday Life." It was later published several times in book form.

4. This was the Dora case, published in 1905 as "Fragment of an Analysis of a Case of Hysteria."

5. This quotation (The world is so full of spookiness . . .) was in fact used as the motto. It comes from Goethe's *Faust*, Part 2, scene 5. As Schönau (1968, p. 85) points out, Freud's associations must have included the rest of the verse (translated by Bayard Taylor):

Ere in the obscure I sought it, such was I,—
Ere I had cursed the world so wickedly.
Now fills the air so many a haunting shape,
That no one knows how best he may escape.
What though one day with rational brightness beams,
The night entangles us in webs of dreams.

6. The review, by Ludwig Karell, appeared in the *Beilage zur [Münchener] allgemeinen Zeitung*. It is not critical and is composed almost entirely of quotations from the book. The reviewer comments that children often wish the death of their parents for "trivial causes, such as refusing them a treat."

October 23, 1900
IX., Berggasse 19

Dear Wilhelm,

Only my very best wishes, a friend's handshake across the distance Berlin-Vienna; no gift such as last year, when I was able to greet you with the firstborn of the dream book. May everything and everyone around you thrive and compensate you for the unavoidable decline of the older generations. Your work, as an organically growing creation, is included in this wish!

I am having a quieter time, enlivened by Martin's throat infection and Minna's return.

Most cordially,

Your
Sigm.

---

November 21, 1900
IX., Berggasse 19

Dear Wilhelm,

You will find several items of interest in the recently published *Geschlechtstrieb und Schamgefühl* by Havelock Ellis; [for example,] p. 113:[1] "It is somewhat curious, however, that at the same time as Fliess, though in apparent independence, and from a different point of view, another worker also suggested that there is a 23-day physiological cycle (John Beard, *The Span of Gestation and the Cause of Birth*, Jena, 1897). Beard approaches the question from the embryological standpoint, and argues that there is what he terms an 'ovulation unit' of about $23\frac{1}{2}$ days, in the interval from the end of one menstruation to the beginning of the next. Two 'ovulation units' make up one 'critical unit,' and the length of pregnancy, according to Beard, is always a multiple of the 'critical unit'; in man, the gestation period amounts to six critical units."

I have not heard from you and yours for an eternally long time. As for me, nothing but monotony, not without worries.

Cordial greetings.

Your
Sigm.

1. I have substituted the original English passage, rather than retranslate the German. See Havelock Ellis, *Studies in the Psychology of Sex*, vol. 1, *The Evolution of Modesty*, . . . (Philadelphia: J. A. Davis, 1900). The quotation is from p. 113 in the English also. The sentence before it reads, "Although Fliess brings forward a number

of minutely-observed cases, I cannot say that I am yet convinced of the reality of this 23-day cycle."

---

Vienna, November 25, 1900
IX., Berggasse 19

Dear Wilhelm,

My suspicion that your long silence meant bad news was correct after all. I am accustomed to this from past times when it used to mean that you yourself were feeling *very* bad. Fortunately it is no longer that!

I myself would not have waited so long with my inquiry if I had not promised myself at the beginning of this year's exchange of letters to refrain under all circumstances from complaining to you so much. You see how quickly we then lose track of each other; after all, you yourself write, "I did not reply because I had nothing to report, at least nothing pleasant." If one had to wait for that! So perhaps something in between: just a little complaining, but writing more frequently.

Your news caused me great pain. So it does not recede, but comes and goes periodically and probably adds something with each new phase of advance. I believe that is always the case with paranoia. There is no cure for it other than its subsidence with the preservation of repression. In comparison to this, its periodic nature is a blessing.

With regard to the other matter, which provides just as little cause for good humor (the maternal on the other side), I know most of it *au fur et à mesure* [as it happens]. I see Oscar very frequently because Minna has chosen him as her physician. And you know him in this respect — and we are in agreement about him in this respect — that his reliability and dedication leave nothing to be desired. So we are really exploiting him thoroughly now. Not everything about her condition is entirely clear, nor is the degree to which worries are justified. I do not want to fill this letter with the details; after all, we shall soon have the answer. The most striking feature is that her pulse rate is 130 and beyond.

In my work I am not exactly at a standstill; on a subterranean level it is probably proceeding quite well, but it is certainly not a time of harvest, of conscious mastery. There probably will be no more surprising findings at all. The [main] viewpoints probably have been put together. All that is missing is the organization and the detailed elaboration. I do not see any prospect of substantially shortening the duration of treatment; it will scarcely be possible to widen the scope of indications.

It is completely uncertain when I shall get to the presentation, if ever. This time there must be no errors in it, nothing provisional; thus I shall go by Horace's rule: *Nonum prematur in annum.*[1] Moreover, who is interested in it? Who is asking for it? *Cui bono* [For whose benefit] should I undertake this work? I have already resigned myself to living like someone who speaks a foreign language or like Humboldt's parrot.[2] Being the last of one's tribe—or the first and perhaps the only one—these are quite similar situations.

I shall not fail to welcome your dear wife here in December. Let me hear more from you and cordial greetings from

Your
Sigm.

1. From the *Ars Poetica:* "Let it be kept quiet to the ninth year."

2. In a chapter of *Ansichten der Natur* titled "Über die Wasserfälle des Orinoco," Alexander von Humboldt refers to the story of a parrot. According to an old legend of the Guareca Indians, the Aturi Indians, threatened by a cannibalistic tribe, sought refuge on a cliff and died out. The sole survivor, an ancient parrot, could not be understood because he spoke the language of the extinct tribe. The legend became the subject of a poem by Ernst Curtius. Freud might have had the following line in mind:

> Einsam ruft er, unverstanden,
> in die fremde Welt hinein.
>
> (Alone, he calls out, not understood,
> To the alien world.)

---

Vienna, January 1, 1901
IX., Berggasse 19

My dear one,

I am tossing the "Psychopathology of Everyday Life" aside so as to answer you immediately, now that your letter has at last broken the alarming silence. I could not make up my mind to press you once more for news when you had shown so clearly that writing was burdensome for you and that you were not moved by a need to communicate. I explained the otherwise inexplicable phenomenon correctly to myself and therefore tolerated my deep loneliness with relative calm. I can well imagine how greatly your mother's illness must have affected you—all logic notwithstanding, because I know you have not been close to each other for a long time, but precisely for this reason you were affected even more deeply.

I am quite content now that I did not come to Berlin at Christmas.

I will gladly bring you up to date on what can be reported from here. It is not very much. The monotony is interrupted by the writing of "Everyday Life," which has progressed rather nicely and gathers all sorts of private matters. My few patients are doing well. The children are thriving, with the exception of an occasional poem by Martin, one of which I enclose, since you have always been one of his admirers. No striking change in Minna. Now and then there are disturbances of her general condition by slight fluctuations of temperature. Otherwise she feels well if she rests and has an ice bag. The same tachycardia with pain when she gets up; no other neurotic symptoms. I am very much opposed to the diagnosis of Basedow, even its *formes frustissimes.*[1] Oscar functions as a caring observer, who does not know what the matter is either. That is about all.

I certainly cannot easily forget your wife's visit and the few fifteen-minute talks I had with her. It is therefore all the more sad that I have to base my hope of seeing her again on an "unfortunately." Let me just ask you: Should we wait with our exchange of letters until a time when neither of us has any hardships? And would this not mean asking too much and showing too little friendship?

Cordial greetings to you, wife, and children from all my family, who have shared my concerns during these past weeks.

Your
Sigm.

*Winter*[2]

The streets are shining so fluffy* and white
And the squares are covered with snow,
The pond, the pool, and the lake
Are frozen to shiny ice.
The wind is blowing so eerie and cold,
It blows from the East and the North.
Many a poor child is crying because of the bitter cold
And seeks shelter and refuge.
  I cheerfully† go to school,
  Am not going for the first time today.
  On my back rests the satchel
  And between my arms lies the ruler.

* The first snow this year came, of course, only last evening.
† A lie, of course. He thoroughly dislikes going.

1. Formes frustes are atypical forms of a disease.
2. In the German, Martin's verse rhymes.

January 10, 1901
IX., Berggasse 19

Dear Wilhelm,

The enclosed letter of appreciation, which incidentally I honestly earned for myself, deserves to be put in your hands because your share in this matter was decisive. I thank you very much for it.

I am not very busy, mentally rather lively, and for this reason am writing two essays simultaneously, that is, in competition: in addition to "Everyday Life," "Dreams and Hysteria: Fragment of an Analysis." Have not yet decided where to publish it.[1]

Once the clouds have passed, I hope to hear from you again.

*Wenn auch die Wolke sie verhüllt . . .* [2]

Most cordially,

Your
Sigm.

1. See note 4 to letter of October 14, 1900.

2. "Though the clouds obscure it . . ." Gerhard Fichtner has pointed out to me that this is adapted from Friedrich Kind's libretto of Carl Maria von Weber's opera *Der Freischütz*, written in 1817. The quotation comes from the aria by Agathe:

Und ob die Wolke sie verhülle,
Die Sonne bleibt am Himmelszelt!
Es waltet dort ein heilger Wille,
Nicht blindem Zufall dient die Welt!
Das Auge, rein und ewig klar,
Nimmt aller Wesen liebend wahr!

(Though the clouds obscure it,
The sun remains in the firmament.
A holy will reigns there;
The world is not the servant of blind chance!
God's eye, pure and ever clear
Perceives all creatures lovingly.)

---

Vienna, January 25, 1901
IX., Berggasse 19

Dear Wilhelm,

Yes, you have now become a great man in Vienna and the surrounding hamlets. Arthur Schiff[1] has made you into that and is almost even greater than you, because he is ready with an explanation of what you merely discovered. Of course I did not attend the meetings, but I have heard and read about them. But by now you know all that from other sources. Deuticke placed seven copies of your once despised *Beziehungen* next to one another to revive the memory of the reading public as they gaze into the store window.

If it took about three and a half years for people to duplicate your cocaine experiment in dysmenorrhea, you now have a unit of measurement to calculate when they will check the product of 28 × 23. At that point I shall no longer write to you; that is, I mean by that time I shall already have been relieved of the obligation.

A veil has lifted from Minna's illness. In connection with a strophanthus[-induced] diarrhea she developed stomach and abdominal pains last week; during one of the following nights she had an especially severe attack of pain localized in the left transverse colon, so that the whole thing reminded me of an awful case of embolism of the mesenteric artery that I once saw in a cardiac patient. The next day, and since then, she has had bloody stools—and now, in addition, bits of mucus and what looks like shreds of tissue. There is no doubt of the existence of an intestinal ulcer. But was it really an embolism? Rie claims to have noticed impure heart sounds throughout those days. She takes only milk now; pain rules her days. I have all sorts of fears about what the future will bring.

I finished "Dreams and Hysteria" yesterday, and today I already miss a narcotic. It is a fragment of an analysis of a case of hysteria in which the explanations are grouped around two dreams; so it is really a continuation of the dream book. In addition, it contains resolutions of hysterical symptoms and glimpses of the sexual-organic foundation of the whole. It is the subtlest thing I have written so far and will put people off even more than usual. Still, one does one's duty and does not write for the day alone. The essay has already been accepted by Ziehen, who does not realize that I shall soon inflict the "Psychopathology of Everyday Life" on him as well. How long Wernicke will put up with these cuckoo's eggs is his business.

My cordial greetings, and I hope to hear soon that the pressure has been lifted from you.

Your faithful
Sigm.

1. See note 2 to letter of January 30, 1901.

Vienna, January 30, 1901
IX., Berggasse 19

Dear Wilhelm,

I have much to reply to, and that has not happened for a long time. As to Minna's condition, I know the following: without doubt there is an ulcer; but nothing whatsoever indicates that it is duodenal. In view of the blood and the pain, Oscar's consultant, B. Hammerschlag (who, by the way, is confused by all this), even wanted to induce us to localize it in the rectum. I believe it is in the colon (flexus). It started with an embolism; but a tbc [tubercular] ulcer apparently can be excluded. Throughout these days Oscar has heard impure sounds; a few days earlier there was a slight, but otherwise not ascertainable increase in temperature. That is all the material we have. No one really has a clear picture, but it is beginning to dawn on us that it might be a cardiac affliction, the origin and significance of which are still unknown, but which could involve endocardiac changes. Several typical stool samples were lost because of domestic mishaps, but since then Oscar has recognized fibrin clots in the admixtures [stool samples] in question.

Her general condition has greatly improved during the past days and consequently we are in better spirits. A functional or neurotic illness surely cannot be diagnosed. The whole business is uncanny.

"Dreams and Hysteria," if possible, should not disappoint you. The main thing in it is again psychology, the utilization of dreams, and a few peculiarities of unconscious thought processes. There are only glimpses of the organic [elements], that is, the erotogenic zones and bisexuality. But bisexuality is mentioned and specifically recognized once and for all, and the ground is prepared for detailed treatment of it on another occasion. It is a hysteria with tussis nervosa and aphonia, which can be traced back to the character of the child's sucking, and the principal issue in the conflicting thought processes is the contrast between an inclination toward men and an inclination toward women.

In the meantime "Everyday Life," half finished, has been taking a rest but will soon be continued. I even have a third [essay], something small, in mind; I have a lot of free time on my hands just now and need to occupy myself. This year I have three to four fewer daily sessions, and therefore feel much better,[1] but suffer a certain financial discomfort.

I did not make too much of a mistake about the date. I was tolerant enough to credit the public only with the time since the publication of *Beziehungen*, which I gave as 1897, and it was published in 1896 at Christmas(?), after all. So, it has been more than four years.—The second discussion in Vienna, I hear, was even more disgraceful than the first.[2] These people are incorrigible. In the same breath with which they should be ashamed to have to admit that they so wrongly dismissed what could easily be proved and yet was quite extraordinary in your book, they now scoff at its more difficult part; and no self-criticism tells them that if they were proved to be wrong and the author right, there might even be something to the other part that they should first reflect on.[3] Incorrigible and therefore enough of it!

Grossmann[4] in Vienna is as disgusting as G. in Berlin. The matter is correct, very old, and has *no* connection with your findings. He once showed me an epileptic brother-in-law of his who could not breathe because his nose was obstructed and I advised him to clear the nose, to see if this might not have a positive influence on the attacks as well. I was permitted to observe the operations(!) on several occasions and was appalled by his clumsiness, helplessness, and lack of foresight.

Do you not think that this would be the right moment to put together on some three pages the few additions you have to the current topic—Head's zones, the effect of herpes zoster, and whatever else you may have, and have them published? Keeping your name before the plebeians would, after all, be a way of assuring a certain amount of attention later on for the big biological things that are more important to you. People follow only authority, after all, and that can be acquired only by doing something that is within their comprehension.

In the midst of the present and material depression I am tormented by the temptation to spend this year's Easter week in Rome. There is no justification for it whatsoever—nothing has been accomplished, and external circumstances will probably also make it impossible. Let us hope for better times. I ardently wish that you may soon have such times to report.

Most cordially yours,

Sigm.

1. The German text in *Anfänge* reads *psychisches,* but the original letter clearly says *physisches.*

2. This is a reference to a paper by Arthur Schiff, "Über die Beziehungen zwischen Nase und weiblichen Sexualorganen," which was given at the Gesellschaft der Ärzte in Vienna on January 25, 1901, and reported in the *Wiener klinische Rundschau* of January 27. The first discussion includes comments by Emil Redlich, Moriz Weil, Benjamin Gomperz, and Michael Grossmann. The discussion Freud refers to was reported by Ottokar von Chiari in no. 5, p. 76, and is critical. Chrobak, however, was "completely convinced of Schiff's observations." The article by Schiff supported

Fliess's views, and especially his 1897 book, *Die Beziehungen*; hence Freud's comment. See note 6 to letter of January 30, 1898.

3. The complexity of this sentence is undoubtedly the result of Freud's attempt to say something positive to Fliess.

4. Michael Grossmann (1848–1927), Viennese laryngologist. See Lesky (1978, pp. 561–563).

---

Vienna, February 15, 1901
IX., Berggasse 19

Dear Wilhelm,

I shall no more get to Rome at Easter than you will. It was only your remark that explained the meaning of what otherwise was for me an unintelligible interpolation in my last letter. Behind it was surely a reminder of the promise you gave in better times to hold a congress with me on classical soil. I knew very well that such a reminder was quite out of place at the moment. I was only escaping from the present into the most beautiful of my former fantasies, and I myself noticed which one it was. Meanwhile the congresses themselves have become relics of the past; I myself am doing nothing new and, as you write, have become totally estranged from what you are doing.

All that is left for me to do is rejoice from a distance when you announce that the presentation of the great solutions is close at hand and express satisfaction with the progress of your work. So you are absolutely right to reserve all further communication on the nasal relationships for this wider context [that is, Fliess's book].

The "Psychology of Everyday Life" will also be finished in a few days, and then both essays will be corrected, sent off, and so on. All of it has been written with a certain gloomy heaviness,[1] traces of which it will not be possible to hide. The third piece I have started is something quite harmless—really a thin soup of the poor. I am collecting my notes on neurotics that I have seen during consulting hours to show what even such necessarily superficial observation reveals about the connections between *vita sexualis* and neurosis and to comment on them. In other words, I am doing roughly the same thing Gattel did at the time he made himself so unpopular in Vienna. Since I need new cases and my practice is very sparse indeed, I have only six examples in my collection so far and those are not the best. I have also introduced testing for left-handedness—with the dynamometer [for testing hand strength] and threading needles.

I cannot give you any further explanations of Minna's illness. No new insights have turned up; the intestinal ulcer seems to have healed properly; she is eating solids again; her general condition fluctuates; her pulse is still quite variable and can rise to 130 merely from talking. I perceive no trace of anything neurotic. On the whole, there is a definite improvement over the last weeks.

I did not give the lecture announced last Monday in the *Neue freie Presse*. It was again a good deed of Breuer who, badgered by the Philosophical Society, set them on me. I agreed very reluctantly and later, while preparing for it, realized that I would have to present all sorts of intimate and sexual matters, which would be quite unsuitable for a mixed audience of people who were strangers to me. So I wrote a letter calling it off (first week). Thereupon two delegates called on me and urged me to give it after all. I strongly advised against it and invited them to come and hear the lecture themselves one evening at my house (second week). In the third week I gave the two of them the lecture and was told it was wonderful, their audience would be able to handle it without objection, and so forth. The lecture was therefore set to take place in the fourth week. A few hours beforehand, however, I received an express letter to the effect that some members had raised objections after all. I was asked to start by illustrating my theory with inoffensive examples, then announce that I was now coming to risqué matters and call for an intermission so that the ladies could leave the hall. Of course I immediately canceled, but at least the letter in which I did so was spicy and salty. Such is scientific life in Vienna!

Hoping to have good news from you soon,

Your faithful
Sigm.

1. Freud uses *Dumpfheit*, a word that has many connotations and calls up associations such as staleness, somberness, mustiness, sullenness, numbness.

---

Vienna, March 3, 1901
IX., Berggasse 19

Dear Wilhelm,

A week ago Oli went to bed with something that soon proved to be measles; yesterday Ernst and Sophie and today Anna came down with it, so we now have quite a nice hospital. It went off rather well for Oli; for the others, we shall have to wait and see. We immediately sent Martin to Mrs. A., a very dear friend and patient whose only son attends the same high school, so that Martin will not have to miss school for weeks on end. He has been doing much better in school lately. Mathilde must stay at home. Minna is distinctly better; she is up and around for a few hours every day, without her pulse rising much above 100; afterward she usually has severe cardiac and intercostal pains.

I have just completed the second treatise, shall be able to correct and patch up both of them during the coming weeks, and shall then attend to arranging simultaneous publication. At his request I let Oscar read "Dreams and Hysteria," but I derived little joy from it.[1] I shall make no further attempt to break through my isolation. Otherwise these are very bleak times, outstandingly bleak!

There is a vague prospect of my arriving in Berlin next Sunday to see a patient from Vienna who is in a private sanatorium about half an hour away from the city. I plan to stay for two days. So I hope to spend a few hours in the evening with you and at last get to see the children whom I have not yet met. I shall not have as much free time as I had on previous visits to Berlin. I will have to go out to the sanatorium on the second day as well in order to properly earn my consultation fee. My sister, with whom I shall stay, also has claims on me. Consequently there will be little time left for the two of us, and I ask you not to let your work and other business be disturbed on my account. Nevertheless, I look forward to this visit as something very enjoyable. However, it is still rather uncertain; the patient's father has not yet made up his mind; and the rub of the whole business, as a *proton pseudos*,[2] is that my medical intervention is rather superfluous. I am writing about it precisely because of this uncertainty; if I knew for sure, I should have liked to surprise you. So I am letting you have the pleasure of anticipation, with which I am also prepared to make do. If I told you of this prospect only after it had come to naught, there would be nothing but disappointment. In case it materializes, I shall of course send you further details.

My cordial greetings to you and your dear wife in expectancy of the near future.

Your
Sigm.

1. A reference to the Dora case. See note 1 to letter of March 11, 1902.

2. See "Project for a Scientific Psychology" (*S.E.* 1:352), where Strachey says: "The term occurs in Aristotle's *Prior Analytics* (Book 2, Ch. 18, 66I, 16), a work dealing with the theory of the syllogism which was later included in what came to be called the *Organon.* The chapter deals with false premises and false conclusions, and the particular sentence asserts that a false statement is the result of a preceding falsity (*'proton pseudos'*)."

Two of Freud's three daughters: Anna, left, and Sophie, ages about four and six. According to a caption on the back of the photo, this is the first attempt at "feminine" needlework.

The three Freud sons. From left to right, Ernst (born 1892), Martin (born 1889), and Oliver (born 1891). The photograph was probably taken around 1900.

Vienna, March 9, 1901
IX., Berggasse 19

Dear Wilhelm,

Many thanks for your kind offer, but the opportunity seems to have passed. I have not heard since from the party concerned.

The measles have taken quite a bad turn. The day before yesterday at noon Sophie developed alarming toxic manifestations, enormous acceleration of pulse, cardiac dyspnea, arrhythmias, and septic confusion. She has improved since yesterday afternoon, except for a kind of toxic mania which has greatly changed this gentle child. The other two, Ernst and Anna, are beginning to recover from their exhaustion today. Next will be earaches and the like.

Mathilde, moreover, is in bed and today is going through her worst day. Yesterday I hired a nurse to help us. Oscar once again is marvelous. My indebtedness is becoming quite onerous.

I just heard from Ziehen in Utrecht that he will accept both works. On Thursday I concluded that nothing would come of my trip [to Berlin] and the following night (Thursday/Friday) I dreamed that I was in Berlin and saw your children, of course mixing in all sorts of things from my house.

Most cordial greetings.

Your
Sigm.

---

March 24, 1901
IX., Berggasse 19

Dear Wilhelm,

You are, of course, the sender of the *Tag* [Day]?[1] After the *Zeit* [Time] and the *Tag*, I am now hoping for the *Woche* [Week]. The reviewer, incidentally, is a man who knows how to spin out a simile and give it a twist. I was very surprised because not a single newspaper, much less a scientific periodical, has paid any attention to the year-and-a-half-old book since the reviews you are familiar with were published. Does this mean that perhaps its "day" has come? The experience you had with the *Deutsche Rundschau* really put me in a very resigned mood.[2]

We are having a cold spring. Mathilde and Sophie still are rather miserable; the others are again lively and better than before. Minna will go to Edlach for hydrotherapy at the beginning of April to speed her recovery. One becomes gradually accustomed to a new realization of the nature of "happiness": one has to assume happiness when fate does not carry out all its threats simultaneously.[3] I have heard some rumors of a brief visit of yours to Vienna. I am hoping for more.

With many thanks,

Your
Sigm.

1. *Der Tag* of March 22 contained a review entitled "Eine neue Theorie des Traumes," by Fr. Mero. The review was positive, calling Freud's work "one of the most ingenious psychological theories of the present," and saying that it was written in a highly elegant fashion. The passage that Freud may have had in mind reads: "What remains of critical attentiveness then acts only as a guardian of morals who takes pains to hang a fig leaf on the frighteningly naked, brutal drives through condensation and disguise."

2. See letter of March 23, 1900, which indicates that Fliess had told Freud he would try to get Freud's book reviewed in the *Rundschau.*

3. Possibly a reference to Alphonse Karr (1808–1890), from *Les Guêpes,* January 1842: "Des malheurs évités le bonheur se compose" (Happiness consists in misfortune that has been avoided).

---

Vienna, May 8, 1901
IX., Berggasse 19

Dear Wilhelm,

You may certainly take my birthday as an occasion to wish for yourself the continuation of your energetic mood and the repetition of such invigorating periods in between, and I shall unselfishly support this wish. Your letter lay on the birthday table with other presents that gave me pleasure and were partly connected with you, though I had asked that the wretched in-between number [of my birthdays] be overlooked. It is too small for a jubilee and much too large for a birthday boy. Your letter gave me by no means the least pleasure, except for the part about magic, which I object to as a superfluous plaster to cover your doubt about "thought reading." I remain loyal to thought reading and continue to doubt "magic."

I seem to remember having heard somewhere that only dire need brings out the best in man. I have therefore pulled myself together, as you wished—in fact, even a few weeks before you did—and have made peace with my circumstances. A basket of orchids gives me the illusion of splendor and glowing sunshine; a fragment of a Pompeiian wall with a centaur and faun transports me to my longed-for Italy.

*Fluctuat nec mergitur!*[1]

My sister-in-law is feeling better at Edlach. The cardiac changes are now readily apparent, but she is cheerful and can walk a little. So far I have been to see her twice, once with Oscar who is really a friend in need. The children decided to get out of the habit of being ill for a while, which offers the prospect of a very pleasant change. I am at present correcting the first pages of "Everyday Life," which turned out to be a hefty sixty pages. I *dis*like it tremendously and hope others will do so even more. The essay is entirely without structure and contains all sorts of forbidden † † † things.[2] I have not yet made up my mind to send off the other essay. A new patient, a young woman who was jilted, filled the gap left by the departure of Miss R., and her care is of course resolving itself just as one would wish. In other respects, too, things are no longer as quiet as they were a few weeks ago. In eight or fourteen days I am expecting a visit from the G. parents, who can be very satisfied with their daughter.

Progress in my work is apparently to be expected only by a more-than-thousandfold repetition of the very same impressions, and I am quite ready to submit to them. So far everything proves to be correct, but I cannot yet survey the full extent of the riches and cannot master them intellectually.

The Bresgen article[3] will find an attentive reader. You cannot have avoided including some new things.

Cordial greetings from

Your
Sigm.

1. "It floats but it does not sink." Expression used also in letter of September 21, 1899.

2. Freud mocks making the sign of the cross three times to protect oneself from evil. See letter of November 5, 1899.

3. Maximilian Bresgen was editor of the monthly *Sammlung zwangloser Abhandlungen aus dem Gebiete der Nasen, Ohren, Mund und Halskrankheiten.*

Vienna, June 9, 1901
IX., Berggasse 19

Dear Wilhelm,

I am using this strange Sunday to write to you once again. It is the first Sunday I have been completely free, with nothing to remind me that at other times I am a physician. My ancient lady, whom I have been visiting twice a day regularly, was taken to the country yesterday, and I am looking at the clock every fifteen minutes to see whether I am not keeping her waiting too long for her injection. Thus we still feel our shackles even after they have been removed and do not really know how to enjoy our freedom.

To answer your questions: we have not yet decided where we shall spend the summer. I think it will be somewhere near Salzburg. The negotiations with the boardinghouse on the Salzberg near Berchtesgaden have become somewhat protracted because of the slowness of these good people. At Whitsun I went with my brother to find a place in Vorarlberg. The proximity of Switzerland and the moderate prices were tempting, but nothing came of it. The cost of traveling there would cancel what we would save in the boardinghouse, and what the landscape has to offer does not justify the expense. In any event, it was more of a pretext for a Whitsun excursion than a serious intent; we spent one day at the Bodensee.

"Everyday Life" will appear in the July issue of the *Monatsschrift*. If I were to abstain from forming an opinion of my works, only your favorable opinion of them would be left. "Dreams and Hysteria" has been sent off and will probably not come to the attention of the astounded public until fall.

Your Bresgen article will certainly be welcome.

My sister-in-law left the sanatorium at Edlach yesterday and will go to her mother in Reichenhall tomorrow morning. She is feeling better; that is, she can walk for about three-quarters of an hour without difficulties. She has intermittent attacks of ulcer pains; according to her doctors' report (Oscar and Dr. Konried), the defect has now become evident. I know that one has to regard this as a favorable outcome. Since I did not take it for granted, I am very satisfied.

My wife and children have been well. The heat has been unbearable. Today we are literally longing for a thunderstorm or rain. We are to spend the evening with Oscar and Mela before their move, together with Miss G., whose parents will arrive tomorrow morning and who also hang over me like a storm cloud—but not one I long for.

You have reminded me of that beautiful and difficult time when I had reason to believe that I was very close to the end of my life, and it was your confidence that kept me going. I certainly behaved neither very bravely nor very wisely. I was too young, my instincts still too hungry, my curiosity still too great to be able to remain indifferent. But I have always lacked your optimism. It is certainly foolish to want to banish suffering and dying from this world, as we do in our New Year's wishes; it was not for this that we did away with our dear Lord God, only to lift them both from us and from our dear ones and dump them on strangers.

So I am more humble now, and more ready to bear what will come. There is no doubt that not all wishes can be fulfilled. Some things for which I fervently strove have already become impossible; why should I not have to bury a new hope each year? If you do not agree, this may be an attempt at appeasement. It may also be a judgment led astray by friendship.

It is true that it is hard to put up with complainers. This, too, I have learned to realize. I have been quite satisfied with my mood for many weeks now.

I hope to hear good news about you and your family soon. Cordial greetings to you.

Your
Sigm.

---

Vienna, July 4, 1901
IX., Berggasse 19

Dear Wilhelm,

Since my interest in you and your family is no longer being fully satisfied by our correspondence, I usually inquire at Oscar's and in this way learned about the threat of measles. I hope they pass comfortably. I have no objections whatsoever if my theoretically hardly tenable optimism proves to be right in practice as frequently as possible.

You ask so many questions that this reply is bound to be long. So my consulting hour will be a letter-writing hour.

I still am unable to tell you for certain where we are going. After a variety of plans miscarried, we hit on something improvised that will *probably* come off. During the two-day holiday at the end of June I visited Mama and Minna in Reichenhall, took a carriage ride to nearby Thumsee, and fell in love with the little place: Alpine roses right down to the road, the small green lake, glorious woods all around, with strawberries, flowers, and (I hope) mushrooms as well. So I inquired about the possibility of getting accommodations at the only inn. They are letting rooms there for the first time this year because the owner, a physician and proprietor from Bad Kirchberg who used to live there himself, died. And now the negotiations are being conducted from Reichenhall and will probably be satisfactorily concluded. Apart from the attractions of the place, it is especially important for me to stay close to my dear patient [Minna], who will probably go to the Salzberg near Berchtesgaden when Reichenhall becomes too hot.

On my return trip Sunday evening I came into unexpectedly intimate contact with Robert Breuer: we shared a compartment in the sleeping car. He was quite embarrassed, but behaved perfectly correctly.

July 5. I have just sent off a telegram confirming our arrangements at Thumsee. I shall still send you a postcard the day we depart.

L.G. is in high spirits and has turned out to be an outstanding success. She still has sensations and visions, but this "shabby remnant" does not bother her at all. You know that during my therapy the patient's general condition changes in every respect; in the process the symptoms, which require a certain degree of attention to subsist, gradually begin to shrink. Her parents were here and behaved amicably. Her father is too complicated a character to hit upon the right thing in each and every instance; the mother is hard to stomach, but a "character" in the full meaning of the word.

Papa G. is assiduously sending me newspaper clippings and articles in which either my name or the dream book is mentioned; among them was an essay on "Dream and Fairytale," published in *Lotse*—which the author, a lecturer in Munich, subsequently also sent to me.[1] He [Mr. G.] is now corresponding with me about what can be made public about the treatment in the interest of "propaganda." Whether much, little, or nothing at all comes of it, at any rate it all goes back to the moment when you mentioned my name to him.

Mr. L. was easy to diagnose: *no* actual sexual cause, not a psychological case, but neurasthenia; so earlier realities must have been retained by way of the alterations of the nose. A Viennese would of course not have followed the advice to which he will owe his recovery. But this remains a modest present in return for G.

My other clients are doing extremely well this year, though there were fewer than last year. Thanks to less drudgery, I feel incomparably better than at the same time [last year], but my brain is very tired all the same. I no longer have any new ideas, nor do I really know how to fill my free hours.

Dr. von der Leyen from Munich has called my attention to a book by L. Laistner, *The Riddle of the Sphinx* (1889), which very forcefully maintains that myths go back to dreams.[2] So far I have read its delightful preface, but my laziness has kept me from reading on. I see that he knows nothing of what is *behind* dreams; on the other hand, he appropriately seems to focus on the *anxiety* dream.

There will be no "journey south" this year; I lack my travel companion for this — Minna's illness forces Martha to stay put as well.

"Everyday Life" will see the light of day in a few days, but probably only half of it will be born, so that I cannot send you an offprint until August. It is too long for a single issue of the *Monatsschrift*.

Martin writes few poems now, but draws and paints, mostly animal fantasies with good-natured humor, and is beginning to represent movements and the like. What is perhaps more important is that he has advanced to second grade in his school with a relatively good report. Oli's entrance exam will keep us here until the 15th of this month. All my big children will also have to wait until then.

I am of course well informed about the sad changes in Kaltenleutgeben.[3] We shall go there next week and at the same time visit Königstein, whose daughter is expecting her first child. "Birth and death . . . "[4]

Your mother must really be going through agony. I imagine, given your hints, that your presentation of why some people suddenly die at the height of their powers, while others deteriorate to the very last, will be very interesting. Strangely enough, we are dissatisfied with either course.

Have you read that the English excavated an old palace in Crete (Knossos), which they declare to be the real labyrinth of Minos? Zeus seems originally to have been a bull. Our old god, too, is said to have been worshiped as a bull prior to the sublimation imposed by the Persians. This is cause for all sorts of thoughts too premature to write down.

Cordial greetings to you, and my best wishes for an easy time for you and your children during these days of imminent illness. The little one, I trust, will still be spared the infection?

Faithfully,
Your
Sigm.

1. The article, by F. von der Leyen, is a long-winded, "Germanic," romanticized discussion of dreams, with little reference to Freud's book. For a different view see Decker (1977, pp. 285–287), who gives a summary of von der Leyen's piece. See also *Origins*, p. 332n1.

2. Ludwig Laistner, *Das Rätsel der Sphinx: Grundzüge einer Mythengeschichte*, 2

vols. (Berlin: Wilhelm Hertz, 1889). Leyen, who wrote the review cited earlier in this letter, mentions this book in the review.

3. The summer residence of Fliess's in-laws.

4. Goethe's *Faust*, Part 1, scene 1.

---

Thumsee, August 7, 1901,[1]

Dear Wilhelm,

For the first time in three weeks the weather is disagreeable today and precludes any other activity; tomorrow we are going to Salzburg fór a performance of *Don Giovanni*, to which Ferstel got us tickets; that is how I come to be answering you at once today, or at any rate begin to answer.

First, business; then something serious; and pleasure at the end.

Mrs. D. would be an excellent substitute for L.G. To judge from your earlier reports, she would certainly be a suitable person for this treatment and therefore a better-than-average success could be anticipated. But I am not going back into harness before September 16 for the sake of any patient, known or unknown, and by then she may no longer have her paroxysm. I do not count on anyone until I have my hands on him. My clients are sick people, hence especially irrational and suggestible. Incidentally, the next season interests me especially. I have only one patient, a youth with obsessional neurosis, who is, so to speak, certain; and my nice old lady, who was a small but sure source of income, died during the vacation.

I enclose a testimonial by Father G. on the explicit wish of Martha, who sees that I am writing to you.

Winternitz[2] is an opportunist, a regular turncoat, and therefore especially interesting from a symptomatic viewpoint. It has always greatly astonished me that you should have the large success that dazzles people only *after forty.* It really could have come to you earlier without doing any psychic damage to you. I would like to have it myself because of the material gains, but it has failed to come about and, I suspect, will ultimately fail to come about.

I am continuously and with sympathy following the sad state of affairs in Kalt[enleutgeben] by corresponding with Oscar. I have always feared that the two of you would have very little in common after the death of the parents; but I cannot really with all my heart take your side, that is, the side of both of you. Oscar and Mela are touchingly eager to make sacrifices and are selfless in this period of illness; Oscar, whom I have known longer, has always been that way and has just demonstrated it to me once again. I cannot disregard my indebtedness to him and therefore forgive him most of his lack of understanding for my findings — an attitude in which he is not unique, after all. Nor would it have to be that way between you and him. "They are not really human beings" appears to me to be a characterization that just does not apply to these two, because they indeed behave correctly and well as human beings.

There is no concealing the fact that the two of us have drawn apart to some extent. In this or that I can see how much. So, too, in the judgment of Breuer. I no longer despise him and have not for some time; I have felt his strength. If he is dead as far as you are concerned, then he is still exerting his power posthumously. What is your wife doing other than working out in a dark compulsion the notion that Breuer once planted in her mind when he told her how lucky she was that I did not live in Berlin and could not interfere with her marriage? In this you too have come to the limit of your perspicacity; you take sides against me and tell me that "the reader of thoughts merely reads his own thoughts into other people," which renders all my efforts valueless.

If that is what you think of me, just throw my "Everyday Life" unread into the wastepaper basket. It is full of references to you — manifest ones, for which you supplied the material, and concealed ones, for which the motivation goes back to you. The motto, too, was a gift from you. Apart from anything that might remain of the content, you can take it as a testimonial to the role you have played for me up to now. Having announced it in this way, I feel I can send you the essay when it comes into my hands without further words.

As to Breuer, you are certainly quite right about *the* brother, but I do not share your contempt for friendship between men, probably because I am to a high degree party to it.[3] In my life, as you know, woman has never replaced the comrade, the friend. If Breuer's male inclination were not so odd, so timid, so contradictory — like everything else in his mental and emotional makeup — it would provide a nice example of the accomplishments into which the androphilic current in men can be sublimated.

I promised that I would also write to you about "pleasure." Thumsee really is a little paradise, especially for the children who are fed wildly here, and fight with one another and the other guests over the boats in which they then vanish from their parents' anxious eyes. Keeping company with the fish has already made me thoroughly stupid, but in spite of that I do not yet have the carefree spirit that I usually get on vacations, and I have a hunch that it will not be possible to do without eight to twelve days of olive oil and wine. My brother, perhaps, will be my travel companion. I cannot report any real improvement in my sister-in-law, but at least she maintains the status quo. She does not move about much; her mood is uneven and depressed. The intestinal ulcer causes continuous discomfort.

And now, the main thing! As far as I can see, my next work will be called "Human Bisexuality." It will go to the root of the problem and say the last word it may be granted me to say—the last and the most profound. For the time being I have only one thing for it: the chief insight which for a long time now has built itself upon the idea that repression, my core problem, is possible only through reaction between two sexual currents. I shall need about six months to put the material together and hope to find that it is now possible to carry out the work. But then I must have a long and serious discussion with you. The idea itself is yours. You remember my telling you years ago, when you were still a nose specialist and surgeon, that the solution lay in sexuality. Several years later you corrected me, saying that it lay in bisexuality—and I see that you are right. So perhaps I must borrow even more from you; perhaps my sense of honesty will force me to ask you to coauthor the work with me; thereby the anatomical-biological part would gain in scope, the part which, if I did it alone, would be meager. I would concentrate on the psychic aspect of bisexuality and the explanation of the neurotic. That, then, is the next project for the immediate future, which I hope will quite properly unite us again in scientific matters as well.

Most cordial greetings to you and your family. Let me hear something from you.

Your
Sigm.

1. Marie Bonaparte recorded in her notebook that when she showed this letter to Freud, he told her it was a "very important letter."

2. Probably Wilhelm Winternitz (1834–1917). See Lesky (1965, p. 336).

3. *Weil ich in hohem Grade Partei bin.*

# End of the Relationship

September 19, 1901
IX., Berggasse 19

Dear Wilhelm:

I received your card a few hours before my departure. I should write to you about Rome now, but that is difficult. It was overwhelming for me too and, as you know, the fulfillment of a long-cherished wish. As such fulfillments are if one has waited too long for them, this one was slightly diminished, yet a high point of my life. But while I was totally and undisturbedly absorbed in antiquity (I could have worshiped the abased and mutilated remnant of the Temple of Minerva near the forum of Nerva), I found I could not freely enjoy the second [the medieval, Christian] Rome; the atmosphere troubled me. I found it difficult to tolerate the lie concerning man's redemption, which raises its head to high heaven — for I could not cast off the thought of my own misery and all the other misery I know about.

I found the third, the Italian, Rome full of promise and likable.

I was frugal in my pleasures, though, and did not try to see everything in twelve days. I not only bribed the Trevi [fountain], as everyone does, I also — and I invented this myself — dipped my hand in the Bocca della Verità at Santa Maria Cosmedin and vowed to return. The weather was hot, but quite tolerable until one day — luckily not until the 9th — the sirocco came up, knocking me out. I did not recover at all. After I returned home, I developed a gastroenteritis which I believe I got on the day of the journey and from which I am still suffering now, though without complaining. My family returned home one night earlier than I; I am still minimally occupied.

Your last letter actually did me some good. I can now understand the attitude you have expressed in your letters to me over the past year. This was, incidentally, the first time you have told me anything but the truth.

Within myself I know that what you say about my attitude toward your big work is unjust. I know how often I have thought about it with pride and trepidation and how disturbed I have been when I was unable to follow you in this or that conclusion. You know that I lack any mathematical talent whatsoever and have no memory for numbers and measurements; this may perhaps have given you the impression that I do not retain anything of what you told me. All that can be gathered from numbers in the way of viewpoints and qualities has not, I think, been wasted on me. Perhaps you have been too quick to give up on me as a confidant. A friend who has a right to contradict, who because of his ignorance can scarcely ever become dangerous, is not without value to one who takes such dark paths and associates with very few people, all of whom admire him unconditionally and uncritically.

The only thing that hurt me was another misunderstanding in your letter: that you connected my exclamation "But you are undermining the whole value of my work!" with my therapy. In this context I really was not thinking of whitewashing! I was sorry to lose my "only audience," as our Nestroy called it. For whom do I still write? If as soon as an interpretation of mine makes you uncomfortable, you are ready to agree that the "reader of thoughts" perceives nothing in the other,[1] but merely projects his own thoughts, you really no longer are my audience either and must regard my entire method of working as being just as worthless as the others do.

I do not comprehend your answer concerning bisexuality. It is obviously very difficult to understand each other. I certainly had no intention of doing anything but working on my contribution to the theory of bisexuality, elaborating the thesis that repression and the neuroses, and thus the independence of the unconscious, presuppose bisexuality.

You will by now have seen from the relevant reference to your priority in "Everyday Life" that I have no intention of expanding my role in this insight. But the establishment of some link to the general biological and anatomical aspects of bisexuality would be, after all, indispensable in any such work. Since almost everything I know about it comes from you, all I can do is cite you or get this introduction entirely from you. Right now I am not at all eager to appear in print. Meanwhile we will no doubt have a chance to discuss it. One cannot simply say, "The conscious is the dominant, the unconscious the underlying sexual factor," without grossly oversimplifying the very much more complicated matter, even though that is of course the basic fact. I am working on a more psychological essay, "Forgetting and Repressing," which, however, I shall also keep to myself for a long time to come.[2]

The date of your lecture for Bresgen's [journal] has passed. I await it eagerly; has it been postponed?

I greet you cordially and am, in the expectation of good news of you and yours,

Your
Sigm.

1. Freud uses the singular, *am anderen*. He could mean patients in general or Fliess in particular.

2. This paper was, in fact, never published.

---

September 20, 1901
IX., Berggasse 19

Dear Wilhelm:

*Tableau!* [Amazing!] Our letters crossed! Only yesterday I inquired about your essay and here it is. I read through it the first time and am glad to say you have never before produced anything so clear, so concise, and so rich in substance. And what a blessing that there is no doubt about its truth! Thank you also for reserving a spot for me.[1] I was very pleased too about the herpes. And throughout one can sense that you have still more material, but are able to put your riches aside and know how to limit yourself. I believe that characterizes the classical style.

Doesn't the title fall strangely short of the "causal" connection between nose and sexual organ? [Is it] an abbreviation for "Changes in the Nose and Sex Organ"? But it really doesn't matter; I don't want to be pedantic.

My cordial thanks.

Your
Sigm.

1. The reference is to Fliess's *Über den ursächlichen Zusammenhang von Nase und Geschlechtsorgan.* There is a passage that reads, "The typical cause of neurasthenia in young people of both sexes is masturbation (Freud), which in the case of older people is frequently replaced by conjugal [mutual] masturbation" (1st ed., p. 7).

Vienna, October 7, 1901
IX., Berggasse 19

Dear Wilhelm:

It is three weeks since Mrs. D., whom you referred, arrived here; so I ought to have reported to you about her some time ago.

She is, of course, just the person I need; a difficult constitutional case, in which all the keys fit and all the strings respond. Painless work with her is hardly possible; for this she is too fond of having pain and of giving pain, but I expect that success is certain and will last.

Unfortunately there are other things in the way. Her husband, who with all his artistry appears to be seriously *meschugge* (he came here with her), has not yet agreed. He released her for three months only, which I of course rejected, but even this concession was not real because he wanted to pack her off the very same evening and she is daily expecting him to come and fetch her. If he does, she will go with him. Already she can no longer stand being without him.

If this is how things are in relation to time, they appear to be no more certain in relation to money. Is everything really so unfavorable, or has *she* already succeeded in confounding me? Briefly, it is by no means impossible that I shall shortly declare that it is better not to start building on so shaky a foundation. It is very improbable that she will achieve anything of value in three months in spite of her intelligence. But the husband approached me with such obvious, jealous mistrust that I cannot hope to make any impression on him by arguing this out.

Perhaps everything will still turn out all right. I only wanted to prepare you for the possibility that you may see her again sooner than you expected, and to justify myself in advance if that is how I must respond to the great trouble you have taken.

Since we now write to each other so rarely, I have not been able to thank you before.

With cordial greetings,

Your
Sigm.

Vienna, November 2, 1901
IX., Berggasse 19

Dear Wilhelm:

You are surely entitled to hear from time to time how matters stand with your patient, and I write about her the more gladly because I am in no mood for anything else.

You have indeed selected a case for me that is made to order for this therapy. I can say that so far it has gone extremely well—perhaps also because it is easy for me to take an interest in this type of character. I shall no doubt give you more of the details verbally sometime when I can violate discretion with impunity. Once again, however, everything falls into place, at least according to my more recent conceptualization, and the instrument responds willingly to the instrumentalist's sure touch. Not that she does not make enough attempts to make my life difficult; she has already made them and will do so again. My dispirited letter, to which you responded with valid information, was a consequence of my being taken in by the mountains of difficulties she piled in front of me. I shall be less easily fooled a second time—at least, that is my intention. She is at any rate an interesting and worthwhile person.

I am glad to be able to tell you this and greet you cordially.

Your
Sigm.

---

Vienna, December 7, 1901
IX., Berggasse 19

Dear Wilhelm:

Mrs. D. has just said good-bye. The concerns I expressed to you after the first two weeks were not wholly unjustified. As you know, her husband forcibly interfered with the treatment, giving considerations of time and money as his reasons, although—entirely in accord with your explanations—these may have been put forward only to mask his jealousy. Finally he sent a letter that made it impossible to utilize the extension he had conceded until the 19th of this month. I myself advised her to return home immediately. In general, the man behaved so offensively toward me that it took a good deal of effort on my part to go through with it as long as I did.

The treatment was so short—ten weeks—that any permanent cure is out of the question. Nor can I predict how things will go with the patient in the immediate future. On the other hand, the matter went so splendidly that the work cannot possibly fail to bear some fruit. When the storm now unleashed has run its course, it should be possible to assess the achievement.

In any event, she was the most suitable and most interesting patient you have referred to me, for which I thank you. It is not the fault of either of us that things did not turn out better. Professor D. just did not succeed in transferring to me his trust in you. I am going through a difficult series of chance events, in which predominantly unpleasant things are happening to me. I am continuously practicing endurance.

Again, then, my cordial thanks.

Your
Sigm.

---

Vienna, January 17, 1902
IX., Berggasse 19

Dear Wilhelm:

I thank you for your inquiry to which I am replying forthwith. Scarlet fever broke out with Ernst and Anna on the first day of Christmas, still very light, and so far has run its course without complications. I see the patients in the morning before I take my bath and find them cheerful, although palefaced and subdued.

It was not possible to send the other children out of the house because of the well-known uncertainties. So we isolated them as much as possible in the house, and so far there is no suspicion of any new illness. Since they are not allowed to go to school, they are enjoying life and are thriving magnificently.

My sister, too, is seriously ill. We are having highly abnormal weather and on the whole peculiarly bad times.

Further thanks for Lubarsch.[1] Miss G.R. had already sent me the two issues. So far I have found only two reviews in professional journals, *Zeitschrift für Psychologie und Physiologie der Sinnesorgane*[2] and *Monatsschrift für Neurologie und Psychiatrie* [*sic*]; naturally both are shocked by the intrusion into science.[3]

I know nothing of you and hope I may assume that all is well.

Cordial greetings.

Your
Sigm.

1. A positive review/article, "Schlaf und Traum," by O. Lubarsch that appeared in *Die Woche* ("There can be no doubt that Freud's work is extraordinarily rich for the understanding of dreams"). Lubarsch ends by saying that the dream is, as Freud

recognizes, of great value in therapy and for the understanding of symptoms, and "we recognize that nothing moves us in a dream that does not hold meaning for us in life." The dream thus "permits a glimpse into the deepest folds of our own hearts."

2. The review, by W. Stern of Breslau, appeared in 1901. It is particularly disagreeable in tone: "A special tendency, namely, to see sexual meaning in all possible and impossible dream contents, is made so much of in the book that it would serve no purpose to cite a single example: the fact that the material comes primarily from hysterics probably is responsible. The unacceptability of this kind of dream interpretation as a scientific method must be emphatically stressed, for the danger is great that uncritical minds might take pleasure in this interesting fantasy game and thereby drag us into complete mysticism and chaotic arbitrariness — one can then prove anything with anything."

3. The review is by a Herr Liepmann of Berlin and also appeared in 1901. It too is unpleasant and ends with these words: "In brief, in this work the clever manipulator of thought triumphs over the scientific researcher. There is a danger that in less gifted minds his example will unleash a fantastical psychology of the anus, which, wallowing in the joys of interpretation, will burrow into the dark recesses of emotional life and throw to the winds the painstakingly gained insights of scientific psychological research."

---

March 8, 1902
IX., Berggasse 19

Dear Wilhelm:

I am glad to be able to let you know that finally the long-withheld and recently rather desirable professorship has come about. Next week the *Wiener Zeitung* will announce it to the public who, I expect, will honor such a seal of official approval. It has been a rather long time since you received any news from me that could be associated with pleasant expectations.

I greet you cordially.

Your
Sigm.

---

Vienna, March 11, 1902
IX., Berggasse 19

Dear Wilhelm:

Just imagine what an "excellency" can accomplish! He can even bring it about that I once again hear your dear voice in a letter. But since you connect such nice things with the news — recognition, mastery, and the like — my usual, harmful urge to honesty obliges me to tell you exactly how it finally came about.

It was my doing, in fact. When I came back from Rome, my enjoyment of life and work was somewhat heightened and that of martyrdom somewhat diminished. I found my practice had almost melted away; I withdrew my last work[1] from publication because just a little earlier I had lost my last audience in you.* I could foresee that waiting for recognition might take up a good portion of my life and that in the meantime none of my fellow men would bother about me. And I did want to see Rome again, take care of my patients, and keep my children in good spirits. So I made up my mind to break with strict virtue and take appropriate steps, as other humans do. One must look somewhere for one's salvation, and I chose the title as my savior. For four whole years I had not put in a single word about it, but now I called on my old teacher, Exner. He was as disagreeable as could be, almost rude, did not want to disclose anything about the reasons for my having been passed over, and assumed completely the role of the functionary. Only after I had really roused him by a few disparaging remarks about the activity of the ministry's high officials did he let fall something obscure about personal influences being at work against me with His Excellency, and he advised me to seek a personal counterinfluence. I was able to tell him that I could approach my old friend and former patient, the wife of Hofrat Gomperz. He seemed to like the idea. Frau Elise was very gracious and warmly took up the cause. She paid a visit to the minister and got a look of astonishment for a reply: "Four years! And who is he?" The old fox acted as though I were unknown to him. In any case, a new proposal would have to be made. So I wrote to Nothnagel and Krafft-Ebing, who was about to retire, and asked them to renew their previous proposal. Both responded wonderfully. Nothnagel wrote a few days later, "I have talked with K.E.," and the latter wrote after a few more days, "We *sent in* the proposal." But the minister doggedly avoided Gomperz, and it looked again as if nothing was going to come of it.

Then another force was applied. One of my patients, Marie Ferstel (who in a few weeks will move to Berlin with her husband, who has been appointed consul general), heard of the matter and began to agitate on her own. She did not rest until she had made the minister's acquaintance at a party, ingratiated herself with him, and secured his promise through a mutual friend that he would give a professorship to her doctor, who had cured her. But being sufficiently well informed that an initial promise from him meant nothing at all, she cornered him in person, and I believe that if a certain Böcklin had been in her possession instead of that of her aunt, Ernestine Thorsch, I would have been appointed three months earlier. As it is, His Excellency will have to be content with a modern painting for the gallery he intends to establish—naturally not for himself. In the end, when the minister had dinner at my patient's home, he graciously informed her that the formal papers had gone to the emperor and that she would be the first to hear when they had been signed and the appointment finalized.

One day, then, she came to her session, beaming and waving an express letter from the minister. So it was accomplished. The *Wiener Zeitung* has not yet publicized the appointment, but the news that it was imminent quickly spread from the official headquarters. Public acclaim was immense. Congratulations and flowers already are pouring in, as though the role of sexuality has suddenly been officially recognized by His Majesty, the significance of the dream certified by the Council of Ministers, and the necessity of a psychoanalytic therapy of hysteria carried by a two-thirds majority in Parliament.

I have obviously become reputable again; my most reluctant admirers greet me in the street from afar.

I myself would still gladly exchange every five congratulations for one decent case suitable for extensive treatment. I have learned that the old world is ruled by authority, as the new is by the dollar. I have made my first bow to authority and so may hope to be rewarded. If the effect on wider circles is as great as it is on the closer ones, I may be hopeful with good reason.

In the whole affair there is one person with very long ears who has not been sufficiently appreciated in your letter, and that is myself. If I had taken the few steps three years ago, I would have been appointed three years earlier and been spared all sorts of things. Others are that clever without first having to go to Rome. That, then, is the glorious course of events to which , among other things, I also owe your kind letter. Please keep the contents of this letter to yourself.

I thank you and greet you cordially.

Your
Sigm.

*Nestroy, looking through a peephole before a benefit performance and seeing only two people in the house is said to have exclaimed: "The one 'audience' I know; he has a complimentary ticket. Whether the other 'audience' has one too, I do not know."

1. This is no doubt a reference to the Dora case ("Fragment of an Analysis of a Case of Hysteria"), which was finished in 1901 but not published until 1905. Strachey (*S.E.* 7:4) notes that Freud wrote on June 9, 1901, that the case history would be published

that autumn. Strachey adds, "We have no information as to how it happened that Freud once more changed his mind and deferred publication for another four years." (Further details, including the fact that Freud told Ferenczi in 1909 that the editor of the *Monatsschrift für Psychiatrie und Neurologie* had originally turned down the paper, can be found in Jones, *Life* 2:286–287).

The present passage, especially in view of the earlier reference to Rie's dislike of the paper (letter of March 3, 1901) allows us to understand what may be the real reason Freud did not wish the article published: with the loss of Fliess's friendship and interest in his work, Freud felt that there was no one who would care about what he was writing.

---

[picture postcard of the Temple of Neptune, Paestum]

September 10, 1902

Cordial greetings from the high point of the trip.

Your
Sigm.

---

December 7, 1902
IX., Berggasse 19

Dear Wilhelm:

To my deep regret I learned of the misfortune that befell your house and can only hope that you will soon get over the distress.[1] Of all the horrible kinds of calamities, it is after all the very least severe test.

Cordial greetings.

Your
Sigm.

1. Michael Schröter informs me that on November 28 Ida Fliess gave birth to a stillborn daughter. See Fliess, *Der Ablauf des Lebens*, p. 34.

# Aftermath

THE LETTERS that follow are the sad aftermath of a passionate friendship. It is difficult to reconstruct, from these few documents, what actually happened. But it seems clear that the impetus to end the relationship came from Fliess, and that Freud only slowly came to realize that his friend was withdrawing from him. Without Fliess's letters it is impossible to know whether Freud overlooked the first signs of the break, or whether Fliess gave no hint of what was to follow.

One document that has recently come to light is relevant. In the Library of Congress are several pages of a paper by Fliess that was never published. It is entitled "Die Entdeckung der dauernden Doppelgeschlechtigkeit: Eine geschichtliche Darstellung." Fliess quotes from a letter he wrote to Freud, unfortunately without date, but which obviously belongs to the time of the break—hence, in Fliess's judgment, to 1900. The portion of the letter that Fliess reproduces in his article reads: "In this case you are, in my opinion, no more responsible for the relapse than for your quick and brilliant success: for I have often observed that a period of euphoria lasting many months precedes the outbreak of malignant tumors. During that period neurotic symptoms recede as well. Later they return with astounding suddenness, simultaneously with the first symptoms of the neoplasm." Fliess continues, "Freud was appalled by this communication." No doubt he was. It meant, very simply, that there was no need for Freud to engage in psychotherapy; a patient got better or worse according to strictly biological periods. Fliess's view undermined all of Freud's work. Estrangement was inevitable.

Another facet of the breakup is that Freud initially shared not only Fliess's views about his own importance for biology, but agreed that he, Freud, had attempted to rob Fliess of his prominence. Freud openly acknowledged this in a passage from the *Psychopathology of Everyday Life* (*S.E.* 6:143–144):

> One day in the summer of 1901 I remarked to a friend with whom I used at that time to have a lively exchange of scientific ideas: "These problems of the neuroses are only to be solved if we base ourselves wholly and completely on the assumption of the original bisexuality of the individual." To which he replied: "That's what I told you two and half years ago at Br[eslau] when we went for that evening walk. But you wouldn't hear of it then." It is painful to be requested in this way to surrender one's originality. I could not recall any such conversation or this pronouncement of my friend's. One of us must have been mistaken, and on the "*cui prodest?*" principle it must have been myself. Indeed, in the course of the next week I remembered the whole incident, which was just as my friend had tried to recall it to me; I even recollected the answer I had given him at the time: "I've not accepted that yet; I'm not inclined to go into that question." But since then I have grown a little more tolerant when, in reading medical literature, I come across one of the few ideas with which my name can be associated, and find that my name has not been mentioned.

This excerpt, in conjunction with the final letters from Freud to Fliess, attests to Freud's feelings of guilt toward his colleague and his conviction that he had been rightfully accused of an indiscretion. Posterity will perhaps be more gentle with Freud than he was with himself, and more inclined to admire his honesty in this awkward situation. In retrospect, Freud's harsh opinion of his own behavior seems nothing more than a remnant of his initial overvaluation of Fliess's scientific achievements. He emerges from this bisexuality episode as the more generous individual, both emotionally and intellectually.

---

April 26, 1904[1]

Dear Wilhelm:[2]

If I am writing to you again after such a long interval, you surely will assume that I am prompted not by an emotional impulse but by a practical motive. And so it is. I should like for us to hear about each other again in the following way: several competent young physicians who — I do not want to be secretive with you — belong to the circle of my pupils plan in the near future to attempt publication of a scientific journal that will be devoted to the "biological and psychological exploration of sexuality." They will ask you to collaborate, and, anticipating them, I should like to ask you not to deny them your name and your contributions. They believe the time is right, because everywhere the signs of agreement with my views are increasing. I recently found an absolutely stunning recognition of my point of view in a book review in the *Münchener medizinische Wochenschrift*[3] by an official psychiatrist, Bleuler, in Zurich. Just imagine, a full professor of psychiatry and my † † †[4] studies of hysteria and the dream, which so far have been labeled disgusting! It now no longer seems impossible that I shall myself still witness part of the change. I have never doubted the posthumous victory.

You must have received a work by Dr. Swoboda,[5] of which I am in more than one respect the intellectual originator, though I would not want to be its author. Type: Gattel.[6] But I believe that I am beginning to have better student material at my disposal.

I am of course looking forward as eagerly as ever before to the explanations you will give us in your new book.

With cordial greetings,

Your
Sigm.

1. This letter, and those of July 23 and July 27, 1904, were partially incorporated by Fliess into his pamphlet *In eigener Sache*. Published here for the first time in their entirety, the original letters are in the Jewish National and University Library, Jerusalem.

2. Freud uses the more usual "Lieber Wilhelm" rather than "Teurer Wilhelm."

3. In a review of L. Löwenfeld's *Die psychischen Zwangserscheinungen*, which appeared in *Münchener medizinische Wochenschrift*, 51 (1904):718, Eugen Bleuler writes: "Freud, in his studies on hysteria and on dreams, has shown us part of a new world, though by no means all of it. Our consciousness sees in its theater only the puppets; in the Freudian world, many of the strings that move the figures have been revealed."

It would seem that Freud did not know that Bleuler had already reviewed his *Studies on Hysteria* in the *Münchener medizinische Wochenschrift* in 1896. That review, primarily a summary of the book, ends with these positive words: "Be that as it may, the fact that the book brings an entirely new view into the workings of the psyche makes this book one of the most important additions of past years in the field of normal or pathological psychology."

Another 1904 review by Bleuler would have given Freud as much pleasure as the one about which he wrote to Fliess. Bleuler's discussion of Emil Raimann, *Die hysterischen Geistesstörungen* (Leipzig: Deuticke, 1904), in the *Münchener medizinische Wochenschrift*, ends with these words: "It is true that this reviewer does not believe in the exclusive significance of sexuality, that he has insufficient understanding for the concept of conversion, etc.; nevertheless, he considers Freud's method to be indispensable for a deeper understanding of the healthy as well as the ill psyche."

These are probably the earliest positive evaluations of Freud's work by a leading academic psychiatrist.

4. See letters of November 5, 1899, and May 8, 1901.

5. Hermann Swoboda, *Die Periode des menschlichen Organismus in ihrer psychologischen und biologischen Bedeutung* (Leipzig and Vienna: Franz Deuticke, 1904).

6. *Gattung* means type, category, genus; Gattel was Freud's early pupil. This is an untranslatable play on words.

---

Berlin, April 27, 1904[1]

Dear Sigmund:

I was very glad to hear from you, even though, by your own statement, your lines were not motivated by any emotional impulse. I was especially pleased about the news that you are gaining more recognition.

Bleuler is not unknown to me. I have retained a favorable memory of the nice study on color vision following acoustic impressions that he did many years ago with Lehmann. For the time being I shall not be able to write anything at all for the new journal (I have declined all other invitations also), because I have my hands full with the writing of my book. And until the last piece is brought to completion I cannot devote myself to other tasks.

That you must figure as the intellectual originator of Swoboda's book I really regret—not because the author does not have the slightest idea of where the problem of periods is located, nor because of the many factual errors, but rather because of the trait of deep dishonesty that runs through the book. You yourself intimate this by referring to Gattel. I noticed it only when I read it more closely; otherwise my note thanking the author for sending me the book would have been written in a different tone. Swoboda did not once reveal the year in which he made his observations and in which he became acquainted with my book. Incidentally, have you finished *Jokes*, the material for which you showed me exactly a year ago?[2]

I would have preferred to answer you verbally, but we are not going to Vienna right now (as has been rumored by unreliable sources), so I send you this handshake with best regards!

Your
Wilhelm

1. I found this letter, in Fliess's hand, in Maresfield Gardens. It has not been previously published.

2. Freud did publish this book in 1905 as *Jokes and Their Relation to the Unconscious.*

---

July 15, 1904
IX., Berggasse 19

Dear Wilhelm:

I use today's date to congratulate you on your sister-in-law Marie's impending marriage. Your presence in Vienna will bring me nothing because I leave for my vacation at Königsee the evening before. Wishing you and yours the best for the summer,

Your
Sigm.

---

Hotel Meissl & Schadn
Vienna, July 20, 1904

Dear Sigmund:

I have come across a book by Weininger,[1] in the first biological part of which I find, to my consternation, a description of my ideas on bisexuality and the nature of sexual attraction consequent upon it — feminine men attract masculine women and vice versa. From a quotation in it I see that Weininger knew Swoboda — your pupil — (before the publication of his book), and I learned here that the two men were *intimi.* I have no doubt that Weininger obtained knowledge of my ideas via you and misused someone else's property. What do you know about it? Would you kindly give me a frank reply (to my Berlin address, because I am leaving Vienna on the evening of the 23rd).

With cordial greetings,

Your
Wilh.

1. Otto Weininger, *Geschlecht und Charakter: Eine prinzipielle Untersuchung* (Vienna: Wilhelm Braumueller, 1903).

V. Sonnenfels
July 23, 1904
IX., Berggasse 19[1]

Dear Wilhelm:

I too believe that the late Weininger was a burglar with a key he picked up.

Herewith everything I know about it. Swoboda, who was an intimate friend of his and who had learned about bisexuality (which comes up for discussion in every treatment) from me, mentioned the word "bisexuality"—as he tells it—when he found Weininger preoccupied with sexual problems. Whereupon Weininger clapped his hand to his forehead and rushed home to write his book. I am in no position to judge whether this report is correct.

Moreover, I believe that Weininger, who allegedly killed himself out of fear of his criminal nature, could have gotten the idea of bisexuality elsewhere, because it has figured in the literature for some time. The correspondence of details can no doubt be explained as follows: once introduced to the idea, he deduced some of the inferences correctly—a larger portion no doubt incorrectly. For Swoboda maintains that he did not give him any further information; nor did he have any to give, because he did not learn from me any more than what comes up in treatment—that a strong homosexual current is found in every neurotic.

Swoboda is not, as you write, *my pupil.* He came to me as a severely ill patient, was given the same help and learned the same things as every other [patient]; I have no part whatsoever in his discovery, which deals rather with your ideas. I did not read his book before its publication; when I read it, I was very astonished by the kind of neurotic gratitude it displays, that is, the way he uses his findings to attack my dream theory. He simply exploited me, finally even for the purpose of finding him a publisher, which I did, and in view of his qualities as a worker, explicitly declining any responsibility for his work. I am always prepared to do such things, with the intention never to regret them later on.

At present I am finishing "Three Essays on the Theory of Sexuality," in which I avoid the topic of bisexuality as far as possible. At two places I cannot do so: in the explanation of sexual inversion—there I go as far as the literature permits (Krafft-Ebing and predecessors, Kiernan, Chevalier, and the others); furthermore, when I mention the homosexual current in neurotics. There I plan to add a note that I had been prepared for the necessity of this finding by certain remarks of *yours.* Or you may want to propose a comparable formulation to me.

The rest deals with infantile sexual life and the components of the sexual drives.

With cordial greetings,

Your
Sigm.

1. See note 1 to letter of April 26, 1904.

---

Berlin, July 26, 1904

Dear Sigmund:

So what Oscar Rie told me in all innocence when I mentioned Weininger was incorrect: he said that Weininger went to you with his manuscript and you, after looking at it, advised him against publication because the content was nonsense. I believe that in this case you should have called his attention and mine to the "burglary." Weininger himself obviously did not believe — as you do — that he *could* have gotten the idea of persistent and inevitable bisexuality of all living beings (not merely the predisposition to bisexuality) elsewhere. For on page 10 he states that the idea in this form is entirely new. I would be much obliged to you if you could list for me the other sources about which you wrote — Krafft-Ebing, Kiernan, Chevalier, and so on — in such a way that I could easily find them, for I am not well acquainted with the literature.

Moreover, in his arrhenoplasma and thelyplasma Weininger also stole the idea that the living substance is both feminine *and* masculine in all living beings — which I deduced from the regular occurrence of 28 *and* 23 in both men *and* women.

Until now I did not know what I learned from your letter — that you are using [the idea of] persistent bisexuality in your treatments. We talked about it for the first time in Nuremberg while I was still lying in bed, and you told me the case history of the woman who had dreams of gigantic snakes. At the time you were quite impressed by the idea that undercurrents in a woman might stem from the masculine part of her psyche. For this reason I was all the more puzzled by your resistance in Breslau to the assumption of bisexuality in the psyche. In Breslau I also told you about the existence of so many left-handed husbands among my acquaintances, and from the theory of left-handedness I developed for you an explanation which down to *every detail* corresponds to Weininger's (who knows nothing about left-handedness). To be sure, you rejected left-handedness itself and, as you yourself admitted most candidly, forgot our bisexual discussion for some time.

Because I did not know that your treatment requires mentioning bisexuality, I did not suspect that Weininger's intimate friend, Dr. Swoboda, was your patient — least of all when you compared him with Gattel in your letter to me and added, "But I believe that I am beginning to have better student material at my disposal."

Both of us would no doubt have wished for a better reason to correspond than arguing about a *robber*. May the future bring it to us.

With cordial greetings,

Wilhelm

---

July 27, 1904
IX., Berggasse 19[1]

Dear Wilhelm:

I see that I have to concede to you more right than I originally was prepared to; I am taken aback by my having forgotten how much I had complained about my pupil Swoboda and by my glossing over Weininger's visit to me (which, however, I had not forgotten). The latter is precisely as Rie related it to you; the manuscript shown to me, though, had an entirely different wording than the printed book; I was also quite alarmed by the chapter on hysteria, which was written *ad captandam benevolentiam meam* [to capture my favor], but the underlying theme of bisexuality was of course recognizable, and I must have regretted at the time that via Swoboda, as I already knew, I had handed over your idea to him. In conjunction with my own attempt to rob you of your originality, I better understand my behavior toward Weininger and my subsequent forgetting.

I do not believe, on the other hand, that I should have shouted "Stop, thief" at that time. Above all, it would have been no use because the thief can just as well claim it was his own idea; nor can ideas be patented. One can withhold them — and does so advisedly if one sets great store by one's right of ownership. Once they have been let loose, they go their own way. Furthermore, at that time I was already familiar with the references in the literature in which the idea of bisexuality is used to explain inversion. You must admit that a resourceful mind can on its own easily take the step from the bisexual disposition of some individuals to extending it to all of them, though this step is your *novum*. For me personally you have always (since 1901) been the author of the idea of bisexuality; I fear that in looking through the literature, you will find that many came at least close to you. The names I mentioned to you are in my manuscript; I did not take books along with me, so I cannot give you more precise documentation. You will certainly find it in *Psychopathia sexualis* by Krafft-Ebing.

Furthermore, I was certain (and still am) that I did not give Swoboda any details from your communications. The universality of the bisexual disposition is all that is mentioned in treatment, and that I need there. Since the experience I candidly reported in "Everyday Life," I have suspected that one of us might come to regret our formerly unrestrained exchange of ideas and have striven successfully to forget the details of your communications. At that time I evidently reproached myself dimly, as I do today in complete clarity, for my generosity or carelessness with your property. I now may assume that the harm done you by Weininger is very slight, because no one will take his shoddy piece of work seriously and you can, if it is worth your while, clear up the circumstances. Stealing is not as easy as Weininger imagined it to be — with this I console myself and would like you to be consoled as well.

You are not alone in regretting — I do too — that this incident in which you reproach me has reawakened a long-dormant correspondence. It is not my fault, however, if you find the time and the inclination to exchange letters with me again only on the occasion of such petty incidents. The fact is that in the past few years — "Everyday Life" is the dividing line — you have no longer showed an interest in me or my family or my work. By now I have gotten over it and have little desire for it any longer; I am not reproaching you and ask you not to reply to this point.

I have a different request. Throughout my life I have freely scattered suggestions without asking what will come of them. I can without feeling diminished admit that I have learned this or that from others. But I have never appropriated something belonging to others as my own — only people like Gärtner can say that. So now, with regard to bisexuality, I also do not want to be in such a position vis-à-vis you, least of all since in precisely the same matter you have chosen to express your appreciation of another [person and] your disapproval of me (the case of Swoboda). I trust you will still be so kind as to help me out of my present predicament by reading the remarks on bisexuality in the proofs of my just completed "Essays on the Theory of Sexuality" and changing them to your satisfaction. It would be easier to postpone publication until you have surrendered your biology to the public. But I do not know when this will be. You will scarcely hurry for my sake. In the meantime I can do nothing, not even finish the *Jokes*, which in a crucial point is partially based on the theory of sexuality. I also do not gain anything by waiting for your publication, because then I could not possibly avoid the topic of bisexuality, as I do now; I would have to take a stand and eventually prepare new works. On the other hand, there is so little of bisexuality or of other things I have borrowed from you in what I say, that I can do justice to your share in a few remarks. I must only be sure that you agree with them and do not find grounds in them for reproaches later on.

I ask you to reply to *this*.

With cordial greetings,

Your
Sigm.

P.S. Möbius has devoted a pamphlet, "Sex and Immodesty,"[2] to Weininger's book; of course, I did not bring it along either. He claims various ideas of Weininger's as his own. It will certainly be of interest to you to look up which ones.

1. See note 1 to letter of April 26, 1904.

2. Paul J. Möbius, *Geschlecht und Unbescheidenheit* (Halle a.S.: Carl Marhold, 1904).

Appendix

Principal Works Cited

Index

# Appendix
# Comparative List of Documents Included

The tabulation that follows indicates which of the letters in this volume appeared previously in *Anfänge* and in *Origins*, either in full or with excisions, and which are presented for the first time. A dagger (†) in the "In part" column indicates that the new material here adds only a phrase or at most a brief sentence to the earlier version; an asterisk (*) indicates that at least half the document was omitted previously.

| Date of letter or name of document | Appears in *Anfänge* and *Origins* | | | |
|---|---|---|---|---|
| | In full | In part | New here | Page |
| 11.24.87 | • | | | 15 |
| 12.28.87 | • | | | 16 |
| 2.4.88 | | † | | 18 |
| 5.28.88 | | • | | 21 |
| 8.29.88 | • | | | 23 |
| 7.21.90 | | | • | 26 |
| 8.1.90 | | † | | 27 |
| 8.11.90 | • | | | 27 |
| 5.2.91 | • | | | 28 |
| 8.17.91 | | | • | 29 |
| 9.11.91 | | | • | 30 |
| 5.25.92 | | | • | 30 |
| 6.28.92 | | • | | 31 |

| Date of letter or name of document | Appears in *Anfänge* and *Origins* In full | In part | New here | Page |
|---|---|---|---|---|
| 7.12.92 | | | • | 31 |
| 10.4.92 | | • | | 33 |
| 10.21.92 | | | • | 33 |
| 10.24.92 | | | • | 35 |
| 10.31.92 | | | • | 35 |
| 11.3.92 | | | • | 36 |
| 12.18.92 | • | | | 36 |
| Draft A | • | | | 37 |
| 1.5.93 | | | • | 39 |
| Draft B | • | | | 39 |
| Draft C | | • | | 45 |
| 5.14.93 | | | • | 47 |
| 5.15.93 | | | • | 48 |
| 5.30.93 | | * | | 49 |
| 7.10.93 | | • | | 50 |
| 7.24.93 | | | • | 52 |
| 8.13.93 | | | • | 53 |
| 8.20.93 | | | • | 53 |
| 9.14.93 | | | • | 55 |
| 9.29.93 | | | • | 56 |
| 10.6.93 | | • | | 57 |
| 10.18.93 | | | • | 59 |
| 11.27.93 (date corrected from 11.17.93) | | * | | 61 |
| 12.11.93 | | | • | 62 |
| 1.4.94 | | | • | 64 |
| 1.16.94 | | | • | 64 |
| 1.30.94 | | | • | 65 |
| 2.7.94 | | • | | 65 |

| Date of letter or name of document | Appears in *Anfänge* and *Origins* In full | In part | New here | Page |
|---|---|---|---|---|
| 4.19.94 | | • | | 67 |
| 4.25.94 | | | • | 69 |
| 5.6.94 | | | • | 70 |
| 5.21.94 | | • | | 73 |
| Draft D | • | | | 76 |
| Draft E | • | | | 78 |
| 6.22.94 | | * | | 83 |
| undated | | | • | 86 |
| 7.14.94 | | | • | 87 |
| 7.25.94 | | | • | 88 |
| 8.7.94 | | | • | 89 |
| 8.18.94 | | * | | 89 |
| Draft F (part previously with letter of 8.23.94) | | † | | 90 |
| 8.23.94 | | | • | 91 |
| 8.29.94 | | * | | 95 |
| 9.13.94 | | | • | 97 |
| 12.17.94 | | | • | 98 |
| Draft G | | • (text complete; one new figure) | | 98 |
| 1.24.95 | | | • | 106 |
| Draft H | • | | | 107 |
| 2.25.95 | | | • | 112 |
| 3.4.95 | | * | | 113 |
| 3.8.95 | | | • | 116 |
| 3.13.95 | | | • | 119 |
| 3.23.95 | | | • | 121 |
| 3.28.95 | | | • | 122 |

| Date of letter or name of document | Appears in *Anfänge* and *Origins* | | | |
| --- | --- | --- | --- | --- |
| | In full | In part | New here | Page |
| 4.11.95 | | | • | 123 |
| 4.20.95 | | | • | 125 |
| 4.26.95 | | | • | 126 |
| 4.27.95 | | • | | 127 |
| 5.25.95 | | • | | 128 |
| 6.12.95 | | * | | 131 |
| 6.17.95 | | | • | 132 |
| 6.22.95 | | | • | 133 |
| 7.13.95 | | | • | 133 |
| 7.24.95 | | | • | 134 |
| 8.6.95 | | † | | 134 |
| 8.16.95 | | • | | 135 |
| 8.28.95 | | | • | 136 |
| 9.15.95 | | | • | 137 |
| 9.23.95 | | † | | 139 |
| 10.8.95 | | • | | 140 |
| Draft I | • | | | 142 |
| 10.15.95 | | † | | 144 |
| 10.16.95 | | • | | 145 |
| 10.20.95 | | • | | 146 |
| 10.31.95 | | • | | 147 |
| 11.2.95 | • | | | 149 |
| 11.8.95 | • | | | 150 |
| 11.29.95 | | • | | 152 |
| 12.3.95 | • | | | 153 |
| 12.8.95 | | • | | 154 |
| Draft J | • | | | 155 |
| 1.1.96 | | • | | 158 |
| Draft K | • | | | 162 |

| Date of letter or name of document | Appears in *Anfänge* and *Origins* In full | In part | New here | Page |
|---|---|---|---|---|
| 2.6.96 | | • | | 170 |
| 2.13.96 | | • | | 172 |
| 2.23.96 | | | • | 173 |
| 3.1.96 | | • | | 173 |
| 3.7.96 | | | • | 176 |
| 3.16.96 | | • | | 178 |
| 3.29? 96 | | | • | 179 |
| 4.2.96 | | • | | 179 |
| 4.16.96 | | | • | 180 |
| 4.26.96 | | | • | 183 |
| 5.4.96 | | * | | 185 |
| 5.17.96 | | * (as part of 5.4.96 letter) | | 186 |
| 5.30.96 | | • | | 187 |
| 6.4.96 | | * | | 191 |
| 6.9.96 | | | • | 192 |
| 6.30.96 | | • | | 193 |
| 7.15.96 | | | • | 194 |
| 8.12.96 | | | • | 195 |
| 8.17.96 | | | • | 197 |
| 8.29.96 (postcard) | | | • | 197 |
| 9.29.96 | | | • | 198 |
| 10.9.96 | | | • | 199 |
| 10.26.96 | | • | | 201 |
| 11.2.96 | | • | | 202 |
| 11.22.96 | | | • | 203 |
| 12.4.96 | | • | | 204 |
| 12.6.96 | | • | | 207 |

| Date of letter or name of document | Appears in *Anfänge* and *Origins*: In full | In part | New here | Page |
|---|---|---|---|---|
| 12.17.96 | | * | | 215 |
| 12.22.96 | | | • | 218 |
| 1.3.97 | | • | | 219 |
| 1.11.97 | | † | | 221 |
| 1.12.97 | | | • | 223 |
| 1.17.97 | | • | | 224 |
| 1.24.97 | | • | | 226 |
| 2.8.97 | | • | | 229 |
| 3.7.97 | | | • | 232 |
| 3.29.97 | | | • | 233 |
| 4.6.97 | | * | | 234 |
| 4.12.97 | | | • | 235 |
| 4.28.97 | • | | | 236 |
| 5.2.97 | | * | | 238 |
| Draft L | • | | | 240 |
| 5.16.97 | | • | | 243 |
| 5.25.97 | | * | | 245 |
| Draft M | • | | | 246 |
| 5.31.97 | | • | | 249 |
| Draft N | • | | | 250 |
| 6.18.97 | | | • | 252 |
| 6.22.97 (date corrected from 6.12.97) | | † | | 253 |
| 7.7.97 | | • | | 254 |
| 7.20.97 | | | • | 256 |
| 8.5.97 | | | • | 257 |
| 8.8.97 | | | • | 258 |
| 8.14.97 | | * | | 259 |
| 8.18.97 | | • | | 261 |

| Date of letter or name of document | Appears in *Anfänge* and *Origins*: In full | Appears in *Anfänge* and *Origins*: In part | New here | Page |
|---|---|---|---|---|
| 9.6.97 | | | • | 263 |
| 9.21.97 | | • | | 264 |
| 9.27.97 | | | • | 267 |
| 10.3.97 | | • | | 267 |
| 10.15.97 | | • | | 270 |
| 10.27.97 | | • | | 273 |
| 10.31.97 | | • | | 275 |
| 11.5.97 | | • | | 277 |
| 11.14.97 | • | | | 278 |
| 11.15.97 | | | • | 282 |
| 11.18.97 | | † | | 283 |
| 12.3.97 | | • | | 284 |
| 12.12.97 | | • | | 285 |
| 12.22.97 | | • | | 287 |
| 12.29.97 | | • | | 290 |
| 1.4.98 | | • | | 291 |
| 1.16.98 | | * | | 294 |
| 1.22.98 | | | • | 295 |
| 1.30.98 | | | • | 296 |
| 2.9.98 | | • | | 298 |
| 2.23.98 | | | • | 300 |
| 3.5.98 | | | • | 301 |
| 3.10.98 | | • | | 301 |
| 3.15.98 | | • | | 303 |
| 3.24.98 | | • | | 304 |
| 4.3.98 | | * | | 306 |
| 4.14.98 | | • | | 307 |
| 4.27.98 | | | • | 310 |
| 5.1.98 | | * | | 312 |

| Date of letter or name of document | Appears in *Anfänge* and *Origins*: In full | In part | New here | Page |
|---|---|---|---|---|
| 5.18.98 | | | • | 313 |
| 5.24.98 | | | • | 314 |
| 6.9.98 | | • | | 315 |
| 6.20.98 | | • | | 317 |
| 7.7.98 | | • | | 319 |
| 7.30.98 | | | • | 320 |
| 8.1.98 | | | • | 322 |
| 8.20.98 | | † | | 322 |
| 8.26.98 | | • | | 323 |
| 8.31.98 | • | | | 325 |
| 9.22.98 | • | | | 326 |
| 9.27.98 | | • | | 327 |
| 10.9.98 | | • | | 330 |
| 10.23.98 | | † | | 331 |
| 10.30.98 | | | • | 332 |
| 11.6.98 | | | • | 333 |
| 11.16.98 | | | • | 334 |
| 11.30.98 | | | • | 335 |
| 12.5.98 | | • | | 335 |
| 12.7.98 | | | • | 336 |
| 12.20.98 | | | • | 337 |
| 1.3.99 | | • | | 338 |
| 1.16.99 | | • | | 340 |
| 1.30.99 | | • | | 342 |
| 2.6.99 | | • | | 343 |
| 2.19.99 | | • | | 344 |
| 3.2.99 | | † | | 346 |
| 3.19.99 | | | • | 348 |
| 3.27.99 | | | • | 349 |

| Date of letter or name of document | Appears in *Anfänge* and *Origins* In full | In part | New here | Page |
|---|---|---|---|---|
| 4.13.99 | | | • | 350 |
| 4.24.99 | | | • | 350 |
| 5.25.99 | | | • | 351 |
| 5.28.99 | | • | | 352 |
| 6.9.99 | | • | | 354 |
| 6.16.99 | | | • | 355 |
| 6.27.99 | | * | | 356 |
| 7.3.99 | | • | | 358 |
| 7.8.99 | | | • | 359 |
| 7.13.99 | | | • | 360 |
| 7.17.99 | | • | | 360 |
| 7.22.99 | | • | | 362 |
| 8.1.99 | | • | | 363 |
| 8.6.99 | | • | | 365 |
| 8.20.99 | | • | | 366 |
| 8.27.99 | | • | | 367 |
| 9.6.99 | • | | | 369 |
| 9.11.99 | | • | | 370 |
| 9.16.99 | | | • | 372 |
| 9.21.99 | | † | | 373 |
| 9.27.99 | | | • | 375 |
| 10.4.99 | | | • | 376 |
| 10.9.99 | | • | | 377 |
| 10.11.99 | | † | | 379 |
| 10.17.99 | | | • | 380 |
| 10.27.99 | | • | | 380 |
| 11.5.99 | | • | | 381 |
| 11.7.99 | | | • | 382 |
| 11.9.99 | | | • | 384 |

| Date of letter or name of document | Appears in *Anfänge* and *Origins*: In full | In part | New here | Page |
|---|---|---|---|---|
| 11.12.99 | | • | | 385 |
| 11.19.99 | | | • | 386 |
| 11.26.99 | | | • | 388 |
| 12.9.99 | | • | | 390 |
| 12.21.99 | | • | | 391 |
| 12.24.99 | | | • | 393 |
| 12.29.99 | | | • | 393 |
| 1.8.00 | | • | | 394 |
| 1.12.00 | | | • | 396 |
| 1.26.00 | | • | | 396 |
| 2.1.00 | | | • | 397 |
| 2.12.00 | | • | | 399 |
| 2.22.00 | | | • | 400 |
| 3.1.00 | | | • | 400 |
| 3.11.00 | | • | | 402 |
| 3.23.00 | | • | | 404 |
| 4.4.00 | | † | | 407 |
| 4.16.00 | | • | | 408 |
| 4.25.00 | | | • | 410 |
| 5.7.00 | | • | | 412 |
| 5.16.00 | | * | | 413 |
| 5.20.00 | | * | | 415 |
| 5.26.00 | | | • | 416 |
| 6.12.00 | | • | | 417 |
| 6.18.00 | | | • | 418 |
| 7.1.00 | | | • | 420 |
| 7.10.00 | | • | | 421 |
| 9.5.00 (postcard) | | | • | 422 |

| Date of letter or name of document | Appears in *Anfänge* and *Origins* | | New here | Page |
|---|---|---|---|---|
| | In full | In part | | |
| 9.14.00 | | | • | 422 |
| 9.24.00 | | | • | 425 |
| 10.14.00 | | * | | 426 |
| 10.23.00 | | | • | 428 |
| 11.21.00 | | | • | 428 |
| 11.25.00 | | | • | 429 |
| 1.1.01 | | | • | 430 |
| 1.10.01 | | | • | 432 |
| 1.25.01 | | * | | 432 |
| 1.30.01 | | * | | 434 |
| 2.15.01 | | • | | 436 |
| 3.3.01 | | | • | 437 |
| 3.9.01 | | | • | 439 |
| 3.24.01 | | | • | 439 |
| 5.8.01 | | • | | 440 |
| 6.9.01 | | | • | 441 |
| 7.4.01 | | • | | 443 |
| 8.7.01 | | • | | 446 |
| 9.19.01 | | † | | 449 |
| 9.20.01 | • | | | 451 |
| 10.7.01 | | † | | 452 |
| 11.2.01 | • | | | 453 |
| 12.7.01 | | † | | 453 |
| 1.17.02 | | | • | 454 |
| 3.8.02 | • | | | 455 |
| 3.11.02 | | • | | 455 |
| 9.10.02 (postcard) | • | | | 458 |
| 12.7.02 | | | • | 458 |

| Date of letter or name of document | Appears in *Anfänge* and *Origins* | | New here | Page |
|---|---|---|---|---|
| | In full | In part | | |
| 4.26.04 | | | • | 460 |
| 4.27.04 (Fliess to Freud) | | | • | 462 |
| 7.15.04 | | | • | 463 |
| 7.20.04 (Fliess to Freud) | | | • | 463 |
| 7.23.04 | | | • | 464 |
| 7.26.04 (Fliess to Freud) | | | • | 465 |
| 7.27.04 | | | • | 466 |

# Principal Works Cited

Freud's works are entered alphabetically under their German title and under the English translation of the title, with full publication data at the German entry. If the work was published separately in English, those publication data are given at the English entry; works included in *S.E.* are identified by volume number and pages in that edition. If there was no publication in English, an English translation of the title has been supplied and is cross-referenced to the German entry. Fliess's works are listed alphabetically by German title, with the English translation given in parentheses. Reviews of both men's works appear chronologically under the German entry for the item reviewed. Works by other writers are given alphabetically by author.

## Works by Sigmund Freud


"Abstracts of the Scientific Writings of Dr. Sigmund Freud, 1877–1897." *S.E.* 3:225–257. See also "Inhaltsangaben der wissenschaftlichen Arbeiten des Privatdozenten Dr. Sigm. Freud, 1877–1897."

"Abwehr-Neuropsychosen, Die." *Neurologisches Centralblatt*, 13 (1894): 362–364, 402–409.

"Analyse der Phobie eines fünfjährigen Knaben." *Jahrbuch für psychoanalytische und psychopathologische Forschungen*, 1 (1909):1–109.

"Analysis of a Phobia in a Five-Year-Old Boy." *S.E.* 10:5–149. See also "Analyse der Phobie eines fünfjährigen Knaben."

"Autobiographical Study." *S.E.* 20:7–70. See also "Selbstdarstellung."

"Beobachtung einer hochgradigen Hemianaesthesie bei einem hysterischen Manne." *Wiener medizinische Wochenschrift*, 36 (1886):1633–38.

*Beyond the Pleasure Principle. S.E.* 18:7–64. See also *Jenseits des Lustprinzips.*

"Bruchstück einer Hysterie-Analyse." *Monatsschrift für Psychiatrie und Neurologie*, 18 (1905):285–310, 408–467.

"Charcot," an obituary. *Wiener medizinische Wochenschrift*, 43 (1893): 1513–20; *S.E.* 3:9–23.

*Civilization and Its Discontents. S.E.* 21:59–145. See also *Das Unbehagen in der Kultur.*

"Clinical Study in Hemiplegia in Children, A," with Oscar Rie. See "Klinische Studie über die halbseitige Cerebrallähmung der Kinder."

"Contribution to the Knowledge of Cerebral Diplegias in Childhood (in Connection with Little's Disease)." Abstract, *S.E.* 3:245. See also "Zur Kenntnis der cerebralen Diplegien des Kindesalters (im Anschluss an die Little'sche Krankheit)."

"Critical Introduction to the Pathology of the Nervous System." See "Kritische Einleitung in die Nervenpathologie."

*Drei Abhandlungen zur Sexualtheorie.* Leipzig and Vienna: Franz Deuticke, 1905.

"Entwurf einer Psychologie." *Anfänge,* 373–456.

"Erfüllte Traumahnung, Eine." *G.W.* 17:21–23.

*Five Lectures on Psycho-Analysis. S.E.* 11:3–56. See also *Über Psychoanalyse.*

"Forgetting and Repressing." See "Vergessen und Verdrängen."

"Fragment of an Analysis of a Case of Hysteria." *S.E.* 7:3–122. See also "Bruchstück einer Hysterie-Analyse."

"Further Remarks on the Neuro-Psychoses of Defence." *S.E.* 3:159–185. See also "Weitere Bemerkungen über die Abwehrneuropsychosen."

*Group Psychology and the Analysis of the Ego. S.E.* 18:67–143. See also *Massenpsychologie und Ich-Analyse.*

"L'hérédité et l'étiologie des névroses." *Revue neurologique,* 4 (1896): 161–169.

"Heredity and the Aetiology of Neuroses." *S.E.* 3:142–156. See also "L'hérédité et l'étiologie des névroses."

"Hysteria." *S.E.* 1:39–57. See also "Hysterie."

"Hysterie." In *Handwörterbuch der gesamten Medizin,* edited by Albert Villaret, 1:886–892. Stuttgart: 1888.

"Infantile Cerebrallähmung, Die." In *Specielle Pathologie und Therapie,* edited by Hermann Nothnagel, vol. 9, pt. 2, sec. 2. Vienna: Alfred Hölder, 1897.

Review by Mann. *Monatsschrift für Psychiatrie und Neurologie,* 2 (1897):247–251.

"Infantile Cerebral Paralyses." See "Die infantile Cerebrallähmung."

"Inhaltsangaben der wissenschaftlichen Arbeiten des Privatdozenten Dr. Sigm. Freud, 1877–1897." Privately printed by Franz Deuticke.

*Interpretation of Dreams, The.* Translated by James Strachey. New York: Basic Books, 1955; *S.E.* 4,5. See also *Die Traumdeutung.*

*Introductory Lectures on Psycho-Analysis. S.E.* 15, 16. See also *Vorlesungen zur Einführung in die Psychoanalyse.*

*Jenseits des Lustprinzips.* Leipzig, Vienna, and Zurich: Internationaler Psychoanalytischer Verlag, 1920.

*Jokes and Their Relation to the Unconscious. S.E.* 8:3–238. See also *Der Witz und seine Beziehung zum Unbewussten.*

"Klinische Studie über die halbseitige Cerebrallähmung der Kinder," with Oscar Rie. In *Beiträge zur Kinderheilkunde*, edited by M. Kassowitz, vol. 3. Vienna: Perles, 1891.

"Kritische Einleitung in die Nervenpathologie." 1887 (unpublished).

*Letters of Sigmund Freud, 1873–1939*. Edited by Ernst L. Freud; translated by Tania Stern and James Stern. London: Hogarth Press, 1961. See also *Sigmund Freud Briefe, 1873–1939*.

*Massenpsychologie und Ich-Analyse*. Leipzig, Vienna, and Zurich: Internationaler Psychoanalytischer Verlag, 1921.

*Neue Studien über Hypnotismus, Suggestion und Psychotherapie*, by Hippolyte Bernheim. Translated from the French by Freud. Leipzig and Vienna: Franz Deuticke, 1892. Originally published as *Hypnotisme, suggestion, psychothérapie: Études nouvelles*. Paris, 1892.

*Neue Vorlesungen über die Krankheiten des Nervensystems insbesondere über Hysterie*, by Jean Martin Charcot. Translated from the French by Freud. Leipzig and Vienna: Töplitz & Deuticke, 1886. Originally published as *Leçons sur les maladies du système nerveux*. Paris, 1887.

"Neuro-Psychoses of Defence, The." *S.E.* 3:45–61. See also "Die Abwehr-Neuropsychosen."

*New Lectures on Diseases of the Nervous System, Especially Hysteria*. See *Neue Vorlesungen über die Krankheiten des Nervensystems insbesondere über Hysterie*. Preface, *S.E.* 1:19–22.

*New Studies on Hypnotism, Suggestion and Psychotherapy*. See *Neue Studien über Hypnotismus, Suggestion und Psychotherapie*.

Obituary of Samuel Hammerschlag. *Neue freie Presse*, November 11, 1904, 8; *S.E.* 9:255–256.

"Observation of a Severe Case of Hemi-anaesthesia in a Hysterical Male." *S.E.* 1:24–31. See also "Beobachtung einer hochgradigen Hemianaesthesie bei einem hysterischen Manne."

"Obsessions and Phobias: Their Psychical Mechanism and Their Aetiology." *S.E.* 3:71–82. See also "Obsessions et phobies (leur mécanisme psychique et leur étiologie)."

"Obsessions et phobies (leur mécanisme psychique et leur étiologie)." *Revue neurologique*, 3 (1895):33–38.

*On Aphasia*. See *Zur Auffassung der Aphasien: Eine kritische Studie*.

"On a Symptom Frequently Accompanying Nocturnal Enuresis." See "Über ein Symptom, das häufig die Enuresis nocturna der Kinder begleitet."

"On Bernhardt's Disturbance of Sensibility in the Thigh." See "Über die Bernhardt'sche Sensibilitätsstörungen am Oberschenkel."

*On Dreams*. *S.E.* 5:631–686. See also *Über den Traum*.

"On Hemianopsia in Early Childhood." See "Über Hemianopsie im frühesten Kindesalter."

"On the Aetiology of Hysteria." *S.E.* 3:189–221. See also "Zur Ätiologie der Hysterie."

"On the Grounds for Detecting a Particular Syndrome from Neurasthenia under the Description 'Anxiety Neurosis.'" *S.E.* 3:87–117. See also "Über die Berechtigung, von der Neurasthenie einen bestimmten Symptomen-Komplex als 'Angstneurose' abzutrennen."

"A Reply to Criticisms of My Paper on Anxiety Neurosis" (translation of Freud's response to Löwenfeld review of "Über die Berechtigung"). *S.E.* 3:121–139.

"On the History of the Psycho-Analytic Movement." *S.E.* 14:3–66. See also "Zur Geschichte der psychoanalytischen Bewegung."

"On the Mechanism of Obsessional Neuroses and Phobias." See "Über den 'Mechanismus der Zwangsvorstellungen und Phobien.'"

"On the Psychical Mechanism of Hysterical Phenomena: A Preliminary Communication," with Josef Breuer. *S.E.* 2:3–17. See also "Über den psychischen Mechanismus hysterischer Phänomene: Vorläufige Mitteilung."

*Origins of Psycho-Analysis, The: Letters to Wilhelm Fliess, Drafts and Notes, 1887–1902, by Sigmund Freud.* Edited by Marie Bonaparte, Anna Freud, and Ernst Kris; translated by Eric Mosbacher and James Strachey; introduction by Ernst Kris. New York: Basic Books, and London: Imago Publishing Company, 1954.

"Premonitory Dream Fulfilled, A." *S.E.* 5:623–625. See also "Eine erfüllte Traumahnung."

"Project for a Scientific Psychology." *S.E.* 1:283–387; *Origins*, 347–445. See also "Entwurf einer Psychologie."

"Psychical Mechanism of Forgetfulness, The." Also called by Freud "The Painting by Signorelli." *S.E.* 3:289–297. See also "Zum psychischen Mechanismus der Vergesslichkeit."

*Psychopathology of Everyday Life.* *S.E.* 6:1–279. See also "Zur Psychopathologie des Alltagslebens."

"Quelques considérations pour une étude comparative des paralysies motrices organiques et hystériques." *Archives de neurologie*, 26 (1893):29–43.

Review by L. Camuset. *Annales médicopsychologiques*, 54 (1896):265.

Review by Freud of Paul J. Möbius, *Migraine. Wiener klinische Rundschau*, 9 (1895):140–141.

"Screen Memories." *S.E.* 3:301–322. See also "Über Deckerinnerungen."

"Selbstdarstellung." In *Die Medizin der Gegenwart in Selbstdarstellungen*, edited by L. R. Grote, 4:1–52. Leipzig: Meiner, 1925.

"Sexualität in der Ätiologie der Neurosen, Die." *Wiener klinische Rundschau*, 12 (1898):21–22, 55–57, 70–72, 103–105.

"Sexuality in the Aetiology of the Neuroses." *S.E.* 3:261–285. See also "Die Sexualität in der Ätiologie der Neurosen."

*Sigmund Freud, Aus den Anfängen der Psychoanalyse. Briefe an Wilhelm Fliess, Abhandlungen und Notizen aus den Jahren 1887–1902.* Edited by Marie Bonaparte, Anna Freud, and Ernst Kris; introduction by Ernst Kris. London: Imago Publishing Company, 1950.

*Sigmund Freud Briefe, 1873–1939.* Frankfurt: S. Fischer Verlag, new and enlarged edition, 1980 (1st ed., 1960).

*Sigmund Freud, Gesammelte Werke.* 18 vols. Edited by Anna Freud, with the collaboration of Marie Bonaparte, E. Bibring, W. Hoffer, E. Kris, and O. Isakower. London: Imago Publishing Company, 1940–1952.
"Some Elementary Lessons in Psycho-Analysis." *S.E.* 23:281–286; *G.W.* 17:141–147.
"Some Points for a Comparative Study of Organic and Hysterical Motor Paralyses." *S.E.* 1:157–172. See also "Quelques considérations pour une étude comparative des paralysies motrices organiques et hystériques."
*Standard Edition of the Complete Psychological Works of Sigmund Freud, The.* 24 vols. Edited by James Strachey; translated in collaboration with Anna Freud, assisted by Alix Strachey and Alan Tyson. London: Hogarth Press and the Institute of Psycho-Analysis, 1953–1974.
*Studien über Hysterie,* with Josef Breuer. Leipzig and Vienna: Franz Deuticke, 1895.
Review by Adolf von Strümpell. *Deutsche Zeitschrift für Nervenheilkunde,* 8 (1895–1896):159–161.
Review by Alfred Freiherr von Berger. "Chirurgie der Seele." *Morgenpresse,* February 2, 1896. Reprinted in part in *Psychoanalytische Bewegung,* 4 (1932):73–76.
Review by Eugen Bleuler. *Münchener medizinische Wochenschrift,* 43 (1896):524–525.
Review by Eugen Bleuler of Emil Raimann, *Die hysterischen Geistesstörungen. Münchener medizinische Wochenschrift,* 51 (1904):2241. Some discussion of *Studien über Hysterie* included.
*Studies on Hysteria,* with Josef Breuer. *S.E.* 2. See also *Studien über Hysterie.*
*Suggestion and Its Therapeutic Effects.* See *Die Suggestion und ihre Heilwirkung.* Preface, *S.E.* 1:73–87.
*Suggestion und ihre Heilwirkung, Die,* by Hippolyte Bernheim. Translated from the French by Freud. Leipzig and Vienna: Franz Deuticke, 1888. Originally published as *De la suggestion et de ses applications à la thérapeutique.* Paris, 1886.
*Three Essays on the Theory of Sexuality. S.E.* 7:125–245. See also *Drei Abhandlungen zur Sexualtheorie.*
*Traumdeutung, Die.* Leipzig and Vienna: Franz Deuticke, 1900.
Review by Carl Metzentin. "Über wissenschaftliche Traumdeutung." *Gegenwart,* 50 (1899):386–389.
Review by Jacob Julius David. *Die Nation,* 17 (1900):238–239.
Review by Max Burckhard. "Ein modernes Traumbuch." *Die Zeit,* 22 (1900): no. 275, p. 911, and no. 276, pp. 25–27.
Review by C. Oppenheimer. *Umschau,* 4 (1900):218–219.
Review in *Berliner Tageblatt und Handels-Zeitung,* June 6, 1900, p. 19.
Review by Ludwig Karell. *Beilage zur [Münchener] allgemeinen Zeitung,* October 12, 1900, pp. 4–5.
Review by Paul J. Möbius. "Über den Traum." *Schmidt's Jahrbücher der in- und ausländischen gesamten Medizin,* 269 (1901):271.

Review by Fr. Mero. "Eine neue Theorie des Traumes." *Der Tag*, March 22, 1901, pp. 5–6.
Review by W. Stern. *Zeitschrift für Psychologie und Physiologie der Sinnesorgane*, 26 (1901):131–133.
Review by O. Lubarsch. "Schlaf und Traum." *Die Woche*, 3 (1901): 2243–46, 4:17–19.
Review by Liepmann. *Monatsschrift für Psychiatrie und Neurologie*, 10 (1901):237–239.
Article by F. von der Leyen. "Traum und Märchen." *Der Lotse: Hamburgersche Wochenschrift für deutsche Kultur*, 1 (1901):382–390.
"Über Deckerinnerungen." *Monatsschrift für Psychiatrie und Neurologie*, 6 (1899):215–230.
"Über den 'Mechanismus der Zwangsvorstellungen und Phobien.'" *Wiener klinische Wochenschrift*, 8 (1895):496. See also expanded version entitled "Obsessions et phobies (leur mécanisme psychique et leur étiologie)."
"Über den psychischen Mechanismus hysterischer Phänomene: Vorläufige Mitteilung," with Josef Breuer. *Neurologisches Centralblatt*, 12 (1893):4–10, 43–47.
Review by Paul J. Möbius. *Schmidt's Jahrbücher der in- und ausländischen gesamten Medizin*, 239 (1893):236.
*Über den Traum*. In *Grenzfragen des Nerven- und Seelenlebens*, edited by L. Löwenfeld and H. Kurella, pp. 307–344. Wiesbaden: J. F. Bergmann, 1901.
"Über die Berechtigung, von der Neurasthenie einen bestimmten Symptomen-Komplex als 'Angstneurose' abzutrennen." *Neurologisches Centralblatt*, 14 (1895):50–66.
Review by Leopold Löwenfeld. "Über die Verknüpfung neurasthenischer und hysterischer Symptome in Anfallsform nebst Bemerkungen über die Freudsche Angstneurose." *Münchener medizinische Wochenschrift*, 42 (1895):282–285.
"Zur Kritik der 'Angstneurose'" (Freud's response to the above review). *Wiener klinische Rundschau*, 9 (1895):417–419, 435–437, 451.
"Über die Bernhardt'sche Sensibilitätsstörungen am Oberschenkel." *Neurologisches Centralblatt*, 14 (1895):491–492.
"Über ein Symptom, das häufig die Enuresis nocturna der Kinder begleitet." *Neurologisches Centralblatt*, 12 (1893):735–737.
"Über Hemianopsie im frühesten Kindesalter." *Wiener medizinische Wochenschrift*, 38 (1888):1081–86, 1116–21.
Review by Höltzke. "Über Hemianopsie im frühesten Kindesalter." *Archiv für Kinderheilkunde*, 12 (1891):444–445.
*Über Psychoanalyse*. Leipzig and Vienna: Franz Deuticke, 1910.
*Unbehagen in der Kultur, Das*. Vienna: Internationaler Psychoanalytischer Verlag, 1930.
"Vergessen und Verdrängen." 1901 (presumably never published).
*Vorlesungen zur Einführung in die Psychoanalyse*. Leipzig and Vienna: Heller, 1916–1917.

"Weitere Bemerkungen über die Abwehrneuropsychosen." *Neurologisches Centralblatt,* 15 (1896):434–448.
*Witz und seine Beziehung zum Unbewussten, Der.* Leipzig and Vienna: Franz Deuticke, 1905.
"Zum psychischen Mechanismus der Vergesslichkeit." *Monatsschrift für Psychiatrie und Neurologie,* 4 (1898):436–443.
"Zur Ätiologie der Hysterie." *Wiener klinische Rundschau,* 10 (1896):379–381, 395–397, 413–415, 432–433, 450–452.
*Zur Auffassung der Aphasien: Eine kritische Studie.* Leipzig and Vienna: Franz Deuticke, 1891.
"Zur Geschichte der psychoanalytischen Bewegung." *Jahrbuch der Psychoanalyse,* 6 (1914):207–260.
"Zur Kenntnis der cerebralen Diplegien des Kindesalters (im Anschluss an die Little'sche Krankheit)." *Beiträge zur Kinderheilkunde,* Neue Folge 3 (1893):1–158. Leipzig and Vienna: Franz Deuticke.
"Zur Psychopathologie des Alltagslebens." *Monatsschrift für Psychiatrie und Neurologie,* 10 (1901):1–32, 95–143.
"Zwangsvorstellungen und Phobien: Ihr psychischer Mechanismus und ihre Ätiologie." Translated from the French by Arthur Schiff. *Wiener klinische Rundschau,* 9 (1895):262–263, 276–278.

## Works by Wilhelm Fliess

*Ablauf des Lebens, Der: Grundlegung zur exakten Biologie* (The course of life: foundation for an exact biology). Leipzig and Vienna: Franz Deuticke, 1906; 2nd ed., 1923.
"Aus der Diskussion über die Vorträge des Herrn Siegmund: Heads Felder und weibliche Geschlechtsorgane, und des Herrn Koblanck: Über nasale Reflexneurosen" (From the discussion of the paper by Siegmund: Head's zones and female sexual organs, and the paper by Koblanck: On the nasal reflex neuroses). *Zeitschrift für Geburtshilfe und Gynäkologie,* 43 (1900):601–604.
*Beziehungen zwischen Nase und weiblichen Geschlechtsorganen, Die: In ihrer biologischen Bedeutung dargestellt* (The relationship between the nose and the female sexual organs: presented from the point of view of its biological significance). Leipzig and Vienna: Franz Deuticke, 1897.
Review by Ry. *Wiener klinische Rundschau,* 12 (1898):240.
Review essay by Arthur Schiff. "Über die Beziehungen zwischen Nase und weiblichen Sexualorganen." *Wiener klinische Wochenschrift,* 14 (1901):57–65.
"Entdeckung der dauernden Doppelgeschlechtigkeit, Die: Eine geschichtliche Darstellung" (The discovery of permanent bisexuality: a historical presentation). Unpublished manuscript in the Library of Congress.
*In eigener Sache: Gegen Otto Weininger und Hermann Swoboda* (In my own defense: against Otto Weininger and Hermann Swoboda). Berlin: Emil Goldschmidt, 1906.

"Magenschmerz und Dysmenorrhöe in einem neuen Zusammenhang" (Stomachaches and dysmenorrhea in a new context). *Wiener klinische Rundschau,* 9 (1895):4–6, 20–22, 37–39, 65–67, 115–117, 131–133, 150–152.

*Nasale Fernleiden* (Remote symptoms attributable to the nose). Leipzig and Vienna: Franz Deuticke, 1926. See also *Über den ursächlichen Zusammenhang von Nase und Geschlechtsorgan.*

"Nasale Reflexneurose, Die" (The nasal reflex neurosis). *Verhandlungen des Congresses für innere Medizin, 12. Congress,* pp. 384–394. Wiesbaden: J. F. Bergmann, 1893.

Summary in French by Fliess. "Les réflexes d'origine nasale" (Travail lu au Congrès de médecine interne de Wiesbaden). *Archives de laryngologie* (also known as the *Archives internationales d'otologie et de rhinologie),* 6 (1893):266–269.

*Neue Beiträge zur Klinik und Therapie der nasalen Reflexneurosen* (New contributions to the theory and therapy of the nasal reflex neuroses). Leipzig and Vienna: Franz Deuticke, 1893.

Review by Arthur Schnitzler. *Internationale klinische Rundschau,* 7 (1893):1098.

Review by O. Chiari. *Wiener klinische Wochenschrift,* 6 (1893):462.

Review by Schech in *Münchener medizinische Wochenschrift,* 41 (1894):55.

*Über den ursächlichen Zusammenhang von Nase und Geschlechtsorgan: Zugleich ein Beitrag zur Nervenphysiologie* (On the causal connection between the nose and the sexual organ, as well as a contribution to the physiology of the nervous system). Halle a.S.: Carl Marhold, 1902; 2nd ed., 1910; 3rd ed., as *Nasale Fernleiden,* Leipzig and Vienna: Franz Deuticke, 1926.

"Über Dysmenorrhöe und Wehenschmerz" (On dysmenorrhea and labor pain). *Zeitschrift für Geburtshilfe und Gynäkologie,* 36 (1897):356–371.

*Vom Leben und Tod: Biologische Vorträge* (Of life and death: biological essays). Jena: Eugen Diederichs, 1909.

*Zur Periodenlehre: Gesammelte Aufsätze* (On periodicity: collected essays). Jena: Eugen Diederichs, 1925.

## Works by Other Authors

Becker, Hortense Koller. "Carl Koller and Cocaine." *Psychoanalytic Quarterly,* 32 (1963):309–373.

Bernfeld, Siegfried. "Sigmund Freud, M.D., 1882–1885." *International Journal of Psycho-Analysis,* 32 (1951):1–14.

Bernfeld, Siegfried. "Freud's Studies on Cocaine, 1884–1887." *Journal of the American Psychoanalytic Association,* 1 (1953):581–613.

Bernfeld, Siegfried, and Suzanne Cassirer Bernfeld. "Freud's First Year in Practice, 1886–1887." *Bulletin of the Menninger Clinic,* 16 (1952):37–49.

Brückner, Peter. "Sigmund Freuds Privatlektüre." *Psyche,* 15 (1961–62):881–902; 16 (1962–63):721–743.

Decker, Hanna S. *Freud in Germany: Revolution and Reaction in Science, 1893–1907.* New York: International Universities Press, 1977.
Eissler, Kurt R. *Goethe: A Psychoanalytic Study.* 2 vols. Detroit, Michigan: Wayne State University Press, 1963.
Eissler, Kurt R. *Sigmund Freud und die Wiener Universität: Über die Pseudo-Wissenschaftlichkeit der jüngsten Wiener Freud-Biographik.* Bern and Stuttgart: Hans Huber, 1966.
Ellenberger, Henri F. *The Discovery of the Unconscious: The History and Evolution of Dynamic Psychiatry.* New York: Basic Books, 1970.
Gicklhorn, Josef, and Renée Gicklhorn. *Sigmund Freuds akademische Laufbahn im Lichte der Dokumente.* Vienna and Innsbruck: Urban & Schwarzenberg, 1960.
Grinstein, Alexander. *On Sigmund Freud's Dreams.* New York: International Universities Press, rev. ed., 1980; 1st ed., 1968.
Grinstein, Alexander. "Freud and Count Oerindur: A Preliminary Communication." Unpublished; presented to the Michigan Association for Psychoanalysis on September 23, 1980.
Hirschmüller, Albrecht. *Physiologie und Psychoanalyse im Leben und Werk Josef Breuers.* Bern: Hans Huber, 1978.
Jones, Ernest. *Sigmund Freud: Life and Work.* 3 vols. New York: Basic Books, 1954–1957.
Krüll, Marianne. *Freud und sein Vater: Die Entstehung der Psychoanalyse und Freuds ungelöste Vaterbindung.* Munich: C. H. Beck, 1979.
Lebzeltern, G. "Sigmund Freud und Theodor Meynert." *Wiener klinische Wochenschrift,* 85 (1973):417–422.
Lesky, Erna. "Die Entwicklung der wissenschaftlichen Kosmetik in Österreich." *Ästhetische Medizin,* 9 (1960):199–210.
Lesky, Erna. *Die Wiener medizinische Schule im 19. Jahrhundert.* Graz and Cologne: Hermann Böhlaus, 1965; 2nd ed., 1978.
Masson, Jeffrey Moussaieff. *The Assault on Truth: Freud's Suppression of the Seduction Theory.* New York: Farrar, Straus and Giroux, 1984.
Meynert, Dora Stockert. *Theodor Meynert und seine Zeit: Zur Geistesgeschichte Österreichs in der 2. Hälfte des 19. Jahrhunderts.* Vienna and Leipzig: Österreichischer Bundesverlag, 1930.
Prevost, Claude M. *Janet, Freud et la psychologie clinique.* Paris: Petite Bibliothèque Payot, 1973.
Pschyrembel, Willibald. *Klinisches Wörterbuch mit klinischen Syndromen.* Berlin: Walter de Gruyter, 1964.
Sablik, K. "Sigmund Freud und die Gesellschaft der Ärzte in Wien." *Wiener klinische Wochenschrift,* 80 (1968):107–110.
Sajner, Josef. "Sigmund Freuds Beziehungen zu seinem Geburtsort Freiberg und zu Mähren." *Clio Medica,* 3 (1968):167–180.
Schönau, Walter. *Sigmund Freuds Prosa: Literarische Elemente seines Stils.* Stuttgart: J. B. Metzler, 1968.
Schur, Max. Editor's introduction, "Marie Bonaparte, 1882–1962." In *Drives, Affects, Behavior,* edited by Max Schur, 2:9–20. New York: International Universities Press, 1965.

Schur, Max. "Some Additional 'Day Residues' of the Specimen Dream of Psychoanalysis." In *Psychoanalysis, A General Psychology: Essays in Honor of Heinz Hartmann,* edited by Rudolph M. Löwenstein, Lottie M. Newman, Max Schur, and Albert J. Solnit, pp. 45–85. New York: International Universities Press, 1966.

Schur, Max. *Freud: Living and Dying.* New York: International Universities Press, 1972.

Sulloway, Frank J. *Freud, Biologist of the Mind: Beyond the Psychoanalytic Legend.* New York: Basic Books, 1979.

Vogel, Paul. "Eine erste, unbekannt gebliebene Darstellung der Hysterie von Sigmund Freud." *Psyche,* 7 (1952–53):481–500.

Zilboorg, Gregory. *A History of Medical Psychology.* New York: W. W. Norton, reprint ed., 1967; 1st ed., 1941.

# Index

Library of Congress Cataloging in Publication Data

Freud, Sigmund, 1856–1939.
The complete letters of Sigmund Freud to
Wilhelm Fliess, 1887–1904.

Bibliography: p.
Includes index.
1. Freud, Sigmund, 1856–1939. 2. Fliess, Wilhelm,
1858–1928. 3. Psychoanalysts—Correspondence.
4. Psychoanalysis. I. Masson, J. Moussaieff (Jeffrey
Moussaieff), 1941– . II. Fliess, Wilhelm, 1858–1928.
III. Title.
BF173.F85A4 1985 150.19'52 84-24516
ISBN 0-674-15420-7 (alk. paper)